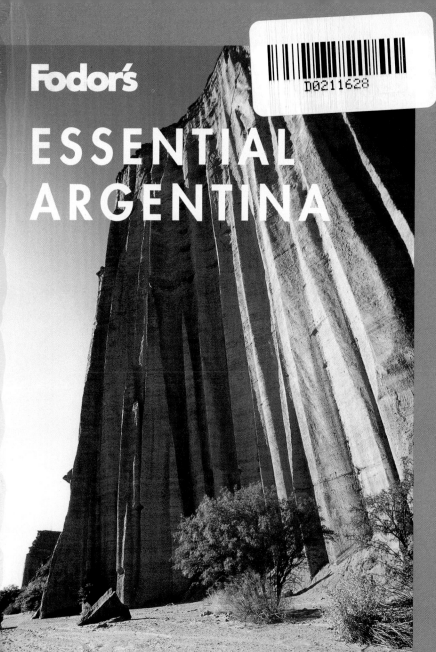

Fodor's

ESSENTIAL
ARGENTINA

WELCOME TO ARGENTINA

Argentina's magnificent landscapes create memorable backdrops for amazing experiences. Wine lovers can sample world-class Malbecs at Mendoza's high-altitude vineyards with Andes Mountain views; adventure seekers revel in the colorful canyons of the Northwest; and nature lovers marvel at the thundering torrents of Iguazú Falls. In Patagonia, top-notch outdoor activities beckon, from scaling translucent glaciers to spotting penguins and whales. Urban adventures also await in Buenos Aires, with its thriving foodie scene, chic shopping districts, and vibrant nightlife.

TOP REASONS TO GO

★ **Stunning Landscapes:** From Iguazú Falls to the Perito Moreno glacier, beauty reigns.

★ **Buenos Aires:** The capital city combines European glamour with Latin American verve.

★ **Food:** Modern Andean cuisine, Patagonian seafood, and some of the world's best beef.

★ **Tango:** On packed dance floors or at ritzy shows, people move to the 2/4 beat.

★ **Mendoza Wineries:** Flavorful vintages flourish in vineyards along the Andean foothills.

★ **Outdoor Adventures:** Riding in the pampas and fly-fishing are just a few top options.

20 ULTIMATE EXPERIENCES

Argentina offers terrific experiences that should be on every traveler's list. Here are Fodor's top picks for a memorable trip.

1 Iguazú Falls

These tremendous waterfalls, which separate Argentina from Brazil, make the world's most spectacular border crossing. Peer into this enormous cascade from the Garganta del Diablo, the "devil's throat," or literally soak them in from a speedboat tour at the bottom. *(Ch. 3)*

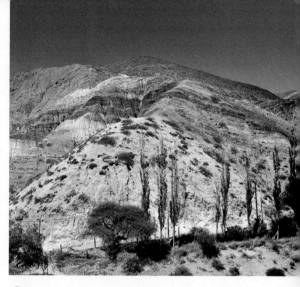

2 Quebrada de Humahuaca

Famous for its colors—from creamy white and burnished gold, to flaming red and dusky purple—this UNESCO heritage site is one of Argentina's most fascinating geological formations. *(Ch. 5)*

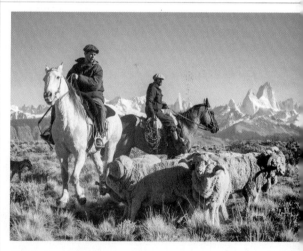

3 Gauchos

Visit an estancia to see Argentina's proud gauchos demonstrate traditional skills and then join them on horseback as they ride across the pampas to check the cattle. *(Ch. 3)*

4 Route of the Seven Lakes

Linking Bariloche and San Martin de los Andes, this partly paved route winds along seven beautiful bodies of water ringed by pine forests and overlooked by the Andes. *(Ch. 7)*

5 Cerro Fitz Roy

Called Chaltén in the native dialect, which means "smoking mountain," this famed peak is surrounded in a white frenzy of ice and cloud, which adds to its photogeneity. *(Ch. 8)*

6 Perito Moreno Glacier

Trek over this glacier's 1,000-year-old ice or just stand and listen as it groans and crackles, with chunks breaking and thunderously crashing into the milky blue waters. *(Ch. 8)*

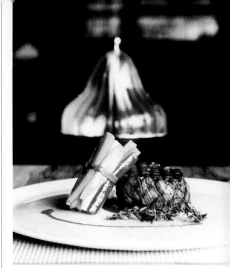

7 Whales at Peninsula Valdes

While the Southern right whale is literally the big ticket at this Atlantic coastal nature reserve, other locals include orcas, penguins, seals, and sea lions. *(Ch. 8)*

8 Grass-Fed Beef

Locals proudly boast that the grass-fed cattle of the pampas produce the world's tastiest beef. Eat your fill at a traditional *asado* (BBQ) at an estancia or at a *parilla* (Argentine steak house). *(Ch. 2)*

9 Sail the Beagle Channel

Take a boat tour on the Beagle Channel for spectacular scenery, hikes, and up-close views of penguins, sea lions, and Les Eclaireurs Lighthouse. *(Ch. 8)*

10 Tango in San Telmo

One of the oldest and most charming parts of Buenos Aires, San Telmo's bohemian barrio is home to several tango parlors and is one of the best places to catch Argentina's infamously seductive dance. *(Ch. 2)*

11 Watch Fútbol in La Boca

Whether you catch Buenos Aires' two teams in hallowed La Bombonera stadium or a local street game in the football-mad neighborhood of La Boca, a soccer match is a must. *(Ch. 2)*

12 Penguins!

The best spots to waddle with Argentina's tuxedoed amigos are Martillo Island, Punta Tombo, and Puerto San Julián. Come December to January to spot fuzzy little penguin chicks. *(Ch. 8)*

13 Weekend in Uruguay

Uruguay is a popular weekend destination for well-heeled porteños who flock to the glitzy resort city of Punta del Este for its beautiful beaches, bars, and nightlife. *(Ch. 4)*

14 Experience a Peña

Clap and dance the night away at one of Salta's peñas—an informal session with traditional guitar music, folk dancing, regional food, and plenty of wine. *(Ch. 5)*

15 Fossils in Patagonia

Some of the world's largest dinosaur fossils were discovered in Patagonia. Dust off your own fossils or walk with life-size replicas in a paleontology park. *(Ch. 8)*

16 Wine Country

Not far from Mendoza's city center, you can reach Maipu, Lujan de Cuyo, and the Uco Valley to explore the past, present, and future of Argentine wine. *(Ch. 6)*

17 Recoleta Cemetery

Featuring art nouveau, art deco, and modernist mausoleums, this beloved cemetery is the resting place of many notable political figures and elites in Argentine history. *(Ch. 2)*

18 MAAM's Mummies

Among other Inca wonders, Salta's High Mountain Archaeological Museum (MAAM) houses the gruesome but fascinating mummies of three sacrificed Inca children. *(Ch. 5)*

19 Hike Aconagua

More than 3,000 climbers attempt to summit this Andean giant every year, but its wild beauty can be just as fully appreciated from short hikes in its foothills. *(Ch. 6)*

20 Polo/Pato

Stamp the divots with Argentina's elite each November, when the polo pros descend on the Campo Argentino de Polo in Buenos Aires, known locally as the Cathedral of Polo. *(Ch. 1)*

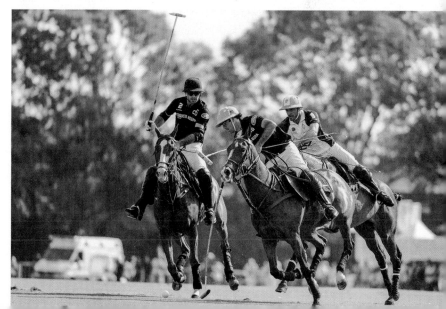

Fodor's ESSENTIAL ARGENTINA

Editorial: Douglas Stallings, *Editorial Director*; Margaret Kelly, Jacinta O'Halloran, *Senior Editors*; Kayla Becker, Alexis Kelly, Amanda Sadlowski, *Editors*; Teddy Minford, *Content Editor*; Rachael Roth, *Content Manager*

Design: Tina Malaney, *Design and Production Director;* Jessica Gonzalez, *Production Designer*

Photography: Jill Krueger, *Senior Photo Editor*

Maps: Rebecca Baer, *Senior Map Editor*; Mark Stroud (Moon Street Cartography) and David Lindroth, *Cartographers*

Production: Jennifer DePrima, *Editorial Production Manager*; Carrie Parker, *Senior Production Editor*; Elyse Rozelle, *Production Editor*

Business & Operations: Chuck Hoover, *Chief Marketing Officer*; Joy Lai, *Vice President and General Manager*; Stephen Horowitz, *Director of Business Development and Revenue Operations;* Tara McCrillis, *Director of Publishing Operations*

Public Relations and Marketing: Joe Ewaskiw, *Manager;* Esther Su, *Marketing Manager*

Writers: Amanda Barnes, Melissa Kitson, Sorrel Moseley-Williams, Victoria Patience

Editors: Jacinta O'Halloran, Kayla Becker, Caroline Trefler

Production Editor: Jennifer DePrima

1st Edition

ISBN 978-1-64097-072-4

ISSN 2576–9316

Library of Congress Control Number 2018950369

SPECIAL SALES

This book is available at special discounts for bulk purchases for sales promotions or premiums. For more information, e-mail SpecialMarkets@fodors.com.

PRINTED IN THE UNITED STATES OF AMERICA

10 9 8 7 6 5 4 3 2 1

CONTENTS

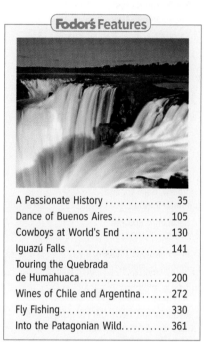

CONTENTS

ABOUT
THIS GUIDE

Fodor's Recommendations
Everything in this guide is worth doing— we don't cover what isn't—but exceptional sights, hotels, and restaurants are recognized with additional accolades. **Fodor'sChoice★** indicates our top recommendations. Care to nominate a new place? Visit Fodors.com/contact-us.

Trip Costs
We list prices wherever possible to help you budget well. Hotel and restaurant price categories from $ to $$$$ are noted alongside each recommendation. For hotels, we include the lowest cost of a standard double room in high season. For restaurants, we cite the average price of a main course at dinner or, if dinner isn't served, at lunch. For attractions, we always list adult admission fees; discounts are usually available for children, students, and senior citizens.

Hotels
Our local writers vet every hotel to recommend the best overnights in each price category, from budget to expensive. Unless otherwise specified, you can expect private bath, phone, and TV in your room. For expanded hotel reviews, facilities, and deals visit Fodors.com.

Top Picks	Hotels &
★ **Fodor'sChoice**	**Restaurants**
	⊡ Hotel
Listings	⇄ Number of
⊠ Address	rooms
⊠ Branch address	⫠⦶⫠ Meal plans
☎ Telephone	✕ Restaurant
⌸ Fax	⚲ Reservations
⊕ Website	⋔ Dress code
✉ E-mail	⊟ No credit cards
⊠ Admission fee	$ Price
☉ Open/closed	
times	**Other**
Ⓜ Subway	⇨ See also
⊹ Directions or	☞ Take note
Map coordinates	⚑ Golf facilities

Restaurants
Unless we state otherwise, restaurants are open for lunch and dinner daily. We mention dress code only when there's a specific requirement and reservations only when they're essential or not accepted. To make restaurant reservations, visit Fodors.com.

Credit Cards
The hotels and restaurants in this guide typically accept credit cards. If not, we'll say so.

EUGENE FODOR

Hungarian-born Eugene Fodor (1905–91) began his travel career as an interpreter on a French cruise ship. The experience inspired him to write *On the Continent* (1936), the first guidebook to receive annual updates and discuss a country's way of life as well as its sights. Fodor later joined the U.S. Army and worked for the OSS in World War II. After the war, he kept up his intelligence work while expanding his guidebook series. During the Cold War, many guides were written by fellow agents who understood the value of insider information. Today's guides continue Fodor's legacy by providing travelers with timely coverage, insider tips, and cultural context.

EXPERIENCE
ARGENTINA

WHAT'S WHERE

1 Buenos Aires. Elegant boulevards and cobbled streets give the capital a European air, but the chaotic traffic and frequent protest marches are distinctly Latin American. The birthplace of tango is *the* place to take in a show. Also visit Argentina's biggest selection of boutiques, restaurants, and museums.

2 Side Trips from Buenos Aires. Varied scenery lies a few hours' drive from Buenos Aires. Traditional *estancias* (ranches) dot the Pampas, lush waterways crisscross the Tigre delta, and windswept dunes and resort towns line the Buenos Aires coast. A two-hour flight transports you to mind-blowing Iguazú Falls, on the border with Brazil.

3 Side Trips to Uruguay. Cobbled lanes and colonial buildings define Colonia del Sacramento. East along the Río de la Plata lies Montevideo, known for its eclectic architecture and down-home dining. Beautiful beaches and beautiful people are what the glamorous resort town of Punta del Este is all about.

4 The Northwest. Deep red gorges, verdant valleys, cloud forests, Inca ruins, and the arid landscape of the Puna: the backdrop in the Northwest changes constantly. Rich Andean traditions live on in the region's food and folk music, beautiful Salta city has a colonial feel, and wines from nearby high-altitude vineyards are the latest thing.

5 Mendoza and the Wine Regions. Argentina's vintners use desert sun, mountain snow, and extreme altitudes to craft distinctive wines— especially Malbec. Mendoza's wineries enjoy the greatest reputation. The Pan-American Highway passes through hot springs, Inca ruins, and incomparable views of Mount Aconcagua.

6 The Lake District. Alpine scenery on a gigantic scale is one way to describe this region's pine forests and snowcapped peaks. Posh resort towns like San Martín de los Andes and Bariloche are Argentina's best ski spots. In summer, you can climb, hike, and bike in the region.

7 Patagonia. Patagonia really is the end of the world. The monumental natural beauty of the Perito Moreno glacier alone is worth the trip south, but on the Chilean side of the Andes, Parque Nacional Torres del Paine competes in grandeur. Penguins, whales, and sea lions are the natural attractions on the windswept, wave-battered Atlantic coast.

NEED TO KNOW

Pacific Ocean

Buenos Aires ★

ARGENTINA

Atlantic Ocean

AT A GLANCE

Capital: Buenos Aires

Population: 43,847,430

Currency: Peso

Money: ATMs common; cash and credit cards common

Language: Spanish

Country Code: 54

Emergencies: 101

Driving: On the right

Electricity: 220v/50 cycle; plugs are either standard European with two round prongs or standard Australian with two- or three-angled flat prongs

Time: One hour ahead of New York during daylight savings; two hours ahead otherwise

Documents: Up to 90 days with valid passport

Mobile Phones: GSM (850 and 1900 bands)

Major Mobile Companies: Movistar, Claro, and Personal

GETTING AROUND

✈ **Air Travel:** International flights arrive at Ezeiza airport, southwest of Buenos Aires; downtown Aeroparque connects to destinations throughout Argentina.

🚌 **Bus Travel:** Comfortable long-distance buses connect cities all over Argentina and in neighboring countries.

🚗 **Car Travel:** Argentina's long highways and fabulous scenery make it a great place for road trips. No need to rent a car if you're only going to be staying in Buenos Aires.

⛴ **Ferry Travel:** There are frequent ferries between Buenos Aires and the Uruguayan cities of Colonia and Montevideo.

PLAN YOUR BUDGET

	HOTEL ROOM	MEAL	ATTRACTIONS
Low Budget	900 pesos	200 pesos	Recoleta Cemetery, Free
Mid Budget	1600 pesos	600 pesos	Entry to Iguazú National Park, 500 pesos
High Budget	5500 pesos	1000 pesos	Ice-trekking trip on the Perito Moreno glacier, 5500 pesos

WAYS TO SAVE

Order from the set menu. Pricey restaurants often offer affordable set menus (*menúes ejecutivos*).

Pay cash. Keeping credit cards out of the equation can score you hefty discounts on lodging and shopping—often as much as 25%.

Take a self-guided wine tour in wine country. Each area has its own unique *caminos del vino* (wine routes). Mendoza's are featured on several maps; you can choose your own adventure, avoid prepackaged tours, and have more money for vino.

PLAN YOUR TIME

Hassle Factor	Medium. Flights from several U.S. cities arrive daily in Buenos Aires. Frequent services from the domestic airport connect the city center to the rest of the country. Delays are commonplace.
3 days	Explore the main sights in Buenos Aires.
1 week	Combine a longer trip to Buenos Aires with a day-trip to Colonia and a night or two at Iguazú Falls.
2 weeks	Explore Buenos Aires, Iguazú Falls, and the Wine Regions before heading south to the Lake District or El Calafate, or north to Salta and Jujuy.

WHEN TO GO

High Season: City sightseeing in Buenos Aires is most pleasant during September to November (spring) and March to June (fall). For Wine Regions, it's late spring and summer (October through April). Iguazú Falls is best August through October, when temperatures are lower and the falls are fuller. Late September to February is high season in Patagonia.

Low Season: Buenos Aires is least crowded in January and February, when locals beat the stifling city heat at resorts along the Atlantic and in Córdoba Province. In Atlantic Patagonia, many properties close in April and May; Southern Patagonia shuts down in the winter months of June through August. Between December and February prepare to melt at Iguazú falls.

Value Season: If you're heading to the Lake District or Patagonia, visit during the shoulder seasons of December and March for savings. Late March through April is a good time for value in the Wine Regions. Prices shoot up everywhere over the long holiday weekends known as *puentes*.

BIG EVENTS

February: Carnival brings drum-banging troupes in Buenos Aires and traditional Andean costumes and rites in the Northwest.

February and March: Toast parades, folk dancing, and grape-stomping at the Mendoza Grape Harvest Festival.

August: Buenos Aires' Tango World Cup and Festival is a two-week celebration of everything Tango.

READ THIS

■ *Collected Fictions,* Jorge Luis Borges. Short stories from Argentina's most famous literary son.

■ *Santa Evita,* Tomás Eloy Martínez. Fictional look at Eva Perón's life and death.

■ *In Patagonia,* Bruce Chatwin. Critically acclaimed lyrical journey many consider among the greatest travel books of all time.

WATCH THIS

■ *Wild Tales.* Passion and revenge fuel the six shorts in Damián Szifron's often-hilarious look at the Argentinean psyche.

■ *The Summit.* Latin American presidents come to blows in a hotel in the Andes in Santiago Mitre's political drama.

EAT THIS

■ *Alfajor*: dulce de leche sandwiched between two cornflour cookies

■ *Humitas*: fist-size balls of maize meal stuffed with cheese and steamed in a corn husk

■ *Choripán con chimichurri*: a barbequed beef sausage sandwich, served smothered in a garlicky parsley sauce

ARGENTINA TODAY

The only thing certain in life is change, and no one knows it like Argentineans. Recession and growth, busts and booms, they've seen it all. Though their country's economic star rises, falls, and occasionally sputters out with alarming regularity, the things that really matter in Argentina don't seem to change. The beef and wine-laden table of a family asado; a penalty kick at a fútbol match; the rhythms of tango, cumbia, and chacarera—these are what make locals' hearts beat faster. They might just win yours over, too.

Political Divisions

Since the country hit rock-bottom in 2001–02, Argentines have taken increasingly vehement positions on their presidents. The political needle swung left during the 12-year Kirchner administration (one term led by the late Néstor Kirchner and two by his wife Cristina Fernández). Critics accused them of corruption, populism, and cutting Argentina off from the global market, while their social spending and renationalization projects earned them many supporters. The scales tipped to the right in 2015, when former Buenos Aires mayor Mauricio Macri's promises to modernize Argentina and reopen the economy to the world brought electoral victory.

For many, soaring inflation and a plummeting peso are causes for concern, as are rising levels of unemployment and violent crime. Argentines feel strongly about politics, and they show it, often by taking to the streets. City avenues and highways are regularly blocked by drum- and banner-toting crowds, and large-scale strikes are becoming common. Sometimes demonstrators are protesting a law; at others they're celebrating political or sporting victories, or commemorating a historical event.

Going Global

Spanish-speakers come to Buenos Aires expecting to hear the sing-song intonation of porteño Spanish. But talk to shop assistants or wait staff in Buenos Aires these days and you might think you're nearer to the Caribbean than the Río de la Plata. Young Colombians and Venezuelans are pouring into Argentina's major cities, where university education is much cheaper than at home. Fast-food joints selling *arepas* and fried plantains are now competing with *empanadas* and *lomitos*. Growing immigrant communities from South Korea, China, Senegal,

WHAT'S HOT IN ARGENTINA

Being out. In 2010 Argentina became the first country in Latin America—and only the ninth in the world—to fully legalize same-sex marriage, sealing Argentina's claim to the title of Latin America's gay capital. The annual Marcha del Orgullo Gay (Gay Pride March) attracts tens of thousands of revelers in Buenos Aires each November.

Green Is the New Black. After years playing second fiddle to other social causes, the medioambiente (environment) is suddenly making headlines in Argentina. The local green movement is rallying around issues like fracking and dam construction in Patagonia, open-pit mining in San Juan and Catamarca, and GM crops in the Pampas. In Buenos Aires, two wheels are now cooler than four, thanks to and Sierra Leone are also changing the cultural and culinary landscape.

Comparatively low property prices and a favorable exchange rate mean that many European and North American visitors are also staying on. Tango enthusiasts are snapping up old apartments in Buenos Aires, wine aficionados are investing in vineyards, outdoors enthusiasts are buying chunks of Patagonia, and early retirees from abroad have opened B&Bs all over the country.

Girls Just Wanna Have Equal Rights

Before #MeToo there was #NiUnaMenos, a homegrown social movement protesting violence against women and other gender-related issues. The slogan means "Not one woman less," a reference to the wave of femicides that has been sweeping the country. Since 2015, the campaign has grown from smallish protests to hashtag-driven media prominence and massive demonstrations. The largest and most colorful is International Women's Day, March 8, when feminist organizations, the women's branches of labor unions and political parties, celebrities, and thousands of supporters of all genders fill the streets of downtown Buenos Aires and other big cities. Argentinean men think twice now before calling out the *piropos* (catcalls) they once prided themselves on, but real change is still slow in coming: the average gender pay gap is still 20%.

Foodie Culture

Foodie culture has hit Argentina in a big way. Celebrity chefs are enthralling TV audiences, and former table-wine drinkers now debate varietals and name-drop boutique vineyards. Their beer-drinking peers are turning from the ubiquitous bottles of Quilmes lager to local craft beers. Instagram feeds alert locals and visitors to the dishes and cocktails of the day, often found behind the unmarked doors of clandestine restaurants and speakeasies. The food scene is rife with contradiction, however. Argentina is one of the world's largest producers of organic fruits and vegetables, but nearly all of it gets exported. A small slow-food and farm-to-table movement is fighting back at farmers' markets in big cities. Saddest of all, the growth of GM soy farming is pushing Argentina's famed grass-fed cattle from the Pampas and into feedlots—these days only very high-end restaurants can guarantee you a grass-fed and -finished steak.

miles of new cycle lanes and a free bike-share program.

Tourism with a Conscience. More visitors to Argentina are stepping off the tourist trail to learn about—or even help change—the country's social and environmental problems. In Buenos Aires, tour worker cooperatives inside one of the city's *villas* (slums) or experience the harrowing history of the 1976–82 dictatorship at the Museo de la Memoria. Choose an ethical homestay when visiting the Andean Northwest or opt for eco-accommodation in Los Esteros de Iberá or Puerto Pirámides. Also, shop for fair-trade crafts made by indigenous communities, textiles from artisan cooperatives, and designer homewares made from recycled materials.

IF YOU LIKE

Nature Writ Large

Argentina's climates range from tropical to subantarctic, and altitudes descend from 22,000 feet to below sea level, so natural environments here vary hugely. Along the south Atlantic coast, orca, whales, and seals mate and give birth on empty beaches and in protected bays. To the north, guanaco, rhea, and native deer travel miles over Andean trails and across windswept plains, while birds pass above in clouds of thousands or descend on lagoons like blankets of feathers.

Glaciar Perito Moreno, Patagonia. Tons of ice regularly peel off the 60-meter-tall (197-foot-tall), 4-km-long (3-mile-long) front of this advancing glacier and crash into Lago Argentino.

Cataratas de Iguazú, Northeast. Iguazú Falls National Park protects 275 waterfalls and countless species of animals. Trails disappear into a greenhouse of creepers, epiphytes, orchids, and bromeliads.

Laguna de los Pozuelos, Jujuy. Thousands of Andean flamingos turn this remote lake near Argentina's border with Bolivia salmon pink.

Península Valdés, Patagonia. Small boats bring you alongside southern right whales as they feed, mate, give birth, and nurse their offspring.

Parque Nacional Nahuel Huapi, Bariloche. Rich forest surrounds the sapphire-blue waters of Lago Nahuel Huapi. Smaller bodies of water nearby make this area Argentina's lake district.

Esteros del Iberá, Corrientes. Alligators, capybara, marsh deer, and long-legged maned wolves are some of the animals you may spot from your boat in this 5,000-square-mile wetland reserve in northeast Argentina.

Reserva Faunística Punta Tombo, Patagonia. This Atlantic peninsula is home to the world's largest colony of Magellanic penguins.

Adrenaline Rushes

If an eyeful of natural beauty doesn't make your heart race in the way you'd like, why not try an adventure sport? Argentina is great for winter rushes—skiing, snowboarding, and dogsledding among them. When temperatures soar, you can cool down by white-water rafting or leaping (with a parachute) into the breeze.

Ice Trekking on the Glaciar Perito Moreno. You can trek over the glacier's 1,000-year-old ice, then celebrate your ascent with cocktails served over cubes of it.

White-water rafting in the Río Mendoza. This river's medium-to-difficult rapids course through Andean foothills. You can combine one- or two-day descents with horseback riding in the mountains.

Skiing and snowboarding at Las Leñas, Catedral, and Chapelco ski areas. Las Leñas near Mendoza, Catedral near Bariloche, and Chapelco near San Martín de los Andes offer groomed runs, open bowls, and trails that follow the fall line to cozy inns or luxurious hotels.

Paragliding, La Cumbre. Reliable thermal winds make the rocky outcrops of La Cumbre, northwest of the city of Córdoba, the best place in Argentina to jump off a cliff.

Mountain climbing at Aconcagua, Mendoza Province. Close to the Chilean border, this 6,959-meter (22,831-foot) peak is the highest in the Western and Southern hemispheres and is surrounded by a host of other climbable mountains.

Time Travel

Your trip to Argentina can cover vast distances in time as well as space. Long before cows and horses, dinosaurs and giant armadillos grazed the plains. Discover massive fossils at natural history museums in Buenos Aires and Patagonia and Argentina's pre-Columbian past in museums and archaeological sites in the Andean Northwest. Jesuit missions, colonial churches, and Italianate townhouses are some of the architectural marks that European settlers have left.

Museo de Arqueología de la Alta Montaña, Salta. The rich pre-Columbian heritage of Argentina's Northwest is explored here.

Museo Paleontológico, Trelew. Meet some of Argentina's oldest inhabitants at this impressive dinosaur museum.

San Ignacio Mini, Misiones. Not far from Iguazú Falls, lush vegetation enshrouds the red stone ruins of this Jesuit mission.

San Telmo, Buenos Aires. Read up on the city's history at the Museo Histórico Nacional, then experience it up close in the tunnels under El Zanjón de Granados or walking the barrio's cobbled streets.

Púcara de Tilcara, Jujuy. Cacti stand sentinel over the low-stone buildings at this partially reconstructed pre-Inca fortress.

Instagram Backdrops

Ice-blue lakes and glaciers in Patagonia. Muted golds and greens rippling the endless fields of the Pampas. Acid-bright aerosol on buildings in downtown Buenos Aires. Brick-red earth and lush green jungle in Iguazú. Argentina's kaleidoscopic landscapes (and streetscapes) will blow your mind, and your social media feed. #nofilter

Quebrada de Humahuaca, Jujuy. Vibrant pinks, yellows, and greens color the walls of this northwestern canyon like giant swaths of paint.

Caminito, Buenos Aires. The bright color-block facades of this street museum in La Boca pay homage to the Italian immigrants who used leftover paint from the shipyards on their houses.

Cueva de las Manos, Santa Cruz. Around 10,000 years ago, early Patagonians used natural red and black pigments to create stenciled handprints and animal paintings on the walls of this southern cave.

Graffitimundo street art tour, Buenos Aires. The brightest stars of the BA art scene eschew canvas for cement: you talk tags and marvel at their murals on these insightful walking tours.

Modern and contemporary art in San Telmo, Buenos Aires. Geometric abstractions and far-out installations are some of the eye-popping creations on display at the MAMBA and MACBA, two edgy art museums on the same San Telmo street block. Hit the neighborhood's many hip galleries to take a slice of color home with you.

The Sporting Life

Few things unite and divide Argentineans as much as their passion for sports. Unsurprisingly for the country that gave the world Diego Maradona and Lionel Messi, the national game is unquestionably soccer. Local teams are the subject of fiery dispute and serious rivalry; the national team brings the country together for displays of unparalleled passion and suicidal despair, especially during the World Cup. You can join the screaming fans at a game—or if fútbol's not your bag, basketball, tennis, hockey, and rugby are also hugely popular. If you'd rather work up a sweat yourself, there are plenty of options for which you don't need to make the national team to take part.

Kick off, Buenos Aires. Every weekend, roaring crowds toting drums and banners pile into the city's soccer stadiums, filling the air with confetti and flares in their team's colors, which—together with the play on the field—makes for a sporting spectacle second to none. Agencies like Tangol ⊕ *www.tangol.com* can set you up with a ticket.

Chukker on, Buenos Aires. Argentina's landed elites breed the world's best polo ponies—and the players to ride them. Watch the pros at the Campo Argentino de Polo or get to grips with a mallet yourself with a lesson at a polo-focused estancia like Puesto Viejo.

Cast a line, Northern Patagonia. Trout species and Atlantic salmon are the prime catches in the chilly (and spectacularly beautiful) rivers and lakes around Junín de los Andes and Bariloche.

Freewheelin', Mendoza. The views of the Andes will take your breath away—and so will some of the gradients on routes like Uspallata to Villavicencio or the trails through the Potrerillos Valley. Cruising the vineyards in Maipú or Luján de Cuyo is an easier ride.

Music

There's no question as to what the soundtrack of Buenos Aires is: the city and the tango are inseparable. Although visitors associate tango with dance, it's more about the music and lyrics for the older generation of locals that are still into it. Their children and grandchildren dance to a very different drum: reggaeton and electrocumbia shake up the city's clubs. Beyond the capital, other folk genres are alive and well, particularly in the Northwest.

Festival de Tango, Buenos Aires. The world's most important tango festival is a two-week extravaganza culminating in a huge milonga along Avenida Corrientes.

Carnaval. Brazilian-style feathers and sequins characterize February parades in Entre Ríos and Corrientes provinces, but pre-Columbian rituals mark celebrations in Salta and Jujuy provinces. In Buenos Aires, neighborhood troupes take to the streets to sing and dance murga.

***Peñas folkóricas*, Salta and Jujuy.** Part restaurant, part bar, and part music hall, these establishments are the best place to hear the romantic strains of zamba or the bracing beat of *chacarera*. Expect your fellow diners to whip out their guitars and join in the choruses or take to the dance floor to swirl their skirts and handkerchiefs and stamp their boots.

ZZK Cumbia Tour, Buenos Aires. The curators of cool behind Buenos Aires' edgiest record label take you on an all-night clubbing pilgrimage to the city's temples of cumbia.

Milongas, Buenos Aires. Watch tango enthusiasts foreign and local kick up a storm at these classic dance halls. Sign up for a class or two before slinking onto the floor yourself.

Staying Somewhere Special

Booming visitor numbers have sparked dozens of new accommodation options in Argentina. There's plenty of variety, whether you're looking for a tried-and-tested international chain, a boutique property, the old-world charm of an estancia, local hospitality at a family-run B&B, or a cheap hostel that's not only clean but stylish, too.

Boutique hotels, Buenos Aires. In Palermo and San Telmo, scores of late 19th-century townhouses have been upcycled into small but luxurious hotels. Soaring ceilings, claw-foot baths, antique furnishings, and wrought iron balconies are common period features.

Community-based tourism, Salta. You get unparalleled insight into organic growing practices and the indigenous culture of the Andean Northwest when you stay at a family farm that's part of the Argentine Network of Rural Community Tourism.

Estancias, **Buenos Aires Province.** For a taste of how Argentina's landed elite once lived, book a night at an *estancia*. Accommodation is usually in grandiose, European-inspired country mansions and rates include activities such as horseback riding and four generous daily meals.

Vineyard hotels, Mendoza. Spectacular views of the Andes and award-winning tipples come as standard at the growing number of Mendoza wineries that operate on-site villas, cabins, or rooms.

Jungle lodges, Iguazú. Birds and butterflies fly out of the dense vegetation around the many lodges within an hour or two of Iguazú National Park. Sustainably sourced wood, stone, and local crafts give most a rustic air, but the elaborate jungle-themed menus, guided excursions, and private plunge pools are anything but.

Horsing Around

Argentina's vast, varied, and sparsely populated landscapes are ideal for exploring on horseback, gaucho-style. Organized riding outfits operate the length of the country, from Salta to Ushuaia. Gauchos aren't the only local equestrian heros: Argentina is home to some of the world's best polo players, many of whom run estancia-based schools.

Polo Open Championship, Buenos Aires. Stamp the divots with Argentina's elite each November, when the polo pros descend on the Campo Argentino de Polo in Buenos Aires, known locally as the Cathedral of Polo. ⊕ *www.aapolo.com*

Don Manuel Polo School, Cañuelas. Combine an estancia stay with some serious polo tuition at this ranch southwest of Buenos Aires. ⊕ *www.poloschoolargentina.com*

Huecachue, Northern Patagonia. On this working ranch, you can spend a day rounding up cattle with gauchos or a whole week riding in the foothills of the Patagonian Andes. ⊕ *www.huechahue.com*

Día de la Tradición, San Antonio de Areco. "Gaucho rodeo" is one way to describe the November festivities in this traditional town: expect folk dancing, buggy rides, and plenty of horseback action from gauchos in full regalia.

Cross the Andes on Horseback, Mendoza. A four-day riding expedition takes you through mountain passes 13,000 feet up in the Andes and down into Chile. ⊕ *www.macdermottsargentina.com*

FLAVORS OF ARGENTINA

Argentina's food traditions begin with wild foods native to the region and crops cultivated since pre-Columbian times. Today's main staples, however, were brought by the European colonizers: first the wheat and cattle that built the country's reputation as the granary—and slaughterhouse—of the world; then the wines, pastas, and ice creams brought by 20th-century immigrants from Spain and Italy. In the last decade, the flavor palette has broadened thanks to new immigrant communities from Korea, China, Venezuela, and Colombia.

Compared with other Latin American fare, Argentine cuisine is found bland by some. And while there are parts of the country that love their spices, the local food philosophy is more about letting top-notch ingredients speak for themselves. Here are some of the flavors that might cross your plate.

Beef

Admit it: a juicy steak comes to mind when you think of Argentina. Locals proudly boast that the grass-fed cattle of the pampas produce the world's tastiest beef. Although the exponential growth of soy farming is elbowing the cows off the pampas and increasing local beef prices, Argentina's inhabitants still manage to consume 120 pounds of carne per capita per year, second only to neighboring Uruguay and well ahead of the U.S.'s 80 pounds. Sunday *asados* (barbecues) are a sacred national ritual. Whether they're grilling in the garden or ordering a *parrillada* (mixed grill) at a restaurant, Argentines typically go for at least two cuts of beef, one on the bone and one off. *Tira de asado* (prime ribs) and *vacío* (flank steak) are the standard selections, and are usually slow-roasted in huge pieces weighing

5 to 10 pounds. Choicer cuts like *bife de chorizo* (porterhouse) or *lomo* (tenderloin) are more likely to be cooked and ordered as individual steaks.

The preludes to the meat include chorizo, *morcilla* (blood sausage), and grilled offal: crispy curls of *chinchulines* (chitterlings) and rich *mollejas* (sweetbreads) are especially popular.

Cow culture doesn't end at the barbecue. Mildly spiced ground or sliced beef is the most traditional filling for *empanadas* (a pastry turnover), the country's star snack. Another local favorite is the *milanesa*, a plate-sized breaded beef cutlet served with fries or a salad, in a sandwich, or topped with tomato sauce and melted cheese (*a la napolitana*).

Andean Ingredients

Maize is the backbone of Andean fare and comes in an impressive range of sizes and colors. The most ubiquitous corn-based dishes are *humitas* and *tamales*, fist-size balls of maize meal stuffed with cheese or ground beef, respectively, and steamed in corn husks. Sweet corn spiced and mixed with goat's cheese is also a popular filling for the area's tiny but incredibly addictive empanadas. Large, nutty-tasting ears of rehydrated dried white maize are popular additions to salads and stews. You can even drink maize: it's fermented into a dangerously powerful alcoholic beverage called *chicha*. Bucketfuls of the soupy-looking concoction fuel the action during the long nights of carnaval, Pachamama, and other traditional festivals.

The Andes are the spiritual home of the potato. Forget big fluffy brown spuds: Andean potato varieties (of which there are scores) are tiny and dense, and might be purple, crimson, green, or rich yellow. Fresh, they're a common side dish, and form part of spicy stews. They're also preserved by being left to freeze outside and then dehydrated. The resulting starchy balls (or a flour ground from them) are known as *chuño* and are a common addition to soups and stews.

Once a staple of the Incas, quinoa continues to grow in these parts. This nutty, protein-rich seed was traditionally incorporated into stews, but these days it's just as common to find it in salads or served as a risotto. Llama steak is more fibrous than beef and has a sweet, gamey edge to it. *Charqui* (the local word for jerky or dried salted meat) is also commonplace in stews. At dessert, don't pass up a plate of *quesillo* (raw goat cheese or stringy fresh white cheese) with *dulce de cayote* (a sweet preserve made of a stringy squash). It's usually served with a handful of nuts and dribbled with *arrope* (a thick, dark fruit syrup).

Patagonian Wild Foods

In the southern half of Argentina the cow plays second fiddle to wilder fare. The star catch along the Atlantic coast is *centolla* or king crab, but mussels, clams, octopus, and shrimp are also regional specialties, as are freshly caught sole, salmon, hake, cod, or silverside. Fish is on the menu in Andean Patagonia, too, which is famous for its wild river trout. Avoid the cheesy sauces local chefs favor and go for something simple that lets you appreciate the star ingredient—*manteca negra* (browned butter) is a fail-safe choice.

If you're feeling game, *jabalí* (wild boar), *ciervo colorado* (red deer), and *liebre* (hare) are the land-lubbing southern specialties. They're usually served roasted or in stews, often accompanied by sauces made from berries or craft beer (or even

berry-flavored beer), some of the other products for which Patagonia is famous.

Best of all, you can take it all away with you. Boar, venison, hare, trout, and seafood are sold pickled and canned (a product known as *escabeche*), and there's a roaring trade in homemade jams and jellies concocted from *rosa mosqueta* (rosehip), *guindas* (morello cherries), and all manner of berries.

Dulce de Leche

Milk, sugar, and not a whole lot else go into this rich brown milk caramel, which is practically a food group in Argentina. Get your first hit each day by spreading some on your toast at breakfast, where you may also find dulce de leche oozing out of cylindrical millefeuille pastries known as *cañoncitos* (little cannons) or long, ridged doughnuts called *churros*. Midmorning or midafternoon you might encounter it sandwiched between two cookies to form an *alfajor,* the nation's favorite sweet snack.

Dulce de leche is a standard flavor for ice cream; you'll also find chocolate-chip dulce de leche, or dulce de leche with swirls of—you guessed it—extra dulce de leche. Diners think nothing of asking for a dollop of dulce de leche on the side of already sugar-laden desserts like *flan* (crème caramel) or flambéed pancakes. Supersweet chocolate cakes filled with dulce de leche are a common fixture in bakery windows.

Connoisseurs insist that the best way to appreciate it is on a spoon straight from the pot. Line up some jars of brands like La Salamandra, Chimbote, and Poncho Negro, and do a dulce de leche tasting of your own.

GREAT ITINERARIES

THE BIG CITY, WATERFALLS, AND WINE

Argentina is a very big country. This whistle-stop tour takes in three of its main attractions—Buenos Aires, Iguazú Falls, and wine country—in 10 days. Although it's technically possible to squeeze all these destinations in, a single flight delay could throw all your plans out of step. Consider adding a day or two's padding here and there to be on the safe side.

Day 1: Arrival

Arrive in Buenos Aires and pick up a city map from the tourist office right before you enter the main airport terminal. Ignore the drivers asking if you need a cab; head straight for the taxi booth, pay up front for your ticket (about 500 pesos), and let staffers assign you a driver. Treat your eyes to an afternoon of visual riches in swanky Recoleta. Stroll past Parisian-style mansions as on Avenida Alvear then visit the equally palatial tombs in Recoleta Cemetery, whose permanent residents include Eva Perón. The world's largest Argentinian art collection is in the nearby Museo de Bellas Artes. Sneak in a power nap to get your body used to the late dinner hours: steak (a bife de chorizo or lomo) is the obvious first-night choice.

Day 2: Plaza de Mayo, San Telmo, La Boca, and Costanera Sur

Have your morning coffee and croissants at an ultratraditional café like Gran Café Tortoni. Stroll down Avenida de Mayo to take in Plaza de Mayo, including a quick look round the Casa Rosada museum. Hop a taxi to La Boca, the port neighborhood where tango was born. The main strip is Caminito, which, though colorful and iconic, is too touristy to merit more than an hour. Lunch at El Obrero is a classic.

Another characteristic old neighborhood, San Telmo, is a short taxi ride back toward downtown. Set aside an hour to get up close to its history with a visit to El Zanjón de Granados, a fascinating house loaded with history. After coffee (or a beer) at one of San Telmo's many cafés, you could spend the rest of the afternoon wandering through the antiques and clothes shops, get a history, or do your walking in greener surroundings at the Costanera Sur Ecological Reserve, a 10-minute taxi ride away.

Day 3: Palermo

After a leisurely breakfast, head for a stroll, skate, or cycle through the Parque 3 de Febrero, and linger at the Jardín Japonés or the Rosedal. Walk or take a short taxi ride to MALBA, which opens at noon, and work up an appetite viewing Latin American art.

Hop a cab to the perennially trendy Palermo Viejo neighborhood, where you can lunch on gourmet salads and sandwiches or far-out fusion. Afterward, browse the city's coolest clothing, shoe, and homeware stores or stray a few blocks west into Palermo Hollywood for antiques and vintage finds at the Mercado de Pulgas (flea market). When night falls, have coffee or a cocktail near Plaza Serrano, and finish with dinner at a modern restaurant. If you're up for a nightcap, you're already where all the action is.

Day 4: Buenos Aires to Puerto Iguazú

Catch an early-morning flight up to Puerto Iguazú. After a quick stop at your hotel, head straight for the Argentine side of Parque Nacional Iguazú. Spend the rest of the day wandering the trails and catwalks and getting soaked on a Zodiac ride through some of the spectacular waterfalls.

Day 5: Iguazú Falls: the Brazilian Side

Spend your second morning at the falls at the Parque Nacional Foz do Iguaçu, Brazil's national park, for amazing views of the Garganta del Diablo (Devil's Throat). (Note that to enter Brazil, U.S. citizens need to have obtained a tourist visa in advance, which costs US$160 and takes three days to process in person, or US$45 and five days via the online service ⊕ *www.vfsglobal.com/brazil-evisa*. In Buenos Aires the Brazilian consulate is open weekdays 9–3.)

Days 6–8: Mendoza

Catch an early flight to Mendoza via Buenos Aires. Spend your afternoon on the first day wandering through the stately city streets of Mendoza and people-watching in its main square, Plaza Independencia.

Divide your next two days between Mendoza's main wine-producing valleys: Uco and Luján de Cuyo. The wisest way to go is with a wine tour, which will help you make the most of your time, not to mention avoid drinking and driving. Let the wining and dining spill over into the evening with dinner at some of the city's excellent restaurants. And if raising your glass isn't your idea of exercise,

TIPS

1. The Big City, Waterfalls, and Wine itinerary works best if Day 1 (arrival) falls on a Thursday or Friday.

2. A 10-day apartment rental in Buenos Aires could save you money, even if you aren't spending all your time there.

3. Most flights to and from Puerto Iguazú and Mendoza use the Aeroparque Jorge Newbery in Palermo, although some also operate from Ezeiza, the airport for all international flights, which is about 40 minutes from downtown. If you can't avoid same-day arrival and departure, allow at least four hours between landing at one airport and leaving from the other.

spend the day rafting, hiking, horseback-riding, biking, or kayaking in fabulous natural settings only an hour or two from downtown.

Days 9 and 10: To Buenos Aires and Home

Catch a morning flight to Buenos Aires and head to your favorite neighborhood for a late lunch.

You could spend the rest of your last day finding out more about *fútbol* at the Museo de la Pasión Boquense, history at the Museo Evita, or street art on a tour with Graffittimundo. Later, try out your footwork with a tango class and a visit to a milonga, or see the pros in action at an evening show.

If you need to do some last-minute shopping, choose from the clothing outlets on Gurruchaga, high-end mall Paseo Alcorta, and the boutiques in Palermo. On your last day, allow at least an hour to get to Ezeiza for your flight home.

ALTERNATIVES

You could combine this 10-day itinerary with a day or two in gaucho country. The town of San Antonio de Areco, in the heart of the pampas, is home to several estancias, country houses-turned-hotels where gauchos tend to the horses. Most estancias include four meals per day in the room price, along with horseback riding or buggy rides. You can also visit just for the day, including a huge midday meat fest, often accompanied by a musical performance with whooping gauchos—cheesy, but fun. Set aside a couple of hours to browse the silversmiths' and artisans' stores that San Antonio is famous for, check out the gaucho museum, and wander the sleepy streets.

Another add-on or replacement side trip is to Uruguay. The port town of Colonia del Sacramento makes an easily accessible day trip. You could stay on for a night at a nearby estancia or catch a bus to Montevideo. In summer the beach resort of Punta del Este is another option. Spending two or three days in Uruguay isn't just a fun way to get an extra passport stamp—it's a window into a country whose cultural differences from Argentina (their heightened obsession with *mate,* for instance) are readily apparent.

BARILOCHE TO PATAGONIA

Day 1: Arrival and on to Bariloche

It's a long trip to Patagonia. After you arrive at Buenos Aires' Ezeiza International you need to transfer to the downtown Aeroparque for your flight to Bariloche. Rent a car at the airport, and drive to your hotel (consider a place on the Circuito Chico outside town). If you could use a beer after all that, choose a laid-back downtown pub to enjoy a local craft brew.

Day 2: Bariloche and Circuito Chico

Spend the day exploring the Circuito Chico and Peninsula Llao Llao. Start early so you have time for a boat excursion from the dock at Puerto Pañuelo on the peninsula's edge as well as for some late-afternoon shopping for homeware and chocolate back in Bariloche. Spend the evening devouring Patagonian lamb *a la cruz* (spit-roasted over an open fire).

Day 3: Circuito Grande to Villa La Angostura

Villa La Angostura is a tranquil lakeside retreat that marks the beginning of the legendary Circuito Grande. Driving there is a gorgeous experience, as you hug the shores of Lago Nahuel Huapi on Ruta 237 and Ruta 231. Relax to the full by checking into a hotel in quiet Puerto Manzano, about 10 minutes outside Villa La Angostura.

Day 4: Villa La Angostura

Spend your second day in Villa La Angostura skiing at Cerro Bayo if it's winter and that's your thing. In warmer weather, explore the Parque Nacional Los Arrayanes, the only forest of these myrtle trees in the world, or simply relax by the lake—if you're staying at Puerto Sur, this might be the most appealing option.

Day 5: Ruta de los Siete Lagos to San Martín de los Andes

Head out of Villa La Angostura onto the unbelievable Seven Lakes Route (Ruta 234), which branches right and along the way passes a string of beautiful lakes. The official seven that give the route its name are Correntoso, Espejo, Villarino, Falkner, Hermoso, Machónico, and Lácar. If you leave early, add the hour-long detour to Lago Traful, where you can stop for lunch. Another detour after Lago Machónico takes you to Lago Meliquina. The route brings you to smart San Martín, where you can spend the late afternoon shopping, trying rainbow trout and other delicacies at the smoke shops, then enjoying them all over again for dinner. Note that the Seven Lakes Route is closed during particularly heavy winter snowfall, when you have to go through Junín de los Andes to get to San Martín.

Day 6: San Martín de los Andes

In winter, skiers should plan on at least one full day at Cerro Chapelco, near San Martín. Otherwise, spend the day relaxing on the beach, fishing, horseback riding, rafting, or just strolling the town.

Day 7: Flight to El Calafate

Get an early start from San Martín de los Andes for the four-hour drive back to Bariloche and then the two-hour flight to El Calafate, the base for exploring Parque Nacional Los Glaciares. From San Martín, be sure to take the longer but faster route through Junín to Bariloche (Ruta 234 and Ruta 237). If you follow the Ruta de los Siete Lagos, you'll have little chance of making an early afternoon flight.

In El Calafate, grab a taxi to your hotel, have dinner, and get some sleep in preparation

for glacier-viewing tomorrow. If money is no object, stay at Hostería Los Notros, the only hotel within the park and in view of the glacier. The sky-high rates include all meals and excursions. Otherwise, stay at a hotel in El Calafate and book your Day 8 glacier visits through El Calafate tour operators (preferably before 7 pm).

Day 8: El Calafate and Perito Moreno Glacier

Spend two days taking in Perito Moreno from different angles. Devote today either to the Upsala Glacier tour, which traverses the lakes in view of an impressive series of glaciers, or the hour-long Safari Nautico on a boat that sails as close as possible to the front of the glacier. Enjoy a well-deserved dinner back in El Calafate. Make arrangements for a Day 9 ice trek by 7 pm.

Day 9: El Calafate and Perito Moreno Glacier

Don crampons and trek across Perito Moreno's icy surface. The trip is expensive, but worth every penny. You crawl through ice tunnels and hike across ice ridges that seem to glow bright blue. After all this, dinner—and everything else—will seem insignificant.

Day 10: Departure

Board a bus or taxi for the airport and take a flight back through Buenos Aires and home. Note that if you are not connecting to another Aerolíneas flight home, you may have to spend an additional night in Buenos Aires on the way back.

ALTERNATIVES

Sports and outdoors enthusiasts can really customize this itinerary. Skiers, for example, can skip southern Patagonia, spending a day or two in Cerro Catedral, near Bariloche, and a day at Cerro Chapelco. Rafters can work with

Bariloche operators to create trips that range from floats down the Río Manso—an eight-hour outing with easy rapids through a unique ecosystem—to 13-hour excursions to the Chilean border. And serious hikers can boat across Lago Mascardi to Pampa Linda, then hike to the black glaciers of Tronador, continuing up above the timberline to Refugio Otto Meiling, spending the night, walking along the crest of the Andes with glacier views, then returning to Pampa Linda. Day hikes to the foot of Tronador leave more time for a mountain-bike or horseback ride in the same area.

The most adventurous travelers drive from Bariloche to El Calafate instead of flying. It adds about a week to the itinerary, but it involves an unforgettable trip down the largely unpaved Ruta Nacional 40. Don't attempt this route without a four-wheel-drive vehicle equipped with two spare tires. And pack plenty of extra food and water as well as camping gear. Getting stuck in a place where cars and trucks pass only a few times a day is guaranteed to ruin your trip.

TIPS

1. In the dead of winter limit yourself to the ski resorts in the Lake District. That said, Bariloche is teeming with kids on high-school vacation trips July through September.

2. Book your flight to Argentina and your round-trip ticket to Bariloche at the same time. Booking a separate flight with another carrier will mean you won't be able to check your luggage through, and you'll have to time things very carefully to avoid missing your connection.

3. It's difficult to tour the Lake District without a rental car. If you don't want to drive, confine your visit to southern Patagonia, spending more time in El Calafate or extending into Tierra del Fuego.

Continued on page 42

A PASSIONATE HISTORY by Victoria Patience

If there's one thing Argentinians have learned from their history, it's that there's not a lot you can count on. Fierce—often violent—political, economic, and social instability have been the only constants in the story of a people who seem never to be able to escape that famous Chinese curse, "May you live in interesting times."

Although most accounts of Argentinian history begin 500 years ago with the arrival of the conquistadors, humans have been living in what is now Argentina for around 13,000 years. They created the oldest recorded art in South America—a cave of handprints in Santa Cruz, Patagonia (c. 7500 BC)—and eventually became part of the Inca Empire.

Spanish and Portuguese sailors came in the early 16th century, including Ferdinand Magellan. The Spanish were forced out 300 years later by locals hungry for independence. Though autonomous on paper, in practice the early republic depended heavily on trade with Europe.

Conflict and civil war wracked the United Provinces of the South as the region struggled to define its political identity and the economic model it would follow.

Spanish and Italian immigrants arrived in the 20th century, changing Argentina's population profile forever. Unstable politics characterized the rest of the century, which saw the rise and fall of Juan Perón and a series of increasingly bloody military dictatorships. Nearly 30 years of uninterrupted democracy have passed since the last junta fell, an achievement Argentinians value hugely.

(left) Ferdinand Magellan (c. 1480–1521)
(right) Stamp featuring Evita

TIMELINE

Magellan sails down
Argentinian coast

Juan de Garay
founds Buenos Aires

PRE-1500s   INCA INVASION   1500   1600

(top left) Cave paintings, Cueva de las Manos,
Santa Cruz; (top right) Río de la Plata aboriginals,
pictured by Hendrick Ottsen; (bottom) Relief detail,
San Ignacio Miní Mission, Misiones Province.

PRE-CONQUEST/INCA

PRE-1500

Argentina's original inhabitants were a diverse group of indigenous peoples. Their surroundings defined their lifestyles: nomadic hunter-gatherers lived in Patagonia and the Pampas, while the inhabitants of the northeast and northwest were largely farming communities. The first foreign power to invade the region was the Inca Empire, in the 15th century. Its roads and tribute systems extended over the entire northwest, reaching as far south as some parts of modern-day Mendoza.

BIRTH OF THE COLONY

1500–1809

European explorers first began to arrive at the River Plate area in the early 1500s, and in 1520 Ferdinand Magellan sailed right down the coast of what is now Argentina and on into the Pacific. Buenos Aires was founded twice: Pedro de Mendoza's 1536 attempt led to starving colonists turning to cannibalism before running for Asunción; Juan de Garay's attempt in 1580 was successful. Conquistadors of Spanish origin came from what are now Peru, Chile, and Paraguay and founded other cities. The whole area was part of the Viceroyalty of Peru until 1776, when the Spanish king Carlos III decreed present-day Argentina, Uruguay, Paraguay, and most of Bolivia to be the Viceroyalty of the Río de la Plata. Buenos Aires became the main port and the only legal exit point for silver from Potosí. Smuggling grew as fast as the city itself. In 1806–07 English forces tried twice to invade Argentina. Militia from Buenos Aires fought them off with no help from Spain, inciting ideas of independence among *criollos* (Argentinian-born Spaniards, who had fewer rights than those born in Europe).

(left) Julio Roca
(right) Monument to
General San Martín;

BIRTH OF THE NATION: INDEPENDENCE AND THE CONSTITUTION

1810—1860s

Early-19th-century proto-Argentinians were getting itchy for independence after the American Revolution. On May 25, 1810, Buenos Aires' leading citizens ousted the last Spanish viceroy. A series of elected juntas and triumvirates followed while military heroes José de San Martín and Manuel Belgrano won battles that allowed the Provincias Unidas de América del Sur to declare independence in Tucumán on July 9, 1816. San Martín went on to liberate Chile and Peru.

Political infighting marked the republic's first 40 years. The conflict centered on control of the port. Inhabitants of Buenos Aires wanted a centralist state run from the city, a position known as *unitario*, but landowners and leaders in the provinces wanted a federal state with greater Latin American integration. The federal side won when Juan Manuel de Rosas came to power: he made peace with indigenous leaders and gave rights to marginal social sectors like gauchos, although his increasingly iron-fisted rule later killed or outlawed the opposition. The centralist constitution established on his downfall returned power to the land-owning elite.

RISE OF THE MODERN STATE

1860—1942

Argentina staggered back and forth between political extremes on its rocky road to modern statehood. Relatively liberal leaders alternated with corrupt warlord types. The most infamous of these was Julio Roca, whose military campaigns massacred most of Argentina's remaining indigenous populations in order to seize the land needed to expand the cattle ranching and wheat farming. Roca also sold off services and resources to the English and started the immigration drive that brought millions of Europeans to Argentina between 1870 and 1930.

(top left) Juan Perón and his wife Eva Duarte attend Independence Day ceremonies, May 30, 1951; (top right) Juan Perón addressing the congress, Buenos Aires, May 6, 1949; (bottom) Perón in discussion c. 1950

THE RISE AND FALL OF PERONISM

1942–1973

A 1943 coup ended a decade of privatization that had caused the gap between rich and poor to grow exponentially. One of the soldiers involved was a little-known general named Juan Domingo Perón. He rose through the ranks of the government as quickly as he had through those of the army. Uneasy about Perón's growing popularity, other members of the military government imprisoned him, provoking a wave of uprisings that led to his release and swept him to the presidency as head of the newly formed labor party in 1946.

Mid-campaign, he quietly married the young B-movie actress he'd been living with, Eva Duarte, soon to be known universally as "Evita." Their idiosyncratic, his'n'hers politics hinged on a massive personality cult. Together, they rallied the masses with their cries for social justice, political sovereignty, economic independence, and Latin American unity. Then, while he was busy improving worker's rights and trying to industrialize Argentina, she set about press-ganging Argentina's landed elite into funding her social aid program. Their tireless efforts to close the gap between rich

and poor earned them the slavish devotion of Argentina's working classes and the passionate hatred of the rich. But everything began to go wrong when Evita died of uterine cancer in 1952. By 1955, the Marshall Plan in Europe reduced Argentina's export advantage, and the dwindling economy was grounds for Perón being ousted by another military coup. For the next 18 years, both he and his party were illegal in Argentina—mentioning his name or even whistling the Peronist anthem could land you in prison.

IN FOCUS A PASSIONATE HISTORY

(top left) Leopoldo Galtieri led the last military dictatorship in Argentina. (top right) Argentina military junta during the Falkland's War; (bottom right) Argentine prisoners of war—Port Stanley;

DICTATORSHIP, STATE TERRORISM & THE FALKLANDS

1973–1983

The two civilian presidencies that followed both ended in fresh military coups until Perón was allowed to return in 1973. Despite falling out with left-wing student and guerrilla groups who had campaigned for him in his absence, he still won another election by a landslide. However, one problematic year later, he died in office. His farcical successor was the vice-president, an ex-cabaret dancer known as Isabelita, who was also Perón's third wife. Her chaotic leadership was brought to an end in 1976 by yet another military coup widely supported by civil society. The succession of juntas that ruled the country called their bloody dictatorship a "process of national reorganization"; these days it's referred to as state-led terrorism.

Much of the world seemingly ignored the actions of Argentina's government during its six-year reign of terror. Throughout the country, students, activists, and any other undesirable element were kidnapped and tortured in clandestine detention centers. Many victims' children were stolen and given up for adoption by pro-military families after their parents' bodies had been dumped in the River Plate. More than 30,000 people "disappeared" and thousands more went into exile. Government ministries were handed over to private businessmen. Massive corruption took external debt from $7 million to $66 million. In 1982, desperate for something to distract people with, the junta started war with Britain over the Islas Malvinas, or Falkland Islands. The disastrous campaign lasted just four months and, together with increasing pressure from local and international human rights activitsts, led to the downfall of the dictatorship.

(top) President Carlos Menem mobbed by the public; (right) a revitalized economy brings new construction.

1982—1999 RETURN OF DEMOCRACY

Celebrations marked the return to democracy. The main players in the dictatorship went on trial, but received relatively small sentences and were eventually pardoned. Inflation reached a terrifying 3,000% in 1988 and only stabilized when Carlos Menem became president the following year. Menem pegged the peso to the dollar, privatized services and resources, and even changed the constitution to extend his mandate. But despite an initial illusion of economic well-being, by the time Menem left office in 1999 poverty had skyrocketed, and the economy was in tatters.

2000—PRESENT CRISIS & THE K YEARS

The longer-term results of Menem's policies came in December 2001, when the government tried to prevent a rush on funds by freezing all private savings accounts. Thousands of people took to the streets in protest; on December 20, the violent police response transformed the demonstrations into riots. President Fernando de la Rúa declared a state of emergency, then resigned, and was followed by four temporary presidents in almost as many days. When things finally settled, the peso had devaluated drastically, many people had lost their savings, and the future looked dark.

However, under the center-leftist government of Argentina's following president, Néstor Kirchner, the economy slowly reactivated. Kirchner reopened trials of high-ranking military officials and championed local industry. In a rather bizarre turn of political events, he was succeeded by his wife, Cristina Fernández. Her fiery speeches have inspired both devotion and derision, but her social and economic policies ensured her landslide re-election in 2011. Times may be better than a few years ago, but Argentinians have lived through so many political ups and downs that they never take anything for granted.

MADE IN ARGENTINA

There's no doubt that Argentinians are an inventive lot. And we're not talking about their skill in arguing their way out of parking tickets: several things you might not be able to imagine life without started out in Argentina.

Una *birome* (ballpoint pen)

BALLPOINT PEN

Although László Jósef Bíró was born in Hungary and first patented the ballpoint pen in Paris, it wasn't until he launched his company in Argentina in 1943 that his invention began to attract attention. As such, Argentinians claim the world's most useful writing instrument as their own.

BLOOD TRANSFUSION

Before ER there was Luis Agote, an Argentinian doctor who, in 1914, was one of the first to perform a blood transfusion using stored blood (rather than doing a patient-to-patient transfusion). The innovation that made the process possible was adding sodium citrate, an anticoagulant, to the blood.

Luis Agote was one of the first to perform a nondirect blood transfusion, in Buenos Aires on November 9, 1914.

FINGERPRINTING

In 1891, Juan Vucetich, a Croatian-born officer of the Buenos Aires police force, came up with a system of classifying fingerprints. He went on to make the first-ever criminal arrest based on fingerprint evidence. Although his method has since been refined, it is still used throughout Latin America.

Huellas digitales (fingerprints)

■ Other useful Argentinian claims to fame include the first working helicopter (1916); the first one-piece floor mop (1953); and the first one-use-only hypodermic syringe (1989).

ARGENTINA LODGING PRIMER

Booming visitor numbers have sparked dozens of new accommodation options. There's plenty of variety, whether you're looking for a tried-and-tested international chain, a boutique property, the Old World charm of an estancia, local hospitality at a family-run B&B, or a cheap hostel that's not only clean but stylish, too. All hotels include breakfast in the room price.

Estancias

For a taste of how Argentina's landed elite live, book a few nights on an *estancia* (ranch). Most estancia accommodation is in grandiose, European-inspired, century-old country mansions. Rates include activities such as horseback riding and four generous daily meals, usually shared with your hosts and other guests.

Estancias vary greatly: some are still working cattle or sheep farms, but many have switched entirely to tourism. At traditional establishments you'll be hosted by the owners and stay in rooms that once belonged to family members. Accommodations are usually old-fashioned and tastefully furnished, but rarely luxurious: you might have to share a bathroom, and some rural locations don't have round-the-clock electricity.

Other estancias still belong to their original owners, but a private company runs the accommodation side of things. These properties are hit-and-miss: some are more luxurious and professional than traditional establishments, while others have become bland and generic. Many properties that advertise themselves as estancias are actually redevelopments of old rural houses, which may not have been estancias originally. These emulate traditional estancia style but are generally more luxurious and have modern amenities.

Apartments and Cabins

Self-catering options are plentiful in Argentina and increasingly popular with visitors. The savings are especially significant if you're traveling as a family or group. In Buenos Aires and other big cities you can rent furnished apartments (and sometimes houses) daily, although weekly and monthly rates are usually cheaper. Some properties are in new buildings with pools, gyms, and 24-hour concierges; others are in atmospheric, but less luxurious, older buildings.

Cabañas (cabins) often outnumber hotels in destinations popular with Argentinean holiday-makers, such as the Atlantic coast or Bariloche. Some are independent holiday houses, most form part of vacation complexes and include maid service and breakfast. Being outside busy town centers in natural surroundings is a boon, but you usually need your own vehicle to reach properties comfortably.

Bed-and-Breakfasts

In many smaller destinations large mid-range hotels tend to be impersonal, institutional set-ups aimed at passing business travelers. If you're looking for local flavor, consider a smaller hotel or bed-and-breakfast. Some are simple family-run affairs, others are boutique properties; many are housed in recycled old buildings that pack plenty of charm. Friendly, personalized service is another major appeal. Although many now use the term "B&B," you may also find them labeled *posada* or *petit hotel*. Hotels with fewer than 10 rooms are very common outside of Buenos Aires—as hotels in Argentina always include breakfast, these properties could be considered B&Bs, even if they don't actively advertise themselves as such.

BUENOS AIRES

WELCOME TO BUENOS AIRES

TOP REASONS TO GO

★ **Dance the Night Away:** This is the capital of tango, that most passionate of dances. But porteños also dance to samba, salsa, and DJ mixes until the wee hours.

★ **Shop 'Til You Drop:** High-quality silver and leather goods as well as fashionable clothing and accessories are available at world-class boutiques and malls. Open-air markets carry regional and European antiques and provincial handicrafts.

★ **Get Your Culture On:** The architecture, wining-and-dining, and arts activities rival similar offerings in any major capital. But the lifestyle, lower prices, and warm locals are more typical of Latin America.

★ **Meat Your Destiny:** Beefy B.A. has more parrillas (steak houses) than you'll be able to sample.

★ **The Beautiful Game:** Top fútbol matches play out in Buenos Aires' colorful stadiums, stuffed to bursting with screaming sports addicts.

1 Centro. The heart of the city is filled with bars, cafés, and bookstores—not to mention crowds.

2 Puerto Madero. An elegant boardwalk and the Museo Fortabat are top draws here. Its high-rise towers are flanked by a sprawling nature reserve.

3 San Telmo. Antiques shops and hip clothing stores compete for space along cobbled streets. Relax at cafés and wander world-class museums.

4 La Boca. Come to gritty La Boca for the colorful Caminito area, and for soccer at the Boca Juniors stadium.

5 Recoleta. The elite live, dine, and shop along Paris-inspired streets (and they're buried in its elegant cemetery). Art galleries and museums are also draws.

6 Almagro. Peruvian restaurants, fringe theater, a lively tango scene, and sprawling mall distinguish Almagro.

7 Palermo. If it's cool, chances are it's in Palermo Soho: bars, restaurants, boutiques, galleries, and hotels line the streets surrounding Plaza Serrano.

Updated
by Sorrell
Moseley-
Williams

For 500 years, Buenos Aires has been in the throes of a powerful identity crisis. The unlikely lovechild of a troubled marriage between Europe and Latin America, Argentina's capital has never wholly aligned itself with either of the cultures that spawned it. Then, each wave of immigration has brought new flavors to the mix, and the resulting fusion — or creative confusion — is attracting more visitors to this capital than any other in South America.

There's no denying Buenos Aires' architectural appeal: the graceful stone facades of its 19th-century town houses and civic constructions speak of Paris or Madrid, so just wandering the streets is a memorable experience. The shopping is world-class, too, whether you covet contemporary couture or quality handicrafts; and the electric nightlife further heightens B.A.'s cosmopolitan ambience. Many of the city's classic cultural institutions have been renovated, while plenty of old-school buildings are being turned into up-and-coming spaces. Traditional dance floors, moreover, have come back to life thanks to a booming tango — and tango tourism — revival. Meanwhile, marriage and equal rights for same-sex partnerships plus a thriving LGBTQ scene have made the city a popular gay destination.

But grit still offsets the glamour. Crumbling balconies, uneven sidewalks, and fresh layers of photo-worthy graffiti are reminders of your real coordinates. The weak peso means that Buenos Aires is still relatively cheap for anyone with hard currency, despite rising prices due to inflation — though growing numbers of homeless people and ever-expanding shanty towns within the city limits speak of tough times to come for on-the-edge residents. In the face of so much change, though, some things do remain the same. Food, family, and fútbol are still the holy trinity for most *porteños* (as the locals are called), and they still approach life with as much dramatic intensity as ever.

BUENOS AIRES PLANNER

2

WHEN TO GO

Remember that when it's summer in the United States, it's winter in Argentina, and vice versa. Winters (July to September) are chilly. Summer's muggy heat (December to March) can be taxing at midday but makes for pleasantly warm nights. During these months Argentineans crowd resorts along the Atlantic and in Uruguay.

Spring (September to December) and autumn (April to June), with their mild temperatures—and blossoms or changing leaves—are ideal for urban trekking. It's usually warm enough for just a light jacket, and it's right before or after the peak (and expensive) seasons.

The best time for trips to Iguazú Falls is August through October, when temperatures are lower, the falls are fuller, and the spring colors are at their brightest.

GETTING HERE AND AROUND

Intriguing architecture, an easy-to-navigate grid layout (a few diagonal transverses aside), and ample window-shopping make Buenos Aires a wonderful place to explore on foot. SUBE, a rechargeable swipe card, can be used on the subway, all city bus lines, and commuter trains.

PUBLIC TRANSIT

Service on the *subte* (subway) is quick, but trains are often packed and strikes are common. Four of the six underground lines (A, B, D, and E) fan out west from downtown; north–south lines C and H connect them. Single-ride tickets cost 10 pesos. Monday through Saturday, the subte opens at 5 am and shuts down between 11 and 11:30 pm, depending on the line. On Sunday, trains run between 8 am and 10–10:30 pm.

Colectivos (city buses) connect the city center with its barrios and the greater Buenos Aires area. You can only pay by SUBE card, and fares within the city cost 8 to 10 pesos. Bus stops are roughly every other block and the MetroBus rapid transit system has dedicated traffic lanes. You may have to hunt for the small, metal route-number signs on regular routes: they could be stuck on a shelter, lamppost, or even a tree. Stop at a news kiosk and buy the *Guía T,* a route guide.

TAXIS

Black-and-yellow taxis fill the streets and will take you anywhere in town and short distances into greater Buenos Aires. Fares start at 30 pesos, with 2.72 pesos for each click of the meter. You can hail taxis on the street or ask hotel and restaurant staffers to call for them.

SAFETY

Although Buenos Aires is safer than most Latin American capitals, petty crime is a concern. Pickpocketing and muggings can happen, so avoid wearing flashy jewelry, be discreet with money and cameras, and be mindful of bags and wallets. Phone for taxis after dark. Police patrol most areas where you're likely to go, but they do have a reputation for corruption.

Buenos Aires Metro Network

KEY

Ⓐ Metro lines
○ Station
◉ Transfer Service

Protest marches are a part of life in Buenos Aires: most are peaceful, but some end in confrontations with the police. They often take place in the Plaza de Mayo, in the square outside the Congreso, or along Avenida de Mayo.

TOURS

Known for superlative customer service, Buenos Aires Tours arranges everything from city walking tours to multiweek Argentine vacations aimed at different budgets. Informed young historians from the University of Buenos Aires lead private tours that highlight the city's art and architecture as well as its intriguing past at Eternautas. Academics also serve as guides at Cultour: the highbrow history- and culture-oriented excursions are complemented by general city tours and boat trips.

For a different take on local life, contact the Cicerones de Buenos Aires. Its resident volunteers take groups of up to six visitors on informal outings, providing a true porteño perspective along the way. The experience is free, but donations are welcome. For serious insight into the city's Jewish community, sign on for one of the full- or half-day outings organized by Deb Miller's company, Travel Jewish. Meanwhile, BA Cultural Concierge, run by Maryland transplant Madi Lang, plans trips for families and groups, specializing in off-the-beaten track tours.

B.A.'s growing network of bicycle lanes has led to a surge in two-wheel travel. La Bicicleta Naranja has scheduled tours led by bilingual guides; it will also supply do-it-yourselfers with excellent route maps and deliver rental equipment to your hotel. Graffiti and street art are the focus of one unusual tour run by Biking Buenos Aires; another includes live performances by actors recreating key moments in civic history.

Large onboard screens make the posh minibuses used by Opción Sur part transport and part cinema. Each stop on the city itinerary is introduced by relevant historical footage (picture Evita rallying the masses at Plaza de Mayo); trips to outlying areas are available, too. If you would rather rely on public transit and foot power, try Buenos Aires Local Tours, a popular pay-what-you-like service (advance online registration is required).

Tour Companies BA Cultural Concierge. ☎ 11/15–3876–5937 ⊕ www.baculturalconcierge.com. **Biking Buenos Aires.** ☎ 11/4300–5373 ⊕ www.bikingbuenosaires.com. **Buenos Aires Local Tours.** ☎ 11/5254–1354 ⊕ www.buenosaireslocaltours.com. **Buenos Aires Tours.** ☎ 11/4785–2753 ⊕ www.buenosaires-tours.com.ar. **Cicerones de Buenos Aires.** ☎ 11/4141–9362 ⊕ www.cicerones.org.ar. **Cultour.** ☎ 11/6365–6892 ⊕ www.cultour.com.ar. **Eternautas.** ☎ 11/5031–9916 ⊕ www.eternautas.com. **La Bicicleta Naranja.** ☎ 11/4362–1104 ⊕ www.labicicletanaranja.com.ar. **Opción Sur.** ☎ 11/4777–9029 ⊕ www.opcionsur.com.ar. **Travel Jewish.** ☎ 949/307–9231 in U.S. only ⊕ www.traveljewish.com.

VISITOR INFORMATION

The civic tourism board—Turismo Buenos Aires—operates information outlets with English-speaking staff at both airports and seven other locations around the city, including Centro, Recoleta, and Puerto Madero. Hours can be erratic, but the booth at the intersection of Florida and

Marcelo T. de Alvear (near Plaza San Martín) is usually open weekdays from 10 to 5 and weekends from 9 to 6.

Visitor Information Turismo Buenos Aires. ⊕ *www.turismo.buenosaires.gob.ar.*

EXPLORING BUENOS AIRES

Unlike most other Latin American cities, where the architecture reveals a strong Spanish influence, little remains of Buenos Aires' colonial days. This is due in part to the short lifespan of the *adobe* (mud and straw) used to build the city's first houses, and also to the fact that Buenos Aires' elite have always followed Europe's architectural trends closely. The result is an arresting hodgepodge of building styles that hints at many far-off cities—including Rome, Madrid, Paris, and Budapest. With their boulevards lined with palatial mansions and spacious parks, the neighborhoods of Palermo, La Recoleta, and some parts of the downtown area are testament to days of urban planning on a grandiose scale (and budget), whereas San Telmo and La Boca have a more working-class Italian feel.

CENTRO AND NEARBY

Porteños love to brag that Buenos Aires has the world's widest avenue (Avenida 9 de Julio), its best steak, and its most beautiful women. The place to decide whether they're right is the city's heart, known simply as "Centro." It contains the oldest and newest districts as well as many other superlatives. Cross Santiago Calatrava's sleek and curvaceous Puente de la Mujer (Bridge of the Woman) and you're in the upscale waterfront neighborhood of Puerto Madero.

CENTRO

The historic heart of Buenos Aires, Centro is still the focus of contemporary civic and commercial life. Plaza de Mayo is the original main square, and civic buildings both past and present are clustered between it and Plaza Congreso. Many of Argentina's most historic events—including revolutions, demonstrations, and terrorist attacks—took place on this square. Bullet-marked facades, sidewalks embedded with plaques, and memorials where buildings once stood are reminders of all this history, and the protesters who fill the streets regularly are history in the making. The city's most highbrow cultural events are hosted a few blocks away in the spectacular Teatro Colón, and high-grossing theatrical productions line Avenida Corrientes. Microcentro is the financial district tucked into Centro.

PLANNING YOUR TIME

Crowds and traffic can make touring this area draining: try to do a few short visits rather than one long marathon. Half a day in Centro is enough to take in the sights, though you could spend a lot more time caught up in the shops and boutiques. Office workers on lunch breaks make Centro even more hectic than usual between noon and 2. If you're planning on hard-core shopping, come on a weekend. The area is quiet at night, and a little dangerous in its desolation.

TOP ATTRACTIONS

Casa Rosada. The eclectic Casa de Gobierno, better known as the Casa Rosada or Pink House, is at Plaza de Mayo's eastern end. The building houses the government's executive branch—the president works here but lives elsewhere—and was built in the late 19th century. Its curious hue dates from the presidency of Domingo Sarmiento, who ordered it painted pink as a symbol of unification between two warring political factions: the *federales* (whose color was red) and the *unitarios* (white). Legend has it that the original paint was made by mixing whitewash with bull's blood.

The balcony facing Plaza de Mayo is a presidential podium. From this lofty stage Evita rallied the *descamisados* (the shirtless—meaning the working class), Maradona sang along with soccer fans after winning one World Cup and coming second in another, and Madonna belted out her movie rendition of "Don't Cry for Me Argentina." Look for a small banner hoisted alongside the nation's flag, indicating "the president is in."

On weekends, hour-long guided tours in English leave at 12:30 and 2:30 (book in advance), taking in some presidential offices and the newly opened *Galería de los Patriotas Argentinos del Bicentenario* (Bicentennial Gallery of Patriots), a pictorial who's who of Argentina's national heroes. The country's heroines have a room of their own here, the *Salón Mujeres Argentinas*, where an impassioned Evita presides over black-and-white photographs of Argentina's other great dames. ⊠ *Balcarce 50, Plaza de Mayo* ☎ *11/4344–3804* ⊕ *https://visitas.casarosada.gob. ar* 🖻 *Free, but reservations are essential* Ⓜ *A to Plaza de Mayo, D to Catedral, E to Bolívar.*

La Manzana de Las Luces (*The Block of Illumination*). A heap of history is packed into this single block of buildings southwest of Plaza de Mayo. Its name, "the Block of Lights," is a metaphorical nod to the "illuminated" scholars who once worked within. Guided tours are led by excellent historians, and though regular tours are in Spanish, English summaries are offered at each stage.

The site's earliest occupant was the controversial Jesuit order, which began construction in 1661. The only surviving building from then is the galleried **Procuraduría,** the colonial administrative headquarters for the Jesuits' land holdings. Secret tunnels linked it to area churches, the Cabildo, and the port. After the Jesuits' expulsion from Argentina in 1767 (the simple brick-and-mud structure housed the city's first school of medicine and then the University of Buenos Aires). Fully restored, it's now home to a school for stringed instrument makers and a somewhat tacky crafts market.

The Jesuits honored their patron saint at the **Iglesia de San Ignacio de Loyola** (Church of Saint Ignatius of Loyola), at the intersection of Alsina and Bolívar. You can visit without taking a tour.

Argentina's first congress convened in another building on the site, the **Casas Virreinales** (Viceroyal Residences)—ironic, given that it was built to house colonial civil servants. The remaining historic building is the neoclassical **Colegio Nacional,** a high-caliber public school that replaced

Getting Oriented

TOP EXPERIENCES

Reflecting: on Argentina's indigenous history at the Museo Ftnográfico Juan B. Ambrosetti.

Witnessing: demonstrations in Plaza de Mayo, where Evita addressed crowds.

Listening: to opera singers in the glittering Teatro Colón or to the equally talented songbirds in the Reserva Ecológica.

Wandering: along Juana Manuela Gorriti and Pierina Dealessi to see Puerto Madero's "recycled" warehouses; Avenida de Mayo for 19th-century style; or Calle Florida for hustle, bustle, and souvenirs.

THE TERRITORY

The Microcentro—the small banking district within Microcentro—runs between avenidas L.N. Alem and 9 de Julio and north of Avenida de Mayo. There are two axes: Avenida Corrientes (east–west) and pedestrian-only shopping street Florida (north–south). Florida's northern end leads into Plaza San Martín in Retiro. South of the Microcentro lies Plaza de Mayo. From here Avenida de Mayo runs 12 blocks west to Plaza del Congreso. Puerto Madero borders the Centro to the east. The main thoroughfares, avenidas Alicia M. de Justo and Olga Cossentini, run parallel to the river.

SAFETY AND PRECAUTIONS

Be especially alert for "stain scammers" downtown: they squirt foul-smelling liquid on you surreptitiously, then "helpfully" offer to clean it off (as they pick your pocket). Use ATMs only during bank hours (weekdays 10–3); thieves target them after hours.

Centro and Nearby

KEY

✕ *Quick bites*

Ⓜ *Subte stops*

GETTING AROUND

The quickest way into Centro is by subte. For Microcentro, get off at Florida (Línea B) or Lavalle (C). Retiro and Plaza San Martín have eponymous stations on Línea C. Stations Avenida de Mayo (A), Catedral (D), and Bolívar (E) all serve Plaza de Mayo. Línea A has stops along de Mayo, including at Congreso. Líneas B, C, and D intersect at Carlos Pellegrini/Diagonal Norte/9 de Julio. Only change lines here if you're going more than one stop. Otherwise, walking is quicker. Puerto Madero is close to L.N. Alem on Línea A.

You can take a taxi or bus to the Microcentro, but walking is the best way to move within it. Bus No. 17 connects Centro and Recoleta; so do Bus Nos. 59 and 93. No. 130 connects these areas with Puerto Madero. Bus Nos. 22 and 24 run between San Telmo and Microcentro. A MetroBus system opened in 2016, making moving around a lot faster.

QUICK BITES

Chan Chan. Peruvian dishes at bargain prices have made a name for Chan Chan. The deep-fried corn kernels they bring while you wait are almost a meal in themselves. ✉ *Hipólito Yrigoyen 1390, Congreso* ☎ *11/4382–8492* ▭ *No credit cards* Ⓜ *A to Sáenz Peña.*

La Morada. Local office workers know where to find the best empanadas. Vintage adverts, 1960s LPs, and photos of late, great Argentine celebrities are hung so close together you can barely see the walls. ✉ *Hipólito Yrigoyen 778, Plaza de Mayo* ☎ *11/4343–3003* ⊕ *www.lamorada.com.ar* ▭ *No credit cards* ☾ *Closed weekends* Ⓜ *A to Plaza de Mayo, D to Catedral, E to Bolívar.*

La Giralda. Don't let the small tables or surly waiters put you off—La Giralda's signature *chocolate con churros* (hot chocolate with crisp cigar-shape doughnuts) are to die for. ✉ *Av. Corrientes 1453, Centro* ☎ *11/4371–3846* ▭ *No credit cards* Ⓜ *B to Uruguay.*

a Jesuit-built structure. The president often attends graduation ceremonies, and Einstein gave a lecture here in 1925. ⊠ *Entrance at Perú 272, Plaza de Mayo* ☎ *11/4342–9930* 🎫 *65 pesos* Ⓜ *A to Plaza de Mayo, D to Catedral, E to Bolívar.*

Museo Casa Rosada. Today, the River Plate is nowhere in sight, but the humming traffic circle that overlooks this underground museum behind the Casa Rosada was once on the waterfront. The brick vaults, pillars, and wooden pulley mechanisms are the remains of the 1845 Taylor Customs House and jetty discovered after being buried for almost a century. In honor of Argentina's 2010 bicentenary celebrations the structure was restored and capped with a glass roof.

Formerly known as the bicentenary museum, each vault covers a portion of Argentina's political history, recalling it through artifacts (many are personal possessions of those who governed from the house overhead), paintings, photographs, film reels, and interactive screens. Temporary art exhibitions run on the other side of the museum courtyard.

The large glass structure in the center contains the star attraction: a 360-degree masterpiece by Mexican muralist David Alfaro Siqueiros. When that house was demolished in the early 1990s, the mural was carefully removed in pieces, though it then languished in a shipping container for 17 years

A café at the back of the museum offers coffee, sandwiches, salads, and a set lunch menu. ⊠ *Paseo Colón 100, at Hipólito Yrigoyen, Plaza de Mayo* ☎ *11/4344–3802* ⊕ *https://www.casarosada.gob.ar/la-casa-rosada/museo* 🎫 *Free* ☉ *Closed Mon. and Tues.* Ⓜ *A to Plaza de Mayo, D to Catedral, E to Bolívar.*

Museo Etnográfico Juan B. Ambrosetti (*Ethnographic Museum*). Until 2012, the 100-peso bill still honored General Roca—the man responsible for the massacre of most of Patagonia's indigenous population—so it's not surprising that information on Argentina's original inhabitants is sparse. This fascinating but little-visited museum is a welcome remedy.

Begun by local scientist Juan Bautista Ambrosetti in 1904, the collection originally focused on so-called exotic art and artifacts, such as Australasian sculptures and a Japanese temple altar. The real highlights here, however, are the Argentine collections: if you're planning to visit Argentina's far north or south, they'll provide an eye-opening introduction.

The ground-floor galleries trace the history of human activity in Patagonia, underscoring the tragic results of European arrival. Dugout canoes, Mapuche silver jewelry, and scores of archival photos and illustrations are the main exhibits. Ask for a photocopied sheet with English versions of the texts.

In the upstairs northwestern Argentina gallery the emphasis is archaeological. Displays chronicle the evolution of Andean civilization, the heyday of the Inca empire, and postcolonial life. Artifacts include ceramics, textiles, jewelry, farming tools, and even food.

⊠ *Moreno 350, Plaza de Mayo* ☎ *11/5287–3050* ⊕ *www.museoetnografico.filo.uba.ar* 🎫 *30 pesos suggested donation* ☉ *Closed Sat.–Mon.* Ⓜ *A to Plaza de Mayo, D to Catedral, E to Bolívar.*

Museo Histórico Nacional del Cabildo y de la Revolución de Mayo (*Cabildo*). Plaza de Mayo's only remaining colonial edifice was built in 1765 as the meeting place for the city council, now based in the ornate wedge-shaped building on the southwest corner of the square. The epicenter of the May Revolution of 1810, where patriotic citizens gathered to vote against Napoleonic rule, the hall is one of Argentina's national shrines. However, this hasn't stopped successive renovations to its detriment, including the demolition of the whole right end of the structure to make way for the new Avenida de Mayo in 1894 and of the left end for Diagonal Julio Roca in 1931. The small museum of artifacts and documents pertaining to the events of the May Revolution is less of an attraction than the building itself. Thursday and Friday from 11 to 6, a tiny craft market takes place on the patio behind the building. ⊠ *Bolívar 65, Plaza de Mayo* ☎ *11/4334–1782* ⊕ *www.cabildonacional.gob.ar* ⊘ *Closed Mon. and Tues.* Ⓜ *Line A to Plaza de Mayo, Line D to Catedral, Line E to Bolívar.*

Fodor'sChoice ★ **Plaza de Mayo.** Since its construction in 1580, this has been the setting for Argentina's most politically turbulent moments, including the uprising against Spanish colonial rule on May 25, 1810—hence its name. The square was once divided in two by a *recova* (gallery), but this reminder of colonial times was demolished in 1883 and the square's central monument, the Pirámide de Mayo, was later moved to its place. The pyramid you see is a 1911 extension of the original (which is hidden inside), erected in 1811 on the anniversary of the Revolution of May. The bronze equestrian statue of General Manuel Belgrano, the designer of Argentina's flag, dates from 1873.

The plaza remains the traditional site for ceremonies, rallies, and protests. Thousands cheered for Perón and Evita here; anti-Peronist planes bombed the gathered crowds in 1955; there were bloody clashes in December 2001 (hence the heavy police presence and crowd-control barriers); but the mood was jubilant for the nation's bicentenary in 2010. The white head scarves painted around the pryamid represent the Madres de la Plaza de Mayo (Mothers of May Square) who have marched here every Thursday at 3:30 for nearly four decades. Housewives and mothers–turned–militant activists, they demand justice for *los desaparecidos*—the people who were "disappeared" during Argentina's dictatorial military government (1976–83). ⊠ *Centro* Ⓜ *A to Plaza de Mayo, D to Catedral, E to Bolívar.*

Fodor'sChoice ★ **Teatro Colón.** Its magnitude, magnificent acoustics, and opulence earn the Teatro Colón a place among the world's top five opera houses and an ever-changing stream of imported talent bolsters the well-regarded local lyric and ballet companies.

After an eventful 18-year building process involving the death of one architect and the murder of another, the sublime Italianate structure was inaugurated in 1908 with Verdi's *Aïda*. It has hosted the likes of Maria Callas, Richard Strauss, Arturo Toscanini, Igor Stravinsky, Enrico Caruso, and Luciano Pavarotti, who said that the Colón has only one flaw: the acoustics are so good that every mistake can be heard.

The theater's sumptuous building materials—three kinds of Italian marble, French stained glass, and Venetian mosaics—were imported from Europe. The seven-tier main theater is breathtaking, and has a grand central chandelier with 700 lights to illuminate the 3,000 mere mortals in its red-velvet seats.

The opera and ballet seasons run from April through December, and performances include symphonic cycles, chamber music concerts, and avant-garde music, opera, and dramatic performances at the ultraminimal Centro Experimental.

You can get in on the behind-the-scenes action on a guided tour, which takes you up and down innumerable staircases to rehearsal rooms and to the costume, shoe, and scenery workshops, before letting you gaze at the stage from a sought-after box. (Tours are daily 9–5, every hour on the hour; arrive at least a half hour before the tour starts, as they fill up quickly.)

Buy performance tickets from the box office on Pasaje Toscanini. If seats are sold out—or beyond your pocket—you can buy 50-peso standing-room tickets on the day of the performance. These are for the lofty upper-tier *paraíso*, from which you can both see and hear perfectly. ⊠ *Main entrance: Libertad between Tucumán and Viamonte, box office: Pasaje Toscanini 1180, Centro* ☎ *11/4378–7100 tickets, 11/4378–7127 tours* ⊕ *www.teatrocolon.org.ar* ✉ *Guided tours 300 pesos* Ⓜ *D to Tribunales.*

WORTH NOTING

Calle Florida. Nothing sums up the chaotic Microcentro better than this pedestrian axis, which has fallen from grace and risen from the ashes at least as many times as Argentina's economy. It's a riotous spot on weekdays, when throngs of office workers eager for a fast-food or high-street retail fix intermingle with buskers and street vendors. You can wander it in less than an hour: start at the intersection with Av. de Mayo, and a bench or patch of grass in shady **Plaza San Martín** will be your reward at the other end.

En route, take in the surrounding buildings. At the ornate **Edificio Bank Boston** (No. 99) attention tends to focus on the battered, paint-splattered 4-ton bronze doors—unhappy customers have been taking out their anger at *corralitos* (banks retaining their savings) since the economic crisis of 2001–02.

The restoration process at **Galería Güemes** has left the soaring marble columns and stained-glass cupola gleaming, and the tacky shops that fill this historic arcade do nothing to lessen the wow factor. Witness Buenos Aires' often cavalier attitude to its architectural heritage at Florida's intersection with Avenida Corrientes, where the neo-Gothic **Palacio Elortondo-Alvear** is now home to Burger King. Go upstairs to check out the plaster molding and stained glass.

Milan's Galleria Vittorio Emanuele served as the model for **Galerías Pacífico** , designed during Buenos Aires' turn-of-the-20th-century golden age. Once the headquarters of the Buenos Aires–Pacific Railway, it's now a posh shopping mall and cultural center. Head to the central stairwell to see the allegorical murals painted by local greats Juan Carlos

Castagnino, Antonio Berni, Cirilo Colmenio, Lino Spilimbergo, and Demetrio Urruchúa. The **Centro Cultural Borges,** which hosts small international exhibitions and musical events, is on the mezzanine level.

Past the slew of leather shops in the blocks north of Avenida Córdoba is **Plaza San Martín,** where you'll see a bronze statue of the namesake saint atop a rearing horse. It's overlooked by several opulent Italianate buildings and South America's tallest art deco structure, the **Edificio Kavanagh.** ✉ *Microcentro* Ⓜ *A to Plaza de Mayo, D to Catedral, or B to Florida (southern end); C to Plaza San Martín (northern end).*

Catedral Metropolitana. The columned neoclassical facade of the Metropolitan Cathedral makes it seem more like a temple than a church, and its history follows the pattern of many structures in the Plaza de Mayo area. The first of six buildings on this site was a 16th-century adobe ranch house; the current structure dates from 1822, but has been added to several times.

There's been a surge of interest in the building since February 2013, when Cardinal Jorge Bergoglio, then archbishop of Buenos Aires, was elected Pope Francis. The sanctuary now includes a small commemorative display of the pope's personal objects, watched over by a grinning life-size fiberglass statue of the pontiff in full regalia.

The embalmed remains of another local hero, General José de San Martín—known as the Liberator of Argentina for his role in the War of Independence—rest here in a marble mausoleum lighted by an eternal flame. Soldiers of the Grenadier Regiment, an elite troop created and trained by San Martín in 1811, permanently guard the tomb. Guided tours (in Spanish) of the mausoleum and crypt leave Monday to Saturday at 11:45 am. ✉ *San Martín 27, at Rivadavía, Plaza de Mayo* ☎ *11/4331–2845* ⊕ *www.catedralbuenosaires.org.ar* 💲 *Free* Ⓜ *A to Plaza de Mayo, D to Catedral, E to Bolívar.*

Centro Cultural Borges. There's something very low-key about this cultural center, despite its considerable size and prime location above the posh Galerías Pacífico mall. With a minimum of pomp and circumstance it has hosted exhibitions of Warhol, Kahlo and Rivera, Man Ray, Miró, Picasso, Chagall, and Dalí, as well as local greats Seguí, Berni, and Noé. Occasional group shows focus on new local artists and art students. Small, independent theater and dance performances are also staged here. ✉ *Viamonte 525, at San Martín, Centro* ☎ *11/5555–5359* ⊕ *www.ccborges.org.ar* 💲 *150 pesos* Ⓜ *B to Florida.*

Museo de Arte Hispanoamericano Isaac Fernández Blanco (*Isaac Fernández Blanco Hispanic-American Art Museum*). The distinctive Peruvian neocolonial-style Palacio Noel is the perfect backdrop for this colonial art and craft museum, which was built in 1920 as the residence of architect Martín Noel. He and museum founder Fernández Blanco donated most of the exquisite silver items, religious wood carvings, inlaid furnishings, and paintings from the Spanish colonial period that are on display. Guided tours in English can be arranged by calling ahead. Shaded benches in the lush walled gardens are a welcome respite, and the rustling leaves and birdcalls almost filter out the busy Retiro traffic noise. ✉ *Suipacha 1422, at Av. Libertador, Retiro* ☎ *11/4327–0272*

⊕ *www.buenosaires.gob.ar/museofernandezblanco* 🖃 *10 pesos, free Weds.* ⊘ *Closed Mon.* Ⓜ *C to San Martín.*

PUERTO MADERO

A forest of skyscrapers designed by big-name architects like Sir Norman Foster and César Pelli has sprouted up in Puerto Madero, a onetime port area that's now notable for its chic hotels, restaurants, and boutiques. Original dockland structures have been repurposed: former grain silos now house luxury lodgings, and high-end cafés line the waterside walkways where cargo was once offloaded.

The neighborhood's upswing has also extended to the 865-acre Reserva Ecológica, a nature preserve built on land reclaimed from the river using rubble from major construction projects in the 1970s and '80s.

PLANNING YOUR TIME

Puerto Madero has a few sights but the best reason to come here is for a leisurely stroll along the waterfront. You might want to enjoy a morning excursion to Puerto Madero, then cross the Puente de la Mujer to spend your afternoon in Centro.

TOP ATTRACTIONS

Colección de Arte Amalia Lacroze de Fortabat. The late Amalia Fortabat was a cement heiress, so it's not surprising that the building containing her private art collection is made mostly of concrete. It was completed in 2003, but after-effects from Argentina's 2001–02 financial crisis delayed its opening until 2008. Amalita (as she was known locally) was closely involved in the design, and her personal touch continues into the collection, which includes several portraits of her—a prized Warhol among them—and many works by her granddaughter, Amalia Amoedo. In general, more money than taste seems to have gone into the project. The highlights are lesser works by big names both local (Berni, Xul Solar, Pettoruti) and international (Brueghel, Dalí, Picasso), hung with little aplomb or explanation in a huge basement gallery that echoes like a high-school gym. The side gallery given over to Carlos Alonso's and Juan Carlos Castagnino's figurative work is a step in the right direction, however, and so are the luminous paintings by Soldi in the glass-walled upper gallery. They're rivaled by the view over the docks below—time your visit to end at sunset when pinks and oranges light the redbrick buildings opposite. The views from the dockside café are also excellent. ⊠ *Olga Cossettini 141, Puerto Madero* ☎ *11/4310–6600* ⊕ *www. coleccionfortabat.org.ar* 🖃 *80 pesos* ⊘ *Closed Mon.* Ⓜ *B to L.N. Alem (10 blocks away).*

WORTH NOTING

Buque Museo Fragata A.R.A. Presidente Sarmiento (*President Sarmiento Frigate Museum*). The navy commissioned this frigate from England in 1898, and meant for it to be used as an open-sea training vessel. The 280-foot boat used up to 33 sails and carried more than 300 crew members. The beautifully restored cabins include surprisingly luxurious officers' quarters with parquet floors, wood paneling, and leather armchairs; cadets had to make do with hammocks. ⊠ *Dique 3, Alicia M. de Justo 980, Puerto Madero* ☎ *11/4334–9386* ⊕ *www.ara.mil.ar/ pag.asp?idItem=112* 🖃 *10 pesos* Ⓜ *B to L.N. Alem (9 blocks away).*

Fodor's Choice

★

Puente de la Mujer. Tango dancers inspired the sweeping asymmetrical lines of Valencian architect Santiago Calatrava's design for the pedestrian-only Bridge of the Woman. Puerto Madero's street names pay homage to famous Argentine women, hence the bridge's name. (Ironically its most visible part—a soaring 128-foot arm—represents the man of a couple in mid-tango.) The $6-million structure was made in Spain and paid for by local businessmen Alberto L. González, one of the brains behind Puerto Madero's redevelopment; he was also for building the Hilton Hotel here. Twenty engines rotate the bridge to allow ships to pass through. ⊠ *Dique 3, between Pierina Dealessi and Manuela Gorriti, Puerto Madero* Ⓜ *A to Plaza de Mayo, B to L.N. Alem, D to Catedral, E to Bolívar (9 to 13 blocks away).*

Reserva Ecológica. Built over a landfill, the 865-acre Ecological Reserve is home to more than 500 species of birds and a variety of flora and fauna. On weekends thousands of porteños vie for a spot on the grass, so come midweek if you want to bird-watch, sunbathe, or use the jogging and cycling tracks in peace. A monthly guided "Walking under the Full Moon" tour in Spanish begins at 7:30 pm April through October and at 8:30 pm November through March. Even if you don't speak Spanish it's still a great way to get back to nature at night; otherwise avoid the area after sunset. (There are guided daytime visits in Spanish on weekends at 10:30 and 3:30.) The main entrance and visitor center is across from the traffic circle where Avenida Tristán Achával Rodríguez intersects with Avenida Elvira Rawson de Dellepiane, a short walk from the south end of Puerto Madero; you can also enter and leave the reserve at its northern end, across from the intersection of Mariquita Sánchez de Thompson and Avenida Hernán M. Giralt. ⊠ *Av. Tristán Achával Rodríguez 1550, Puerto Madero* ☎ *11/4315–4129, 11/4893–1853 tours* ⊕ *www.buenosaires.gob.ar/ciudadverde/espacios-verdes/reservaecologica* ☐ *Free* ⊗ *Closed Mon.*

SAN TELMO AND LA BOCA

"The south also exists," quip residents of the bohemian neighborhoods of San Telmo and La Boca, which historically played second fiddle to posher northern barrios. No more. The hottest designers have boutiques here, new restaurants are booked up, an art district is burgeoning, and property prices are soaring. The south is also a hotbed for the city's tango revival, appropriate given that the dance was born in these quarters.

SAN TELMO

San Telmo, Buenos Aires' first suburb, was originally inhabited by sailors, and takes its name from their wandering patron saint. All the same, the mariners' main preoccupations were clearly less than spiritual, and San Telmo became famous for its brothels.

That didn't stop the area's first experience of gentrification: wealthy local families built ornate homes here in the early 19th century, but ran for Recoleta when a yellow-fever epidemic struck in 1871. Newly arrived immigrants crammed into their abandoned mansions, known as *conventillos* (tenement houses). Today these same houses are fought

Getting Oriented

CENTRO
AV. DE MAYO
PIEDRAS
CATEDRAL
PERÚ
PLAZA DE MAYO
Av. de Mayo
BOLÍVAR
Adolfo Alsina
Moreno
BELGRANO
Av. Belgrano
Venezuela
SAN TELMO
México
Chile
INDEPENDENCIA
El Zanjón de los Granados
Av. Independencia
El Desnivel
Estados Unidos
Carlos Calvo
Bar El Federal
Plaza Dorrego
Humberto 1
Pasaje Defensa
Museo de Arte Contemporáneo de Buenos Aires
Av. San Juan
Museo de Arte Moderno de Buenos Aires (MAMBA)
Autopista 25 de Mayo
Cochabamba
Av. Juan de Garay
Museo Histórico Nacional
Av. Caseros
Parque Lezama
ESTACIÓN FERROVIARIA CONSTITUCIÓN
Playa de Maniobras
Aristóbulo del Valle
Pinzón
Brandsen
Suárez
Olavarría
Estadio Boca Juniors
Museo de la Pasión Boquense
La Perla
LA BOCA
Calle Museo Caminito
Caminito
Fundación Proa
Proa Café
Vuelta de Rocha

Puente de la Mujer
PUERTO MADERO
Dique 3
Reserva Ecológica
Azucena Villaflor
Marta Salotti
Petrona Eyle
Encarnación Ezcurra
Dique 2
Rosario Vera Peñaloza
Padre M. L. Mignone
Dique 1
Av. Brasil
Autopista La Plata - Buenos Aires
Av. Pedro Mendoza

KEY

✕	Quick bites
Ⓜ	Subte stops

1/4 mile

1/4 kilometer

San Telmo and La Boca

2

TOP EXPERIENCES

Descending: into El Zanjón de Granados's restored tunnels for a different perspective.

Drinking: in the atmosphere—and a cortado coffee—at a time-honored café like Bar El Federal or La Perla.

Watching: the sun set from Fundación Proa's roof café.

Wandering: Caminito (and adjacent Garibaldi and Magallanes), to tick the sightseeing boxes, or Defensa to cruise antiques stalls (on Sunday) and boutiques.

THE TERRITORY

San Telmo, south of the Centro, is bordered by Avenida Madero to the east, avenidas Brasil and Caseros to the south, Piedras to the west, and—depending on whom you ask—Chile or Belgrano to the north. The main drag is the north–south Defensa, part of which is pedestrian-only and forms one side of Plaza Dorrego, the area's tourist hub.

South of Avenida Brasil lies La Boca, whose westernmost edge is Avenida Patricios. The Riachuelo River forms a curving border; Avenida Don Pedro de Mendoza runs beside it.

GETTING AROUND

The subte takes you within about half a mile of San Telmo. The closest stations to the southern end are Independencia (Línea C or E) and San Juan (Línea C). Be prepared to walk nine blocks east along Avenidas Independencia, Estados Unidos, or San Juan to get to Defensa, the main street. To approach San Telmo from the north, get off at Bolívar (Línea E) or Catedral (Línea D) and walk eight blocks south along Bolívar. Bus Nos. 22, 24, 26, and 28 connect San Telmo to Centro. The same route by taxi costs 50–70 pesos.

There's no subte to La Boca, so taxi travel is a good bet, especially after dark: expect to pay 100–1300 pesos to or from the Centro. Bus No. 29 runs between La Boca and the Centro; so do Nos. 64 and 152, which continue to Palermo. Bus No. 53 connects La Boca and San Telmo.

SAFETY AND PRECAUTIONS

San Telmo's popularity with visitors has led to increased police presence in the busiest areas (especially near Defensa). Still, instances of petty crime are common. After dark, stick to busy, well-lighted streets close to Defensa.

La Boca is far sketchier, and you'd do best not to stray from the Caminito area. Avoid the neighborhood after dark; take radio taxis if you must visit then.

QUICK BITES

El Desnivel. At this classic *parrilla* (steak house) the trimmings don't go beyond a mixed salad and fries, and surly waiters are part of the experience. ✉ *Defensa 855, San Telmo* ☎ *11/4307–2489* ▭ *No credit cards* ☉ *Closed Mon. lunch* Ⓜ *C or E to Independencia.*

La Perla. This colorful old-time café is *the* place for a *licuado* (milk shake) or *tostado mixto* (a local *croque monsieur*). ✉ *Av. Pedro de Mendoza 1899, La Boca* ☎ *11/4301–2985* ▭ *No credit cards.*

Proa Café. Gorgeous port views await here along with fresh juices, smoothies, salads, and pastas. ✉ *Fundación Proa, Av. Pedro de Mendoza 1929, La Boca* ☎ *11/4104–1003* ▭ *No credit cards* ☉ *Closed Mon.*

over by foreign buyers dying to ride the wave of urban renewal—the *reciclaje* (recycling), as porteños call it—that's sweeping the area and transforming San Telmo into Buenos Aires' hippest 'hood.

Although San Telmo does have its share of sites, the barrio itself is the big attraction. Simply watching the world go by as you linger over coffee is one quintessential experience. Soaking up some history by wandering down cobbled streets edged with Italianate town houses is another. You can get closer to the past at two small museums, or even take a piece of it home from the shops and stands selling antiques and curios. However, there's plenty of contemporary culture on offer in the neighborhood's art museums, cutting-edge galleries, and bars.

PLANNING YOUR TIME

San Telmo thrives on Sunday, thanks to the art and antiques market in Plaza Dorrego. During the week a leisurely afternoon's visit is ideal. Start with lunch in a café at the northern or southern end of San Telmo, then spend an hour or two wandering the cobbled streets. You'll still have time for some shopping before winding up with a coffee or a drink.

TOP ATTRACTIONS

Fodor'sChoice ★ **El Zanjón de Granados.** All of Buenos Aires' history is packed into this unusual house. The street it's on was once a small river—the *zanjón*, or gorge, of the property's name—where the first, unsuccessful attempt to found Buenos Aires took place in 1536. When the property's current owner decided to develop it, he discovered all sorts of things below: pottery and cutlery, the foundations of past constructions, and a 500-foot network of tunnels that has taken over 25 years to excavate. With the help of historians and architects, they've now been restored, and the entire site has been transformed into a private museum. Excellent hour-long guided tours in English and Spanish take you through low-lighted sections of the tunnels. Expect few visitors and plenty of atmosphere on weekdays; cheaper, shorter tours on Sunday draw more people. ✉ *Defensa 755, San Telmo* ☎ *11/4361–3002* ⊕ *www.elzanjon.com.ar* 🎫 *Guided tours 250 pesos (1 hr, weekdays only); 200 pesos (30 min, Sun. only)* ⊗ *Closed Sat.* Ⓜ *C or E to Independencia.*

Museo de Arte Moderno de Buenos Aires (MAMBA) (*Museum of Modern Art of Buenos Aires*). Some 7,000 contemporary artworks make up the permanent collection at this block-long museum. Formerly the site of a tobacco company, the MAMBA retains its original exposed-brick facade and fabulous wooden doors with wrought-iron fixtures. Inside, galleries showcasing a carefully curated selection of paintings, sculptures, and new media are complemented by large temporary exhibitions of local or Latin American works as well as smaller installations. Recent highlights include the unusual portraits of superstar collective Grupo Mondongo, who eschew paint in favor of materials like crackers, sliced ham, and chewing gum. ✉ *Av. San Juan 350, San Telmo* ☎ *11/4342–3001* ⊕ *www.buenosaires.gob.ar/museoartemoderno* 🎫 *30 pesos, Tues. free* ⊗ *Closed Mon.* Ⓜ *C to San Juan.*

Pasaje Defensa. Wandering through this well-preserved house affords a glimpse of life in San Telmo's golden era. Behind an elegant but narrow stone facade, the building extends deep into the block, around a series of internal courtyards. This type of elongated construction—known as a *casa chorizo* or "sausage house"—is typical of San Telmo. Once the private residence of the well-to-do Ezeiza family, it became a *conventillo* (tenement), but is now a picturesque spot for antiques and curio shopping. ⊠ *Defensa 1179, San Telmo* Ⓜ *C to San Juan.*

Plaza Dorrego. During the week a handful of craftspeople and a few scruffy pigeons are the only ones enjoying the shade from the stately trees in the city's second-oldest square. Sunday couldn't be more different: scores of stalls selling antiques and collectibles move in to form the Feria de San Pedro Telmo (San Pedro Telmo Fair). Tango dancers take to the cobbles come late afternoon, as do hundreds of shoppers (mostly tourists) browsing the tango memorabilia, antique silver, brass, crystal, and Argentine curios. Note that prices are high at stalls on the square and astronomical in the shops surrounding it. ⚠ **Pickpockets work as hard as stall owners on Sundays, so keep a firm hold on bags and purses or—wiser still—leave them at home.** More affordable offerings—mostly handicrafts and local artists' work—are on the ever-growing web of stalls along Calle Defensa. ■ **TIP→ Look out for antique glass soda siphons that once adorned every bar top in Buenos Aires. Classic colors are green and turquoise.** Be sure to look up as you wander Plaza Dorrego, as the surrounding architecture provides an overview of the influences—Spanish colonial, French classical, and ornate Italian masonry—that shaped the city in the 19th and early 20th centuries. ⊠ *Defensa and Humberto I, San Telmo* Ⓜ *C to San Juan.*

WORTH NOTING

Museo de Arte Contemporáneo de Buenos Aires. Geometric abstraction is the guiding principle for both the collection and the construction of Buenos Aires' contemporary arts museum. Sharply sloped walkways connect four floors of concrete-walled galleries, creating an austere backdrop for the bright lines and shapes of local financier Aldo Rubin's private collection. Regularly changing exhibitions may include pieces by contemporary local stars like Pablo Siquier and Guillermo Kuitca. ⊠ *Av. San Juan 328, San Telmo* ☎ *11/5263–9988* ⊕ *www.macba.com. ar* 🖼 *70 pesos, Wed. 40 pesos* ⊘ *Closed Tues.* Ⓜ *C to San Juan.*

Museo Histórico Nacional. What better place for the National History Museum than overlooking the spot where the city was supposedly founded? Once owned by entrepreneur and horticulturalist Gregorio Lezama, the beautiful chestnut-and-white Italianate mansion that houses it also did duty as a quarantine station during the San Telmo cholera and yellow-fever epidemics before it became a museum in 1922. Personal possessions and thoughtful explanations (in Spanish) chronicle the rise and fall of Argentina's liberator José de San Martín. Other galleries celebrate the heroes of independence and foreign forces' unsuccessful attempts to invade Argentina. ⊠ *Calle Defensa 1600, San Telmo* ☎ *11/4300–7540* ⊕ *museohistoriconacional.cultura.gob.ar* ⊘ *Closed Mon. and Tues.* Ⓜ *C to Constitución (10 blocks).*

LA BOCA

Although La Boca is more touristy than San Telmo, it shares much of that neighborhood's gritty history. La Boca sits on the Riachuelo River, where rusting ships and warehouses remind you that this was once the city's main port. The immigrants who first settled here built their houses from corrugated metal and brightly colored paint left over from the shipyards. Today you'll see imitations of these vibrant buildings forming one of Buenos Aires' most emblematic sights, the Caminito.

The waterfront near the iconic Caminito area may be the most unashamedly touristy part of town, but the neighborhood surrounding it is the most fiercely traditional. Cafés, pubs, and general stores that once catered to passing sailors (and now reel in vacationers) dot the partially renovated area. For high-brow hipsters, the gallery of the Fundación Proa is the main draw.

What has also made La Boca famous internationally are the blue and gold of the Boca Juniors soccer team, whose massive home stadium is the barrio's unofficial hub. For many local soccer devotees, the towering Boca Juniors stadium makes La Boca the center of the known world.

PLANNING YOUR TIME

In La Boca, allow two or three hours to explore Caminito and visit a museum or two. It's busy all week, but expect extra crowds on weekends.

TOP ATTRACTIONS

Calle Museo Caminito. Cobblestones, tango dancers, and haphazardly constructed, colorful *conventillos* have made Calle Museo Caminito the darling of Buenos Aires' postcard manufacturers since this pedestrian street was created in 1959. Artists fill the block-long street with works depicting port life and the tango, said to have been born in La Boca. These days it's commercial, but it can make a fun outing if you embrace it. The name "Caminito" comes from a 1926 tango by Juan de Dios Filiberto. It was chosen by local artist Benito Quinquela Martín, who helped establish the street as an open-air museum.

Many tenements are now souvenir stores such as Centro Cultural de los Artistas (*Magallanes 861, Monday–Saturday 10:30–6*), where the uneven stairs hint at what a conventillo interior was like. Visit **Museo Conventillo de Marjan Grum** (*Garibaldi 1429, 50 pesos, 11/4302-2472, daily 10:30–5:30*), which the eponymous sculptor-owner has converted into an art gallery.

Painters peddle their creations from stalls along Caminito. Quality varies considerably; focus on the mosaics set into the walls, such as Luis Perlotti's *Santos Vega*. Brightly colored scrollwork known as *fileteado* adorns many store fronts; another highlight here are the tango dancers. Expect to be canvassed aggressively by rival restaurant owners touting overpriced menus near the start of Caminito. ⊠ *Caminito between Av. Pedro de Mendoza (La Vuelta de Rocha promenade) and Gregorio Aráoz de Lamadrid, La Boca* ⊡ *Free.*

Fundación Proa. This thoroughly modern art museum continues to nudge traditional La Boca into the present. Its facade alone reads like a manifesto of local urban renewal: part of the original 19th-century Italianate housefront has been cut away and huge plate-glass windows accented by unfinished steel stand alongside it. The space behind them now includes three adjacent properties. The luminous main gallery retains the building's original Corinthian-style steel columns, artfully rusted, but has sparkling white walls and polished concrete floors. With every flight of stairs you climb, views out over the harbor and cast-iron bridges get better. On the roof, an airy café serves salads, sandwiches, and cocktails. Grab one of the outdoor sofas around sunset and your photos will rival the work below. English versions of all exhibition information are available. The museum also runs guided tours in English, with two days' notice. ⊠ *Av. Pedro de Mendoza 1929, La Boca* ☎ *11/4104–1000* ⊕ *www.proa.org* ⊠ *80 pesos, free Tues.* ☉ *Closed Mon.*

Museo de la Pasión Boquense. Inside Estadio Boca Juniors (aka La Bombonera or "the candy box"), this modern, two-floor museum is heaven for *fútbol* fans. It chronicles Boca's rise from a neighborhood club in 1905 to its current position as one of the best teams in the world. Among the innovative exhibits is a giant soccer ball that plays 360-degree footage of an adrenaline-fueled match, recreating all the excitement (and the screaming) for those too faint-hearted to attend the real thing. A huge mural of Maradona (the team's most revered player), a hall of fame, jerseys, and trophies complete the circuit. For the full-blown experience, buy a combo ticket that includes museum entry plus an extensive tour of the beloved stadium. Lighthearted exhibits take you all over the stands as well as to press boxes, locker rooms, underground tunnels, and the emerald grass of the field itself. Everything you need to Boca up your life—from official team shirts to school folders—is available in the on-site gift store (shops outside La Bombonera sell cheaper copies). ⊠ *Brandsen 805, La Boca* ☎ *11/4362–1100* ⊕ *www.museoboquense. com* ⊠ *200 pesos, 260 pesos with stadium tour.*

RECOLETA AND ALMAGRO

For Buenos Aires' most illustrious families, Recoleta's boundaries are the borders of the civilized world. The local equivalents of the Vanderbilts are baptized and married in the Basílica del Pilar, throw parties in the Alvear Palace Hotel, live in spacious 19th-century apartments nearby, and wouldn't dream of shopping anywhere but avenidas Quintana and Alvear. Ornate mausoleums in the Cementerio de la Recoleta promise an equally stylish afterlife.

RECOLETA

Recoleta wasn't always synonymous with elegance. Colonists, including city founder Juan de Garay, farmed here. So did the Franciscan Recoleto friars, whose 1700s settlement inspired the district's name. Their church, the Basílica del Pilar, was almost on the riverbank then: tanneries grew up around it, and Recoleta became famous for its *pulperías* (taverns) and brothels. Everything changed, though, with the 1871 outbreak of yellow fever in the south of the city.

The elite swarmed to Recoleta, building the *palacios* and stately Parisian-style apartment buildings that are now the neighborhood's trademark. They also laid the foundations for Recoleta's concentration of

DID YOU KNOW?

Graffiti here can be political, whimsical, inspirational, or controversial, but it's technically always illegal. Popular targets like the Congreso building now sport graffiti-resistant paint for quick cleanup, reducing the incentive for *artistas*.

intellectual and cultural activity: the Biblioteca Nacional (National Library), a plethora of top-notch galleries, and three publicly run art museums are based here. Combine all of that with Recoleta's exclusive boutiques and its beautiful parks and squares—many filled with posh pooches and their walkers—and sightseeing becomes a visual feast. An unofficial subdistrict, Barrio Norte, is one step north of Recoleta proper and one small step down the social ladder. Shopping is the draw in Barrio Norte: local chains, sportswear flagships, and mini-malls of vintage clothing and clubwear line Avenida Santa Fe between 9 de Julio and Puerreydón.

PLANNING YOUR TIME

Despite the luxury around you, many of Recoleta's sights are free. Blitz through the main ones in half a day, or spend a full morning or afternoon in the cemetery or museums alone. Come midweek for quiet exploring, or on the weekend to do the cemetery and crafts market on Plaza Francia in one fell swoop.

TOP ATTRACTIONS

Fodor'sChoice **Cementerio de la Recoleta.** The ominous gates and labyrinthine paths of ★ the city's oldest cemetery, founded in 1822, is the final resting place for the nation's most illustrious figures. Covering 13½ acres and said to be the most expensive real estate in town, the cemetery has more than 6,400 elaborate vaulted tombs and majestic mausoleums, 70 of which have been declared historic monuments. Architectural styles run the gamut from chapels to Greek temples to pyramids to art deco and miniature mansions. The biggest name is Eva Duarte de Perón, after 17 years of posthumous wandering, found in the Duarte family vault. Other highlights include the tombs of landowner Dorrego Ortíz Basualdo, who resides in Recoleta's most monumental sepulcher, complete with chandelier, and Rufina Cambaceres, the girl who died twice. Entombed on her 19th birthday in 1902 she awoke inside her casket and clawed the top open, dying of a heart attack before she could be rescued. The names of many key players in Argentina's history are chiseled over other sumptuous mausoleums: Alvear, Quintana, Sáenz Peña, Lavalle, Sarmiento. There are guides for hire at the entrance or the administrative office can provide a free photocopied map if you wish to wander at your own pace. On weekends catch the open-air market known as La Feria de Artesanos de Plaza Francia outside the cemetery. It's usually teeming with shoppers eager to stock up on quality crafts. ⊠ *Junín 1760, Recoleta* ☎ *11/4803–1594* Ⓜ *H to Las Heras, 6 blocks.*

Floralis Genérica. The gleaming steel and aluminum petals of this giant flower look very space age, perhaps because they were commissioned from the Lockheed airplane factory by architect Eduardo Catalano, who designed and paid for the monument. The 66-foot-high structure opens at dawn and closes at dusk, when the setting sun turns its mirrored surfaces a glowing pink. The flower stands in the Plaza Naciones Unidas (behind El Museo Nacional de Bellas Artes over Avenida Figueroa Alcorta). ⊠ *Plaza Naciones Unidas at Av. Figueroa Alcorta and J.A. Biblioni, Recoleta.*

Getting Oriented

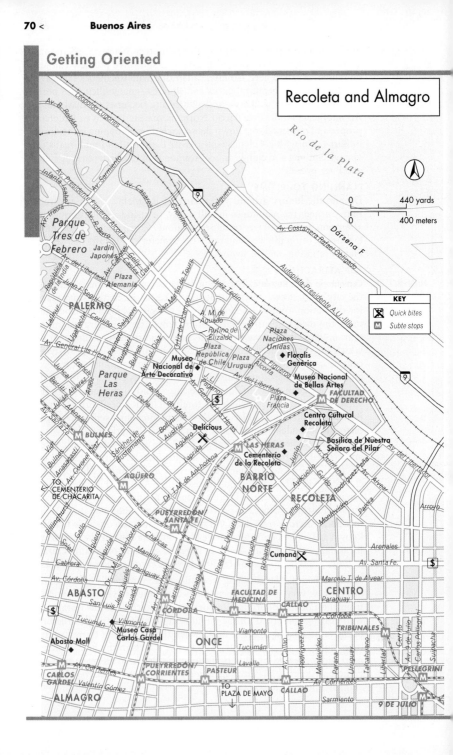

Recoleta and Almagro

Río de la Plata

KEY

✕ Quick bites

Ⓜ Subte stops

Parque Tres de Febrero

Jardín Japonés

Plaza Alemania

PALERMO

A. M. de Aguado

Rufino de Elizalde

Plaza República de Chile

Plaza Naciones Unidas

♦ Floralis Genérica

Museo Nacional de Arte Decorativo

Plaza Uruguay

Museo Nacional de Bellas Artes

Parque Las Heras

Plaza Francia

FACULTAD DE DERECHO

Delicious ✕

Centro Cultural Recoleta

Basílica de Nuestra Señora del Pilar

BULNES

LAS HERAS

Cementerio de la Recoleta

AGÜERO

BARRIO NORTE

RECOLETA

TO CEMENTERIO DE CHACARITA

PUEYRREDÓN/ SANTA FE

Arroyo

Cumaná ✕

Arenales

Av. Santa Fe

Av. Córdoba

ABASTO

FACULTAD DE MEDICINA

CALLAO

CENTRO

Marcelo T. de Alvear

Paraguay

CÓRDOBA

Museo Casa Carlos Gardel

ONCE

TRIBUNALES

Abasto Mall

CARLOS GARDEL

Valentín Gómez

PUEYRREDÓN/ CORRIENTES

PASTEUR

TO PLAZA DE MAYO ↓

Av. Corrientes

CALLAO

PELLEGRINI

ALMAGRO

Sarmiento

9 DE JULIO

THE TERRITORY

The Río de la Plata borders Recoleta to the north. Uruguay and Montevideo join to form the eastern border, and the jagged western edge is made up of Mario Bravo, Coronel Díaz, and Tagle. The area between Juncal and Córdoba—Recoleta's southern boundary—is known as Barrio Norte, whose main thoroughfare is Santa Fe. In Recoleta proper, avenidas Alvear and Quintana are the key streets.

Almagro is officially bordered by avenidas Córdoba and Estado de Israel to the north, Río de Janeiro to the west, Independencia to the south, and Sánchez de Bustamante and Gallo to the east. The Abasto subdistrict, which centers on Gallo and Corrientes, stretches a few blocks farther east into neighboring Balvanera.

GETTING AROUND

True to its elite roots, Recoleta has no subway, so taxis are your best option. Expect to pay around 70 pesos from downtown or 90 from Palermo. Bus Nos. 17 and 59 run to Recoleta from Palermo, San Telmo, and Centro; Nos. 92 and 108 connect Retiro and Recoleta, then continues to central Palermo and Almagro, and the west respectively.

Heavy traffic means Almagro is best reached by subte. Línea B runs along Avenida Corrientes through Almagro; Carlos Gardel station leads right into the Abasto mall. Bus No. 24 connects Almagro with Centro and San Telmo; No. 168 goes west down Avenida Córdoba past Palermo Viejo.

SAFETY AND PRECAUTIONS

Recoleta and Barrio Norte are relatively safe in the daytime, but stick to well-lighted streets at night. Bag snatching is opportunist rather than systemic here: keep a firm grip on your purse in the crowded weekend market and in busy restaurants. Although Almagro is on the upswing, many streets near the Abasto mall are still run-down. Wander with caution.

TOP EXPERIENCES

Seeking: unusual statues and elaborate mausoleums in Cementerio de la Recoleta.

Window-shopping: on Avenida Quintana for Argentine designs but buying more affordable ones on Avenida Santa Fe or in the Abasto mall.

Comparing: 19th-century Argentine and European art on the first floor of the Museo Nacional de Bellas Artes.

Wandering: Avenida Alvear for the gorgeous late 19th- and early 20th-century mansions.

QUICK BITES

Cumaná. The hearty stews, steaks, and empanadas at chaotic Cumaná are a far cry from Recoleta's European pretensions. Skip dessert, though (nearby ice-cream parlors are better). ✉ *Rodríguez Peña 1149, Barrio Norte* ☎ *11/4813–9207* 🚫 *No credit cards* Ⓜ *D to Callao.*

Delicious. It's a hard name to live up to, but there's no doubt this casual café pulls it off, with super fresh sandwiches, salads, and smoothies, which you can eat in or pack into your picnic basket. A shot of espresso and a slice of cheesecake provide the perfect dose of caffeine and sugar to get you back in the sightseeing saddle. ✉ *Laprida 2015, Recoleta* ☎ *11/4803–1151* 🚫 *No credit cards* ⊘ *Closed Mon.* Ⓜ *D to Agüero.*

Museo Nacional de Arte Decorativo. The harmonious, French neoclassical mansion that houses the National Museum of Decorative Art is as much a reason to visit as the period furnishings, porcelain, and silver within it. Ornate wooden paneling in the Regency ballroom, the imposing Louis XIV red-and-black-marble dining room, and a lofty Renaissance-style great hall are some of the highlights in the only home of its kind open to the public here. There are excellent English descriptions of each room, and they include gossipy details about the original inhabitants, the well-to-do Errázuriz-Alvear family. The museum also contains some Chinese art. Guided tours include the Zubov Collection of miniatures from Imperial Russia. ⊠ *Av. del Libertador 1902, Recoleta* ☎ *11/4801–8248* ⊕ *museoartedecorativo.cultura.gob.ar* 🖲 *25 pesos (suggested donation); guided tours in English 25 pesos* ☽ *Closed Mon.*

Fodor'sChoice ★ **Museo Nacional de Bellas Artes.** The world's largest collection of Argentine art is contained in this neoclassical wine-color building, which once housed the city's waterworks. Here, you can see many lesser works by big-name European artists from the 12th through 20th centuries, and the MNBA also hosts high-profile temporary exhibitions on its refurbished second floor. The European collection and 19th-century Argentine works are on display in the 24 ground-floor galleries; highlights include Cándido López's panoramic battle scenes, which he painted with his left hand after losing his right arm in the 1870s during the War of the Triple Alliance. His work spearheaded contemporary primitive painting and is showcased in Gallery 23. A whole room (Gallery 8) is given over to European master Goya's dark, disturbing works. The room behind the entrance hall (Gallery 10) contains Rodin sculptures. The right wing includes paintings by Manet, Degas, Monet, Pissarro, Gaugin, and Toulouse-Lautrec. The large modern pavilion behind the museum also hosts excellent temporary exhibitions, often showcasing top local artists little known outside Argentina. Free one-hour guided visits in English are offered on Tuesday, Thursday, and Friday at 12:30, and Saturday at 2. ⊠ *Av. del Libertador 1473, Recoleta* ☎ *11/5288–9900* ⊕ *www.mnba.gob.ar* ☽ *Closed Mon.* Ⓜ *H to Las Heras, 7 blocks.*

WORTH NOTING

Basílica de Nuestra Señora del Pilar. This basilica beside the famous Cementerio de la Recoleta is where Buenos Aires' elite families hold weddings and other ceremonies. Built by the Recoleto friars in 1732, it is a national treasure for its six German baroque–style altars. The central one is overlaid with Peruvian engraved silver; another, sent by Spain's King Carlos III, contains relics. The basilica's cloisters house the **Museo de los Claustros del Pilar** , a small museum that displays religious artifacts as well as pictures and photographs documenting Recoleta's evolution. There are excellent views of the cemetery from upstairs windows. ⊠ *Junín 1898, Recoleta* ☎ *11/4806–2209* ⊕ *www.basilicadelpilar.org.ar* ☽ *Museum closed Sun.* Ⓜ *H to Las Heras, 6 blocks.*

Centro Cultural Recoleta. Art exhibitions, concerts, fringe theater performances, and workshops are some of the offerings at this cultural center; one must-visit is Fuerza Bruta, a fantastic water and acrobatics collective that pops up in summer and for one-off shows. The rambling building it occupies was converted from the cloister patios of the

Cementerio de la Recoleta

Vicente López

Guido

Pueyrredón

Azcuénaga

Luis Ángel Firpo ◆

Roque
Sáenz Peña ◆

Juan Lavalle ◆

Vicente López

Evita ◆

Dorrego Ortiz
Basualde ◆

Domingo ◆
Faustino
Sarmiento

Rufina ◆
Cambaceres

Nuestra
Señora
de Pilar

Facundo Quiroga ◆
Carlos M. de Alvear ◆◆

Office   Capilla   Administration

Junín

ENTRANCE   Junín

Plaza Intendente
Torcuato de Alvear

Pres. Roberto M. Ortiz

Guido

Av. Alvear

Ayacucho

0   50 yards

0   50 meters

Franciscan monks. ✉ *Junín 1930, Recoleta* ☎ *11/4803–1040* ⊕ *www.centroculturalrecoleta.org* ⊗ *Closed Mon.* Ⓜ *H to Las Heras, 8 blocks.*

ALMAGRO

Almagro lies southwest of Recoleta but feels like a different world. Traditionally a gritty, working-class neighborhood, it spawned many tango greats, including the legendary Carlos Gardel. The Abasto subdistrict has long been the heart of the barrio: it centers on the massive art deco building (at Corrientes and Agüero) that was once the city's central market. The abandoned structure was completely overhauled and reopened in 1998 as a major mall, spearheading the redevelopment of the area, which now has several top hotels and an increasing number of restaurants and tango venues. More urban renewal is taking place a few blocks away at Sarmiento and Jean Jaurés, where the Konex Foundation has transformed an old factory into a cutting-edge cultural venue.

PLANNING YOUR TIME

In Almagro a couple of hours will suffice if you want to pay homage to Carlos Gardel—tango's greatest hero—and get a feel for the district.

TOP ATTRACTIONS

Museo Casa Carlos Gardel. Hard-core tango fans must visit the home of tango's greatest hero, Carlos Gardel. The front rooms of this once-crumbling *casa chorizo* (sausage house—that is, a long, narrow house) contain extensive displays of Gardel paraphernalia—LPs, photos, and old posters. The maestro's greatest hits play in the background. The back of the house has been restored with the aim of re-creating as closely as possible the way the house would have looked when Gardel and his mother lived here, right down to the placement of birdcages on the patio. Concise but informative texts in Spanish and English talk you through the rooms and the history of tango in general. Guided visits are available in Spanish weekdays at 1 and 4, and on weekends at 11, 3, and 5. English tours are usually available on request on weekdays. ✉ *Jean Jaurés 735, Almagro* ☎ *11/4964–2015* ⊕ *www.buenosaires.gob.ar/museocasacarlosgardel* 💲 *30 pesos; free Wed.* ⊗ *Closed Tues.* Ⓜ *B to Carlos Gardel.*

PALERMO

Trendy shops, bold restaurants, elegant embassies, acres of parks—Palermo really does have it all. Whether your idea of sightseeing is ticking off museums, flicking through clothing racks, licking your fingers after yet another long lunch, or kicking up a storm on the dance floor, Palermo can oblige. The city's largest barrio is subdivided into various unofficial districts, each with its own distinct flavor.

Some say Palermo takes its name from a 16th-century Italian immigrant who bought land here, others say it's named after the abbey honoring Saint Benedict of Palermo. Either way, the area was largely rural until the 1830s, when national governor Juan Manuel de Rosas built an estate in Palermo. After the dictatorial Rosas was overthrown, his property north of Avenida del Libertador was turned into a huge patchwork of parks. Known as Los Bosques de Palermo (the Palermo Woods), the green space provides a peaceful escape from the rush of downtown. The botanical gardens are at its southern end. High-brow culture is provided by the gleaming MALBA (Museo de Arte Latinoamericano de Buenos Aires, or the Museum of Latin American Art of Buenos Aires), whose clean stone lines stand out on Avenida Figueroa Alcorta. The streets around the intersection of avenidas Santa Fe and Coronel Díaz are home to mainstream clothing stores and the Alto Palermo mall, while more upscale alternatives abound in Palermo Viejo. Top boutiques—along with minimalist lofts, endless bars, and the most daring restaurants in town—have made Palermo Viejo (and its unofficial subdistrict, Palermo Soho) the epicenter of Buenos Aires' design revolution.

PLANNING YOUR TIME

Palermo is so big that it's best to tackle it in sections. An even-paced ramble through Parque Tres de Febrero should take no more than two hours, though you could easily spend an entire afternoon at the Japanese Garden and Botanical Garden. In architectural and geographic terms, Palermo Chico and the MALBA tie in nicely with a visit to Recoleta: allow at least a couple of hours for that.

TOP ATTRACTIONS

FAMILY **Jardín Japonés** (*Japanese Garden*). Like the bonsais in the nursery within it, this park is small but perfectly formed. A slow wander along the arched wooden bridges and walkways is guaranteed to calm frazzled sightseeing nerves. A variety of shrubs and flowers frame ornamental ponds that are filled with friendly koi carp—you can actually pet them if you feel so inclined (kids often do). The restaurant, where you can enjoy sushi, adzuki-bean sweets, and tea, overlooks the zen garden. ⊠ *Av. Casares at Av. Figueroa Alcorta, Palermo* ☎ *11/4804–4922* ⊕ *www. jardinjapones.org.ar* 🎟 *120 pesos.*

Fodor's Choice **MALBA.** Comprising works of 19th- and 20th-century Latin American
★ art collected by founder Eduardo Constantini, the fabulous Museum of Latin American Art of Buenos Aires (MALBA) is one of the cornerstones of the city's cultural life. Early works in the permanent collection reflect the European avant-garde experiences of artists such as Diego Rivera, Xul Solar, Roberto Matta, and Joaquín Torres García. These, in turn, gave rise to paintings like *Abaporu* (1928) by Tarsila do Amaral, a Brazilian involved in the "cannibalistic" Movimento Antropofágico. Geometric paintings and sculptures from the 1940s represent movements such as Arte Concreto, Constructivism, and Arte Madí. Argentina's undisputed modern master, Antonio Berni, is represented by a poptastic collage called *The Great Temptation* (1962) and the bizarre sculpture *Voracity or Ramona's Nightmare* (1964). Pieces by local greats Liliana Porter, Marta Minujín, Guillermo Kuitca, and Alejandro Kuropatwa form the end of the permanent collection. The MALBA also hosts world-class temporary exhibitions—recent examples include Yoko Ono and Jeff Koons—and two small basement galleries show art by cutting-edge Argentines. ⊠ *Av. Presidente Figueroa Alcorta 3415, Palermo* ☎ *11/4808–6500* ⊕ *www.malba.org.ar* 🎟 *120 pesos, Wed. half price* ⊙ *Closed Tues.* Ⓜ *D to Bulnes.*

Getting Oriented

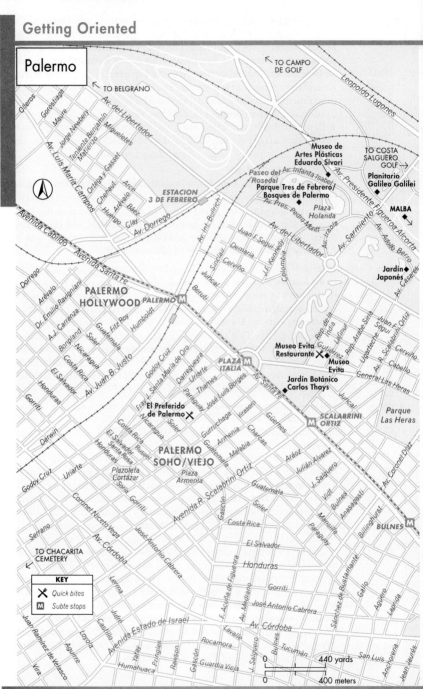

Palermo

TO CAMPO
DE GOLF

Leopoldo Lugones

TO BELGRANO

Olleros
Gorostiaga
Maure
Jorge Newbery
Tenante Benjamín Matienzo
Miguelettes
Av. del Libertador
Av. Luis María Campos
Ortega y Gasset
Arce
Cheñaut
Arévalo
Báez
Huelgo
Clay
ESTACION
3 DE FEBRERO
Av. Dorrego

Museo de
Artes Plásticas
Eduardo Sívori

TO COSTA
SALGUERO
GOLF

Av. Infanta Isabel
Paseo del
Rosedal
Parque Tres de Febrero/
Bosques de Palermo

Planitario
Galileo Galilei

Av. Presidente Figueroa Alcorta

Plaza
Holanda

MALBA

Av. Pres. Pedro Montt
Av. del Libertador
Av. Intl. Bullrich

Av. Iraola
Av. Sarmiento
Av. Adolfo Berro

Avenida Cabildo
Avenida Santa Fe

Juan F. Seguí
Demaría
Cervino
Sinclair
Juncal
Berutti

J. F. Kennedy
Colombia
Rep. de la India

Jardín
Japonés

Av. Casares

Dorrego
Arévalo
PALERMO
HOLLYWOOD
PALERMO M

Dr. Emilio Ravignani
A. J. Carranza
Bonpland
Guatemala
Fitz Roy
Humboldt
Soler
Nicaragua
Costa Rica
El Salvador
Av. Juan B. Justo
Honduras
Gorriti

Godoy Cruz
Fray J. Santa María de Oro
Darregueyra
Uriarte
Thames
Paraguay
José Luis Borges
PLAZA
ITALIA M
Av. Santa Fe

Latinur
Rep. Árabe Siria
Ugarteche

Juan F. Ortiz
Seguí
Scalabrini
Cervino
Cabello
General Las Heras

Museo Evita
Restaurante ✕
Museo
Evita

Jardín Botánico
Carlos Thays

Gutiérrez

Juncal

Parque
Las Heras

Darwin
El Preferido
de Palermo ✕
Nicaragua
Soler

Gorriti
Godoy Cruz
Uriarte
Costa Rica
El Salvador Russel
El Salvador
Santa Rosa
Honduras
Plazoleta
Cortázar
Soria

PALERMO
SOHO/VIEJO

Gurruchaga
Armenia
Guatemala
Malabia
Charcas
Thames

SCALABRINI
ORTIZ M

Aráoz
Julián Álvarez
J. Salguero
Vidt
Bulnes
Anasagasti
Billinghurst

Av. Coronel Díaz

BULNES M

Serrano
TO CHACARITA
CEMETERY

Av. Córdoba
José Antonio Cabrera
Coronel Niceto Vega
Av. Niceto Vega

Plaza
Armenia
Avenida R. Scalabrini Ortiz
Gascón
Costa Rica
Guatemala
Soler
El Salvador
Honduras
Gorriti
José Antonio Cabrera

Mansilla
Paraguay

Sánchez de Bustamante
Gallo
Agüero
Laprida

Juan Ramírez de Velasco
Aguirre
Vera
Lerma
Julián
Castillo
Loyola
Yatay
Av. Acuña de Figueroa
Av. Medrano
Avenida Estado de Israel
Pringles
Rawson
Gascón
Guardia Vieja
Humahuaca
Rocamora
Lavalle
J. Salguero
Av. Córdoba
Bulnes
Tucumán
San Luis
Anchorena
Jean Jaurès

0   440 yards
0   400 meters

THE TERRITORY

The city's biggest barrio stretches from Avenida Costanera R. Obligado, along the river, to Avenida Córdoba in the west. Its other boundaries are jagged, but include Avenida Coronel Díaz to the east and La Pampa and Dorrego to the north. Avenida Santa Fe cuts the neighborhood roughly in half. Palermo's green spaces and Palermo Chico lie east of it. To the north are Palermo Viejo and Palermo Hollywood, south and north of Avenida Juan B. Justo, respectively.

GETTING AROUND

Subte Línea D runs along Avenida Santa Fe, but doesn't always bring you to the doorstep of Palermo's attractions, so you may need to combine it with a taxi or some walking. Indeed, weekday traffic makes this combination a better idea than coming all the way from Centro by cab (which costs 130–160 pesos). Get off the subte at Bulnes or Scalabrini Ortíz for Palermo Chico; Plaza Italia for Palermo Viejo and the parks; and Ministro Carranza for Palermo Hollywood.

A more scenic route to Palermo Viejo and Hollywood from Centro is Bus No. 39 (Route 3, usually with a windshield sign "Palermo Viejo"). It takes 30 to 60 minutes, running along Honduras on the way to Palermo and along Gorriti on the way back. Bus No. 59 serves Palermo via Centro, San Telmo, and Recoleta. Nos. 29 and 64 link La Boca, San Telmo, and Centro with the northern end of Palermo; No. 152 connects La Boca and Palermo more directly.

SAFETY AND PRECAUTIONS

Pickpocketing is the biggest threat, especially on crowded streets on weekends. Palermo Viejo's cobbled streets aren't always well illuminated at night, so avoid walking along any that look lonely. Although locals usually hail cabs on the street, it's safer to ask a restaurant or bar to call one for you. The usual caveats about parks apply to the Palermo woods.

TOP EXPERIENCES

Appreciating: the early works in the permanent collection of the MALBA, featuring painters like Diego Rivera, Xul Solar, and Joaquín Torres García.

Exercising: your arms in Palermo Soho carrying bags on a boutique crawl.

Visiting: with Evita; understanding the phenomenon that she was by taking in the Museo Evita.

Wandering: on the winding paths of Parque Tres de Febrero to smell the roses, or along Honduras—east of Juan B. Justo for boutiques, west of it for bars and restaurants.

QUICK BITES

El Preferido de Palermo. Trends come and go, but nothing changes the tall Formica tables of 1960s-general-store-meets-snack-bar El Preferido de Palermo. A plate of cold cuts and pickles or basic (but delicious) sandwiches are the way to go. ⊠ *Jorge L. Borges 2108, Palermo Viejo* ☎ *11/4774–6585* ▭ *No credit cards* ⊗ *Closed Sun.* Ⓜ *D to Plaza Italia.*

Museo Evita Restaurante. The checkered floors and glossy black tables of Museo Evita Restaurante are as stylish as the great lady herself. Sticky and flaky, the *medialunas* here are some of the best in town. ⊠ *J.M. Gutiérrez 3926, Palermo Botánico* ☎ *11/4803–1617* ⊕ *www.museoevitaresto.com. ar* Ⓜ *D to Plaza Italia.*

Museo Evita. Eva Duarte de Perón, known as Evita, was the wife of populist president Juan Domingo Perón. Revered by working-class followers and despised by the Anglophile oligarchy, the Museo Evita shies from pop culture clichés and conveys facts about Evita's life and works. Exhibits include family photos that document Evita's humble origins, and mannequins wearing some of her fabulous designer outfits. The Evita myth can be baffling to the uninitiated but excellent guided visits shed light on the phenomenon and are available in English for groups of six or more, but must be arranged by phone in advance. Exhibits include 1952 film footage showing hundreds of thousands of mourners lined up to view their idol's body, family photos that document Evita's humble origins and time as a B-list actress, and a set of mannequins wearing some of her fabulous designer outfits. A video chronicles the fate of Evita's cadaver after dying of cancer at age 33: embalmed by Perón, stolen by political opponents, and moved and hidden for 17 years before being returned to Argentina, where it now rests in Recoleta Cemetery. Knowledgeable staffers are on hand to answer questions. The on-site restaurant is good for coffee or lunch, and there's also a small gift shop. ⊠ *Lafinur 2988, 1 block north of Av. Las Heras, Palermo* ☎ *11/4807–0306* ⊕ *web.museoevita.org.ar* 🖃 *90 pesos* ☉ *Closed Mon.* Ⓜ *D to Plaza Italia.*

FAMILY **Parque Tres de Febrero.** Known locally as Los Bosques de Palermo (Palermo Woods), this 400-acre green space is actually a crazy quilt of smaller parks. A stroll along the paths takes you through the Jardín de los Poetas (Poets' Garden), dotted with statues of literary figures, and to the enchanting **Patio Andaluz** (Andalusian Patio), where majolica tiles and Spanish mosaics sit under a vine-covered pergola. Near the lakes in the northwestern part, some 12,000 rosebushes (more than 1,000 different species) bloom seasonally in the **Paseo del Rosedal.**

You can jog or rent bikes, in-line skates, and pedal boats. The park gets crowded on sunny weekends, as this is where families come to play and have picnics. If you like the idea of the latter, take advantage of the street vendors who sell refreshments and *choripán* (chorizo sausage in a bread roll) within the park. There are also several posh cafés lining the Paseo de la Infanta (running from Libertador toward Sarmiento in the park). ⊠ *Bounded by Avs. del Libertador, Sarmiento, Leopoldo Lugones, and Dorrego, Palermo* Ⓜ *D to Plaza Italia.*

WORTH NOTING

FAMILY
Fodor'sChoice
★
Jardín Botánico Carlos Thays. Wedged between three busy Palermo streets, this unexpected haven has 18 acres of gardens filled with 5,500 varieties of exotic and indigenous flora. Different sections re-create the environments of Asia, Africa, Oceania, Europe, and the Americas. An organic vegetable garden aims to teach children healthy eating habits, and winding paths lead to hidden statues and a brook. The central area contains an exposed-brick botanical school and library, plus a beautiful greenhouse brought from France in 1900 but unfortunately not open to the public. ⊠ *Av. Santa Fe 3951, Palermo* ☎ *11/4831–4527* ⊕ *www.buenosaires.gob.ar/ambienteyespaciopublico/mantenimiento/espacios-verdes/jardinbotanico* ☉ *Closed Mon.* Ⓜ *D to Plaza Italia.*

Museo de Artes Plásticas Eduardo Sívori (*Eduardo Sívori Art Museum*). If you're looking for a respite from the sun or sports in Parque Tres de Febrero, check out this sedate museum. Focused on 19th- and 20th-century Argentine art, the collection includes paintings by local masters like Emilio Petorutti, Lino Eneo Spilimbergo, Antonio Berni, and the museum's namesake Sívori. The shaded sculpture garden is the perfect combination of art and park. ⊠ *Av. Infanta Isabel 555, Palermo* ☎ *11/4774–9452* ⊕ *museos.buenosaires.gob.ar/sivori.htm* 🗹 *30 pesos, free Wed.* ⊙ *Closed Mon.* Ⓜ *D to Plaza Italia.*

Planetario Galileo Galilei (*Galileo Galilei Planetarium*). One of the city's most iconic buildings, the Planetario Galileo Galilei is a great orb positioned on a massive concrete tripod in the middle of Palermo's Parque Tres de Febrero. Built in the early 1960s, it looks like something out of *Close Encounters of the Third Kind*—especially at night, when the dome glows with eerie blue and red lighting. Tickets for the twice-daily sky shows (five times on weekends), narrated in Spanish, go on sale at 9:30 am Tuesday through Friday and at noon on weekends; note that they usually sell out fast. Three meteorites that landed in northern Argentina 4,000 years ago guard the entrance. The nearby pond with swans, geese, and ducks—also lit up at night—is always a hit with kids. ⊠ *Avs. Sarmiento and Figueroa Alcorta, Palermo* ☎ *11/4771–6629* ⊕ *www.planetario.gob.ar* 🗹 *120 pesos* Ⓜ *D to Plaza Italia.*

WHERE TO EAT

Visitors may flock to Buenos Aires for the steak and Malbec, but the food scene goes far beyond those two attractions. Over the past decade, the city has burst onto the international food scene with gusto.

Three things have come together to create a truly modern cuisine: diverse cultural influences, high culinary aspirations, and a relentless devotion to aesthetics, from plate garnishes to room decor. Tradition dictates late dining, and the majority of restaurants don't open until 8 or 9 pm for dinner and don't get busy until after 10. Dinner is a leisurely affair, and the *sobremesa*, or after-dinner chat over coffee or digestifs, is nearly obligatory. Rushing from the table is frowned on—anyway, where would you go? Bars and clubs often don't open until well after midnight.

The core of the population is of Italian and Spanish heritage, and pizza, pasta, paella, and *puchero* (beef boil) are as common as the *parrilla* (steak house). Argentines have taken the classics and made them their own with different techniques and ingredients, but they're still recognizable to the international traveler. Pizzas and empanadas are the favored local snack food, the former piled high with cheese, the latter typically filled with beef or chicken. And while steak is indisputably king in this town, it has competition in tender Patagonian lamb, game meats, fish, and shellfish. In contrast to much of Latin America, Argentine cuisine is not known for its spice, and *picante* dishes are not common except in the northwest of the country.

Cafés are also an important part of the culture, and locals will stop in at their favorite for a *cafecito* at least once a day, not only to knock back a little caffeine, but also to see friends and catch up on the latest news and gossip.

Use the coordinate (✛ 2:C5) at the end of each listing to locate a site on the corresponding Where to Eat and Stay map.

WHAT IT COSTS (IN ARGENTINE PESOS)			
	$	$$	$$$	$$$$
Restaurants	Under 180 pesos	180 pesos–250 pesos	251 pesos–350 pesos	over 350 pesos

Restaurant prices are the average cost of a main course at dinner or, if dinner is not served, at lunch.

CENTRO

The area around Centro has something for everyone, from traditional to trendy. At lunchtime, the city's bustling downtown is the place where business deals are negotiated over leisurely lunches of steak, potatoes, salad, and wine; a younger crowd heads for the array of burger joints that have sprouted up. In the evening the neighborhood gets quiet except for the pedestrian strip along Avenida Reconquista, which is jammed with bars and restaurants.

$$ ✕ **Café Tortoni.** Take a seat amid the Tiffany lamps and marble-topped
CAFÉ tables, and contemplate the fact that you may be sitting in a chair once occupied by a former president, a renowned tango singer, or a world-famous artist or writer while they nibbled an exquisite pastry. The place and setting are from another age, thankfully well preserved, but you may have to wait for a table. **Known for:** tango; blast from the past; submarino (hot chocolate) and churros. ⑤ *Average main: 200 pesos* ⊠ *Av. de Mayo 825, at Piedras, Centro* ☎ *11/4342–4328* ⊕ *www. cafetortoni.com.ar* Ⓜ *A to Perú* ✛ *1:D4.*

$$ ✕ **Dadá.** An intimate and artsy setting are the backdrop for a short but
ECLECTIC creative menu, which includes house specialties like phyllo-wrapped Morbier cheese salad as a starter and the perfectly cooked *ojo de bife* (rib-eye steak). Relax, enjoy a glass of wine, read the paper, and eat well. **Known for:** classy bistro fare; intimate setting; buzzy. ⑤ *Average main: 220 pesos* ⊠ *San Martín 941, Retiro* ☎ *11/4314–4787* ⊘ *Closed Sun.* Ⓜ *C to San Martín* ✛ *1:D3.*

$$ ✕ **El Cuartito.** This iconic pizza parlor is frequented by porteños who
PIZZA worship the pies topped with fresh tomato sauce and a mile-high pile
Fodor's Choice of oozing mozzarella. Every square inch of wall space is dedicated to
★ memorabilia of sports legends, musicians, tango dancers, and actors, and every local has their cherished dining spot. **Known for:** old-school atmosphere; pizza; frequented by locals. ⑤ *Average main: 200 pesos* ⊠ *Talcahuano 937, Centro* ☎ *11/4816–1758* ⊟ *No credit cards* ⊘ *Closed Mon.* Ⓜ *D to Tribunales* ✛ *1:C3.*

COFFEE IN BUENOS AIRES

Coffee is taken seriously in Argentina. A morning and evening caffeine jolt gets many porteños through their long days and nights. Here's how to order it:

Café: Same as an American espresso

Café con leche: Half coffee and half milk, served in a larger cup

Cortado: A café topped or "cut" with hot foamy milk

Filtro: Brewed coffee

Lágrima: Hot foamy milk with a "tear drop" of coffee

Ristretto: A small, strong shot of espresso

Submarino: A tall glass of hot milk served with a chocolate bar submerged in the milk (aka hot chocolate)

Unless you specify otherwise, your café will be served in a short espresso glass. If you want a larger coffee, order en *jarrito*, or medium. If you want an American-size coffee, order a *doble*, or double espresso.

$$
ITALIAN
✕ **Filo.** Crowded and lively, particularly at lunch, Filo is the place for pasta and wood-oven pizza in the downtown area. The Neapolitan-style pies with thin, charred crusts are among the best in the city. **Known for:** cheap and cheerful; Italian fare; busy. $ *Average main: 200 pesos* ⊠ *San Martín 975, between Alvear and Paraguay, Retiro* ☎ *11/4311–1871* ⊕ *www.filo-ristorante.com* Ⓜ *C to San Martín* ✛ *1:D3.*

$$$
WINE BAR
✕ **Gran Bar Danzón.** The city's longest established wine bar is a dimly lit lounge that attracts the local wine-geek set as well as cocktail aficionados. They serve some of the best lounge food in town, including great sushi (don't miss the crispy prawn rolls), appetizers such as ceviche, and a great selection of wines by the glass. **Known for:** loungey ambience; great wine list; attracts a cool crowd. $ *Average main: 280 pesos* ⊠ *Libertad 1161, 2nd fl., Retiro* ☎ *11/4811–1108* ⊕ *www.granbardanzon. com.ar* ⊘ *No lunch* Ⓜ *C to San Martín* ✛ *1:C2.*

$$$
ARGENTINE
✕ **Sabot.** A classic landmark for more than 40 years, this lunch-only spot where behind-the-scenes negotiations take place over French-influenced local fare. The *centolla* (king crab) or *langostino* (prawn) salad is a throwback to another age, but it's perfectly prepared. **Known for:** business lunch crowd; French cuisine; semolina gnocchi. $ *Average main: 280 pesos* ⊠ *25 de Mayo 756, between Córdoba and Viamonte, Centro* ☎ *11/4313–6587* ⊘ *Closed weekends. No dinner* Ⓜ *B to L.N. Alem* ✛ *1:E3.*

$$$$
ARGENTINE
Fodor's Choice
★
✕ **Tomo I.** One of the city's more sophisticated dining rooms, Tomo I is a bastion of modern French-Argentine cooking. Dishes lean towards less-is-more, and truly shine with updated versions of classic French dishes, like kid with broad beans. **Known for:** sophisticated; ideal for business meetings; upscale service. $ *Average main: 450 pesos* ⊠ *Hotel Panamericano, Carlos Pellegrini 521, Centro* ☎ *11/4326–6695* ⊕ *www. tomo1.com.ar* ⊘ *Closed Sun. No lunch Sat.* Ⓜ *B to Carlos Pellegrini, D to 9 de Julio* ✛ *1:C3.*

PUERTO MADERO

A magnet for tourists, Puerto Madero's restaurants charge amounts that would make restaurant owners in other parts of the city blush with shame. Unless you're on an expense account, the food is generally far better and far less expensive elsewhere. The riverside views are always appealing, though.

$$$$
STEAKHOUSE

✕ **Cabaña Las Lilas.** The beef and pork are sourced from the owner's own ranch at this well-known—and expensive—steak house that attracts a crowd of mostly international travelers to the docklands. Service is impeccable, as are the steaks; of note are the *ojo de bife* and *bife de lomo,* aka the rib eye and the sirloin. **Known for:** tender beef; impeccable service; fantastic wine list. $ *Average main: 600 pesos* ⊠ *A.M. de Justo 516, at Corrientes, Puerto Madero* ☎ *11/4313–1336* ⊕ *www. restaurantlaslilas.com.ar* Ⓜ *B to L.N. Alem* ✛ *1:E3.*

$$$$
ARGENTINE

✕ **Chila.** With a prime harborside location and a carefully curated tasting menu, Chila is worth the splurge. Book a table on the water and allow the exemplary team (helmed by one of Argentina's brightest young culinary stars, Pedro Bargero), work its magic. **Known for:** fine-dining tasting menu; great wine list; upscale service. $ *Average main: 2000 pesos* ⊠ *Av. Alicia Moreau de Justo 1160, Puerto Madero* ☎ *11/4343–6067* ⊕ *www.chilaweb.com.ar* ☾ *Closed Sun. and Mon.* Ⓜ *B to L.N. Alem (10 blocks)* ✛ *1:E5.*

SAN TELMO

San Telmo has an artsy, bohemian vibe and there are plenty of inexpensive dining spots. There are some true gems among the mix and be sure to check out the indoor Mercado de San Telmo for great coffee, Vietnamese food, and handmade burgers.

$
CAFÉ

✕ **Bar Plaza Dorrego.** This atmospheric corner building with greenery tumbling over wrought-iron balconies has the best view of Plaza Dorrego. It's busy any time of day so stop by for coffee and a pastry or a beer and a dish of peanuts, then sit back and people-watch. $ *Average main: 140 pesos* ⊠ *Defensa 1098, at Humberto I, on Plaza Dorrego, San Telmo* ☎ *11/4361–0141* ▭ *No credit cards* Ⓜ *C or E to Independencia* ✛ *1:E6.*

$$$
BRASSERIE

✕ **Brasserie Petanque.** One of the few classic French brasseries in Buenos Aires, Petanque is a place to enjoy hearty French fare accompanied by local wines. The ambience is lively, with marble-topped tables so close to each other that you may find yourself participating in neighboring conversations, though service can be snooty. **Known for:** bistro fare; quality wine list; lunchtime specials. $ *Average main: 350 pesos* ⊠ *Defensa 596, at Mexico, San Telmo* ☎ *11/4342–7930* ⊕ *www.brasseriepetanque.com* ☾ *Closed Mon.* Ⓜ *E to Bolivar* ✛ *1:D5.*

$$
STEAKHOUSE
FAMILY

✕ **Desnivel.** Don't expect any frills here, just great steaks, and side dishes such as the *papas fritas provençal,* golden french fries tossed in fresh parsley and garlic. Take a table in the cavernous dining room, or grab something to go—steak sandwiches and empanadas fly out the door as fast as they can make them. **Known for:** casual ambience; large portions; cheap and cheerful. $ *Average main: 190 pesos* ⊠ *Defensa 855,* *at Giuffra, San Telmo* ☎ *11/4307–2489* ▭ *No credit cards* ⊘ *No lunch Mon.* Ⓜ *E to Independencia* ✛ *1:D6.*

LA BOCA

La Boca was the dock and warehouse district, and much of that is still in evidence—meaning the area can be dicey so you should always take a taxi in and out after dark.

$$$
STEAKHOUSE

✕ **El Obrero.** Big, juicy steaks that are perfectly cooked, massive helpings of side dishes, and more ambience than you can shake a stick at make El Obrero a movie director's dream of an Argentine steak house. The neighborhood is iffy, particularly at night—take a taxi to and from (they'll call one for you). **Known for:** authentic-style canteen; abundant portions; friendly service. ⑤ *Average main: 280 pesos* ✉ *Augustín R. Caffarena 64, at Don Pedro Mendoza, La Boca* ☎ *11/4362–9912* ▭ *No credit cards* ⊘ *Closed Sun.* ✛ *1:F6.*

RECOLETA

Arguably Buenos Aires' poshest neighborhood, Recoleta is the epicenter for high-end shopping, museum-going, and white-tablecloth dining. It's home to most of the swankier hotels, many with excellent restaurants, but there are also a number of classic spots that have been serving high-quality fare for decades.

$$
ARGENTINE

✕ **BIS.** A romantic bistro located down a secluded Recoleta lane, chef Gonzalo Aramburu's BIS deals in classy comfort food with contemporary twists. Expect dishes such as rabbit terrine, wood-grilled octopus, and a steak tartare that comes with mustard ice cream. **Known for:** efficient service; great wine list; excellent brunch. ⑤ *Average main: 250 pesos* ✉ *Vicente López 1661, local 12, Recoleta* ☎ *11/4813–5900* ⊕ *www.aramburubis.com.ar* ⊘ *Closed Sun. dinner* Ⓜ *C to Retiro* ✛ *2:H5.*

$$
AMERICAN
Fodor'sChoice
★

✕ **Buller Brewing Company.** The city's first microbrewery is in a prime position opposite Recoleta Cemetery, and it's a prince among frogs in a saturated craft beer market. There are seven different styles of beer (the Porter is highly recommended), and you can have a sampler of the whole range. **Known for:** craft beer; pub grub; happy hour. ⑤ *Average main: 180 pesos* ✉ *Junín 1747, Recoleta* ☎ *11/4806–0556* ⊕ *www.bullerpub.com* Ⓜ *H to Las Heras* ✛ *1:B1.*

$$$$
MODERN
ARGENTINE

✕ **Duhau Restaurante & Vinoteca.** An oasis of elegance and grace in the heart of Recoleta, French cooking techniques dominate this kitchen, though the seafood and meat are sourced from South American destinations such as Patagonia. Standout dishes include butter-soft Angus tenderloin, crispy sweetbreads, and a decadent molten chocolate cake. **Known for:** sophisticated ambience; great wine list; white-tablecloth service. ⑤ *Average main: 500 pesos* ✉ *Park Hyatt Palacio Duhau, Av. Alvear 1661, at Montevideo, Recoleta* ☎ *11/5171–1340* ⊕ *www.hyatt.com/en-US/hotel/argentina/palacio-duhau-park-buenos-aires/bueph/dining* ⊘ *No lunch* Ⓜ *C to Retiro* ✛ *1:C1.*

$
ARGENTINE
Fodor'sChoice
★

✕ **El Sanjuanino.** It may be cramped, crowded, and kitschy—and very warm in hot weather due to the roaring wood-fired ovens—but the empanadas are delicious and they serve the city's best *locro* (corn, squash, and meat stew) as well as delicious and iconic game dishes. Ignore the wine list and opt for the house *vino* served in pitchers, which is just as good and half the price. **Known for:** laid-back ambience; solid fare from the north; cheap and cheerful. ⑤ *Average main: 130 pesos* ✉ *Posadas 1515, at Callao, Recoleta* ☎ *11/4804–2909* ⊕ *www.elsanjuanino.com.ar* Ⓜ *C to Retiro* ⊹ *1:C1.*

$$$
ARGENTINE

✕ **La Biela.** A blast from the past, this traditional café is one of the best spots in Recoleta for people-watching and celebrity-spotting. For the most part, it's a place to linger over coffee and a pastry, or perhaps a savory sandwich at midday, but there's also a full menu of local specialties. **Known for:** old-school vibe; teatime crowd; outdoor dining. ⑤ *Average main: 280 pesos* ✉ *Quintana 600, at Junín, Recoleta* ☎ *11/4804–0449* ⊕ *www.labiela.com* Ⓜ *H to Las Heras* ⊹ *1:B1.*

$$$$
FRENCH

✕ **La Bourgogne.** This elegant dining room in the Alvear Palace Hotel turns out brilliant French classics from chef Jean-Paul Bondeaux, updated for modern sensibilities. Service is impeccable, and the best value is the seven-course tasting menu that includes six wines. **Known for:** sophisticated ambience; French fare; excellent service. ⑤ *Average main: 600 pesos* ✉ *Alvear Palace Hotel, Ayacucho 2023, at Alvear, Recoleta* ☎ *11/4805–3857* ⊕ *www.alvearpalace.com/en/restaurants-bars/la-bourgogne-restaurant/* ☉ *Closed Sun. No lunch* Ⓜ *H to Las Heras* ⊹ *1:B1.*

$$
ITALIAN
FAMILY

✕ **La Parolaccia Trattoria.** A family-run and family-friendly Italian eatery of the sort you might find in any big city, La Parolaccia stands out for its excellent homemade pastas—particularly good are the hand-rolled fusilli. And don't overlook the three-course lunch specials, which can be a great deal. ⑤ *Average main: 250 pesos* ✉ *Riobamba 1046, Recoleta* ☎ *11/4812–1053* ⊕ *www.laparolaccia.com* Ⓜ *C to Congreso, B to Callao* ⊹ *1:B4.*

$$$$
SEAFOOD
Fodor'sChoice
★

✕ **Oviedo.** In a meat-centric city like Buenos Aires, excellently cooked seafood is a welcome change, and Oviedo turns out beautifully plated fillets of fish—don't miss the daily catch with pickled baby vegetables or the pristine shellfish. Top it all off with wine from the city's finest cellar and you're in for a memorable lunch or dinner. **Known for:** great wine list; knowledgeable service; sophisticated ambience. ⑤ *Average main: 400 pesos* ✉ *Beruti 2602, at Ecuador, Recoleta* ☎ *11/4821–3741* ⊕ *www.oviedoresto.com.ar* ☉ *Closed Sun. dinner* Ⓜ *D to Pueyrredón* ⊹ *1:A2.*

$$$
MODERN
ARGENTINE
Fodor'sChoice
★

✕ **Restó SCA.** A haunt for foodies who adore the creative, contemporary Argentine cuisine and beautiful presentation, there's nowhere better in the neighborhood for lunch or an atmospheric dinner. The star of the lineup is the roasted, stuffed whole quail with squash. **Known for:** romantic; low key; great wine list. ⑤ *Average main: 350 pesos* ✉ *Sociedad Central de Arquitectos, Montevideo 938, between M.T. Alvear and Paraguay, Recoleta* ☎ *11/4816–6711* ☉ *No dinner Mon.–Wed. No lunch Sat.* Ⓜ *D to Callao* ⊹ *1:B3.*

$$$ ✕ **Roux.** French techniques applied to Argentine ingredients, accompa-
ARGENTINE nied by efficient service, make this cozy corner bistro a fantastic spot
for relaxed business lunches or special occasions. Try the Patagonian
king crab ravioli or perfectly cooked venison steak, paired with a recom-
mendation from the sommelier. **Known for:** great seafood; intimate set-
ting; great wine list. $ *Average main: 350 pesos* ✉ *Peña 2300, Recoleta*
☎ *11/4805–6794* ⊕ *www.rouxresto.com* ⊘ *Closed Sun. and Mon.* Ⓜ *H
to Las Heras* ✛ *2:G4.*

PALERMO

The city's largest neighborhood, Palermo offers something for every
taste, style, and budget. It's the city's undisputed culinary hot spot, with
enclaves that have their own distinct styles and vibes. If you want the
tastiest, most cutting-edge, most traditional, most ethnic, most daring,
and most fashionable food in Buenos Aires, then head to Palermo. It's
that simple.

$ ✕ **Chori.** This bright yellow corner shop has given the humble sau-
ARGENTINE sage sandwich called choripán a radical and much-needed makeover,
Fodor'sChoice turning it from basic street food to a sleek fast-food meal. All the
★ chorizos that are the base of the sandwich—from lamb to mushroom
and even fish—are produced in house, and there are side dishes like
sweet potato fries as well as beer, wine and cocktails. **Known for:**
upmarket street food; sausage specialist; budget-friendly. $ *Average
main: 130 pesos* ✉ *Thames 1653, Palermo Soho* ☎ *11/3966–9857*
Ⓜ *D to Plaza Italia* ✛ *2:B4.*

$$$ ✕ **Don Julio.** One of Buenos Aires' top steak houses features cowhide
STEAKHOUSE tablecloths, wagon-wheel lighting fixtures, an indoor grill, and rows of
Fodor'sChoice empty wine bottles signed by satisfied customers. A mix of locals and
★ expats packs the place at lunch and dinner to feast on the fantastic *ojo
de bife* (rib eye) and *cuadril* (rump). **Known for:** tender rib eye; excellent
attention and service; fantastic wine list. $ *Average main: 300 pesos*
✉ *Guatemala 4691, at Gurruchaga, Palermo Soho* ☎ *11/4831–9564*
⊕ *www.parrilladonjulio.com* Ⓜ *D to Plaza Italia* ✛ *2:C4.*

$$$$ ✕ **La Cabrera.** Huge slabs of meat for sharing are cooked to perfection
STEAKHOUSE at this classic parrilla, and they're always accompanied by a variety
of small side dishes, so there's little need to order anything other than
french fries, though *provoletas* (gooey, slightly crispy grilled cheese
slabs) are a must to start. The same menu is served down the block at
La Cabrera Norte, at 5127 Cabrera, which opened to handle the over-
flow. **Known for:** casual ambience; friendly service; happy hour 6:30
to 8. $ *Average main: 400 pesos* ✉ *Cabrera 5099, at Thames, Palermo
Soho* ☎ *11/4832–5754* ⊕ *www.lacabrera.com.ar* Ⓜ *D to Plaza Italia,
10 blocks* ✛ *2:B5.*

$$$ ✕ **Las Pizarras.** The chalkboard-covered walls *(las pizarras)* at this
ECLECTIC appealing spot list the market-driven menu of a dozen or so creative
Fodor'sChoice dishes. The wine list is equally intriguing. **Known for:** relaxed ambience;
★ classy bistro fare; great wine list. $ *Average main: 300 pesos* ✉ *Thames
2296, at Charcas, Palermo* ☎ *11/4775–0625* ⊕ *www.laspizarrasbistro.
com* ⊘ *Closed Mon. No lunch* Ⓜ *D to Plaza Italia* ✛ *2:C4.*

$$$$
ISRAELI
Fodor'sChoice
★
×**Mishiguene.** The first purveyor of contemporary Jewish cuisine in the city, Mishiguene brings classic Middle Eastern, Polish, and Russian dishes such as baba ghanoush, varenikes, pastrami, and borscht up-to-date. Vibrant Klezmer music, efficient service, and a party atmosphere add to the reason why these are some of the hottest tables around. **Known for:** innovative concept; classic dishes brought up-to-date; fun ambience. $ *Average main: 400 pesos* ⊠ *Lafinur 3368, Palermo Botánico* ☎ *11/3969–0764* ⊕ *www.mishiguene.com* ☉ *Closed Sun. dinner* Ⓜ *D to Plaza Italia* ✛ *2:E3.*

$$$$
JAPANESE
FUSION
×**Osaka.** A bamboo facade gives way to a slick setting with plenty of black lacquer, creating a sleek ambience for Buenos Aires' first modern Japanese-Peruvian fusion spot. The sushi is excellent, though pricey, and the service is spot-on, particularly at the gleaming sushi bar. **Known for:** fusion cuisine; great cocktails; smart clientele. $ *Average main: 385 pesos* ⊠ *Soler 5608, at Fitz Roy, Palermo* ☎ *11/4775–6964* ⊕ *www. osaka.com.pe* Ⓜ *D to Palermo* ✛ *2:B3.*

$$$$
STEAKHOUSE
×**Río Alba.** This venerable steak house has waiters in bow ties and vests who maneuver around the farmhouse-style dining room, serving flavorful, tender cuts of meat including *entraña* (hanger steak) and *matambrito* (pork flank). Although the menu appears pricey, portions are massive, and they know it: the steaks are set atop small hibachis to keep them hot. **Known for:** casual ambience; friendly service; abundant portions. $ *Average main: 400 pesos* ⊠ *Cerviño 4499, at Fray J.S. de Oro, Palermo* ☎ *11/4773–5748* Ⓜ *D to Plaza Italia* ✛ *2:D3.*

$$$
PIZZA
×**Siamo nel Forno.** After spending a year studying traditional techniques in Naples, *pizzero* Néstor Gattorna imported a wood-burning oven, specially milled flour, and extra-virgin olive oil to reproduce the best Neapolitan-style pizza. Italophiles looking for an alternative to pizza *porteña* piled up with cheese jam into the place for his smoky, perfectly charred pies and equally good calzones. **Known for:** casual ambience; fast turnaround; traditional Neopolitan pies. $ *Average main: 280 pesos* ⊠ *Costa Rica 5886, Palermo Hollywood* ☎ *11/5290–9529* ☉ *Closed Mon. No lunch* Ⓜ *D to Ministro Carranza* ✛ *2:A3.*

$$$
ASIAN
×**Sunae Asian Cantina.** The city's finest purveyor of southeast Asian food started out as a closed-door restaurant in the chef's home but these days Christina Sunae's name is on the door of a prime Palermo Hollywood location. *Adobo pao* (steamed pork buns) from her beloved Philippines and delicious Thai yellow curry are two musts, best accompanied by a lemongrass and vodka cocktail. Book a table under the banana trees out back for a romantic dinner. **Known for:** authentic flavors; spicy food; chilled-out ambience. $ *Average main: 350 pesos* ⊠ *Humboldt 1626, Palermo Hollywood* ☎ *11/4776–8122* ⊕ *www.sunaeasiancantina.com* ☉ *Closed Sun.* Ⓜ *D to Palermo (10 blocks)* ✛ *2:B5.*

$$$$
ECLECTIC
Fodor'sChoice
★
×**Tegui.** For a sublime eight-course tasting experience, head to Tegui, helmed by chef Germán Martitegui, who regularly ranks in the top 10 of Latin America's 50 Best Restaurants list. Martitegui has a deft hand with fish, in particular, and is fond of using fruit in his savory dishes. **Known for:** molecular gastronomy; excellent service; attention to detail across the board. $ *Average main: 700 pesos* ⊠ *Costa Rica 5852, between Carranza and Ravignani, Palermo Hollywood*

MAP 1: Where to Eat and Stay in Centro, Puerto Madero, San Telmo, La Boca, and Recoleta

E F G H

1
2
3
4
5
6

Av. Ramon S. Castillo

Dársena B

Dársena A

Av. Ant. Argentina

0   1/2 mi
0   1/2 km

Antepuerto

Dársena Norte

Sabot

Av. Córdoba

Av. Leandro N. Alem

Dique 4

Av. Costanera Carlos Noel

PUERTO MADERO

Cabaña Las Lilas

Macacha Guemes

Juana Manso

Av. Eduardo Madero

25 de Mayo

CASA ROSADA

Av. Dávila

Dique 3

Reserva Ecológica

Moreno Hotel

Balcarce

Chila

Azucena Villaflor

Av. Ing. Huerza

Av. Paseo Colón

Dique 2

Faena Hotel

Av. Costanera Carlos Noel

Hotel Babel

Zapiola

Vera Peñaloza

Hotel Madero

Bar Plaza Dorrego

Av. Dávila

Dique 1

El Obrero

Balcarce

KEY

■ Restaurants
□ Hotels
Ⓜ Subte stops
✛ following dining and lodging reviews indicates a map-grid coordinate

E F G H

Restaurant parrillas like this one offer everything from classic bife de lomo to all manner of offal.

📠 11/4770–9500 ⊕ *www.tegui.com.ar* 🕙 *Closed Sun. and Mon. No lunch* Ⓜ *D to Carranza* ✛ *2:A3*.

$$
ITALIAN
FAMILY
Fodor's Choice
★

✕ **Trattoria Olivetti.** Casual style, fantastic service and atmosphere, and a prime location in Palermo Chico make this one of the city's top Italian restaurants. For the more adventurous, don't miss the "surf and turf" of *gamberi e animelle* (perfectly grilled prawns and sweetbreads), or *guanciola* (beautifully braised pork cheeks). **Known for:** casual ambience; excellent wine list; genuine Italian fare. ⓢ *Average main: 250 pesos* ✉ *Cerviño 3800, República Arabe Siria, Palermo Botánico* 📠 *11/4802–4075* ⊕ *www.trattoriaolivetti.com* Ⓜ *D to Plaza Italia* ✛ *2:E3*.

WHERE TO STAY

In Buenos Aires, neighborhoods each have their own energy and spirit, and hotels tend to both mimic the identity of their neighborhood and help to shape it. The lodging options here are some of the most impressive of any international, cosmopolitan locale. From luxurious, majestic hotels (many with recognizable chain names) to boutique hotels operating a handful of rooms and injected with local flair, one thing is certain: you're bound to encounter plenty of attractive lodging options.

Though prices have climbed in Argentina in recent years, the city is still highly affordable for international visitors on the dollar, euro, or real. Many visitors, having discovered the intoxicating energy of the city, return again and again. Hotel owners and staff are some of the key players in helping people to fall in love with the city or lure them back.

WHERE SHOULD I STAY?

NEIGHBORHOOD	VIBE	PROS	CONS
Centro and Puerto Madero	The center of it all; you have a little bit of everything here, from history (Retiro and Congreso) to modernity (Puerto Madero). It buzzes by day, but is quiet at night.	Close to all major city sights and good transportation options. If you're only in town briefly, this is your place.	Certain areas are loud, chaotic, dirty, and deserted at night, which can make them dangerous. Don't walk around alone.
La Boca and San Telmo	The oldest barrios in the city; you can get a real feel for how Buenos Aires has operated for the past 100-plus years.	Old-world charm: cobblestone streets, corner cafés, tango music. You're sure to meet some interesting characters in this area.	Streets are dark and not well policed. Limited public transportation options. Locals have been known to target tourists.
Recoleta and Almagro	The most upscale area of the city, home to Argentina's high society. Certain enclaves will convince you you're in Paris.	Proximity to sights in Centro. It's safe, friendly, and chic. Great eating options; high-end stores and art galleries abound.	Prices are sometimes inflated for foreigners. Streets and sights are often crowded with tourists.
Palermo	The biggest neighborhood in the city; it's a mix of old family homes, soaring new towers, and renovated warehouses.	It's the undisputed hot spot of Buenos Aires' gastronomic scene. The city's biggest park, polo field, horse track, and casino are also here.	The übercool attitude of some locals is a turn-off. Some quality-of-life issues like clean sidewalks have been ignored in recent property developments.

Downtown—in Centro and Puerto Madero—you'll find sleek, soaring hotel properties; inch toward Recoleta and you can choose from some of the ritziest hotels in town, especially around Avenida Alvear and the Recoleta Cemetery. Boutique hotels are where Buenos Aires' options really shine, and while intimate, stylish spots dot most of the city's neighborhoods, they are found in greatest concentration in the vast, hip barrio of Palermo. Each neighborhood offers visitors the chance to experience a different facet of the buzzing, intriguing city of Buenos Aires.

WHAT IT COSTS IN U.S. DOLLARS				
	$	$$	$$$	$$$$
Hotels	under $115	$115–$175	$176–$250	over $250

Hotel prices are for two people in a standard double room in high season.

Use the coordinate (✛ 2:C5) at the end of each listing to locate a site on the corresponding Where to Eat and Stay map.

For expanded hotel reviews, visit Fodors.com.

CENTRO

$$$ ⚏ **Alvear Art Hotel.** The sleek Alvear Art Hotel is set back behind some
HOTEL trees on a pedestrian-only street in the heart of the city's business dis-
trict. **Pros:** gorgeous views from the sky-high pool; well-appointed gym;
quiet location. **Cons:** pool and gym areas open only until 9 pm; rooms
lack personality; buffet lunch can be hit-and-miss. $⑤ Rooms from:
US$250 ⊠ Suipacha 1086, Centro ☎ 11/4114–3477 ⊕ www.alvearart.
com ↴ 141 rooms *○* No meals* Ⓜ C to San Martín ✛ 1:D2.*

$$$ ⚏ **Casa Calma.** This "wellness hotel" in the heart of downtown Buenos
HOTEL Aires has taken the concept of in-house spa to a new level, equipping
Fodor'sChoice each of its 17 rooms with jetted tubs—six deluxe rooms also have
★ saunas where you can relax after a day of exploring the city. **Pros:**
gorgeous design; serene atmosphere; convenient downtown location.
Cons: on a chaotic city street; views aren't great on lower floors; sauna
is small; some balconies are very tiny. $⑤ Rooms from: US$180 ⊠ Suipacha 1015, Centro ☎ 11/4312–5000 ⊕ www.casacalmahotel.com ↴ 17
rooms *○* No meals* Ⓜ C to San Martín ✛ 1:C2.*

$$ ⚏ **Design cE.** Kudos go to the architect for this sleek space with spacious,
HOTEL loftlike rooms. **Pros:** supermodern suites; great location; breakfast is
served 24 hours a day. **Cons:** common areas are on the small side; lim-
ited breakfast; just a few drawers to put your clothes. $⑤ Rooms from:
US$147 ⊠ Marcelo T. Alvear 1695, Centro ☎ 11/5237–3100 ⊕ www.
designce.com ↴ 20 rooms, 8 suites *○* Breakfast* Ⓜ D to Callao ✛ 1:B2.*

$$ ⚏ **Hotel NH City & Tower.** Topped with an eye-catching rooftop pool and
HOTEL patio, this enormous art deco showplace is a reminder of an earlier era.
Pros: central location; amazing views from the roof; transports you back
to another era. **Cons:** the gym could do with an upgrade; area can be
sketchy at night; quite far from Recoleta and Palermo. $⑤ Rooms from:
US$170 ⊠ Bolívar 160, Centro ☎ 11/4121–6464 ⊕ www.nh-hotels.
com/hotel/nh-buenos-aires-city ↴ 369 rooms *○* Breakfast* Ⓜ A to Perú,
E to Bolívar ✛ 1:D5.*

PUERTO MADERO

$$$$ ⚏ **Faena Hotel.** Argentine fashion impresario Alan Faena and famed
HOTEL French architect Philippe Starck have created a universe unto itself
Fodor'sChoice with this hotel: rooms are feng-shui perfect, with rich reds and crisp
★ whites, sporting velvet curtains and blinds opening electronically to
river or city views. **Pros:** quite simply, one of the most dramatic hotels
on the planet; luxury abounds; celebrity magnet. **Cons:** an "are you cool
enough?" vibe is ever-present; extremely pricey to eat in; bar clientele
can be tacky. $⑤ Rooms from: US$380 ⊠ Martha Salotti 445, Puerto
Madero ☎ 11/4010–9000 ⊕ www.faena.com ↴ 110 rooms, 16 suites
○ Breakfast* Ⓜ D to Catedral, then a 20-min walk ✛ 1:F5.*

$$ ⚏ **Hotel Madero.** A favorite for visiting British rock stars, television per-
HOTEL sonalities, and fashion photographers, this slick hotel is within walk-
ing distance of downtown as well as the riverside ecological reserve.
Pros: the lobby bar attracts a cool after-office crowd; see-and-be-seen
clientele; central location. **Cons:** the gym and pool are a bit cramped;
subway far away. $⑤ Rooms from: US$200 ⊠ Rosario Vera Peñaloza

360, Puerto Madero ☎ 11/5776–7777 ⊕ www.hotelmadero.com ⤵ 169 rooms, 28 suites ⦿ Breakfast Ⓜ C to Independencia, 13 blocks ✥ 1:F6.

SAN TELMO

$
B&B/INN
🏠 **Hotel Babel.** This 200-year-old former home of the late Argentine president Juan Manuel de Rosas is on one of the city's most historic streets, in the heart of San Telmo. **Pros:** beautiful and welcoming lobby; complimentary glass of Argentine wine upon arrival; local artists display their works throughout the hotel and hold monthly events. **Cons:** it's an old house: rooms are close together; open-air patio can lead to noise—and sometimes rainwater—outside your door; decor can seem dark. $ *Rooms from: US$90 ⊠ Balcarce 946, San Telmo ☎ 11/4300–8300 ⊕ www.hotelbabel.com.ar ⤵ 9 rooms ⦿ Breakfast Ⓜ E to Belgrano ✥ 1:E6.*

$
B&B/INN
🏠 **Mansión Dandi Royal.** For a glimpse of early-20th-century high society, look no further than this mansion-turned-hotel, where exquisite rooms are decorated with classic wood furnishings and period murals. **Pros:** a tango junkie's heaven; stunning interiors; slice of local history. **Cons:** the surrounding streets are often populated with unsavory characters. $ *Rooms from: US$90 ⊠ Piedras 922, San Telmo ☎ 11/4307–7623 ⤵ 26 rooms, 4 suites ⦿ Breakfast Ⓜ C to San Juan ✥ 1:D6.*

$
HOTEL
🏠 **Moreno Hotel.** When they were reviving this art deco masterpiece, the architects ably met the challenge of restoring the 1929 building without disturbing its original elements, like mosaic tiling and stained-glass windows. **Pros:** designed to the max; plenty of charm; great views. **Cons:** some rooms are just steps away from the main lobby and elevator; no breakfast; room service only available in evenings from the restaurant next door. $ *Rooms from: US$90 ⊠ Moreno 376, San Telmo ☎ 11/6091–2000 ⊕ www.morenobuenosaires.com ⤵ 39 rooms ⦿ No meals Ⓜ A to Plaza de Mayo ✥ 1:E5.*

RECOLETA

$
B&B/INN
🏠 **A Hotel.** This lodging has an impressive ground-floor gallery where exhibits of paintings, photographs, and sculptures by acclaimed Argentine artists change monthly—you may run into art aficionados sipping wine and admiring the creations. **Pros:** its bohemian vibe will make you feel like you've joined an artists' colony; great location without the price tag; on-site gallery is fun. **Cons:** hotel is a bit antiquated; rooms could use a makeover. $ *Rooms from: US$100 ⊠ Azcuénaga 1268, Recoleta ☎ 11/4821–4744 ⊕ www.ahotel.com.ar ⤵ 34 rooms ⦿ Breakfast Ⓜ D to Pueyrredón ✥ 1:A2.*

$$$$
HOTEL
🏠 **Algodon Mansion.** Every detail of this hotel, one of the ritziest properties in the city, makes it clear that your comfort is of the utmost importance. **Pros:** unparalleled service; luxe location; each room comes with a complimentary bottle of wine. **Cons:** not much buzz to the place; pricey; terrace is small. $ *Rooms from: US$400 ⊠ Montevideo 1647, Recoleta ☎ 11/3530–7777 ⊕ www.algodonhotels.com/mansion ⤵ 10 suites ⦿ Breakfast Ⓜ D to Callao ✥ 1:C2.*

$$$$ ⌂ **Alvear Palace Hotel.** The standard-bearer for upscale sophistication
HOTEL since 1932, the Alvear Palace is undoubtedly the shining star of the
city's hotel scene: scores of dignitaries, celebrities, and VIPs have passed
through its doors over the years, and they keep coming back for the
world-class service and refined atmosphere. **Pros:** in-house French restaurant La Bourgogne is one of the city's best; top-notch service; beautiful spa features a sauna and steam rooms. **Cons:** bathrooms are on
the small side; one of the country's most expensive hotels; some rooms
could use a makeover. $ *Rooms from: US$515* ✉ *Av. Alvear 1891,
Recoleta* ☎ *11/4807–7777, 800/448–8355 in U.S.* ⊕ *www.alvearpalace.
com* ⇆ *191 rooms* ¡○¡ *No meals* Ⓜ *H to Las Heras* ✛ *1:C1.*

$$$$ ⌂ **Four Seasons Hotel Buenos Aires.** One of the city's swankiest lodg-
HOTEL ings, the Four Seasons is a magnet for famous folk. **Pros:** all the class
you'd expect from this brand; wonderful eateries in Elena and Nuestro
Secreto; swanky bar. **Cons:** the pool is outdoors, so unusable in winter; room aesthetics can seem impersonal; the bar can seem too cool
to hang out at. $ *Rooms from: US$565* ✉ *Posadas 1086, Recoleta*
☎ *11/4321–1200* ⊕ *www.fourseasons.com/buenosaires* ⇆ *165 rooms*
¡○¡ *No meals* Ⓜ *C to Retiro* ✛ *1:C2.*

$$$ ⌂ **Hotel Bel Air.** Given the frilly French-style facade, you could mis-
HOTEL take the Bel Air for a neighborhood hotel somewhere in Paris. **Pros:**
great location on one of the city's poshest streets; attractive rooms;
a legit "Paris of the South" hotel. **Cons:** the staff is easily distracted;
hallways and common areas are cramped; basic aesthetics. $ *Rooms
from: US$180* ✉ *Arenales 1462, Recoleta* ☎ *11/4021–4000* ⊕ *www.
hotelbelair.com.ar* ⇆ *77 rooms* ¡○¡ *Breakfast* Ⓜ *D to Tribunales* ✛ *1:B1.*

$$$$ ⌂ **Mio Buenos Aires.** The Catena family owns this luxurious boutique
HOTEL hotel, and all the rooms come stocked with wines straight from their
own Mendoza vineyards. **Pros:** on one of the most picturesque streets in
Recoleta; mixes rustic and modern elements; open and airy feel. **Cons:**
the ground-floor common areas feel elegant but somewhat somber; the
pool is good for swimming lengths but shallow; dining in the basement
is a bit glum. $ *Rooms from: US$260* ✉ *Av. Pres. Manuel Quintana
465, Recoleta* ☎ *11/5295–8500* ⊕ *www.miobuenosaires.com* ⇆ *30
rooms* ¡○¡ *Breakfast* Ⓜ *Linea D to Callao* ✛ *1:B1.*

$$$$ ⌂ **Palacio Duhau Park Hyatt Buenos Aires.** This landmark hotel ups the
HOTEL ante for elegance in Buenos Aires—its two buildings, a restored 1930s-
Fodor's Choice era mansion and a 17-story tower, are connected by an underground
★ art gallery and an expansive, leafy garden that's among the city's most
attractive outdoor areas. **Pros:** understated splendor; two great restau-
rants; has the city's largest indoor pool. **Cons:** a long walk from one
side of the hotel to the other; far from the subway; elevators are small.
$ *Rooms from: US$400* ✉ *Av. Alvear 1661, Recoleta* ☎ *11/5171–1234*
⊕ *www.hyatt.com/en-US/hotel/argentina/palacio-duhau-park-hyatt-
buenos-aires/bueph* ⇆ *165 rooms* ¡○¡ *No meals* Ⓜ *C to San Martín or
H to Las Heras* ✛ *1:C1.*

PALERMO

$$
B&B/INN
Duque Hotel Boutique & Spa. As the name suggests, this 1920s French-style hotel is fit for a duke—or even a president, as the mansion once served as an Argentine president's private residence. **Pros:** gorgeous entrance; spacious and inviting common areas; an enclosed patio means many guests use rooms only for sleeping. **Cons:** some rooms are small; swimming-pool and deck area are small; far from central Soho fun. $ *Rooms from: US$160* ✉ *Guatemala 4364, Palermo Soho* ☎ *11/4832–0312* ⊕ *www.duquehotel.com* ➷ *14 rooms* ❍| *Breakfast* Ⓜ *D to Scalabrini Ortiz* ✛ *2:D4.*

$$
HOTEL
Fodor's Choice
★
Fierro Hotel. A choice lodging for travelers looking for a five-star stay in a boutique package, all rooms boast top-of-the-line beds, spacious living areas with chaise lounges, and flat-screen TVs. **Pros:** among the city's best dining and drinking; rooftop pool with skyline views; helpful staff. **Cons:** common areas are small; pool is not large; the back patio is a bit sterile. $ *Rooms from: US$160* ✉ *Soler 5862, Palermo* ☎ *11/3220–6800* ⊕ *www.fierrohotel.com* ➷ *22 rooms, 5 suites* ❍| *Breakfast* Ⓜ *D to Carranza* ✛ *2:B3.*

$$
HOTEL
Fodor's Choice
★
The Glu Hotel. Attention to detail is key at this small boutique hotel where all of the spacious rooms are stylishly modern and minimalist and equipped with low-slung furnishings, bright wooden floors, and small bar areas. **Pros:** sought-after location; sleek interior decor; excellent concierges provide highly personalized and attentive service. **Cons:** its location on a happening street means constant traffic, though rooms are soundproofed; roof terrace has a Jacuzzi rather than a pool; the breakfast room is cramped. $ *Rooms from: US$150* ✉ *Godoy Cruz 1733, Palermo* ☎ *11/4831–4646* ⊕ *www.thegluhotel.com* ➷ *11 rooms* ❍| *Free Breakfast* Ⓜ *D to Plaza Italia, 10 blocks* ✛ *2:B4.*

$$
B&B/INN
Home Hotel Buenos Aires. Run by an Anglo-Argentinean couple, the Home Hotel oozes coolness and class. **Pros:** hip and fun; eclectic mix of people stay here; great pool area. **Cons:** lots of nonguests come here to hang out; breakfast is good, lunch is less exciting; some guests might not feel cool enough. $ *Rooms from: US$165* ✉ *Honduras 5860, Palermo Hollywood* ☎ *11/4779–1006* ⊕ *www.homebuenosaires.com* ➷ *14 rooms, 4 suites, 2 apartments* ❍| *Breakfast* Ⓜ *D to Ministro Carranza* ✛ *2:A3.*

$$$
B&B/INN
Legado Mítico. Blessed with the city's most gorgeous sitting room, the Legado Mítico also has an enormous library with plush leather couches, antique furnishings, a fireplace, and bookshelves stocked with English- and Spanish-language classics. **Pros:** exquisitely decorated rooms; welcoming; an authentic and unique Argentine experience. **Cons:** common areas and hallways are very dark; the upstairs terrace disappoints for a property of this quality; not much ambience. $ *Rooms from: US$250* ✉ *Gurruchaga 1848, Palermo* ☎ *11/4833–1300* ⊕ *www.legadomitico. com* ➷ *11 rooms* ❍| *Breakfast* Ⓜ *D to Plaza Italia* ✛ *2:C4.*

$$
B&B/INN
Fodor's Choice
★
Magnolia Hotel Boutique. This boutique lodging feels like home—if home were a high-ceilinged, lavishly decorated Palermo town house dating from the 1890s. **Pros:** top-floor terrace is the perfect urban escape; lots of cozy common areas; homemade baked goods at breakfast. **Cons:** some rooms require walking outdoors; quite far from the Soho buzz.

2

$ *Rooms from: US$150* ⊠ *Julián Alvarez 1746, Palermo* ☎ *11/4867–4900* ⊕ *www.magnoliahotelboutique.com* ➲ *8 rooms* ⊗ *Breakfast* Ⓜ *D to Scalabrini Ortiz* ✛ *2:C5.*

$$
B&B/INN
Fodor'sChoice
★

Ⓣ **Miravida Soho Hotel & Wine Bar.** This enchanting boutique hotel offers thoughtful and personalized service starting the minute you walk in the door. **Pros:** charm to spare; breakfast includes options like homemade granola; very helpful staff. **Cons:** if street noise is a concern, request a room in the back; this road is a bit dark and quiet at night; some rooms are small. $ *Rooms from: US$160* ⊠ *Darregueyra 2050, Palermo* ☎ *11/4774–6433* ⊕ *www.miravidasoho.com* ➲ *7 rooms* ⊗ *Breakfast* Ⓜ *D to Palermo* ✛ *2:C4.*

NIGHTLIFE AND PERFORMING ARTS

Preparing for a night out in Buenos Aires has an element of marathon training to it. Rest up with a siesta, fortify yourself with some protein, and drink plenty of fluids before, during, and after. That's right, the key to *porteño* nightlife is longevity—after all, an early night means hailing a cab at 6 am.

The scene here rivals that of any capital city, so you'll find something to suit every taste. Trendy cocktail bars, secret speakeasies, classic tango haunts, artsy watering holes, and packed dance floors await. To make the most of them, try following the locals' lead.

Painting Buenos Aires red means looking sharp, going with the flow as you bar-hop, and not challenging your new B.A. buddies to raucous drinking games. *Porteños* adore going out with their friends, but it's not uncommon to see a large group sharing a liter bottle of beer or lingering over a warm pint of IPA. Latino lightweights? Not at all. This is just how Argentineans roll—and once a night gets really rocking, they'll move onto their favorite tipple, Fernet y Cola.

Hours are relaxed, but there are general guidelines. The smartest bars kick off an evening with happy hours that begin around 8 pm and often stretch way beyond 60 minutes; downtown drinking establishments start even earlier to lure workers to part with hard-earned pesos, spawning the "after-office" across the city, which is now a nightlife fixture most days of the week.

CENTRO

BARS

La Cigale. Take advantage of happy hour until 10 pm at La Cigale's curvaceously seductive first-floor bar, which leads to the street-side balcony and smokers' corner. Another flight of stairs winds up to the stage, ready and waiting for local indie, jazz, and acoustic bands any night of the week. The first Monday of the month sees a popular pub quiz frequented by expats. ⊠ *25 de Mayo 597, Centro* ☎ *11/4893–2332* ⊕ *www.lacigalebar.wixsite.com/microcentro* Ⓜ *B to L.N. Alem.*

Florería Atlántico. Behind the fridge door of this florist shop and wine store lies a trendy basement bar that fills up quickly with the after-office crowd, and stays packed with cool locals after drinks and dinner seven nights a week. The cocktails are elaborate and carefully crafted, and many incorporate the gin produced by the bar's mixologist. Famous DJs sometimes pop in to get the crowd going. ⊠ *Arroyo 872, Retiro* ☏ *11 /4313–6093* ⊕ *www.floreriaatlantico.com.ar* Ⓜ *C to Retiro.*

DANCE CLUBS

Fodor'sChoice **Bahrein.** This sheik—er, *chic* and stylish—party palace is located in a
★ former bank, and the Funky Room is where beautiful, tightly clothed youth groove to pop, rock, and funk, while the basement Excess Room has electronic beats and dizzying wall visuals. For a more sophisticated dinner-before-dancing vibe, head upstairs to the Yellow Room. This is a great spot to catch local DJs, though there are also big nights with international artists. ⊠ *Lavalle 345, Centro* ☏ *11/4315–2403* ⊕ *www. bahreinba.com* Ⓜ *B to Alem.*

Cocoliche. This happening spot enjoys cult status in both the straight and gay communities. Upstairs is a diverse art gallery big on young locals; downstairs, underground house and techno drives one of the city's darkest dance floors, while DJs with huge followings are frequently on rotation. ⊠ *Rivadavia 878, Centro* ☏ *11/4342–9485* Ⓜ *A to Piedras.*

GAY AND LESBIAN

Flux. It took a couple of expats to realize the gap in the market for early-evening gay bars. Their creation, Flux, is a smart, friendly, and sociable basement club that gets going for happy hour at 7 pm and keeps on until after midnight with decent pop music and an ample cocktail menu. ⊠ *Marcelo T. de Alvear 980, Centro* ☏ *11/5252–0258* ⊕ *www.fluxbar. com.ar* Ⓜ *C to San Martín.*

LIVE MUSIC

ND/Ateneo. This spacious theater and cultural space mainly showcases midlevel local bands, showmen, and comedians, with a few big Argentine names thrown in for good measure. Get tickets at the box office (open Monday–Saturday, from noon to 8) or through Ticketek (*www. ticketek.com.ar*). ⊠ *Paraguay 918, Centro* ☏ *11/4328–2888* ⊕ *www. ndteatro.com.ar* Ⓜ *C to San Martín.*

TANGO

El Beso. The standard of dancing is usually high at this club, which belongs to La Academia del Tango Milonguero, one of the city's best tango schools. Beginners should consult the online schedule for classes. ⊠ *Riobamba 416, Congreso* ☏ *11/4951–2535* ⊕ *www.elbeso.com.ar* Ⓜ *B to Callao.*

PUERTO MADERO

TANGO

Fodor'sChoice **Rojo Tango.** Five-star food, musicians, choreography, and glamour: you
★ wouldn't expect anything less from the Faena Hotel + Universe. Crimson velvet and gold trim line everything from the walls to the menu at El Cabaret, and tables often hold celebs both local and global. The implausibly good-looking troupe puts on a tango-through-the-ages show, which includes jazz-tango, semi-naked numbers, and even the

Don't forget your best dancing shoes: nightclubs, like this one in Palermo, are a stylish affair.

tango version of Roxanne from *Moulin Rouge*. It's worth the splurge. ✉ *Martha Salotti 445, Puerto Madero* ☎ *11/4952–4111* ⊕ *www.rojo-tango.com* Ⓜ *D to Catedral.*

SAN TELMO

BARS

Fodor's Choice ★ **Bar Británico.** Opened in 1928, this traditional corner bar opposite Parque Lezama is an iconic spot. Day and night it's full of characters who engage in passionate discussions or simply watch the world unfold through the oversized windows. Imbued with nostalgia, Bar Británico has a cinematic appeal—which may explain why it has appeared in movies like *The Motorcycle Diaries* and Francis Ford Coppola's *Tetro.* ✉ *Brasil 399, at Defensa, San Telmo* ☎ *11/4361–2107* Ⓜ *C to San Juan.*

Doppelgänger. With a list of 100 cocktails and an excellent menu to match, this corner bar on the edge of San Telmo is a hidden gem. The fancy glassware and quotations in the menu show that the "double" concept has been thought through down to the finest details. Happy hour runs from 7 to 9, Tuesday through Friday. ✉ *Av. Juan de Garay 500, San Telmo* ☎ *11/4300–0201* ⊕ *www.doppelganger.com.ar* Ⓜ *C to San Juan.*

DANCE CLUBS

Rey Castro. This Cuban restaurant-bar may get a little wild on weekends but never out of hand: the bouncers look like NFL players. It's a popular spot for birthday parties and great mojitos. After the nightly live dance show, DJs crank up the Cuban rhythms; you're likely to learn some sexy new moves. ✉ *Perú 342, San Telmo* ☎ *11/4342–9998* ⊕ *www. reycastro.com* Ⓜ *A to Perú.*

LIVE MUSIC

Centro Cultural Torquato Tasso. Classic trios and quartets share the stage with young musicians performing hip tango and folk sets here. There are also milongas on weekends. ✉ *Defensa 1575, Montserrat* ☎ *11/4307–6506* Ⓜ *C to San Juan.*

La Trastienda. A San Telmo institution, this cabaret-style club is one of Buenos Aires' most popular venues, so grab a table and enjoy an intimate performance for 900. La Trastienda is the place to catch electrotango or new tango groups, although it takes pains to promote other genres as well. Check out national pop and rock legends, as well as local rock, reggae, and funk. ✉ *Balcarce 460, Montserrat* ☎ *11/4342–7650* ⊕ *www.latrastienda.com* Ⓜ *A to Bolívar.*

TANGO

Buenos Ayres Club. Rousing live orchestras keep even nondancers entertained at the nontraditional *milongas* that are this club's hallmark. La Orquesta Típica el Afronte provides the music for Maldita Milonga (☎ *11/2189–7747*) on Sunday, Monday, and Wednesday, while El Toque Cimarron Salsa (☎ *11–15/3827–7786*) takes charge on Thursday. Tuesday's Tango Queer (☎ *11–15/3252–6894*, ⊕ *www.tangoqueer. com*) draws both gay and straight dancers looking to escape the confines of more conservative dance floors; and Friday takes a different turn with Latin American music. ✉ *Perú 571, San Telmo* ☎ *11/4331–1518* Ⓜ *D to Catedral.*

El Viejo Almacén. This place was founded by legendary tango singer Edmundo Rivero, though he wouldn't recognize the slick outfit his bar has become. Inside the colonial building a tireless troupe of dancers and musicians perform showy tango and folk numbers. ✉ *Independencia 299, at Balcarce, San Telmo* ☎ *11/4307–7388* ⊕ *www.viejoalmacen. com.ar* Ⓜ *C to Independencia.*

RECOLETA

BARS

Milión. One of the city's most stunning bars is spread across three floors of a perfectly restored French-style mansion. A cool vibe and cooler drinks (try the frozen basil daiquiri) keep this place packed on weekends. When the back garden fills on balmy summer nights, squeeze onto the marble steps with the beautiful people. ✉ *Paraná 1048, Recoleta* ☎ *11/4815–9925* ⊕ *www.milion.com.ar* Ⓜ *D to Callao.*

Fodor'sChoice ★ **Pony Line.** No expense has been spared at the polo-themed Pony Line, a cool watering hole in the Four Seasons hotel. Creative cocktails, its own line of craft beer, luxury bar snacks, and great tunes have made this a go-to spot for sassy ladies, suave gentlemen, and models. ✉ *Posadas 1086/88, Recoleta* ☎ *11/4321–1728* ⊕ *www.elenaponyline.com* Ⓜ *C to San Martín.*

Shoeless Joe's El Alamo. From the outside, the signs asking patrons to leave quietly are the only hint that this isn't the demure bar it appears

DID YOU KNOW?

The uniquely porteño style of decorative sign art seen here is called *fileteado*. It's generally used in association with well-loved, nostalgia-inducing things, like tango halls, old *collectivos* (city buses), or a really good cortado.

NIGHTCLUB TIPS

Don't be afraid to stand in line outside. Lines are generally quick and painless—and if there isn't one, the place might not be worth visiting.

Buy a ticket or make a reservation. For concerts, shows, and club events, people often buy tickets in advance, as many fill up or sell out, especially international offerings.

Go late—really. Otherwise you'll miss out on the atmosphere and find it a bit boring. If necessary, help smooth the adjustment with a *merienda* (a snack of coffee and croissants at around 6 pm) and a "disco siesta."

Find out what's on and where. Scour flyers, websites, ticket agencies, and magazine listings for up-to-date information. There's a lot more going on than you can find out from any single source.

Dress to impress. *Porteños* like fine clothes, though their style tends to be on the conservative side. So skip the shorts and flip-flops (both social no-nos) in favor of something fashionable. With the exception of one or two scruffy bars in San Telmo, you'll never feel overdressed.

Never imagine you've seen it all. Private parties and last-minute underground events are where it's at. Finding out about them isn't easy, but keep an ear out and tell people you're looking, and you might luck out.

to be. The generous drinks promotions (ladies drink free until midnight on Friday) add substantial rowdiness, and it turns into a raucous party zone on weekends. A sports bar at heart, El Alamo also hosts bikini competitions—just so you know. There's a sister branch in Palermo at Córdoba 5267. ⊠ *Uruguay 1177, Recoleta* ☎ *11/4813–7324* Ⓜ *D to Tribunales.*

DANCE CLUBS

The Basement. Owned by an Irish father-and-son duo, this vibrant downstairs nightspot is popular with expats and young upwardly mobile *porteño* party people. Stop first for a pint at the ground floor Shamrock pub, where you can yap away in English and easily forget you're in South America; then, following the techno beats, descend to the dance club where Argentina's finest DJs burn up the decks. ⊠ *Rodríguez Peña 1220, Recoleta* ☎ *11/4812–3584* Ⓜ *D to Callao.*

GAY AND LESBIAN

Zoom. Half a block from the very cruisey section of Santa Fe, between avenidas Callao and Coronel Díaz, Zoom offers a lounge bar, a maze, video cabins, and plenty of dark corners. It can get pretty intense, but there's good security. ⊠ *Uriburu 1018, Recoleta* ☎ *11/4827–4828* ⊕ *www.zoombuenosaires.com* Ⓜ *D to Pueyrredón.*

LIVE MUSIC

Clásica y Moderna. An older, artsy crowd gathers here for live jazz complemented by dinner, drinks, and a dash of philosophy. Musicians make good use of the vintage venue's grand piano, while singers offer their take on the bossa nova, tango, and bolero. Bibliophiles will appreciate the on-site bookshop that stocks great Argentine literature. ⊠ *Av. Callao 892, Recoleta* ☎ *11/4812–8707* Ⓜ *D to Callao.*

Notorious. A jazz bar, restaurant, and record shop rolled into one, Notorious often hosts top musicians. You can also listen to the club's extensive music collection on the CD players at each table. ⊠ *Av. Callao 966, Recoleta* ☎ *11/4813–6888* ⊕ *www.notorious.com.ar* Ⓜ *D to Callao.*

ALMAGRO

LIVE MUSIC

Ciudad Cultural Konex. A mixed bag of live music, film screenings, fun parties, and interactive theater makes for an interesting line-up at this huge converted factory. The outdoor space morphs into an inner-city beach complete with hammocks in summer; the winter months see DJs and bands hash it out indoors. The Konex is also home to percussion band Bomba de tiempo, who play every Monday evening. ⊠ *Sarmiento 3131, Abasto* ☎ *11/4864–3200* ⊕ *www.cckonex.org* Ⓜ *B line to Carlos Gardel.*

TANGO

La Catedral. This former grain factory has been converted into a hip club where the tango is somehow very rock. There are classes and milongas every evening, although Tuesdays are the most popular. It's a cool night out even if you're not planning to dance, as you can watch aficionados in action over a beer or a bottle of wine. Note that the real pros tend not to come here because of the uneven floorboards. ⊠ *Sarmiento 4006, Almagro* ☎ *15/5325–1630* Ⓜ *B to Carlos Gardel.*

PALERMO

BARS

Antares. It started in Mar del Plata, southeast of Buenos Aires, in 1999, and it's now a successful national brewer making seven of its own ales. The spacious bar attracts a cosmopolitan group of drinkers who keep it packed from after-office until the small hours. Service is friendly and efficient, the music is feel-good, and the bar snacks are tasty. Also check out the newer outposts in Las Cañitas at Arévalo 2876 and San Telmo at Bolívar 491. ⊠ *Armenia 1447, Palermo Soho* ☎ *11/4833–9611* ⊕ *www.cervezaantares.com* Ⓜ *B to Malabia.*

Bangalore. A pub and curry house in Buenos Aires? You bet, and the Bangalore has it all—right down to a blazing log fire in winter. There's limited seating at the bar and in the tiny restaurant upstairs, and the place is often packed from early evening on, spilling out onto the street. Service is friendly, and there's a wide range of draft beers. Revelers spill out onto the street with their pints in the warmer months. ⊠ *Humboldt 1416, Palermo Hollywood* ☎ *11/4779–2621* Ⓜ *B to Dorrego.*

Congo. Beautiful people—in faded fitted jeans, hipster sneakers, and leather jackets—frequent this hangout postdinner and preclub. Browse the great cocktail list at Congo's lengthy bar, or head for the large back patio: either way, you'll easily be able to convince new friends to stick

Continued on page 110

The Dance of Buenos Aires

by Victoria Patience

"THE TANGO IS MACHO, THE TANGO IS STRONG. IT SMELLS OF WINE AND TASTES LIKE DEATH."

So goes the famous tango "Why I Sing Like This," whose mix of nostalgia, violence, and sensuality sum up what is truly the dance of Buenos Aires. From its beginnings, tango and its two-four beat marked and reflected the character of Buenos Aires. You may hear strains of tango on the radio while sipping coffee in a café, see high-kicking sequined dancers in a glitzy dinner show, or listen to musicians in a darkened cabaret. But one of the most memorable ways to experience the best of this broody, melancholic, impassioned art form is through dancing it yourself.

DANCING THE TANGO

Many milongas now kick off with group dance classes which usually last an hour or two and cost 15–20 pesos; some lessons are free, though chaotic. These classes are great for getting over nerves and getting you in the mood. However, most *milongueros* (people who dance at *milongas*, or tango dance halls) take tango very seriously and don't look kindly on left-footed beginners crowding the floor. We recommend you take a few private classes first—they can make a huge difference to your technique.

English-speaking private teachers abound in Buenos Aires; classes generally last 1½ hours and prices can range from $20 to $80 a class. Complete beginners should plan on at least three or four classes before hitting a milonga. Many private instructors organize milonga outings with groups of their students (usually for a separate fee). Others even offer a so-called "taxi dance service": you pay for them to dance with you all night. See the end of this feature for a rundown of some of the best options for lessons and milongas.

DANCE STYLES
Tango milonguero, the style danced at milongas and taught in most classes in Buenos Aires, is quite different from the so-called salon or ballroom tango danced in Hollywood movies and in competitions outside Argentina. Ballroom tango is all fixed steps and staccato movements, and dancers' backs arch away from each other in a stiff embrace. Tango milonguero is a highly improvised style built around a variety of typical movements, not fixed steps. Dancers embrace closely, their chests touching. There are other, historical tango styles, but it's

less common to see them on milonga floors. (Confusingly, "milonga" refers both to traditional tango dance halls and to a style of music and dance that predates the tango; though similar to tango, it has a more syncopated beat and faster, simpler steps.)

AT THE MILONGA
Dancers of all ages sit at tables that edge the floor, and men invite women to dance through *cabeceo* (subtle eye contact and head-nodding), a hard art to master. Note that women sitting with male partners won't be asked to the floor by other men.

Dances come in sets of three, four, or five, broken by a *cortina* (obvious divider of non-tango music), and it's common to stay with the same partner for a set. Being discarded in the middle is a sign that your dancing's not up to scratch, but staying for more than two sets with the same partner could be interpreted as a come-on.

To fit in seamlessly, move around the floor counterclockwise without zigzagging, sticking to the inside layers of dancers if you're a beginner. Respect other dancers' space by avoiding collisions and keeping your movements small on crowded floors. Don't spend a long time doing showy moves on the spot: it holds up traffic. Finally, take time to sit some out, catch your breath, and watch the experts.

TANGO TALK

Abrazo: the embrace or stance dancers use; in tango, this varies from hip-touching and loose shoulders to close chests and more fluid hips, depending on style.

Abrazo

Barrida

Barrida: literally, "a sweep"; one partner sweeps the other's foot into a position.

Caminada: a walking step that is the basis of the tango.

Canyengue: style of tango dancing with short and restricted steps; from the 1910s and '20s when tight hobble skirts were popular.

Ocho: eight; a criss-crossing walk.

Parada: literally a "stop"; the lead dancer stops the other's foot with his own.

Petitero: measured style of tango developed after the 1955 military coup, when large tango gatherings were banned and the dance relegated to small cafés.

Caminada

MILONGA STYLE

Wearing a fedora hat or fishnet stockings is as good as a neon sign reading "beginner." Forget what on-stage tango dancers wear and follow a few basic rules.

Go for comfortable clothes that allow you to move freely; a sure bet are breathable, natural fabrics with a bit of stretch. Be sure it's something that makes you feel sexy. If in doubt, wear black. Avoid showy outfits: it's your footwork that should stand out. It's also smart to steer clear of big buckles, studs, stones, or anything that might catch on your partner. Try not to wear skirts that are too long or too tight. Also a bad idea are jeans or gymwear.

A good example of what to wear for men would be black dress pants and a black shirt; for women, two of many options are a simple halter-neck dress with a loose, calf-length skirt or palazzo pants with a fitted top.

As for your feet: look for dance shoes with flexible leather or suede soles that allow you to glide and pivot. The fit should be snug but comfortable. Note that rubber-soled street shoes or sneakers mark the dance floor and are often forbidden. High heels are a must for women; the most popular style is an open-toed sandal with an ankle strap (which stops them coming off). Black lace-ups are the favorite among men, so leave your two-tone spats at home.

TANGO THROUGH TIME

The tango and modern Buenos Aires were born in the same place: the *conventillos* (tenement houses) of the port neighborhood of La Boca in the late 19th century, where River Plate culture collided with that of European immigrants. The dance eventually swept from the immigrant-quarter brothels and cabarets to the rest of the city; rich playboys took the tango to Paris on their grand tours, and by the 1920s the dance had become respectable enough to fill the salons and drawing rooms of the upper class in Argentina and abroad. In the 1930s, with the advent of singers like Carlos Gardel, tango music became popular in its own right. Accordingly, musical accompaniment started to come from larger bands known as *orquestas típicas*.

Carlos Gardel

By the '40s and '50s, *porteños* (people from Buenos Aires) celebrated tango as the national music of the people, and tango artists lent Evita and Perón their support. The military coup that ousted Perón in 1955 forbade large tango dances, which it saw as potential political gatherings, and (bizarrely) encouraged rock 'n' roll instead. Young people listened, and tango fell out of popular favor.

The '90s saw a huge revival in both traditional *milongas* (dance halls) and a more improvised dance style. Musical offerings now include modern takes on classic tangos and electrotango or *tangofusión*. Even local rock stars are starting to include a tango or two in their repertory. And since 1998, thousands of people from around the world have attended the annual fortnight-long Festival de Tango in Buenos Aires (⊕ *www.tangobuenosaires.gob.ar*), held late winter or spring.

Whether you decide to take in a show or take up dancing yourself, sit down for a classic concert or groove at an electrotango night, there are more ways to experience tango in Buenos Aires than anywhere else on earth.

DID YOU KNOW?

■ Tango so horrified Kaiser Wilhelm and Pope Pius X that they banned the dance.

■ In 1915, before he was famous, Carlos Gardel was injured in a barroom brawl with Ernesto Guevara Lynch, Che's father.

■ One of Gardel's most famous numbers, "Por Una Cabeza," is the tango featured in *Schindler's List, Scent of a Woman*, and *True Lies*.

■ The coup of 1930 prompted composers like Enrique Santos Discépolo to write protest tangos.

■ Finnish tango has been a distinct musical genre since at least mid-century and is still one of the most popular in Finland; there's even an annual *Tangomarkkinat* (tango festival) in Seinäjoki, complete with the crowning of a Tango King and Queen.

around for another drink or three. ✉ *Honduras 5329, Palermo Soho* ☎ *11/4833–5857* ⊕ *www.congoclubcultural.com.ar* Ⓜ *to Plaza Italia.*

Fodor's Choice ★ **878.** B.A.'s original speakeasy has spawned a spate of followers over the past few years, but it remains a classic for cocktail lovers: 878 has an extensive drinks list, armchairs to sink into, plus a supercool clientele. Be sure to stick your head around the more private back bar. ✉ *Thames 878, Villa Crespo* ☎ *11/4773–1098* ⊕ *www.878bar.com.ar* Ⓜ *B to Malabia.*

The Harrison Speakeasy. One of the finest speakeasies around, the Harrison is inspired by the Prohibition-era and the time-warped cocktails have earned a cluster of awards, so you're in expert hands. Membership is required; alternatively, you can dine at the shop-front sushi restaurant, then ask "to see the bodega" to gain access. ✉ *Malabia 1764 and Costa Rica, Palermo Soho* ⊕ *www.nicky-harrison.com* Ⓜ *D to Scalabrini Ortiz.*

Isabel. Glamour is the name of the game at Isabel, one of Palermo's posher watering holes. You can feel like a star sipping a cocktail under the twinkling ceiling lights, while actually star spotting if you're up to date with your Argentine models and polo players. Hip DJs spin tunes for a bling-y crowd, so booking is essential—as is a bottomless wallet. ✉ *Uriarte 1664, Palermo Soho* ☎ *11/4834–6969* ⊕ *www.isabelbar.com* Ⓜ *D to Plaza Italia.*

Fodor's Choice ★ **Verne Club.** Themed around Jules Verne's *Twenty Thousand Leagues Under the Sea*, Verne Club runs a tight ship thanks to it's top-notch mixologists. This old-school cocktail bar serves innovative offerings that are often inspired by the eponymous author's characters, including a Phileas Fogg Martini. ✉ *Medrano 1475, Palermo* ☎ *11/4822–0980* ⊕ *www.vernecocktailclub.com* Ⓜ *D to Scalabrini Ortiz.*

DANCE CLUBS

Club Aráoz. A serious party crowd is found at Club Aráoz. Bump and grind it at Thursday's block-rocking hip-hop night; Friday and Saturday see DJs spinning rock and electronic dance music for a relatively laid-back bunch of Buenos Aires youth. ✉ *Aráoz 2424, Palermo* ☎ *11/5977–9922* ⊕ *www.clubaraoz.com.ar* Ⓜ *D to Bulnes.*

Kika. Right in the heart of Palermo and next door to Congo, Kika is much bigger than you'd guess from the outside. Thanks to its funky musical orientation, its two dance floors fill up quickly. The back room sometimes hosts live bands while Tuesdays are all about Hype, an all-in-one electro, hip-hop, indie, and dubstep night that gets the student-heavy crowd moving till dawn. ✉ *Honduras 5339, Palermo Soho* ☎ *11/4833–9171* ⊕ *www.kikaclub.com.ar* Ⓜ *D to Palermo.*

Fodor's Choice ★ **Niceto.** One of the city's best venues for two decades features everything from demure indie rock to the outrageous and legendary Club 69 on Thursday (think underdressed cross-dressers). Check out live bands and dancing on the A Side, while something contrasting and chill simultaneously takes place in the back B Side room. ✉ *Cnel. Niceto Vega 5510, Palermo Hollywood* ☎ *11/4779–9396* ⊕ *www.nicetoclub.com* Ⓜ *B to Dorrego.*

GAY AND LESBIAN

Amerika. This immense gay disco has three floors of high-energy action and shows. Friday and Saturday are fun and frivolous verging on hectic thanks to its one-fee, all-you-can-drink-entry. Thursday and Sunday are quieter, with greater emphasis on the music. Amerika remains the city's gay club to check out—and be checked out in. ✉ *Gascon 1040, Palermo* ☎ *11/4865–4416* ⊕ *www.ameri-k.com.ar* Ⓜ *B to Medrano.*

LIVE MUSIC

Thelonious Club. The best *porteño* jazz bands (and occasional foreign imports) play at this upscale spot. Arrive early for a good seat, as it's a long, narrow bar and not all tables have good views; on weekends there are usually two shows per night. ✉ *Nicaragua 5549, Palermo* ⊕ *www. thelonious.com.ar* Ⓜ *D to Palermo.*

Virasoro Bar. This is an intimate art deco venue for local jazz maestros and appreciative audiences. It's a great space and you can get up close and personal with the musicians, who draw from a deep well of talent and cover a lot of ground, from improv to standards and experimental. ✉ *Guatemala 4328, Palermo* ☎ *11/4831–8918* ⊕ *www.virasorobar. com.ar* Ⓜ *D to Scalabrini Ortiz.*

TANGO

Fodor'sChoice ★ **Salón Canning.** Several milongas call this large dance hall home. The coolest is Parakultural (⊕ *www.parakultural.com.ar*), which takes place late on Monday, Tuesday, and Friday. Reservations are essential for the last of these—the dance floor is totally packed by midnight, so get here early. Originally an alternative, "underground" milonga, it now attracts large numbers of locals, including longtime expats. ✉ *Av. Scalabrini Ortíz 1331, Palermo* ☎ *11/4833–3224* ⊕ *www.parakultural. com.ar* Ⓜ *B to Malabia.*

SHOPPING

Whether you're looking for a unique handicraft, a cowhide chair, the latest boutique-vineyard Malbec, a one-off pair of rhodochrosite earrings set in silver, or jeans no one's got back home, you're sure to leave Buenos Aires with your bags full. Ever since Argentina's economic collapse in 2001, designers have had to inject a new level of creativity into their wares in order to survive. Innovation is key, and it can be found on many corners, at street fairs, and at upmarket boutiques.

If you love the hustle and bustle, elbow your way through the stalls at the city's outdoor markets. Many artisans set up around squares such as plazas Francia and Armenia, and Plazoleta Cortazar, also known as Plaza Serrano. On weekends in Palermo Soho, some artisans simply lay out handcrafted leather mate gourds or colorful aguayo hair clips on the sidewalk, while Sunday at San Telmo's Plaza Dorrego turns into an outdoor theater show, with living statues and tango dancers jostling for space among the antiques.

CENTRO

JEWELRY AND ACCESSORIES

Fodor's Choice
★

Autoría Bs As. Fashion meets art at Autoría Bs As. After browsing the ready-to-wear women's collections, head to jewelry and accessories, where creative necklaces may be made of coiled silver or crochet. Some handbags have been fashioned from car tires, others from top-quality leather or organic wool. This is one of the few places to pick up a daring one-of-a-kind item, perhaps a handwoven coat in luminous colors in northern Argentina by Manto Abrigo. ☒ *Suipacha 1025, Microcentro* ☎ *11/5252–2474* ⊕ *www.autoriabsas.blogspot.com.ar* Ⓜ *C to San Martín.*

Plata Nativa. Tucked into an arcade, this tiny shop is filled with delights for both boho chicks and collectors of singular ethnic jewelry. Complex, chunky necklaces with turquoise, amber, and malachite—all based on original Araucanian (ethnic Argentine) pieces—and Mapuche-style silver earrings and brooches are some of the offerings. Happy customers include Sharon Stone, Pedro Almodóvar, and the Textile Museum in Washington, D.C. ☒ *Galería del Sol, Shop 41, Florida 860, Centro* ☎ *11/4312–1398* ⊕ *www.platanativa.com* Ⓜ *C to San Martín.*

SHOES, HANDBAGS, AND LEATHER GOODS

Carpincho. As its name suggests, this spot specializes in supersoft, stippled *carpincho* leather from the capybara—the world's largest rodent, native to Argentina. Gloves (which also come in more conventional kidskin) are the main attraction, and there's a wide variety of lengths and colors to choose from. ☒ *Esmeralda 775, Centro* ☎ *11/4322–9919* Ⓜ *C to Lavalle.*

Casa López. Don't let the drab storefront put you off: you're as likely to find a trouser suit in floral-print suede as a staid handbag for grandma at this two-part shopping spot. The right-hand store (No. 658) has totes in chestnut- and chocolate-color leather, as well as classic jackets. More unusual fare—including fur sacks with wool fringe, black cowhide baguettes, and tangerine purses—are sold next door at No. 640. ☒ *Marcelo T. de Alvear 640 and 658, Centro* ☎ *11/4311–3044* ⊕ *www.casalopezcuero.com* Ⓜ *C to San Martín.*

SAN TELMO

ANTIQUES AND COLLECTIBLES

Gabriel del Campo Anticuario. Gabriel's good taste means 50-year-old Louis Vuitton trunks don't look out of place beside wooden church statues or scale-model ships with canvas sails. Ceramic rubber-glove molds, one of his specialties, are some of the more accessible conversation pieces. The flagship store takes up a sizable patch of the Plaza Dorrego shop front. ☒ *Bethlem 427, on Plaza Dorrego, San Telmo* ☎ *11/4307–6589* Ⓜ *C to San Juan (walk 6 blocks along Humberto I).*

Gil Antigüedades. Sequined flapper dresses, dashing white-linen suits, and creamy lace wedding veils are some of the items you might stumble across in this *casa chorizo*, a typical multiroom property that stretches back to the next block. Period accessories include Castilian hair combs

Soda syphons for sale in the San Telmo flea market in Plaza Dorrego

and lacy fans that beg you to bat your lashes from behind them. ✉ *Humberto I 412, San Telmo* ☎ *11/4361–5019* ⊕ *www.gilantiguedades. com.ar* ☾ *Closed Mon.* Ⓜ *C to San Juan (walk 6 blocks along Av. San Juan).*

GIFTS AND SOUVENIRS

Artepampa. An artist-and-architect duo is behind these singular works, which are inspired by native Argentine art. They use an unusual papier-mâché technique to create boxes, frames, tapestries, and freestanding sculptures. The primitive-looking pieces, a vision of rich rusts and earthy browns, make highly original gifts. ✉ *Defensa 917, on Plaza Dorrego, San Telmo* ☎ *11/4362–6406* Ⓜ *C to San Juan.*

Juan Carlos Pallarols Orfebre. Argentina's legendary *orefebre* (silversmith) has made pieces for a mile-long list of celebrities including Frank Sinatra, Sharon Stone, Antonio Banderas, Bill Clinton, Nelson Mandela, and the king and queen of Spain. A set of ornate silver-handled steak knives is the perfect memento of cow country, although it will set you back several grand. ✉ *Defensa 1039, San Telmo* ☎ *11/4362–0641* ⊕ *www.pallarols.com.ar* Ⓜ *C or E to Independencia (walk 6 blocks along Estados Unidos).*

Fodor'sChoice
★

Marcelo Toledo. Sunlight and the smell of solder fill the rooms of this old San Telmo house, which doubles as a store and open workshop for celebrity silversmith Marcelo Toledo. A huge silver mosaic of Evita gives away who Toledo's main muse is: he has created replicas of her own jewelry (he is the only silversmith authorized by her estate to do so) as well as pieces inspired by her. Eva Duarte Perón isn't the only crowd-pleasing politician Toledo's been associated with: a local magnate commissioned cuff links as an inauguration gift for President Obama. He also designed a *mate* gourd especially for Prince William and his bride, the Duchess of Cambridge. ⊠ *Humberto I 458, San Telmo* ☎ *11/4362–0841* ⊕ *www.marcelotoledo.net* ☉ *Closed Sat.* Ⓜ *C to San Juan (6 blocks away).*

JEWELRY AND ACCESSORIES

Abraxas. "Yes" is pretty much guaranteed if you propose with one of the period engagement rings that dazzle in the window of this antique jeweler. If you're not planning on popping the question any time soon, surely you can find a home for a pair of art deco earrings with the tiniest of diamonds or a gossamer-fine bracelet? ⊠ *Defensa 1092, San Telmo* ☎ *11/4361–7512* ⊕ *www.abraxasantiques.com* Ⓜ *C to San Juan (walk 6 blocks along Humberto I).*

MARKETS

Fodor'sChoice **Feria de San Pedro Telmo.** Plaza Dorrego is the heart of the Feria de San
★ Pedro Telmo—an open-air market that stretches for more than a kilometer (0.6 mile) along Calle Defensa each Sunday. Thrust your way through the crowds to pick through antiques and curios of varying vintages as well as tango memorabilia, or watch professional tango dancers perform on the surrounding cobbled streets. The unofficial "stalls" (often just a cloth on the ground) of young craftspeople stretch several blocks up Defensa, away from the market proper. As it gets dark, the square turns into a milonga, where quick-stepping locals show you how it's done. ⊠ *Plaza Dorrego, Humberto I and Defensa, San Telmo* ⊕ *www.feriadesantelmo.com* ☉ *Closed Mon.–Sat.* Ⓜ *C to San Juan.*

RECOLETA

JEWELRY AND ACCESSORIES

Fodor'sChoice **Celedonio.** Local design hero Celedonio Lohidoy has created pieces—
★ often with frothy bunches of natural pearls—for Kenzo and Emanuel Ungaro and his work has even been slung around Sarah Jessica Parker's neck on *Sex in the City.* He favors irregular semiprecious stones, set in asymmetrical, organic-looking designs such as butterflies and daisies. ⊠ *Av. del Libertador 1774, Recoleta* ☎ *11/4803–7598* ⊕ *www.celedonio.com.ar* ☉ *Closed weekends* Ⓜ *H to Las Heras.*

Fahoma. This small boutique has enough accessories to make the rest of your outfit a mere formality. Berry-size beads go into chunky but affordable necklaces, which take flora and fauna as their inspiration, while all manner of handbags line the back wall. Need a royal seal of approval? Argentina-born Queen Máxima of the Netherlands has been photographed wearing their fun, oversize earrings. ⊠ *Libertad 1169, Recoleta* ☎ *11/4813–5103* ⊕ *www.fahoma.es* ☉ *Closed Sun.* Ⓜ *D to Tribunales (5 blocks away).*

MARKETS

Feria de Artesanos de Plaza Francia (*Feria Plaza Francia*). Each weekend, artisans sell handmade clothes, jewelry, and housewares as well as traditional crafts at this sprawling open-air market that winds through several linked squares outside the Recoleta Cemetery. ⊠ *Avs. Libertador* *and Pueyrredón, Recoleta* ⊕ *www.feriaplazafrancia.com* ⊗ *Closed weekdays* Ⓜ *H to Las Heras.*

SHOES, HANDBAGS, AND LEATHER GOODS

Guido. In Argentina loafers mean Guido, whose retro-looking logo has been the hallmark of quality footwear since 1952. Try on timeless handmade Oxfords and wing tips; there are also fun items like a tomatored handbag or a cow-skin tote. Accessories include simple belts and suede wallets. ⊠ *Av. Quintana 333, Recoleta* ☎ *11/4811–4567* ⊕ *www. zapateriaguido.com* ⊗ *Closed Sat. afternoon, Sun.* Ⓜ *C to San Martín (10 blocks away).*

WINE

Grand Cru. Savvy staff, some trained as sommeliers, will guide you through Grand Cru's peerless selection; the vast range is dominated by high-end wines from small wineries. ⊠ *Rodríguez Peña 1886, Recoleta* ☎ *11/4816–2223* ⊕ *www.grandcru.com.ar* ⊗ *Closed Sun.* Ⓜ *D to Callao.*

ALMAGRO

MALLS

FAMILY **Abasto Shopping.** The soaring art deco architecture of what was once the city's central market is as much a reason to come here as the 250 shops spread over its three levels. Abasto has many top local chains, so it isn't as exclusive as other malls, so bargains await at retailers like Ver, Yagmour, and Markova. Women can dress up at Paula Cahen d'Anvers, Akiabara, and Rapsodia, while men can hit trendy shops such as Bensimon, Prototype, and Old Bridge, or go for the *estanciero* look with smart La Martina polo wear. There's a food court on the top floor. The mall is also home to Museo de los Niños (a hands-on children's museum) and a 12-screen cinema; you can pick up tickets for entertainment elsewhere in town at the Ticketek booth near the food court, too. ⊠ *Av. Corrientes 3247, Almagro* ☎ *11/4959–3400* ⊕ *www. abasto-shopping.com.ar* Ⓜ *B to Carlos Gardel.*

PALERMO

CLOTHING: MEN

La Dolfina. Being a number-one polo player wasn't enough for Adolfo Cambiaso—he founded his own team in 1995, then started a clothing line that he also models for. If you think polo is all about kneehigh boots and preppy chinos, think again: Cambiaso sells some of the best urban menswear in town and this store includes a café. The Italian-cotton shirts, sharp leather jackets, and to-die-for totes are perfect for any occasion. ⊠ *Av. Figueroa Alocrta 3301, Palermo Botánico* ☎ *11/4806–3233* ⊕ *www.ladolfina.com.*

GIFTS AND SOUVENIRS

Elementos Argentinos. A fair-trade agreement links this luminous Palermo town house to a team of craftswomen in northwest Argentina who spin, dye, and weave the exquisite woolen goods sold here. Some of the handmade rugs, blankets, and throws follow traditional patterns and use only natural pigments (such as *yerba mate* or beetroot juice); others are contemporary designs using brighter colors. Packable souvenirs include sheep-wool table runners, alpaca scarves, and knitted cacti. Ask about designing your own rug. ⊠ *Gurruchaga 1881, Palermo Viejo* ☎ *11/4832–6299* ⊕ *elementosargentinos.com.ar* Ⓜ *D to Plaza Italia.*

JEWELRY AND ACCESSORIES

María Medici. Industrial-looking brushed silver rings and necklaces knit from fine stainless-steel cables are some of the attractions at this tiny shop. Architect and sculpturist María Medici also combines silver with primary-color resin to make unusual-looking rings. ⊠ *Niceto Vega 4619, Palermo Viejo* ☎ *11/4773–2283* ⊕ *mariamedici.blogspot.com.ar* Ⓜ *B to Malabia.*

SHOES, HANDBAGS, AND LEATHER GOODS

Fodor'sChoice
★

Humawaca. Thanks to its innovative shapes and funky colors, Humawaca is the hippest name in leather in town. Cowhide is a favorite here, as are lively combinations like chocolate-brown leather and moss-green suede, or electric blue nubuck with a floral lining. Along with the expected bags and purses, you can pick up stylish laptop or travel totes. Price tags will make you gulp, but there are wallets, gloves, and pencil cases for more demure budgets. There's a branch at Posadas 1380, in Palermo. ⊠ *El Salvador 4692, Palermo Viejo* ☎ *11/4832–2662* ⊕ *www. humawaca.com* Ⓜ *D to Plaza Italia.*

Fodor'sChoice
★

28Sport. These Argentine leather bowling sneakers and boxing-style boots are the heart and, er, sole of retro. All the models are variations on a classic round-toed lace-up, but come with different-length legs. Plain black or chestnut uppers go with everything, but equally tempting are the two-tone numbers—in chocolate and orange, or black with white panels, for example. Even the store is a nod to the past, kitted out like a 1950s living room. ⊠ *Gurruchaga 1481, Palermo Viejo* ☎ *11/4833–4287* ⊕ *www.28sport.com* Ⓜ *D to Plaza Italia (10 blocks away).*

Uma. Light, butter-soft leather takes very modern forms here, with geometric stitching the only adornment on jackets and asymmetrical bags that might come in rich violet in winter and aqua-blue in summer. The top-quality footwear includes teetering heels and ultrasimple boots and sandals. Ultratight jeans, leather boots, and tops are also on offer. There's a branch in the Galerías Pacífico Mall, at Florida 753, in Microcentro. ⊠ *Paseo Alcorta Mall, Shop 1049, Jerónimo Salguero 3172, at Av. Figueroa Alcorta, Palermo* ☎ *11/5777–6535* ⊕ *www.uma. com.ar* ☉ *Closed Sun.* Ⓜ *D to Bulnes.*

WINE

Fodor'sChoice
★

Terroir. Wine lovers' dreams come true inside this white-stone town house. Expert English-speaking staffers are on hand to help you make sense of the massive selection of Argentine wine, which includes collector's gems such as the 1999 Angélica Zapata Cabernet Sauvignon. They even arrange private wine-tasting courses to get you up to speed on local vintages: call a week or two before you arrive. ⊠ *Buschiazzo 3040, Palermo* ☎ *11/4778–3443* ⊕ *www.terroir.com.ar* Ⓜ *D to Palermo.*

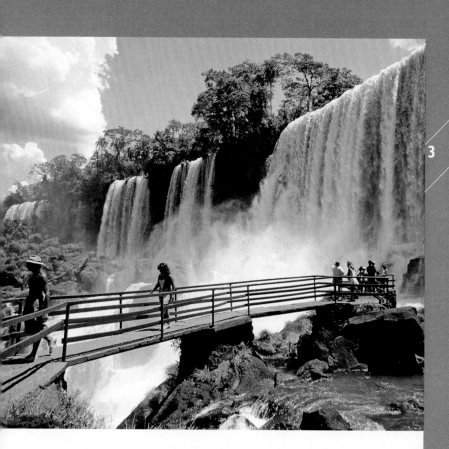

3

SIDE TRIPS

Buenos Aires Province and Iguazú Falls

Visit Fodors.com for advice, updates, and bookings

WELCOME TO SIDE TRIPS

TOP REASONS TO GO

★ **Wall of Water:** Nothing can prepare you for the roaring, thunderous Cataratas del Iguazú (Iguazú Falls). We think you'll agree.

★ **Cowboy Culture:** No visit to the pampas (grasslands) is complete without a stay at an *estancia,* a stately ranch house, like those around San Antonio de Areco. Sleep in an old-fashioned bedroom and share meals with the owners for a true taste of the lifestyle.

★ **Delta Dreaming:** Speeding through the Paraná River Delta's thousands of kilometers of rivers and streams, we'll forgive you for humming "Ride of the Valkyries"—it does feel very Mekong.

Argentina's famous pampas begin in Buenos Aires Province—an unending sea of crops and cattle-studded grass that occupies nearly one-quarter of the country's landscapes. Here are the region's most traditional towns, including San Antonio de Areco.

Suburban trains connect Buenos Aires to Tigre, close to the labyrinthine waterways of the Paraná Delta, explorable only by boat. On Argentina's northeastern tip, readily accessible by plane, are the jaw-dropping Cataratas del Iguazú.

1 Buenos Aires Province. An hour's drive from Buenos Aires leads to varied sights. The gaucho town of San Antonio de Areco lies northwest of other sites, such as the semitropical delta of the Paraná River, near the town of Tigre, and the provincial capital La Plata.

2 Iguazú Falls (Cataratas del Iguazú). The grandeur of this vast sheet of white water cascading in constant cymbal-banging cacophony makes Niagara Falls and Victoria Falls seem sedate. Allow at least two full days to take in this magnificent sight.

Updated by Sorrell Moseley-Williams

To hear *porteños* (inhabitants of Buenos Aires) talk of their city, you'd think Argentina stops where Buenos Aires ends. Not far beyond it, however, the skies open up and the *pampas*—Argentina's huge flat grasslands—begin. Pampean traditions are alive and well in farming communities that still dot the plains that make up Buenos Aires Province.

The best known is San Antonio de Areco, a well-preserved provincial town that's making a name for itself as gaucho central. You can ride across the pampas and get a taste of country life (and lots of grass-fed beef) by visiting—or staying at—a traditional *estancia* (ranch).

Ranchland gives way to watery wonders. The quiet suburban town of Tigre is the gateway to the network of rivers and tributaries that form the delta of the Paraná River, lined with luscious tropical vegetation. Low wooden launches speed along its waterways to the houses, restaurants, and lodges built on stilts along the riverbanks.

If you like your natural wonders supersized, take a short flight or a long bus ride to Iguazú Falls, northeast of Buenos Aires in semitropical Misiones Province. Here, straddling the border between Argentina and Brazil, two natural parks contain and protect hundreds of roaring falls and a delicate jungle ecosystem. The spectacle caused Eleanor Roosevelt to exclaim "Poor Niagara!" but most people are simply left speechless by the sheer size and force of the Garganta del Diablo, the grandest falls of them all.

PLANNING

WHEN TO GO
Temperatures in Buenos Aires Province rarely reach extremes. Note that some hotels and restaurants in areas popular with local tourists open *only* on weekends outside of peak season—this coincides with school holidays in summer (January and February), winter (July), and the Easter weekend. You'll get great discounts at those that open midweek in winter.

Early November's a good time to visit San Antonio de Areco, which holds its annual gaucho festival then. Like Buenos Aires, it feels curiously empty in January, when everyone decamps to the coast.

Though Iguazú Falls is thrilling year-round, seasonal rainfall and upstream Brazilian *barrages* (minidams) can affect the amount of water. If you visit between November and March, booking a hotel with air-conditioning and a swimming pool is as essential as taking mosquito repellent.

BORDER CROSSINGS

Crossing into Brazil from Argentina can be a thorny issue. By law, all U.S. citizens need a visa to enter Brazil. Visas can sometimes be issued in as little as three hours from the Brazilian consulate in Puerto Iguazú (as opposed to the three days they take in Buenos Aires) but can take up to two days. So it's best to secure your visa, which costs $160, well before you expect to cross. The Buenos Aires consulate also has a reputation for refusing visas to travelers who don't have onward tickets from Brazil.

If you stay in Foz do Iguaçu, travel on to other Brazilian cities, or do a day trip to Brazil by public bus or through an Argentine company, you'll need a visa. There have been reports of getting around this by using a Brazilian travel agent or by using local taxis (both Argentine and Brazilian) that have "arrangements" with border control. Though the practice is well established (most hotels and travel agents in Puerto Iguazú have deals with Brazilian companies and can arrange a visa-less visit), it *is* illegal. Enforcement of the law is generally lax, but sudden crackdowns and on-the-spot fines of hundreds of dollars have been reported.

CAR TRAVEL

Argentina has one of the world's worst records for traffic accidents, and the busy highways of Buenos Aires Province are often where they happen. January and February are the worst times, when drivers anxious to get to and from their holiday destination speed, tailgate, and exercise illegal maneuvers even more alarmingly than usual. If you're driving, do so very defensively and avoid traveling on Friday and Sunday, when traffic is worst.

Expressways and interprovincial routes tend to be atrociously signposted, so take a map. Getting a GPS-equipped rental car costs an extra 35 pesos or so per day: devices usually work well in cities, but the calibration is often a couple of hundred yards off in rural areas. Major routes are usually privately owned, which means frequent tolls. There are sometimes alternative roads to use, but they're generally smaller, slower, and in poor condition. On main roads the speed limit is 80 kph (50 mph), while on highways it's 130 kph (80 mph), though Argentinean drivers rarely pay heed to this.

SAFETY

Provincial towns like San Antonio de Areco are usually extremely safe, and the areas visited by tourists are well patrolled. Puerto Iguazú is fairly quiet in itself, but mugging and theft are common in nearby Foz do Iguaçu in Brazil, especially at night, when its streets are deserted.

WHAT IT COSTS IN ARGENTINE PESOS			
	$	$$	$$$	$$$$
Restaurants	under 300 pesos	300–500 pesos	501–750 pesos	over 750 pesos
Hotels	under 1,500 pesos	1,500–2,000 pesos	2,001–3,000 pesos	over 3,000 pesos

Restaurant prices are per person for a main course at dinner. Hotel prices are for a standard double room in high season.

BUENOS AIRES PROVINCE

Plains fan out where the city of Buenos Aires ends: this is the beginning of the pampas, which derive their name from the native Quechua word for "flat field." All over this fertile earth are signs of active ranch life, from the grazing cattle to the modern-day gauchos. The region is also noted for its crops, although these days the traditional alfalfa, sunflowers, wheat, and corn have largely been replaced by soy.

While Argentina was still a Spanish colony, settlers gradually began to force indigenous tribes away from the pampas near Buenos Aires, making extensive agriculture and cattle breeding possible. (In 1880, during the bloody Campaign of the Desert, the southern pampas were also "cleared" of indigenous tribes.) By the latter half of the 19th century the region had become known as the grain supplier for the world. From 1850 to 1950 more than 400 important estancias were built in Buenos Aires Province alone. Some of these have been modified for use as guest ranches and provide the best glimpse of the fabled pampean lifestyle.

TIGRE AND THE PARANÁ DELTA

30 km (19 miles) northwest of Buenos Aires on the Ruta Panamericana, 35 km (22 miles) northwest of Buenos Aires on Avenida Libertador.

A coastal train ride or a drive through the shady riverside suburbs of Buenos Aires takes you to the riverport town of Tigre, the embarkation point for boats that ply the Delta del Paraná. A couple of hours is plenty of time to visit the town itself from Buenos Aires; allow a whole day if you also plan to explore the delta—a vast maze of canals, tributaries, and river expanding out like the veins of a leaf. Heavy vegetation and rich birdlife (as well as clouds of mosquitoes) make the network of rivers feel tropical. The delta's many islands hide peaceful luxury getaways and cozy riverside restaurants accessible only by boat.

The waterways and close-packed islands that stretch northwest of Tigre are the most accessible part of the 14,000 square km (5,400 square miles) that make up the delta, where roads are replaced by rivers. Churning brown waters and heavy vegetation are vaguely reminiscent of Southeast Asia, though the chic houses and manicured gardens that line the rivers of the Primera Sección (closest to Tigre) are a far cry from Mekong River settlements.

If you want to take in more of the delta than a short boat trip allows, do as porteños do and combine it with a day's wining and dining at an island restaurant or a weekend at one of the hotels or luxury lodges a little farther afield. Many offer private transportation. The delta gets very hot and humid in summer, and the mosquitoes are ferocious, so bring insect repellent.

GETTING HERE AND AROUND

The cheapest way to get to Tigre by train is on the suburban commuter train from Estación Retiro to the central Estación Tigre. There are about four departures an hour on the Ramal Tigre (Tigre Branch) of the Línea Mitre; round-trip tickets cost 2.70 pesos. Alternatively, take the slick, tourist-oriented Tren de la Costa. It meanders through some of Buenos Aires' most fashionable northern suburbs and along the riverbank, stopping at nine stations before arriving at Estación Delta, near the Río Luján and Puerto de Frutos market. It starts halfway between Buenos Aires and Tigre, so you'll have to first take Línea Mitre, Ramal Mitre from Retiro to Estación Bartolomé Mitre, where you can change to the Tren de la Costa's Maipú Station. Round-trip fare is 40 pesos. The center of Tigre is small enough to walk around easily, but there are also taxis outside both train stations.

The most comfortable—and the most touristy—way to travel the delta's waterways is aboard the two-story catamarans that leave from docks on the Luján River, inside the Puerto de Frutos market. Rio Tur catamarans meander through 14 miles of waterways in about 90 minutes. They're a great way to glimpse delta life, and you'll see houses on stilts and boats piled high with provisions for towns upriver. | ■TIP→ **The last boat of the day usually catches the sunset.**

The low-slung wooden *lanchas colectivas* (boat buses) are the cheaper and more authentic way to explore the waterways; locals use them to get around the delta. These leave from the Estación Fluvial (Boat Station), on the other side of the round-about from Estación Tigre, the main train station. The main transport company for the delta is Interisleña, which serves all of the closest islands to the Tigre. Round-trip tickets start at 56 pesos. Líneas Delta Argentino uses similar boats but also runs one-hour tourism-oriented trips every couple of hours on weekends and holidays, which cost 60 pesos. Buy tickets from Booth 6, opposite the jetty. Touts offering private boat trips loiter outside the Tigre tourist board offices at the train and boat stations, but it's best to stick with recognized companies. As the boats leave the delta, they pass the magnificent turn-of-the-20th-century buildings of Tigre's heyday and colorfully painted houses built on stilts to protect them from floods.

> ### WORD OF MOUTH
>
> "We took two subways and a train to get to Tigre in the Delta area, north of BA. We had lunch along the river, strolled through Tigre, then got tickets on a 'lancha colectiva'—a public water bus that serves the Delta area. It was a fun, cheap way to spend an hour boating through the river system. I was surprised at the number of large homes along the river; apparently they are getaways for the wealthy who live in BA. The craft fair in Tigre was disappointing." –sbackus

ESSENTIALS

Boat Contacts Interisleña. ⊠ *Estación Fluvial, Mitre 345, Tigre* ☎ *11/4749–0900.* **Líneas Delta Argentino.** ⊠ *Estación Fluvial, Mitre 345, Tigre* ☎ *11/4731–1236* ⊕ *www.lineasdelta.com.ar.*

Train Contacts Línea Mitre. ☎ *0800/222–8736* ⊕ *www.trenmitre.com.ar.* **Tren de la Costa.** ☎ *11/4002–6000* ⊕ *www.trendelacosta.com.ar.*

Visitor and Tour Info Río Tur. ⊠ *Sarmiento and Buenos Aires, on the Río Luján, Tigre* ☎ *11/4731–0280* ⊕ *www.rioturcatamaranes.com.ar.* **Tigre Tourist Board.** ⊠ *Estación Fluvial, Bartolome Mitre 305, Tigre* ☎ *11/4512–4497* ⊕ *www.vivitigre.gob.ar.*

EXPLORING

TOP ATTRACTIONS

Fodor's Choice ★ **Museo de Arte de Tigre.** An arcade of Doric columns leads from the Luján River to this ornate building, built in 1909 to house a social club and casino. It contains a modest collection of Argentine paintings by artists like Quirós, Castagnino, Soldi, and Quinquela Martín, as well as works portraying life in the delta. The real showstopper, however, is the beautifully restored architecture: a sweeping marble staircase, stained-glass windows, gilt-inlaid columns, and soaring ceilings conspire to form a microcosm of the *fin de siècle* European style adored by the porteño elite. A trim sculpture garden and flower-filled park surround the museum, which is best reached by walking along Paseo Victorica. ⊠ *Paseo Victorica 972, Tigre* ☎ *11/4512–4528* ⊕ *www.mat. gov.ar* ✍ *50 pesos* ☉ *Closed Mon. and Tues.*

Museo del Mate. *Mate* drinking in Argentina is even more deeply culturally rooted than drinking coffee in the United States or tea in the United Kingdom. The *mate* gourd and the accompanying flask of hot water is ubiquitous throughout all social classes and age groups, whether one is sipping alone or sharing with a group of friends. The Museo del Mate is a great place to learn about the history of *mate yerba*—the shrub from which the bitter tea is made—and the sometimes very stylish mate gourds from which it's drunk. Many *mate* gourds, both antique and modern, are made from beautifully crafted porcelain or metal. Tours are available in English. ⊠ *Lavalle 289, Tigre* ☎ *11/4506–9594* ⊕ *www. elmuseodelmate.com* ✍ *60 pesos* ☉ *Closed Mon.–Wed.*

Museo Naval de la Nación. Although most visitors are into naval, military, or nautical history, this museum's collection will fascinate even those whose interests point elsewhere. The interior of the building, which looks like a hangar-size barn, is filled with paintings, statues, uniforms, and beautifully crafted model ships. On the grounds are long-retired planes from Argentina's aviation history, including a great example of a North American AT-6 "Texan" from 1939. ⊠ *Av. Victorica 602, Tigre* ☎ *11/4506–09332* ✍ *25 pesos* ☉ *Closed Mon.*

Puerto de Frutos. The center of the action at Tigre is its picturesque market. Hundreds of stalls selling furniture, handicrafts, and reasonably priced souvenirs fill the area around the docks along the Río Luján. It's particularly busy on weekends (indeed, many stalls are closed midweek). Grab a quick lunch from stands selling steak and chorizo sandwiches. ⊠ *Sarmiento at Buenos Aires, Tigre* ⊕ *www.puertodefrutos.gob.ar.*

WORTH NOTING

Paseo Victorica. Italianate mansions, museums, restaurants, and several rowing clubs dot this picturesque paved walkway and waterside park that curves alongside the Río Luján for about 10 blocks. To reach it, cross the bridge next to the roundabout immediately north of Estación Tigre, then turn right and walk five blocks along Avenida Lavalle, which runs along the Río Tigre. ⊠ *Along Río Luján between Río Tigre and Río Reconquista, Tigre.*

WHERE TO EAT

$$
MODERN
ARGENTINE

✕ **Almacén de Tigre.** About 100 yards west of the Estación Fluvial, this cozy eatery is seemingly miles away from the automobile and boat traffic. In a quiet quarter among a scattering of shops and cafés with bohemian flair, it's a great place to get away from the weekend crowds and enjoy a freshly made salad or sandwich. **Known for:** good salads; peaceful setting; trendy spot. ⑤ *Average main: 250 pesos* ⊠ *Bul. Saenz Peña 1336, Tigre* ☎ *11/5197–4009.*

$$$$ ✕ **Il Novo María del Luján.** An expen-
ARGENTINE   sive terrace overlooking the river
is the appropriate backdrop for
Tigre's best fish dishes. The kitchen
favors elaborate preparations:
some are so packed with unlikely
ingredients that the fish gets lost;
others, such as the sole in lemon-
infused cream, are spot-on. **Known
for:** outdoor dining; seafood; lively
atmosphere. ⑤ *Average main: 380
pesos* ⊠ *Paseo Victorica 511, Tigre*
☎ *11/4731–9613* ⊕ *www.ilnovo-
mariadellujan.com.*

WHERE TO STAY

The city of Tigre is so close to Buenos Aires that there's little reason to
stay overnight there. However, a night or two in the Paraná Delta is a
rewarding experience.

$$$ 🏨 **Bonanza.** Thick vegetation surrounds the tomato-red 19th-century
B&B/INN   country house that's the center of the eco-action at Bonanza. **Pros:** very
back-to-nature; great home cooking; lots of sports. **Cons:** remote; no
pool; minimal luxury. ⑤ *Rooms from: 2600 pesos* ⊠ *Río Carapachay
km 13, Tigre* ☎ *11/5245–9929* ⊕ *www.bonanza.com.ar* ⇆ *4 rooms*
⟊⃝ *All-inclusive.*

$$$$ 🏨 **La Becasina Delta Lodge.** Wooden walkways connect the luxurious bun-
RESORT   galows—each with a private riverside deck. **Pros:** peace and quiet; lots
of creature comforts; wild delta surroundings. **Cons:** expensive; nothing
else nearby; no kids under 14. ⑤ *Rooms from: 5300 pesos* ⊠ *Arroyo las
Cañas, San Fernando* ☎ *11/4728–1253* ⊕ *www.labecasina.com* ⇆ *15
bungalows* ⟊⃝ *All-inclusive.*

SAN ANTONIO DE ARECO

110 km (68 miles) west of Buenos Aires.

There's no better place to experience traditional provincial life in the
pampas than this well-to-do farming town. Grand estancias dot the
land in and around San Antonio. Many of the families that own them,
which form a sort of local aristocracy, mix lucrative soy farming with
estancia tourism. The gauchos who were once ranch hands now cook
up huge *asados* (barbecues) and lead horseback expeditions for the ever-
growing numbers of foreign tourists. You can visit one for a day—*un
día de campo*—or immerse yourself with an overnight visit.

Porteño visitors tend to base themselves in the town itself, which is
becoming known for its B&Bs. The fiercely conservative inhabitants
have done a good job of preserving the turn-of-the-20th-century Itali-
anate buildings that fill the sleepy *casco histórico* (historic center). Many
contain bars and general stores, which maintain their original fittings;
others are the workshops of some of the best craftspeople in the country.

In summer the banks of the Río Areco (Areco River), which runs through town, are teeming with picnickers—especially near the center of town, at the Puente Viejo (Old Bridge), which is overlooked by the open-air tables of various riverside parrillas. Nearby is the Museo Gauchesco y Parque Criollo Ricardo Güiraldes, which celebrates historical gaucho life. During the week surrounding November 10, the Día de la Tradición (Day of Tradition) celebrates the gaucho with shows, community barbecues, riding competitions, and a huge crafts fair. It's more fun to visit San Antonio on weekends, as many restaurants are closed Monday to Thursday.

GETTING HERE AND AROUND

To drive to San Antonio de Areco, leave Buenos Aires on RN9, crossing to RN8 when it intersects at Km 35 (total tolls of 15.60 pesos). There are more than 20 buses daily from Buenos Aires' Retiro Station to San Antonio; most are run by Nueva Chevallier, and some by Pullman General Belgrano. Each company operates from its own bus stop in San Antonio. Once you've arrived, the best way to get around is on foot, but you'll need a *remis* (radio taxi) to get to most estancias, though some have their own shuttle service.

ESSENTIALS

Bus Contacts Nueva Chevallier. ☎ 11/4000–5255 ⊕ www.nuevachevallier. com. **Pullman General Belgrano.** ☎ 11/4018–0010 ⊕ www.gralbelgrano.com. ar. **Terminal de Ómnibus Retiro.** ☎ 11/4310–0700 ⊕ www.tebasa.com.ar.

Taxi Contacts Remis Centro. ☎ 2326/456–225.

Visitor Info San Antonio de Areco Tourist Board. ⊠ Bul. Zerboni, at Arellano ☎ 2326/453–165 ⊕ www.sanantoniodeareco.com.

EXPLORING
TOP ATTRACTIONS

Museo Gauchesco y Parque Criollo Ricardo Güiraldes. Gaucho life of the past is celebrated—and idealized—at this quiet museum just outside town. Start at the 150-year-old *pulpería* (the gaucho version of the saloon), complete with dressed-up wax figures ready for a drink. Then head for the museum, an early-20th-century replica of a stately 18th-century *casco de estancia* (estancia house). Polished wooden cases contain a collection of traditional gaucho gear: decorated knives, colorful ponchos, and elaborate saddlery and bridlery. The museum is named for local writer Ricardo Güiraldes (1886–1927), whose romantic gaucho novels captured the imagination of Argentinean readers. Several rooms document his life in San Antonio de Areco and the real-life gauchos who inspired his work. ⊠ Camino Ricardo Güiraldes ☎ 2326/455–839 ✉ Free.

Museo Las Lilas de Areco. Although iconic Argentinean painter Florencio Molina Campos was not from San Antonio de Areco, his humorous paintings depict traditional pampas life. The works usually show red-nosed, pigeon-toed gauchos astride comical steeds, staggering drunkenly outside taverns, engaged in cockfighting or folk dancing, and taming bucking broncos. The collection is fun and beautifully arranged, and your ticket includes coffee and croissants in the jarringly modern café, which also does great empanadas and sandwiches. Behind its

San Antonio
de Areco

Parque
San Martín

Puente
Viejo

TO
BUENOS AIRES

Plaza
Arellano

Plaza
Gómez

Plaza
Belgrano

0   1/4 mile
0   1/4 kilometer

KEY

❶ Exploring sights

① Hotels & Restaurants

curtained walls lie huge theme park–style re-creations of three paintings. The lively and insightful voice-over explaining them is in Spanish
only. ⊠ *Moreno 279* ☏ *2326/456–425* ⊕ *www.museolaslilas.org* 🎫 *130
pesos* ☾ *Closed Mon.–Wed.*

WORTH NOTING

Museo Draghi Plateros Orfebres. San Antonio is famed for its silversmiths,
and the late Juan José Draghi was the best in town. This small museum
adjoining his workshop showcases the evolution of the Argentine silver-
work style known as *platería criolla*. Pieces are ornate takes on gaucho-
related items: spurs, belt buckles, knives, stirrups, and the ubiquitous
mate gourds, some dating from the 18th century. Also on display is
the incredibly ornate work of Juan José Draghi himself; you can buy
original pieces in the shop. His son keeps the family business alive—he's
often at work shaping new pieces at the back of the museum. ⊠ *Lavalle
387* ☏ *2325/15–650–600* ⊕ *www.marianodraghi.com* 🎫 *100 pesos.*

WHERE TO EAT

$$ ✕ **Almacén de Ramos Generales.** Airy and charming, this traditional eat-
ARGENTINE   ery's classic Argentine fare is consistently delicious. You can snack on
Fodor'sChoice cheeses, olives, prosciutto, salami, and eggplant *en escabeche* (pickled).
★   **Known for:** timewarp tavern; generous portions; genuine rural ambience.

⑤ *Average main: 240 pesos* ✉ *Zapiola 143, between Lavalle and Sdo. Sombra* ☎ *2326/456–376* ⊕ *www.ramosgeneralesareco.com.ar.*

WHERE TO STAY

$$$$
B&B/INN
🛏 **La Bamba de Areco.** Dating from the 1830s, the venerable La Bamba de Areco was once an important stop along the road from Buenos Aires to the northern reaches of Argentina. **Pros:** peace and quiet; gorgeous decor; great for outdoors lovers. **Cons:** might be too isolated for some; staff can seem harried; pricey. ⑤ *Rooms from: 22153 pesos* ✉ *Ruta 31* ☎ *2326/454–895* ⊕ *www.labambadeareco.com* ⇆ *11 rooms* ⦿ *All meals.*

$$$
HOTEL
🛏 **Patio de Moreno.** Being in the pampas doesn't mean you have to forget about slick design: this 1910-built town house has been transformed into the coolest hotel around. **Pros:** two blocks from main street; beautifully designed rooms and lobby; spacious bathrooms. **Cons:** rooms overlooking street can be noisy; families might be uncomfortable with very adult vibe; service is professional but impersonal. ⑤ *Rooms from: 2400 pesos* ✉ *Moreno 251, at San Martín* ☎ *2326/455–197* ⊕ ⇆ *11 rooms* ⦿ *Breakfast.*

NIGHTLIFE

"Pulpería," "*almacén*" (general store), and "*despacho de bebidas*" (drinks counter) are some of the labels you might find on San Antonio's many traditional bars. Some genuinely haven't changed in 50 years (neither have their clientele), and others are well-intentioned re-creations; all provide truly atmospheric surroundings for a coffee or a drink.

La Cervecería. Silver and leather aren't the only hand-crafted products in San Antonio. Seven varieties of artisanal beer, brewed on-site, have made a name for La Cervecería. The amber-colored Scottish ale packs a punch in winter; the paler pilsner's ideal for cooling off in summer. Pizzas, sandwiches, and other snacks accompany them. ✉ *Zapiola 76* ☎ *2326/1543–5712* ⟳ *Closed Mon.*

La Esquina de Mertí. Candy jars, old bottles, and a gleaming antique cash register sit atop the decades-old zinc-topped bar at La Esquina de Mertí, a gorgeous old café on Plaza Arellano. Stick with drinks—mugs of icy beer or vermouth and soda are the local favorites. ✉ *Arellano 149, at Segundo Sombra* ☎ *2326/456–705.*

SHOPPING

San Antonio de Areco is an excellent place to pick up high-quality handicrafts and gifts, especially traditional silverware and leather goods. Workshops that double as stores fill the old houses lining Calle Alsina and other streets leading off Plaza Arellano, the main square.

Cristina Giordano. The handwoven belts and ponchos Cristina Giordano creates in soft, naturally dyed fibers are fit to hang on the wall as art, and have justifiably made her San Antonio's best-known traditional weaver. ✉ *Sarmiento 112* ☎ *2326/452–829* ⊕ *www.telarcriolloypampa.com.ar.*

Gustavo Stagnaro. Gustavo Stagnaro is a big name in San Antonio silversmithing. His majestic corner store sells gaucho knives,

Continued on page 137

THE COWBOYS at WORLD'S END

by Victoria Patience

Along a country road, you may come across riders herding cattle. Dressed in baggy pants and shirts, a knife stuck in the back of their belts, these are the descendants of the gauchos, Argentina's cowboys. These men of few words symbolize honor, honesty, and courage— so much so that a favor or good deed is known locally as a *gauchada*.

WHAT'S IN A NAME?

No one can agree on where the word "gaucho" comes from. Some say it's derived from the native Quechua-language word *guachu*, meaning "orphan" or "outcast"; others attribute similar meanings to the French word *gauche*, another suggested source. Yet another theory traces it (via Andalusian Spanish) to the Arabic word *chaouche*, a kind of whip for herding cattle.

Gauchos were the cattle-herding settlers of the pampas (grasslands), renowned for their prowess as horsemen. Most were criollos (Argentina-born descendants of Spanish immigrants) or mestizos (of mixed Spanish and native Argentine descent). They lived in villages but spent much of their time riding the plains, much like North American cowboys.

With the establishment of big estancias (ranches) in the early- and mid-19th century, landowners began taking on gauchos as hired hands. The sheer size of these ranches meant that the gaucho's nomadic lifestyle remained largely unchanged, however.

In the 1860s Argentina's president Domingo Faustino Sarmiento encouraged massive settlement of the pampas, and branded gauchos as barbaric, potentially criminal elements. (Despite being of humble origins, Sarmiento as a snob about anything he saw as uncivilized.) Laws requiring travelers to carry passes ended the gaucho's right to roam. Many more than ever signed on as permanent ranch hands; others were drafted into military service, at times becoming deserters and outlaws.

Vindication came in the late-19th and early-20th century, when a wave of literary works like José Hernández's Martín Fierro and Ricardo Güiraldes's Don Segundo Sombra captured the national imagination with their dramatic, romantic descriptions of gauchos and their nomadic lifestyle. The gaucho—proud, brave, and melancholy—has been a national icon ever since.

Gaucho on an estancia near El Calafate, Patagonia, Argentina

GAUCHO GEAR

SOMBRERO
Although a sombrero (flat-crowned, wide-brimmed hat) is the most typical style, conical felt hats (shown), berets, flat caps, and even top hats are also worn.

CAMISA
Traditionally smocked shirt with baggy sleeves. Modern gauchos wear regular long-sleeved cotton shirts.

BOMBACHA
Baggy pants cinched at the ankle; the story goes that after the Crimean War, surplus Turkish-style army pants were sold to Argentina by Britain and France. The fashion caught on: no gaucho is seen without these.

BOTAS
Early gauchos wore rough, rawhide boots with open toes or a flip-flop-style thong. Today, gauchos in colder parts of Argentina wear flat-soled, tapered boots, usually with a baggy pirate-style leg.

PAÑUELO
Large, brightly colored kerchief, worn knotted around the neck; some gauchos drape them under their hats to protect their necks from the sun or cold.

CHAQUETA
Jacket; often kept for special occasions, and usually worn short and unbuttoned, to better display the shirt and waistcoat underneath.

CHIRIPÁ
Before bombachas arrived, gauchos used to wind a large swathe of woven fabric (like an oversize loincloth) over thin, long underpants.

FAJA
A long strip of colorful woven fabric once worn to hold the pants up, now mainly decorative and often replaced by a leather belt. Either way, gauchos stick their knives in the back.

ESPUELAS
Spurs; most gauchos favor those with spiked wheel-like designs.

Gaucho traditionally dressed

SUPER GAUCHOS

REBENQUE
A short rawhide crop, often with a decorative metal handle.

PONCHO
Woven from sheep's or llama's wool, usually long and often vertically striped. Some colors denote certain provinces.

ALPARGATAS
Spanish immigrants in the 18th century popularized flat, rope-soled espadrilles in warmer parts of Argentina. Today, rubber-soled versions are more common.

BOLEADORAS
Gauchos adopted this native Argentinian device for catching animals. It's made of two or three stones wrapped in cowhide and mounted at the end of a cowhide cord. You whirl the boleadora then release it at the animal's legs.

LAZO
A braided rawhide lasso used for roping cattle.

CUCHILLO OR FACÓN
No gaucho leaves home without his knife. Indeed, most Argentine men have one to use at barbecues (early gauchos used theirs for fighting, too). Handles are made of wood or horn, blades are triangular.

Unsigned mural of Gauchito Gil, a saint-like character in popular Argentine belief (supposedly a Robin Hood-type outlaw called Antonio Mamerto Gil Núñez).

EL GAUCHITO GIL: legend has it that this gaucho from Corrientes Province was hunted down by a sheriff over a woman. He was hung by his feet from a tree but, just before his throat was cut, he predicted that the sheriff would find his son at home mortally ill and only able to recover if the sheriff prayed to Gil. The prediction came true, and the repentant sheriff spread the word. Today, roadsides all over Argentina are dotted with red-painted shrines to this folk saint. Superstitious locals leave offerings, hoping for help with their problems.

MARTÍN FIERRO: the fictional hero of an eponymous 19th-century epic poem written by José Hernández. Fierro is a poor but noble gaucho who's drafted into the army. He deserts and becomes an outlaw. His pride, independence, and love of the land embody the national ideal of what a man should be. Writer Jorge Luis Borges so loved the poem that he started a literary magazine with the same name.

JUAN MOREIRA: a real-life gaucho who married the daughter of a wealthy landowner, provoking the wrath of a jealous local judge. Wrongly accused of various crimes, Moreira became a fugitive and a famed knife-fighter, killing 16 men before eventually dying in a police ambush in 1874 in the town of Lobos in Buenos Aires Province. A 1973 biographical film by arty local director Leonardo Favio was a box-office smash.

3

IN FOCUS THE COWBOYS AT WORLD'S END

UN DIA DE CAMPO

Gaucho on an estancia near El Calafate, Patagonia, Argentina

In the late 19th century, well-to-do European families bought huge blocks of pampas land on which to build estancias, often with luxurious houses reminiscent of the old country. The advent of industrial agriculture has led many estancias to turn to tourism for income; others combine tourism with small-scale farming.

The gauchos who once herded cows now have a new sideline shepherding visitors, putting on riding shows or preparing large-scale *asados* (barbecues). You can visit an estancia for a *día de campo* (day in the country) or to stay overnight or for a weekend. There are estancias for most budgets: some are ultraluxurious bed-and-breakfasts, others are homey, family-run farms.

A day at an estancia typically involves a late breakfast; horseback riding or a long walk; a full-blown asado accompanied by Argentine red wine; and afternoon tea. Longer stays at upscale establishments might also include golf or other sports; at working farms you can feed animals or help with the milking. Estancia accommodation generally includes all meals, and although some estancias are close to towns, it's rare to leave the grounds during a stay.

HORSEMANSHIP

During a visit to an estancia, you may see gauchos demonstrating traditional skills and games such as:

Zapateo Criollo: a complicated, rhythmic, foot-stomping dance.

Jineteada or Doma: rodeo, gaucho-style.

La Carrera de Sortija: riders gallop under a bar from which metal rings are hung, trying to spear a ring on a stick as they pass.

Carrera Cuadrera: a short horseback sprint that riders start from a standstill.

Boleadas and Pialadas: catching an animal using boleadoras or a lasso, respectively.

La Maroma: participants hang from a bar or rope and jump onto a horse that gallops beneath them.

GAUCHO GRUB

When gauchos were out on the pampas for weeks, even months, at a time, their diet revolved around one food—beef—and one drink—mate (a type of tea). Times may have changed, but most Argentinians still consume a lot of both.

MAKING THE MOST OF AN ASADO

Whether you're just at someone's home or out on an estancia, a traditional Argentinian asado is a drawn-out affair. All sorts of meats go on the grill initially, including chorizo sausage, black pudding, and sweetbreads. These are grilled and served before the larger cuts. You'll probably also be served a picada (cheese, salami, and other snacks). Follow the local example and go easy on these starters: there's lots more to come.

The main event is, of course, the beef. Huge, grass-fed chunks of it, roasted for at least two hours over hot coals and flavored with little more than salt. While the asador (barbecuer) does his stuff, it's traditional to admire his or her skills; interfering (criticism, touching the meat, or the like) is not part of this tradition. The first meat to be served is often thick-cut ribs, accompanied simply by a mixed salad and bread. Then there will be a pause for digestion, and the asador will serve the choicest cuts: flank or tenderloin, usually. All this is washed down with a robust red wine and, not surprisingly, followed by a siesta.

Gaucho *asado* (barbecue), Argentina

MATE FOR BEGINNERS

Mate (mah-tay) is a strong tea made from the dried leaves of *Ilex paraguariensis*, known as yerba. It's drunk from a gourd (also called a mate) through a metal straw with a filter on the end (the *bombilla*).

A gaucho drinking mate, at the estancia La Cina, Buenos Aires Provence

Mate has long been a traditional drink for the Guaraní people native to Argentina's northeast. They introduced it to Jesuit missionaries, who learned to cultivate it, and today, most yerba mate is still grown in Misiones and Corrientes provinces. The drink eventually became popular throughout Argentina, Uruguay, and southern Brazil.

Much like tea in England, mate serves as the basis of social interaction: people drink it at any hour of the day. Several drinkers share the same gourd, which is refilled and passed round the group. It's often extended to strangers as a welcoming gesture. If you're shown this hospitality be sure to wait your turn, drink all the mate in the gourd fairly quickly, and hand the gourd directly back to the *cebador* (server). Don't pour yourself a mate if someone else is the cebador, and avoid wiping or wiggling the straw around. Also, you don't say "gracias" until you've had your fill.

WHAT'S IN A MATE?

Caffeine: 30 mg per 8-oz serving (versus 47 mg in tea and 100 mg in coffee)

Vitamins:
A, C, E, B1, B2, B3, B5, B complex

Minerals:
Calcium, manganese, iron, selenium, potassium, magnesium, phosphorus, zinc

Antioxidant properties:
similar to green tea

SERVING MATE

1) Heat a kettle of water to just before boiling (176°F/80°C)—boiling water ruins yerba.

2) Fill ⅔ of the gourd with yerba.

3) Without the bombilla in place, cover the gourd with your hand, and turn it quickly upside down (to get rid of any fine yerba dust that can block the bombilla).

4) For some reason, yerba never sits flat in the gourd; pour some hot water in the empty space left by the slightly slanting yerba leaves. Let the yerba swell a little, cover the top of the bombilla with your thumb, and drive it firmly into the leaves.

5) Finish filling the gourd with water, pouring it in slowly near the bombilla's base. (Some people also add sugar at this point.)

6) Drink all the mate in the gourd (the cebador traditionally drinks first, so the mate isn't so bitter when brewed for others) and repeat Step 5, passing the gourd to the next drinker—and so on—until the yerba mate loses its flavor.

no-nonsense silver jewelry, and mate paraphernalia. ⊠ *Arellano at Matheu* ☎ *2326/454–801* ⊕ *www.stagnaro.com.ar.*

La Olla de Cobre. All the mouthwatering chocolates and *alfajores* (dulce de leche sandwich cookies) at La Olla de Cobre are handmade on the premises. Best of all, you can sample before you buy. ⊠ *Matheu 433* ☎ *2326/453–105* ⊕ *www.laolladecobre.com.ar* ☉ *Closed Tues.*

Platería de Campo. All the gaucho accessories you can think of—including knives, belt buckles, and kerchief rings—are exquisitely made in silver at Platería de Campo. ⊠ *Alsina 86* ☎ *2326/456–825* ⊕ *www. plateriadecampo.com.ar* ☉ *Closed Sun.*

IGUAZÚ FALLS

1,358 km (843 miles) north of Buenos Aires; 637 km (396 miles) west of Curitiba; 544 (338 miles) west of Vila Velha.

Iguazú consists of some 275 separate waterfalls—in the rainy season there are as many as 350—that plunge more than 200 feet onto the rocks below. They cascade in a deafening roar at a bend in the Iguazú River (Río Iguazú in Spanish, Rio Iguaçu in Portuguese) where the borders of Argentina, Brazil, and Paraguay meet. Dense, lush jungle surrounds the falls: here the tropical sun and the omnipresent moisture produce a towering pine tree in two decades instead of the seven it takes in, say, Scandinavia. By the falls and along the roadside, rainbows and butterflies are set off against vast walls of red earth, which is so ubiquitous that eventually even paper currency in the area turns red from exposure to the stuff.

The falls and the lands around them are protected by Argentina's Parque Nacional Iguazú (where the falls are referred to by their Spanish name, the Cataratas de Iguazú) and by Brazil's Parque Nacional do Iguaçu (where the falls go by the Portuguese name of Cataratas do Iguaçu).

To visit the falls, you can base yourself in the Argentine town of Puerto Iguazú, or its sprawling Brazilian counterpart, the city of Foz do Iguaçu. The two cities are 18 km (11 miles) and 25 km (15 miles) northwest of the falls, respectively, and are connected by an international bridge, the Puente Presidente Tancredo Neves.

PUERTO IGUAZÚ, ARGENTINA

Originally a port for shipping wood from the region, Puerto Iguazú now revolves around tourism. This was made possible in the early 20th century when Victoria Aguirre, a wealthy visitor from Buenos Aires, funded the building of a road to the falls. Despite the constant stream of visitors from Argentina and abroad, Puerto Iguazú remains small and sleepy. Many of its secondary roads still aren't paved.

Many travelers to the falls—including those from Brazil—opt to stay on the Argentine side of the border because it's less expensive than the Brazilian side. The town is also a good place to wind down after a day or two of high-energy adventure before heading back to Buenos Aires. So spare some time to experience being surrounded by hummingbirds in a garden, or just grab some *helado* (ice cream) and meander to el Hito Tres Fronteras.

GETTING HERE AND AROUND

Aerolíneas Argentinas flies four to five times daily between Aeroparque Jorge Newbery in Buenos Aires and the Aeropuerto Internacional de Puerto Iguazú, which is about 20 km (12 miles) southeast of Puerto Iguazú; the trip takes 1¾ hours. LAN does the same trip two or three times daily. Normal rates start at about 800 pesos each way. Four Tourist Travel runs shuttle buses from the airport to hotels in Puerto Iguazú. They leave after every flight lands and cost 25 pesos. Taxis to Puerto Iguazú cost 100 pesos.

Vía Bariloche operates several daily buses between the Retiro bus station in Buenos Aires and the Puerto Iguazú Terminal de Omnibus in the center of town. The trip takes 16–18 hours, so it's worth paying the little extra for *coche cama* (sleeper) or *cama ejecutivo* (deluxe sleeper) services, which cost about 903 pesos one-way (regular semi-cama services cost around 410 pesos). You can travel direct to Rio de Janeiro (22 hours) and São Paolo (15 hours) with Crucero del Norte; the trips cost 1,035 and 904 pesos, respectively.

From Puerto Iguazú to the falls or the hotels along RN12, take El Práctico from the terminal or along Avenida Victoria Aguirre. Buses leave every 15 minutes from 7 to 7 and cost 20 pesos round-trip.

There's little point in renting a car around Puerto Iguazú: daily rentals start at 260 to 300 pesos, more than twice what you pay for a taxi between the town and the falls.

Crucero del Norte runs an hourly cross-border public bus service (60 pesos) between the bus stations of Puerto Iguazú and Foz do Iguaçu. Locals don't have to get on and off for immigration, but be sure you do so. To reach the Argentine falls, change to local minibus service El Práctico at the intersection with RN12 on the Argentine side. For the Brazilian park, change to a local bus at the Avenida Cataratas roundabout.

Argentinean travel agency Sol Iguazú Turismo organizes door-to-door transport to both sides of the falls, and can reserve places on the Iguazú Jungle Explorer trips.

Bus Contacts Crucero del Norte. ☎ *0810/777–2725* ⊕ *www.crucerodelnorte. com.ar.* **Four Tourist Travel.** ☎ *3757/420–681* ⊕ *www.ftt.tur.ar.* **Vía Bariloche.** ☎ *0810/333–7575 in Buenos Aires, 3757/420–854 in Puerto Iguazú* ⊕ *www. viabariloche.com.ar.*

Visitor Info Cataratas del Iguazú Visitors Center. ⊠ *Off Ruta Nacional 101, Puerto Iguazú* ☎ *3757/491–469* ⊕ *www.iguazuargentina.com.* **Puerto Iguazú Tourist Office.** ⊠ *Av. Victoria Aguirre 311, Puerto Iguazú* ☎ *3757/420–800* ⊕ *www.iguazuturismo.gob.ar.* **Sol Iguazú Turismo.** ⊠ *Av. Victoria Aguirre 237, Puerto Iguazú* ☎ *3757/421–008* ⊕ *www.soliguazu.com.ar.*

EXPLORING

The falls are not the only sites to see in these parts, though few people actually have time (or make time) to go see others.

TOP ATTRACTIONS

Güira Oga. Although Iguazú Falls is home to around 450 bird species, the parks are so busy these days that you'd be lucky to see so much as a feather. It's another story at Güira Oga, which means "House of the Birds" in Guaraní. Birds that were injured, displaced by deforestation, or confiscated from traffickers are brought here for treatment. The large cages also house species you rarely see in the area, including the gorgeous red macaw. The sanctuary is in a forested plot halfway between Puerto Iguazú and the falls. Entrance includes a 90-minute guided visit (in English and Spanish). ⊠ *RN12, Km 1638, Puerto Iguazú* ☎ *3757/423–980* ⊕ *www.guiraoga.com.ar* 🖭 *200 pesos.*

WORTH NOTING

Jardín de los Picaflores. With more than 400 species of birds in the national parks surrounding Iguazú Falls, bird-watchers will be kept happily busy. This tiny garden north of Puerto Iguazú serves as more of a feeding station than a refuge, but it's busy with the little powerhouses zipping about. ⊠ *Fray Luis Beltran 150, Puerto Iguazú* ☎ *3757/424–081* 🖭 *80 pesos.*

Hito Tres Fronteras. This viewing point west of the town center stands high above the turbulent reddish-brown confluence of the Iguazú and Paraná rivers, which also form the Triple Frontera, or Triple Border

Landmark. A mini pale-blue-and-white obelisk reminds you you're in Argentina. Take binoculars to see Brazil's green-and-yellow equivalent across the Iguazú River; across the Paraná is Paraguay's, painted red, white, and blue. A row of overpriced souvenir stalls stands alongside the Argentine obelisk. ⊠ *Av. Tres Fronteras, Puerto Iguazú.*

La Aripuca. It looks like a cross between a log cabin and the Pentagon, but this massive wooden structure—which weighs 551 tons—is a large-scale replica of a Guaraní bird trap. La Aripuca officially showcases different local woods, supposedly for conservation purposes—ironic, given the huge trunks used to build it and the overpriced wooden furniture that fills the gift shop. ⊠ *RN12, Km 4.5, Puerto Iguazú* ☎ *3757/423–488* ⊕ *www.aripuca.com.ar* ⌑ *110 pesos.*

WHERE TO EAT

$$$$
MODERN
ARGENTINE

✕ **Aqva.** Locals are thrilled: finally, a date-night restaurant in Puerto Iguazú. Although the high-ceilinged split-level cabin seats too many to be truly intimate, the owners make up for it with well-spaced tables, discreet service, and low lighting. **Known for:** local ingredients; great service; excellent fish dishes. ⑤ *Average main: 380 pesos* ⊠ *Av. Córdoba at Carlos Thays, Puerto Iguazú* ☎ *3757/422–064* ⊕ *www.aqvarestaurant.com.*

$$$
ARGENTINE

✕ **La Rueda.** This parrilla is so popular that it starts serving dinner at 6 pm—teatime by Argentine custom. The local beef isn't quite up to Buenos Aires standards, but La Rueda's perfectly cooked *bife de chorizo* is one of the best in town. **Known for:** good grilled fish and steak; efficient service gets diners in and out quickly; well priced. ⑤ *Average main: 350 pesos* ⊠ *Av. Córdoba 28, Puerto Iguazú* ☎ *3757/422–531* ⊕ *www.larueda1975.com.ar* ⊙ *No lunch Mon.*

WHERE TO STAY

$$$$
RESORT
FAMILY

▦ **Iguazú Grand.** A full-on resort designed with families in mind, Iguazú Grand is bursting with facilities to keep every family member satisfied. **Pros:** spacious rooms and comfy beds; indoor and outdoor pools; courteous and helpful staff. **Cons:** downtown is a 20-minute walk or pricey cab ride away; slow elevators; passageways reverberate noise. ⑤ *Rooms from: 4400 pesos* ⊠ *Ruta 12, Km 1640, Puerto Iguazú* ☎ *3757/498–050* ⊕ *www.iguazugrand.com* ⌑ *134 rooms* ❍❘ *Free Breakfast.*

$$$
B&B/INN

▦ **Posada 21 Oranges.** You'll get a warm welcome at this rootsy B&B, which is surrounded by a lush garden. **Pros:** helpful and attentive owners; peaceful surroundings; abundant homemade breakfasts served on the garden terrace. **Cons:** too far to walk to town center; low on luxury; some rooms are cramped. ⑤ *Rooms from: 2200 pesos* ⊠ *Montecarlo s/n, near RN12, Km 5, Puerto Iguazú* ☎ *3757/494–014* ⊕ *www.21oranges. com* ⊟ *No credit cards* ⌑ *10 rooms* ❍❘ *Breakfast.*

$$$
B&B/INN

▦ **Secret Garden Iguazú.** Dense tropical vegetation overhangs the wooden walkway that leads to this tiny guesthouse's three rooms, tucked away in a pale-blue clapboard house. **Pros:** wood deck overlooking the back-to-nature garden; owner's charm and expert mixology; home-away-from-home vibe. **Cons:** the three rooms book up fast; no pool; comfortable but not luxurious. ⑤ *Rooms from: 3000 pesos* ⊠ *Los Lapachos 623, Puerto Iguazú* ☎ *3757/423–099* ⊕ *www.secretgardeniguazu.com* ⊟ *No credit cards* ⌑ *3 rooms* ❍❘ *Breakfast.*

Continued on page 148

By Victoria Patience

IGUAZÚ FALLS

Big water. That's what *y-guasu*—the name given to the falls by the indigenous Guaraní people—means. As you approach, a thundering fills the air and steam rises above the trees. Then the jungle parts. Spray-soaked and speechless, you face the Devil's Throat, and it's clear that "big" doesn't come close to describing this wall of water.

Taller than Niagara, wider than Victoria, Iguazú's raging, monumental beauty is one of nature's most awe-inspiring sights. The Iguazú River, on the border between Argentina and Brazil, plummets 200 feet to form the Cataratas de Iguazú (as the falls are known in Spanish) or Foz do Iguaçu (their Portuguese name). Considered to be one waterfall, Iguazú is actually made up of around 275 individual drops, that stretch along 2.7 km (1.7 mi) of cliff-face. Ranging from picturesque cascades to immense cataracts, this incredible variety is what makes Iguazú so special. National parks in Brazil and Argentina protect the falls and the flora and fauna that surround them. Exploring their jungle-fringed trails can take two or three days: you get right alongside some falls, gaze down dizzily into others, and can take in the whole spectacle from afar. You're sure to come across lizards, emerald- and sapphire-colored hummingbirds, clouds of butterflies, and scavenging raccoonlike coatis. You'll also glimpse monkeys and toucans, if you're lucky.

GEOLOGY 101

Over 100 million years ago, lava surged up through cracks in the earth's crust near Iguazú. It spread out over the surrounding area, forming three layers of basalt (a dark, fine-grained rock) tens of meters high. The Iguazú River, which starts 1,200 km (745 mi) east, flowed over this. Later, the movement of tectonic plates raised parts of the surface, which became stepped. As the river flowed over these steps it eroded the rock surface it fell on even more, and over the next few million years, the waters carved out what are now the falls.

WHEN TO GO

Time of year	Advantages	Disadvantages
Nov.–Feb.	High rainfall in December and January, so expect lots of water.	Hot and sticky. December and January are popular with local visitors. High water levels stop Zodiac rides.
Mar.–Jun.	Increasingly cooler weather. Fewer local tourists. Water levels are usually good.	Too cold for some people, especially when you get wet. Occasional freak water shortages.
Jul.–Oct.	Cool weather.	Low rainfall in July and August—water levels can be low. July is peak season for local visitors.

WHERE TO GO: ARGENTINA VS. BRAZIL

Argentines and Brazilians can fight all day about who has the best angle on the falls. But the two sides are so different that comparisons are academic. To really say you've done Iguazú (or Iguaçu), you need to visit both. If you twist our arm, we'll say the Argentine side is a better experience with lots more to do, but (and this is a big "but") the Brazilian side gives you a tick in the box and the best been-there-done-that photos. It's also got more non-falls-related activities (but you have to pay extra for them).

	ARGENTINA	BRAZIL
Park Name	Parque Nacional Iguazú	Parque Nacional do Iguaçu
The experience	Up close and personal (you're going to get wet).	What a view!
The falls	Two-thirds are in Argentina including Garganta del Diablo, the star attraction.	The fabulous panoramic perspective of the Garganta do Diablo is what people really come for.
Timing	One day to blitz the main attractions. Two days to explore fully.	Half a day to see the falls; all day if you do other activities.
Other activities	Extensive self-guided hiking and Zodiac rides.	Organized hikes, Zodiac rides, boat rides, helicopter rides, rafting, abseiling.
Park size	67,620 hectares (167,092 acres)	182,262 hectares (450,379 acres)
Animal species	80 mammals/450 birds	50 mammals/200 birds

VITAL STATISTICS

Number of falls: 160—275*	Total length: 2.7 km (1.7 mi)	Average Flow: 396,258 gallons per second Peak Flow: 1,717,118 gallons per second
Major falls: 19	Height of Garganta del Diablo: 82 m (270 feet)	Age: 120—150 million years

*Depending on water levels

IGUAZÚ ITINERARIES

LIGHTNING VISIT. If you only have one day, limit your visit to the Argentine park. Arrive when it opens, and get your first look at the falls aboard one of Iguazú Jungle Explorer's Zodiacs. The rides finish at the Circuito Inferior: take a couple of hours to explore this. (Longer summer opening hours give you time to squeeze in the **Isla San Martín**.) Grab a quick lunch at the Dos Hermanas snack bar, then blitz the shorter Circuito Superior. You've kept the best

Tren Ecologico de la Selva

for last: catch the train from **Estación Cataratas** to **Estación Garganta del Diablo**, where the trail to the viewing platform starts (allow at least two hours for this).

BEST OF BOTH SIDES. Two days gives you enough time to see both sides of the falls. Visit the Brazilian park on your second day to get the panoramic take on what you've experienced up-close in Argentina. If you arrive at 9 AM, you've got time to walk the entire trail, take photos, have lunch in the Porto Canoas service area, and be back at the park entrance by 1 PM. You could spend the afternoon doing excursions and activities from Macuco Safari and Ma-

KEY

♿	*Wheelchair-accessible*
🍴	*Restaurant*
🍁	*Scenic Viewpoint*
- - -	*Walking/Hiking Trails*
🚢	*Ferry Lines*
⊢⊢⊢	*Rail Lines*

Estación Garganta
del Diablo

Garganta
del Diablo ♿

*Garganta
del Diablo*

ARGENTINA

*Parque Nacional
do Iguaçu*

Isla San Martín

BRAZIL

Río Iguazú

Walkway view at
Garganta del Diablo

cuco EcoAventura, or visiting the Itaipú dam. Alternatively, you could keep the visit to Brazil for the afternoon of the second day, and start off with a lightning return visit to the Argentine park and see the **Garganta del Diablo** (left) with the sun rising behind it.

SEE IT ALL. With three days you can explore both parks at a leisurely pace. Follow the one-day itinerary, then return to the Argentine park on your second day. Make a beeline for the Gar-

ganta del Diablo, which looks different in the mornings, then spend the afternoon exploring the **Sendero Macuco** (and Isla San Martín, if you didn't have time on the first day). You'll also have time to visit Güira Oga bird sanctuary or La Aripuca (both on RN 12) afterwards. You could spend all of your third day in the Brazilian park, or just the morning, giving you time to catch an afternoon flight or bus.

Estación
Central

Estación
Cataratas

Circuito
Superior

Parque Nacional
Iguazú

Circuito
Inferior

Dos Hermanas

VISITING THE PARKS

Visitors gaze at the falls in Parque Nacional Iguazú.

Argentina's side of the falls is in the **Parque Nacional Iguazú,** which was founded in 1934 and declared a World Heritage Site in 1984. The park is divided into two areas, each of which is organized around a train station: Estación Cataratas or the Estación Garganta del Diablo. (A third, Estación Central, is near the park entrance.)

Paved walkways lead from the main entrance past the **Visitor Center,** called *Yvyrá Retá*—"country of the trees" in Guaraní (☎ 3757/49-1469 ⊕ www.iguazuargentina. com ⊙ Mar.–Aug. 8–6; Sept.–Feb. 8–8). Colorful visual displays provide a good explanation of the region's ecology and human history. To reach the park proper, you cross through a small plaza containing a food court, gift shops, and ATM. From the nearby Estación Central, the gas-propelled Tren de la Selva (Jungle Train) departs every 20 minutes.

In Brazil, the falls can be seen from the **Parque Nacional Foz do Iguaçu** (☎ 45/3521-4400 ⊕ www.cataratasdoiguacu. com.br ⊙ Apr.–Sep 9–5; Oct.–Mar. 9–6). Much of the park is protected rain forest—off-limits to visitors and home to the last viable populations of panthers as well as rare flora. Buses and taxis drop you off at a vast, plaza alongside the park entrance building. As well as ticket booths, there's an ATM, a snack bar, gift shop, and information and currency exchange. Next to the entrance turnstiles is the small **Visitor Center,** where helpful geological models explain how the falls were formed. Double-decker buses run every 15 minutes between the entrance and the trailhead to the falls, 11 km (7 mi) away; the buses stop at the entrances to excursions run by private operators Macuco Safari and Macuco Ecoaventura (these aren't included in your ticket). The trail ends in the **Porto Canoas** service area. There's a posh linen-service restaurant with river views, and two fast-food counters the with tables overlooking the rapids leading to the falls.

VISAS

U.S. citizens don't need a visa to visit Argentina as tourists, but the situation is more complicated in Brazil. ⇨ See the planning section at the beginning of the chapter.

EXCURSIONS IN AND AROUND THE PARKS

A Zodiac trip to the falls.

Iguazú Jungle Explorer (☎ 3757/42–1696 ⊕ iguazujungle.com) runs trips within the Argentine park. Their standard trip, the Gran Aventura, includes a truck ride through the forest and a Zodiac ride to San Martín, Bossetti, and the Salto Tres Mosqueteros (be ready to get soaked). The truck carries so many people that most animals are scared away: you're better off buying the 75-peso boat trip—Aventura Nautica—separately.

You can take to the water on the Brazilian side with **Macuco Safari** (☎ 045/3574–4244 ⊕ www.macucosafari.com.br). Their signature trip is a Zodiac ride around (and under) the Salto Tres Mosqueteros. You get a more sedate ride on the Iguaçu Explorer, a 3½ hour trip up the river.

It's all about adrenaline with **Iguazú Forest** (☎ 3757/42–1140 ⊕ www.iguazuforest.com). Their full day expedition involves kayaking, abseiling, waterfall-climbing, mountain-biking, and canopying all within the Argentine park.

In Brazil, **Cânion Iguaçu** (☎ 045/3529–6040 ⊕ www.campodedesafios.com.br) offers rafting and canopying, as well as abseiling over the river from the Salto San Martín. They also offer wheelchair-compatible equipment.

Argentine park ranger Daniel Somay organizes two-hour Jeep tours with an ecological focus through his Puerto Iguazú–based **Explorador Expediciones** (☎ 3757/42–1632 ⊕ www.rainforest.iguazuargentina.com). The tours cost 120 pesos and include detailed explanations of the Iguazú ecosystem and lots of photo ops. A specialist leads the birdwatching trips, which cost US$100 and include the use of binoculars and hotel pick-up and drop-off.

Macuco Ecoaventura (☎ 045/3529–6927 ⊕ www.macucoecoaventura.com.br) is one of the official tour operators within the Brazilian park. Their Trilha do Pozo Negro combines a 9-km guided hike or bike ride with a scary boat trip along the upper river (the bit before the falls). The aptly-named Floating trip is more leisurely; shorter jungle hikes are also offered.

ON THE CATWALK

You spend most of your visit to the falls walking the many trails and catwalks, so be sure to wear comfortable shoes.

FOZ DO IGUAÇU, BRAZIL

The construction of the Itaipú Dam (now the world's second largest) in 1975 transformed Foz do Iguaçu into a bustling city with seven times more people than nearby Puerto Iguazú. It's precisely because of the city's size that many visitors to the falls arrange accommodations in or near Foz do Iguaçu. After daytime adventures in the national park, the city's nightlife extends the fun. Aside from pubs, clubs, and all kinds of live music, there's even a samba show.

GETTING HERE AND AROUND

There are direct flights between Foz do Iguaçu and São Paulo (1½ hours; $230), Rio de Janeiro (2 hours; $260), and Curitiba (1 hour; $280) on TAM, which also has connecting flights to Salvador, Recife, Brasilia, other Brazilian cities, and Buenos Aires. Low-cost airline GOL operates slightly cheaper direct flights on the same three routes.

The Aeroporto Internacional Foz do Iguaçu is 13 km (8 miles) southeast of downtown Foz. The 20-minute taxi ride should cost R$40 to R$50; the 45-minute regular bus ride about R$2.60. Note that several major hotels are on the highway to downtown, so a cab ride from the airport to these may be less than R$30. A cab ride from downtown hotels directly to the Parque Nacional in Brazil costs about R$70.

Via bus, the trip between São Paolo and Foz do Iguaçu takes 15 hours (R$153). The Terminal Rodoviário in Foz do Iguaçu is 5 km (3 miles) northeast of downtown. There are regular buses into town; they stop at the Terminal de Transportes Urbano (local bus station, often shortened to TTU) at Avenida Juscelino Kubitschek and Rua Mem de Sá. From platform 2, Bus No. 120 (labeled "Parque Nacional") also departs every 15 minutes (from 7 to 7) to the visitor center at the park entrance; the fare is R$2.60. The buses run along Avenida Juscelino Kubitschek and Avenida Jorge Schimmelpfeng, where you can also flag them down.

There's no real reason to rent a car in Foz do Iguaçu, as you can't cross the border in a rental car. There are *pontos de taxi* (taxi stands) at intersections all over town. Hotels and restaurants can call you a cab, but you can also hail them on the street.

Bus Contacts Pluma. ☎ *045/3522–2988 in Foz do Iguaçu* ⊕ *www.pluma.com.br.*

Visitor Info Foz do Iguaçu Tourist Office. ✉ *Praça Getúlio Vargas 69, Foz do Iguaçu* ☎ *045/3521–1455* ⊕ *www.iguassu.tur.br.*

EXPLORING

TOP ATTRACTIONS

Itaipú Dam and Hydroelectric Power Plant. It took more than 30,000 workers eight years to build this 8-km (5-mile) dam, voted one of the Seven Wonders of the Modern World by the American Society of Civil Engineers. The monumental structure, which produces roughly 17% of Brazil's electricity and 75% of Paraguay's, was the largest hydroelectric power plant in the world until China's Three Gorges Dam was completed.

You get plenty of insight into how proud this makes the Brazilian government—and some idea of how the dam was built—during the

KEY

❶ *Exploring sights*

① *Hotels & Restaurants*

Foz do Iguaçu

30-minute video that precedes the hour-long guided panoramic bus tours of the complex. Although commentaries are humdrum, the sheer size of the dam is an impressive sight. To see more than a view over the spillways, consider the special tours, which take you inside the cavernous structure and into the control room. Night tours—which include a light-and-sound show—begin at 8 on Friday and Saturday, 9 during the summer months (reserve ahead). ⊠ *Av. Tancredo Neves 6702, Foz do Iguaçu* ☎ *800/645–4645, 0800/645–4645* ⊕ *www.turismoitaipu. com.br* 🎫 *Panoramic tour R$26, special tour R$64.*

Parque das Aves (*Bird Park*). Flamingos, parrots, and macaws are some of the more colorful inhabitants of this privately run park. Right outside the Parque Nacional Foz do Iguaçu, it's an interesting complement to a visit to the falls. A winding path leads you through untouched tropical forest and walk-through aviaries containing hundreds of species of birds. One of the amazing experiences is the toucan enclosure, where they are so close you could touch them. Iguanas, alligators, and other nonfeathered friends have their own pens. ⊠ *Rodovia das Cataratas, Km 17.1, Foz do Iguaçu* ☎ *045/3529–8282, 045/3529–8282* ⊕ *www.parquedasaves.com. br* 🎫 *R$24 for Brazilians, R$34 for international visitors.*

WORTH NOTING

Ecomuseu de Itaipú (*Itaipú Eco-Museum*). At the Ecomuseu de Itaipú you can learn about the geology, archaeology, and efforts to preserve the flora and fauna of the area since the Itaipú Dam was built. This museum is funded by the dam's operator, Itaipú Binacional, so the information isn't necessarily objective. ⊠ *Av. Presidente Tancredo Neves 6731, Foz do Iguaçu* ☎ *045/3529–2892* ⊕ *www.turismoitaipu.com.br* ⊠ *R$10.*

WHERE TO EAT

$$$$ ✕ **Búfalo Branco.** The city's finest and largest churrascaria does a killer
BRAZILIAN   *rodizio* (all-you-can-eat meat buffet). The *picanha* (beef rump cap) stands out among the dozens of meat choices, but pork, lamb, and chicken find their way onto the metal skewers they use to grill the meat. Ⓢ *Average main: R$75* ⊠ *Av. Rebouças 530, Foz do Iguaçu* ☎ *045/3523–9744* ⊕ *www.bufalobranco.com.br.*

$$$$ ✕ **Tempero da Bahia.** If you're not traveling as far as Salvador and the
BRAZILIAN   state of Bahia, you can at least check out its flavors at this busy restaurant. It specializes in northeastern fare like *moquecas* (a rich seafood stew made with coconut milk and palm oil). Ⓢ *Average main: R$80* ⊠ *Rua Marechal Deodoro 1228, Foz do Iguaçu* ☎ *045/3025–1144* ⊕ *www.restaurantetemperodabahia.com* ☾ *No lunch Mon.–Sat. No dinner Sun.*

$$$ ✕ **Zaragoza.** On a tree-lined street in a quiet neighborhood, this tra-
SPANISH   ditional restaurant's Spanish owner is an expert at matching Iguaçu's fresh river fish to authentic Spanish seafood recipes. Brazilian ingredients sneak into some dishes—the *surubi à Goya* (catfish in a tomato and coconut-milk sauce) definitely merits a try. Ⓢ *Average main: R$50* ⊠ *Rua Quintino Bocaiúva 882, Foz do Iguaçu* ☎ *045/3028–8084* ⊕ *www.restaurantezaragoza.com.br.*

WHERE TO STAY

$$$$ ▦ **Hotel das Cataratas.** Not only is this stately hotel *in* the national
RESORT   park, with views of the smaller falls from the front-side suites, but
Fodor'sChoice   it also provides the traditional comforts of a colonial-style establish-
★   ment: large rooms, terraces, vintage furniture, and hammocks. **Pros:** right inside the park, a short walk from the falls; serious colonial-style charm; friendly, helpful staff. **Cons:** rooms aren't as luxurious as the price promises; far from Foz do Iguaçu so you're limited to the on-site restaurants; only the most expensive suites have views of the falls. Ⓢ *Rooms from: R$960* ⊠ *Rodovia das Cataratas, Km 32, Foz do Iguaçu* ☎ *045/2102–7000, 0800/726–4545* ⊕ *www.belmond.com/ hotels/south-america/brazil/iguassu-falls/belmond-hotel-das-cataratas* ⇌ *197 rooms, 5 suites* ⦿⃒ *Breakfast.*

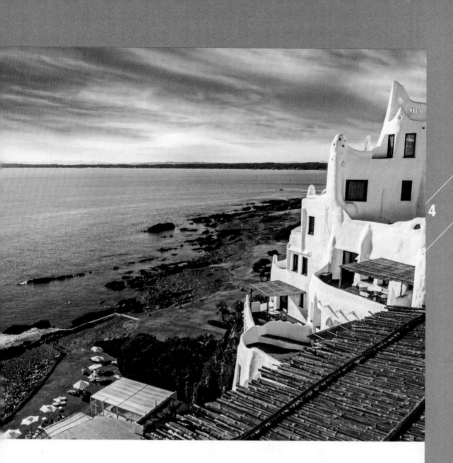

4

SIDE TRIPS TO
URUGUAY

WELCOME TO SIDE TRIPS TO URUGUAY

TOP REASONS TO GO

★ **Bask in Colonial Splendor:** There's little that could be called old in this modern, progressive country—except for the once-walled 1680 Portuguese settlement of Colonia del Sacramento. Flowers spill over balconies, balladeers serenade their sweethearts, and lanterns illuminate the streets of this well-preserved colonial city.

★ **Frolic with the Rich and Famous:** One visit to Uruguay's tony Punta del Este, and Brazil's beaches will forever seem a tad too déclassé. From December through February, fun-in-the-sun crowds flock here.

★ **Ride 'Em, Cowboy:** The *gaucho* embodies the country's spirit, and these rugged cowboys still mount their trusty horses to round up livestock on vast ranges. If your time is limited, you don't even need to leave urban Montevideo to see the spectacle: the capital's El Prado district is the site of the best rodeos.

Uruguay is one of South America's smallest countries, both in area (it's roughly the size of England) and population. Montevideo anchors the coast, and most of the population and action hugs the water line. Vast ranches and farms fill the hilly, sparsely developed interior. Uruguay's elite beach destination Punta del Este attracts beachgoers from across South America and beyond while historic Colonia del Sacramento offers a quiet getaway for many Buenos Aires residents who take a quick ferry ride across the Río de la Plata. Ferries also reach Montevideo from Buenos Aires in a couple hours, making Uruguay a favorite and easy trip from Argentina's capital.

1 Montevideo. True to developing-country patterns, all roads, literal and figurative, lead to Montevideo. Uruguay's friendly capital strings for miles along the southern coast with an odd positioning that means you can walk south, north, or west from the center city to reach the water.

2 Colonia del Sacramento. It's hard not to fall in love with Colonia. The picturesque town has a six-by-six-block old city with wonderfully preserved architecture, rough cobblestone streets, and a sleepy grace. Tranquility reigns here—bicycles and golf carts outnumber cars.

3 Punta del Este. One of the world's trendiest beach communities, Punta del Este is a glitzy destination that doesn't sleep in peak season. Every summer, families and the celebrity jet-set flock to its shore for sun, good food, and luxury.

BRAZIL

Artigas

Rivera

Salto

CUCHILLA DE HAEDO

Tacuarembo

26

26

Paysandu

5

Melo

Lago Artificial
de Baygorria

6

Lago Artificial
de Rincón del Bonete

CUCHILLA GRANDE

Laguna
Merín

8

Fray Bentos

3

Treinta
Y Tres

Mercedes

Durazno

7

2

Trinidad

URUGUAY

3

Florida

8

Colonia del
Sacramento

2

San José de Mayo

2

Aguas Dulces

Minas

Rocha

Canelones

Las Piedras

Ciudad
de la Costa

San Carlos

MONTEVIDEO

1

Punta
Ballena

La Barra de Maldonado

3

Punta del Este

ARGENTINA

Río de la Plata

ATLANTIC OCEAN

4

0   50 mi

0   50 km

Updated
by Sorrell
Moseley-
Williams

It used to be that Uruguay missed out on the touristic attention it deserved, dwarfed by its larger neighbors Argentina and Brazil. That has changed dramatically in recent years, though, as many around the world have turned their attention to this serene, welcoming country. The government has mounted concerted efforts to advertise Uruguay and its offerings to international travelers, and there is plenty to show: Colonia del Sacramento, one of South America's most historic cities; tony resort town Punta del Este; and the coastal capital city Montevideo. Many travelers come away impressed and inspired with Uruguay's tranquil beauty and laid-back vibe.

On a continent with a turbulent past, Uruguayans have parlayed their human and natural resources into a history of success. A strong middle class, a high standard of living, relative prosperity, and a long tradition of peace, good government, and democracy have defined Uruguay (although that last feature did disappear for a dozen years in the last century). The country has enacted landmark legislation that made it the first in South America to sever relations between church and state, to grant women the right to vote, to permit same-sex civil unions, to legalize cannabis, and to enact a generous social-welfare system. The *Economist* even named Uruguay its "country of the year in 2013" for its landmark legislation.

Today about half the country's population lives in Uruguay's capital city. The country takes pride in the number of famous artists it produces, and Uruguayans like to claim their country as the birthplace of the internationally renowned tango singer Carlos Gardel, although the Argentineans and French also vie for this honor. As in Argentina, the legendary *gaucho* is Uruguay's most potent cultural fixture, and it's difficult to pass a day without some reference to these cowboys who once roamed the country singing their melancholy ballads or, of course, to drive without seeing grazing cows or horses. You can still see remnants of the gaucho lifestyle on active ranches throughout the country.

PLANNING

WHEN TO GO

Between October and March the temperatures are pleasant—it's warm and the country is in bloom. Unless you're prepared to tangle with the multitude of tourists that overwhelm Punta del Este in January and February, late spring (November–December) and late winter (March) are the most appealing months to lounge on the beach.

Uruguay's climate has four distinct seasons. Summer (January–March) can be hot and humid, with temperatures as high as 90°F. Fall (April–June) is marked by warm days and evenings cool enough for a light sweater. Winter (July–September) is cold and rainy, with average temperatures generally below 50°F. Although it seldom reaches freezing, the wind off the water can give you quite a chill. Spring (October–December) is much like the fall, except that the trees will be sprouting, rather than dropping, their leaves.

GETTING HERE AND AROUND
AIR TRAVEL

Most international flights land at Montevideo's Aeropuerto Internacional de Carrasco, about 24 km (15 miles) east of downtown. Nearly all Montevideo-bound flights are routed through Buenos Aires. Aerolíneas Argentinas, LAN, GOL, TAM, and Avianca run regular flights to Latin American metropolises like Buenos Aires and São Paulo, and there also is a nonstop American Airlines flight from Miami as well as direct flights to Paris and Madrid.

If you fly a strictly Argentina–Uruguay itinerary, you'll likely depart from Buenos Aires' domestic airport, the Aeroparque Jorge Newbery. Through flights on American Airlines use the capital's international airport at Ezeiza.

Service to the Aeropuerto Internacional de Punta del Este is frequent from many South American cities during the resort's December–March high season, but almost nonexistent the rest of the year.

BOAT TRAVEL

Ferries cross the Río de la Plata between Argentina and Uruguay several times daily. They travel to Montevideo or Colonia, where you can get a bus to Montevideo and Punta del Este. The best companies are Aliscafos, Buquebus, Ferrylíneas Argentina, and Ferry Tur.

BUS TRAVEL

You can go almost anywhere in Uruguay by bus. Some are quite luxurious, with air-conditioning, movies, and snack service. Departures are frequent and fares low. Most companies are based in Montevideo and depart from its state-of-the-art Terminal Tres Cruces. The station's website (⊕ *www.trescruces.com.uy*) lists all bus schedules to and from Montevideo.

CAR TRAVEL

From Argentina you can transport your car across the Río de la Plata by ferry. Alternatively, you can cross the Argentina–Uruguay border in three places: Puerto Unzue-Fray Bentos, Colón-Paysandu, or Concordia-Salto.

Roads between Montevideo and Punta del Este or Colonia del Sacramento are quite good, as are the handful of major highways. In the countryside, roads are usually surfaced with gravel. If you want to leave the main roads, it's best to speak with locals about current conditions before setting off. Trips will often take longer than expected, so budget extra time. On the upside, country roads often have little traffic and spectacular scenery.

Car-rental rates are often higher in Uruguay than in the United States because of the value-added tax. For an economy-size car, expect to pay around US$55 per day. Uruguayans tend to drive carefully, but visitors from Argentina have the reputation of driving with wild abandon. Since almost all roads have only two lanes, keep an eye out for passing vehicles.

HEALTH AND SAFETY

It's a good idea to avoid tap water, as pipes in many older buildings are made of lead. Almost everyone drinks locally bottled *agua mineral* (mineral water), which is available *con gas* or *sin gas* (with or without carbonation).

Uruguay would win most "Safest South American Country" competitions, but standard travel precautions apply. Keep an eye on your purse or wallet, avoid unnecessary displays of wealth, and avoid wandering back streets of Montevideo at night.

RESTAURANTS

Argentina may leap to mind when discussing South American beef, but some 12 million cattle, primarily Hereford and Angus, graze Uruguay's open, vast grasslands—this in a nation of roughly 3 million people. Beef is the staple of the Uruguayan diet. It's quality, cheap, abundant, and often grilled in a style borrowed from the gauchos, and known as *parrillada*. A meal in a Uruguayan steak house should be on your agenda. Beef is also made into sausages, such as *chorizo* and *salchicha*, or is combined with ham, cheese, bacon, and peppers to make *matambre*.

Seafood is also popular here—and it's fresh and delicious, especially the *lenguado* (flounder), *merluza* (hake), and *calamar* (squid). Try the *raya a la manteca negra* (ray in blackened butter). If you are not up to a full meal, order what is often considered the national sandwich, *chivito*, a steak sandwich with thin strips of beef.

Uruguayan wines under the Bouza, Santa Rosa, and Calvinor labels are available in most restaurants. As Uruguayan wines also have raised their profile in the past decade, a vineyard visit or wine tasting is highly recommended. *Clericó* is a mixture of white wine and fruit juice, while *medio y medio* is part sparkling wine, part white wine.

Lunch is served between noon and 3; restaurants begin to fill around 12:30 and are packed by 1:30. Many restaurants do not open for dinner until 8 pm, and often don't start to get crowded until 9:30. Most pubs and *confiterías* (cafés) are open all day. Formal dress is rarely required. Smart sportswear is acceptable at even the fanciest establishments.

HOTELS

Hotels here are generally comfortable and good value for your money. Most include breakfast in their rates. All but the most basic hotels have air-conditioning—you'll appreciate it during the hot summers. *Hosterías* are country inns that not only offer modest rooms but are open for dinner as well. Menus tend to be limited, though the food served is unfailingly hearty.

Lodging at the beach requires reservations no matter what the time of year. Rooms fill up quickly (and prices increase dramatically) during the December–February high season. Rates go down during the shoulder months of November and March, but you can still count on good weather. Many hotels close for a few weeks between Easter and late May and/or in September. *Hotel reviews have been shortened. For full information, visit Fodors.com.*

WHAT IT COSTS IN URUGUAYAN PESOS				
	$	$$	$$$	$$$$
Restaurants	Under 301	301–450	451–600	over 600
Hotels	Under 1,501	1,501–3,000	3,001–4,500	over 4,500

Restaurant prices are the average cost of a main course at dinner or, if dinner is not served, at lunch. Hotel prices are the lowest cost of a standard double room in high season.

MONTEVIDEO

Uruguay's capital city hugs the eastern bank of the Río de la Plata. A massive coastal promenade (*malecón*) that passes fine beaches, restaurants, and numerous parks recalls the sunny sophistications of the Mediterranean and is always dotted with Montevideans strolling, exercising, and lounging along the water. Montevideo has its share of glitzy shopping avenues and modern office buildings, balanced with its historic old city and sumptuous colonial architecture, as well as numerous leafy plazas and parks. It is hard not to draw comparisons to its sister city Buenos Aires across the river, and indeed Montevideo strikes many as a calmer, more manageable incarnation of Argentina's capital.

When the weather's good, La Rambla, a 22-km (14-mile) waterfront avenue that links the Old City with the eastern suburbs and changes names about a dozen times, gets packed with fishermen, ice-cream vendors, and joggers. Around sunset, volleyball and soccer games wind down as couples begin to appear for evening strolls. Polls consistently rate Montevideo as having the highest quality of life of any city in Latin America. After one visit here, especially on a lovely summer evening, you probably will agree.

GETTING HERE AND AROUND

AIR TRAVEL

Uruguay's principal airport, Aeropuerto Internacional de Carrasco (MVD), is 24 km (15 miles) east of Montevideo. A taxi to downtown costs about 1400 pesos; plan on 1600 pesos to reach the Ciudad Vieja. A city bus (marked Ciudadela) is cheap—about 29 pesos—but the drawback is that it takes an hour to get downtown.

WHAT'S IN A NAME?

Stories abound about the origin of Montevideo's unusual name. The generally accepted account holds that Magellan, traveling along the coast from Brazil in 1520, counted off six hills from the Brazilian border and thus named the city Monte (mountain) vi (roman numeral six) de (from) eo (este a oeste, or east to west).

Air Contacts Aerolíneas Argentinas.
✉ *Plaza Independencia 818* ☎ *598/2902–3691* ⊕ *www.aerolineas.com.ar.*
Aeropuerto Internacional de Carrasco. ✉ *Ruta 101, km 19.950, Ciudad de la Costa* ☎ *598/2604–0329* ⊕ *www.aeropuertodecarrasco.com.uy.* **American Airlines.** ✉ *Carrasco International Airport* ☎ *598/2916–3929* ⊕ *www.aa.com.*

BOAT AND FERRY TRAVEL

Buquebus operates ferry service between Buenos Aires and the ports at Montevideo and Colonia. The trip takes less than three hours to Montevideo and less than four hours to Colonia. A round-trip ticket between Buenos Aires and Montevideo costs about 3,000 pesos. A package that includes a round-trip ticket between Buenos Aires and Colonia and a shuttle bus to or from Montevideo costs about 2,400 pesos.

Boat Contacts Buquebus. ☎ *+54 11/4316–6530* ⊕ *www.buquebus.com.*

BUS TRAVEL

Montevideo's public buses are a great alternative to taxis, which can be difficult to find during peak hours. Buses crisscross the entire city 24 hours a day. You don't need exact change, and the price for any trip within Montevideo is only 29 pesos.

Colonia is serviced by several regional bus lines, including COT and Turil. The three-hour ride costs 500 pesos.

Bus Contacts COT. ☎ *2409–4949 in Montevideo* ⊕ *www.coturuguay.com.*
Terminal Tres Cruces. ✉ *Bulevar General Artigas 1825, Centro* ☎ *2401–8998* ⊕ *www.trescruces.com.uy.* **Turil.** ☎ *4622–4163 in Montevideo* ⊕ *www.turil.com. uy.*

CAR TRAVEL

Because La Rambla, Montevideo's riverside thoroughfare, extends for dozens of miles, driving is a good way to see the city. Roads are well maintained and drivers obey the traffic laws—a rarity in South America. It's easy to rent a car, both downtown and at the airport. In Montevideo you can rent from several major international companies, including Avis, Budget, and Dollar, and from smaller companies such as Inter Car and Multicar.

Car-Rental Contacts Avis. ☎ *21700* ⊕ *www.avis.com.uy.* **Dollar.** ☎ *2682–8350 at Aeropuerto de Carrasco* ⊕ *www.dollar.com.uy.*

TAXI TRAVEL

All cabs have meters that count *fichas,* or pulses, each 1/10 km (1/20 mile). When you arrive at your destination, the driver will take out an official chart that calculates the fare from the number of fichas elapsed. You can hail taxis on the street with ease, or call one to pick you up at your hotel. A ride to the airport from the Old City costs about 1700 pesos, and 1550 pesos from downtown.

Taxi Contacts Taxi Aeropuerto Internacional de Carrasco. ☎ *2604–0323* ⊕ *www.taxisaeropuerto.com.*

SAFETY AND PRECAUTIONS

Although Montevideo doesn't have the problems with crime that larger cities in South America do, it's best to watch your wallet in crowded markets and to avoid walking down deserted streets at night. Most of Montevideo's residents stay up late, so the streets are usually full of people until 1 am. The city bus authority discourages boarding empty buses at night. Look for the helpful tourist police decked out in blue berets and yellow vests that say *policía turística.* They patrol Avenida 18 de Julio, Ciudad Vieja, and the Mercado del Puerto.

ESSENTIALS

Visitor Information Ministry of Tourism and Sport. ✉ *Rambla 25 de Agosto 1825, Ciudad Vieja* ☎ *2/1885* ⊕ *www.uruguaynatural.com.*

EXPLORING

Modern Montevideo expanded outward from the peninsular Ciudad Vieja, the Old City, still noted for its narrow streets and mix of elegant colonial and art deco architecture. El Prado, an exclusive enclave a few miles north of the city center, is peppered with lavish mansions and grand parks. When you remember that these mansions were once summer homes for aristocratic Uruguayans who spent most of the year elsewhere, you'll get some idea of the wealth this small country once enjoyed.

CIUDAD VIEJA

Ciudad Vieja is fairly compact, and you could walk from one end to the other in about 15 minutes. Take care at night, when the area is fairly deserted.

TOP ATTRACTIONS

Fodor's Choice
★

Mercado del Puerto. For Montevideo's quintessential lunch experience, head to the old port market, a restored 1868 building of vaulted iron beams and colored glass, and a terrific example of urban renewal at its best. The market shields 14 stalls and eateries where, over large fires, the best *asado* (barbecue) in the city is cooked. It's a mix of casual lunch-counter places and sit-down restaurants. The traditional drink here is *medio y medio* (champagne mixed with white wine). Other eateries congregate outside around the perimeter of the building and are open for dinner as well as lunch. ✉ *Rambla 25 de Agosto, between Av. Maciel and Av. Pérez Castellano, across from port, Piedras 237, Ciudad Vieja* ☎ *27/116–801* ⊕ *www.mercadodelpuerto.com.*

Montevideo

TO EL PRADO ↖

TO BODEGA BOUZA ↗
19 – 22

ARROYO SECO

Martin García
Isidoro de María
Av. Agraciada

Coronel Francisco Tajes

Gen. Manuel Freire

César Díaz

Paraguay
Colombia

Panamá

Guatemala

Venezuela

Nicaragua

Lima

Asunción

Nueva York

Valparaíso

La Paz

Galicia

Cerro Largo

Paysandú

Av. Uruguay

Mercedes

Colonia

Bahía de Montevideo

Breakwater

FERRY TO
BUENOS AIRES

Ferry
Terminal

7

1
2

7

Rambla 25 de Agosto de 1825

Piedras

Cerrito

Maciel

Guaraní

Juan Lindolfo Cuestas

Juan Carlos Gómez

Zabala

Sol

Piedras

3
5
6

4

Treinta y Tres

25 de Mayo

Rincón

7
8

9

10

11

CIUDAD VIEJA

Sarandí

Buenos Aires

Reconquista

Rambla Francia

Plaza España

Cerrito
Washington

Rambla Gran Bretaña

Florida

Ciudadela

Andes

Convención

12

13

Palacio Estévez

Avenida 18 de Julio

San José

14

15

Soriano

Canelones

Maldonado

Durazno

Carlos Gardel

BARRIO SUR

Rambla República Argentina

Río de la Plata

Rambla Sur América

18

17

AGUADA

Nicaragua

Lima

Asunción

Nueva York

Miguelete

Galicia

Cerro Largo

Río Negro

Yí

Yaguarón

Cuareim

Av. Gral Flores

Marcelino Sosa

Rocha

Av. Libertador Brigadier Gral Lavalleja

Arturo Lezama

Gral Lima

15

14

CENTRO

16

Ejido

Av. Gral Rondeau

Paraguay

Río Negro

Andes

Florida

Dr. Aquiles R. Lanza

Zelmar Michelini

Carlos Quijano

Av. Gonzalo Ramírez

Santiago de Chile

Ejido

La Cumparsita

TO PARQUE
RODÓ AND
PLAYA DE
LOS POCITOS

0 — 1,000ft
0 — 500m

Museo del Carnaval. Move over, Rio. Montevideo's annual Carnaval celebration may be more low-key than that of its northern neighbor, but it lasts for a full 40 days. This museum next to the Mercado del Puerto celebrates and honors the pre-Lenten festivities year-round with displays featuring the elaborate costumes and photos of processions. Guided tours are available. ⊠ *Rambla 25 de Agosto de 1825 No. 218, Ciudad Vieja* ☎ *2916–5493* ⊕ *www.museodelcarnaval.org* 🎫 *100 pesos.*

> ### CRIOLLAS
>
> Also known as *jineteadas,* the Uruguayan-style rodeos called *criollas* are held all over the country, but the most spectacular one takes place in Montevideo's El Prado neighborhood every Easter. Gauchos from all over the country come to display their skill in riding wild horses.

Fodor'sChoice ★ **Plaza Independencia.** Connecting Cuidad Vieja and the Centro, Independence Square is the heart of Montevideo. All that remains of the original walls of the Spanish fort is the Puerta de la Ciudadela, the triumphal gate to the Old City. In the center stands a 30-ton statue of General José Gervasio Artigas, the father of Uruguay and founder of its 19th-century independence movement. At the base of the monument, polished granite stairs lead to an underground mausoleum that holds Artigas's remains, open daily 9–6. The mausoleum is a moving memorial: bold graphics chiseled in the walls of this giant space detail the feats of Artigas's life. There's a changing of the guard every Friday at noon. ⊠ *Plaza Independencia.*

WORTH NOTING

Cabildo de Montevideo. The original City Hall is where the Uruguayan constitution was signed in 1830. This two-story colonial edifice houses an impressive collection of paintings, antiques, costumes, and rotating history exhibits. Fountains and statuary line the interior patios. English-speaking guides are available. ⊠ *Calle Juan Carlos Gómez 1362, Ciudad Vieja* ☎ *2915–9685* ⊕ *cabildo.montevideo.gub.uy* 🎫 *Free* ☉ *Closed Sun.*

Casa de Lavalleja Museum. This Spanish neoclassical home was built in 1783 and later became the home of General Juan A. Lavalleja, who distinguished himself in Uruguay's war for independence. This pristine colonial home with lovely wrought-iron balconies displays manuscripts and historical memorabilia. ⊠ *Calle Zabala 1469, Ciudad Vieja* ☎ *2915–1051* 🎫 *Free* ☉ *Closed Mon. and Tues.*

Casa de Fructuoso Rivera. Once the home of General Fructuso Rivera, Uruguay's first president, this neoclassical Rivera House from the early 1800s was acquired by the government in 1942 and opened as a national history museum. Exhibits inside this pale yellow colonial house with an octagonal cupola document the development of Uruguay and showcase daily life in Montevideo of the 1900s. ⊠ *Calle Rincón 437, Ciudad Vieja* ☎ *2915–1051* ⊕ *www.museohistorico.gub.uy* 🎫 *Free* ☉ *Closed Mon. and Tues.*

Club Uruguay. Uruguay's most prestigious private social club, founded in 1888, is headquartered in this eclectic, three-story neoclassical national monument on the south side of Plaza Matriz. Formed for high society of

The Plaza Independencia is the heart of Montevideo, a great place for history lovers and people-watchers.

European descent, today it opens to the public. Friendly, English-speaking guides bring visitors up the marble staircases so they can marvel at the elegant salons. The club also hosts cultural events, including music performances and art shows, throughout the year. Nonmembers are welcome at the on-site bar and restaurant, but full access to the club's luxe facilities, including a library and billiards room, is reserved for its exclusive members. ⊠ *Calle Sarandí 584 CP, Ciudad Vieja* ☎ *2915–7820* ⊕ *www.cluburuguay.com.uy* ✉ *Free* ☉ *Closed weekends.*

Iglesia Matriz. It's officially the Cathedral of the Immaculate Conception and St. Phillip and St. James, but it is known to Montevideans as the Matriz ("head") Church, as well as the Catedral Metropolitana de Montevideo. The cathedral is the oldest public building in Montevideo, with a distinctive pair of dome-cap bell towers that stand guard over the plaza below. Besides its rich marble interior, colorful floor tiling, stained glass, and dome, the Matriz Church is notable as the final resting place of many of Uruguay's most important political and military figures. ⊠ *Calle Ituzaingó 1373, at Calle Sarandí, Ciudad Vieja* ☎ *2915–8127* ⊕ *www.icm.org.uy.*

Palacio Estévez. On the south side of Plaza Independencia, Estévez Palace, one of the most beautiful old buildings in the city, was the seat of government until 1985, when the president's offices were moved to a more modern building. This building, unfortunately closed to the public, is used on occasion for ceremonial purposes. ⊠ *Plaza Independencia, Ciudad Vieja.*

Palacio Taranco/Museo de Artes Decorativas. Built in 1907, the ornate Taranco Palace in the Ciudad Vieja is representative of the

French-inspired architecture favored in fin-de-siècle Montevideo. Even the marble for the floors was imported from France. Today you can survey that bygone glory in the palace's new incarnation as the Museo de Artes Decorativas (Museum of Decorative Arts). Its rooms are filled with period furniture, statuary, draperies, clocks, and portrait paintings. A cultural center within has a calendar of performances and live music. ⊠ *Museo de Artes Decorativas, Calle 25 de Mayo 376, Ciudad Vieja* ☎ *2915–1101* ⊕ *www.cultura.mec.gub.uy/taranco* ⊠ *Free* ⊘ *Closed Sun.*

Plaza Constitución. This plaza, also known as Plaza Matriz, is the heart of Montevideo's Ciudad Vieja. An ornate cantilever fountain in the center of this tree-filled square was installed in 1871 to commemorate the construction of the city's first water system. ⊠ *Montevideo* ☎ *1950–7052.*

Plaza Zabala. At this charmed spot in the heart of the Ciudad Vieja it's easy to image the splendor of the old Montevideo. Around the fountain and flowers of the park are the turn-of-the-century Palacio Taranco and a bank headquarters in a renovated older building—a refreshing sight in the Old City. ⊠ *Circunvalacion Durango.*

FodorsChoice
★

Teatro Solís. Named in honor of the discoverer of the Río de la Plata, Juan Díaz de Solís, the 1856 Solís Theater is famed for its fine acoustics. Informative guided tours of the building are offered in Spanish; call ahead to arrange one in English. (The afternoon tours are occasionally canceled if the theater is in use for rehearsals.) The theater maintains an active calendar of concerts, dance, and plays, all in Spanish, and all for prices much lower than you'd pay for a comparable evening back home. ⊠ *Reconquista at Bartolomé Mitre, Ciudad Vieja* ☎ *1950–3323* ⊕ *www.teatrosolis.org.uy* ⊠ *90 pesos (free Wed.).*

CENTRO

Montevideo's main street, the Avenida 18 de Julio, runs through the heart of the city's center. You'll find everything here—shops and museums, cafés and plazas, bustling traditional markets, chrome-and-steel office towers, and places to change money. The avenue runs east from Plaza Independencia, away from the Ciudad Vieja, passing through bustling Plaza Fabini and tree-lined Plaza Cagancha.

It's a 20-minute walk from Plaza Independencia to the Palacio Municipal. If shopping is your main interest, you may want to devote an entire afternoon to browsing and buying along the avenue.

TOP ATTRACTIONS

FodorsChoice
★

Museo del Gaucho y la Moneda (*Cowboy and Coin Museum*). This museum is in Palacio Heber Jackson, a rococo 19th-century mansion near Calle Julio Herrera y Obes, four blocks east of Plaza Independencia. Here you'll find articles from the everyday life of the gauchos, from traditional garb to the detailed silver work on the cups used for *mate* (an indigenous herb from which tea is brewed). Ancient South American and European coins are on the first floor. Tours in English are available with a couple days' notice. ⊠ *Av. 18 de Julio 998, Centro* ☎ *29/008–764* ⊠ *Free* ⊘ *Closed weekends.*

Museo de Historia del Arte (MuHAr). In the Palacio Municipal (an ambitious name for this unremarkable brick city hall) you'll find the Museum of

Art History, which has the country's best collection of pre-Columbian and colonial artifacts. You'll also find Greek, Roman, and Middle Eastern art, including ceramics and other antiquities. On the street level is the **Biblioteca de Historia del Arte** (Art History Library), worth a stop if you're a student of the subject matter. ⊠ *Calle Ejido 1326, Centro* ☎ *19/502–191* ⊕ *muhar.montevideo.gub.uy* ✉ *Free* ☽ *Closed Mon.*

WORTH NOTING

Plaza Fabini. In the center of this lovely, manicured square is the Monumento del Entrevero, a large sculpture depicting a whirlwind of gauchos, *criollos* (mixed-blood settlers who are half native, half European), and native Uruguayans in battle. It's one of the last works by sculptor José Belloni (1882–1965). An open-air market takes place here every morning. ⊠ *Surrounded by Av. 18 de Julio and Calles Río Negro, Colonia, and Julio Herrera y Obes, Centro.*

EL PRADO

The district known as El Prado lies roughly 6 km (4 miles) north of Plaza Independencia. You could make the long uphill walk along the busy Avenida Agraciada, but it's a lot easier in a taxi. It is pleasant to walk along Avenida Buschental in fall and spring when the trees are in full color. The Jardín Botánico (Botanical Garden) inside the Parque del Prado is a worthwhile stop, where you can admire thousands of plant species, many of which were brought to Uruguay in the 19th century by Charles Racine.

TOP ATTRACTIONS

Museo de Bellas Artes Juan Manuel Blanes (*Museum of Fine Arts*). Known locally as the Blanes Museum, the Museum of Fine Arts is housed in an elegant colonial mansion that once belonged to Uruguay's foremost 19th-century painter, Juan Manuel Blanes. He was entirely self-taught, and did not begin painting until he was in his fifties. His realistic portrayals of gauchos and the Uruguayan countryside compose the core of the museum's collection. ⊠ *Av. Millán 4015, Prado* ☎ *2336–2248* ⊕ *blanes.montevideo.gub.uy* ✉ *Free* ☽ *Closed Mon.*

Palacio Legislativo. Almost 50 different types of native marble were used in the construction of the Legislative Palace, the seat of Uruguay's bicameral legislature. Free Spanish- and English-language tours are available when the congress is in session; passes are available inside at the information desk. ⊠ *Av. De las Leyes s/n, Prado* ☎ *2400–9111* ⊕ *www.parlamento.gub.uy* ✉ *90 pesos* ☽ *Closed Mon.*

Parque del Prado. The oldest of the city's parks is also one of the most popular. Locals come to see El Rosedal, the rose garden with more than 800 different varieties, and the fine botanical garden. Also in the 262-acre park you'll find the statue called *La Diligencia,* by sculptor José Belloni. ⊠ *Av. Delmira Agustini, Prado* ☎ *1950–2003.*

WORTH NOTING

Museo del Fútbol. "Other countries have their history," Helenio Herrera, Uruguay's most famous soccer coach once said. "We have our fútbol." Indeed, *fútbol*—that's "soccer" to U.S. readers—is played anywhere there's space, by kids of all ages. Uruguay both hosted and won the first World Cup competition in 1930 here at the Estadio Centenario.

In the pits of the stadium is this museum (the AUF) dedicated to the country's soccer heritage. It's worth a detour if you're a big fan of the sport. ✉ *Av. Dr. Americo Ricaldoni, Prado* ☎ *2480–1259* ⊕ *www.auf. org.uy* ✍ *100 pesos* ☉ *Closed weekends.*

Museo de la Memoria. The question still pains Uruguayans who remember the era: How did South America's strongest democracy dissolve into 12 years of brutal military dictatorship? This museum documents the history of the 1973–85 period that people here call simply the *dictadura,* during which an astounding 2% of the population experienced arrest for "political crimes" at some time or other. (The government did not begin investigating abuses by the military government until 2011.) The museum won't be a stop on most visitors' Montevideo itineraries, but if you're a student of Latin American history and politics, it's worth a look. ✉ *Av. Las Instrucciones 1057, Prado* ⊕ *Esq. Bvar. José Batlle and Ordoñez.* ☎ *2355–5891* ⊕ *mume.montevideo.gub.uy* ✍ *Free* ☉ *Closed Sun.*

4

Sagrada Familia. Too tiny to require flying buttresses, the ornately Gothic Holy Family Church, also known as Capilla Jackson, is complete in all other respects. A troop of gargoyles peers down at you from this Jesuit house of worship, and the finely wrought stained-glass windows become radiant when backlit by the sun. ✉ *Calle Luis Alberto de Herrera 4246, Prado* ☎ *2203–3686.*

GREATER MONTEVIDEO

FAMILY **Parque Rodó.** This park has a little something for everyone, with two amusement parks, a number of decent eateries, and the National Museum of Visual Arts. The park also has an outdoor theater and hosts an open-air *feria* (fair) on Sunday. ✉ *Julio Maria Sosa, Punta Carretas.*

FAMILY

Fodor's Choice

★

Playa de los Pocitos. This stretch of sand is the city's most attractive beach, and surprisingly tranquil. Throughout the day you'll see locals running, biking, strolling, and rollerblading along the *rambla* (boardwalk) here. Snap a picture with the sculpture spelling out "Montevideo" for a classic tourist shot. **Amenities:** food and drink; lifeguards; showers; toilets. **Best for:** solitude; sunrise; sunset; swimming; walking. ✉ *Rambla Perú at Gabriel A. Pereira, Pocitos* ☎ *4141–9285.*

OFF THE
BEATEN
PATH

Bodega Bouza. Argentina and Chile grab all the attention in discussions of South American wines, but Uruguay has a number of impressive wineries of its own. It's worth stopping by the Bodega Bouza outside of Montevideo for a tour and sampling; it's one of the few wineries open for daily visits. For a real treat (3,000 pesos), reserve the works: a tour, tasting, and extravagant lunch with, of course, wines to accompany each course and that all-important transfer to and from Montevideo. It's worth visiting the winery for its standout restaurant alone. ✉ *Camino la Redención 7658* ☎ *2323–7491* ⊕ *www.bodegabouza.com* ✍ *Winery tour 600 pesos; tasting and tour 1200 pesos* ☉ *Closed Sun.*

WHERE TO EAT

Montevideo was not long ago a city that almost exclusively subsisted on steak and potatoes and pastas, but the city's restaurant scene has experienced a slow-but-sure emergence the past decade. You still can find all the tasty steak you want, but offerings have diversified with an increasing number of international and fusion restaurants. From fine dining to quality chivito joints, you'll have your share of memorable meals in Montevideo.

CIUDAD VIEJA

$ ╳ **Café Bacacay.** This small and smartly designed restaurant facing Teatro
SOUTH Solís inhabits a building that dates to 1844 and attracts a young, hip
AMERICAN crowd. The owner takes special care in preparing the excellent salads, such as the Bacacay (spinach, raisins, carrots, nuts, grilled eggplant) or the Sarandí (celery, chicken, apples, carrots). **Known for:** unique and historic space; great wine list; streetside tables. *⑤ Average main: 220 pesos ✉ Bacacay 1306, at Calle Buenos Aires, Ciudad Vieja ☎ 2916–6074 ⊕ www.bacacay.com.uy ⊘ Closed Sun.*

$$$ ╳ **Jacinto.** The smell of fresh-baked bread wafts through this pleasant,
SOUTH sunny spot off Plaza Zabala. Plates are fresh, inspired, and expertly
AMERICAN prepared, from the soup of the day to desserts like panna cotta with red
Fodor'sChoice grapes and a sweet orange sauce. Jacinto is a favorite among the city's
★ foodie crowd and stylish set. **Known for:** seasonal menu; efficient service; trendy space. *⑤ Average main: 600 pesos ✉ Sarandí 349, Ciudad Vieja ☎ 2915–2731 ⊕ www.jacinto.com.uy ⊘ Closed Sun.*

$$$$ ╳ **Rara Avis.** Located in a wing of the Teatro Solis theater building, Rara
FRENCH Avís is one of Montevideo's best restaurants. Both the food—such as a black oyster risotto with smoked salmon or duck magret in baby greens with a pepper sauce—and the setting are sophisticated. **Known for:** fancy fare; great wine list; best to book ahead. *⑤ Average main: 900 pesos ✉ Buenos Aires 652, Ciudad Vieja ☎ 2915–0330 ⊕ www.raraavis.com.uy ⊘ Closed Sun.*

CENTRO

$$ ╳ **Viejo Sancho.** What draws the post-theater crowds to this friendly
STEAKHOUSE but plain restaurant near Plaza Cagancha are gargantuan portions of smoked pork chops and fried potatoes. **Known for:** cheap and cheerful; bustling ambience; friendly staff. *⑤ Average main: 350 pesos ✉ Calle San José 1229, Centro ☎ 2900–4063 ▭ No credit cards ⊘ Closed Sun.*

GREATER MONTEVIDEO

$$ ╳ **Expreso Pocitos.** This classic and beloved diner-style establishment has
ITALIAN been around for more than a century, and it is clear that some of the
Fodor'sChoice customers have been frequenting it for almost as long. Many congregate
★ here for a coffee or beer, and the *chivito*, which is made with fresh, fluffy bread, is considered one of the best in town. **Known for:** local institution; traditional decor; chivito bread. *⑤ Average main: 350 pesos ✉ Juan Benito Blanco 956 at Av. Brasil, Pocitos ☎ 2708–0496.*

$$$$ ╳ **La Casa Violeta.** Meats are the specialty at this beautiful restaurant
STEAKHOUSE facing Puerto del Buceo, one of the prettiest spots in the city. You can opt for a steak-tasting menu that is served in the method called *espeto corrido*, with meat brought to your table on a long skewer. **Known for:** steak-tasting menu; salad bar; marina views. *⑤ Average main: 750 pesos ✉ Rambla Armenia 3667, Pocitos ✛ Corner of 26 de Marzo, Puerto del Buceo ☎ 2628–7626 ⊕ www.lacasavioleta.com.*

$$$$ ✕ **Restaurant Francis.** This bright, upscale restaurant is a local favorite
SEAFOOD   and always filled, yet the efficient, friendly staff manages to keep up.
Fodor's Choice   The menu is gourmet and extensive, ranging from sushi to paella to cuts
★   of meat on the grill. **Known for:** excellent wine list; chipirones (baby
cuttlefish); extensive menu. $ *Average main: 750 pesos* ⊠ *Luis de la
Torre 502, Punta Carretas* ☎ *2711–8603* ⊕ *francis.com.uy.*

$$$$ ✕ **Tandory.** With Tandory, French-Uruguayan chef and owner Gabriel
ASIAN FUSION   Coquel has created an intimate yet convivial restaurant with top-level
Fodor's Choice   service. Fusion dishes harmoniously blend Asian, Latin American, and
★   European flavors, and the eclectic decor includes heirlooms and sou-
venirs from his travels around the world. **Known for:** eclectic menu;
seasonal, local ingredients; great wine list. $ *Average main: 800 pesos*
⊠ *Ramon Masini at Libertad, Pocitos* ☎ *2709–6616* ⊕ *www.tandory.
com.uy* ⊗ *Closed Sun.*

WHERE TO STAY

Many downtown hotels are grouped around the big three squares:
Plaza Independencia, Plaza Fabini, and Plaza Cagancha. In the weeks
before and after Carnaval in February, rooms become hard to come by.
Otherwise, rooms are plentiful in summer, when beach-bound residents
desert the city.

CENTRO

$$ 🏨 **Oxford Hotel.** Glass walls, broad windows, and mirrors give the small
HOTEL   lobby an open but intimate feel, much like that of the hotel itself. **Pros:**
central location; attentive staff; fast Wi-Fi. **Cons:** some oddly configured
rooms; small bathrooms; basic breakfast. $ *Rooms from: 1680 pesos*
⊠ *Paraguay 1286, Centro* ☎ *2902–0046* ⊕ *www.hoteloxford.com.uy*
↪ *125 rooms* �‖ *Breakfast.*

GREATER MONTEVIDEO

$$ 🏨 **Armon Suites.** This hotel in a quiet neighborhood east of down-
HOTEL   town is an all-suites hotel, and the spaces are huge. **Pros:** good value;
ample-size suites; courteous staff. **Cons:** far from sights; slow Internet
access; uninteresting breakfast. $ *Rooms from: 2700 pesos* ⊠ *21 de
Setiembre 2885, Pocitos* ☎ *2712–4120* ⊕ *www.armonsuites.com.uy*
↪ *40 rooms* ❘‖ *Breakfast.*

$ 🏨 **Hostería del Lago.** On a beautiful lake about 12 km (7 miles) east
of downtown, this sprawling Spanish colonial hotel is the kind of
place that encourages relaxation. **Pros:** secluded site; beautiful lake.
Cons: requires a car, not immediately convenient to city. $ *Rooms
from: 1100 pesos* ⊠ *Av. Arizona 9637, Carrasco* ☎ *2601–2210* ↪ *60
rooms* ❘‖ *Breakfast.*

$$ 🏨 **Hotel Ermitage.** The Ermitage is in an unprepossessing, sandstone-
HOTEL   front building overlooking the lovely Plaza Tomás Gomensoro, and
is a good, affordable choice if you want to be near the shore. **Pros:**
great location in attractive Pocitos; wonderful historic building; good
value. **Cons:** far from sights; some rooms need updating; road-facing
rooms are noisy. $ *Rooms from: 1800 pesos* ⊠ *Calle Juan Benito
Blanco 783, Pocitos* ☎ *2710–4021* ⊕ *www.ermitagemontevideo.com*
↪ *78 rooms* ❘‖ *Breakfast.*

4

Where to Eat and Stay in Montevideo

KEY

❶ *Restaurants*

① *Hotels*

TO EL PRADO

ARROYO SECO

Martín García

Isidoro de María

Rocha

Av. Agraciada

Marcelino Sosa

Av. General Flores

Coronel Francisco Tajes

Gen. Manuel Freire

César Díaz

Paraguay

Colombia

Arturo Lezama

Panamá

Palacio Legislativo

Guatemala

Venezuela

Nicaragua

Nicaragua

Lima

Lima

Asunción

Asunción

Nueva York

AGUADA

Nueva York

Valparaíso

Miguelete

La Paz

Galicia

Galicia

Cerro Largo

Cerro Largo

Río Negro

Paysandú

Av. Uruguay

Mercedes

Colonia

Plaza Fabini

CENTRO

②

Avenida 18 de Julio

④

San José

①

Soriano

Canelones

Maldonado

BARRIO SUR

Durazno

Carlos Gardel

Rambla República Argentina

Av. Gonzalo Ramírez

La Cumparsita

Bahía de Montevideo
Breakwater

FERRY TO BUENOS AIRES

Ferry Terminal

Rambla 25 de Agosto de 1825

Piedras

Pérez Castellano

Maciel

Solís

25 de Mayo

Rincón

Juan Carlos Gómez

Bme. Mitre

Juncal

Ituzaingó

Ciudadela

Florida

Andes

Convención

Plaza Independencia

②

③

Plaza Zabala

Cerrito

❶

Sarandí

CIUDAD VIEJA

Buenos Aires

Reconquista

Plaza España

Rambla Francia

Florida

Andes

Río Negro

Paraguay

Carlos Quijano

Zelmar Michelini

Carlos Lanza

Dr. Aquiles R. Lanza

Santiago de Chile

Eduardo

Av. General Rondeau

Cuareim

Yí

Yaguarón

Ejido

Juan Lindolfo Cuestas

Juan Lindolfo Cuestas

Guaraní

Av. Libertador Brigadier Gen. Lavalleja

Rambla Sud América

Río de la Plata

❺-❽
③-⑥

| 0 | | 1,000ft |
| 0 | | 500m |

Restaurants ▼

Café Bacacay	2
Expreso Pocitos	8
Jacinto	1
La Casa Violeta	6
Rara Avis	3
Restaurant Francis	5
Tandory	7
Viejo Sancho	4

Hotels ▼

Armon Suites	5
Hostería del Lago	2
Hotel Ermitage	6
Oxford Hotel	1
Sheraton Montevideo	4
Sofitel Montevideo Casino Carrasco & Spa	3

$$$$
HOTEL **Sheraton Montevideo.** Removed from the Old City and attached to the flashy Punta Carretas shopping center, the Sheraton Montevideo is one of the city's biggest hotels. **Pros:** good amenities; convenient to beach and shopping; city views from rooftop pool. **Cons:** cab ride to downtown and sights; some rooms need an update; water pressure can be inconsistent. ⑤ *Rooms from: 6200 pesos* ⊠ *Victor Soliño 349, Punta Carretas* ☎ *2710–2121* ⊕ *www.sheratonmontevideo.com* ⟳ *207 rooms* ⊙l *Breakfast.*

$$$$
HOTEL **Sofitel Montevideo Casino Carrasco & Spa.** Originally opened in 1921 as a summer escape for the Uruguayan elite, this stunning Belle Epoque waterfront building, known as the "palace on the sand," underwent an intensive restoration process. **Pros:** attractive casino, restaurant, and bar on-site; inspired spa treatments; open river views from many rooms. **Cons:** a lengthy taxi ride to the sights of Montevideo; showing wear and tear in places; service could be sharper. ⑤ *Rooms from: 5400 pesos* ⊠ *Rambla República de México 6451* ☎ *2604–6060* ⊕ *www.sofitel.com* ⟳ *116 rooms* ⊙l *No meals.*

NIGHTLIFE

Montevideo's nightlife scene is a smattering of pubs, bars, clubs, and tango and folk music venues. With few exceptions, bars and clubs come to life around 1 am and don't close until it's time for breakfast. Still, "after office" outings are popular, which is essentially happy hour with groups hitting the bars on an earlier-than-usual schedule.

BARS AND PUBS

Riff Gallery Pub. Riff Gallery Pub is the only bar in the city devoted to jazz, with live shows on Thursday and Saturday. ⊠ *Bul. España 2511, Centro.*

La Pasiva. For an ice-cold beer, this popular pub is a late-night favorite. Specialties are frankfurters, chivitos, and other bar food. In good weather you can socialize at the outdoor tables in Plaza Matriz. This Montevideo staple has an array of franchises throughout the city, including a prominent location on Plaza Fabini. ⊠ *Calle Sarandí at Calle J.C. Gómez, Ciudad Vieja* ☎ *2903–1790* ⊕ *www.lapasiva.com.uy* ⊙ *Closed Sun.* ⌁ *Reservations not accepted.*

Volvé Mi Negra. Lines form frequently outside this nightlife spot on weekends, where locals come for generous-size drinks. While it's technically a pub complete with wood paneling, bar stools, and pool tables, live DJs get people dancing and give it a club vibe. ⊠ *Francisco Muñoz 3177, Pocitos* ☎ *97/087–922.*

DANCE CLUBS

Fodor'sChoice **Lotus Club.** Located in Montevideo's World Trade Center, this club for
★ years has been considered one of Montevideo's best. The red-and-black
color scheme gives the place an upscale feel, and Montevideans dance
until the wee hours under shimmering disco balls. ⊠ *Lecuender at
Bonavita, Pocitos* ☎ *2628–1379* ⊕ *www.lotus.com.uy.*

TANGO SHOWS

Joventango. If you're itching to try out your dance steps, Joventango is
the best place in the city to learn tango. Shows and classes are frequent;
call or check the website for times. ⊠ *Aquiles Lanza 1290 esq. Saint
Joseph, Centro* ☎ *2908–6813* ⊕ *www.joventango.com* ⌑ *225 pesos.*

SHOPPING

Let's face it: Montevideans head to Buenos Aires when they want to
go on an extra-special shopping excursion. But quality and selection
are decent here, and prices often are lower than in Argentina. Stores in
Centro, along Avenida 18 de Julio, offer the standard selection of urban
merchandise. The truly fun shopping experience is to be found in the
city's markets, which are vibrant and numerous.

ANTIQUES

Calle Tristán Narvaja north of Avenida 18 de Julio is packed with
antiques shops. In the Old City, the streets north of Plaza Constitución
are also lined with such stores.

Louvre. This antiques store is the only source for handmade and
painted trinket boxes—the perfect *recuerdos* (souvenirs). It also offers
an impressive selection of jewelry and silver. ⊠ *Sarandí 652, Ciudad
Vieja* ☎ *2916–2686* ⊕ *www.louvreantiguedades.com.uy* ☉ *Closed Sat.
afternoon and Sun.*

HANDICRAFTS

Fodor'sChoice **Manos del Uruguay.** With six locations total in Montevideo and Punta
★ del Este, Manos del Uruguay stock a wide selection of woolen wear
and locally produced ceramics crafted by women's artisan cooperatives
around the country. ⊠ *Punta Carretas Shopping, José Ellauri 350, Centro* ☎ *2710–6108* ⊕ *www.manos.com.uy.*

LEATHER

Montevideo is a good source for inexpensive leather. Shops near Plaza
Independencia specialize in hand-tailored coats and jackets made out
of nutria (fur from a large semiaquatic rodent).

Pecarí. Soft lamb leather goes into making classic jackets, handbags, and
footwear at this ladies' leather store. ⊠ *Juan C. Gómez 1412, Ciudad
Vieja* ⊕ *www.pecari.com.uy* ☉ *Closed. Sat. afternoon and Sun.*

MARKETS

Weekend *ferias* (open-air markets) are the best place for leisurely browsing among a warren of crafts stalls. Government regulations dictate
that all ferias must close in the early afternoon, so make sure to arrive
by 10 am.

El Mercado de la Abundancia. Dating back to 1836, El Mercado de la Abundancia is a fun indoor market in Centro, a few blocks from the Palacio Municipal. Inside are a tango dance center, a handful of good choices for a lunchtime *parrillada*, and a crafts fair. ⊠ *San José 1312, and Aquiles Lanza, Centro* ⊘ *Closed Sun. morning.*

Fodor'sChoice ★ **Feria Tristán Narvaja.** Started in the early 1900s by Italian immigrants, Feria Tristán Narvaja is Montevideo's top attraction on Sunday and one of the city's largest and most popular fairs. (It operates only on Sunday, a day when all other markets, and much of the city, are closed. Hours run about 9–3.) The fair, a 5- to 10-minute walk from the Old City and in the Centro district, is plentifully stocked with secondhand goods and antiques. ⊠ *Dr. Tristán Narvaja 1545, Centro* ⊘ *Closed Mon.–Sat.*

Parque Villa Biarritz. The Saturday morning market at Parque Villa Biarritz in the neighborhood of Pocitos sells crafts, clothes, and some antiques. You can find some vendors set up other days of the week, as well. The small park also has a recreational center, Club Biguá, with tennis courts and other sports facilities. ⊠ *José Vazquéz de Ledesma, Punta Carretas.*

Plaza Cagancha. Between Avenida 18 de Julio and Calle Rondeau in Centro, Plaza Cagancha regularly has vendors set up in the area at all hours selling trinkets and crafts. ⊠ *Av. 18 de Julio between Av. Gral Rondeau and Pasaje de los Derechos Humanos, Punta Carretas.*

SHOPPING CENTERS

Montevideo Shopping. There are three major shopping centers in Montevideo, offering everything from designer clothing to gourmet foods to art supplies. Montevideo Shopping is the oldest along the Rio de la Plata and has more than 175 stores and entertainment options including a movie theater. ⊠ *Luis Alberto de Herrera 1290, Punta Carretas* ☎ *2622–1005* ⊕ *www.montevideoshopping.com.uy.*

Portones Shopping. Adjacent to the Portones terminal, Portones Shopping is an indoor mall with more than 130 stores and a movie theater. ⊠ *Av. Italia 5775, Carrasco* ☎ *2601–7733, 0800–1807* ⊕ *www.portones.com.uy.*

Fodor'sChoice ★ **Punta Carretas Shopping.** Housed in a former prison, Punta Carretas Shopping is the city's largest and most upscale mall, measuring in at around 200 stores mixing local and international brands. It's in a pleasant residential area near the Sheraton Montevideo, a 10-minute cab ride from the Old City. ⊠ *José Ellauri 350, Punta Carretas* ☎ *2711–6940.*

COLONIA DEL SACRAMENTO

The peaceful cobbled streets of Colonia are just over the Río de la Plata from Buenos Aires, but they seem a world away. Charm might be an overused descriptor, but Colonia, with its old-world architecture, serenity, and water lapping at sandy shores is a place that redefines it.

The best activity in Colonia is walking through its peaceful Barrio Histórico (Old Town), a UNESCO World Heritage Site. Porteños come to Colonia for romantic getaways or for a break from the city. If you like

Cobblestones abound in the Old Town section of Colonia del Sacramento, Uruguay.

to keep busy on your travels, a late-morning arrival and early-evening departure give you plenty of time to see the sights and wander at will. To really see the city at its own pace, spend the night in one of its many colonial-style bed-and-breakfasts: This offsets travel costs and time and makes a visit here far more rewarding.

GETTING HERE AND AROUND

Hydrofoils and ferries cross the Río de la Plata between Buenos Aires and Uruguay several times a day. Boats often sell out, particularly on summer weekends, so book tickets at least a few days ahead. The two competing companies that operate services—Buquebus and Colonia Express—often wage a reduced-rates war in the low season.

Buquebus provides two kinds of service for passengers and cars: the quickest crossing takes an hour by hydrofoil and the slower ferry takes around three hours. The Buquebus terminal in Buenos Aires is at the northern end of Puerto Madero at the intersection of Avenida Alicia M. de Justo and Avenida Córdoba (which changes its name here to Bulevar Cecilia Grierson). It's accessible by taxi or by walking seven blocks from L.N. Alem subte station along Trinidad Guevara.

Colonia Express operates the cheapest and fastest services to Colonia but has only four daily services in each direction. There often are huge discounts on the 50-minute catamaran trip if you buy tickets in advance. The Colonia Express terminal in Buenos Aires is south of Puerto Madero on Avenida Pedro de Mendoza, the extension of Avenida Huergo. It's best reached by taxi, but Bus No. 130 from Avenidas Libertador and L.N. Alem also stops outside it.

The shortest way to the Barrio Histórico is to turn left out of the port parking lot onto Florida—it's a six-block walk. Walking is the perfect way to get around this part of town; equally practical—and lots of fun—are golf carts and sand buggies that you can rent from Thrifty.

Ferry Contacts Buquebus. ✉ *Av. Antartida Argentina 821, Puerto Madero* ☎ *11/4316–6530* ⊕ *www.buquebus.com.* **Colonia Express.** ✉ *Ticket office at Av. Córdoba 753, Microcentro, Av. Pedro de Mendoza 330, La Boca* ☎ *11/4317–4100 in Buenos Aires* ⊕ *www.coloniaexpress.com.*

Rental Cars Thrifty. ✉ *Av. Gral. Flores 172* ☎ *4522–2939* ⊕ *www.thrifty.com.uy.*

Taxi Contact Taxis Colonia. ☎ *598/4522–2920.*

ESSENTIALS

Visitor Information Colonia del Sacramento Tourism Office. ✉ *At ferry terminal, Also at Manuel Lobo, between Ituzaingó and Paseo San Antonio* ☎ *4522–6886* ⊕ *www.coloniaturismo.com.*

EXPLORING

Begin your tour at the reconstructed Portón de Campo or city gate, where remnants of the old bastion walls lead to the river. A block farther is Calle de los Suspiros, the aptly named Street of Sighs, a cobblestone stretch of one-story colonials that can rival any street in Latin America for sheer romantic effect. It runs between a lookout point on the river, called the Bastión de San Miguel, and the Plaza Mayor, a lovely square filled with Spanish moss, palms, and spiky, flowering *palo borracho* trees. The many cafés around the square are ideal places to take it all in. Clusters of bougainvillea flow over the walls here and in the other quiet streets of the Barrio Histórico, many of which are lined with art galleries and antiques shops.

Another great place to watch daily life is the Plaza de Armas Manoel Lobo, where you can find the Iglesia Matriz, the oldest church in Uruguay. The square itself is crisscrossed with wooden catwalks over the ruins of a house dating to the founding of the town. The tables from the square's small eateries spill from the sidewalk right onto the cobblestones: they're all rather touristy, but give you an excellent view of the drum-toting *candombe* (a style of music from Uruguay) squads that beat their way around the Old Town each afternoon.

You can visit all of Colonia's museums with the same ticket, which you buy from the Museo Portugués or the Museo Municipal for about $2.50. Most take only a few minutes to visit, but you can use the ticket on two consecutive days.

TOP ATTRACTIONS

Faro (*Lighthouse*). Towering above the Plaza Mayor is the lighthouse, which was built in 1857 on top of a tower that was part of the ruined San Xavier convent. The whole structure was engulfed in flames in 1873 after a lighthouse keeper had an accident with the oil used in the lamp at the time. Your reward for climbing it are great views over the Barrio Histórico and the River Plate. ✉ *Plaza Mayor* 🎟 *25 pesos.*

Museo Portugués. The museum that's most worth a visit is this one, which documents the city's ties to Portugal. It's most notable for its collection of old map reproductions based on Portuguese naval expeditions. A small selection of period furnishings, clothes, and jewelry from Colonia's days as a Portuguese colony complete the offerings. Exhibits are well labeled, but in Spanish only. ⊠ *Plaza Mayor between Calle de los Suspiros and De Solís* ☎ *50 pesos* ⊗ *Closed Sun.*

WORTH NOTING

Museo del Azulejo. A small collection of the beautiful handmade French majolica tiles that adorn fountains all over Colonia are on display at the tile museum, housed in a small 18th-century building near the river. The 50-peso entry fee is good for all Colonia's museums. ⊠ *Misiones de los Tapies 104, at Paseo San Gabriel* ☎ *4522–1056* ⊕ *www.museoscolonia. com.uy* ☎ *50 pesos* ⊗ *Closed Thurs.*

Museo Municipal Dr. Bautista Rebuffo. A sundry collection of objects related to the city's history is housed here. ⊠ *Plaza Mayor at Misiones de los Tapies* ☎ *50 pesos* ⊗ *Closed Tues.*

Nacarello Museum. A colonial Portuguese residence has been lovingly re-created inside this 17th-century structure. The simple bedroom and kitchen furnishings are period pieces, but the real attraction is the house itself, with its thick whitewashed walls and low ceilings. For 50 Uruguayan pesos you gain access to all Colonia's museums, including this one. ⊠ *Plaza Mayor at Henríquez de la Peña* ⊕ *www.museoscolonia. com.uy* ☎ *50 pesos* ⊗ *Closed Fri.*

OFF THE
BEATEN
PATH

Narbona Wine Lodge. For an upscale, indulgent Uruguayan wine experience, Narbona Wine Lodge in Carmelo, an hour's drive from Colonia, is worth a visit. The peaceful property includes a vineyard, a restaurant with exposed brick walls that serves Italian-influenced dishes featuring the wines and products like cheeses made on-site, and a luxurious tasting room. If you find yourself unable to leave at the end of the day, book a stay at one of property's five sophisticated, bright, yet rustic rooms named after grape varietals. Your stay includes a vineyard tour, mountain bikes for borrowing, and access to Narbona's private beach. ⊠ *Ruta 21, Km 268, Carmelo* ☎ *4544–6831* ⊕ *www.narbona.com.uy.*

WHERE TO EAT

In Colonia, both dollars and Uruguayan pesos are accepted. Uruguayan food is as beef-based as Argentine fare, and also has a notable Italian influence. Here, enticing cafés and restaurants with plaza and riverfront views are numerous.

$$
SOUTH
AMERICAN

✕ **El Drugstore.** The colorful, eclectic decor has turned this restaurant into a notorious spot in tranquil Colonia. You'll find Uruguayan standby dishes like pastas and *chivito* on the menu, all of which come in generous portions. **Known for:** great old town location; decent size portions; well priced for the area. ⑤ *Average main: 450 pesos* ⊠ *Portugal 174* ☎ *4522–5241.*

$$$
MEDITERRANEAN

✕ **El Mesón de la Plaza.** Simple dishes—many steak-based—made with good-quality ingredients have made this traditional restaurant a favorite with porteño visitors to Colonia. The comprehensive wine list showcases Uruguayan vineyards hard to sample anywhere outside the country. **Known for:** outdoor dining; great Uruguayan wine list; live music. ⑤ *Average main: 550 pesos* ✉ *Vasconcellos 153* ☎ *598/4522–4807* ⊗ *No dinner Mon.*

$
SOUTH
AMERICAN
✕ **La Bodeguita.** This hip restaurant serves delicious, crispy pizza, sliced into bite-size rectangles. The backyard tables overlook the river, and inside is cozy, with warm walls. **Known for:** lovely views; casual spot; well priced. ⑤ *Average main: 230 pesos* ✉ *Calle del Comercio 167* ☎ *598/4522–5329* ⊕ *www.labodeguita.net* ▬ *No credit cards* ⊗ *Closed Mon. during winter, no lunch Tues.–Fri.*

$$$$
LATIN AMERICAN
Fodor'sChoice
★
✕ **La Florida.** The black-and-white photos, lace tablecloths, and quaint knickknacks that clutter this long, low house belie the fact that it was once a brothel. It still has private rooms, but the politicians and occasional celebs rent them for dining these days. **Known for:** dishes for sharing; kingfish, sole, and salmon; plenty of ambience. ⑤ *Average main: 800 pesos* ✉ *Odriozola 215* ☎ *598/9429–3036* ▬ *No credit cards* ⊗ *Closed Wed.; Apr.–Nov. dinner by reservation only.*

$$
CAFÉ
Fodor'sChoice
★
✕ **Lentas Maravillas.** There's no spot more perfect in Colonia to while away an afternoon with a leisurely salad for lunch or tea than this café nestled along the water. Don't miss the baked goods—the *redondos* (rich, round cheesecakes) are particularly heavenly. **Known for:** adorable setting; great lunch spot; lovely views. ⑤ *Average main: 320 pesos* ✉ *Santa Rita 61* ☎ *4522–0636* ▬ *No credit cards* ⊗ *Closed Wed. No dinner.*

WHERE TO STAY

Since Colonia is the consummate day trip from Montevideo or Buenos Aires, few visitors actually spend the night here. Consider breaking that mold; there's no shortage of homey lodgings to choose from, and an overnight stay really gives you the opportunity to unwind and adopt the relaxed Colonia pace.

$$$$
RESORT
▦ **Carmelo Resort & Spa, in the Unbound Collection by Hyatt.** Serenity pervades this harmoniously decorated resort an hour west of Colonia del Sacramento, reachable by car, boat, or a 25-minute flight from Buenos Aires and a destination in and of itself. **Pros:** all rooms are spacious bungalows; personalized service; on-site activities compensate for distance to sights and restaurants. **Cons:** despite copious netting and bug spray, the mosquitoes can get out of hand; food quality is erratic; popular with groups and families. ⑤ *Rooms from: 10,000 pesos* ✉ *Ruta 21, Km 262, Carmelo* ☎ *4542–9000* ⊕ *carmelo.hyatt.com* ⇲ *20 bungalows, 24 duplex suites* ⦿ *Breakfast.*

$$
B&B/INN
▦ **Posada de la Flor.** This colonial-style hotel is on a quiet street leading to the river and is arranged around a sunny courtyard. **Pros:** peaceful location near river and the Barrio Histórico; gorgeous breakfast area and roof terrace; great value. **Cons:** standard rooms are cramped; ground-floor rooms open onto the courtyard and can be noisy. ⑤ *Rooms from: 1725 pesos* ✉ *Calle Ituzaingó 268* ☎ *52/30794* ⊕ *www.posada-delaflor. com* ▬ *No credit cards* ⇲ *14 rooms* ⦿ *Breakfast.*

Colonia del Sacramento

6 9

Campo Municipal

Coronet Arroyo

Rambla Cristóbal Colón

Doctor Daniel Fosalba

8

Rivadavia

1

8 de Octubre

San José

Santa Rita

España

Virrey Cebattos

7

Ituzaingó

Washington Barbot

Intendente Suárez

Plaza 25 de Agosto

Lavalleja

Alberto Méndez

General Rivera

Avenida General Flores

Paseo de San Gabriel

Colegio

Comercio

Real

Portugal

Iglesia Matriz

4

5

Plaza de Armas Manuel Lobo

18 de Julio

2

la Playa

3

Misiones de los Tapes

Plaza Mayor

Manuel de Lobo

1

2

3

Flores

San Francisco

Solís

5

Suspiros

Odriozola

4

De San Pedro

6

Av. Buenos Aires

10

Río de la Plata

Ferry Terminal

Puerto

KEY

1 *Exploring sights*

(1) *Hotels & Restaurants*

0   500ft

0   200m

FERRY TO BUENOS AIRES

$$$

HOTEL

🏨 **Posada Don Antonio.** Long galleries of rooms overlook an enormous split-level courtyard at Posada Don Antonio, the latest incarnation of a large, elegant building that has housed one hotel or another for close to a century. **Pros:** sparkling turquoise pool, surrounded by loungers; two blocks from the Barrio Histórico; rates are low, but there are proper hotel perks like poolside snacks. **Cons:** ill-fitting doors let in courtyard noise; some rooms open onto the street. $ *Rooms from: 3500 pesos* ✉ *Ituzaingó 232* ☎ *598/4522–5344* ⊕ *www.posadadonantonio.com* 🔑 *38 rooms* ⧏◎⧐ *Breakfast.*

$$$

B&B/INN

🏨 **Posada Plaza Mayor.** A faint scent of jasmine fills the air at this lovely old hotel, where all the rooms open onto a large, plant-filled courtyard complete with a bubbling fountain. **Pros:** beautiful green spaces; on a quiet street of the Barrio Histórico; cheerful, accommodating staff. **Cons:** cramped bathrooms; the three cheapest rooms are small. $ *Rooms from: 3500 pesos* ✉ *Calle del Comercio 111* ☎ *598/4522–3193* ⊕ *www.posadaplazamayor.com* 🔑 *17 rooms* ⧏◎⧐ *Breakfast.*

$$$

RESORT

🏨 **Sheraton Colonia Golf & Spa Resort.** Materials like copper, terra-cotta, and golden-color stone add warm touches to the airy, light-filled atrium as does the massive wood-fronted fireplace, which is always lit in winter. **Pros:** peaceful location with river views from many rooms; great spa; rooms are often discounted midweek. **Cons:** it's a 10-minute drive or taxi ride north of the Barrio Histórico; can be noisy on weekends. $ *Rooms from: 4200 pesos* ✉ *Cont. Rambla de las Américas s/n* ☎ *4522–9000* ⊕ *www.sheraton.com* 🔑 *96 rooms, 8 suites* ⧏◎⧐ *Breakfast.*

PUNTA DEL ESTE

134 km (83 miles) east of Montevideo.

Fodor'sChoice ★ Often likened to the Hamptons or St-Tropez, Punta del Este is a flashy destination where parties run nonstop in peak season. But it is also a destination that draws a range of beachgoers to its shores, from summering families to the celebrity jet-set. There's a bustling city on the beach downtown, as well as quiet countryside populated solely with upscale ranches called *chacras* or *estancias,* and creative, buzzing hamlets like La Barra and José Ignacio. Though it's pricey and at times a logistical challenge to get around, everyone finds something about Punta to love.

The resort takes its name from the "east point" marking the division of the Río de la Plata on the west from the Atlantic Ocean to the east. It also lends its name to the broader region encompassing the nearby communities of Punta Ballena and La Barra de Maldonado. These days even José Ignacio, some 20 miles away, is grouped in. It's usually a given that Argentina's upper class spends at least part of the summer in Punta, soaking in the ample rays.

GETTING HERE AND AROUND

Most visitors headed to the beach fly into Montevideo's Aeropuerto Internacional de Carrasco (MVD). Flights arrive from many South American cities, in high season only, directly to the Aeropuerto Internacional de Punta del Este (PDP), about 24 km (15 miles) east of town.

Many bus lines travel daily between Montevideo's Terminal Tres Cruces and Punta del Este's Terminal Playa Brava. Two companies that serve the entire region are Copsa and Cot. Buquebus also offers flights, and ferries with a bus connection to Punta.

To get to Punta del Este from Montevideo, follow Ruta 1 east to the Ruta 93 turnoff. The road is well maintained and marked, and the trip takes about 1½ hours. Rental agencies, such as Avis, Budget, and Dollar, are in downtown Punta del Este.

Airport Contact Aeropuerto Internacional de Punta del Este. ⊠ *Ruta 93, Km 113* ☎ *4255–9777* ⊕ *www.puntadeleste.aero.*

Bus Contacts COT. ☎ *2409–4949 in Montevideo* ⊕ *www.coturuguay.com.* **Copsa.** ☎ *2902–1818* ⊕ *www.copsa.com.uy.* **Terminal de Omnibus.** ⊠ *Rambla Artigas and Calle 32.*

SAFETY AND PRECAUTIONS
For such a touristy locale, Punta maintains a reassuring level of security. Nevertheless, it pays to watch your things. Swimming is not safe at several of the beaches, especially those on the Atlantic side of the point. Never swim alone, and gauge your abilities carefully.

ESSENTIALS
Visitor and Tour Information Maldonado Tourist Office. ⊠ *Parada 1, Calles 31 and 18* ☎ *4222–1921* ⊕ *www.maldonadoturismo.com.uy.* **Punta del Este Tourist Office.** ⊠ *Av. Gorlero* ☎ *4244–6510* ⊕ *www.turismo.gub.uy.*

EXPLORING

TOP ATTRACTIONS
Avenida Gorlero. Punta del Este is circled by the Rambla Artigas, the main coastal road that leads past residential neighborhoods and pristine stretches of beach. You can find everything on Avenida Gorlero, Punta's main commercial strip. The thoroughfare runs northeast–southwest through the heart of the peninsula and is fronted with cafés, restaurants, boutiques, and casinos. ⊠ *Av. Gorlero.*

Casapueblo. A hotel and museum at the tip of a rocky point with tremendous views of the Río de la Plata is the main draw in Punta Ballena. Uruguayan abstract artist Carlos Páez Vilaró created his work as a "habitable sculpture" and it defies architectural categorization. With allusions to Arab minarets and domes, cathedral vaulting, Grecian whitewash, and continuous sculptural flourishes that recall the traceries of a Miró canvas, this curvaceous 13-floor surrealist complex climbs a hill and is highly unique.

The spaces include an excellent series of galleries dedicated to the artist's work and peruse copies of his books: one book tells the true story of his son Carlos Miguel, who survived a plane crash in the Andes, which was made into the 1993 film *Alive*. ⊠ *Punta Ballena* ☎ *4257–8041* ⊕ *www. clubhotelcasapueblo.com* 🗐 *240 pesos.*

Isla de Lobos. This island is a government-protected natural reserve and national park home to one of the world's largest colonies of sea lions. You can view them from tour boats that leave regularly from the marina. Its 1907 lighthouse stands nearly 190 feet tall. ⊠ *Punta del Este.*

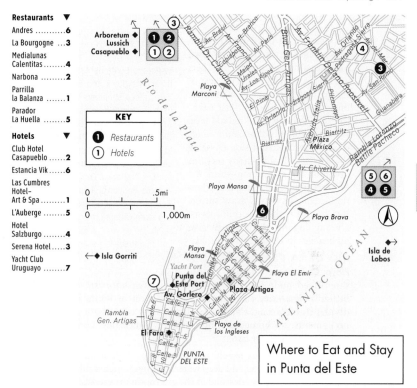

Where to Eat and Stay in Punta del Este

Restaurants ▼

Andres **6**

La Bourgogne ...**3**

Medialunas
Calentitas **4**

Narbona **2**

Parrilla
la Balanza **1**

Parador
La Huella **5**

Hotels ▼

Club Hotel
Casapueblo **2**

Estancia Vik **6**

Las Cumbres
Hotel–
Art & Spa **1**

L'Auberge **5**

Hotel
Salzburgo **4**

Serena Hotel **3**

Yacht Club
Uruguayo **7**

WORTH NOTING

Arboretum Lussich. Naturally perfumed with the scent of eucalyptus, this huge arboretum is one of the most important botanical gardens in the world. Its creation was the labor of love of Croatian-Uruguayan botanist Antonio Lussich (1848–1928). The approximate 474 acres contain more than 350 species of trees from outside Uruguay as well as 70 domestic species. Guided tours are in Spanish only. ⊠ *Av. Antonio Lussich* ☎ *4257–8077* ⌨ *Free.*

Isla Gorriti. Once the site of a prison, Isla Gorriti now attracts a different type of exclusive crowd. High-end residents with their own boats often set Gorriti as their destination to play and party for the day. You can catch a ferry ride from the marina, though, and make a day trip of it. Note that the island is reachable only by boat. (The *parador,* or beach club, has a good restaurant.) ⊠ *Punta del Este.*

Punta del Este Port. Punta's sunsets seem even more spectacular when witnessed over its port, with sails and boats dotting the bay. Stop for a drink at any one of the many restaurants lining the street, or make it your destination for a leisurely walk or scenic run. ⊠ *2 de Febrero at Mareantes.*

BEACHES

This stretch of coast has a dozen or so beaches, each with its own high-season personality. All bets are off on activity levels the rest of the year, and remember: what's hot one season may be so "last year" the next. Punta is that kind of place. Locals frequently shorthand things to the *mansa* (calm) side fronting the Río de la Plata—many sections are fine for swimming—and the *brava* (rough) side lining the Atlantic Ocean—its waves draw surfers but should make you think twice about going into the water. By law, all beaches in Uruguay are public.

> ### A CAVALCADE OF STARS
>
> Visitors to Punta del Este during its first heyday in the '50s and '60s rubbed shoulders with the likes of Ingmar Bergman and Yul Brynner. Even Brigitte Bardot, that then-icon of similarly themed St-Tropez, appeared here periodically. Recently celebrities such as Shakira, Madonna, Enrique Iglesias, Antonio Banderas, Ralph Lauren, Bob Dylan, Eric Clapton, and Leonardo DiCaprio have done the Punta circuit. You never know who you might see—in season, that is.

RÍO DE LA PLATA SIDE

Playa Chihuahua. Uruguay's only sanctioned nude beach—look for the *playa naturista* ("naturalist beach") sign—sits out near the airport west of Punta Ballena and divides into a straight and a gay section. Be cool about it if you go: no cameras, no binoculars, no gawking. **Amenities:** none. **Best for:** nudists. ⊠ *Punta del Este.*

Playa El Chiringo. This beach, just east of Punta Ballena, can be a bit rough, with gritty sand and deep water. Chiringo catches full sun at midmorning, but shadows descend as the afternoon progresses, and the sun sets behind Punta Ballena. The wind and waves make swimming risky here. **Amenities:** lifeguards. **Best for:** solitude; sunrise. ⊠ *Punta del Este.*

Playa El Chileno. The wind gusts dramatically at Playa El Chileno, making this beach a favorite among windsurfers. **Amenities:** toilets; showers. **Best for:** surfing; windsurfing. ⊠ *Punta del Este.*

Playa Pinares. A continuation of Playa Mansa, Playa Pinares has deep water and rocky sand that make this a beach you'll likely have to yourself. Expect little in the way of facilities. **Amenities:** none. **Best for:** sunrise; sunset; walking. ⊠ *Punta del Este.*

FAMILY
Fodor'sChoice
★
Playa Mansa. The waters are calm at Punta's longest beach and one of its most popular. Good sand, shallow water, many food stands, and proximity to the center of town make it the area's most family-oriented stretch of coast. Catch good sunset views here, and take in one of the late-afternoon beach aerobics classes, too. **Amenities:** food and drink; lifeguards; parking; showers; toilets; water sports. **Best for:** sunset; swimming; walking. ⊠ *Punta del Este.*

Playa Solanas. The famous Casapueblo museum and hotel sit above this calm beach, also called Portezuelo, at Punta Ballena. Its shallow water shielded from the wind makes it a favorite of families with small children. Great sunset views are a plus here, too. **Amenities:** lifeguards; showers; toilets. **Best for:** sunrise; sunset; swimming; walking. ⊠ *Punta del Este.*

In high season, people come to see and be seen at Punta del Este's glamorous beaches.

ATLANTIC SIDE

Fodor's Choice ★ **La Barra.** The La Barra hamlet is both artistic and trendy, with a number of popular boutiques, restaurants, and nightlife spots that spring into life in January. A mostly locally patronized beach sits here, too, where the Río Maldonado spills into the ocean. Keep in mind that swimming is risky. **Amenities:** food and drink; lifeguards; parking; toilets. **Best for:** partiers; sunrise; sunset; surfing; walking. ⊠ *Punta del Este.*

SUNRISE, SUNSET

How many beach resorts let you enjoy spectacular sunrises *and* sunsets over the water? Punta's orientation on a narrow north–south peninsula allows you to take in both.

Fodor's Choice ★ **José Ignacio.** This hamlet with a vibrant art community and some of the most jaw-dropping properties for miles is the choice beach for Punta's most well-heeled and stylish visitors. José Ignacio sits on a miniature peninsula and has beaches with both calm and rough waters. Because it's just enough outside the downtown Punta orbit, visiting is a day trip for most. **Amenities:** food and drink; lifeguards; toilets. **Best for:** partiers in the know; sunrise; sunset; surfing; swimming; walking; windsurfing. ⊠ *Punta del Este.*

Playa Brava. The golden sand and numerous food stands here draw a young crowd that mostly stays on the beach rather than braving the rough water (*brava* means "rough"). Brava is one of the most frequented beaches—largely thanks to *La Mano de Punta del Este,* a giant sculpture with the fingers of an enormous hand appearing to reach out of the sand—where many visitors will surely be snapping photos. This work by Chilean artist Mario Irarrázabal gives the beach its colloquial name, Playa de los Dedos (Beach of the Fingers). **Amenities:** food and drink; lifeguards; showers; toilets. **Best for:** sunrise; sunset; walking. ⊠ *Punta del Este.*

Playa de los Ingleses. While this beach has fine sand, the wind and waves are strong here. Venture into the water at your own risk. You're still close to the center of Punta, meaning this beach sees many nonswimming visitors. Restaurants lining this so-called Englishmen's Beach were the spots for afternoon tea in a bygone era. **Amenities:** none. **Best for:** walking. ⊠ *Punta del Este.*

Playa El Emir. This beach is named for an eccentric Middle Eastern emir who vacationed here and built a house near this stretch of sand. High waves make this beach popular with surfers but somewhat dangerous for swimmers. **Amenities:** food and drink; lifeguards; showers; toilets. **Best for:** surfing; walking. ⊠ *Punta del Este.*

Fodor'sChoice
★
Playa Manantiales. Locals have dubbed this trendy stretch of sand Bikini Beach. The swimwear skews a tad more daring here, where people come to see and be seen, as well as swim or play volleyball. During peak season DJs often spin through sunset. If you're looking for a party beach, this is where you want to be. **Amenities:** food and drinks; lifeguards; parking; showers; toilets. **Best for:** partiers; sunrise; sunset; surfing; swimming; windsurfing. ⊠ *Punta del Este.*

Playa Montoya. Just east of La Barra beach (but still belonging to La Barra) is this stretch of sand, where a young, attractive crowd mostly stays dry but always seems to have volleyball or soccer games going. Montoya also is the site of a number of surf competitions. **Amenities:** lifeguards; showers; toilets. **Best for:** partiers; sunset; surfing; swimming; walking. ⊠ *Punta del Este.*

WHERE TO EAT

$$$
SEAFOOD
✕**Andres.** Bearing the name of its founder, this small restaurant on the Rambla Artigas, the oceanside promenade, offers fine dining at moderate prices—its successful recipe for attracting clientele for more than 40 years. You can't beat the view, and in the summer you can appreciate the excellent service while enjoying the sea breeze. **Known for:** oceanside location and breeze; surf and turf; spinach and cheese soufflés. $ *Average main: 600 pesos* ⊠ *Parada 1, Rambla Williman, Edificio Vaguardia* ☏ *4248–1804* ⊕ *www.restaurantandres.com.uy/en* ☽ *Closed Mon.–Thurs. Mar.–Nov.*

$$
FRENCH
Fodor'sChoice
★
✕**La Bourgogne.** A shaded terra-cotta terrace gives way to a breezeway with arched windows at this restaurant, considered one of Latin America's finest, and opens onto a large split-level dining room with antique sideboards. French chef Jean Paul Bondoux is at the helm, and the food, served by impeccably clad waiters, is prepared with only the finest and freshest ingredients. **Known for:** fine dining; French family at the helm; excellent service and wine list. $ *Average main: 2500 pesos* ⊠ *Av. del Mar at Calle Pedragosa Sierra* ☏ *4248–2007* ⊕ *labourgogne. uy* ☽ *Closed Mon.–Thurs. May–Nov.*

$ ✕**Medialunas Calentitas.** People flock to this classic Punta spot at all
CAFÉ hours for their piping-hot *medialunas,* which are crescent moon–
Fodor'sChoice shape pastries that taste like fluffy croissants and come brushed
★ with a sweet syrup. Many patrons profess they're the best medialunas to be found anywhere. **Known for:** pastries and teatime treats;
takeaway; popular bakery. $ *Average main: 240 pesos* ⊠ *Ruta 10
at Camino del Cerro Eguzquiza* ☎ *4277–2347* ⊕ *www.medialunas-
calentitas.com.*

$$$$ ✕**Narbona.** Set inland from Barra's center on an expansive, rolling
ITALIAN property is the upscale, rustic Narbona restaurant. The property is so
tranquil and removed from the Punta frenzy that the restaurant provides
GPS coordinates as their address. **Known for:** beautiful setting; Italian
fare; uses own products such as olive oil. $ *Average main: 1350 pesos*
⊠ *Punta del Este* ☎ *4410–2999* ⊕ *www.narbona.com.uy.*

$$$$ ✕**Parador La Huella.** *Huella* means footprint, and this now-legendary
SOUTH restaurant certainly has left its mark. Built right on the sand, La Huella
AMERICAN takes beach dining to an unrivaled level with exquisite grilled seafood
Fodor'sChoice and meats—the octopus is not to be missed—as well as fresh sushi,
★ pastas, and pizzas. **Known for:** delectable seafood; very trendy; cool and
relaxed vibe. $ *Average main: 700 pesos* ⊠ *Calle de los Cisnes, Brava
Beach* ☎ *4486–2279* ⊕ *www.paradorlahuella.com* ☉ *Closed Apr.–Nov.,
Mon.–Thurs. and Sun. night.*

$$$ ✕**Parrilla la Balanza.** It's a bit hard to believe a place as low-key and
STEAKHOUSE affordable as this traditional Uruguayan steak house exists in chic Punta
del Este, but it does—and that's precisely why locals love it. Your best
bet is to stick to steak and sides to share, including the platter of mini
provoleta (grilled cheese) with a bottle of wine to wash it all down.
Known for: cheap and cheerful; open all year round; great beef. $ *Av-
erage main: 490 pesos* ⊠ *25 de Mayo y Santa Teresa* ☎ *4225–3909*
⊕ *www.parrillalabalanza.com.*

$$ ✕**Rex.** In peak season this laid-back, Americana-style diner serving up
SOUTH classic Uruguayan fare in La Barra is open 24 hours a day to accommo-
AMERICAN date everyone's beach and partying hours. The atmosphere is lively no
matter when you come, and the fried calamari and chivito—they claim
to have the best in town—are popular menu items. **Known for:** fast and
fun food; diner-style ambience; abundant sandwiches. $ *Average main:
350 pesos* ⊠ *Ruta 10, Km 161* ☎ *4277–1504* ⊕ *www.rexbestchivitoin-
town.com* ⊟ *No credit cards.*

$ ✕**Yacht Club Uruguayo.** Loved by locals, this small eatery has a great view
SEAFOOD of Isla Gorriti. The menu includes a bit of everything, but the specialty
is seafood. **Known for:** fish and seafood; outdoor tables; great waitstaff.
$ *Average main: 300 pesos* ⊠ *Rambla Artigas between Calles 6 and 8*
☎ *4244–1056* ⊕ *www.ycu.org.uy.*

WHERE TO STAY

Punta hotels operate on a multi-tier rate system. Prices go through the
roof during Christmas and Easter weeks. Standard high-season rates
apply in January and go slightly lower in February. March and December see prices a bit lower still, and then November creeps down a bit

more, with some real bargains to be found the rest of the year. On the "rest of the year" topic, lodgings may close for a few weeks in the off-season. Always check ahead. Renting also is popular for long-term stays, and listings are available on sites like ⊕ *www.apuntavamos.com*.

$$$$ 🏨 **Club Hotel Casapueblo.** It would be hard not to feel like an artist in
HOTEL this whitewashed marvel. **Pros:** secluded location; conversation-starting architecture; interesting adjoining museum. **Cons:** far from the Punta action; difficult to procure space in summer; pricey. ⑤ *Rooms from: 6000 pesos* ⊠ *Punta Ballena* 📞 *4257–8611* ⊕ *www.clubhotelcasapueblo.com* 🛏 *72 rooms* ⦿ *Breakfast.*

$$$$ 🏨 **Estancia Vik.** This luxe yet bohemian 12-suite ranch property set on
HOTEL 4,000 acres in José Ignacio offers guests the best of both a countryside and beach retreat. **Pros:** tranquil; impressive amenities; stylish and bespoke rooms. **Cons:** 4-mile walk to the beach; quite remote; expensive. ⑤ *Rooms from: 32,000 pesos* ⊠ *Camino Eugenio Saiz Martinez, Km 8* 📞 *598/9460–5212, 598/9460–5314* ⊕ *www.estanciavik.com* 🛏 *12 suites* ⦿ *Breakfast.*

$$$ 🏨 **Hotel Salzburgo.** This delightful hotel occupies a white-stucco, three-
HOTEL story chalet with polished slate floors and exposed beams. **Pros:** friendly owner; secluded neighborhood; great price. **Cons:** removed from the beach; breakfast could be more abundant; rooms could be updated. ⑤ *Rooms from: 3800 pesos* ⊠ *Calle Pedragosa Sierra at El Havre* 📞 *4248–8851* ⊕ *www.hotelsalzburgo.com* 🛏 *36 rooms* ⦿ *Breakfast.*

$$$$ 🏨 **Las Cumbres Hotel–Art & Spa.** At this alluring, un-Punta-like lodging
HOTEL up a 160-meter (520-foot) hill north of Punta Ballena, you can expect great views and a wooded, away-from-it-all vibe. **Pros:** quiet location; attentive staff; cooler temperatures than in town. **Cons:** far from Punta; need car to stay here; open weekends only during off-season. ⑤ *Rooms from: 5400 pesos* ⊠ *Ruta 12, Km 3.5, Laguna del Sauce* 📞 *4257–8689* ⊕ *www.cumbres.com.uy* ⊗ *Closed Mon.–Thurs., Apr.–Nov.* 🛏 *18 rooms, 10 suites* ⦿ *Breakfast.*

$$$$ 🏨 **L'Auberge.** At this hotel in the heart of Parque del Golf, one of Punta's
HOTEL chicest neighborhoods, a stone water tower, which now contains guest rooms, rises from a double-wing chalet and affords spectacular Punta panoramas. **Pros:** secluded neighborhood; great restaurant; friendly staff. **Cons:** not on beach; not close to downtown; some rooms are poky. ⑤ *Rooms from: 6500 pesos* ⊠ *Pda. 19 Brava. Carnoustie y Av. del Agua* 📞 *4888–8888* ⊕ *www.laubergehotel.com* 🛏 *34 rooms, 2 suites* ⦿ *Breakfast.*

$$$$ 🏨 **Serena Hotel.** While few Punta hotels actually sit on the beach, this
HOTEL is the rare exception: a stay here puts you steps from tranquil Playa Mansa and all its amenities. **Pros:** right on beach; attended by owner; lovely pool area with double sunbeds. **Cons:** not an option for families with young children; some rooms are cramped; service could be friendlier. ⑤ *Rooms from: 6800 pesos* ⊠ *Rambla Williman Parada 24* 📞 *4223–3441* ⊕ *www.serenahoteles.com* 🛏 *32 rooms* ⦿ *Breakfast.*

NIGHTLIFE

Nightlife and tastes change capriciously from season to season. Expect fast-paced evenings in bars and nightclubs that might open as late as 1 am and reach a fever pitch around sunrise. Many places are open only in high season and have steep covers.

BARS AND PUBS

Moby Dick. Punta del Este's most classic and popular pub sits right across from the city's port. While most other establishments close or slow in low season, Moby Dick keeps whistles wet year-round until 5 am every day of the week. ✉ *Rambla de Artigas 650* ☎ *4244–1240* ⊕ *www. mobydick.com.uy.*

Negroni. During peak season the sunset party at nearby Bikini Beach invariably migrates to Negroni, anchoring the Manantiales strip along Punta's main artery, Ruta 10. Bartenders serve up top-notch cocktails while DJs spin. ✉ *Ruta 10, Km 164.5* ☎ *9436–3400* ⊕ *www.negroni-bistrobar.com* ☾ *Closed March–Nov.*

LIVE ENTERTAINMENT

Enjoy Punta del Este Casino. For many visitors, Enjoy PDE—formerly known as the Conrad—defines nightlife in Punta with its casino and a year-round slate of Las Vegas–style shows by some of the biggest stars in Latin entertainment. Even if you don't recognize the names, taking in a performance at the area's largest hotel is *de rigueur.* ✉ *Rambla Claudio Williman at Parada 4* ☎ *4249–1111* ⊕ *www. enjoy.cl/puntadeleste/casino/.*

SPORTS AND THE OUTDOORS

Not everyone is in Punta for beach bumming—many spend their time in the water. Surfing is popular on the brava side, as is swimming on the mansa side.

GOLF

Cantegril Country Club. This country club has welcomed visitors to its golf course since 1947. At its main location on Salt Lake and Avenida Mauricio Litman, it offers tennis, and at Honorato de Balzac y Calderón de la Barca, it has rugby and soccer fields and tennis courts. ✉ *Av. San Pablo s/n* ☎ *4222–3211* ⊕ *www.cantegrilcountry-club.com.uy* ☛ *$150 in high season; $50 in low season* ⚑ *18 holes, 6412 yards, par 71.*

Club del Lago Golf. You can play a round of golf at the challenging Club del Lago Golf, the only green in Punta del Este with 20 holes. As the course is popular in peak season, reservations are recommended, as well as confirming hours during off-season. ✉ *Ruta Interbalnearia, Km. 116.5* ☎ *4257–8423* ⊕ *www.clubdellagogolf.com* ☛ *$100* ⚑ *20 holes, 6823 yards, par 82.*

POLO

From December 15 to February 28 there are several polo tournaments in Punta del Este, the most famous of which are the Medellín Polo Cup and the José Ignacio Tournament, attended by some of the best players from South America and Europe.

SHOPPING

Feria Artesanal. An essential part of visiting Punta is exploring the colorful Feria Artesanal on the town's central Plaza Artigas. It's open weekend evenings all year; between Christmas and Easter it's open weekday evenings as well. Popular items include gourds for sipping *mate* (local green tea) and leather and silver crafts. ⊠ *Plaza Artigas*.

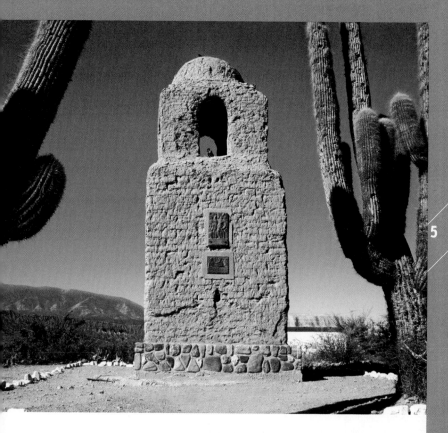

THE NORTHWEST

WELCOME TO THE NORTHWEST

TOP REASONS TO GO

★ **The Quebrada:** In this vast, mountainous, color-splashed landscape, gaze up at an eternity of stars or the otherworldly carved walls of the gorge.

★ **Sports and the Outdoors:** Rivers deep, mountains high, valleys, lakes, and plains all play their part in tempting the adventurous to hike, ride, raft, fish, and rock climb. Take a spin in a kite buggy on the Salinas Grandes or try trekking with a llama.

★ **Folk Music:** Dive into the fabled Argentine folk scene by spending a night out at one of Salta's *peñas* (halls of food, music, and dancing). Wind instruments, diverse percussion, and soaring harmonies define the evocative high-Andean soundtrack.

★ **Wine:** Vintners from the Northwest—especially the Cafayate region of Salta—are gaining world-wide recognition for their cépages grown at great heights. The area is part of Argentina's Wine Trail and offers ample touring opportunities for oenophiles.

The landscape in Argentina's northwestern reaches is incredibly varied—from 22,000-foot Andean peaks to the high, barren plateau known as La Puna, from subtropical jungles to narrow sandstone canyons. Much of the area is desert, cut and eroded by raging brown rivers that wash away everything in sight during summer rains. The region's inhabitants have a tough, resilient quality. Here you'll find some of the country's most vibrant cities—but even they grind to a halt each afternoon for a siesta.

1 Jujuy. A province of varied histories and geographies, Jujuy (pronounced "hoo-hoo-wee") combines a respect for ancestral customs with stunning high-altitude landscapes—its most famous, the Quebrada de Humahuaca, is a UNESCO World Heritage Site.

2 Salta. The colonial city of Salta is a perfect base for exploring the wonders of the eponymous province. Chief among them is the Calchaqui Valley, which follows the Inca Trail and Ruta 40 through improbably charming towns in a dusty, cactus-studded wilderness. And in the midst of this are the world's highest vineyards.

Updated by
Sorrel
Moseley-
Williams

This region flourished under the Inca, then attracted trea-
sure-seeking Spaniards during colonial times; now it's luring
an international contingent of tourists—and rightly so. The
Northwest is notable for diverse locales, ranging from colonial towns to thriving vineyards and arid Andean deserts. It
appeals to diverse types of travelers, too. Hikers converge
on colorful canyons; oenophiles satisfy their wine cravings
in Cafayate; and history buffs get their fix at ancient ruins
and archaeology museums. Visitors who swoon over scenery, meanwhile, ascend to the clouds on the Tren a las
Nubes: a day-long trip that's literally and figuratively
breathtaking.

Despite their proximity, the provinces of Jujuy and Salta are at oppos-
ing ends of the cultural and geographical spectrum. The capital of the
former is San Salvador de Jujuy. A quiet business-oriented city with
a historic center, it serves as the provincial gateway. To the north is
the Quebrada de Humahuaca, a stunning UNESCO-designated valley
poised 3,000 meters (9,843 feet) above sea level; colorful mineral deposits make its sandstone walls particularly photogenic, and small towns
like Purmamarca, Tilcara, and Humahuaca that are rich in indigenous
culture as well as natural beauty give it added appeal. Llama-trekking
through the foothills and a visit to a well-preserved pre-Inca settlement
are among the highlights here. The Quebrada is also a great base for
exploring the vast salt flats known as Salinas Grandes.

Salta Province, to the south, is anchored by its capital city—also called
Salta. The jewel in Argentina's colonial crown is blessed with bright,
beautiful religious architecture, interesting museums, and atmospheric
streets. More sophisticated than San Salvador de Jujuy but still a world
away from Buenos Aires, the city has an array of restaurants specializing

in local dishes, plus a lively nightlife scene led by folk-music peñas. Continuing south to the vineyard-studded Calchaquí Valley, you can sample wares at the bodegas in and around Cafayate, where wine tourism opportunities abound. This region is proud of its own spectacular canyon, dubbed Quebrada de Las Conchas. Looping back from it to Salta on fabled Ruta 40, you'll encounter the picturesque Andean villages of Cachi and Molinos, as well the cactus-capped hills of Parque Nacional Los Cardones.

PLANNING

WHEN TO GO
January and February are Argentina's summer vacation months, meaning hotels get booked up and prices rise. Ironically, these two months coincide with rainy season, when flooding and/or landslides can block mountain roads. (The Salta–Cachi route is notorious for this.) Other busy times are winter break (July), Easter week, and moveable feasts such as Carnaval in the Quebrada de Humahuaca. Most facilities remain open year-round.

GETTING HERE AND AROUND
AIR TRAVEL
Aerolíneas Argentinas/Austral (⊕ *www.aerolineas.com.ar*) has direct flights from Buenos Aires to Jujuy and Salta, as well as connecting flights between Salta and Iguazú or Mendoza. LATAM (⊕ *www.latam.com*), Andes Líneas Aéreas (⊕ *www.andesonline.com*), and Flybondi (⊕ *www.flybondi.com*) fly from Buenos Aires to Salta. All flights between Buenos Aires and the Northwest use the capital's Aeroparque Jorge Newbery, about 15 minutes north of downtown.

BUS TRAVEL
Buses are reliable, affordable, and well used, though certain routes require a little advance planning. Some companies offer roadside pickup; others have luxury double-decker vehicles offering overnight services and maybe even a glass of sparkling wine and a game of bingo. Tourist offices can advise which companies go where. In peak season, buy tickets a day or two in advance.

CAR TRAVEL
Traveling outside of urban centers is often easiest by car. However, picking up a rental vehicle in one city and dropping it off in another incurs significant extra costs, so plan to drive for only parts of your journey or commit to a round trip. Roads are generally good and not very crowded, but be prepared for paved roads turning *ripio* (unpaved) and bumpy for long stretches. Very few routes require a 4X4 (apart from in wet weather).

Two main roads cross the area: the legendary Ruta 40, winding its unpaved way through small towns nearly 3,000 miles to the country's southern tip, and Ruta 9, the ancient road of the Inca, which takes you from Bolivia through San Salvador de Jujuy, Salta, and on toward Córdoba. Before you set out, visit an Automóvil Club Argentino (⊕ *www.*

5

aca.org.ar) office for maps and information, especially during the January–March rainy season.

REMIS TRAVEL

For short trips (e.g., Salta to Cafayate), consider taking a *remis* (a hired car with driver). Some routes have shared services, where you split the cost with others making the same journey; sometimes you have to wait for the car to reach capacity. You can find a remis at airports, bus stations, and on main plazas—or your hotel can call one for you. Be sure to agree on a price before setting off.

HEALTH AND SAFETY

Visitors unaccustomed to traveling at great heights may be susceptible to *soroche,* or altitude sickness, resulting in shortness of breath and headaches. Walk slowly, eat light meals, and drink plenty of fluids (but avoid alcohol). Locals swear by the *coqueando* remedy: sucking on coca leaves (sold at corner groceries and street vendors for around 30 pesos). Tear off the stems and stuff several leaves into the space between your teeth and cheek; leave them in for an hour or so, neither chewing nor spitting, but swallowing when you salivate.

Aside from being sold an overpriced tour (recommended rates are listed in Salta's tourism office), you're unlikely to encounter crime, and local people are happy to receive visitors. Many hotels pride themselves on not needing safety deposit boxes.

The many roadside shrines marking car accidents, especially on winding mountain routes, are a reminder to check your speed. Also take care on the many bumpy, unpaved roads. And wear your seatbelt, as it is the law.

RESTAURANTS

The Northwest's indigenous heritage still influences its cuisine: corn, grains, beans, and potatoes are common ingredients stemming back to the days of the Inca. Dishes worth trying include *locro,* a spicy soup with corn, beans, and red peppers that becomes a rich stew when meat is added; *tamales,* ground corn baked with potatoes and meat and tied up in a corn husk; and *humita,* grated corn with melted cheese cooked in a corn husk. Grilled *cabrito* (goat) is also a regional specialty. For dessert you may come across *cayote,* an interesting concoction of green-squash marmalade served with walnuts and local goat cheese.

HOTELS

Hotels in the Northwest's major cities tend to be modern and comfortable. Most accept credit cards; if you are paying in cash, however, do ask whether a discount is offered. Many *estancias* (ranches) in the foothills welcome guests and are listed with local tourist offices. Although the whole region has really started to open up to local and foreign tourism, chain hotels are few and far between. Instead, take advantage of a dazzling array of boutique hotels and estancias built—or reinvented—to reflect history and ever mindful of their location. *Hotel reviews have been shortened. For full information, visit Fodors.com.*

	$	$$	$$$	$$$$
WHAT IT COSTS IN ARGENTINE PESOS				
Restaurants	Under 120 pesos	121 pesos–200 pesos	201 pesos–300 pesos	over 300 pesos
Hotels	Under 900 pesos	901–1,500 pesos	1,501–2,500 pesos	over 2,500 pesos

Restaurant prices are the average cost of a main course at dinner or, if dinner is not served, at lunch. Hotel prices are the lowest cost of a standard double room in high season.

SAN SALVADOR DE JUJUY

1,643 km (1,020 miles) northwest of Buenos Aires; 92 km (57 miles) north of Salta on RN9.

Founded by Spaniards in 1593, San Salvador de Jujuy (known as Jujuy to most Argentineans and as "S.S. de Jujuy" on signs) is a compact city. Its focal point is Plaza General Belgrano, in the city center between the Río Grande and Río Xibi Xibi. The square is home to a number of key sights, the 18th-century cathedral and grand Casa de Gobierno among them.

The city's quarter-million inhabitants—including a large indigenous population—busy themselves with administering the province's main sources of income (tobacco, mining, and sugarcane), although more are now dealing with tourism. Jujuy may lack nearby Salta's colonial dreaminess and ample hotel selection, but it has a laid-back, unadulterated local culture plus a touch of frontier-town charm. It also makes a great stop-off point and touring base (although staying in the Quebrada's small towns is infinitely more pleasing on the eye). Just outside town you can ride horses along mountain paths in the jungle or go boating in valley waterways.

GETTING HERE AND AROUND

Aerolíneas Argentinas (⊕ *www.aerolineas.com.ar*) flies six times a day from Buenos Aires, as does Andes (⊕ *www.andesonline.com*) and Flybondi (⊕ *www.flybondi.com*), making the trip in two hours and 15 minutes. Jujuy's Aeropuerto Dr. Horacio Guzmán is 30 km (19 miles) southeast of town. La Veloz del Norte, Balut, and Panamericano buses travel between Salta and Jujuy; the latter two continue north to Purmamarca, Tilcara, Humahuaca, and La Quiaca at the Bolivian border. La Quiaqueño buses also depart for La Quiaca nine times a day. Other bus companies serving Jujuy include Andesmar, Crucero del Norte, and El Quiaqueño.

The city's one-way grid system is easy to navigate in a rental car or cheap red cab, although traffic builds up a bit around the beginning and end of the siesta. Proceeding on foot is an alternative because Jujuy is flat despite the altitude. Most attractions, restaurants, and hotels are within easy walking distance of Plaza Belgrano; the exception is the Alto de la Viña district, which is worth the 70-peso taxi fare to reach.

ESSENTIALS

Bus Contacts Andesmar. ☎ 0810/122–4300 ⊕ www.andesmar.com. **Balut.** ☎ 0810/888–2258 ⊕ www.balutsrl.com.ar. **Crucero del Norte.** ☎ 0810/777–2925 ⊕ www.crucerodelnorte.com.ar. **El Quiaqueño.** ☎ 388/428–0041 ⊕ www.elquiaqueño.com. **La Veloz del Norte.** ☎ 388/423–5272 ⊕ www.lavelozdelnorte.com.ar. **Panamericano.** ☎ 388/425–4336. **Terminal de Omnibus.** ✉ Ruta 9 and Autopista 66 ☎ 388/498–3337.

Medical Assistance

Rental Cars Hertz. ✉ Balcarce 578 ☎ 388/422–9582 ⊕ www.hertz.com.ar.

Taxis Parada Uno. ☎ 388/425–6500.

Visitor and Tour Information Secretaría de Turismo y Cultura de la Provincia de Jujuy. ✉ Gorriti 295 ☎ 388/422–1326 ⊕ www.turismo.jujuy.gov.ar.

TOURS

Paisajes del Noroeste. This Jujuy specialist runs a range of tours and day trips, including minibus outings to the remote village of Iruya and excursions to Hornocal (an impressive 21-colored hill near Humahuaca). ✉ San Martín 132 ☎ 388/423–7565 ⊕ www.paisajesdelnoroeste.tur.ar 💰 From 750 pesos.

Tawantinsuyo. The efficient, friendly Tawantinsuyo agency can organize local transfers and custom tours of Jujuy city and to the Quebrada. ✉ *Belgrano 566* ☎ *388/424-4658* ⊕ *www.evttawantinsuyo.tur.ar* 🗐 *From 450 pesos per person for a Jujuy city tour.*

EXPLORING

TOP ATTRACTIONS

Fodor'sChoice **Casa de Gobierno.** The 1907 Casa de Gobierno (Government House)
★ fronts the plaza on San Martín and contains the provincial government offices. A first-floor hall, the Salón de la Bandera, displays the original Argentine flag donated by General Belgrano in 1813, a gift to the city after it cooperated with the Belgrano-headed Exodus of Jujuy during the War of Independence. Entry is on Sarmiento street. The flag was replaced a few years later by the current white and sky-blue stripe version, and the one here is now used as the national coat of arms. ✉ *San Martín 450* ☎ *388/423-9400* ⊕ *www.jujuy.gov.ar* 🗐 *Free.*

Catedral de Jujuy. The cathedral dates from 1765 and was the first building constructed in the city; however, it has been augmented and remodeled so many times that it's now a hodgepodge of architectural styles. The interior contains an ornately carved, gold-plated pulpit, said to be the finest in South America. A close look reveals an intricate population of carved figures, biblical and otherwise. It was inspired by the Cusqueña school of art from Cuzco, Peru, as were the building's ornate doors and confessionals. The cathedral museum next door houses a wealth of religious art. ✉ *West side of Plaza General Belgrano* ☎ *388/423-5333* ⊕ *www.catedraldejujuy.blogspot.com.ar* 🗐 *Free; museum 20 pesos* ⊗ *Closed Sun.*

Iglesia de San Francisco. An ornate 18th-century wooden pulpit with dozens of figures of monks is the centerpiece of the Church of St. Francis, two blocks west of Plaza General Belgrano. There's some debate about who carved the pulpit: it may have been local artisans, or the pulpit may have been transported from Bolivia. Although the church and bell tower look colonial, they date from 1930. Also stop by the bijou museum here (entrance on Belgrano) to see religious art dating back to the 17th century. ✉ *Lavalle 325* 🗐 *Free; museum 20 pesos* ⊗ *Closed weekends.*

Fodor'sChoice **Plaza General Belgrano.** Orange trees and vendors populate the cen-
★ tral square, which is surrounded by colonial buildings—including the imposing government palace. It's empty by day, but starts to fill with gossiping *jujeños*, old and young, by late afternoon. ■ TIP→ **The plaza benefits from free Wi-Fi.** ✉ *San Salvador de Jujuy.*

Fodor'sChoice **Quebrada de Humahuaca.** About 60 km (37 miles) north of San Salva-
★ dor de Jujuy, the inimitable Ruta 9 runs into the Quebrada de Humahuaca—a riotously colorful gorge that ranks among Argentina's most distinctive landscapes. Running alongside the Río Grande, variegated tones of pink, red, and gray brighten canyon walls.

As the gorge deepens approaching Humahuaca on its northern tip, the colors become more vibrant. Brilliant-green alamo and willow trees surround villages, contrasting with the red hues in the background.

In summer and fall, torrential rains mixed with mud and snowmelt from the mountains rush down, carving ravines before pouring into the chalky gray river.

WORTH NOTING

Museo Histórico Provincial Juan Lavalle. Arms, trophies, and military memorabilia collected from the 25 years of fighting for independence are on display at the Juan Lavalle Provincial History Museum. In this adobe building General Juan Lavalle, a hero of the War of Independence and an enemy of the dictator Juan Manuel de Rosas, was assassinated. A replica of the door through which Lavalle was shot in 1746 is part of the exhibit. ⊠ *Lavalle 256* ☎ *388/422–1355* ⌨ *20 pesos* ☉ *Closed Sun.*

Museo y Centro Cultural Culturarte. Drop into Culturarte to get a quick hit of contemporary art and photography. After seeing the exhibits, you can order a coffee and pull up a breezy balcony seat for a different side-on view of Government House. ⊠ *Sarmiento and San Martín* ☎ *388/431–4657* ⌨ *Free.*

WHERE TO EAT

$$ ✕ **Manos Jujeñas.** Ponchos on the walls, old paintings, native artifacts,
ARGENTINE stucco archways, and Andean background music are clues that this
might be one of the best places to sample authentic Northwestern cuisine. Try the *locro*: a stew of maize, white beans, beef, chorizo, pancetta, and a wonderful red pepper–oil glaze, all of which come together in a mélange of savory, starchy flavors. **Known for:** traditional dishes; busy atmosphere drawing locals; great place to try locro. $ *Average main: 140 pesos* ⊠ *Senador Pérez 379* ☎ *388/424–3270* ▭ *No credit cards* ⊙ *Closed Mon.*

$$ ✕ **Pan de Azúcar.** For *jujeña* classics with an eclectic twist, head to Pan
ARGENTINE de Azúcar, where an ample menu offers original concoctions of the local staple, llama—think curry, carpaccio, grilled fillet, or stuffed in ravioli. House specialties also include quinoa, pork, and pasta. **Known for:** regional ingredients; relaxed ambience; llama dishes. $ *Average main: 160 pesos* ⊠ *Senador Perez 110* ☎ *388/423–2392* ▭ *No credit cards* ⊙ *Closed Sun.*

$$ ✕ **Viracocha.** The menu at this unassuming *picanteria* (restaurant spe-
ARGENTINE cializing in spicy foods) has everything from trout to rabbit, but llama
Fodor'sChoice or quinoa are the dishes to try: give them a go as an *empanada* starter.
★ Less adventurous eaters can sample one of the pasta dishes. **Known for:** Northwestern cuisine; buzzy atmosphere; spicy food. $ *Average main: 160 pesos* ⊠ *Independencia 994, corner of Lamadrid* ☎ *0388/423–3554* ▭ *No credit cards* ⊙ *Closed Mon. No dinner Sun.*

WHERE TO STAY

$$$ ▦ **Altos de la Viña.** This former state-owned hotel, a short ride out of
HOTEL town, has comfortable rooms and recreational facilities that invite you
FAMILY to linger; the view from the swimming pool takes in most of the city
Fodor'sChoice and the mountains beyond. **Pros:** great pool; good for families; helipad.
★ **Cons:** very little within walking distance; own transport is useful; some rooms could do with an update. $ *Rooms from: 2500 pesos* ⊠ *Pasquini López 50, Alto La Viña* ☎ *388/426–2626* ⊕ *hotelaltosdelavina.com.ar* ⤳ *60 rooms* ◯│ *Breakfast.*

$$$ ▦ **Gregorio 1.** This downtown boutique hotel has sober rooms with par-
HOTEL quet floors and all the modern conveniences. **Pros:** close to everything; attentive service; comfy rooms. **Cons:** few in-hotel services; isn't quite "boutique"; breakfast isn't very imaginative. $ *Rooms from: 1900 pesos* ⊠ *Independencia 829* ☎ *388/424–4747* ⊕ *www.gregoriohotel. com* ⤳ *19 rooms* ◯│ *Breakfast.*

$$$$ ▦ **Termas de Reyes.** Built on the edge of a spectacular river valley, this
HOTEL countryside complex has natural thermal baths—both indoor and out—
that bubble up from underground hot springs. **Pros:** the chance to take the cure and find inner peace; fantastic views; good in-house restaurant. **Cons:** located 19 km (12 miles) outside of Jujuy on a partially paved road; rooms could do with an update. $ *Rooms from: 3000 pesos* ⊠ *R4, Km 19* ☎ *388/492–2522* ⊕ *www.termasdereyes.com* ⤳ *60 rooms* ◯│ *Breakfast.*

5

Head to Jujuy Province to see Puna architecture—like this church in Tafna—as stark as the landscape.

NIGHTLIFE

El Bodegón. This popular *peña* with hundreds of vinyl records on the walls calls itself "the cathedral of Jujuy folklore." It's predominantly filled with a young crowd of locals who have no qualms about taking to the small stage, and is a great space to see up-and-coming musicians. ⊠ *Sarverri, at José Peres, Alto La Viña* ☎ *388/504–3215.*

La peña de Carlitos. This restaurant on the main plaza doubles up as a spot for live regional music and local bands. ⊠ *Lavalle 397, at Rivada-via, Tilcara* ☎ *11/5483–7278* ☞ *Closed Wed.*

SHOPPING

Paseo de los Artesanos. The modest Paseo de los Artesanos on Plaza General Belgrano has reasonable prices on all kinds of woven and hand-crafted souvenirs. And those *coca* tea bags, imported from Bolivia, are a curiosity that's hard to resist. The small café at the back is ideal for a quick *empanada* pitstop. ⊠ *Sarmiento 240.*

SPORTS AND THE OUTDOORS

With its jungles, lakes, waterfalls, and wild rivers, the area around San Salvador de Jujuy is great for hiking and horseback riding. There are a number of companies offering excursions, but only a handful have an online presence, which makes things hard, as most trips must be booked a few days in advance. Check the Jujuy tourism board's website (⊕ *www.turismo.jujuy.gov.ar*) for a complete list of operators.

JUJUY PROVINCE

San Salvador de Jujuy is both the capital of Argentina's northernmost province and the region's gateway; the star attraction here, however, is the 161-km (100-mile) Quebrada de Humahuaca, which has been used as a trade route for more than 10,000 years. The gorge is breathtaking, and each of its three noteworthy towns—Purmamarca, Tilcara, and Humahuaca—has a unique feel. Most of the region's attractions are within day-trip distance of these bases; in fact, there are few visitor facilities elsewhere.

By far the largest part of Jujuy is the area known as the Puna: vast, high-altitude desert plains that merge into the Andes. Except for some villages built around exquisite adobe churches (most notably Yavi, near the Bolivian border), this area is pristine and tough, baked by day and chilly at night. The easiest way to experience it is on a trip to the Salinas Grandes (Great Salt Plains) from Purmamarca, a two-hour drive offering spectacular views as you scale the Cuesta de Lipan range.

For an otherworldly adventure, head to Laguna de los Pozuelos, with its exotic year-round colony of pink flamingos. Note, though, that it's a long way from the nearest hotel. The best approach is via Abra Pampa, the town where Ruta 9 and Ruta 40 meet, a 97-km (60-mile) drive from Humahuaca.

PURMAMARCA

65 km (40 miles) north of San Salvador de Jujuy.

Nestled in the shadow of craggy rocks and multicolor, cactus-studded hills—with the occasional low-flying cloud floating by—the colonial village of Purmamarca is one of the best bases from which to explore the Quebrada. Its 2,195-meter (7,200-foot) altitude, dry air, and dearth of artificial light also make it a great spot for stargazing.

Here blazing red adobe replaces the white stucco used in architecture elsewhere, and the simple, square buildings play off the matching red rock. Come quick, before it's completely transformed from a two-horse town with basic stores and artisans selling their wares in the pleasant, tree-shaded plaza into a more exclusive destination.

GETTING HERE AND AROUND

Located on Ruta 52, Purmamarca is just a 3-km (2-mile) detour from Ruta 9. Balut buses traveling between Jujuy and Humahuaca run through about 10 times a day. Almost no place here has its own street number (they're marked *s/n* or *sin número* ["no number"] in addresses), but the town is so small that everything is either on or within one block of the main square, Plaza 9 de Julio. There's no bank or hospital, but there is a cash machine next to the tourist information office.

ESSENTIALS

Bus Contacts Balut. ☎ *0810/885–2258* ⊕ *www.balutsrl.com.ar.*

Taxi Contacts Taxi. ☎ *388/490–8030.*

Continued on page 209

TOURING THE
QUEBRADA DE HUMAHUACA

by Andy Footner, updated by Sorrel Moseley-Williams

This rugged, windswept canyon connects Argentina's desert-like Puna near Bolivia with the city of San Salvador de Jujuy 150 km (93 mi) further south. It's a natural passage through the surrounding mountains, so it's no surprise that thousands of years of history have played out between its sandstone walls. For many, those very walls are the main attraction: colorful minerals, seismic activity, and a powerful river continue to shape one of Argentina's most fascinating geological formations.

Cardones, or cacti, and sandstone formations are a major part of the landscape in Argentina's northwest

HISTORY OF THE QUEBRADA

Jujuy Province, Quebrada de Humahuaca landscape near Purmamarca village

The Quebrada de Humahuaca continues to be carved into existence by the ever-changing Rio Grande. A roaring, splashing force in summer, the river in winter reduces to barely a trickle in its wide, dry riverbed. You'll have a good view wherever you are in the main canyon of the Quebrada; Route 9, the main north-south road through here, runs parallel to it. Like the river, people have come through this canyon in both trickles and torrents over the centuries—but unlike the river, the sense of history is strong whenever you visit.

PEÑAS

Clubs, restaurants, and *peñas* attract both locals and tourists, who come to hear regional folk bands give it their all on small, cramped stages. Adding to the rowdy, dinner-theater atmosphere are the local dancers who entice (and often entrap) foreigners into strutting their stuff on stage; it's always a good laugh, no matter what language you speak.

PRE-INCAN TO THE CAMINO INCA

Ten thousand years ago, the first humans to inhabit the Southern Cone came from the north through this very canyon. Some stayed, becoming this area's original indigenous peoples. In the 15th and 16th centuries, the Incan Empire left its mark on the valley and the culture; the single road through this protected canyon became part of the hugely important Camino Inca—the Inca Trail, a system of roads used to travel through the empire which eventually spanned much of the Andes. Because of this unique Andean history, the culture here can seem to share more with those of Bolivia and Peru than with other parts of Argentina; keep your ears open in town squares: in this part of Argentina you can still hear people speaking Quechua and Aymara, two of the main languages of the Incas.

Tilcara, Children's carnival, Quebrada de Humauaca

JESUITS AND VICEROYALTIES

The Incans weren't the only conquering force that found the protected valley appealing: in the 17th century, Jesuit priests used Aymara and Quechua to convert the locals to Catholocism, which helped the Spanish eventually use the Quebrada to connect the Viceroyalties (administration center) of Peru in Lima and La Plata in what would later become Buenos Aires. Today, the local mix of pre-Incan, Incan, and Christian traditions and symbols are reflected in everything from dress to architecture to the kinds of items you'll find for sale.

WORLD HERITAGE

Traditions and festivals celebrated along the Quebrada include a unique combination of ancient Andean rites and European religious celebrations. In 2003, UNESCO added the Quebrada to its World Heritage list for its continued legacy of pre-Hispanic and pre-Incan settlements in the area.

SHOPPING CULTURE

The best shopping is in Humahuaca. Numerous small shops sell tourist trinkets, and there's a daily handicrafts market on the steps leading up the hill to the monument. Most of the items for sale will be familiar to anyone who has traveled in the central Andean region, and there are a few artisans making jewelery and other items in more modern Argentine styles.

5

IN FOCUS TOURING THE QUEBRADA DE HUMAHUACA

GEOLOGICAL COLORS: A TIMELINE

white composed
of limestone

purple/violet colored
by lead and calcium

yellow composed
of iron hydroxides

400 MILLION YEARS

80–90 MILLION YEARS

The hills in the Quebrada de Humahuaca are famous for their colors—caused by mineral deposits formed from 1 to 400 million years ago. The two best places to see the colors are the Paleta del Pintur (Painter's Palette, pictured) and the Cerro de los Siete Colores (Hill of Seven Colors).

| red composed of clay and iron oxide | light orange composed of red clay, mud, and sand | green colored by copper oxides | brown colored by manganese oxides and hydroxides |

3-4 MILLION YEARS — 1-2 MILLION YEARS

ITINERARY

Salinas Grandes

DAY ONE

MORNING: Purmamarca

The smallest and most picturesque town in the Quebrada, Purmamarca is about two hours north of Salta or over an hour north of San Salvador de Jujuy on R9. The turnoff (left side) onto RA52 is well marked. Arrive as early as possible for the morning light. Get your bearings with a view of the Cerro de Los Siete Colores (Hill of Seven Colors) from a popular viewpoint on the north side of RA52; the trailhead is on your right as you approach town. You can also walk along Paseo de los Colorados, a dirt road (watch for vehicles) that winds around the base of hill itself; to get to it from Plaza 9 de Julio, head west on Florida for 3 blocks.

AFTERNOON: Siesta or Salinas Grandes

Purmamarca goes from quiet to dead during the afternoon siesta; take a siesta yourself, or head out on a half-day side trip. Drive farther west on RA52 as it winds its way up the **Cuesta de Lipan** (the Lipan Slope, the Quebrada's mountainous western barrier) and on to the **Salinas Grandes** (Big Salt Flats). If you're without your own transport, there are plenty of taxis, remises, or guides to take you. Technically, the Salinas Grandes themselves are outside of the Quebrada, but the drive there takes you through a dramatic mountain pass—and the highest driveable point in the Quebrada; look for a sign marking your altitude of 4170 m (13,681 ft). After an hour or two (depending on your vehicle's horsepower and photo stops), you'll take unpaved EX-RN40 south to the turnoff (right side) for the Salinas Grandes. Drive until you're on the salt flats themselves—this is the parking lot. This is a working salt flat; don't miss gazing into the clear blue harvesting pools.

NIGHT: Purmamarca

Once back in Purmamarca, explore some nouveau Andean cuisine in town. After dinner, head to a peña where musicians offer renditions of folk songs about the Quebrada.

DAY TWO

MORNING: Tilcara

Set out early and take R9 north to Tilcara; head straight to the **Pucará de Tilcara**. This partially reconstructed pre-Columbian fort shows one of the most complex ruins in Argentina. Make time to visit the botanical garden next door. Wander through the central square's market, one of the best in the region. Leave to arrive in Humahuaca before noon.

AFTERNOON: Humahuaca to Maimara

Every day at noon at San Francisco Solano church, a statue of the church's namesake pops out of the clock tower and, as the story goes, delivers a blessing. Catch this if you can, then have lunch and explore the market near the monument steps. Stop in at the small yet atmospheric folklore museum. On your way back to Salta or Jujuy, make brief photo stops at the **Tropic of Capricorn** at Huacalera, the church at Uquia (known for its Cuzco School angel paintings), and the photogenic cemetery of the town of Maimara. If sunset is approaching, however, simply head straight for Maimara—visible behind the cemetary is the Painter's Palette. This flat segment of the east canyon wall contains colored layers of mineral deposits that attain stunningly rich hues as the light shines in from the west.

Pucará de Tilcara

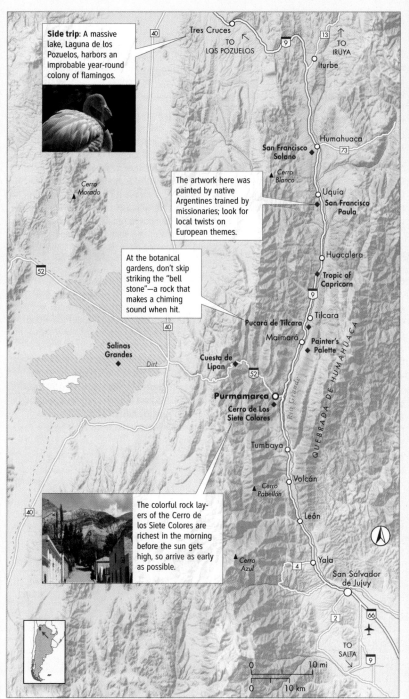

Side trip: A massive lake, Laguna de los Pozuelos, harbors an improbable year-round colony of flamingos.

The artwork here was painted by native Argentines trained by missionaries; look for local twists on European themes.

At the botanical gardens, don't skip striking the "bell stone"—a rock that makes a chiming sound when hit.

The colorful rock layers of the Cerro de los Siete Colores are richest in the morning before the sun gets high, so arrive as early as possible.

Tres Cruces

TO LOS POZUELOS

TO IRUYA

Iturbe

Humahuaca

San Francisco Solano

Cerro Blanco

Uquía
San Francisco Paula

Cerro Morado

Huacalera

Tropic of Capricorn

Salinas Grandes

Pucará de Tilcara

Tilcara

Maimará

Painter's Palette

Cuesta de Lipan

Dirt

Purmamarca

Cerro de Los Siete Colores

QUEBRADA DE HUMAHUACA

Tumbaya

Cerro Pabellón

Volcán

León

Cerro Azul

Yala

San Salvador de Jujuy

Río Grande

TO SALTA

5

IN FOCUS TOURING THE QUEBRADA DE HUMAHUACA

| 0 | | | 10 mi |
| 0 | | | 10 km |

PLANNING YOUR VISIT

PUBLIC TRANSIT

A good and frequent bus system and shared taxis between the main towns mean hitchhiking isn't common or necessary. However, although buses reach all destinations described, renting a car or going with a guide mean you can stop at any point to explore, take pictures, and admire the views.

SELF-DRIVE LOGISTICS

Cars can be rented in Salta and Jujuy. Check the conditions for off-road driving and the options for crossing a pass into Chile—these are not automatically included in the rental.

Good to Know:

■ Car hire agencies like to calculate the price on the spot and there's little transparency in their calculations. Many destinations from Salta and San Salvador de Jujuy involve unpaved roads that are punishing on cars, so it might help to let them know your itinerary if you're only visiting the Quebrada (where all the roads are paved). Pricing systems favor round trips (i.e. there's a big surcharge for dropping off a car in another city).

■ Gas stations can be found in most of the towns, but they don't all take credit cards. Except for in Humahuaca (ACA—the Automovil Club Argentino) and San Salvador de Jujuy, plan for cash only. As well as providing gas and good maps, ACA is the Argentine equivalent of the AAA and can help you out if your car breaks down somewhere.

■ The roads in the Quebrada are better than most in the area—they're well marked and have clear passing lanes—but during the rainy season (between October and February), falling rocks or mudslides can block the roads.

GUIDED TOURS

Personal guides, with their own cars or ones owned by their companies, can be found through the tourism offices of Salta and Jujuy.

For Indigenous Culture:

When you pull into the town of Humahuaca, you'll see a group of locals waiting under the main sign. These are tour guides; if you know a little Spanish, they're a wealth of information on how Wichí and other indigenous peoples live and work in Humahuaca today. Even if you're here with a tour guide of your own, he or she might hire one of these guides—they're part of an initiative to provide career alternatives in a place where drug smuggling (Bolivia is just a few clicks north, after all) has in the past been one of the only decent-paying jobs available.

For Getting Out Into the Landscape:

Caravana de Llamas (☎ 0388/408–8000 ⊕ www.caravanadellamas.com.ar), out of Tilcara, offers an experience you won't get at home: llama treks along trails that have been used for thousands of years. You lead the llamas along; they carry everything you need for trips that can last from 1 to 10 days. On overnight excursions, you're hosted by the inhabitants of remote mountain huts.

Crias, or baby llamas, Jujuy Province

Visitor and Tour Information Tourist Office. ✉ *Florida casi Rivadavia* ☎ *388/490–8443.*

EXPLORING

Fodor's Choice
★
Bodega Fernando Dupont. On the lovely grounds of this bodega, cardon cacti mingle with Malbec, Cabernet Sauvignon, and Syrah vines, which thrive at 2,500 meters (8,202 feet) thanks to hot days and very cool nights. The Paleta del Pintor hill provides a stunning backdrop. You can call ahead for a brief yet interesting tour; try the Rosa de Maimará Rosé or the Sikuri Syrah. Reaching the winery is impossible when the river floods in summer, though a new bridge has been in the pipeline for several years. ✉ *RN9, Km 1776, 19 km (12 miles) north of Purmamarca, Maimará* ☎ *388/15–473–1918* ⊕ *www.bodegafernandodupont. com* ✉ *Free tour; 3-wine tasting 500 pesos* ☉ *Closed Sun.*

Fodor's Choice
★
Cerro de Siete Colores. Looming above Purmamarca is the brightly tinted Cerro de Siete Colores (Hill of Seven Colors). Look closely and see if you can find all seven—most people can pick out only four. The best way to see the hill is by walking a 3-km (2-mile) loop called the **Paseo de Siete Colores,** which starts to the left of the church on the main square. This one-lane gravel road winds through bizarre, humanlike formations of bright, craggy, red rock, before passing a series of stark, sweeping, Mars-like vistas with stands of trees in the river valley. The road then passes a few family farms and ends with a striking view of the Cerro itself before bringing you back to the center of Purmamarca. ■TIP→ The colors are most clearly visible in the morning. The tourist office on Florida Street has a map showing the best points for photos. ✉ *Purmamarca.*

Iglesia de Santa Rosa de Lima. The most notable landmark downtown on the central plaza is Iglesia de Santa Rosa de Lima. Dating from 1648, it was constructed from adobe and thistle wood. ✉ *Plaza 9 de Julio.*

Fodor's Choice
★
Salinas Grandes. West of Purmamarca you can ogle one of the area's most eye-popping sights: the Salinas Grandes, more than 200 square km (80 square miles) of dazzling salt flats at the top of a mountain. Take the sinuous Ruta 52 for 64 km (40 miles) over the majestic Cuesta de Lipan (Lipan Rise)—which tops out at 4,170 meters (13,700 feet) above sea level—and cross Ruta 40. The salty landscape is surreal, and it's made even more so by a building constructed entirely out of slabs of salt turned a brownish color and salt furniture set up like church pews, complete with lectern. A series of small pools have been cut out of the salt flats' surface, revealing a layer of water and freshly forming crystals underneath. For 200 pesos, you can contract a guide from the kiosk at the entrance to lead you in your vehicle through the flats. ■TIP→ Remember to carry a camera, a hat, some water, and sunblock. ✉ *Purmamarca.*

WHERE TO EAT

$$$
ARGENTINE
✗ **La Posta.** Empanadas, llama dishes, and other regional specialties dominate the menu at this eatery on the main square. Take a seat by the window and watch the scene at the market stalls outside while enjoying *jujeño* staples such as *picante de pollo* (spicy chicken) or regional stews, or avoid the bustle on the airy back patio. **Known for:** traditional

dishes; attracting families; lively atmosphere. $ *Average main: 230 pesos* ⊠ *Rivadavia s/n, on Plaza 9 de Julio* ☎ *388/490–8040* ⊕ *terrazasdelaposta.com* ⊟ *No credit cards.*

$$ ✕ **Los Morteros.** For a more contemporary spin on regional delicacies,
ARGENTINE   head to Los Morteros. The llama in Malbec, fresh grilled trout, and
Fodor's Choice   succulent lamb stew are all noteworthy picks; this busy spot also cooks
★   up a sizzling barbecue worth ordering for its smell alone. **Known for:**
regional cuisine; good wine list; barbecue. $ *Average main: 200 pesos*
⊠ *Salta s/n* ☎ *388/490–8063* ⊟ *No credit cards.*

WHERE TO STAY

$ 🏠 **El Cardon.** It's small and no-frills, but if you're just looking for a
B&B/INN   place to sleep in between excursions, this friendly lodging a short walk
from the main square is a good bet. **Pros:** a reliable, in-town option;
budget-friendly; great terrace. **Cons:** few, basic facilities; often full in
high season; staff can be cross. $ *Rooms from: 800 pesos* ⊠ *Belgrano
s/n* ☎ *388/490–8672* ⊕ *www.hostal-elcardon.com* ⊟ *No credit cards*
⤳ *7 rooms* ⦿ *Breakfast.*

$$$$ 🏠 **El Manantial del Silencio.** At this tranquil retreat, weeping willows, red
HOTEL   rocks, and gardens filled with birdsong are hemmed in by the craggy
Fodor's Choice   Quebrada and its utter calm; inside the colonial-style stucco mansion,
★   local artifacts and earth tones make things warm and harmonious
throughout. **Pros:** one of the grandest lodgings in the Quebrada; great
gardens, restaurant, spa, and pool; welcoming shared areas. **Cons:** one
of the most expensive lodgings in the area; noise reverberates down
hallways; friendly staff aren't necessarily on the ball. $ *Rooms from:
6600 pesos* ⊠ *RN52, Km 3.5* ☎ *388/490–8080* ⊕ *www.hotelmanantialdelsilencio.com* ⤳ *20 rooms* ⦿ *Breakfast.*

$$$$ 🏠 **La Comarca.** The various rooms, cabins, and houses here surround a
HOTEL   garden of flowers and cacti; all accommodations are built with traditional local materials—adobe, cane, wood—and are decorated with a
contemporary eye. **Pros:** heated pool has a view of the Siete Colores;
good restaurant; houses can sleep up to six guests. **Cons:** showers not
designed for tall people; a little way out of town; hallways are noisy in
high season. $ *Rooms from: 3770 pesos* ⊠ *RN52, Km 3.8* ☎ *388/490–
8098* ⊕ *www.lacomarcahotel.com.ar* ⤳ *18 rooms* ⦿ *Breakfast.*

$$$$ 🏠 **Los Colorados.** All the reddish adobe walls of the cabins at Los Colo-
B&B/INN   rados, on the Cerro de Siete Colores, have rounded corners, giving the
whole place a look of having been sculpted straight from the earth;
it's a perfect spot for kicking back, whether you're curled up by the
fireplace in your room or stargazing on the common terrace. **Pros:**
quiet; cozy; six-person Jacuzzi. **Cons:** small bathrooms; slow Wi-Fi;
staff can be inattentive. $ *Rooms from: 2550 pesos* ⊠ *El Chapacal
511* ☎ *388/490–8182* ⊕ *www.loscoloradosjujuy.com.ar* ⤳ *7 rooms/
cabins* ⦿ *Breakfast.*

NIGHTLIFE

Don Heriberto. You'll meet a mix of locals and visitors at the town's only
late-night bar, which also doubles up as a *peña*, where folk musicians
and singers gather to perform. In high season, it opens at 10 pm and

closes at 5 am or when the last customer leaves—whichever comes first.
✉ *Sarmiento s/n, close to corner of Libertad* ☎ *388/490–8026.*

SPORTS AND THE OUTDOORS

Purmamarca Trekking. Local guide Carlos Prado leads excursions in
and around the Quebrada. Choices include a half-day trip to see
10,000-year-old cave paintings near Humahuaca and a full-day outing
that involves driving to the Salinas Grandes, then hiking back down to
Purmamarca. ✉ *Maimará* ☎ *388/590–7100* ⊕ *www.purmamarcatrek-
king.com.ar* ✆ *From 700 pesos.*

TILCARA

*85 km (53 miles) north of San Salvador de Jujuy; 18 km (11 miles)
northeast of Purmamarca via RN9.*

Founded in 1600 and witness to many battles during the War of Independence, Tilcara is on the eastern side of the Río Grande at its confluence with the Río Huasamayo. Purveyors of local crafts crowd the
main plaza, and artists and musicians escaping the big cities fill the cafés
and bars. There are several reasons to stop off in this 2,469-meter-high
(8,100-foot-high) Quebrada town: an interesting museum; nearby Inca
ruins, caves, and waterfalls; and a good selection of accommodations
and restaurants.

GETTING HERE AND AROUND

Tilcara is well served by buses running between Jujuy and Humahuaca
or La Quiaca. Taking a shared taxi from San Salvador de Jujuy's bus
station is another option; the cost is about the same. Arriving from the
south, look out for the surprisingly large cemetery of Maimará, which
sprawls on either side of the road outside town.

ESSENTIALS

Bus Contacts Balut. ☎ *0810/888–2258* ⊕ *www.balutsrl.com.ar.*

Visitor Information Tourist Office. ✉ *Belgrano s/n, at Padilla.*

EXPLORING

La Garganta del Diablo. Seven km (4 miles) west of town is La Garganta
del Diablo (The Devil's Throat), a red-rock gorge with waterfalls (the
number depends on the season). The tourist office in Tilcara can point
you in the right direction; ask about the path that knocks about half
the distance off the journey. Ask, too, for directions to the wind-eroded
caves that are a similar distance east of town. ✉ *Tilcara.*

Museo Arqueológico. Exhibits at the Museo Arqueológico, run by the
University of Buenos Aires, can be a little confusing due to a lack of
explanatory labels. The two mummies here are considerably less well
cared for than those in Salta's MAAM (Museum of High Altitude
Archaeology), but no less fascinating. The clothes, hair, and skin of
the first, which was found in San Pedro de Atacama in Chile, are well
preserved. Other rooms display Nazca, Inca, Moche, and other remains
from the past 2,000 years. ■ TIP→ Keep your ticket stubs, as they'll
get you into the nearby Pucará de Tilcara ruins, where some of this

"Rectangles have been dug out [of Salinas Grandes] to allow the water to seep through and salt to crystallize...The clearest water and the whitest salt I have ever seen." —Clive Ellston, Fodors.com member

museum's artifacts were discovered. ⊠ *Belgrano 445* ☎ *388/495–5006* ⊕ *tilcara.filo.uba.ar* 🖅 *80 pesos.*

Fodor's Choice
★
Museo en los Cerros. You'll find this surprising photography gallery by following a stony road that runs alongside the River Huichaira up into the mountains. The brainchild of photographer Lucio Boschi, the "museum in the hills" has two spaces displaying permanent collections as well as a temporary exhibit room. For the ultimate in artsy tranquility, kick back in the library while browsing coffee table books with a coca leaf tea. ⊠ *Huichaira, 4 km (3 miles) off R9* ☎ *0388/156–863–013* ⊕ *www.museoenloscerros.com.ar* 🖅 *Free.*

Fodor's Choice
★
Pucará de Tilcara. Set on a hill above the left bank of the Río Grande, this fortified, pre-Inca *pucará* (settlement) is the best-preserved of several in the Quebrada de Humahuaca and the only one that can be visited. Its different areas (some of which have been rebuilt) can be clearly discerned. Allow at least 90 minutes to walk around the site, where an estimated 2,000 Omaguaca once lived, worshipped, and kept their animals. On your way out, turn right at the entrance to the fort for the Jardín Botánico (Botanical Garden): inside you can admire a large array of cacti and other plants. Don't miss the chance to strike the Piedra Campana with a mallet disguised as a stick—true to its name (Bell Stone) it rings like a bell. ■TIP→ Ticket stubs from a visit to the Museo Arqueológico in town get you free entrance to both the ruins and the botanical garden. ⊠ *About 1½ km (1 mile) south of Tilcara* 🖅 *80 pesos.*

WHERE TO EAT

$$$ ✕ **El Nuevo Progreso.** The food, from steak to quinoa salad, is superb; the
ARGENTINE wine list is fairly priced; and the wooden floors, whimsical lights, and
Fodor'sChoice artwork make the space appealing. What's more, some evenings around
★ 9:30 there's live music, generally performed by friends of the owners.
Known for: traditional dishes with a modern twist; friendly, on-the-ball
service; abundant portions. ⑤ *Average main: 220 pesos* ✉ *Lavalle 351*
☎ *388/495–5237.*

$$ ✕ **El Patio.** With three dining rooms, a patio out back, a location just
ARGENTINE yards from the central plaza, and well-priced regional cuisine, El Patio
is one of Tilcara's most popular restaurants. The menu is an unpretentious yet delectable mix of regional specialties and standard Argentinian
fare, and service is friendly. **Known for:** local dishes; good wine list; a
cool atmosphere that attracts locals and visitors. ⑤ *Average main: 190*
pesos ✉ *Lavalle 352* ☎ *388/495–5044* ☾ *Closed Tues.*

$$$ ✕ **Los Puestos.** A poetic narrative in the menu describes this place as
ARGENTINE "a haven for parched travelers," along the lines of the watering holes
used for centuries by local shepherds. Top picks include empanadas
baked in the oven right by the entrance and a llama fillet served with
orange sauce and Andean new potatoes. **Known for:** empanadas; asado;
buzzy vibe. ⑤ *Average main: 240 pesos* ✉ *Belgrano, corner of Padilla*
☎ *388/495–5100* ⊕ *www.lospuestostilcara.com.ar.*

$$ ✕ **Yacón.** The warm service, wooden tables and chairs, cane roof, and
ARGENTINE stone walls all suggest tradition. Yet Yacón's kitchen shows some inno-
vation by serving up llama meat on skewers and a shepherd's pie made
with quinoa. **Known for:** friendly service; llama dishes; handy central
location. ⑤ *Average main: 180 pesos* ✉ *Rivadavia 222* ☎ *388/495–5611*
☾ *No dinner Sun.*

WHERE TO STAY

$$$ ⛫ **El Refugio del Pintor.** The building that houses this hotel was formerly
HOTEL used by the painter Medardo Pantoja from Jujuy, hence the name (Ref-
uge of the Painter) and the artwork adorning the walls. **Pros:** great
views; plenty of common spaces; good breakfast with homemade bread.
Cons: small rooms; staff could be more attentive. ⑤ *Rooms from: 1900*
pesos ✉ *Alverro 660, between Jujuy and Ambroseti* ☎ *388/4271–432*
⊕ *www.elrefugiodelpintor.com* ⇥ *13 rooms* ⑩ *Breakfast.*

$$$ ⛫ **Hotel Huacalera.** This hotel, on the main road in the heart of the
HOTEL Quebrada de Humahuaca, has recently undergone a substantial refit;
Fodor'sChoice the result is a stunning colonial-style property, complete with a spa, an
★ outdoor swimming pool, and spacious, well-appointed guest rooms.
Pros: courteous staff; good restaurant; large breakfast. **Cons:** trucks on
the main drag can be noisy; the restaurant lacks atmosphere; echoing
in hallways. ⑤ *Rooms from: 2400 pesos* ✉ *R9, Km 1790, Huacalera*
☎ *388/155–813–417* ⊕ *www.hotelhuacalera.com* ⇥ *32* ⑩ *Breakfast.*

$$$$ ⛫ **Las Terrazas.** A few blocks from the square in a quieter area, Las Ter-
B&B/INN razas has nine spacious rooms, each with its own balcony. **Pros:** good-
size rooms and bathrooms; great views; swimming pool and bar on-site.
Cons: not very central; some rooms are dated; lots of stairs. ⑤ *Rooms*
from: 2700 pesos ✉ *Calle de la Sorpresa s/n, at San Martín* ☎ *388/495–*
5589 ⊕ *www.lasterrazastilcara.com.ar* ⇥ *9 rooms* ⑩ *Breakfast.*

Cardones (cacti) grow amid the ruins of the Pucará de Tilcara in Jujuy Province.

$$$
B&B/INN
 Uwa Wasi. The name of this B&B means "a house with grapes," and it does, indeed, have a few vines in its rambling back garden, where there's also space to relax, cook your own steak, and get to know your hosts (one of whom works for the tourism office). **Pros:** good location; friendly service; nice garden and communal areas. **Cons:** compact rooms; some shared bathrooms; few facilities. ⑤ *Rooms from: 1800 pesos* ✉ *Lavalle 564* ☎ *388/495–5368* ⊕ *www.uwawasi.com* ⌺ *4 rooms* ⓘⓄⓘ *Breakfast.*

$$$$
HOTEL
Viento Norte. This long, thin, adobe boutique hotel overlooks a decent-size swimming pool; inside, rooms have simple decorations and low lighting. **Pros:** central yet quiet; a good breakfast; great bathrooms. **Cons:** pool is visible from the street; dust can gather at the pool area. ⑤ *Rooms from: 2800 pesos* ✉ *Jujuy 536* ☎ *388/495–5605* ⊕ *www. hotelvientonorte.com.ar* ⌺ *11 rooms* ⓘⓄⓘ *Breakfast.*

SPORTS AND THE OUTDOORS

Fodor'sChoice
★
Caravana de Llamas. For an unforgettable trekking experience, sign on with Caravana de Llamas. You'll lead a team of llamas along trails that have been used for thousands of years. Trips run the gamut from half-day picnics to 10-day adventures: on overnight excursions, you're hosted by the inhabitants of remote mountain huts. ✉ *Calle Corte and Viltipoco* ☎ *388/495–5326* ⊕ *www.caravanadellamas.com.ar* ⌺ *From 1000 pesos.*

HUMAHUACA

126 km (78 miles) north of San Salvador de Jujuy; 42 km (26 miles) north of Tilcara on RN9.

Humahuaca—at an altitude of 2,957 meters (9,700 feet)—is the gateway to the Puna. Its narrow stone streets hark back to pre-Hispanic civilizations, when aboriginals fought Incan marauders from the north. The struggle for survival continued into the 16th century, when the Spanish arrived.

Given its location, the village feels a bit touristy today—especially at midday, when an automated carving of Saint Francisco Solano emerges like a cuckoo from a clock to bless the folks gathered in the main plaza with his mechanized arm. More visitor amenities are slowly becoming available, too: however, the tourist board is less than organized (if you find it open) and lodgings are predominantly hostels. That said, if you're near Humahuaca around the time of Carnaval (40 days before Easter), it's worth putting up with whatever accommodations you can find to participate in the wonderful festivities that are a complicated mix of Catholicism and paganism.

GETTING HERE AND AROUND

Most people visit Humahuaca either on a day trip from Tilcara, Purmamarca, Jujuy, or Salta; or as a stopover en route to Iruya. If you're not coming by car or with a tour group, you can catch a bus. Balut, Panamericano, and other lines serving the San Salvador de Jujuy-to-La Quiaca route have buses running through almost every hour during the day.

ESSENTIALS

Bus Contacts Balut. ☎ 0810/888–2258 ⊕ www.balutsrl.com.ar. **Panamericano.** ☎ 388/423–7330.

Visitor Information Tourist Office. ⊠ Cabildo, central plaza ☎ 388/421–375.

EXPLORING

Cabildo. Humahuaca's *cabildo* (town hall), the most striking building in the village, has a beautifully colored and richly detailed clock tower. Each day at noon crowds fill the small main square outside to watch a life-size mechanized statue of San Francisco Solano pop out of the tower—it's kitschy fun and one of the world's few clock performances. You can't enter the cabildo, but you can peer into the courtyard. ⊠ *Central plaza.*

Iglesia de la Candelaria. The 1631 Iglesia de la Candelaria contains fine examples of Cusqueño art, most notably paintings depicting elongated figures of Old Testament prophets by 18th-century artist Marcos Zapaca. ⊠ *Calle Buenos Aires, west side of central plaza.*

Museo Folklórico Regional. At first glance the Museo Folklórico Regional appears to be a dusty collection of stones and strange objects, but allow a guide to show you around (arrange in advance for an English-speaking one), and you'll learn a lot about the indigenous population. The museum was founded by Sixto Vázquez Zuleta, who invested a huge amount of passion and imagination, and each exhibit—from dolls made of dried apricots to musical instruments made from armadillos—provides a new insight into the carnival spirit of the area. Note that it is only open to groups of three or more. ⊠ *Buenos Aires 447* ☎ *388/421–064* 🖼 *20 pesos* ⊗ *Closed Sun.*

OFF THE BEATEN PATH

Iruya. If you can endure a harrowing five-hour, 50-km (31-mile) ride east from Humahuaca on an unpaved cliffside road, you'll be rewarded with one of Argentina's most stunning settings. (Take the bus from Humahuaca rather than driving yourself; you really have to know the road, as the bus drivers do, to negotiate it safely.) This cobblestoned town, which clings to sheer rock, has become an increasingly popular stop despite its small size. It has just a couple of accommodations, the **Hotel Iruya** (☎ *3887/432–1322*) and **Hostal Milmahuasi** (☎ *3887/445–7994*), but many villagers offer rooms for rent. The busiest times to visit are at Easter and during the first and second weekends in October, when the village celebrates its festival. There are some good hikes from Iruya to even more remote towns like San Isidro, three hours away through the mountains. For more information and guide recommendations, call Adelina López at the **Tourist Office** (☎ *3887/155–094–799*). ⊠ *Humahuaca.*

WHERE TO EAT

$$
ARGENTINE

✗ **K'allapurca.** At lunch the best tables are taken by groups of tourists being serenaded by a band of minstrels, but don't let that put you off. The food is simple, well-presented Andean fare, and the prices are very reasonable. **Known for:** lamb stew; fixed menu; welcoming groups. ⑤ *Average main: 150 pesos* ⊠ *Belgrano 210* ☎ *3887/15–410–5139* ⊕ *www.kallapurcarestobar.com.ar.*

SHOPPING

The shops just east of the plaza are full of the same ponchos, bags, hats, and shirts sold elsewhere in the Quebrada. Though things are reasonably priced, they're more expensive than they would be in Bolivia, which is where most of the stock originates. There are also some interesting souvenirs on sale in the main plaza.

SALTA

92 km (57 miles) south of San Salvador de Jujuy on RN9 or 311 km (193 miles) south of San Salvador de Jujuy on R34 (La Cornisa Road).

It's not just "Salta" to most Argentineans, but "Salta la Linda" ("Salta the Beautiful"). That nickname is actually redundant: "Salta" already comes from an indigenous Aymara word meaning "beautiful." But for the country's finest colonial city, it's worth stating twice. Walking among its well-preserved 18th- and 19th-century buildings, single-story houses, and narrow streets, you could easily forget that this is a city of more than half a million people. But the ever-increasing traffic, the youthful population, and the growing number of international itinerants also give Salta a cosmopolitan edge. All in all, it's a hard place to leave. For its friendliness, its facilities, its connections, and its central location, Salta is also the best base for a thorough exploration of the Northwest.

Do make good use of the tourist office, which has a helpful staff armed with a wealth of maps and information.

GETTING HERE AND AROUND

Salta is two hours by air from Buenos Aires. Aerolíneas Argentinas flies the route six times a day, LATAM twice a day, and Andes once a day. From Aeropuerto El Aybal, it's a 10-km (6-mile) drive southeast into Salta; the trip costs 200 pesos by taxi or 10 pesos by bus. Balut buses connect Salta to Jujuy (15 trips daily) and Humahuaca (six trips daily). El Indio has two daily buses to Cafayate, while Marco Rueda has at least one to Cachi. Buy tickets the day before, as most buses leave early in the morning.

Most city sights are within walking distance of one another, and taxis are cheap and easy to find. Note that some visitors opt to stay in the quieter hillside suburb of San Lorenzo, 10 km (6 miles) northwest and a cooler 299 meters (980 feet) higher. It's a great place if you have a car or are prepared to rely on the half-hourly bus to and from Salta.

ESSENTIALS

Bus Contacts Balut. ☎ *388/422–9393* ⊕ *www.balutsrl.com.ar.* **El Indio.** ☎ *387/432–0846.* **Marcos Rueda.** ☎ *387/421–4447.* **Terminal de Omnibus.** ✉ *Av. Hipólito Yrigoyen 339* ☎ *387/401–1143* ⊕ *www.terminalsalta.com.*

Rental Car Contacts Hertz. ✉ *Caseros 374* ☎ *387/424–0113* ⊕ *www.hertz.com.* **Perfil Rent a Car.** ✉ *Buenos Aires 189* ☎ *387/431–7782* ⊕ *www.perfilrentacar.com.*

Taxi Contacts Taxi Car. ☎ *387/439–0530.*

Visitor and Tour Information Tourist Office. ✉ *Buenos Aires 93* ☎ *0800/222–3752* ⊕ *www.turismosalta.gov.ar.*

TOURS

MoviTrack. This Northwest specialist offers excursions around Salta but is best known for its Safari to the Clouds, an oxygen-equipped vehicle that follows the same route that the Tren a las Nubes used to take. Trips last 16 hours; they depart daily in winter and nearly every day in summer. Check the website for schedules and prices. ✉ *Buenos Aires 68* ☎ *387/431–6749* ⊕ *www.movitrack.com.ar* 🎫 *From 1,010 pesos.*

Uma Travel. Knowledgeable, English-speaking guides at Uma lead day trips to Cafayate or through the Quebrada de Humahuaca. Rafting, riding, and biking tours are also available; if you're more into local culture, there's a folklore circuit as well. ✉ *Güemes 34* ☎ *0387/422–8317* ⊕ *www.umatravel.com.ar* 🎫 *From 840 pesos.*

EXPLORING

TOP ATTRACTIONS

Fodor'sChoice
★
Basílica Menor y Convento San Francisco. Every *salteño*'s soul belongs to the landmark St. Francis Church and Convent, with its white pillars and bright terra-cotta-and-gold facade. The first sanctuary was built in 1625; the second, erected in 1674, was destroyed by fire; the present version was completed in 1882. A 53-meter (173-foot) belfry houses the

DID YOU KNOW?

Iruya, a tiny hillside town tucked in a valley northeast of the Quebrada de Humahuaca, is literally the end of the road. To explore beyond, you'll need to leave your vehicle behind.

Salta

KEY

1 *Exploring Sights*

1 *Hotels & Restaurants*

0   330 yards

0   300 meters

Campaña de la Patria. This bell, made from the bronze cannons used in the War of Independence, sounds once a day at 7:30 pm. In the sacristy, the Museo Convento San Francisco displays religious art. ⊠ *Córdoba 33* ☏ *387/431–0830* ⊕ *www.conventosanfranciscosalta.com* 🖃 *Church free; museum 30 pesos* ⊗ *Museum closed weekends.*

Cabildo. The whitewashed town hall, first constructed in 1582 and rebuilt many times since, used to house Salta's municipal government. Not only a colonial gem in itself, the Cabildo—the most well-preserved council building in Argentina—is home to the Museo Histórico del Norte, which includes a relevant collection of pre-Hispanic stone sculptures, as well as religious artifacts and a rather obscure assortment of vintage cars in the back garden. ⊠ *Caseros 549* ☏ *387/421–5340* 🖃 *30 pesos, free Tues.–Fri. 9 am–10 am* ⊗ *Closed Sun. and Mon.*

Catedral Basílica de Salta. The city's 1882 neoclassical cathedral fronts the central plaza. It's notable for the enormous frescoes portraying the four gospel writers on the portico around the altar and its impressive stained glass windows. Inside the entrance is the Panteón de las Glorias del Norte, enclosing the tombs of General Martín Miguel de Güemes and other heroes from the War of Independence. Wander to the back of the rose-colored cathedral for a peek at the beautiful, jasmine-infused garden. ⊠ *España 558* ☏ *387/431–8206* ⊕ *www.catedralsalta.org* 🖃 *Free.*

Convento de San Bernardo. Salta's oldest religious building served as a chapel first, then a hospital. Today it is home to a cloistered order of Carmelite nuns. The wooden rococo-style door, carved by indigenous craftsmen in 1762, contrasts markedly with the otherwise stark exterior of this 1625 structure. ⊠ *Caseros 73* ☏ *387/431–0092* 🖃 *Free.*

Fodor's Choice ★ **Museo de Árqueología de Alta Montaña.** The fascinating Museum of High Mountain Archaeology (MAAM) holds the mummified remains of three children born into Incan nobility—aged 6, 7, and 15—and the 146 objects buried with them in sacrificial services some 600 years ago. They were discovered at the summit of the 22,058-foot Volcán Llullaillaco, on the Argentine–Chilean border, in 1999. The high altitude and freezing temperatures kept their skin, hair, and clothes in impeccable condition, although the face of one was damaged by lightning. The museum also contains an exhibition about the Qhapaq Ñan Inca trading route from southern Colombia to Mendoza and another mummy, the Reina del Cerro (Queen of the Mountain), which for decades was illegally in the hands of private collectors. ⊠ *Mitre 77* ☏ *387/437–0592* ⊕ *www. maam.gob.ar* 🖃 *150 pesos* ⊗ *Closed Mon.*

Museo de Arte Etnico Americano Pajcha. The small, private Museum of Ethnic American Art Pajcha contains interesting artifacts and illustrations from the pre-Columbian world and later. Enthusiastic tour guides explain exhibits, using religious objects, furniture, jewelry, and the like to illuminate indigenous culture; there's also a well-curated textile collection. There's enough reason to linger here for hours; when you're done, relax with a coffee on the back terrace. ⊠ *20 de Febrero 831* ☏ *387/422–9417* ⊕ *museopajchasalta.com.ar* 🖃 *100 pesos (guided tour an additional 10 pesos)* ⊗ *Closed Sun.*

Museo Folclórico Pajarito Velarde. The two rooms of this museum are stuffed with curiosities and background information pertaining to Guillermo "Pajarito" Velarde Mors—the consummate bohemian who brought tango to Salta and lived here from 1930 to 1965. The space is brimming with his trinkets, artworks, and possessions. Take a look at the hat that Carlos Gardel gave him and the rosewood bed that folk singer Atahualpa Yupanki slept on. Even if you're not well versed in Argentine culture from that period, the museum is a delightful tribute to a real character. ⊠ *Pueyrredón 106* ☎ *387/421–2921* ⊕ *www.pajaritovelarde.com* ⊠ *30 pesos, includes 20-minute guided tour* ☉ *Closed weekends.*

Plaza 9 de Julio. The heart of Salta is quintessential Latin America: a leafy central plaza named after Argentina's date of independence. Arcaded buildings line the streets surrounding it, and some have been converted into cafés, providing perfect spots to while away a warm afternoon. Popular with families who take shade under the palm and jacaranda trees, the square is dotted with craftsmen selling their wares and teens canoodling by the bandstand. ⊠ *Salta.*

Teleférico a Cerro San Bernardo. The Cerro San Bernardo rises east of downtown Salta, a cool 268 meters (880 feet) higher than the city center. This cable car takes you up the hill from a station across from Parque San Martín in 10 minutes. Views of the entire Lerma Valley await at the top; you can also wander the breezy garden and browse around a small crafts market. ■ TIP→ If you're in the mood for a little light exercise, take the winding road back down. ⊠ *San Martín and H. Yrigoyen* ☎ *387/431–0641* ⊕ *www.telefericosanbernardo.com* ⊠ *150 pesos.*

WORTH NOTING

Casa de Hernández/Museo de la Ciudad. The City Museum is in Casa de Hernández, an 1879 neocolonial house. The ground floor displays an exceptional collection of musical instruments. Rooms upstairs document the history of Salta through paintings and photographs. ⊠ *Florida 97* ☎ *387/437–3352* ⊕ *www.museociudadsalta.info* ⊠ *Voluntary donation.*

Museo de Bellas Artes. The Fine Arts Museum's collection of colonial-era religious works includes figures from Argentina's Jesuit missions as well as Cuzco-style paintings from Peru and Bolivia. Another part of the museum highlights 20th-century pieces by Salta artists. ⊠ *Belgrano 992* ☎ *387/422–1745* ⊠ *40 pesos* ☉ *Closed Sun. and Mon.*

Museo Presidente José Evaristo Uriburu. Fine examples of late-colonial architecture—an interior courtyard, thick adobe walls, a reed-and-tile roof—abound in this simple building, the 19th- and 20th-century home of the Uriburu family, which gave Argentina two presidents. Furniture, costumes, paintings, and family documents are on display across six rooms. ⊠ *Caseros 417* ☎ *387/421–8174* ⊠ *20 pesos.*

CLOSE UP

Tren a las Nubes

With a bird's-eye view of its passage over the 64-meter-high (210-foot-high) Viaducto La Polvorilla, the Tren a las Nubes (Train to the Clouds) is one of the Northwest's most famous attractions, though, given that it no longer traverses the complete 217-km (135-mile) circuit, it has had its heyday. A lack of investment in the single railroad means the incredible 16-hour return journey it once made is now a thing of the past.

These days, you can take a snippet of a train ride on a one-hour journey to the high, desolate Puna from the small mining town of San Antonio de los Cobres, the only town of any size in the Puna. Take the bus from Salta or make your own way to San Antonio de los Cobres; you can bargain with locals selling textiles and ceramics next to the railway line, and buy coca leaves to ease the effects of the 4,197-meter (13,770-foot) altitude.

WHAT'S OUT THE WINDOW
An ethereal landscape offers view after spectacular view as the train twists and turns along the route. In San Antonio de los Cobres and on the lookout point at Viaducto La Polvorilla, locals gather round the train for a chat—and to sell handicrafts and trinkets.

SAN ANTONIO DE LOS COBRES
San Antonio, the highest town in Argentina, is as slow-moving as many of the country's small rural communities; it's also heavily battered by sun and wind, and there is little oxygen in the air. Essential accessories for visitors are sunscreen, extra clothes for warmth, and coca leaves—they're chewed as an aide to digestion (which

helps with altitude sickness). All that saliva production promotes swallowing, too, which will pop your ears.

Only in the past couple of years have there been any lodging options: the basic **Hostal del Cielo** (⊠ *Belgrano at Comandante Goulu* ☎ *387/490–9912* ⊕ *www.vivirenloscobres.com. ar*) and the smarter **Hosteria de las Nubes** (⊠ *RN51 s/n* ☎ *387/432–1322* ⊕ *www.hoteldelasnubes.com*) are the best. Renting a room in someone's house is an option, too. A small ethnographic and archaeological museum, ANTAPU, fills in some detail on the town's background, but it needs more work. The main business is making *artesanías*—handmade goods that can be sold to tourists.

RESERVATIONS
Reservations can be made at many agencies in Salta or with **Les Amis** (⊠ *Cerrito 844* ☎ *0810/345–3030* ⊕ *www.lesamisviajes.com*) in Buenos Aires and cost 1,470 pesos (train only) or 2,840 pesos (bus and train). ⊠ *Salta Station, Ameghino and Balcarce* ☎ *387/422–8021* ⊕ *www.trenalasnubes.com.ar*.

EXTENDING YOUR TRIP
Though you can only buy return tickets, you can stay in San Antonio and continue north to the *salinas* (salt flats) and on to Purmamarca in Jujuy. There's no public transport; for the right price, however, drivers will take you in their own cars. Going south to Cachi isn't as easy; the road is narrow and dangerous. Make sure to tell the *gendarmeria* (border guards) in San Antonio if you're going to attempt this route.

WHERE TO EAT

SALTA

$$
DELI
✕**Casa Moderna.** *Picadas*—assorted cured meats and local cheeses, accompanied by home-baked breads—are the star attractions here (be sure to try the smoked boar and trout). Although this deli-wine bar hybrid does get busy, the staff is generally friendly, and you can escape the bustle by retreating to the back terrace. **Known for:** excellent charcuterie; picnic food; wine store. ⑤ *Average main: 180 pesos* ✉ *España 674* ☎ *387/422–0066* ⊟ *No credit cards.*

$$
ARGENTINE
✕**Doña Salta.** This warm, festive, family-friendly locale serves dishes quite typical of Salta and the Northwest such as classics like *humita* (steamed corn husks filled with cheese) or the local *locro* stew, with beans and hunks of beef. You'll dine in a room steeped in local tradition, amid wine jugs and old wooden implements. *Empanadas* and meats are also reliable; the pastas are unremarkable, though. The location, across from Iglesia San Francisco, couldn't be more central. **Known for:** beef empanadas; its popularity, especially with tourists; classic fare from the Northwest. ⑤ *Average main: 170 pesos* ✉ *Córdoba 46* ☎ *387/432–1921* ⊟ *No credit cards.*

$$$
MODERN
ARGENTINE
Fodor's Choice
★
✕**José Balcarce.** A group of chefs launched a restaurant and catering service with high Andean cuisine as its goal—"high" referring to both the altitude and the gourmet techniques. The result is José Balcarce, in a brick-and-wood building with large windows just two blocks from bustling Balcarce Street. **Known for:** creativity with traditional ingredients; sophisticated setting; the most haute cuisine in Salta. ⑤ *Average main: 300 pesos* ✉ *Necochea 590* ☎ *387/421–1628* ⊕ *www.cocinadealtura. com.ar/jose-balcarce.php* ⊟ *No credit cards* ☽ *No lunch. Closed Sun.*

$$$
ARGENTINE
✕**Jovi Dos.** A great-value restaurant on a bustling downtown corner, Jovi Dos has several airy, high-ceilinged rooms with wood beams and plate-glass windows. Noteworthy starters include marinated eggplant and baked beef *empanadas* while grilled meats, seafood, pizza, and pasta have equal billing on the ridiculously long menu. **Known for:** fast service; abundant portions; lunch spot for local businesspeople. ⑤ *Average main: 240 pesos* ✉ *Balcarce 601* ☎ *387/432–9438.*

SAN LORENZO

$$
ARGENTINE
✕**Lo de Andrés.** Folks from Salta and San Lorenzo favor this bright, semi-enclosed brick-and-glass building with a vaulted ceiling for weekend dining. Lo de Andrés prepares a lightly spiced Argentine-style *parrillada*, but if you're not up for a full-on feast, there are *empanadas* and *milanesas* (breaded steak), as well as regional dishes like *humita*. **Known for:** steak and barbecue; quick service; cheap and cheerful. ⑤ *Average main: 150 pesos* ✉ *Juan Carlos Dávalos and Gorriti, San Lorenzo* ☎ *387/492–1600* ⊕ *www.saltaonline.com/andres.*

WHERE TO STAY

SALTA

$$$ **Ayres de Salta.** Conveniently located between the main plaza and
HOTEL Balcarce Street, Ayres de Salta has a small pool and fitness center on
the roof and a good little restaurant on the ground floor; rooms are
large and well equipped. **Pros:** efficient, professional staff can arrange
excursions; good location; buffet breakfast. **Cons:** some rooms look
into the windows of other rooms; street-facing rooms are noisy; could
do with new paint. ⑤ *Rooms from: 2000 pesos* ✉ *General Güemes
650* ☎ *387/422–1616* ⊕ *www.ayresdesalta.com.ar* ⤳ *40 rooms*
⦿ *Breakfast.*

$$$ **Carpe Diem.** Run by a German-Italian couple, this B&B in a heritage
B&B/INN home surrounded by a beautiful garden has an eclectic mix of singles
Fodor's Choice and doubles; rooms fuse antiques sourced from Buenos Aires with eth-
★ nic art, and period details with modern amenities. **Pros:** homemade
bread and cakes at breakfast; greenhouse, back garden, and library
on-site; convenient location. **Cons:** no children under 14; guests with
cat allergies will need to ask the owners to relocate their pets to the
garden, which they'll happily do; eerily quiet at times. ⑤ *Rooms from:
2000 pesos* ✉ *Urquiza 329* ☎ *387/421–8736* ⊕ *bedandbreakfastsalta.
com* ⤳ *8 rooms* ⦿ *Breakfast.*

$$ **Delvino Boutique Hotel.** Oenophiles will appreciate the decor at Del-
HOTEL vino—a remodeled, Spanish-style villa where the airy guest rooms are
painted in grape tones (Malbec red among them) and decorated with
wine-themed artworks. **Pros:** two blocks from Train to the Clouds rail-
way station; glass of wine on arrival; swimming pool. **Cons:** exposed
stairway can be chilly; no elevators; some rooms are poky. ⑤ *Rooms
from: 1500 pesos* ✉ *Ameghino 555* ☎ *387/432–0092* ⊕ *www.delvino-
salta.com.ar* ⤳ *18 rooms* ⦿ *Breakfast.*

$$$ **Hotel del Antiguo Convento.** This charming property in a former
HOTEL convent is run by a cheerful, attentive young staff; rooms are clean,
bright, and well-priced. **Pros:** staffers go out of their way to be helpful;
convenient location; private, apartment-style suites available. **Cons:**
courtyard and pool are small; some rooms are cramped; rooms next
to the courtyard are noisy. ⑤ *Rooms from: 2200 pesos* ✉ *Caseros 113*
☎ *387/422–7267* ⊕ *www.hoteldelconvento.com.ar* ⊟ *No credit cards*
⤳ *15 rooms* ⦿ *Breakfast.*

$$$ **Hotel Salta.** Designated as a National Historic Monument, the Salta
HOTEL occupies a handsome neocolonial building in the heart of the city;
antique furniture and views of either the plaza or the surrounding
mountains make every room attractive. **Pros:** ideal location; access to
Salta Polo Club; decent spa. **Cons:** rooms facing the plaza can be noisy;
corridors can echo; bathrooms are dated. ⑤ *Rooms from: 1750 pesos*
✉ *Buenos Aires 1* ☎ *387/426–7500* ⊕ *www.hotelsalta.com* ⤳ *99 rooms*
⦿ *Breakfast.*

$$$ **Hotel Solar de la Plaza.** The exterior of this beautiful old house belies
B&B/INN the modern comforts within; an elegant lobby leads to a tastefully
appointed sitting room, an airy courtyard, and a good (though expensive) restaurant. **Pros:** rooftop pool with city views; some rooms have
balconies; buffet breakfast. **Cons:** costly in-house dining; doors slam

loudly; rooms facing the square can be noisy. $ *Rooms from: 2500 pesos* ✉ *Leguizamón 669* ☎ *387/431–5111* ⊕ *www.solardelaplaza.com. ar* ↜ *30 rooms* ⦿ *Breakfast.*

$$$$
B&B/INN
Fodor's Choice
★

☷ **Kkala.** This elegant 10-room abode represents Salta, right down to the cardon cactus door panels and hand-stitched headboards depicting Andean landscapes. **Pros:** delightful bilingual staff; stylish en suite rooms; honesty bar. **Cons:** not that close to main attractions; some rooms are compact; some areas could use paint. $ *Rooms from: 3600 pesos* ✉ *Las Higueras 104* ☎ *0387/439–6590* ⊕ *www.hotelkkala.com. ar* ↜ *10 rooms* ⦿ *Breakfast.*

$$$$
B&B/INN
Fodor's Choice
★

☷ **Legado Mítico.** Sister to the Buenos Aires hotel of the same name, the family-run Legado Mítico attends to every detail—from the gorgeous guest rooms named after notable figures from the city's past and individually decorated to suit the titular person right down to the welcome glass of wine. **Pros:** warm and pleasing spaces; the living room and terrace are comfy spots for a moment of relaxation; attractive decor. **Cons:** located on a rather busy main drag; street-facing rooms can be noisy; noisy doors. $ *Rooms from: 5250 pesos* ✉ *Bartolomé Mitre 647* ☎ *387/422–8786* ⊕ *www.legadomitico.com* ↜ *11 rooms* ⦿ *Breakfast.*

$$$
HOTEL

☷ **Provincial Plaza.** This hotel is on a corner, just blocks from Plaza 9 de Julio; standard rooms have had recent renovations—superior and executive floors are spruced up and have good facilities. **Pros:** central location; views from the top floor; rooftop swimming pool. **Cons:** lower floors get street noise; decor in some rooms needs updating; maintenance needs attention. $ *Rooms from: 1900 pesos* ✉ *Caseros 786* ☎ *387/432–2000* ⊕ *www.provincialplaza.com.ar* ↜ *88 rooms* ⦿ *Breakfast.*

SAN LORENZO

$$$$
HOTEL

☷ **Amalinas.** A more contemporary option than Salta's often more traditional hotels, Amalinas' design features poured cement and soothing natural hues adorned with splashes of primary colors, plus airy rooms offering views across leafy San Lorenzo. **Pros:** rooms with a view of rolling hills; quiet and peaceful; restaurant puts fresh spin on local classics. **Cons:** you need a car to get around; check-out time is early at 10; pool isn't heated. $ *Rooms from: 2700 pesos* ✉ *Ruta Provincial 28, Km 11.5, San Lorenzo* ☎ *0387/492–1738* ⊕ *www.amalinashotel.com* ↜ *10 rooms* ⦿ *Free Breakfast.*

$$$
B&B/INN

☷ **Eaton Place.** Despite appearances, this striking Georgian-style mansion only dates from the 1980s, when it was built as a private home; it still feels like one, with bright and airy rooms in the main house and in a guesthouse with huge windows, hardwood floors, and period furniture. **Pros:** well appointed; large breakfast; lovely property with pool and gardens. **Cons:** a long way from the center of Salta; no on-site restaurant; a vehicle is necessary. $ *Rooms from: 1900 pesos* ✉ *San Martín 2457, San Lorenzo* ☎ *387/492–1347* ⊕ *www.eatonplacesalta. com.ar* ▭ *No credit cards* ↜ *9 rooms* ⦿ *Breakfast.*

5

NIGHTLIFE

Salta is a young and lively city, with a bar district along a few blocks of Balcarce Street that can get quite busy. Clubs, restaurants, and peñas attract both locals and tourists, who come to hear regional folk bands perform on small, cramped stages. Adding to the rowdy, dinner-theater atmosphere are the local gaucho dancers who entice (and often entrap) foreigners into strutting their stuff on stage; it's always a good laugh, no matter what language you speak. For a more authentic musical experience, head to La Casona del Molino.

Fodor's Choice
★
La Casona del Molino. Twenty-odd blocks down Caseros Street from the main plaza, La Casona del Molino is an authentic gem renowned for nightly folk performances; join in by clapping or dancing. It also serves great regional food at extremely decent prices. ⊠ *Luis Burela 1* ☎ *387/434–2835.*

La Vieja Estación. The self-proclaimed "home of folklore" stages nightly shows; it's a top spot for regional music, gaucho dancing, and the like. ⊠ *Balcarce 885* ☎ *387/421–7727* ⊕ *www.laviejaestacion.com.ar.*

Macondo. Blues and beer are always on tap at this raucous pub, where you're as likely to meet backpacking Aussies as you are local law students. ⊠ *Balcarce 980* ☎ *387/431–7191.*

Peña Gauchos de Güemes. One of the oldest and most traditional venues in the city, this *peña* retains a genuine gaucho spirit. It's been hosting folkloric nights for more than 50 years. ⊠ *Uruguay 750* ☎ *387/421–7007* ✆ *Closed weekdays.*

SHOPPING

En lo de Carmén. Although it stocks a far smaller selection of products than the Mercado Artesanal, artist Carmén Clerici de Dominguez's store does house a workshop for craftsmen. Pick up reasonably priced ceramic dishes, hand-knitted alpaca socks and gloves, and paintings by local artists. ⊠ *Ameghino 529* ☎ *387/431–3306.*

Feria de la Balcarce. Every Sunday, on Balcarce street between Entre Ríos and Ameghino, around 200 local artisans get together for this weekly handicrafts market. It's considered to be the most important in the north. Pick up ceramics, knitwear, rugs, shawls, and even furry llama toys. ⊠ *Balcarce 700 between Entre Ríos and Ameghino* ⊙ *Closed Mon.–Sat.*

Mercado Artesanal. Although Salta has all the usual high-street shops where you can stock up on sundries, provincial villages are a better bet for souvenirs and regional products. There are, however, a few proud exceptions to that rule—including the huge 1882 Jesuit monastery that holds the Mercado Artesanal and the open stalls across the street. Look for red-and-black *salteño* ponchos, alpaca knitwear and weavings, leather goods, wooden masks, carved animals, and fine silver from around the province. Everything is open daily 9–9. ⊠ *Av. San Martín 2555* ☎ *387/434–2808.*

SPORTS AND THE OUTDOORS

Salta has just a few outfitters, but the options they offer feel fresh and exciting. Horseback riding is growing in popularity, as is rafting.

HORSEBACK RIDING

Finca Lesser. Fifteen km (10 miles) west of Salta, Finca Lesser provides horseback-riding tours on a huge private estate. Trips can last anywhere from a few hours to two days. They can also organize a folk music performance and a tour showing gauchos at work. ⊠ *4 km (3 miles) past Castellanos, San Lorenzo* ☎ *387/492–1155.*

MacDermott's Argentina. Despite being told by local gauchos that he and his horse Pancho wouldn't make it across the Andes, Hugh MacDermott proved the cynics wrong. Now he shares his expertise by leading horse-riding holidays across the Northwest, with options ranging from short breaks to two-week treks. ⊠ *Salta* ☎ *11/4773–2522* ⊕ *www.macdermottsargentina.com* ✉ *From $200.*

Sayta. Rural tourism specialist Sayta offers stays out at a ranch in Chicoana, 40 km (24 miles) south of Salta, and horseback treks lasting from one to five days for riders of all levels. ⊠ *Chicoana* ☎ *387/683–6565* ⊕ *www.saltacabalgatas.com.ar* ✉ *From 1,000 pesos.*

RAFTING

Salta Rafting. This company specializes in whitewater rafting, operating from a base 35 km (21 miles) south of Salta by the Cabra Corral dam. Kayaking excursions, 4X4 adventures, and tandem paragliding are also available. For a breathtaking canopy surfing experience, try its "death slide"—a network of zip-line cables that crosses high above the Río Juramento. ⊠ *Caseros 117* ☎ *387/421–3216* ⊕ *www.saltarafting.com* ✉ *From 790 pesos.*

SALTA PROVINCE

The city of Salta, unofficial capital of the Argentine north, is known for its colonial architecture and its unassuming provincial appeal. It's also a hot spot for international visitors and, compared with its neighbors, really has its act together in terms of tourist infrastructure. The surrounding province of the same name, however, is only slowly being discovered by outsiders. Even the main circuit, the Valles Calchaquíes (Calchaquí Valley), involves long drives on unpaved roads with few other vehicles in sight.

Only the central third of the province has much in the way of population (the east and the west being vast, uninhabitable wilderness), but within that there's plenty of variety. Although new circuits are being opened up that take in the Cabra Corral dam and thermal waters of Rosario de la Frontera, the main destinations outside the city of Salta are Cafayate for its wine, Cachi for its landscape and archaeological sites, and San Antonio de las Cobres—the destination of the Tren a las Nubes.

CACHI

157 km (97 miles) southwest of Salta.

This small colonial village on Ruta 40 is fast becoming a base for exploring the north of Calchaqui Valley. Cachi itself has a charming church, a small archaeological museum, and a couple of decent hotels and restaurants, although there is nothing in the way of nightlife. Watching over it all is the 6,340-meter (20,800-foot) Nevado de Cachi, a few miles away.

The surrounding area is loaded with archaeological sites that have scarcely been explored. El Tero contains the remains of pre-Inca dwellings, and within 15 km (10 miles) are two more important sites: Puerta La Paya to the southwest and Las Pailas to the north (at the foot of the Nevado de Cachi). A little farther north, en route to La Poma, are the Graneros Incaicos, stunning cave-carved granaries from the Inca era.

GETTING HERE AND AROUND

Just one bus company, Ale Hermanos, serves Cachi from Salta, leaving at 7 am daily and in the evening at 8pm every day (except Saturday). You're advised to buy tickets for the journey (which takes just over four hours) a day in advance. For more flexibility, Remis San José runs a fixed-price taxi service four times daily; the cost is about 700 pesos. It also offers area sightseeing tours, plus transfers to Cafayate and the villages in between.

ESSENTIALS

Bus Contacts Ale Hermanos. ☎ *387/421–1588* ⊕ *www.alehnos.com.ar.*

Taxi Contacts Remis San José. ☎ *3868/491–907.*

Visitor Information Tourist office. ✉ *General Güemes s/n* ☎ *3868/491–902.*

TOURS

Turismo Urkupiña. From two-hour walking trips around Cachi to day-long excursions deep into the Salta countryside, this tour company covers most areas from its Cachi base. ✉ *Benjamin Zorrilla s/n* ☎ *387/155–118–396* ⊕ *www.urkupiña.tur.ar* 🖅 *From 120 pesos* 🖅 *From 360 pesos.*

WHERE TO STAY

$$$
HOTEL
🏨 **ACA Hosteria.** Once the only decent place to stay in Cachi, the Argentine Automobile Club hosteria is gaining some stiff competition but is still a practical option thanks to its swimming pool, children's facilities, attractive garden, and reliable restaurant. **Pros:** lovely pool views; buffet breakfast; large play area. **Cons:** compact rooms; rooms can echo; lacks character of other local hotels. ⑤ *Rooms from: 2269 pesos* ✉ *Av. Automóvil Club Argentino s/n* ☎ *3868/491–904* ⊕ *www.hosteriacachi.com.ar* 🛏 *33 rooms* 🍽 *Breakfast.*

$$$
B&B/INN
🏨 **El Cortijo.** Converted from a vintage villa, this boutique hotel stands out for its rustic-chic style and friendly service; the 12 guest rooms are tastefully decorated with traditional antiques and art. **Pros:** artistic decor; charming courtyard and wine cellar; free Wi-Fi. **Cons:** rooms vary in terms of size and views; breakfast is basic; passageways echo. ⑤ *Rooms from: 1800 pesos* ✉ *Av. Automóvil Club Argentino s/n* ☎ *3868/491–034* ⊕ *www.elcortijohotel.com* 🛏 *12 rooms* 🍽 *Breakfast.*

THE NORTHWEST SHOPPING EXPERIENCE

Throughout the Northwest, almost every town has an area where vendors sell *artesenías*—emblematic crafts using local materials and incorporating the culture. Spending time at these markets, which may simply be set up around the main plaza, isn't just a great way to find the perfect souvenir; it's also a real opportunity to interact with locals.

Andean artesanías come in two forms: mass-produced products (generally imported from Bolivia) and locally produced handmade items. Often, stall owners will sell a mix of the two; ask which fall into the latter category and opt for them, as they do more to support the local community. Bolivian goods get cheaper the farther north you go. Some towns such as Humahuaca and Tilcara have shops that are exclusively fair trade, so look out for the signs reading, *comercio justo*.

Also, you'll see lots of dimpled *cardon* (cactus) wood carved into all manner of souvenirs, but there's no system right now for verifying the origin of the wood (only souvenirs carved from already-dead cardones are legal). We encourage you to ask your guide or another local for vendor recommendations.

Alpaca knits. Alpacas look like a cross between a llama and a sheep with a glossy, silky fleece. Textiles from them feel lovely and are unmistakably Andean, with the traditional designs.

Coca. Freely available, coca here is a medicine rather than a narcotic. Coca tea is neatly packaged and tastes better than green tea. Don't try taking it home without checking customs regulations first.

Leather. Unless there's an item that particularly catches your eye, save your leather purchases for the pampas. They do use leather in the Quebrada, but not in the decorative ways of elsewhere in the country.

Masks. If you don't experience Humahuaca at carnival time, you might be surprised by the number of masks—of humans and animals, made of wood or pottery—among the stalls. If you do go during *carnaval*, it'll make more sense.

Musical instruments. Panpipes are easy to play (though harder to play well) and instantly evocative of the windswept Quebrada. There are more intricate instruments available for musicians or the curious. For some tips on how to play, take it to a peña—a musical gathering at a bar—one evening and corner one of the performers.

Ponchos. Made from sheep or llama wool, ponchos go with everything, are useful against the cool cloudless nights in the Quebrada, and make great souvenirs (just resist the temptation to wear one out in Buenos Aires if you want to blend in). You can also pick up hats and gloves in matching patterns.

Silver. It was its position on the road to the Potosí silver mines that made the Quebrada so important in colonial days, but don't count on the silver on sale now being locally sourced. Look for traditional motifs and symbols cast into silver as jewelry and, borrowing traditions from elsewhere, tableware.

$$$$ 🏨 **La Merced del Alto.** Although this stately white-adobe building looks
HOTEL like it's been here forever, it was in fact built in 2006; inside, rooms
Fodor's Choice are huge and comfortable with tasteful wood and iron furniture. **Pros:**
★ expansive grounds with great views; spa, wine cellar, bar, and restaurant
on-site; accessible for people with disabilities. **Cons:** 3 km (2 miles)
from Cachi; echoing corridors; Wi-Fi is flaky. $ *Rooms from: 3100
pesos* ✉ *Fuerte Alto s/n* ☎ *3868/490–030* ⊕ *www.lamerceddelalto.com*
↪ *13 rooms* ¶⨀¶ *Breakfast.*

MOLINOS

*206 km (128 miles) southwest of Salta (via Cachi); 50 km (31 miles)
south of Cachi.*

Molinos, a village with about 6,000 inhabitants, has a photogenic 17th-
century church and a small vicuña-breeding farm (*vicuñas* are similar
to llamas but their fur makes a much finer, more expensive wool). The
main draw, however, is its location on the way to Argentina's oldest
winery (Bodega Colomé) and to many more in Cafayate.

Molinos is also just a few miles from Seclantás' Camino de Artesanos
(Road of the Artisans), where weavers make ponchos and scarves by
the roadside on contraptions improvised from wood and old bicycle
parts. The Laguna de Brealito, 10 km (6 miles) due west of Seclantás,
is a picturesque lake in the middle of nowhere. Eight km (5 miles) east
of Molinos are the pre-Columbian ruins of Chicoana.

GETTING HERE AND AROUND

Ale Hermanos offers daily bus services at 7 am between Salta and
Molinos.

ESSENTIALS

Bus Contacts Ale Hermanos. ☎ *387/421–1588* ⊕ *www.alehnos.com.ar.*

EXPLORING

Fodor's Choice **Bodega Colomé and James Turrell Museum.** Remote wineries and museums
★ are one thing; Bodega Colomé is something else altogether. Yet finally
arriving at this world-class spot puts the miles of driving along bumpy,
unpaved roads firmly into perspective. Established in 1831, Colomé is
Argentina's oldest winery. A visitor center runs daily tours and offers
tastings, while a terrace restaurant serves delectable lunches with views
of one of the world's highest vineyards. Colomé is also home to the
breathtaking and unexpected James Turrell Museum, which showcases
five decades of the artist's works with light and space, and includes a
fun tunnel of color (book in advance). ◼ TIP→ **Turrell's contemporary
art installations are at their most striking at sunset.** ✉ *RP53, Km 20,
20 km (13 miles) west of Molinos* ☎ *387/439–4009* ⊕ *www.bodegaco-
lome.com* ✎ *Winery entrance free, tastings from 200 pesos; museum
free.*

WHERE TO STAY

$$$$ 🏨 **Estancia Colomé.** An ideal stopover between Salta and Cafayate, this
HOTEL stunning lodge is located on the Colomé wine estate 20 km (13 miles)
Fodor's Choice from Molinos. **Pros:** spacious and well-designed rooms; restaurant uses
★ ingredients from its organic garden; authentic experience at a working

vineyard. **Cons:** Wi-Fi is spotty; very remote; not all staff speak English well. $ *Rooms from: 5150 pesos* ⊠ *RP53, Km 20, 20 km (13 miles) west of Molinos* ☎ *3868/494–200* ⊕ *www.bodegacolome.com* ➘ *9 rooms* �‖ *Free Breakfast.*

$$$$
B&B/INN

⚐ **Hacienda de Molinos.** This lovely 18th-century hacienda belonged to the last Spanish governor, its fantastic open courtyard, white adobe walls, and racing green doorways denoting the colonial era. **Pros:** spacious rooms; good restaurant with local wine list; swimming pool. **Cons:** service can be slow at peak times; noisy doors. $ *Rooms from: 3150 pesos* ⊠ *Molinos s/n* ☎ *3868 /494–094* ⊕ *www.haciendademolinos.com.ar* ➘ *18 rooms* �‖ *Free Breakfast.*

WHERE TO EAT

$$
ARGENTINE

✕ **Inti Raymi.** It's an honest little restaurant in Seclantás, with some fine old photos on the walls and good, oven-baked *empanadas*. Other attractions include a delicious goat stew, corn-based dishes, regional breads, and a warm welcome from your host, Alejandro Díaz. **Known for:** typical northwestern fare; good value; traditional decor. $ *Average main: 160 pesos* ⊠ *Abraham Cornejo s/n, opposite police station, Seclantás* ☎ *3868/498–009* ▭ *No credit cards.*

CAFAYATE

185 km (115 miles) southwest of Salta via RN68; 340 km (211 miles) southwest of Salta via R40.

Thanks to a microclimate and fertile soil, Cafayate and the surrounding area is one of Argentina's booming wine regions. The town itself is civilized and orderly, with various bodegas offering tours and tastings, lots of good restaurants, and some exquisite hotels. But wander a couple of blocks from the central plaza and you're back on unpaved roads. Take a bit of a hike, and you're in the mountains—probably enjoying a wine-tasting session at a tiny *finca* and trying hard to get your camera to do justice to the view.

GETTING HERE AND AROUND

Chevallier and Balut both run about 10 buses a day from Salta. It's best to buy your ticket for the four-hour trip a day in advance, especially in summer. In Cafayate, many agencies and hotels rent bikes, which can come in handy when visiting bodegas and sights within a few miles of town.

ESSENTIALS

Bus Contacts Balut. ☎ *0387/422–9393* ⊕ *www.balutsrl.com.ar.* **Nueva Chevallier.** ☎ *387/431–2819* ⊕ *www.nuevachevallier.com.*

Visitor Information Tourist Office. ⊠ *Nuestra Senora del Rosario, at Plaza 20 de Febrero* ☎ *3868/422–224* ⊕ *www.turismosalta.gov.ar.*

EXPLORING

Museo de la Vid y del Vino. This museum, located in a warehouse dating from 1881, has undergone an extensive refurbishment to include more flash and 3D exhibitions. You can learn about wine-making in the Calchaquí Valley. Machinery, agricultural implements, and old photographs also tell the history of wine-making in this area. ⊠ *Guemes Sur and Fermín Perdiguero* ☎ *3868/422–322* ⊕ *www.museodelavidyelvino.gov.ar* ☑ *60 pesos* ⊗ *Closed Mon.*

Museo Regional y Arqueológico Rodolfo Bravo. For 66 years, Rodolfo Bravo collected and cataloged funerary and religious objects from local excavations. These objects, made of clay, ceramic, metal, and textiles, are on display at the private Museo Regional y Arqueológico Rodolfo Bravo (Rudolfo Bravo Regional and Archaeological Museum). Artifacts from the Incas and Diaguitas of the Calchaqui Valley also form part of the collection. ⊠ *Colón 191* ☎ *3868/421–054* ☑ *Voluntary contribution.*

NEED A BREAK

✕ **Heladería Miranda.** For wine-tasting with a difference, stop at Heladaría Miranda in Cafayate. In 1994, at the age of 60, Ricardo Miranda decided that he wasn't going to succeed as a painter. **Known for:** quirky ice cream flavors. ⊠ *Av. Güemes Norte 170* ☎ *3868/421–106.*

Quebrada de las Conchas. The first 50 km (30 miles) of the direct road to Salta (or the last stretch if you don't come via Cachi and Molinos) is known as the Gorge of the Shells, and breathtaking scenery makes it an attraction in its own right. Various rock formations have been eroded into wildly different shapes that have been nicknamed the Windows, the Castles, the Frog, the Friar—each name seems fanciful, that is until the road winds around the corner and you're actually confronted by the formation itself. The climax is the Amphitheater, sometimes used as a venue for proper orchestras thanks to its outstanding natural acoustics; wandering minstrels offer impromptu performances. ■TIP➜ If you've rented a car, keep valuables out of view as thieves have become more prevalent at the Amphitheater. ⊠ *RN68, Km 6–Km 46.*

WINERIES

Although Salta makes only 1.5% of Argentina's wine, the province accounts for 8% of the country's exports. Most of the production is in or around Cafayate, which has a dozen bodegas, ranging from boutique family businesses to small branches of multinational concerns. Book ahead for tastings.

Bodega José L. Mounier. In 1996 there was nothing on the land of Bodega José L. Mounier in El Divisadero, 4 km (2 miles) outside of town. Now this is one of Salta's best boutique wineries with fabulous views down into the valley. Almost half its small line of reds, whites, rosés, and sparklings is sold in the bodega itself. The tour includes sampling three wines, and lunch on the veranda is available if you book ahead. ⊠ *El Divisadero, Km 4* ☎ *3868/422–129* ⊕ *www.bodegamounier.com.ar* ☑ *70 pesos* ⊗ *Closed Sun.*

Bodega Nanni. Nanni has been in the same family and in the same building—just a block from the main square—since 1897. Thanks to its organic certification, much of its small production of Torrontés, Malbec, Cabernet Sauvignon, and Tannat is exported to the United States. Book lunch or dinner at Retoño, the rustic little restaurant in the back garden, for hearty stews and regional cuisine. ⊠ *Silverio Chavarria 151* ☎ *3868/421–527* ⊕ *www.bodegananni.com* ☑ *50 pesos for tour and 3-wine tasting.*

Fodor's Choice
★ **Domingo Molina.** About 2 km (1 mile) north of Cafayate, Domingo Molina has been making Torrontés, a 90-point Malbec, and various blends since 2000. Tastings are available, and you can book in advance for a *picada* or *asado*. A drive leads you high up into the hills, offering stunning views of the wine lands to the east. ■ TIP→ Take a look at Domingo Molina's oldest vine—a 100-year-old Malbec, still providing drinkable grapes. Domingo Hermanos, a sister winery in town, is one of Cafayate's biggest operations, producing 3 million liters a year. ⊠ *RN40, Km 6, Yacochuya Norte* ☎ *3868/1545–2887* ⊕ *www.domingomolina.com.ar* 🖃 *150 pesos.*

Fodor's Choice
★ **El Porvenir de Cafayate.** Old blends with new at Bodega El Porvenir. Founded at the turn of the 20th century by Italian immigrants, the winery was bought by the Romero Marcuzzi family in 2000 and brought up-to-date. The result is a small yet sleek facility surrounded by old carob casks and presses. Drop by the tasting room to sample the Laborum-label Malbec and Torrontés, as well as the top-end Amauta three-grape red blend, or book a private asado at Finca El Retiro, the family's downtown vineyard, for lunch among the vines (600 pesos per person). Ask to see the small olive oil factory, as well. ⊠ *Córdoba 32* ☎ *3868/422–007* ⊕ *www.elporvenirdecafayate.com* 🖃 *100 pesos for 3 wines.*

El Transito. A contemporary building in the center of town houses El Transito's bodega and visitor center, a business run by a family that shares common ancestors with the folks at Bodega Nanni across the street. Pop in for a short tour and the chance to sample Malbec, Cabernet Sauvignon, and Torrontés. ⊠ *Belgrano 102* ☎ *3868/422–385* ⊕ *www.bodegaeltransito.com* 🖃 *50 pesos for 4 wines* ☉ *Closed Sun.*

Piattelli Vineyards. The first winery in Cafayate to be constructed with tourism in mind, Piattelli caused a bit of a flurry with locals when it opened in 2013 thanks to the modern aesthetic conceived by its American owners. The state-of-the-art bodega, halfway up the foothills towards Yacochuya, offers tastings, tours, and fabulous valley views. Kick back on one of the two terraces with a refreshing Torrontés before tucking into slow-roasted lamb or panfried salmon for lunch at the winery's restaurant. ⊠ *R2, on way to Yacochuya* ☎ *3868/1540–5881* ⊕ *www.piattellivineyards.com* 🖃 *150 pesos for tour and four-wine tasting, 300 pesos for premium tasting.*

San Pedro de Yacochuya. Head 8 km (5 miles) northwest of town toward the hills to find Arnaldo Etchart's boutique winery. He established it in 1988, collaborating with star oenologist Michel Rolland to create a trio of award-winning wines. Visits don't require a reservation, so you can simply drop by to sample the Coquena or San Pedro de Yacochuya lines while enjoying stunning views over the valley. ⊠ *Cafayate* ☎ *3868/421–233* ⊕ *www.yacochuya.com.ar* 🖃 *Tastings 150–350 pesos* ☉ *Closed Sun.*

Vasija Secreta. Occupying a grand 1850s building on the northern edge of town, Vasija Secreta has a small museum displaying imported oak barrels and machinery for pumping and bottling wine. Short tours give a historical overview and show how production methods have changed.

Tasty local dishes are served at the rustic on-site restaurant. ⊠ *RN40 s/n* ☎ *3868/421–850* ⊕ *www.vasijasecreta.com* ▭ *Free.*

WHERE TO EAT

$$ ✕ **Destilería Etchart & Argerich.** When you need a break from wine, head
ARGENTINE to this Tolombón distillery to sample an array of grappas—one even made from coca leaves. The former warehouse is covered in signs and distilling memorabilia; there's also a small country store selling local produce including everything from nuts to olive oil. **Known for:** grappa tastings; snacks; country store stocked with local products. $ *Average main: 200 pesos* ⊠ *Ruta 40 Km 4323, Tolombón* ☎ *3868/465–853* ⊕ *www.facebook.com/gargantuadeyacochuya* ▭ *No credit cards.*

$$ ✕ **El Rancho.** Facing the main plaza, this big barn of a restaurant serves
ARGENTINE regional specialties (like baked rabbit and *cabrito al horno*), as well as pastas and classic Argentine steaks. Expect generous portions, a bustling atmosphere, live folk music, and wines from the owner's Bodega Río Colorado, just a block away. **Known for:** bustling atmosphere; traditional fare; efficient service. $ *Average main: 145 pesos* ⊠ *Vicario Toscano 4* ☎ *3868/421–256* ▭ *No credit cards* ⊘ *Closed Mon.*

$$ ✕ **Macacha Gourmet.** A 100-year-old converted school building houses
ARGENTINE one of Cafayate's more ambitious restaurants. Overseen by the friendly
Fodor's Choice owner Matías, it has three dining rooms themed after the Nanni,
★ Domingo Hermanos, and Etchart bodegas, with wine displays and special cutlery. **Known for:** traditional fare such as llama steaks; wine list; jolly ambience. $ *Average main: 170 pesos* ⊠ *Av. Güemes Norte 28* ☎ *3868/422–319* ▭ *No credit cards* ⊘ *Closed Sun.*

$$ ✕ **Peña y Parrillada de la Plaza.** This place makes the list for its music
ARGENTINE rather than its food—though the barbecued meats and *empanadas* are good deals. Singers, musicians, and sometimes dancers bring Peña y Parrillada de la Plaza to life each night. **Known for:** live music; traditional northwestern dishes; fun atmosphere. $ *Average main: 170 pesos* ⊠ *Nuestra Señora del Rosario 96* ☎ *3868/421–043* ⊕ *www.laplazarestaurante.com.ar.*

WHERE TO STAY

$$$$ ⛉ **Altalaluna Boutique Hotel & Spa.** This gorgeous boutique hotel in the vil-
HOTEL lage of Tolombón, 14 km (9 miles) south of Cafayate, occupies an 1892 colonial mansion; there's a wine bar and cellar, an excellent restaurant, a reading room complete with fireplace, and a peaceful spa overlooking endless vines. **Pros:** great facilities; perfect for star-spotting; spacious rooms. **Cons:** the pool isn't heated; a bit far from the town center; passageways can echo. $ *Rooms from: 4300 pesos* ⊠ *RN40, Km 4326* ☎ *387/461–0283* ⊕ *www.altalaluna.com* ⤳ *20 rooms* ⦿ *Breakfast.*

$$$$ ⛉ **Cafayate Wine Resort.** Three km (2 miles) from the plaza on a straight
RESORT dusty road lined with vineyards and in the shadow of San Isidro is a large white adobe building with 22 rooms built around a wide courtyard. **Pros:** spacious shared areas and access to veranda from all rooms; swimming pool with great views; lovely garden surrounded by vines. **Cons:** a little isolated from the town; some noise from hallways. $ *Rooms from: 3000 pesos* ⊠ *25 de Mayo s/n, Camino al Divisadero* ☎ *3868/154–528–883* ⊕ *www.cafayatewineresort.com* ⤳ *22 rooms* ⦿ *Breakfast.*

Drying chilies near Cachi, Calchaquí Valley

$$
B&B/INN
🍴 **El Hospedaje.** This century-old building used to be a youth hostel until the owner got tired of the noise and chaos; rooms are basic, but they're set around a pleasant courtyard or around the inviting swimming pool. **Pros:** quiet and close to center; continental breakfast in a large dining room; friendly staff. **Cons:** few facilities; rooms are basic; rooms next to street are noisy. ⑤ *Rooms from: 1500 pesos* ⊠ *Salta 13, and Camila Quintana de Niño* ☎ *3868/421–680* ⊕ *www.saltaweb.com.ar/elhospedaje* ⊟ *No credit cards* ⇆ *12 rooms* ⟟⊙⟨ *Breakfast.*

$$$$
B&B/INN
🍴 **El Porvenir Casa de Bodega.** For a taste of being a vineyard owner, book a room at this charming, colonial-style B&B located on the working estate that belongs to El Porvenir de Cafayate *bodega.* **Pros:** peaceful despite being three blocks from the main square; great shared spaces including outdoor barbecue area; mountain views. **Cons:** breakfast isn't very exciting; you can't use the kitchen facilities to cook. ⑤ *Rooms from: 2900 pesos* ⊠ *Belgrano, at Jujuy* ☎ *3868/422–007* ⊕ *www.elporvenirdecafayate.com* ⇆ *5 rooms* ⟟⊙⟨ *Free Breakfast.*

$$$$
HOTEL
Fodor'sChoice
★
🍴 **Grace Cafayate.** A contemporary offering in the area, Grace Cafayate isn't just a step away from the local style—it's a whole world away; located within the posh La Estancia de Cafayate residential and recreational complex, its lodging options include suites overlooking vineyards in the main building, as well as stand-alone villas and apartments across the way. **Pros:** infinity pool and spa on-site; supercomfy king beds; spacious communal areas. **Cons:** breakfast is on the small side; it can seem overly quiet; not all staff speak English. ⑤ *Rooms from: 4200 pesos* ⊠ *RN40, Km 4340* ☎ *3868/427–000* ⊕ *www.gracehotels.com/cafayate* ⇆ *52 rooms* ⟟⊙⟨ *Breakfast.*

$$$$ ⊡ **Hotel Asturias.** The swimming pool is terrific, the garden is ample,
HOTEL and this—the biggest and oldest hotel in town—is quite comfortable.
Pros: great garden and pool; central; walking distance to wineries.
Cons: restaurant open only in high season; many staff don't speak
English; breakfast is standard. ⑤ *Rooms from: 3050 pesos* ⊠ *Av.
Güemes Sur 154* ☎ *3868/421–328* ⊕ *www.cafayateasturias.com* ⊅ *57
rooms* ⦿| *Breakfast.*

$$$$ ⊡ **La Casa de la Bodega.** Carob wood and local boulders from the
HOTEL Quebrada de las Conchas were used to construct the little Casa de la
Bodega, a rustic space with most mod cons that feels like peace personi-
fied. **Pros:** total peace and quiet in a beautiful setting; winery attached
to the hotel; restaurant and pool on-site. **Cons:** if it's windy, you'll feel
it here; the piped '80s music gets a bit much; you need a vehicle as it's
isolated. ⑤ *Rooms from: 3000 pesos* ⊠ *RN 68, Km 18.5, 18 km (11
miles) from Cafayate center* ☎ *3868/452–620* ⊕ *www.lacasadelabo-
dega.com.ar* ⊅ *8 rooms* ⦿| *Breakfast.*

$$$$ ⊡ **Patios de Cafayate Wine Hotel.** Creature comforts, a fine restaurant, and
HOTEL rustic-chic rooms overlooking the vineyards make this luxury property
Fodor'sChoice a top choice. **Pros:** exclusive; wonderful pool surrounded by vines;
★ fabulous facilities including wine spa, restaurant, and bodega. **Cons:**
pricey; you'll need a car to get around; large tours can spoil the ambience. ⑤ *Rooms from: 4500 pesos* ⊠ *R40 at RN68, 3 km (2 miles) from
Cafayate center* ☎ *3868/422–229* ⊕ *www.patiosdecafayate.com* ⊅ *31
rooms* ⦿| *Some meals.*

$$$ ⊡ **Portal del Santo.** Just two blocks from the plaza but already on the
B&B/INN edge of town, this place feels like a hideaway; behind the large colo-
nial-style building, with its big guest rooms and its fireplace-warmed
common area, is a garden with a blue-and-white swimming pool and
great views. **Pros:** both central and quiet; good bathrooms; big break-
fast. **Cons:** many guests are families, which tends to disturb the peace;
small communal spaces; rooms look dated. ⑤ *Rooms from: 1900 pesos*
⊠ *Silvero Chavarria 250* ☎ *3868/422–500* ⊕ *www.portaldelsanto.com*
⊅ *13 rooms* ⦿| *Breakfast.*

SHOPPING

Cesteria (weaving with cane), *tejidos* (weaving with fabric), and
cerámica (pottery) are the local specialties. Find these goods in the
Paseo de Artesanos on the main plaza or in individual workshops. The
tourist office opposite the Paseo de Artesanos has details. Cafayate has
also seen a boom in wine stores selling products from local bodegas.

Calchaquitos. Just next to the plaza, Calchaquitos sells cookies
and chocolates, local jams, wine, and clothes. ⊠ *Güemes Sur 118*
☎ *3868/421–799.*

La Ultima Pulpería. For a time-warp trip, just step into this store. La
Ultima Pulpería, which has barely changed since opening in 1923, is an
Aladdin's Cave selling loose herbs and spices, animal hides, and fresh
produce. If you can pry owner Miguel Dioli away from his regular
Salta-brand beer-drinking customers at the makeshift bar, he's good for
a chat in Spanish. ⊠ *Mitre 20* ☎ *3868/421–629.*

Vinoteca La Escalera. Plenty of wine stores have popped up of late in Cafayate but Vinoteca La Escalera is one of the more established ones. It carries a solid selection from around the valley. ⊠ *San Martín 71* ☎ *3868/421–142* ⊘ *Closed afternoons.*

SPORTS AND THE OUTDOORS

Getting active in Cafayate involves the gentler end of adventure tourism: there are lots of opportunities for hikes, horseback rides, and bike excursions, but nothing too extreme. The waterfalls in the Río Colorado make a good excursion on a bike or on foot.

Los Toneles. Biking is a pleasant way to access some of the farther-afield wineries or to explore the countryside. You can rent cycles from Los Toneles hostel. ⊠ *Camila Quintana de Niño 38* ☎ *3868/422–301* ⊕ *los-tonelescafayate.business.site* ⊠ *From 150 pesos.*

MENDOZA AND
THE WINE REGIONS

WELCOME TO
MENDOZA AND THE WINE REGIONS

TOP REASONS TO GO

★ **Majestic Mountains:** Wherever you are in Mendoza, the sight of those towering Andean peaks never ceases to amaze.

★ **Fun in the Sun:** With more than 320 days of sunshine a year, Mendoza is the ultimate sunseekers destination, whether you pedal a bike along flat vineyard roads, ride a horse along Andean trails, or ski down challenging slopes.

★ **Bed and Bodega:** Country inns with gourmet restaurants, vineyard visits and tastings, cooking classes, and discussions with oenologists make wine touring a pure pleasure.

★ **Food and Wine:** Some of Argentina's premier chefs have left coastal resorts and Buenos Aires' bistros behind, choosing to relocate to wine-country inns and bodegas.

★ **Unique Terroir:** Known worldwide for its Malbec, Mendoza's Wine Region is one of the most sought-after in the New World with big international investment and an impressive wine heritage.

The provinces of Mendoza and San Juan, in the central-west portion of Argentina, lie at the foot of the highest Andean ranges along the border with Chile. The city of Mendoza and its surrounding departments are in Mendoza Province's northern portion, 1,040 km (646 miles) from Buenos Aires but only 360 km (224 miles) from Santiago, Chile. The east–west Ruta Nacional 7 (RN7, part of the Ruta Panamericana or Pan-American Highway) crosses the Andes from Mendoza to Chile and links Argentina and neighboring countries (Brazil, Uruguay, Paraguay) with Pacific ports. Ruta Nacional 40 runs north–south the length of the country, passing through San Juan and down to Mendoza, the Valle de Uco, and San Rafael.

1 Gran Mendoza. Gran, or greater, Mendoza refers to the city and the surrounding *departments* (urban areas) of Godoy Cruz, Guaymallén, Maipú, Junín, Luján de Cuyo, and Las Heras—most of which have vineyards, bodegas, small hotels, and restaurants.

2 Valle de Uco. At the foot of the Cordón del Plata, between the towns of Ugarteche and Pareditas, the valley spreads its green mantle of vineyards and fruit orchards for 125 km (78 miles). The Río Tunuyán and its many *arroyos* (streams) create an oasis in this otherwise dry desert region.

3 San Rafael Region. The vineyards and olive groves that ring this burgeoning agricultural town in the southern portion of Mendoza Province are irrigated by the Ríos Atuel and Diamante, which flow from the nearby Andes.

4 San Juan Region. From this historic town surrounded by three important wine-producing valleys—Tulum, Ullum, and Zonda—you can travel west up the Río San Juan into a landscape of mountains, valleys, and desert.

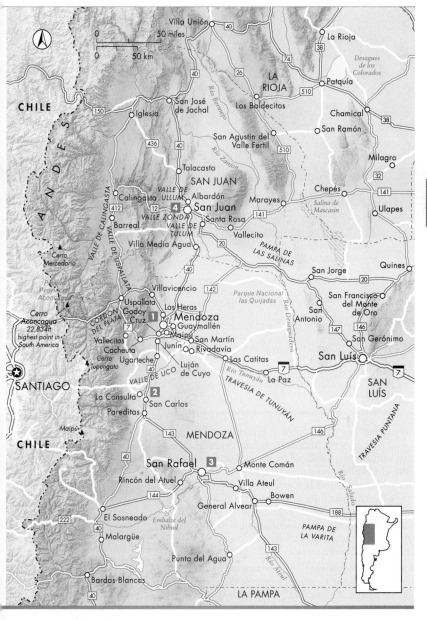

6

CERRO ACONCAGUA VIA THE USPALLATA PASS

At 6,957 meters (22,825 feet), Cerro Aconcagua is the highest mountain in both the Western and the Southern hemispheres. The so-called Giant of America towers over the Andes with its five glaciers gleaming in the sun; and every year, late November through March, thousands try to conquer it.

(above) Sunset on Aconcagua from Plaza de Mulas base camp (top right) Poplar trees en route to the pass (bottom right) Look up: condor sightings are common in this area.

However, you don't have to be a mountaineer to enjoy the wild beauty here. Although guided climbing expeditions require two weeks of hiking and acclimating, a worthy alternative is to park at the rangers' cabin right off Ruta Nacional 7 just beyond the Puente del Inca, pay the park fee, and hike three hours from the Río Horcones to a lagoon. If this seems like a short hike for such a drive out, relax knowing that the journey to this place is as breathtaking as Aconcagua itself.

While fauna isn't thick, sight lines are unobstructed, and you might see foxes or shy guanacos; look up for condors, too. Alpine meadows bloom in the spring, and lichen are up to 500 years old.

DRIVE SAFELY

Ruta Nacional 7 is the only road that connects the Pacific ports of Chile with Argentina, Brazil, and Uruguay. Be prepared for heavy truck traffic.

In winter, icy roads can close for days; mudslides can cause closures in all seasons. The altitude jumps from 762 meters (2,500 feet) in Mendoza to 3,184 meters (10,446 feet) at the top of the pass; winds can sometimes be brutal.

ALONG THE USPALLATA PASS (RN7, THE PANAMERICAN HIGHWAY)

Leaving Mendoza, green vineyards give way to barren hills and scrub brush as you follow the river for 30 km (19 miles). If you find yourself engulfed in fog and drizzle, don't despair: you'll likely encounter brilliant sunshine when you reach the Potrerillos Valley 39 km (24 miles) away. The road passes a long dam and then follows the Río Mendoza for 105 km (65 miles) to Uspallata, the last town before the Chilean frontier.

Along the way, the ríos Blanco and Tambillos rush down from the mountains into the Río Mendoza, and remnants of Inca *tambos* (resting places) marked by signs en route remind you that this was once an Inca trail; if you're traveling with a guide, she or he will stop for you to check them out. At Punta de Vacas, corrals that held cattle on their way to Chile lie abandoned alongside defunct railway tracks. Two km (1 mile) beyond the army barracks and customs office three valleys converge. Looking south, the region's third-highest mountain—Cerro Tupungato, an inactive volcano (6,800 meters/22,310 feet)—reigns above the Valle de Uco.

After passing the ski area at Los Penitentes, you arrive at Puente del Inca (2,950 meters/9,680 feet). Legend has it that long before the Spaniards arrived, an Inca chief traveled here to cure his paralysis in the thermal waters. Today, in addition to the thermal springs, you'll see a natural bridge of red rocks encrusted with yellow sulfur that spans the Río Cuevas; what's left of a spa hotel, built in the 1920s and destroyed in a 1965 flood, is covered in copper and gold sediment below the bridge. A few miles farther west, past the Argentine customs check, are the entrance to the park and the ranger's cabin. Fifteen km (9 miles) farther along, the highway passes Las Cuevas, a settlement where the road forks right to Chile or left to the statue of Cristo Redentor (Christ the Redeemer), commemorating the 1902 peace pact between the two countries.

HIKING GUIDES AND LOGISTICS

November through March, you can sign on for two- or three-day guided treks to the Plaza de Mulas base camp at 4,260 meters (13,976 feet), where there's a *refugio* (cabin with bunk beds).

Guides will often take care of the necessary paperwork *(Hiking and Mountaineering in Uspallata)*; otherwise, you can purchase a permit at the **Parque San Martín Visitor's Center** in Mendoza City (*Las Tipas at Los Robles, Weekdays 8–6, weekends 9–1*). Trekking permits cost upward of 2,000 pesos, depending on the season, level, and number of days; ascent permits cost upwards of 12,000 pesos. Day permits, available at the entrance to Aconcagua Park, cost about 40 pesos.

INTO CHILE

Some tour groups and independent travelers continue on through to Chile to explore the vintages there. Visas, required of U.S. citizens, can be obtained at the border.

Updated
by Amanda
Barnes

Exceptional wine, top-quality cuisine, exhilarating outdoor activities, and the skyscraping Andes framing almost every view: it's easy to see why people come here, and why many stay longer than they'd planned. In the center of Argentina, this region is often referred to as the Cuyo; and the name—passed down from the early indigenous Huarpe people, who called it Cuyum Mapu (Land of Sand)—is a reminder that the terrain is naturally semi-arid.

It is only because of carefully managed snowmelt from the mountains that the provinces are so green and, through irrigation, able to produce more than 90% of the country's wine. *Acéquias* (canals) built by the Huarpes and improved on by the conquering Incas and Spaniards, as well as by modern engineers, continue to capture the flow of the region's great rivers and channel it along the shady streets of the major cities: Mendoza, San Juan, and San Rafael.

Jesuit missionaries crossed the Andes from Chile to plant the first grape vines in 1556. Today more than 200,000 hectares (494,200 acres) of vineyards bask in the sun from the hills of San Juan down to the suburbs of Mendoza City and farther south through the Valle de Uco to San Rafael. The grapes are protected from the humid winds of the Pacific by the Andes, and grow at altitudes between 609 and 2,000 meters (2,000 to 6,500 feet), where they ripen slowly during long, hot summer days, while cool nights maintain acidity for long-lasting taste. Indeed, many vineyards could be classified as organic, as chemicals are seldom used or needed, and vintages are consistent.

Many bodegas offer tours and tastings; some also have atmospheric restaurants that pair fine wine with inspired food. But beyond the wineries, active adventures await. With more than 320 days of annual sunshine, this region is a four-season destination for outdoor enthusiasts. Ski resorts like Las Leñas attract snow bunnies in winter, and Aconcagua, the highest peak outside of the Himalayas, lures ambitious hikers and climbers in summer. At lower altitudes, there are less dizzying activities for all ages year-round, including horseback riding, whitewater rafting, and soaking in thermal baths.

PLANNING

WHEN TO GO

The wine harvest ends in autumn and is celebrated with festivities that culminate in the *vendimia* (wine festival). In Mendoza this takes place during the last days of February and first week of March. A parade circles the Plaza Independencia and ends in San Martín Park with a grand finale of music, dancing, and religious ceremonies to ensure a good harvest. People shop and graze at food stands in the parks and plazas.

Winter is time for pruning and tying vines. Ski season begins in mid-June (depending on the year). July, the month with the best weather, is most favored by Argentineans and Brazilians. August usually has plenty of snow, and September offers spring conditions. Weather in the Andes is unpredictable, though; pack clothes for all conditions, and get up-to-date reports from ski areas. Springtime in the Valle de Uco brings trees covered in pink and white blossoms and new life in the vineyards. The snowcapped Andes form a spectacular backdrop, so bring your wide-angle lens.

GETTING HERE AND AROUND

There are direct flights from Buenos Aires to Mendoza (about two hours) and Santiago in Chile (45 minutes). Flights to nearby cities San Juan and San Rafael are routed through Buenos Aires, making them easier to reach by road. Comfortable buses between the three major cities are cheap, and bus stations are centrally located. On arrival, you'll find that all three cities have car-rental agencies and *remises* (hired cars with drivers), as well as wine-oriented tour companies that will take care of local transportation for you.

Hiring a remis for a full- or half day is a good use of money, as frequent detours, road construction or washed-out roads, and misleading (or nonexistent) signs can make driving yourself frustrating. Further, finding wineries on your own requires not only a good map (most are off the GPS grid) but also a working knowledge of Spanish. That said, if you have the time and the temperament for it, exploring on your own—stopping to snap photos and chat with locals—has its rewards. Driving to Andean villages and the border with Chile is a particularly remarkable experience.

If you are using Mendoza City as a base for independent winery visits, just bear in mind that Maipú is about a 30-minute drive away; reaching Luján de Cuyo by car takes 45 minutes and the Valle de Uco can take upward of an hour. In San Rafael, you can reach many wineries by bike. In San Juan, some are within cycling distance, while others are on quiet, pretty roads that are best accessed by car; driving onward from San Rafael is also a practical solution if you're combining wine tours with a ski vacation in Las Leñas.

6

RESTAURANTS

Most of the region follows national culinary trends—think beef, lamb, chicken, and pork *a la parrilla* (grilled). Malargüe, southwest of San Rafael, famously adds *chivito* (goat) to the mix—whether cooked à la parrilla or *al asador* (skewered on a metal cross stuck in the ground aslant a bed of hot coals). But you don't have to be a carnivore to eat well; after all, more than grapes grow in this part of Argentina. The vineyards are matched by olive groves, vegetable fields, and fruit orchards, which provide local chefs with an abundance of fresh ingredients. You'll taste them in the side dishes served at old-school *asados* (barbecues); in the hearty Spanish-style stews and casseroles that are an edible connection to the region's past; and in the innovative gourmet fare prepared at next-generation winery restaurants.

> **TIP**
>
> Inflation in Argentina is a part of day-to-day life, with annual inflation up to 30% in recent years. Pricing is therefore inconsistent month to month so be sure to check your hotel's website before you travel. Some businesses will quote prices in U.S. dollars (especially hotels) in order to offer some consistency to customers.

HOTELS

Like the altitude, the types of accommodations available here vary widely, so tourist offices can recommend all kinds of lodgings. As you'd expect, Mendoza City has the largest selection, with options including basic hostels, practical "apart-hotels" (furnished units with kitchen facilities), stylish boutique hotels, plus a healthy handful of luxury properties. In the countryside, you'll find everything from traditional *estancias* (ranches) that offer horseback riding and other outdoorsy activities to rustic *cabañas* (cabins), homey *residenciales* (bed-and-breakfasts), and modern ski lodges—all of which are generally well maintained and well priced. Vacationing hedonists can also choose between several posh resorts and *posadas* (country inns), where the on-site amenities include top-notch restaurants, extensive wine cellars, and soothing spas. *Hotel reviews have been shortened. For full information, visit Fodors.com.*

WHAT IT COSTS IN PESOS			
	$	$$	$$$	$$$$
Restaurants	Under 300 pesos	300–500 pesos	501–750 pesos	over 750 pesos
Hotels	Under 1,500 pesos	1,500–2,000 pesos	2,001–3,000 pesos	over 3,000 pesos

Restaurant prices are the average cost of a main course at dinner or, if dinner is not served, at lunch. Hotel prices are the lowest cost of a standard double room in high season.

WINE TOURS

Most wineries require reservations, so it's easiest to arrange visits through your hotel or a local tour operator. Organized tours are particularly good if there isn't a specific bodega you wish to see or if you're traveling alone and/or during busy periods like the harvest. Most last a full day and include transportation from city hotels. If you do head out yourself, remember that many wineries charge for tastings (often redeemable against wine purchases); be sure to ask about fees when making your reservation.

ORGANIZED TOURS

Ampora. This well-established outfit runs full-day group tours (maximum eight people) to Luján de Cuyo and the Valle de Uco. Ampora also has a private wine bar for tastings. ✉ *Sarmiento 647, Mendoza* ☎ *261/429–2931* ⊕ *www.mendozawinetours.com* ✉ *From $185.*

Aventura and Wine (Bacchus Tours). Over the last 10 years this company has been creating private tours for individuals and groups. ☎ *261/420–4230 in Mendoza* ⊕ *www.aventurawine.com* ✉ *From $195.*

Aymará Turismo. In business for more than 20 years, Aymará offers a variety of tours—the most popular of which includes two Maipú wineries and an olive oil producer. Prices are cheap but groups are large. ☎ *261/420–2064 in Mendoza* ⊕ *www.aymaramendoza.com.ar* ✉ *From $25.*

Malbec Symphony. Directed by a sommelier, this agency offers tours in Mendoza and the San Juan region. Each itinerary is custom-made, so you can take a more thematic approach (like organic wine tastings) if you'd like. ☎ *261/429–3696* ⊕ *www.malbecsymphony.com* ✉ *From $180.*

Mendoza Viajes. This big agency offers all sorts of excursions (usually in large groups and in Spanish); wine-themed options include half- or full-day tours. Prices are reasonable, but the service is less personal. ☎ *261/524–4904* ⊕ *www.mendozaviajes.com* ✉ *From $50.*

Mendoza Wine Camp. This company has full- or multiday tours to Luján de Cuyo and Valle de Uco in small private groups. ☎ *261/343–9929* ⊕ *www.mendozawinecamp.com* ✉ *From $195.*

Trout & Wine Tours. Owned by a cheery Irish expat, one of the longest-running, high-end operators in Mendoza offers full-day group tours (eight people maximum) to Luján de Cuyo and the Valle de Uco. Fly-fishing tours are available, too. ☎ *261/425–5613, 261/15–541–3892 cell phone* ⊕ *www.troutandwine.com* ✉ *From $185.*

Uncorking Argentina. This custom-package creator will book the wineries and driver for you. Most clients opt to visit the Valle de Uco or Luján de Cuyo, but the choice is yours. ☎ *261/429–6955 in Mendoza* ⊕ *www. uncorkingargentina.com* ✉ *From $140.*

SELF-GUIDED TOURS

Each area has its own unique *caminos del vino* (wine routes), and the Caminos del Vino de Argentina's Spanish-language website is a valuable trip planning tool (⊕ *www.caminosdelvino.org.ar*). Wineries in San Juan Province have pooled their resources to print a booklet, *Ruta del Vino,* with maps, photos, and information in Spanish. In Mendoza Province, you can pick up the free WINEMAP at bookstores and wineries; it consists of four maps and a guidebook in Spanish. DIY types based in Mendoza City can also take advantage of the convenient, cost-effective Vitivinicola bus service.

Bus Vitivinicola. Mendoza's hop on–hop off Vitivinicola bus is an affordable way to reach area wineries without your own transportation. Tuesday through Saturday, the comfy, air-conditioned vehicle picks up passengers at various points in the city and then starts its run to select venues. ■TIP➜ Because you'll be going without a guide, you'll need to make your own advance reservations for the wineries you wish to visit and pay your own way at each once you arrive. Bus tickets can be purchased online or on-board; they're also sold at visitor information centers and participating hotels. ⊕ *www.busvitivinicola.com* ✉ *Full-day ticket $15.*

GRAN MENDOZA

Mendoza Province, its eponymous capital, and the capital's departments are home to about 1,880,000 people, roughly 130,000 of whom live in Mendoza City. Most of the major vineyards and bodegas are in departments south of the city (such as Maipú and Luján de Cuyo) and farther south across the Río Mendoza, in the regions of Agrelo and Perdriel. Still more vineyards are farther south in the Valle de Uco. Each department has its own commercial areas, with shopping centers, hotels, and restaurants.

MENDOZA CITY

1,060 km (659 miles) southwest of Buenos Aires; 250 km (155 miles) east of Santiago, Chile.

Mendoza's streets are shaded from the summer sun by a canopy of poplars, elms, and sycamores. Water runs along its sidewalks in acéquias, disappears at intersections, then bursts from fountains in the city's 74 parks and squares. Many acéquias were built by the Huarpe Indians and improved upon by the Incas long before the city was founded in 1561 by Pedro del Castillo.

Thanks to the booming wine and tourism industries, Mendoza bustles with innovative restaurants and lodgings that range from slick high-rises with conference rooms for serious wine tasting to low-key inns and B&Bs for serious relaxing. Low-rise colonial buildings with their lofty ceilings, narrow doorways, and tile floors house restaurants and shops. In the afternoon shops close, streets empty, and siesta-time rules—until around 5, when the city comes back to life and goes back to work. Don't expect much to be open on a Sunday either.

GETTING HERE AND AROUND

Mendoza's Aeropuerto Internacional Francisco Gabrielli is 6 km (4 miles) north of town on Ruta Nacional 40. Flights from Buenos Aires operated by Aerolíneas Argentinas (⊕ *www.aerolineas.com.ar*) and LATAM (⊕ *www.latam.com*) take about two hours; flights from Santiago, Chile, operated by LATAM (⊕ *www.lan.com*) and Sky Airline (⊕ *www.skyairline.com*) take 45 minutes. Bus Terminal del Sol is on the outskirts of the city, about a 10-minute drive from downtown. From here buses provide daily service to San Juan (3 hours), Buenos Aires (14 hours), Santiago (8 hours), and other destinations. Never cut it close on timing when it comes to bus connections. If the bus company says a trip will take 10 hours, it may, unfortunately, take 12 or 13. So leave a decent amount of time for extenuating circumstances—especially if you're crossing the Chilean border and have to account for customs queues.

Driving from Buenos Aires (on lonely but paved Ruta Nacional 7, aka the Panamerican Highway) or Santiago (again, on Ruta Nacional 7, which is sometimes closed along this stretch in winter) is an option, provided you have plenty of time and speak some Spanish. There's little need for a car in town, and it can be hard to find wineries in outlying areas on your own—even when you *do* speak Spanish. Furthermore, mendocinos are known for their cavalier attitude toward traffic rules. Pay attention to weather and road information. If you fear getting lost or breaking down in remote areas, hire a remis or arrange a tour. ■TIP→ Downtown streets have ankle-breaking holes, steps, and unexpected obstacles, so watch where you're going.

Bus Contacts Andesmar. ☎ 261/405-0600, 0810/122-1122 ⊕ www.andesmar.com. **CATA Internacional.** ☎ 0800/222-2282 ⊕ www.catainternacional.com. **Chevallier.** ☎ 261/431-0235, 11/4000-5255 ⊕ www.nuevachevallier.com. **El Rápido.** ☎ 261/405-4344 ⊕ www.elrapidoint.com.ar. **Terminal de Ómnibus.** ✉ Av. Gobernador Videla at Av. Acceso Oeste, Mendoza ☎ 261/431-5000.

Car Rentals Avis. ✉ Primitivo de la Reta 914, Mendoza ☎ 261/420-3178 ⊕ www.avis.com.ar. **Hertz.** ✉ Espejo 391, Mendoza ☎ 261/423-0225 ⊕ www.hertz.com. **Localiza.** ✉ Primitivo de la Reta 936, Mendoza ☎ 261/429-6800 ⊕ www.localiza.com.

Taxi Contacts La Veloz del Este. ✉ Alem 439, Mendoza ☎ 261/429-9999.

ESSENTIALS

Visitor Information Mendoza Tourist Board. ✉ Av. San Martín 1143, at Garibaldi, Mendoza ☎ 261/420-1333 ⊕ www.turismo.mendoza.gov.ar.

EXPLORING

After a devastating earthquake in 1861, Mendoza was reconstructed on a grid, making it easy to explore on foot. Four small squares (Chile, San Martín, Italia, and España) radiate from the four corners of Plaza Independencia, the main square. Their Spanish tiles, exuberant fountains, shaded walkways, and myriad trees and flowers lend peace and beauty. Avenida San Martín, the town's major thoroughfare, runs north–south out into the southern departments and wine districts. Calle Sarmiento intersects San Martín at the tourist office and becomes a *peatonal* (pedestrian road) with cafés, shops, offices, and bars. It crosses the Plaza Independencia, stops in front of the Park Hyatt, then continues on the other side of the hotel to a busy restaurant strip.

TOP ATTRACTIONS

Parque General San Martín. Dating back to 1896, this 971-acre park has more than 50,000 trees from all over the world. Fifteen km (9 miles) of paths meander through it. You can stop and smell the roses (a dedicated garden contains hundreds of varieties), observe aquatic competitions from the rowing club's balcony restaurant, or set the kids free on the numerous playgrounds. Scenes of the 1817 Andes crossing by José de San Martín and his army during the campaign to liberate Argentina

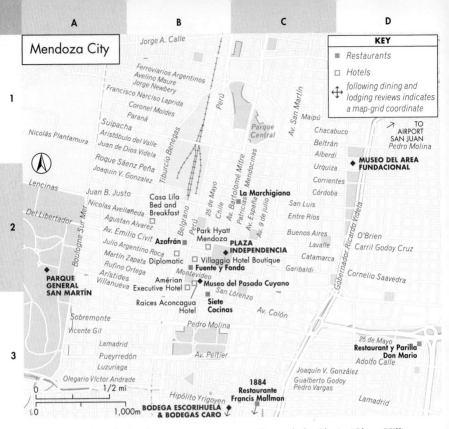

Mendoza City

KEY

■ Restaurants

□ Hotels

✛ following dining and lodging reviews indicates a map-grid coordinate

Jorge A. Calle

Ferroviarios Argentinos

Avelino Maure

Jorge Newbery

Francisco Narciso Laprida

Coronel Moldes

Paraná

Suipacha

Aristóbulo del Valle

Juan de Dios Videla

Roque Sáenz Peña

Joaquín V. Gonzalez

Nicolás Plantamura

Lencinas

Juan B. Justo

Nicolas Avellaneda

Agustan Alvarez

Av. Emilio Civit

Julio Argentino Roca

Martín Zapata

Rufino Ortega

Arístides Villanueva

Del Libertador

Boulogne Sur Mer

Perú

Tiburcio Benegas

Belgrano

25 de Mayo

Chile

Av. Bartolomé Mitre

Patricias Mendocinas

Av. España

Av. 9 de Julio

Av. San Martín

Maipú

Parque Central

Chacabuco

Beltrán

Alberdi

Urquiza

Corrientes

Córdoba

San Luis

Entre Ríos

Buenos Aires

Lavalle

Catamarca

Garibaldi

La Marchigiana

O'Brien

Carril Godoy Cruz

Cornelio Saavedra

Gobernador Ricardo Videla

TO AIRPORT
SAN JUAN
Pedro Molina

◆ MUSEO DEL AREA FUNDACIONAL

Casa Lila Bed and Breakfast

Park Hyatt Mendoza

Azafrán

PLAZA INDEPENDENCIA

Diplomatic

Villaggio Hotel Boutique

Fuente y Fonda

Amérian Executive Hotel

Museo del Pasado Cuyano

Montevideo

San Lórenzo

Raices Aconcagua Hotel

Siete Cocinas

Av. Colón

◆ PARQUE GENERAL SAN MARTÍN

Sobremonte

Vicente Gil

Pedro Molina

Lamadrid

Pueyrredón

Luzuriaga

Av. Peltier

Olegario Víctor Andrade

Hipólito Yrigoyen

1884 Restaurante Francis Mallman

Joaquín V. González

Gualberto Godoy

Pedro Vargas

25 de Mayo

Restaurant y Parilla Don Mario

Adolfo Calle

Lamadrid

0 ——— 1/2 mi

0 ——— 1,000m

BODEGA ESCORIHUELA & BODEGAS CARO

are depicted on a monument atop Cerro de la Gloria (Glory Hill), a steep 20-minute walk up from the park's center. The stadium here (built for the 1978 World Cup, which Argentina won) hosts popular soccer matches; the amphitheater (capacity 22,500) fills to the brim during Vendimia, the annual wine-harvest festival; and there are markets and open aerobics classes on the weekend. ⊠ *Mendoza.*

Plaza Independencia. In Mendoza's main square you can sit on a bench in the shade of a sycamore tree and watch children playing in the fountains, browse the stands at the daily artisan fair, or stroll past the historic Plaza Hotel (now the Park Hyatt) on your way to the shops and outdoor cafés on pedestrian-only Calle Sarmiento, which bisects the square. ⊠ *Mendoza.*

NEED A BREAK

Bonafide. Caffeine fans can get their espresso fix at Bonafide. The Bonafide brand was the first to bring a coffee roasting machine to Argentina in 1917, and it now has locations city-wide. On the corner of Sarmiento and 9 de Julio near the central plaza, enjoy a steaming cup of joe with *medialunas* (sweet croissants) and *alfajores* (cookies with *dulce de leche,* sweet carmelized milk). ⊠ *Peatonal Sarmiento 102, Mendoza* ☎ *261/423-7915* ⊕ *www.bonafide.com.ar.*

WORTH NOTING

Fodor'sChoice ★ **Bodega Escorihuela & Bodegas Caro.** The closest winery to the city—and one of the oldest working wineries in the province—is the historical Bodega Escorihuela, founded in 1884 and now home to two producers: Escorihuela Gascon and Bodegas Caro. Located in Godoy Cruz (a 15-minute cab ride from Mendoza center), you can visit both in an afternoon. Escorihuela Gascon produces a range of bubbles and still wines and includes a peek at Mendoza's largest barrel (it can hold 63,000 liters). Bodegas Caro is a small enterprise between the Catena family from Mendoza and the Rothschild family who own Chateau Lafite Rothschild in Bordeaux. Come in the evening and you might catch tango at Bodegas Caro or pop in for a wine tasting before dinner at Francis Mallmann's restaurant next door. ⊠ *Belgrano 1188, Godoy Cruz* ☎ *261/424–2744 Escorihuela, 261/453–0963 Caro* ⊕ *www.escorihuelagascon.com.ar* ☉ *Closed weekends.*

Museo del Area Fundacional. On the site of the original *cabildo* (town hall), the Foundation Museum explains the region's social and historical development. Of note is the display of a mummified child found on Aconcagua, with photos of his burial treasures. Excavations, made visible by a glass-covered viewing area, reveal layers of pre-Hispanic and Spanish remains. ⊠ *Beltrán and Videla Castillo, Mendoza* ☎ *261/425–6927* 🖾 *60 pesos* ☉ *Closed weekends.*

Museo del Pasado Cuyano. Home of former governor and senator Emilio Civit, this 26-bedroom 1873 mansion was the gathering place of the Belle Epoque elite. Today it's the Museum of the Cuyo's Past with paintings, antiques, history books, and artifacts from Argentina's War of Independence on display. ⊠ *Montevideo 544, Mendoza* ☎ *261/423–6031* 🖾 *Donations accepted.*

NEED A BREAK

Heladerias. Mendoza has no shortage of *heladerias* (ice cream shops) ranging from artisan producers to national chains. It's a favorite pastime of locals to sit down to a few scoops, at any time of the day or night. Try local flavors, including wine ice creams, at Soppelsa (on Belgrano and Civit), Perin (on Sarmiento and Belgrano), Michel (on Belgrano and Montevideo), and Bianco & Nero (on Aristides and Belgrano). ⊠ *Mendoza.*

WHERE TO EAT

$$$ MODERN ARGENTINE ✕ **Azafrán.** This character-filled spot is more than just a restaurant: grocery shelves are stocked with local olive oils, smoked meats, and home-made jams, and more than 80 wineries are represented in the wine shop, where an old press has been converted into a tasting table. Offering a welcome break from *parrilla* fare, the food is fresh, nicely presented, and gives traditional Argentine ingredients a creative twist. **Known for:** creative Argentine cuisine; colorful decor; charcuterie. ⑤ *Average main: 400 pesos* ⊠ *Sarmiento 768, Mendoza* ☎ *261/429–4200* ⊕ *www.azafranresto.com* ✛ *B2.*

$$$$ MODERN ARGENTINE ✕ **1884 Restaurante Francis Mallman.** One of the better known eateries in Mendoza, Francis Mallmann's joint promises good service, handsome surroundings, and tasty fare straight from the flame. The price is steep for Mendoza but if you like fire-cooking and fine wines in a classy

surrounding, this is the spot. **Known for:** steak bigger than your plate; smart presentation; 600-bottle-strong wine list. ⑤ *Average main: 500 pesos* ✉ *Belgrano 1188, Godoy Cruz* ☎ *261/424–2698* ⊕ *1884restaurante.com.ar* ☾ *No lunch* ✛ *C3*.

$$
ARGENTINE
FAMILY
✕ **Fuente y Fonda.** Priding itself on cooking dishes like grandma would, Fuente y Fonda offers hearty Argentine fare designed to be shared in big groups with hands clambering over the table. Expect deep dishes filled with stuffed canneloni, cheese and ham-topped milanesas, or roast meats. **Known for:** big portions; great milanesas; lively family atmosphere. ⑤ *Average main: 280 pesos* ✉ *Montevideo 675, Mendoza* ☎ *261/429–8833* ⊕ *fuenteyfonda.com* ✛ *B2*.

$$$
ITALIAN
FAMILY
✕ **La Marchigiana.** They've been serving homemade pasta at La Marchigiana since 1950, and many of the recipes were passed down from founder Nonna Fernanda; today her descendants carry on the tradition in the kitchen. The original venue burned down in 2006, but a modern version with underground parking is just as popular with Mendocinos looking for a reasonably priced meal (and a great lasagna). **Known for:** Italian; homemade pasta; suited and booted waiters. ⑤ *Average main: 300 pesos* ✉ *Patricias Mendocinas 1550, Mendoza* ☎ *261/423–0751* ⊕ *www.marchigiana.com.ar* ✛ *C2*.

$$$
ARGENTINE
FAMILY
✕ **Restaurant y Parilla Don Mario.** Mendocinos have been coming here for years to get their basic beef fix—*bife de lomo* and *bife de chorizo* are grilled to perfection at this comfortable country-style restaurant. Pastas, grilled vegetables, and salads are also on the menu. **Known for:** carnivore's menu; old-school service; a Mendoza institution. ⑤ *Average main: 320 pesos* ✉ *25 de Mayo 1324, Guaymallén* ☎ *261/431–4838* ✛ *D3*.

$$$$
MODERN
ARGENTINE
Fodor'sChoice
★
✕ **Siete Cocinas.** One of the best restaurants in Mendoza, located in a beautiful old house in the city center, Siete Cocinas prepares a modern tasting menu inspired by the country's seven different food regions. Chef Pablo del Rio's menu is slightly more daring than most in Mendoza, so you can order interesting cuts and meats (like brains and wild boar) in addition to tasty river fish and enormous steaks. **Known for:** innovative regional cuisine; lively wine bar; tasting menu. ⑤ *Average main: 400 pesos* ✉ *Av. Bartolomé Mitre, 794, Mendoza* ☎ *261/423–8823* ⊕ *www.sietecocinas.com.ar* ☾ *Closed Sun.* ✛ *B3*.

WHERE TO STAY

$$
HOTEL
⛻ **Amerian Executive Hotel.** The tall, elegant tower of this downtown hotel looks out on the Plaza Italia, and the rooftop pool gives you a view over the city center. **Pros:** good value in city center; rooftop pool; helpful concierge. **Cons:** windowless bar-restaurant; rooms need a refurb; breakfast buffet disappointing. ⑤ *Rooms from: 2400 pesos* ✉ *San Lorenzo 660, Mendoza* ☎ *261/524–5000* ⊕ *www.amerian.com* ⇥ *74 rooms* ⦿❘ *Breakfast* ✛ *B3*.

$$
B&B/INN
⛻ **Casa Lila Bed and Breakfast.** With only four rooms, this handsome bed-and-breakfast guarantees personalized service within walking distance of the city center, lots of restaurants, and Parque General San Martin. **Pros:** charming, quiet home base; spacious en suite bathrooms; complimentary bikes. **Cons:** meals on request, but no on-site restaurant; not for pet shy (friendly dogs live here); close quarters. ⑤ *Rooms from:*

Difficult choices at Mendoza City's Mercado Central

2600 pesos ✉ Nicolás Avellaneda 262, Mendoza ☎ 261/429–6349 ⊕ www.casalila.com.ar ➾ 4 rooms ❖ Breakfast ✛ B2.

$$
HOTEL
🏨 **Diplomatic.** One of the city center's larger top-end hotels, the Diplomatic often hosts conferences and football teams that each take advantage of the central location, modern facilities, and various event spaces. **Pros:** good location with parking; good amenities; large rooms. **Cons:** not the five stars it claims to be; small swimming pool gets crowded; needs some TLC. $ *Rooms from: 3500 pesos* ✉ *Belgrano 1041, Mendoza* ☎ *261/405–1900, 0810/122–5000 reservations* ⊕ *www.diplomatichotel.com.ar* ➾ *156 rooms* ❖ *Breakfast* ✛ *B2.*

$$
HOTEL
🏨 **Park Hyatt Mendoza.** The Hyatt has preserved the landmark Plaza Hotel's 19th-century Spanish colonial facade: a grand pillared entrance and a wide veranda that extends to either side of the street. **Pros:** ideal location; staff accustomed to accommodating foreign guests; comfortable rooms. **Cons:** small pool with street noise; rooms look onto public areas; impersonal service. $ *Rooms from: 3600 pesos* ✉ *Calle Chile 1124, Mendoza* ☎ *261/441–1234* ⊕ *www.mendoza.park.hyatt.com* ➾ *186 rooms* ❖ *Breakfast* ✛ *B2.*

$
HOTEL
🏨 **Raices Aconcagua Hotel.** Classic gray granite creates a businesslike atmosphere in the lobby of this popular city center hotel. **Pros:** central location; nice suites on top floor; cheap option. **Cons:** public areas are often crowded; rooms could do with an update; basic breakfast. $ *Rooms from: 1400 pesos* ✉ *San Lorenzo 545, Mendoza* ☎ *261/520–0500* ⊕ *www.raicesaconcagua.com* ➾ *150 rooms* ❖ *Breakfast* ✛ *B2.*

$$
HOTEL
🏨 **Villaggio Hotel Boutique.** If you want to stay right in the city but prefer to sidestep the big hotel chains, Villaggio is just one block from the main plaza with attractive guest rooms and two self-catering apartments.

Pros: central location; free Wi-Fi; spa with sauna and Jacuzzi. Cons: needs some TLC; some rooms have views of air shaft; street noise in some rooms. ⑤ *Rooms from: 2200 pesos* ✉ *25 de Mayo 1010, Mendoza* ☎ *261/524–5200* ⊕ *www. hotelvillaggio.com* 🛏 *26 rooms, 2 apartments* 🍽 *Breakfast* ✛ *B2.*

> ### TIP
>
> A change in regulation pushed the nightclubs out of Mendoza's city center. If you want to dance, you'll find the nightclub strip just beyond Chacras on the Panamericana between Guardia Vieja and Gdor. Ortiz crossroads. Doors don't usually open until after midnight.

NIGHTLIFE

BARS AND PUBS

Avenida Arístedes Villanueva. Full of bars, cafés, microbreweries, and restaurants, this avenida begins to wake up around 9 pm (don't even bother going any earlier). As the evening progresses, crowds get bigger, and the music—rock, tango, salsa—gets louder. Action peaks at midnight. ✉ *Mendoza.*

Believe Irish Pub. Every town has one, and Mendoza's Irish bar has been a popular spot for locals and expats since 2005. Expect typical pub grub and beer served till late. ✉ *Av. Colon 241, Mendoza* ☎ *261/429–5567.*

El Mercadito. A pretty bar with a nice patio on busy Arístides Street, El Mercadito plays good music and even serves a decent salad. ✉ *Arístides Villanueva 521, Mendoza* ☎ *261/463–8847* 🕙 *Closed Sun.*

Juan B Justo. Locals are calling Juan B Justo street the "new Aristides" and, only six streets up, it certainly shares a similar vibe. While Aristides is busier, Juan B Justo street has a growing number of (more affordable) pubs, bars, and its own handful of microbreweries. ✉ *Mendoza.*

CASINOS

Regency Casino. Inside the Park Hyatt, this casino has blackjack, stud poker, roulette tables, slot machines, and a bar. ✉ *25 de Mayo and Sarmiento, Mendoza* ☎ *261/441–1234.*

SHOPPING

Pick up leather goods, shoes, and clothing along Sarmiento and its cross streets, or on Avenida Las Heras, where you'll find regional products to eat, drink, wear, or decorate your house with. On summer evenings and weekends Plaza Independencia becomes an artisan market, with stands selling jewelry, handmade sweaters, ponchos, mate gourds, olive oil, and other regional wares.

CLOTHES AND ACCESSORIES

La Matera. Mendocinos shop at La Matera for boots, vests, belts, scarves, and riding gear. ✉ *Villanueva 314, Mendoza* ☎ *261/425–3332.*

FOOD AND WINE

Juan Cedrón. Before your picnic, grab a bottle of Malbec at Juan Cedrón. The store also stocks many older vintages of wine worth collecting (or drinking!). ✉ *Sarmiento 278, Mendoza* ☎ *261/423–9450.*

La Casa del Vino. There's a huge selection of affordable wine and olive oil at La Casa del Vino. ✉ *Aristedes Villanueva 160, Mendoza* ☎ *261/423–5862* 🕙 *Closed siesta (1:30–5 pm).*

Sol y Vino. This spot has a great stock of wines and gourmet food. Handicrafts and other local items are sold as well. ✉ *Sarmiento 664, Mendoza* ☎ *261/425–6005* ⊕ *www.solyvinomendoza.com.*

Fodor'sChoice
★
Wine O'Clock. A wine bar and shop, Wine O'Clock has pretty gardens where you can enjoy wine by the glass or bottle and then take a few home with you. ✉ *Espejo 533, Mendoza* ☎ *261/423–1573.*

MALLS

La Barraca Mall. A 10-minute drive from Mendoza City, La Barraca has lots of local brands, a children's playground, restaurants, and a pharmacy. ✉ *Las Cañas 1833, Dorrego, Guaymallén* ☎ *261/459–8019* ⊕ *labarracamall.com.*

Mendoza Plaza Shopping Center. This mall in Guaymallén, 10 minutes from Mendoza, has more than 160 stores, including an American-style department store, cafés and restaurants, a movie theater, bowling, and an indoor amusement park. ✉ *Lateral Accesso Este 3280, Guaymallén* ☎ *261/449–0100* ⊕ *www.mendozaplazashopping.com.*

Palmares Open Mall. A 15-minute drive south of Mendoza, the Palmares Open Mall has 120 stores, lots of restaurant options, and 10 movie theaters (including one in 3-D). ✉ *Panamericano 2650, Godoy Cruz* ☎ *261/413–9100* ⊕ *www.palmares.com.ar.*

MARKET

Mercado Central. For more than 120 years the Mercado Central has been selling local foods from stalls including butchers, cheese shops, grocers, and a couple of restaurants for a quick bite on the go. ✉ *Av. Las Heras and Patricias Mendocinas, Mendoza.*

SPORTS AND THE OUTDOORS

The high peaks of the Andes provide a natural playground, with miles of trails to hike, bike, or ride on horseback. Rivers invite rafters and kayakers to test the water in the spring. Some of the wildest and most remote mountain areas are made accessible by the Ruta Nacional 7, which crosses the Andes right by Parque Provincial Aconcagua.

HORSEBACK RIDING

Cabalgata (horseback riding) is an enjoyable and natural way to explore the mountains west of Mendoza. You can ride to the foot of Aconcagua or Tupungato, or follow the hoofprints of General San Martín on a multiday trip over the Andes.

Trekking Travel. Offering everything from one-day excursions to eight-day trips that take you across the Andes, this outfitter can accommodate beginner and expert riders alike. ☎ *261/421–0450* ⊕ *www.horseriding.com.ar.*

MULTISPORT TOUR OPERATOR

Argentina Rafting. Whether you want to go rafting, kayaking, climbing, or zip-lining, this company can set you up. Let the adrenaline ease off by sinking a pint at their pool bar by the river. ☎ *262/429–6325* ⊕ *www. argentinarafting.com.*

MAIPÚ

16 km (10 miles) southeast of Mendoza City.

Lying south and slightly east of Mendoza City, Maipú—the province's oldest Wine Region—is spread over the districts of General Gutierrez, Coquimbito, and Cruz de Piedra. While not as glamorous as neighboring Luján de Cuyo, on the other side of the Acceso Sur, Maipú does have its virtues. Thirty-odd bodegas are open to tourism.

GETTING HERE AND AROUND

Acceso Sur (Ruta Nacional 40), the main highway south, is the fastest way to get to the area. Driving yourself here can be a bit of a headache, though, given Maipú's notorious road works and diversions. If you're on a tight budget, you can catch a public bus from Mendoza City, and then rent a bike to visit wineries; alternately, you come by cab (most wineries are only a 20-minute taxi ride from Mendoza City). If you want to drink, the best options are to hire a remis for a day or sign on for a wine tour.

WINERIES

Bodega la Rural. In 1855, Felipe Rutini left the hills of Italy to found a winery in the raw land of Coquimbito, Argentina. His descendants planted the first grapes (Chardonnay and Merlot) in the now-popular Tupungato District of the Valle de Uco. Today, Bodega la Rural is still family-owned and -operated. The winery's well-known San Felipe label was created by Alejandro Sirio, a famous Spanish artist. Inside the original adobe barns the Museo del Vino (Wine Museum) displays leather hoppers, antique pressing machines, vintage carriages, 100-year-old tools, and even an amazing mousetrap. ✉ *Montecaseros 2625, Coquimbito, Maipu* ☎ *261/497–2013* ⊕ *www.bodegalarural.com.ar* ☙ *Closed Sun.*

Bodegas y Viñedos López. Wines up to 60 years old are stored in the main cellar of this traditional winery, established in 1898 and still owned by the same family. Easily accessible by tram from Mendoza, this is a great budget option with free tours and a range of tastings. The upstairs restaurant serves à la carte and fixed-menu lunches, and there's also an on-site museum documenting Mendoza's winemaking history. ✉ *Ozamis 375, Maipu* ☎ *261/497–2406* ⊕ *www.bodegaslopez.com.ar.*

FAMILY **Carinae.** This boutique spot is run by a charming French couple, Philippe and Brigitte, who came to Mendoza to start a new life in wine-making. You can turn up for a tour without booking—there is always someone on hand to take you through the small facility and offer a tasting. ✉ *Videla Aranda, 2899, Cruz de Piedra* ☎ *261/499–0470* ⊕ *www.carinaevinos.com.*

FAMILY **Casa del Visitante.** The Zuccardi family set up here in 1950 and has since
Fodor's Choice expanded to the Valle de Uco, but their location in Maipú remains
★ an important base for producing their popular Santa Julia range. The extensive tourist offerings here include harvest experiences and olive oil-making sessions in season, as well as tastings, cooking classes, and dining at one of two restaurants for lunch. ✉ *RP33, Km 7.5, Maipu* ☎ *261/441–0000* ⊕ *www.casadelvisitante.com.*

Casa El Enemigo. Getting to this boutique winery might require a car, but it is one of Maipú's most celebrated, as the home winery of one

Mendoza
Wineries

Av. San Martín

CIUDAD

50

7

405

40

GODOY
CRUZ

1

LUZURIAGA

2

7

3

Montecaseros

SAN
ROQUE

LA RUNTILLA
CORRODILLA

GUTIÉRREZ

MAIPU

J.A. Ozamis

4

Canal Pescara

Urquiza Ponce

Corredor del Oeste

Av. San Martín

2

5

Alzaga

MAYOR
DRUMMOND

82

Anchorena

60

12

LUNLUNTA

6 7 →

11

40

8

10

9

12

LUJÁN
DE CUYO

Río Mendoza

Saenz Peña

87

13

14

PERDRIEL

84

15

15

Thames

16

7

79

17

18

19

Cobos

Cochabamba

15

AGRELO

20

40

UGARTECHE

21

22

86

16

23

0   5 miles

0   5 kilometers

of Argentina's top winemakers, Alejandro Vigil. There are no tours, but it is a top spot for lunch and the best place to try renowned El Enemigo wines. ⊠ *Videal Aranda 7008, Mendoza* ☎ *261/413–9178* ⊕ *www.enemigowines.com.*

Di Tomasso. A family business founded in 1869, Di Tomasso blends the old and new. Although the roof is made of mud and cane, the machinery inside is shiny and modern. There's a casual on-site restaurant, too, overlooking the vines. ⊠ *Carril Urquiza 8136, Maipu* ☎ *261/524–1829* ⊕ *www.familiaditommaso.com.*

WHERE TO EAT AND STAY

$$$
ARGENTINE
Fodor'sChoice
★

✕ **La Cayetana 1865.** Hidden between the vineyards of Maipú is this historic manor, lovingly restored as an intimate restaurant, which serves a five-course tasting menu of farm-to-table Argentine cuisine (including recipes from a 19th-century cookbook found on the property) paired with the exclusive wines of Ver Sacrum. Wine tastings, cooking classes, and live art shows are all on offer, and the limited lunchtime reservations fill up fast. **Known for:** ingredients picked from the garden; authentic Argentine cooking; delicious wines. ⑤ *Average main: 400 pesos* ⊠ *Manuel Cruz Videla 2605, Mendoza* ☎ *261/639–2757* ⊕ *www. lacayetana1865.blogspot.com.ar* ⊗ *Closed Sun., June–Aug.*

$$
HOTEL

⌂ **Club Tapiz.** Set in a 19th-century mansion surrounded by vineyards and tall trees, Club Tapiz feels like a private villa; guests can lounge in the olive-tree lined garden and gaze at the Andes from the outdoor pool or indoor Jacuzzi before sampling the estate's wines at the informal evening tasting. **Pros:** great restaurant; complimentary perks include Wi-Fi, daily wine tasting, and a visit to Bodega Tapiz (20 minutes away); charming and peaceful setting. **Cons:** close to vineyards but far from shops or town; spa is a little outdated; noise travels between rooms. ⑤ *Rooms from: 3000 pesos* ⊠ *Pedro Molina (RP60) s/n, Maipu* ☎ *261/496–3433, 261/596–6853 (whatsapp)* ⊕ *www.club-tapiz.com. ar* ⇌ *11 rooms* ⦿ *Breakfast.*

NIGHTLIFE

CASINOS

Arena Maipú Casino Resort. The huge Arena Maipú Casino Resort features more than 480 slots, 40 electronic roulette tables, five traditional roulette tables, and six card tables. An on-site stadium, cinema, and hotel—plus several bars and restaurants—make this complex popular with nongamblers, too. ⊠ *Emilio Civit y Maza, Maipu* ☎ *261/481–9800* ⊕ *www.arenamaipu.com.ar.*

DANCE CLUBS

Black Jagger. Late-night dancing and a fun crowd make for good times at the Black Jagger. It's part of the Arena Maipú Casino complex. ⊠ *Emilio Civit y Maza, Maipu* ☎ *261/481–9800* ⊕ *www.arenamaipu. com.ar/black-jagger.*

SPORTS AND THE OUTDOORS

BIKING

Many of Mendoza's back roads lead through the suburbs and vineyards into the Andean foothills and upward to mountain villages—or all the way to Chile.

Maipú Bikes. Bikers are provided with helmets, water, and a free glass of wine on your return at this popular bike rental in Maipú. ⊠ *Urquiza 5175, Maipu* ☎ *261/467–0761* ⊕ *www.maipubikes.com.*

Mr. Hugo Wineries and Bikes. Genial Mr. Hugo owns one of the longest-running bike rental spots on the Maipú wine route. He'll provide water and maps before you head out and lemonade when you return. ⊠ *Urquiza 2288, Maipu* ☎ *261/497–4067.*

LUJÁN DE CUYO

20 km (12 miles) south of Mendoza City.

Bordering both banks of the Mendoza River, Luján de Cuyo is known as the home of Malbec because it was here that the variety first started showing great potential. With more than 50 bodegas, ranging from the traditional to the ultramodern, this is one of the largest Wine Regions in Mendoza—and one of the province's best pastimes is hopping between them (you can expect to visit three or four a day), enjoying tours and tasting great vino along the way. Luján also has a smattering of luxury resorts and boutique hotels should you wish to extend your stay.

GETTING HERE AND AROUND

Some wineries are accessible by public transport (you can catch a bus to ones in Chacras de Coria or on the main San Martín road); however, the large majority—and often the cream of the crop—are best visited by car. A self-driving tour is doable, provided you carry a good map, but hiring a remis or joining a tour group is more convenient.

WINERIES

Achával Ferrer. This winery made its name on single variety Malbec but today it has expanded to a handful of other varieties as well. It's now owned by the same group as Stolichnaya vodka, and you can learn about the evolution of the company and its different single-site Malbecs in Mendoza. ⊠ *Calle Cobos 2601, Perdriel* ☎ *261/481–9205* ⊕ *www. achaval-ferrer.com.*

Bodega Catena Zapata. A faux Mayan pyramid rising from the vineyards fronts the towering Andes at this landmark winery owned by the fourth generation of the Catena family. Descend from a crystal cupola through concentric spaces to the tasting room, which is surrounded by 400 oak barrels. ⊠ *Calle J. Cobos s/n, Alto Agrelo* ☎ *261/490–0214* ⊕ *www. catenawines.com.*

Bodega Lagarde. Built in 1897, Lagarde is one of the oldest and most traditional wineries in Mendoza, and the third generation of the Pescarmona family now cultivates the grapes. At lunchtime, enjoy an *asado*-based tasting menu in the 19th-century *casona* (farm house) or order a picnic in the gardens. ⊠ *San Martín 1745, Mayor Drummond* ☎ *261/498–0011* ⊕ *www.lagarde.com.ar* ☼ *Closed Sun.*

Bodega Norton. In 1895 English engineer Sir Edmund Norton built the first winery in the valley south of the Mendoza River and much of the historical building is still intact. Today production is much larger and there's a wide portfolio. Tours with tastings and other vineyard experiences are available with advance reservations, and the stylish

Bodega Catena Zapata, Luján de Cuyo

on-site restaurant, La Vid ($$$$), welcomes lunch guests for a five-course tasting menu or à la carte dishes. ⊠ *RP15, Km 23.5, Perdriel* ☎ *261/490–9700* ⊕ *www.norton.com.ar.*

Bodegas Nieto y Senetiner S.A. White adobe walls, tile roofs, flower-bed-lined walkways, and huge shade trees welcome you to this historic bodega. Visits typically include a winery tour and either a wine tasting or a chocolate-and-wine pairing. You can also opt for a 2-km (1-mile) horseback ride to a hilltop for a view of the mountains and vineyards. Most activities finish with an *asado* lunch at the bodega. ⊠ *Guardia Vieja, between RN7 and Rosque Sáenz Peña s/n, Vistalba* ☎ *261/496–9099* ⊕ *www.nietosenetiner.com.ar.*

Bodegas Tapíz. When the Ortiz family bought this modern bodega from Kendall Jackson in 2003, CEO Patricia Ortiz and oenologist Fabián Valenzuela decided to make wines that are easier to drink and more food-friendly. Tours begin in the vineyard, followed by tank, barrel, and bottle tastings. In summer, a two-horse carriage driven by a local gaucho takes you on a learning tour of the vineyard and to visit the resident llamas. ⊠ *RP15, Km 32, Agrelo* ☎ *261/490–0202* ⊕ *www.bodega-tapiz.com.ar* � *Closed Sun.*

Carmelo Patti. Carmelo—a legendary garage winemaker—is the passionate owner of this operation. He answers the phone, greets you at the door, and personally conducts tours (in Spanish only), drawing wine from the barrel and entertaining guests with anecdotes and fascinating facts about everything from growing grapes to preserving corks. The winery may be nothing fancy, but Carmelo has a cultlike following. ⊠ *San Martín 2614* ☎ *261/498–1379.*

Chandon. The president of Moët & Chandon was so impressed by Agrelo's *terroir* (the soil, climate, and topography that contribute to making each wine unique) that he decided to build the first foreign branch of his family's company here. Today the winery is producing *vino spumante* (sparkling wine) in great quantities. Chandon is popular, so book ahead for private tours. The pretty restaurant serves a tasting menu paired exclusively with sparkling wine. ⊠ *RN40, Km 29, Agrelo* ☎ *261/490–9968* ⊕ *www.chandon.com.ar.*

Dominio del Plata. Susana Balbo—Argentina's first licensed female winemaker—has been making a name for herself since 2001, when she pioneered the making of a high-quality Torrontés. Today she and her family make reds, whites, and pinks, which you can enjoy in the tasting room or over lunch at one of the two restaurants on-site. ⊠ *Cochabamba 7801, Agrelo* ☎ *261/498–9231* ⊕ *www.susanabalbowines. com.ar* ⌂ *Reservations essential.*

Luigi Bosca. One of the oldest wine dynasties of Mendoza, the Arizú family brought vines from Spain in 1890 and continues the family legacy at this large winery, which has both a big domestic following and impressive exports. A tourist circuit takes in all the production areas of the winery and 14 beautifully carved reliefs depicting the history of wine-making in Argentina. ⊠ *San Martín 2044, Mayor Drummond* ☎ *261/498–0437* ⊕ *www.luigibosca.com.ar.*

Fodor's Choice ★ **Matervini.** This modern winery in the heart of Lujan is Santiago Achával and Roberto Cipresso's personal project. They make a series of exciting, exclusive Malbecs from different wine regions in Argentina. The high price tag (tours start at $50) reflects the exclusive pours and attentive experience. ■ TIP→ Reserve ahead. ⊠ *Cobos 2142* ☎ *261/561–6691* ⊕ *www.matervini.com* ⊘ *Closed Sun.*

Mendel Wines. This modest winery is home to one of Argentina's best-known winemakers, Roberto de la Mota, and quality, not quantity, is the mantra. Informal tours of the unassuming 80-year-old adobe building highlight the loving care grapes receive—from handpicking to hand-crushing to storage. ⊠ *Terrada 1863* ☎ *261/524–1621* ⊕ *www. mendel.com.ar.*

Pulenta Estate. Two brothers from one of the most iconic wine families in Mendoza—the Pulentas—started their own premium winery in 2002. The attractive, modern facility runs excellent tours and tastings (including one of Argentina's best Cabernet Francs) and even offers a sensory aroma class. ⊠ *RP 86, Km 6.5, Alto Agrelo* ☎ *261/15–507–6426* ⊕ *www.pulentaestate.com.*

Ruca Malén. This winery is known not just for its hearty wines but its plentiful lunch—six courses of creative cuisine by Chef Lucas Bustos are paired with predominantly red wines. Vertical tastings of different vintages and wine blending sessions are also on offer in the modern winery. ⊠ *RN7, Km 1059, Agrelo* ☎ *261/553–7164* ⊕ *www.bodegarucamalen.com.*

Séptima. Spanish wine group Codorniú constructed their Argentine winery in the *pirca* style of the Huarpe natives, by piling stones one atop the other. The end result is both practical (it helps keep the winery naturally cool) and visually arresting. A highlight is the panoramic view from the terrace over the vineyards and mountains, where you can have lunch at their restaurant. ⊠ *RN7, Km 6.5, Agrelo* ☎ *261/498–9558* ⊕ *www. bodegaseptima.com* ⚱ *Reservations essential.*

Terrazas de Los Andes. Bare brick walls, high ceilings, and a labyrinth of soaring arches shelter premium wines in stainless-steel tanks and oak barrels in this restored 1898 winery. Everything in the tasting room—from the bar to the tables to the leather chairs—is made with recycled barrels. The restaurant serves a well-paired tasting menu. ⊠ *Thames and Cochabamba, Perdriel* ☎ *261/490–9862* ⊕ *www.terrazasdelosandes.com* ☾ *Closed weekends.*

WHERE TO EAT

Most of the top restaurants in Luján de Cuyo are, in fact, in the wineries. They are rarely open for dinner, but if you have just had a large winery lunch you'll likely only want a light bite in the evening. Chacras de Coria, a small town outside of Mendoza City, is the perfect spot for a drink and bite in the evening with several casual bars, beer gardens, and restaurants around the main square.

$$$$
INTERNATIONAL
Fodor'sChoice
★

✕ **Brindillas.** Partners in life and in the kitchen, Mariano and Florencia traveled the world working in restaurants; they've brought that experience to their own intimate eatery, which offers a sophisticated tasting menu. The space may be small (it sits only 18 people), but you can expect diverse culinary creations with consistently appealing flavors and presentation. **Known for:** five- and seven-course tasting menus; quiet setting; professional service. $ *Average main: 1000 pesos* ⊠ *Guardia Vieja 2898* ☎ *261/496–3650* ⊕ *www.brindillas.com* ☾ *Closed Sun., Mon., and June.*

WHERE TO STAY

$$$$
HOTEL
Fodor'sChoice
★

▦ **Cavas Wine Lodge.** Secluded adobe guesthouses have their own plunge pool, star-gazing roof terrace (with a fireplace), living room, and walk-in shower—a romantic setting that's made this one of the top honeymoon destinations in Mendoza. **Pros:** luxurious and private; wine tastings held in the private cellar every evening; surrounded by vineyards and wineries. **Cons:** expensive; advance reservations needed for most activities; far from other restaurants. $ *Rooms from: 16,000 pesos* ⊠ *Luján de Cuyo* ⬦ *RN40 south, west on RN7, turn off onto Costa Flores just before Ruca Malen Winery. Follow signs for 2.2 km (1.4 miles)* ☎ *261/456–1748* ⊕ *www.cavaswinelodge.com* ⤏ *17 cottages* ❖ *Breakfast.*

$$$$
HOTEL

▦ **Entre Cielos.** Set in the middle of vineyards, this stunning resort has big, beautiful guest rooms with vibrant design, and suites come with private terraces looking out onto the pool, garden, and vineyards. **Pros:** the Swiss founders have impeccable taste; terrific spa; good sunset view. **Cons:** noise travels through hallways; expensive; pool can get crowded. $ *Rooms from: 9000 pesos* ⊠ *Guardia Vieja 1998, Vistalba* ☎ *261/498–3377* ⊕ *www.entrecielos.com* ⤏ *16 rooms* ❖ *Breakfast.*

$$$
HOTEL
Fodor'sChoice
★

▦ **Finca Adalgisa.** Behind tall terra-cotta walls hides one of the best-kept secrets in Chacras: a large, yet intimate estate with regal bedrooms and suites, almost 5 acres of well-kept century-old Malbec vines, a pool set in gardens, and a cozy winery restaurant reserved exclusively for guests to enjoy evening wine tastings and tapas. **Pros:** modern amenities; homemade wine and farm-to-table kitchen; close to everything in

Chacras. **Cons:** some rooms are darker than others; closed in winter; 11 am check-out. ⑤ *Rooms from: 5200 pesos* ⊠ *Finca Adalgisa, Pueyrredon 2222, Chacras de Coria* ☎ *261/496–0713* ⊕ *www.fincaadalgisa. com* ⊘ *Closed June–Sept.* ⑩ *Breakfast.*

$$
HOTEL

⊡ **Lares de Chacras.** This long-running boutique hotel in the heart of little Chacras de Coria has comfortable rooms with stone fireplaces, wood floors, and exposed beams that are at once handsome and homey. **Pros:** good value; pleasant, small-town location with wineries nearby; pool and garden on-site. **Cons:** some street noise; slow restaurant service; bathrooms are a bit dark. ⑤ *Rooms from: 3200 pesos* ⊠ *Larrea 1266, Chacras de Coria* ☎ *261/496–1061* ⊕ *www.LaresdeChacras.com* ⇨ *10 rooms* ⑩ *Breakfast.*

SPORTS AND THE OUTDOORS

Betancourt Rafting. Rafting and adventure packages include trekking, rappelling, biking, and horseback riding, and you can combine with a visit to their outdoor pool area. ☎ *261/15–559–1329, 261/15–559–1328* ⊕ *www.betancourt.com.ar.*

FAMILY

Parque de Agua. Like its sister property, Termas Cacheuta, Parque de Agua takes advantage of the area's hot springs; this spot, though, is focused on family fun rather than adult-only activities. It's a popular water park for its naturally heated water (65–102°F), wave pool, and 270-meter (886-foot) canal through a tunnel and waterfall. In addition to an on-site restaurant, the park has covered eating areas with picnic tables, and you can grill your own *bife* in the many parrillas provided. ⊠ *RP82, Km 38, 24 km (15 miles) west of Luján de Cuyo, Cacheuta* ☎ *2624/490–152* ⊕ *www.termascacheuta.com* ⊠ *370 pesos.*

Fodor'sChoice
★

Termas Cacheuta. Locals have been soaking in the natural hot springs here for centuries; these days they're joined by day-tripping tourists, who come to enjoy both the thermal waters and an attractive spa. The latter features hot and cool indoor and outdoor pools, a steamy grotto sauna, a thermal mud bath, and high-powered showers. Day passes include a huge lunch buffet, with countless salads and all the cuts of a traditional Argentine asado. Dedicated spa-goers can spend the night in one of the 16 all-inclusive rooms at Hotel Termas Cacheuta ($$$). ■TIP➜ **Unlike the Parque de Agua next door, this is a child-free zone.** ⊠ *RP82, Km 38, 24 km (15 miles) west of Luján de Cuyo, Cacheuta* ☎ *261/490–153* ⊕ *www.termascacheuta.com* ⊠ *From 800 pesos* ⊘ *Daily 10–6:30.*

USPALLATA

125 km (78 miles) west of Mendoza City.

At the crossroads of three important routes—Ruta Nacional 7 from Mendoza across the Andes, Ruta 57 from Mendoza via Villavicencio, and Ruta 39 from San Juan via Barreal—this small town lies in the Calingasta Valley between the foothills and the front range of the Andes. Although most people will use Uspallata only as a food- and gas-refill point, it's also a good base for memorable excursions into the mountains by 4X4 or on horseback. Metals have been forged at **Las Bóvedas,** the pointed adobe cupolas a few miles north of town, since

pre-Columbian times. Weapons for San Martín's army were made here, and some of them were melted down to create the Cristo Redentor monument on the Chilean border; other big Andean attractions in the vicinity include Parque Provincial Aconcagua and Puenta del Inca.

GETTING HERE AND AROUND

From Mendoza City, head south on Avenida San Martín to the Ruta Nacional 7 and turn west. You can make this 125-km (78-mile) journey in two to three hours by bus or rental car; the easiest option, though, is to visit Uspallata and nearby attractions on a guided day trip from Gran Mendoza.

SAFETY

An adventurous way to explore the dramatic landscape around Uspallata is by driving yourself. There are things to keep in mind, though, if you want to have a safe, stress-free time. Always leave town with a full tank of gas, as there are few services available, and traffic is minimal. Carry a flashlight if you leave late in the day, be mindful of weather conditions (the drive is not recommended in winter snowstorms), and always keep your lights on while driving.

EXPLORING

Cristo Redentor de los Andes. A steep, bumpy ascent off of Ruta 7 leads to a stunning view of the Andes and a large statue of Christ that was erected to mark the end of the war between Chile and Argentina. Made from melted weaponry when peace was declared in 1902, it's poised right on the border at an altitude of 4,206 meters (13,800 feet). At the top there's a food truck serving coffee and local sweet bites. The gravel path is not for the faint-hearted but can just about be done in a hired car; the drive up from the road takes half an hour. ■TIP→ Bring a jacket! ⊠ *RN7, Puente del Inca.*

Fodor's Choice **Parque Provincial Aconcagua.** Extending 66,733 hectares (164,900 acres)
★ over wild, high country, this provincial park has few trails other than those used by expeditions ascending the impressive Cerro Aconcagua (Aconcagua Mountain). You can get multiday permits for climbing it either through your tour operator or on your own at the Mendoza Tourist Board Visitor's Center in Parque San Martín; it's open weekdays 8–6 and weekends 9–1. Day permits (to visit as a tourist, not trekker) are available at the entrance to Aconcagua Park itself. ⊠ *San Martín Park Office, Las Tipas at Los Robles, Mendoza* 🖃 *Day permits 2 pesos; trekking permits 110–280 pesos, depending on season, permit level, and number of hiking days.*

Puente del Inca. Spanning the Río Cuevas, Puente del Inca is a natural rock bridge that was formed over thousands of years. The abandoned hotel below is a more recent addition, built in the 1920s to accommodate guests who came to soak in the therapeutic hot springs here. Both are now covered in bright yellow sulfur deposits, giving the surreal site an eerie appeal. An artisan market sells unusual souvenirs like healing stones and sulfur-coated bottles or shoes. ⊠ *RN7, 3 km (2 miles) east of Parque Provincial Aconcagua, Puente del Inca.*

Hikers traverse a low portion of the south face of Cerro Aconcagua.

SCENIC DRIVES AND LOOKOUTS

Camino del Año. From Mendoza traveling 47 km (29 miles) north on Ruta Provincial 52, passing through Canota, you arrive at Villavicencio, the source of mineral water sold throughout Argentina. The nearby Hosteria Villavicencio offers a simple lunch menu.

Farther up the road, the Camino del Año begins its ascent around 365 turns to El Balcón atop the pass at Cruz de Paramillo (3,000 meters/9,840 feet). Look for the ruins of a Jesuit mine, the Arucarias de Darwin (petrified trees found by Darwin in 1835), and the 1,000-year-old petroglyphs on Tunderqueral Hill. From the top of the pass you can see three of the highest mountains outside of Asia, all over 6,000 meters (20,000 feet): Aconcagua to the west, Tupungato to the south, and Mercedario to the north.

At Km 67, the road straightens and descends into Uspallata, where you can continue west on Ruta Nacional 7 to Chile or take the lonely road north on Ruta 39 (which turns into Ruta 412) onward to Barreal in San Juan Province, 108 km (67 miles) away. The road to Barreal crosses a high desert valley, where the only sign of life is an occasional ranch obscured by a grove of alamo trees.

At Los Tambillos, about 40 km (25 miles) north of Uspallata, the route is intersected by the Inca road that ran from Cusco, Peru, through Bolivia and into northern Argentina. The site is surrounded by a fence that protects traces of the original road and remains of an Inca *tambo* (resting place). A map shows the route of the Incas.

The mountains to the west get higher and more spectacular as you approach Barreal. At the San Juan Province border, the road becomes Ruta 412, and is paved the remaining 50 km (31 miles) to Barreal. ⊠ *Uspallata.*

Uspallata Pass on Ruta Nacional 7 (*Panamerican Highway*). This route heads west on R13 and then RN7 (also known as the Panamerican Highway) and takes you straight into the mountains. You'll go from vineyards to barren hills until you reach the Potrerillos Valley, then head farther west on R7 into the heart of the Andes. This was a major Inca route, so keep your eyes peeled for Inca tambos. You'll pass the Puente del Inca ancient thermal springs and the ruins of a spa from the 1920s. This is the only route between Chile and Argentina for miles and miles, so if you're self-driving be ready to share the road with cargo trucks.

WHERE TO EAT AND STAY

$ ✕ **El Rancho.** This spit-and-sawdust-style eatery has monster-size steaks,
ARGENTINE   irresistible BBQ smells, and cheap wine by the jug. If you've had a long day in the mountains and need a place to refuel, old-school El Rancho is your best bet: open daily for lunch and dinner, it also serves coffee and snacks outside of mealtimes. **Known for:** big portions; comfort food; reliable choice in the mountains. ⑤ *Average main: 160 pesos* ⊠ *RN7, Km 1147* ☎ *2624/420–134.*

$$ ✕ **La Juanita.** This colorful spot is known for its large dishes of warming
ARGENTINE   pasta, succulent local trout, and king-size milanesas. Decor is minimal
FAMILY   but service is warm, and there are splendid mountain views. **Known for:** mountain views; homemade pasta; empanadas. ⑤ *Average main: 300 pesos* ⊠ *Ruta 52 Uspallata* ☎ *261/15–653–4699* ⊕ *www.lajuanitaresto. com* ▭ *No credit cards.*

$$ ⛉ **Hotel Uspallata.** In spite of the cavernous hallways, minimal decor,
HOTEL   barren walls, and dim lighting (legacies of the Perón era, when the government built hotels for its employees), this grand old hotel offers comfortable refuge en route to Aconcagua, Chile, or Barreal in the opposite direction. **Pros:** big rooms; proximity to outdoor activities including skiing; pool and gardens. **Cons:** impersonal decor; mediocre service; past its heyday. ⑤ *Rooms from: 2300 pesos* ⊠ *RN7, Km 1149* ☎ *2624/420–003* ⊕ *www.granhoteluspallata.com.ar* ⟿ *74 rooms* ⎍⎕⎜ *Breakfast.*

$$ ⛉ **Hotel Valle Andino.** Approaching Uspallata on Ruta Nacional 7, you'll
HOTEL   see this wood-trimmed brick building with a pitched tile roof by the roadside. **Pros:** family-friendly; practical base; scenic vistas in all directions. **Cons:** rooms could use updating; facilities are spread out; basic services. ⑤ *Rooms from: 3600 pesos* ⊠ *RN7* ☎ *2624/420–095, 261/15– 597–7858* ⊕ *www.hotelvalleandino.com.ar* ⟿ *25 rooms* ⎍⎕⎜ *Breakfast.*

SPORTS AND THE OUTDOORS

HORSEBACK RIDING

FAMILY   **El Rincón de los Oscuros.** Gentle horses and experienced guides make riding at this ranch near Potrerillos a pleasure. Two-hour and full-day outings take you to high-altitude sites where condors and guanacos are often seen. ⊠ *Av. Los Cóndores s/n, 50 km (30 miles) southeast of Upsallata, Potrerillos* ☎ *261/15–653–8839* ⊕ *www.rincondelososcuros.com.ar.*

HIKING AND MOUNTAINEERING

November through March is the best time for hiking and climbing. You can arrange day hikes with area tour operators. Of the longer treks, the most popular lasts four to seven days and begins at Puente del Inca (2,950 meters/9,680 feet), where you spend a night to get acclimated, and then set out for Aconcagua's base camp. On the first day, a steady climb takes you to Confluencia, where most people spend two nights and enjoy a day hike to the south wall and its incredible glacier. The hike continues to the Plaza de Mulas (4,260 meters/13,976 feet) and ends at the base camp for climbers making a final ascent on Cerro Aconcagua.

Fernando Grajales. Guiding since 1976, Fernando Grajales is a veteran of many Aconcagua ascents. His company leads 18-day excursions to the summit in season. ☎ *261/15–658–8855 cell* ⊕ *www.grajales.net.*

Inka Expeditions. This outfit has 20 years of experience leading tours both to the base camp and to Aconcagua's summit. Other treks in the area can also be organized. ☎ *261/15–569–4668* ⊕ *www.inka.com.ar.*

SKIING

Los Penitentes. Named for the rock formations that resemble penitent monks, this medium-size ski area attracts mostly Argentines and is a popular day-trip destination for Mendocinos. Despite the elevation—2,580 meters (8,465 feet) at the base and 3,194 meters (10,479 feet) at the top—the snow here is often thin, so check weather reports before coming. The village has restaurants, medical services, a ski school, and Hotel Ayelen ($$) (which also serves as the base hotel for Aconcagua climbing expeditions).

Facilities: 700-meter (2,300-foot) vertical drop; 300 hectares (741 acres); 20% beginner, 30% intermediate, 50% advanced; two double chairs, one T-bar, five surface lifts. Cross-country ski trails.

Lessons and Programs: Ski school.

Lift Tickets: Adults from 1,000 pesos a day in high season

Rentals: Rental shops at the base area.

FAMILY **Los Puquios.** Each winter Los Puquios opens its slopes for family snow activities including skiing, sledding, and tubing. There's a host of evening activities in peak winter when flood lights, bonfires, and live music bring more action to the slopes. ✉ *Ruta 7, Puente del Inca, Puente del Inca* ☎ *261/15–688–6190* ⊕ *www.puquios.com.*

VALLE DE UCO

The Valle de Uco extends south of Mendoza along the foothills of the Cordón de Plata and the Andes, whose two highest peaks—Tupungato Volcano and El Plata—rise over 580 meters (19,000 feet) on the western horizon. Horseback riding, climbing, trekking, and simply savoring the quietude are all popular pastimes here; however, most people are drawn by the prospect of indulging in fabulous wine and fresh food while admiring up-close views of the Andes.

The Ríos Tunuyán in the north and Las Tunas in the south bring mineral-rich melted snow from the glaciers to the garlic fields, apple and cherry orchards, olive groves, and, of course, the vineyards that are planted across this immense valley. Old family ranches that once extended all the way to Chile are being sold off or converted to vineyards in what is now the country's fastest-growing wine area. It's also one of the world's highest wine regions, with approximately 81,000 hectares (200,000 acres) planted at altitudes between 900 and 1,700 meters (2,952 and 5,577 feet). Cool nights and warm days allow grapes to ripen slowly while developing excellent fruit flavor, good acidity in white wines, and the formation of strong tannins in reds.

Wineries vary from traditional family-run spots to ultramodern facilities operated by big international names. Since they tend to be scattered about in infrequently traveled areas, reservations are highly recommended. The easiest way to see them is to take a tour or stay in a local lodge that offers excursions.

TUPUNGATO

78 km (48 miles) south of Mendoza.

Tupungato is a sleepy agricultural town most of the year. During harvest (February and March), though, the roads in and around it overflow with carts and tractors loaded with grapes from many surrounding vineyards. The population doubles from its official number of nearly 30,000 as pickers arrive.

GETTING HERE AND AROUND

The most direct route from Mendoza to the Valle de Uco is south on Ruta Nacional 40 for 37 km (23 miles) to Ugarteche, where you turn west onto Ruta 86 for another 37 km (23 miles), passing through the village of San José just before arriving in Tupungato. Although buses arrive several times a day from Mendoza, the best way to get around the area is to join a tour or rent a car. If you're driving north, turn off Ruta Nacional 40 onto Ruta Provincial 88 at Zapata.

If you have some time and aren't put off by driving on a dirt road, a scenic way here is south on Ruta Nacional 40 from Mendoza and west on Ruta Nacional 7 to the dam at Potrerillos; exiting at the dam, take the unpaved Ruta Provincial 89 south through the villages of Las Vegas and El Salto, where clusters of vacation cottages brim with flowers in summer and are covered with snow in winter. The road climbs steeply out of the canyon and over a pass, then crosses a high valley with a magnificent view of the Andes. Soon the great expanse of the Valle de Uco lies before you, with its miles of vineyards and orchards of peaches, almonds, and chestnuts, adding wide swaths of pink and white blossoms in spring (late September–October). This drive is equally impressive in reverse.

ESSENTIALS

Visitor Information Oficina de Turismo de Tupungato. ⊠ *Av. Belgrano 348* ☎ *2622/488-015* ⊕ *www.tupungato.gov.ar.*

WINERIES

Andeluna. Surrounded by miles of vineyards, with the majestic Andes as a backdrop, this red brick bodega blends beautifully into the scenery. Inside, the large reception and tasting room—with leather furnishings and high ceiling of reeds and open beams—evokes an old Mendocino mansion. The open kitchen at one end serves fine tasting menus and conducts cooking classes with two days' notice. ✉ *R89, Km 11* ☎ *261/15–508–9525* ⊕ *www.andeluna.com.ar.*

Fodor'sChoice ★ **Bodega Atamisque.** The gray adobe building with its uneven slate roof almost disappears against the background of bushes and mountains. This enormous estancia property (the boundaries of which date back to 1658, when the Jesuits owned it) is owned by a French family who named it after a native tree. In addition to the winery, Atamisque includes a trout farm, a 9-hole golf course, a restaurant, and accommodations. ✉ *RP86, Km 30* ☎ *261/15–699–1166* ⊕ *www.atamisque.com.*

Bodega Salentein. On a knoll with an Andean backdrop, this ultramodern winery has remarkable architecture that draws the eye to cavernous winery halls and into the circular barrel room where a grand piano sits center stage. This complex also contains an art museum, a wine bar, a sculpture garden, a pretty chapel, and two restaurants, making it easy to spend a leisurely afternoon here. ✉ *R89 at Elias Videla, Los Árboles, 15 km (9 miles) south of Tupungato* ☎ *2622/429–500* ⊕ *www. bodegasalentein.com.*

La Azul. Exporters of wine as well as peaches, plums, cherries, and apples, this agro-wine complex's vineyard tours demonstrate the different vine-growing methods used over the centuries. Nice lunch options are served at the rustic-chic restaurant, and there's a small guest house with four rooms. ✉ *R89* ☎ *2622/423–593* ⊗ *Closed Mon.*

Passionate Wine. This urban winery is Tupungato's newest and certainly hippest addition—rock music plays as wines are served by the glass, bottle, or jug. The winemaker in charge is one of Argentina's best, Matias Michelini. ✉ *Av. Correa 1221* ☎ *261/15–418–2323* ⊕ *barbarians.wine/passionate-wine-2.*

WHERE TO EAT

If you are in Tupungato, you really ought to be eating at the local wineries for lunch. Andeluna, La Azul, Domaine Bousquet, and Atamisque are top options in the Tupungato Wine Region.

$$ ARGENTINE ✕ **Restaurante Valle de Tupungato.** Traditional grilled meats, homemade pastas, and appetizers featuring locally made cold cuts comprise the hearty fare at this friendly family-style restaurant. On Sunday you can help yourself to steak, lamb, chicken, and goat at the open grill. **Known for:** family-sized portions; weekend buffet; good value. ⑤ *Average main: 300 pesos* ✉ *Belgrano 542* ☎ *2622/488–421* ▭ *No credit cards.*

$$$ ARGENTINE Fodor'sChoice ★ ✕ **Tupungato Divino.** Overlooking Tupungato volcano and the family vineyards, this small restaurant is the perfect spot for a lazy lunch in wine country. The colorful tasting menu is served with flair, from the assortment of starters to the juicy steak and hearty pasta dishes, and the final tasting platter of puddings. **Known for:** sampler of starters and desserts; excellent Valle de Uco cellar; great valley views. ⑤ *Average main:*

Continued on page 280

Wines of Chile & Argentina

The wine regions of both Chile and Argentina are set against the backdrop of the Andes. And while these mountains do play an important role in the making of wine in both countries, Chile and Argentina have very different traditions and strengths.

Although wine-loving Spaniards settled both countries in the 16th century, only Chile's wine industry developed quickly, largely because the land around Santiago was particularly good for growing grapes. Buenos Aires, on the warm and humid Atlantic coast, however, was hardly an ideal place for viticulture. Mendoza, Argentina's present-day wine wonderland, was impossibly far away to be a reliable supplier of wine to the capital until the railroad united it with the coast in the mid-19th century.

Chile also experienced a boom in the 19th century as new, French-inspired wineries sprang up. Both countries continued without significant change for more than 100 years, until the 1990s international wine boom sparked new interest in South American wines. Big investments from France, Spain, Italy, the United States, and elsewhere—plus some extraordinary winemakers—have made this an exciting place for oenophiles to visit.

(left) Bottle of Maradona red wine;
(above) Errazuriz Winery, Chile

NEIGHBORS ACROSS THE ANDES

CHILE

In the early days, the emphasis was on growing cheap wine to consume domestically. Then, in the middle of the 20th century, Chile's political turmoil caused the business to stagnate. It wasn't until the 1980s that wine exports became a major business, and today Chile exports more than it imports.

Chile's appellation system names its valleys from north to south, but today's winegrowers stress that the climatic and geological differences between east and west are more significant. The easternmost valleys closest to the Andes tend to have less fog, more hours of sunlight, and greater daily temperature variations, which help red grapes develop deep color and rich tannins while maintaining bright acidity and fresh fruit characteristics. On the other hand, if you're after crisp whites and bright Pinots, head to the coast, where cool fog creeps inland from the sea each morning and Pacific breezes keep the vines cool all day.

Viña Cousiño Macul, Chile

Interior areas in the Central Valley are less prone to extremes and favor varieties that require more balanced conditions, such as Merlot, and Chile's own rich and spicy Carmenère. Syrah, a relatively new grape in Chile, does well in both cold and warm climates.

BE SURE TO TASTE:

Sauvignon Blanc: Cool-climate vineyards from Elqui to Bío Bío are producing very exciting Sauvignon with fresh green fruit, crisp acidity, and often an enticing mineral edge.

Miguel Torres, Chile

Carmenère: Chile's signature grape arrived in Chile during the mid-19th century from France, where it was usually a blending grape in Bordeaux. Over time Chileans forgot about it, mistaking it for Merlot, but during the Chilean boom times of the 1990s they realized that they had a very unique grape hidden among the other vines in their vineyards.

Cabernet Sauvignon: The king of reds grows well almost anywhere it's planted, but Cabernets from the Alto Maipo are particularly well balanced, displaying elegance and structure.

Bodega Tres Erres, Chile

Syrah: Chile produces two distinct styles of this grape. Be sure to try both: luscious and juicy from Colchagua or enticingly spicy from coastal areas, such as Elqui or San Antonio.

Malbec: True, this is Argentina's grape, but Chile produces award-winning bottlings that have appealing elegance and balance.

ARGENTINA

Unlike Chile, Argentina exports far less wine than it consumes, and much of its wine is produced in accordance with local tastes and wallets. The 1990s wine boom sparked a greater emphasis on export, and following new investments, the country is now widely recognized for the quality of its red wines, particularly its signature Malbec.

Monteviejo Winery, Clos de los Siete, Mendoza

Broad-shouldered Argentina looks west to the Andes for a life-giving force. Its wine regions receive no cooling maritime influence, as Chile's do, and its vineyards rely on the mountain altitudes not only to irrigate its lands, but also to attenuate the effects of the blazing sun. The climate here is capricious, so producers must be ever-prepared for untimely downpours, devastating hailstorms, and scorching, dehydrating Zonda winds.

BE SURE TO TASTE:

Malbec: Just one sip of Argentina's most widely known wine evokes gauchos and tangos. Deep, dark, and handsomely concentrated, this is a must-try on its home turf.

Estancia San Pablo Tupungato

Cabernet Sauvignon: Argentine Cabs are big, bold, and brawny, as is typical of warmer climates. They're perfect with one of those legendary Argentine grilled steaks.

Red Blends: The red blends here may be mixtures of classic Bordeaux varietals with decidedly Argentine results, or audacious combinations that are only possible in the New World.

Torrontés: Argentina's favorite white has floral overtones, grown most often in Cafayate, in the northwestern province of Salta.

Colomé Winery, Molinos, Salta

TASTING TIPS ON BOTH SIDES OF THE BORDER

1. Make reservations! Unlike wineries in the U.S., most wineries are not equipped to receive drop-in visitors.

2. Don't expect wineries to be open on Sunday. Winery workers need a day off too.

3. The distances between wineries can be much longer than they look on the map. Be sure to allot plenty of travel time, and plan on no more than three or four wineries per day.

4. Do contact the wine route offices in the region you're visiting. They can be extremely helpful in coordinating visits to wineries and other local attractions.

5. Hire a driver, or choose a designated driver.

6. Know what you are walking into. Some wineries offer free tours and tastings, others can charge upwards of 150 pesos per person.

6

IN FOCUS WINES OF CHILE & ARGENTINA

GREAT WINE ITINERARIES

SEE CHAPTER FOR WINERY CONTACT INFORMATION

Chile and Argentina are wine paradises in terms of the climate they usually enjoy. On the Argentine side, Mendoza is blessed with over 330 days of sunshine, a dry climate, and a low risk of mold or disease. On the other side of the Andes, Chile enjoys great light and air purity, and a cooling Humboldt current. Its natural fortunes are balanced with natural disasters, though. Chile has been ravaged by some of the world's worst earthquakes; the devastating 2010 quake and tsunami wiped out more than 130 million liters of wine. The greatest frustration for winemakers in Mendoza is the infamous zonda (a burning and dusty foehn wind that burns grapes and tears vines down) and occasional hail storms. Even paradise has its share of difficulties!

Crossing the Andes will be one of the highlights of your trip, especially the series of switchbacks that wind into the mountains just before the border crossing.

Haras de Pirque. Horses are the owners' first love. You'll pass the breeding farm and the race track on the way to this horseshoe-shaped winery tucked up into the Andean hills.

COLCHAGUA ITINERARY

If it's Saturday, book a ride on the Wine Train, which travels from San Fernando to the heart of the Colchagua Valley in Santa Cruz.

Viña Bisquertt. This family-run winery houses several 15-foot-tall wooden casks from the 1940s.

Lapostolle. Viña Casa Lapostolle built this gravity-flow wonder exclusively for their red blend, Clos Apalta.

Viña Santa Cruz. More than just a winery, this is an entire wine complex. Take the a cable car to the "indigenous village."

ALTO MAIPO ITINERARY

Plenty of wineries are a day trip from Santiago. You can go solo and hire a taxi ($70 for a half day), but for around US$160 (full day) a guide provides better access.

Concha y Toro. Start the day at one of Chile's oldest and best known wineries, located just outside of the capital in Pirque.

Antiyal. One of Chile's first boutique-garage wineries, Antiyal only makes two red blends, both of which are organic and biodynamic.

Bodegas Salentein

ARGENTINA ITINERARY

The charming city of Mendoza is the logical home base for exploring Argentine wine country, and the country's finest wineries surround the city.

Ruca Malén. The fame of Ruca Malen's award-winning restaurant has overtaken that of the winery. However, no great meal in Mendoza works without good wines, so it's best to walk off the five-course lunch here with a tour afterward.

Pulenta Estate. Owned by the renowned Pulenta wine dynasty, this modern winery makes a fabulous Cabernet Franc and has a great boutique feel to it. Tours can include a sensory aroma game.

Bodega Catena Zapata. Rising like a Mayan temple from the fertile soil, this winery produces some of Argentina's most memorable blended wines.

Familia Zuccardi, Mendoza

Harvest time at Andeluna

WINERY-ARCHITECTURE ITINERARY

Fans of spectacular architecture will enjoy visiting Argentina's wineries. Big, modern, sometimes whimsical, and often surprising, many of these enormous high-tech facilities have restaurants and even lodgings to make the long distances between them bearable. Plan for a long day in the beautiful Valle de Uco visiting some striking examples.

Salentein. A perfect example of the "winery-plus" experience in South American wine tourism, this property is a work of art set against a natural backdrop of the Andes, complete with an art gallery, restaurant, chapel, and award-winning wines.

Andeluna. With a stellar view of Tupungato and the Cordon del Plata, this stellar winery draws your eyes to the mountains and your nose to the open-plan kitchen serving great food to pair with their full-bodied wines.

O. Fournier. End your day at this highly unusual building that looks, from a distance, like a city of Oz for the new millennium. An enormous, flat roof seems to hover over the building, and the large U-shaped ramp accommodates gravity-flow winemaking.

6

IN FOCUS WINES OF CHILE & ARGENTINA

CROSSING THE ANDES

Mendoza, Argentina; Andean foothills, wine harvest.

■ If you're coming all the way to South America to taste wine, be sure to visit both sides of the Andes. There are frequent hour-long jet flights between Santiago and Mendoza for US$200–$300 that provide a spectacular condor's-eye view of the craggily snow-covered peaks below.

■ If you are visiting in the summer months and have time for the day-long 250 km (155 miles) overland route, by all means take it. Know that you will most likely have to get a roundtrip car rental. Most companies will not allow one-way international crossings. Better to rent a car in Santiago or Mendoza to see the wineries in each country, then fly or catch a bus to cross the border. On the Argentina side, a flight from Buenos Aires to Mendoza can save time.

■ Roads are well-maintained and reasonably marked. Take Ruta 57 north from Santiago to the small city of Los Andes, then head east on Ruta 60 toward the mountains and the Argentine border, where the highway's name changes to Ruta 7, to Mendoza.

■ Crossing the Andes will be one of the highlights of your trip, especially the series of switchbacks that wind into the mountains just before the border crossing some 8,200 feet above sea level. Be aware that the Libertadores Pass is often closed for days at a time during the winter months, so don't risk it unless you're willing to spend several days sleeping in your car while you wait for things to clear up. Be sure to bring a jacket any time of year, as it can be very chilly at that altitude.

■ Plan a couple of stops along the way; make the Portillo Ski Resort your last stop on the Chilean side, where you can visit the Laguna del Inca at nearly 10,000 feet. The ski resort is a great place to stop for lunch. On the Argentine side, stop for gas and a bite to eat in Upsallata, about 100 km (65 miles) before reaching Mendoza.

WINE TASTING PRIMER

Ordering and tasting wine—whether at a winery, bar, or restaurant—is easy once you master a few simple steps.

LOOK AND NOTE

Hold your glass by the stem and look at the wine in the glass. Note its color, depth, and clarity.

For whites, is it greenish, yellow, or gold? For reds, is it purplish, ruby, or garnet? Is the wine's color pale or deep? Is the liquid clear or cloudy?

SWIRL AND SNIFF

Swirl the wine gently in the glass to intensify the scents, then sniff over the rim of the glass. What do you smell? Try to identify aromas like:

- **Fruits**—citrus, peaches, berries, figs, melon
- **Minerals**—earth, steely notes, wet stones
- **Flowers**—orange blossoms, honey, perfume
- **Dairy**—butter, cream, cheese, yogurt
- **Spices**—baking spices, pungent, herbal notes
- **Oak**—toast, vanilla, coconut, tobacco
- **Vegetables**—fresh or cooked, herbal notes
- **Animal**—leathery, meaty notes

Are there any unpleasant notes, like mildew or wet dog that might indicate that the wine is "off?"

SIP AND SAVOR

Prime your palate with a sip, swishing the wine in your mouth. Then spit in a bucket or swallow.

Take another sip and think about the wine's attributes. Sweetness is detected on the tip of the tongue, acidity on the sides of the tongue, and tannins (a mouth-drying sensation) on the gums. Consider the body—does the wine feel light in the mouth, or is there a rich sensation? Are the flavors consistent with the aromas? If you like the wine, try to pinpoint what you like about it, and vice versa if you don't like it.

Take time to savor the wine as you're sipping it—the tasting experience may seem a bit scientific, but the end goal is your enjoyment.

Valle de Uco Wineries

86

SAN JOSÉ
1

VILLA BASTÍAS

ANCHORIS

40

2

TUPUNGATO

88

3

EL ZAMPAL

4

89

99

96

5

LOS ARBOLES

90

VILLA SECA

89

6

LOS SAUCES

7 **8**

93

COLONIA LAS ROSAS

92

TUNUYÁN

94

9 **10**

VISTA FLORES

91

40

CAMPO DE LOS ANDES

92

92

95

LA CONSULTA

SAN CARLOS

Río Tunuyán

EUGENIO BUSTOS

11

13

12

40

TRES ESQUINAS

0   5 miles

0   5 kilometers

400 pesos ✉ *Los Europeos, Ruta 89* ☎ *2622/15–448–948* ⊕ *www. tupungatodivino.com.ar.*

WHERE TO STAY

$$
B&B/INN

⊞ **Posada Salentein.** Tucked into the foothills behind Bodega Salentein, this posada is delightfully off the beaten track, and you can choose between modern en suite rooms or one of the homey 100-year-old cottages, all of which look onto the vineyards, large lawn, and swimming pool. **Pros:** peaceful vineyard setting; best value in the Valle de Uco; intimate, exclusive restaurant. **Cons:** far from it all; pool isn't heated; horse-riding costs extra. ⑤ *Rooms from: 3400 pesos* ✉ *RN89 at Elias Videla, Los Árboles, 15 km (9 miles) south of Tupungato* ☎ *2622/429–500* ⊕ *www.bodega-salentein.com* ⟿ *16 rooms (8 in cottages)* ⍟ *Breakfast; Some meals.*

$$
B&B/INN

⊞ **Tupungato Divino.** This popular posada in the heart of Uco wine land has rustic chalets with sweeping views of the Andes, offering top value lodging near Tupungato's wineries; each is equipped with a woodstove for the winter, plus a private patio looking out onto the property's own biodynamic Syrah vineyard. **Pros:** gorgeous mountain views; quality restaurant; good value. **Cons:** the pool isn't very private when the restaurant fills up at lunchtime; own transport required; in-room decor lacking. ⑤ *Rooms from: 3000 pesos* ✉ *RP89 and Calle Los Europeos s/n* ☎ *2622/1544–8948* ⊕ *www.tupungatodivino.com.ar* ▬ *No credit cards* ⟿ *4 rooms* ⍟ *Breakfast.*

SHOPPING

KDS Hecho a Mano. Five members of the da Silva family have been designing and selling handmade knives and leather cases at KDS Hecho a Mano since the 1970s. You can watch the process and choose the right knife for your next *asado* from many designs in their showroom. ✉ *Ruta 92, KM 5* ☎ *2622/488–852* ⊕ *www.kdscuchillos.com.ar* ☾ *Closed at lunchtime.*

SPORTS AND THE OUTDOORS
HORSEBACK RIDING

You can ride in the foothills of the Andes for a day or cross the Andes on a six-day trip to Chile that takes you through a treeless landscape of rocky trails, roaring rivers, tiny green meadows, and lofty peaks. Argentine horses aren't allowed in Chile, so you'll have to either change horses at the border or return.

Estancia El Puesto. This five-bedroom ranch offers accommodations, meals, and assorted excursions—most notably horseback riding. The owner, Raúl Labat, has made more than 30 crossings to Chile and still finds each trip rewarding. He leads riders there on six-day journeys each summer. ✉ *Los Árboles, off R89* ☎ *261/428–8541* ⊕ *www.estanciaelpuesto.com.ar* ✉ *From 3,000 pesos (booking essential).*

Parque Provincial Volcán Tupungato. Tupungato Volcano rises 6,800 meters (22,310 feet) in snowbound splendor, looming above the high peaks that march along the border between Chile and Mendoza Province. The park that's named for it covers 110,000 hectares (272,000 acres) in the western portion of the departments of Luján de Cuyo, Tupungato, and Tunuyán. There are no roads into the park, but local tour companies lead horseback rides and hikes into the area. Some offer six-day horseback rides to the Chilean border. Mules can be hired to climb to South Glacier at 2,000 meters (6,562 feet). ⊠ *Tupungato.*

TUNUYÁN

81 km (50 miles) south of Mendoza.

Twice the size of Tupungato, Tunuyán makes a good base for touring the Valle de Uco wineries. Downtown consists of two traffic circles on either side of two blocks, where most of the shops are geared to local agricultural pursuits. Along with grape growing, said pursuits include growing cherries, pears, and apples, and making apple cider.

GETTING HERE AND AROUND

There's bus service here from Mendoza, but you'll have a hard time getting around without a car unless you're on a tour. From Mendoza City you can take Ruta Nacional 40 directly to Tunuyán. Wineries are spread out toward the west (in the direction of the Andes) and Ruta 94 and 92 are where you'll find access to the majority. In Vista Flores you'll find Clos de los Siete (a complex of wineries owned by well-known Bordeaux wine families) and the Winemakers Village (a handful of boutique wineries and passion projects owned by some of Argentina's best known winemakers).

ESSENTIALS

Tourist Information Oficina de Turísmo. ⊠ *San Martín at Dalmau* ☎ *2622/422–193* ⊕ *www.tunuyan.gov.ar.*

WINERIES

TUNUYÁN AND NEARBY

Vines of Mendoza. Making hundreds of small labels for different private estate owners, The Vines of Mendoza offers an educative tasting in Tunuyán where you'll learn about the art of blending and working in microlots. ⊠ *Ruta 94* ☎ *261/461–3900.*

Bodega Diamandes. The newest winery in the Clos de los Siete complex, Diamandes has some of the most striking architecture in the valley with a steel diamond in the center of the showpiece winery. Most visits here focus on the four-course pairing menu from which you'll taste the Bordeaux-inspired wine portfolio with local cuisine. ⊠ *Clodomiro Silva* ☎ *261/15–657–5472* ⊕ *www.diamandes.com.*

Bodega Monteviejo. The first winery to be constructed in the Clos de los Siete complex in Vista Flores, Bodega Monteviejo is not only an icon in the local wine scene but also in the cultural scene, boasting rotating art exhibitions, regular concerts, and Mendoza's top rock festival each April. A visit to this winery includes an informative tasting, a tour of the wine-making facilities, and a walk up to the stunning rooftop with jawdropping views over the valley. There is a great restaurant on site, too. ⊠ *Clodomiro Silva s/n, Vistaflores* ☎ *261/15–532–8126* ⊕ *www. monteviejo.com.ar.*

FAMILY **Gimenez Riili.** You can often get Federico Gimenez-Riili or his father to take you around this family-owned boutique operation and offer you a taste of their wines straight from the barrel. If you want to stay for lunch, they'll organize a traditional asado in the vineyard, and there's a small guesthouse for overnight stays. ⊠ *Ruta 94, Vistaflores* ☎ *261/498–7863* ⊕ *www.gimenezriili.com.*

SuperUco. Off-beat and contemporary describes not only the wine style of the Michelini brothers but also SuperUco, their boutique winery in the Winemakers Village. In between the biodynamic vines, the winery rises up like a cement crown. Enter and you'll be greeted by the family offering a pour of their many different wine labels that range from steely Sauvignon Blanc and juicy Bonarda to orange wines and hand-riddled sparkling wine. ■ TIP→ Reserve ahead for a BBQ lunch. ⊠ *Ruta 94* ☎ *261/15–681–9773* ⊕ *www.superucowines.com.*

SAN CARLOS VICINITY

Finca La Celia. Built by Eugenio Bustos in 1890, this winery flourished under his daughter Celia's leadership, producing an excellent Malbec. Now it's owned by a Chilean company that has invested in the latest technology. Tastings, traditional lunches, and tours of the winery and experimental garden are available with advance booking. In season, pruning and harvesting programs are offered in the vineyard as well. ■ TIP→ There is a rustic posada on-site for anyone interested in spending the night. ⊠ *Circunvalación Celia Bustos de Quiroga 374, San Carlos* ☎ *2622/451–193* ⊕ *www.lacelia.com.ar.*

O. Fournier. Approaching this ultramodern winery on a lonely dirt road, you could be forgiven for thinking you'd discovered a flying saucer instead. But, as your tour guide will tell you, every part of the futuristic building has a function—whether it's to make the best use of gravity or to direct the sometimes brutal winds that whip through. The wines here all come from the local estate, which sits at an altitude of 1,200 meters (3,940 feet). ⊠ *Los Indios s/n, La Consulta* ☎ *2622/451–579* ⊕ *www.ofournier.com.*

Piedra Infinita Zuccardi. This showstopping winery was built by the Zuccardi family to celebrate their newfound passion for the Valle de Uco, following the success of their other family winery in Maipú. In the heart of Altamira, this winery has impressive architecture made of natural materials from the area that reflect the wild, rocky landscape while incorporating artistic touches, too, like a colorful cupola and twisted metalwork door. You can taste the family's top wines in the wine bar and excellent restaurant ($$$$). ⊠ *Calle Costa Canal Uco, La Consulta* ☎ *261/441–0090* ⊕ *www.zuccardiwines.com* ☉ *Closed Mon. and Tues.*

WHERE TO EAT AND STAY

$$

BARBECUE

FAMILY

✕ **La Juntada.** Serving a buffet of salads and starters followed by a main course straight from the grill, La Juntada updates the classic *pulperia* (tavern) atmosphere with a good wine list and a fresh lick of paint. Expect typical Argentine fare that's well prepared and well presented. **Known for:** big buffet; BBQ aromas; traditional folk music. ⑤ *Average main: 300 pesos* ⊠ *R92, Vista Flores* ☎ *262/266–6355* ☉ *Closed Mon.–Thurs.*

$$

ARGENTINE

✕ **Posada del Jamón.** This casual, family-run restaurant has been a staple in the valley for more than 25 years, serving up ham cooked in every way imaginable (and some ways you have probably never imagined). There are also a surprising number of vegetarian options available, and all of the wines offered are from the neighborhood wineries. **Known for:**

Bodegas in Argentina's wine region often have restaurants with dedicated chefs and stellar cuisine. Some prepare food using traditional methods, like this charcoal grill.

ham, ham, and more ham; roadside dining; friendly welcome. $ *Average main: 300 pesos* ✉ *Ruta 92, Km 14* ☎ *2622/492–053* ⊕ *www. laposadadeljamon.com.ar.*

$$$$
HOTEL
Fodor's Choice
★

🏨 **Casa de Uco.** You can tell the owner of this luxury hotel is an architect as soon as you enter: majestic views of vineyards and mountains are expertly placed through a series of shapely windows, skylights, and sloping walls, and there's a handsome infinity pool that drops off into the vineyards below. **Pros:** stunning Valle de Uco location; great on-site restaurant; relaxing spa and pool. **Cons:** extras add up; bar stocks run low; lakeside rooms have less impressive views. $ *Rooms from: 8400 pesos* ✉ *Ruta 94 , Km 14.5* ☎ *261/476–9831* ⊕ *www.casadeuco.com* ⤴ *18 rooms* ⫿⊙⫿ *Free Breakfast.*

$$
B&B/INN

🏨 **Postales (Valle de Uco Lodge).** Tucked away on a quiet country road, this casona-style wine lodge has simple but comfortable rooms that each look out onto old vines, distant mountains, and the peaceful garden and pool area. **Pros:** quiet, countryside setting; nice restaurant option; nearby wineries. **Cons:** little to do without a car; poor Wi-Fi; pool can get crowded. $ *Rooms from: 3000 pesos* ✉ *Calle Ezequiel Tabanera, Colonia Las Rosas* ☎ *2622/490–024* ⊕ *www.postalesarg.com* ⤴ *9 rooms* ⫿⊙⫿ *Breakfast.*

$$$$
RESORT

🏨 **The Vines Resort & Spa.** Stunning sunsets, luxury villas, and seven-course flame-grilled dinners are the norm at The Vines Resort & Spa, which has a superb on-site restaurant, pool, and boutique winery. **Pros:** great restaurant and bar; luxury offerings in the remote Valle de Uco; beautiful location. **Cons:** expensive; limited spa (only a pool); hit and miss service. $ *Rooms from: 19,500 pesos* ✉ *Ruta 94* ☎ *261/461–3900* ⊕ *www.vinesresortandspa.com* ⤴ *21 rooms* ⫿⊙⫿ *Free Breakfast.*

SAN RAFAEL REGION

Numerous dams and acres of irrigated land have created a vigorous agro-industrial oasis in the department of San Rafael, one of the country's smallest wine regions to claim a Denominación de Origen (DOC). This is a point of pride for local vintners, and the quality of wine produced here speaks for itself. San Rafael has a nearly perfect climate for growing grapes: low humidity, cold and dry winters, ample temperature variation, and plenty of water from the Ríos Diamante and Atuel. But into every vineyard a little rain must fall—and when it comes in the form of hail *(granizo),* it can be devastating, destroying one year's crop and the next year's tiny buds in one short shower. Most vineyards now protect their crops with expensive heavy netting that lets the water drip through and shades the grapes, aiding ripening.

SAN RAFAEL

240 km (150 miles) south of Mendoza.

San Rafael (population 175,000) is the second largest city in Mendoza. Wide avenues lined with leafy sycamores and tall poplars fed by streetside canals give it a bucolic charm, but the bodegas are reason enough for many visitors to make the trip. Wine-making took off here in the late 19th century when immigrants from Italy, Switzerland, and France came with advanced viticulture skills and new grape varieties. When the railroad arrived in 1903, the fledgling industry was connected to Buenos Aires and the rest of the world. Today the city has about 100 wineries. Although most are small, family-owned operations, a number do have tourist-friendly facilities within walking or cycling distance of the center. If you're looking for more active alternatives, local tour operators can arrange rafting, riding, and hiking excursions in the surrounding mountains and lakes. About 75 km (47 miles) west of San Rafael, the Cañón del Atuel (aka the "other" Grand Canyon) can also be explored.

GETTING HERE AND AROUND

A daily flight makes the two-hour trip from Buenos Aires to San Rafael's airport, located about 15 minutes west of downtown on Ruta 150, but if you want to arrive by air from Mendoza, you'll (frustratingly) have to fly via Buenos Aires. By road, take Ruta Nacional 40 south from Mendoza to Pareditas, where you pick up Ruta Nacional 143 to San Rafael. Coming on a bus (overnight from Buenos Aires) is another option, as it's less expensive than flying.

San Rafael is flat and laid out on a grid, which makes it easy to tour on foot. At Km 0, Avenida Yrigoyen crosses the downtown area (north–south) and becomes Bartolomé Mitre. At this same intersection (east–west), Avenida El Libertador becomes San Martín—the main shopping street. Hotels are scattered on the edge of residential areas, but you can still walk (or take a short cab ride) to downtown. ■TIP→ **Beware of the acéquias—canals between the sidewalks and streets. At night people riding bicycles with no lights or reflectors on narrow dirt roads can also be a hazard.**

San Rafael's wineries are mainly within cycling distance (or a cheap taxi ride) of the city center; if you're driving, note that road signs are scarce in the region, though the municipality is working to correct that. Before heading for the wineries, it's wise to make an appointment as owners are often busy in the vineyard, working in the bodega, testing wine with the oenologist, or tending to customers.

Bus Contacts Andesmar. ☎ *2627/427–720* ⊕ *www.andesmar.com.* **Iselin.** ☎ *260/444–0020* ⊕ *www.iselin.com.ar.* **Terminal de Ómnibus.** ✉ *General Paz 980* ☎ *260/444–5495.*

ESSENTIALS
Visitor and Tour Information San Rafael Tourist Board. ✉ *Av. H. Yrigoyen 1530* ☎ *260/442–4217* ⊕ *www.sanrafaelturismo.gov.ar.*

WINERIES
Goyenechea. One of the country's oldest wineries, Goyenechea was founded in 1868 by a Basque immigrant family that had the foresight to build not only a solid brick winery, but also 60 houses for the working families, a school for their children, a repair shop, and a chapel. As you pass through the arched caves where wine ages in bottles, you can see the *piletas,* huge concrete vats that held 8,976 gallons of wine when the industry was focused on quantity, not quality. Family members often lead tours. ✉ *Sotero Arizú s/n, Villa Atuel* ☎ *260/15–461–7294* ⊕ *www. goyenechea.com* ☉ *Closed Sun.*

Jean Rivier. The Swiss-French brothers who own this winery produce a limited quantity of quality wines from their own grapes. Tours of the spotless facility include crushing, fermentation, and tasting areas. ✉ *Hipólito Yrigoyen 2385, Rama Caída* ☎ *260/443–2675* ⊕ *www.jeanrivier.com.*

La Champañera Valentin Bianchi. Bianchi is the largest of San Rafael's wineries, receiving more than 100,000 visitors per year to its lush, garden setting, which is just a little over 5 km (3 miles) from the center of San Rafael. The fact that La Champañera focuses solely on the production and tasting of sparkling wine also sets it apart. The wine shop sells all of Bianchi's other lines of wines if fizz isn't what you are looking for, and you can trade up to taste other wines and order a bite to eat. ✉ *R143 at Valentin Bianchi, Las Paredes* ☎ *260/444–9600* ⊕ *www.vbianchi.com.*

Suter. In 1900 the Suter family journeyed to Argentina from Switzerland and planted the first Riesling variety in the country. Today the fourth generation of the family continues to produce good value white wines, Malbec, Cabernet Sauvignon, and Espumante. A winery tour leads you through a labyrinth of underground caves filled with huge oak casks—used more to evoke atmosphere than to store wine. ✉ *Hipólito Yrigoyen 2850, near airport, El Toledano* ☎ *260/442–1076* ⊕ *www.bodegasuter.com.ar.*

WHERE TO EAT
$$$$
ARGENTINE
✕ **Al Antojo del Cocinero.** This intimate eatery serves up comforting Argentine cuisine each evening for a maximum of 10 tables in a romantic, candlelit garden. The menu changes regularly but some favorites include homemade gnocchi and shrimp gratin. **Known for:** comforting food; intimate setting; Argentine tasting menu. $ *Average main: 500 pesos* ✉ *Av. Ballofet 173* ☎ *261/15–333–7364* ☉ *Closed Sun. and Mon.*

San Rafael
Wineries

SAN
RAFAEL

Rio Diamante

Tabanera

6

$ ✕ **Bonafide.** A popular gathering place for both locals and visitors just
CAFÉ one block from Km 0 (the very center of town), Bonafide serves up fresh
coffee, sandwiches, cakes, and other goodies for the road. Grab one of
the window seats with leather couches and take advantage of the Wi-Fi.
Known for: coffee; decent Wi-Fi; cheap bites. ⑤ *Average main: 120
pesos* ✉ *San Martín 102* ☎ *260/442–0420* ⊕ *www.bonafide.com.ar.*

$$ ✕ **Chez Gaston at Algodón.** Nestled between a golf green and tennis courts,
ARGENTINE Chez Gaston serves up unpretentious and fresh local cuisine in the smart
Fodor's Choice Algodon Wine Resort. Surrounded by ancient olive groves and vine-
★ yards, you can sit outside on the brick patio where pine-log tables are
surrounded by comfy couches with puffy white cushions. **Known for:**
farm fresh ingredients; Algodon wine pairings; meat straight from the
grill. ⑤ *Average main: 300 pesos* ✉ *RN144, Km 674, Cuadro Benegas*
☎ *260/442–9020* ⊕ *www.algodonwineestates.com.*

$$$ ✕ **L'Obrador-Casa de Campo.** Daniel Ancina, his wife Graciela, and a team
ARGENTINE of cooks will greet you at this typical ranch house, about 20 minutes from
Fodor's Choice town; then they'll fill your wine glass, introduce you to the other guests,
★ and seat you family-style at a long table. Little pots of sauces for spreading on *pan casero* (homemade bread) line the center of the table and out
of the mud-brick oven comes a platter of crisp baked empanadas followed
by some type of meat—goat, lamb, beef, chicken, or chorizo. **Known for:**
everything cooked on the spot; a warm intro to the local cuisine; hard to

find, but worth the effort. $ *Average main: 360 pesos* ⊠ *Camino Bentos 50* ☎ *260/460–1347* ▭ *No credit cards* ☾ *Closed Sun.*

WHERE TO STAY

$$$$
RESORT
Fodor's Choice
★

🔆 **Algodón Wine Resort.** Country casual meets luxury at the Algodón Wine Resort, which combines a remodeled 1920s farmhouse and a modern lodge offering rooms with their own patio and woodstove. **Pros:** relaxing countryside setting; good option for golfers; great restaurant. **Cons:** 20 minutes from downtown San Rafael; closed in winter; expensive for what it is. $ *Rooms from: 7600 pesos* ⊠ *RN144, Km 674, Cuadro Benegas* ☎ *260/4429–020* ⊕ *www.algodonwineestates. com* ☾ *Closed in winter* ↝ *8 rooms* ⦿◯ *Breakfast.*

$$
HOTEL

🔆 **Hotel Tower Inn and Suites.** Across the street from the tourist office, this modern hotel has spacious accommodations with big picture windows that fill the rooms with natural light and provide views of the main street and the mountains in the distance. **Pros:** large rooms; poolside dining in summer; central. **Cons:** street noise can carry; unimpressive breakfast; small pool for quantity of guests. $ *Rooms from: 2600 pesos* ⊠ *H. Irigoyen 774* ☎ *260/442–7190* ⊕ *www.towersanrafael.com* ↝ *111 rooms* ⦿◯ *Breakfast.*

$$
B&B/INN

🔆 **Suter Petit Hotel.** Set in large, historic gardens, Suter winery offers a smart guesthouse with 12 spacious rooms, each en suite looking out onto the grounds. **Pros:** large gardens and pool; homey; attentive service. **Cons:** a little tired around the edges; simple room facilities; a bit out of town. $ *Rooms from: 3000 pesos* ⊠ *Av. Yrigoyen 3003* ☎ *260/443–5924* ⊕ *www.suterhotel.com.ar* ↝ *12 rooms* ⦿◯ *Free Breakfast.*

$
RENTAL

🔆 **Tierra Mora.** This apart-hotel is a compact three-story building overlooking a large park; it's about 14 blocks from downtown but within walking distance of an up-and-coming area with restaurants and shops. **Pros:** large rooms; in a nice part of town with park; free parking. **Cons:** not a lot of amenities; small breakfast; basic services. $ *Rooms from: 1600 pesos* ⊠ *Ameghino 350* ☎ *260/444–7222* ⊕ *www.tierramora.com* ↝ *19 apartments, 17 rooms* ⦿◯ *Breakfast.*

SHOPPING

FOOD

Ketobac. Wines, jams, and homemade goodies (such as chocolate-covered figs, raisins, and dried apricots from the region) are all sold at Ketobac. ⊠ *San Martín 175* ☎ *260/442–2082.*

Yancanelo. An olive oil factory that offers tastings, Yancanelo also sells local olive oil and other regional foods. ⊠ *Hipólito Yrigoyen 4030* ☎ *260/442–3879* ⊕ *www.yancanelo.com* ☾ *Closed Sun. afternoon.*

LAS LEÑAS

200 km (124 miles) south of San Rafael.

Las Leñas is the largest ski area served by lifts in the Western Hemisphere—bigger than Whistler/Blackcomb in British Columbia, and larger than Vail and Snowbird combined. Although it should be thriving, the area has suffered bankruptcies, absentee owners, and several

CLOSE UP

A Recreational Drive

Cañón del Atuel (Atuel Canyon). This has been called the world's second Grand Canyon, as they were both formed at the same time, and their coloring is quite similar. To traverse the photogenic, 160-km (99-mile) route with its four hydro-electric stations along the Atuel River, start at the top of the canyon in the village of El Nihuel, 75 km (47 miles) west of San Rafael. Take Ruta Provincial 144 from San Rafael in the direction of Malargüe, turning south at El Desvío onto 180. At the dam, Ruta 173 descends into a labyrinth of red, brown, and gray sandstone rock formations. Unfortunately, the river disappears into underground pipes—supplying energy for the growing population and the vineyards of Mendoza Province. At Valle Grande the water is collected behind a large dam, after which the river runs freely between sandstone cliffs, beneath shady willows and poplar trees. Swimming holes, sheltered picnic spots, and rafting adventures offer escape from the city on hot summer days. Small hotels, cottages, campsites, and shops that rent rafting and kayaking equipment line the road before it returns across the desert to San Rafael.

management teams. You must go through tour operators and travel agents to book into area hotels, all of which have minimum-stay requirements. Accommodations range from dorm-style houses and apart-hotels—some in disrepair—to hotels with indoor/outdoor pools, decent restaurants, bars, and a ski concierge. Travel offices in Buenos Aires, Mendoza, and San Rafael sell ski packages with lift tickets, equipment, and, in some cases, transportation—which may involve a combination of bus rides and charter flights.

The ski season runs June through October, depending on the year's snow. Most South Americans take their vacation in July, the month to avoid if you don't like crowds and high prices, although the weather is more benign. August has the most reliable snow conditions, September the most varied. Prices for lifts and lodging are lowest in June and from September to closing; rates are highest in July.

GETTING HERE AND AROUND

In high season (July and August) there are two charter flights a day from Buenos Aires to Malargüe, a town 80 km (50 miles) from the resort. A more reliable alternative is to take a 90-minute flight from Buenos Aires to San Rafael, then a three-hour drive onward to Las Leñas. From San Rafael, follow Ruta Provincial 144 for 141 km (88 miles) to El Sosneado, then pick up Ruta Nacional 40 to the turnoff onto Ruta Provincial 222 that passes through Los Molles, 20 km (12 miles) from Las Leñas. This is a dramatically beautiful drive, but carry chains and be aware of weather conditions.

If you want to save your pesos for lift tickets and good lodgings, consider taking the Las Leñas "Coche-cama" from Buenos Aires. This sleeper bus departs on Friday and Sunday evening, making the trip in 11 hours; return tickets (bookable directly through the resort) cost about 4,800 pesos.

ESSENTIALS

Visitor Information Malargüe Tourism Office. ⊠ *Hipólito Yrigoyen 774, San Rafael* 🕾 *260/447–1659* ⊕ *www.malargue.gov.ar* ⊠ *San Martin s/n, Malargüe* 🕾 *260/447–1659.*

WHERE TO STAY

$$$ 🛏 **Aries.** This slope-side luxury hotel has plenty of diversions for stormy
HOTEL   days—including a space for children's games and activities, a piano bar in the lobby, a wine bar serving cheese and regional smoked meats, a movie theater, a heated pool, and a sauna. **Pros:** proximity to slopes; good facilities; post-ski entertainment. **Cons:** no direct reservation service; two-night minimum stay; outdated interiors. ⑤ *Rooms from: 5600 pesos* ⊠ *Las Leñas Ski Resort* 🕾 *11/4819–6060 in Buenos Aires off-season, 260/447–0683 ski season* ⊕ *www.laslenas.com* ↩ *100 rooms* ⦿| *Breakfast.*

$$ 🛏 **Escorpio.** This small, intimate ski lodge is right on the slopes; you can
HOTEL   watch the action from the terrace while having lunch, or hit the cozy
FAMILY   piano bar for après-ski board games with tea or cocktails. **Pros:** ski in, ski out; mountain views; terrace bar. **Cons:** difficult to make reservations directly at times; few facilities; two-night minimum. ⑤ *Rooms from: 3700 pesos* ⊠ *Las Leñas Ski Resort* 🕾 *11/4819–6060 in Buenos Aires off-season, 260/447–0683 in Mendoza ski season* ⊕ *www.laslenas.com* ↩ *46 rooms* ⦿| *Free Breakfast.*

$$$$ 🛏 **Piscis.** This deluxe hotel pampers its guests with spa services, ski-
HOTEL   equipment delivery, and an indoor-outdoor pool. **Pros:** lots of post-ski activity; indoor-outdoor pool; slope-side location. **Cons:** difficult to make direct reservations; two-night minimum stay; outdated interiors. ⑤ *Rooms from: 6400 pesos* ⊠ *Las Leñas Ski Resort* 🕾 *11/4819–6060 in Buenos Aires off-season, 260/447–0683 in Mendoza ski season* ⊕ *www. laslenas.com* ↩ *98 rooms* ⦿| *Free Breakfast.*

SPORTS AND THE OUTDOORS

SKIING

Las Leñas Ski Resort. From the top (3,429 meters/11,250 feet), a treeless lunar landscape of white peaks extends in every direction. There are steep, scary, 610-meter (2,000-foot) vertical chutes for experts; machine-packed routes for beginners; and plenty of intermediate terrain. A terrain park for snowboarders has jumps and a half pipe. There's also a free-style slope. Off-piste skiing can be arranged through the ski school.

Facilities: 3,300 hectares (8,154 acres) skiable terrain; 1,230-meter (4,035-foot) vertical drop; 64 km (40 miles) of groomed runs, the longest is 8 km (5 miles); 15% beginner, 40% intermediate, 45% expert; 1 quad, 6 double chairs, 5 surface lifts. There are no detachable quad chairs or high-speed lifts.

Seasonal Rate Information: Low: September. Medium: June and August. High: July.

Lessons and Programs: Multilingual ski and snowboard instructors give 2½-hour classes or two-hour private lessons for all levels. Good

intermediate skiers to experts can experience untracked slopes with heli-ski and off-piste skiing accompanied by trained guides and avalanche experts.

One-Day Adult Lift Tickets: Low: 1000 pesos, Medium: 1400 pesos, High: 1600 pesos

Rentals: Rentals of boots, skis, snowboards, and poles are readily available. ⊠ *Las Leñas* 🕾 *11/4819–6060 in Buenos Aires* ⊕ *www.laslenas. com.*

SAN JUAN REGION

In the foothills of the Andes, the city of San Juan lies in an oasis of orchards and vineyards, surrounded by mountains to the west and monotonous desert in every other direction. People here work hard in the fields during the day, take long siestas in the afternoon, and head back to the fields until sundown. Although San Juan wineries have been slow to make the shift from quantity to quality, some 160 facilities have converted (or are converting) from producing bulk wine, and a new generation of oenologists and vintners is taking the lead. The province produces some of Argentina's top Syrah and Bonarda and there is a plethora of other steak-worthy red wines, aromatic white wines, and good value sparkling wine on offer.

The Ullum, Tulum, and Zonda valleys are the principal wine-growing areas close to the city of San Juan, and the Río San Juan flows from the mountains into 2,000 km (1,243 miles) of canals to irrigate about 48,500 hectares (120,000 acres) of vineyards. Other growing areas include El Perdenal, southeast near the Mendoza border, and Jachal, to the north.

SAN JUAN

167 km (104 miles) northwest of Mendoza.

Easygoing San Juan makes a good base if you want to combine active pursuits (a good selection of which can be found in and around the Ullum Valley Dam Reservoir) with visits to local bodegas. This small city was founded in 1562 as part of the Chilean viceroyalty, and *sanjuaninos* began making wine almost immediately; however, it wasn't until the 1890s, when Graffigna and other major operations put down roots here, that production increased. At that point wineries began offering varieties other than the sweet white table wines, sherries, and ports that the area had been known for. Today, although the city remains steeped in history and awash in wine, it is surprisingly modern. San Juan was devastated by earthquakes in 1944 and 1977 (the first of these helped establish Juan Perón, who led the relief effort, as a national figure): all of the low-rise buildings, tree-lined plazas, and pedestrian walkways you see are the results of reconstruction.

Antigua Bodega
1929 ....**3**

Bodegas
Santiago
Graffigna S.A. ... **2**

Callia **7**

Champañera
Miguel Ángel
Más **6**

Fabril Alto
Verde **5**

Merced
del Estero **1**

Viñas de
Segísa **4**

San Juan
Wineries

GETTING HERE AND AROUND

San Juan is a 1½-hour drive from Mendoza on Ruta Nacional 40. The trip from Buenos Aires takes 10 hours by car, slightly longer by bus, but daily flights on Aerolíneas Argentinas (⊕ *www.aerolineas.com.ar*) take just 1¾ hour. The Chacritas Airport is 11 km (7 miles) southeast of San Juan; a taxi in takes about 15 minutes and costs about 255 pesos. The city is easy to navigate: there's one main shopping area in a three-block radius around the Plaza 25 de Mayo, and most hotels are within walking distance of it. Some wineries are within cycling distance, whereas others are drive-to destinations. Always try to reserve visits ahead of time.

Bus Contacts Andesmar. ☎ *264/422–2871* ⊕ *www.andesmar.com.* **Autotransportes.** ☎ *264/427–6864* ⊕ *www.atsj.com.ar.* **CATA Internacional.** ☎ *264/427–7600, 800/122–2282* ⊕ *www.catainternacional.com.* **Chevallier.** ☎ *264/422–1388* ⊕ *www.nuevachevallier.com.* **Terminal de Ómnibus.** ✉ *Estados Unidos 492, between Santa Fe and España 985* ☎ *264/422–1604.*

Car Rentals Avis. ✉ *Domingo Sarmiento Sur 164* ☎ *264/420–0571, 264/15–499–1472* ⊕ *www.avis.com.ar.*

Taxis Argentina Remise. ✉ *Gral. Mariano Acha Norte 989* ☎ *264/422–5522.* **Radio Taxi.** ☎ *264/427–2705* ⊕ *www.radiotaxisanjuan.com.ar.*

ESSENTIALS

Visitor Information San Juan Secretaria de Turismo. ✉ *Sarmiento 24 Sur* ☎ *264/421–0004* ⊕ *www.turismo.sanjuan.gob.ar.*

TOURS

Dante Montes Turismo. Anna Maria de Montes and her partners at Dante Montes Turismo are experienced local agents with a full-service agency for lodging and transportation. They offer guided tours to bodegas, Valle Fertí (where they own their own cabins), Ischigualasto Park, and beyond. ✉ *Santa Fe 58 Este, Galeria Estornell, Loc 31* ☎ *264/422–9019, 264/421–5198* ⊕ *www.agenciamontes.com.*

Moneytur. This outfit conducts tours of local bodegas; outings to Ischigualasto, Talampaya, Las Quijades, and Jachal; plus rafting trips on the Río San Juan and horseback trips in the Calingasta Valley. ✉ *Santa Fe Oeste 202* ☎ *264/420–1010* ⊕ *www.moneytur.com.ar.*

EXPLORING

Casa Natal de Sarmiento (*Sarmiento's Birthplace*). This modest house was the birthplace of Domingo Faustino Sarmiento (1811–88), known to Argentines as the Father of Education. Sarmiento was a prolific writer, a skilled diplomat, and a successful politician who served as president from 1869 to 1874. Casa Natal de Sarmiento—Argentina's first designated National Historic Landmark—pays tribute to his achievements and gives an overview of Argentine history during his era. ✉ *Sarmiento 21 Sur* ☎ *264/422–4603* ⊕ *www.casanatalsarmiento.cultura.gob.ar* 🎫 *Free.*

Ullum Dam (*Ullum Valley Dam Reservoir*). Fifteen km (9 miles) west of San Juan, this huge hydroelectric complex—also known as the Ullum Valley Dam Reservoir—offers grand views of the Río San Juan. Windsurfing, sailing, swimming, rowing, fishing, and diving keep San Juaninos cool on hot summer days. You can rent boating equipment just beyond the dam, where you'll also find a café and change cabins. There's a public beach at the Embarcadero turnoff. You can go whitewater rafting and kayaking on the San Juan, Los Patos, and Jachal rivers. Fishing in Las Hornillas River can be arranged through local tour companies. ✉ *San Juan.*

WINERIES

Antigua Bodega 1929. At this landmark bodega and museum, great concrete wine-storage tubs are exposed in a cavernous old building that survived three earthquakes and now functions as part of the museum. Wine and espumante are served in the lovely garden or at a wine bar in the front room. ✉ *Salta 782 Norte, Capital* ☎ *261/459–7777* ⊕ *www.antiguabodega.com.*

Bodegas Santiago Graffigna S.A. Italian wine expert Don Santiago Graffigna, who planted Tulum Valley's first vines, founded this winery in 1870. You can learn the history of his family and their vineyard in the museum nearby. An enormous barrel serves as a sitting area in the tasting room. ✉ *Colón 1342 Norte, Desamparados* ☎ *264/421–4227* ⊕ *www.graffignawines.com.*

Callia. In a hot, dry, wide open valley 35 km (22 miles) from town and with vineyards planted in every direction, Callia produces some of

Argentina's best Syrah. The winery looks modern, but inside its super-structure is the old bodega (albeit with all new equipment). It's owned by Salentein, a formidable Dutch company that also makes wine in the Valle de Uco. ⊠ *Calle de los Ríos s/n, Caucete* ☎ *264/496–0000* ⊕ *www.bodegascallia.com* ⊘ *Closed Sun.*

Champañera Miguel Ángel Más. There's a lot going on at this unassuming little winery. It doesn't run fancy tours, but workers will stop to show you how they make sparkling wine, turning the bottles slowly on the many racks. Everything is certified organic—from the wine to the garlic and tomatoes that grow out back. ⊠ *Calle 11 s/n, 300 meters (984 feet) east of RN40* ☎ *264/660–4901* ⊘ *Closed weekends.*

Fabril Alto Verde. Grapes from this spotless winery are grown organically, and the wine and espumante are stabilized without preservatives or additives. They are made in small quantities, and a great deal of care and control go into the production. ⊠ *RN40, between Calles 13 and 14* ☎ *264/438–5862* ⊕ *www.fabril-altoverde.com.ar.*

Merced del Estero. The same family has been cultivating vines at this finca (estate) since 1897, but it wasn't until the 1990s they started producing varietals, including Cabernet Franc, Cabernet Sauvignon, Malbec, and Syrah. A visit offers a personal tour of the winery and a taste of its modern portfolio. ⊠ *Av. Moron 432* ☎ *264/15–4400–385* ⊕ *www.merceddelestero.com.ar.*

Viñas de Segisa. Segisa claims to be the first boutique winery in San Juan after Don Vicente Perez Ganga settled here in 1925. Several earthquakes have left nothing of the original building, but it's still worth a visit to taste new wines on their daily tours. ⊠ *Aberastain at Calle 15, La Rinconada, Pocito* ☎ *264/492–2000* ⊕ *www.saxsegisa.com.ar.*

WHERE TO EAT

$$$
FRENCH FUSION
Fodor's Choice
★

✕ **La Madeleine.** There's a friendly atmosphere in this small bistro, which started out as a teahouse until the French owners expanded into Argentine-Franco breakfasts, lunch, dinner, and a wine bar. **Known for:** delicious cakes; eclectic wine list; European menu. ⑤ *Average main: 400 pesos* ⊠ *Mitre Oeste 202* ☎ *264/427–7825* ⊕ *www.lamadeleinebistrot.com.ar* ⊘ *Closed Sun.*

$$
ARGENTINE
FAMILY

✕ **Remolacha.** Delicious smells from the outdoor grill lure locals off the streets and into this popular and unpretentious restaurant in the center of town. Saffron-yellow tablecloths throughout brighten the low-ceilinged dining room and add a splash of color to the outdoor patio. **Known for:** Argentine grill; popular with families; laid-back service. ⑤ *Average main: 300 pesos* ⊠ *Av. J.I. de la Roza 199 Oeste, at Sarmiento* ☎ *264/422–7070.*

$$
MEDITERRANEAN
FAMILY

✕ **Restaurante Palito—Club Sirio Libanés.** Tiled walls that look straight out of the Middle East mark the entrance to this eatery, which offers top value Lebanese food. Don't be dismayed by the bright lights; just order a bottle of Malbec, head for the table of appetizers, and fill your plate with crab brochettes, pickled eggplant, fresh tomatoes, and sliced tongue. **Known for:** good value buffet; Middle Eastern flavors; eccentric design. ⑤ *Average main: 300 pesos* ⊠ *Entre Ríos 33 Sur* ☎ *264/422–3841* ⊕ *www.hostaldepalito.com.ar* ⊘ *No dinner Sun.*

6

Taking a rest at Cerro Aconcagua's Camp Two

$ **✕ Soychu.** Dedicated to natural foods, this buffet-style restaurant has
VEGETARIAN lots of vegetarian and even vegan options. The atmosphere is laid-back,
and your meal—which is priced by weight—can be eaten in or taken
out. $ *Average main: 160 pesos* ⊠ *Av. José de la Roza 223* ☎ *264/422–
1939* ⊘ *No dinner Sun.*

WHERE TO STAY

$ **⛲ Albertina.** Bright white walls with colorful art and slick modern fur-
HOTEL niture decorate this central four-story hotel, which offers good value,
if simple, lodgings in San Juan. **Pros:** convenient location; affordable
rates; on-site eatery. **Cons:** tiny windows; basic amenities; lots of
stairs. $ *Rooms from: 1600 pesos* ⊠ *Mitre 202 oeste* ☎ *264/421–4222*
⊕ *www.hotelalbertina.com* ⟿ *36 rooms* ⏇*Breakfast.*

$$ **⛲ Alkazar.** Polished granite floors, chrome, and glass lend this city hotel's
HOTEL lobby a businesslike air. **Pros:** some rooms have mountain views; central
location; lively lobby bar. **Cons:** rooftop pool is small; decor is dated; medi-
ocre service. $ *Rooms from: 2600 pesos* ⊠ *Laprida 82 Este* ☎ *264/421–
4965* ⊕ *www.alkazarhotel.com.ar* ⟿ *96 rooms, 8 suites* ⏇*Breakfast.*

$$ **⛲ Del Bono Park.** Light shines from a skylight four stories above the
HOTEL registration area, lobby, bar, and gathering spaces, and a third-floor
glass bridge connects rooms by spanning the atrium, with a circular
staircase winding around a glass cylinder down into the basement bar,
restaurant, and casino. **Pros:** San Juan's sleekest hotel; lots of light; varied amenities. **Cons:** just off the Circunvalación (Ring Road); breakfast
can get busy; room size varies. $ *Rooms from: 2900 pesos* ⊠ *Av. J.I.
de La Roza 1946* ☎ *264/426–2300* ⊕ *www.delbonohotels.com* ⟿ *100
rooms* ⏇*Breakfast.*

$ **La Deolinda.** The helpful owners of this apart-hotel have created a
RENTAL   cheery complex of cabins with outdoor patios, backyard grills, and a
swimming pool. **Pros:** friendly staff; spacious grounds with open-air
pool; good for families. **Cons:** 15-minute drive from town; no public
transportation; poorly equipped if you plan to cook. $ *Rooms from:*
1400 pesos ⊠ *25 de Mayo and Lateral Este* ☎ *264/422–2923* ⊕ *www.*
ladeolinda.com.ar ⤳ *4 rooms, 20 apartments* ¶◎¶ *Breakfast.*

$ **Villa Don Tomás.** This resort-like hotel on the outskirts of town has
HOTEL   a spacious lawn, pool with swim-up bar, and casual restaurant, giving
FAMILY   children plenty of space to play and offering respite from a busy day
sightseeing. **Pros:** huge lawn; pool; low rates. **Cons:** 15-minute drive
from town; no nearby shops or restaurants; basic accommodation.
$ *Rooms from: 1200 pesos* ⊠ *Comandante Cabot 568 Oeste, 5400*
☎ *264/428–3842* ⊕ *www.villadontomas.com.ar* ⤳ *32 rooms, 11 cot-*
tages, 8 apartments ¶◎¶ *Breakfast.*

BARREAL

6

136 km (85 miles) northwest of San Juan.

Beyond the streets of Barreal, hiding in the shade of *sauce llorones*
(weeping willows) and alamos, lie apple orchards, vineyards, and fields
of mint, lavender, and anise. Using this tranquil village as your headquarters, you can mountain bike, horseback ride, hike, climb, or drive
a 4X4 east into the Sierra Tontal, where at 3,999 meters (13,120 feet)
you can see the highest peaks in the Andes, including Aconcagua (6,957
meters/22,825 feet) and Mercedario (6,770 meters/22,211 feet).

GETTING HERE AND AROUND

You can reach Barreal by bus or car in about three hours. Leave San
Juan on Ruta Nacional 40 driving north, then veer west on 436 to
Talacasto, which becomes 149 to the Calingasta Valley and then continues south to Barreal. Another option is the long, lonely but scenic
drive from Uspallata *(Scenic Drives in Uspallata)* on north–south Ruta
39 (which turns into Ruta 412) all the way to Barreal. The optimal way
to explore the surrounding area is by car, using a 4X4 for forays into
the mountains, or by joining a tour.

ESSENTIALS

Visitor Information Tourist Office. ⊠ *Municipalidad, Presidente Roca*
☎ *264/844–1066.*

EXPLORING

Reserva Natural El Leoncito. Twenty-two km (14 miles) south of Barreal on
Ruta 412 toward Uspallata, a dirt road turns off into Reserva Natural El
Leoncito (Little Lion Natural Reserve), a vast, rocky area with little vegetation. You can continue on this road for 17 km (11 miles) to the CASLEO
observatory ⊕ www.casleo.gov.ar, known for its exceptional stargazing.

Near the turnoff, on the western side of Ruta 412 at Pampa Leoncito,
the sport of *carrovelismo* (land-sailing) is practiced during summer
months in wheeled sand cars called wind yachts that can travel up to
150 kph (93 mph) across a cracked-clay lake bed.

An all-day drive (160 km/100 miles round-trip) in a 4X4 to Las Hornillas at 3,300 meters (9,500 feet) takes you along the Río Los Patos into a red rock–walled canyon. The road narrows, clinging to the canyon walls, as it winds around closed curves, eventually opening into a small valley where, in 1817, General San Martín's troops gathered before crossing the Andes over Los Patos Pass on one of his historic liberation campaigns.

A brief glimpse of Aconcagua looming in solitary splendor about 160 km (100 miles) south is a preview of coming attractions: four peaks over 6,000 meters (20,000 feet) tall are visible in the Ramada Range to the northwest: Polaco, Alma Negra, La Ramada, and Mercaderio. The last of these—rising to 6,770 meters (22,211 feet)—is the fourth highest peak in the Americas. As the road winds ever higher, herds of guanacos graze on the steep slopes, pumas prowl in the bush, and condors soar above. ⊠ *Cordillera de Ansilta.*

WHERE TO STAY

$ · **El Mercadario.** This 1928 adobe farmhouse on the main street is a
B&B/INN gathering place for like-minded lovers of all that Barreal has to offer: good books and music are noticeable in the living room, comfort food comes from the kitchen, and the quaint rooms lead out onto an ample garden. **Pros:** local flavor and friendly owners; good value; bike and 4X4 excursions can be arranged. **Cons:** basic amenities; must preorder dinner; simple breakfast. ⑤ *Rooms from: 1300 pesos* ⊠ *Av. Presidente Roca and Calle Los Enamorados* ☎ *264/15–509–0907* ⊕ *www.elmercedario.com.ar* ⤳ *7 rooms* ⎺⊙⎺ *Breakfast.*

$ · **La Querencia.** Situated just beyond the south end of town, this South-
B&B/INN west-style inn looks west to the Andes and east to the pre-Cordillera. **Pros:** big backyard; mountain views and magnificent sunsets; home cooking. **Cons:** you'll need a car, bike, or horse to get around; basic rooms; poor Wi-Fi. ⑤ *Rooms from: 1900 pesos* ⊠ *Florida s/n* ☎ *264/15–436–4699 cell, 264/15–504–6958 cell* ⤳ *6 rooms* ⎺⊙⎺ *Breakfast.*

$ · **Posada San Eduardo.** A yellow adobe house with green shutters sits on
B&B/INN the shady corner of Calle Los Enamorados (Lover's Lane); inside, spacious rooms decorated with local weavings and rustic pine furniture open on to a colonial patio. **Pros:** peaceful setting; attentive staff and owners; good base for mountain forays. **Cons:** rooms are dark; small bathrooms; basic amenities. ⑤ *Rooms from: 1800 pesos* ⊠ *Av. San Martín at Los Enamorados* ☎ *264/6608–549* ⊟ *No credit cards* ⤳ *14 rooms* ⎺⊙⎺ *Breakfast.*

SPORTS AND THE OUTDOORS

Tour offices in Barreal, San Juan, and as far away as Mendoza City offer assorted activities—including hikes or horseback rides of varying lengths—in the Reserva Natural El Leoncito and the high mountain ranges of the Cordillera Ansilta.

Fortuna Viajes. In business for more than 30 years, this outfit arranges horseback trips lasting from one to nine days—including ones to Valle Colorado, where you'll see six peaks over 6,000 meters (20,000 feet). Hiking, mountaineering, fishing, and 4X4 excursions are also offered. ⊠ *Presidente Roca s/n* ☎ *264/15–404–0913, 264/15–404–0914* ⊕ *www.fortunaviajes.com.ar.*

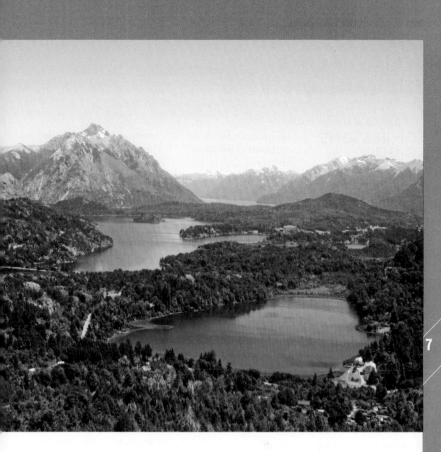

THE LAKE DISTRICT

WELCOME TO THE LAKE DISTRICT

TOP REASONS TO GO

★ **The Great Outdoors:** Hikers following well-marked trails in the national parks will encounter atmospheric forests, camera-ready cascades, and magnificent vistas. Waterways can carry rafters and kayakers all the way to Chile.

★ **Water, Water Everywhere:** 40 different lakes, seven major rivers flowing into two oceans, and you can spend days just staring at Nahuel Huapi Lake with its shoreline disappearing under distant peaks and volcanoes.

★ **Summer Skiing:** In the northern Lake District of Patagonia, June through September is ski season on the slopes of Cerro Catedral, near Bariloche, and Cerro Chapelco, near San Martín de los Andes.

★ **Savage Beauty:** One day a lake is silent, a mirror of the surrounding mountains. Another day waves are crashing on its shores, with wind tearing limbs from trees.

The Lake District lies in the folds of the Andes along the Chilean border in the provinces of Neuquén, Río Negro, and Chubut, where myriad glacial lakes lap at the forest's edge beneath snowcapped peaks.

The area includes three national parks, with towns in each. Bariloche is the base for exploring Parque Nacional Nahuel Huapi, and the departure point for the lake crossing to Chile. North of Bariloche is Parque Nacional Lanín, which contains the town of San Martín de los Andes. South of Bariloche and El Bolsón is Parque Nacional Lago Puelo in the Pacific watershed.

1 Bariloche. Full of sightseers, shoppers, and skiers in winter, this unashamedly touristy city on the southeastern shore of Nahuel Huapi Lake welcomes the world with all levels of lodgings, restaurants, and tour offices. The best part of Bariloche is beyond the city limits.

2 San Martín de los Andes and Nearby. Tourist amenities, combined with the alpine setting and distinctive architecture, make San Martín both a

pretty and practical base for exploring Parque Nacional Lanín. The town's location also makes it a logical stopover on the Seven Lakes Route.

3 Ruta de los Siete Lagos (Route of the Seven Lakes). The highlight of this 105-km (65-mile) drive is the scenic leg between Villa La Angostura and San Martín de los Andes, where the road winds up and around lake after lake—all of them different in shape, size, and setting.

4 Parque Nacional Nahuel Huapi. Founded in 1934, Argentina's oldest national park covers more than 7,050 square km (2,720 square miles): 800,000-plus visitors per year come to explore its high mountain glaciers, endless lakes, and enticing trails in buses, boats, and private vehicles.

5 El Bolsón and Nearby. Known as a refuge for hippies and ex-urbanites, amiable little El Bolsón is a valley town that straddles Ruta Nacional 40 just north of Parque Nacional Lago Puelo on the Chilean border. Hops and berry farms thrive in the microclimate along the Río Azul.

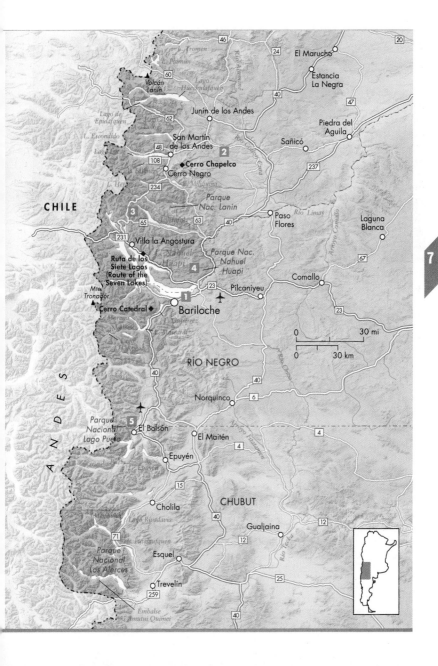

RUTA DE LOS SIETE LAGOS

To fully experience the Lake District, head north of Bariloche past Nahuel Huapi Lake to the Ruta de los Siete Lagos (Route of the Seven Lakes). This excursion has it all: lake after lake, mountains, wildflowers, waterfalls, hiking trails, and small towns along the way.

(above) You'll pass lots of big-leaf lupine, or Lupus polyphyllus—an invasive species here. (top right) Rainbow trout (bottom right) One of many stunning views along the way

The route itself links Bariloche and San Martín de los Andes. Start in Bariloche and follow the Circuito Grande along Ruta 237 and Ruta 231 to Villa La Angostura, then pass Lagos Espejo and Correntoso on Ruta 231 to get to mostly unpaved Ruta 234; take this north to San Martín.

For a day trip, return from San Martín de los Andes through Junín de Los Andes and Alicura (rutas 234, 40, and 237) on 260 km (161 miles) of paved road. If you have the time, though, overnight in San Martín de los Andes, take Ruta Provincial 63 to Confluencia, and then join Ruta 237 south along the Río Limay to Bariloche.

Renting a car is best, but even on a group tour it's spectacular. Buses are available from Bariloche or Villa La Angostura; you can also rent bicycles in these towns and take to the road on two wheels instead of four.

TIPS

Ask about road conditions before you leave Villa La Angostura; the route's unpaved portion north of there is often closed during heavy rains, winter storms, or construction. Best bets for picnic spots or campsites are the beaches of lakes Villarino, Falkner, and Hermoso. For maps, pick up *Guía Busch* and *Viajar Hoy* (tour pamphlets in English and Spanish). There are no gas stations on the Ruta de los Siete Lagos.

HIGHLIGHTS OF THE DRIVE

Rivers. Just past Villa La Angostura, the **Río Correntoso**—one of the world's shortest rivers at 300 meters (984 feet)—flows from the lake of the same name into Nahuel Huapi. This is a classic mouth-of-the-river fishing spot; you can watch the action from the glassed-in deck at the Hotel Correntoso *(see Where to Stay in Villa La Angostura)* or from the old fishing lodge on the shore of Nahuel Huapi Lake.

Lakes. Traveling north from Villa Angostura to San Martín de los Andes is the most scenic part of the drive, and it's no coincidence that this is where you'll find the region's most scenic namesake natural features—lakes. **Lago Correntoso** (Rapid Water Lake) is the first one you'll pass, and you'll do so immediately after you cross over the Río Correntoso. Drive along its northern shore to arrive at an abandoned hotel site; from here you'll see a road that leads to **Lago Espejo Chico** (Little Mirror Lake), with a beach, a campground, and trails. Return to the main road and you'll come to **Lago Espejo** (Mirror Lake)—head to the viewpoint for a good lunch spot, or use the camping area's tables. **Lago Falkner** (east side of the road) has sandy beaches and a popular campground. It is linked by a stream and an isthmus, which you will cross to **Lago Villarino** (west side of the road). **Lago Hermoso** (Beautiful Lake) is a small sheltered lake. A sunny beach faces west, with nearby camping and a few cabins. Finally, before you reach San Martín de los Andes, enjoy **Lago Machónico's** dry landscape via the scenic overlook, or take the short walk to the shore.

Waterfalls. Between Lakes Villarino and Falkner, **Cascada Vulignanco**, a 20-meter (66-foot) waterfall, is visible on the left-hand side of the road, where you can pull off at the *mirador* (overlook).

DETOURS

Four km (3 miles) south of Lago Villarino, jade-green **Lago Escondido** (Hidden Lake) lies veiled in a thick forest. You'll need to park and walk in.

At Pichi Traful, turn east onto a bumpy road for 2 km (1 mile) and walk to the sandy beach at **Pichi Traful Lake** (aka Brazo Norte de Lago Traful). Fishermen, bikers, and hikers enjoy camping or picnicking here.

About 30 km (18 miles) north of the junction of Ruta Provincial 234 and Ruta Provincial 65, look on your left for a sign indicating the trail to **Casacada Ñivinenco** (Whispering Falls). The 2-km (1-mile) trail crosses a river (in November and December the river is high; check conditions ahead of time), then follows the river into a silent forest.

If you pass through **Confluencia**, take Ruta Provincial 65 along the Traful River west a few km to **Cuyín Manzano**, a dirt road that continues along the river into a world of strange caves and limestone rock formations.

7

CIRCUITO CHICO Y CIRCUITO GRANDE

If you're in Bariloche, get out of town to take in some of the spectacular scenery and old-school resort feel of the area on either the Circuito Chico (Small Circuit) or Circuito Grande (Large Circuit) by rental car, hired driver, or tour group.

(above) "We drove the Circuito Chico and stopped at this overlook." –HappyTrvlr (top right) "With flowers in full bloom it couldn't get much better." –Josh Roe (bottom right) Peninsula Llao Llao

The Circuito Chico is a 70-km (44-mile) half-day round-trip from Bariloche along the southern shore of Lago Nahuel Huapi. Visitors head out to the Llao Llao Peninsula to ski or take in the lake views and waterfalls without ever being too far from a cup of tea.

The Circuito Grande covers 250 km (155 miles) and is an all-day excursion across the lake from Bariloche. This drive is more about wooded hikes and hidden lakes, and includes two towns where you could spend a night.

You can do the Circuito Chico on one tank of gas. Circuit Grande, however, has longer unpopulated spans. Leave Bariloche with a full tank and refuel at Confluencia or Villa La Angostura.

WEATHER TIPS

The Circuito Chico has lots of traffic but is otherwise an easy drive whatever the weather. The Circuito Grande is another story. The roads to Villa La Angostura and Confluencia are good, but Ruta Provincial 65 past Lago Traful is unpaved and can be treacherous in bad weather. Always check road conditions with the Automóvil Club Argentino (⊕ www.aca.org.ar), the park office, or your hotel.

CIRCUITO CHICO

From Bariloche's Centro Cívico (Km 0), follow the shore of Lago Nahuel Huapi west on Ruta 237. At Km 7, stop at **Playa Bonita**'s sandy beach. At Km 10, take the chairlift or climb to the top of **Cerro Campanario.** When you reach the Península Llao Llao (Km 25.5), bear right to **Puerto Pañuelo,** where boats embark on lake excursions to Isla Victoria, Puerto Blest, and the boat crossing to Chile. Across from the Puerto Pañuelo, the **Llao Llao Hotel & Resort** *(See Where to Stay in Bariloche)* sits on a lakeside knoll with a backdrop of sheer cliffs and snow-covered mountains. Continue following Ruta 77 to **Bahía Lopez**; you'll approach through a forest of ghostly, leafless *lenga* trees. After Bahía Lopez, the road crosses **Arroyo Lopez** (Lopez Creek); stop to hike to the waterfall or continue on Ruta 77 to **Punto Panorámico,** one of the most scenic overlooks on the peninsula. Just before you cross the Moreno Bridge, an unmarked dirt road off to the right leads to the rustic village of Colonia Suiza, a perfect stop for tea or lunch. Backtrack to cross Moreno Bridge, then leave Ruta 77 for Ruta 237 back to Bariloche.

CIRCUITO GRANDE

Leaving Bariloche on Ruta 237 heading east, follow the Río Limay into the **Valle Encantado** (Enchanted Valley), with its magical red rocks. Before crossing the bridge at Confluencia (where the Río Traful joins the Limay), turn left onto Ruta 65 to Lago Traful. Five km (3 miles) beyond the turnoff, a dirt road to Cuyín Manzano leads to **astounding sandstone formations.** Return to Ruta 65 and follow Lago Traful's shore. When you see the sign indicating a mirador, stop and climb the wooden stairs to one of the loveliest views in the region. Descend to Villa Traful, follow the lakeshore, then dive into a dense forest of *caña colihue* and lenga trees. At the intersection with Ruta 237, turn left and follow the shore of Lago Correntoso to the paved road down to Villa La Angostura. The road skirts Lago Nahuel Huapi back into Bariloche.

NEED A BREAK?

Circuito Chico: Chiado (✉ *Av. Bustillo [R237], Km 18* ☎ *2944/448-152 Closed Wed.*) is a log house with a corrugated metal roof, a stone terrace, and colorful plants hanging out over the lake. Views are through the gnarly branches of a giant *coihué* tree to blue water and mountains. The brie sorrentinos in pear and port sauce are as good as the view.

Circuito Grande: If you visit Lago Traful in the morning, chances are you'll hit Villa Traful in time for lunch at Nancu Lahuen (✉ *Village center, opposite chapel* ☎ *294/447-9017*), a casual spot in the middle of town with home cooking. If you've brought a picnic, continue on past the town to the beach, where the road leaves the lake for Ruta 234 and Villa La Angostura. In Villa La Angostura, head to La Casita de la Oma (✉ *Cerro Inacayal 303* ☎ *2944/494-602*), which serves homemade cakes, pies, and scones. Any dulce de leche item is a sure bet.

Updated by
Melissa Kitson

The northern Lake District has become Patagonia's most popular tourist region. Spread over three states and encompassing more than a million hectares (2½ million acres) of nature preserves, it offers more than natural beauty. The hundreds of sapphire lakes here allow visitors to experience an array of outdoor activities. Lakes such as Lago Nahuel Huapi and Lago Puelo are the focal points of eponymous national parks; at both you can choose between fishing, boating (whether in a kayak, raft, or motor launch), and swimming from a pretty playa.

Back on dry land other recreational opportunities await. In the warmer months, horseback riding, mountain biking, and hiking are popular pastimes; climbing Volcán Lanín for a wraparound view of the sublime landscape is another memorable option. In winter, conversely, snow-sport enthusiasts head for the hills. Cerro Catedral (the continent's oldest ski area) is notable for its size, terrain, and superb setting, while smaller areas like Chapelco attract mostly vacationing Argentineans and Brazilians.

A broad range of accommodations—ranging from rustic refugios and classic ranches to luxe destination hotels—cater to these travelers year-round. Yet despite growing popularity and heightened accessibility from developed towns like San Martín de los Andes and Bariloche, first-time visitors are constantly amazed at how easy it is to lose yourself in a silent forest, on a rugged mountaintop, or by one of the district's beautiful namesake lakes.

PLANNING

WHEN TO GO

June through September the weather is typical of any ski region—blowing snowstorms, rain, and fog punctuated by days of brilliant sunshine. August and September are the best months for skiing, as the slopes are crowded with vacationers in July.

In December the weather can be cool, breezy, overcast, or rainy, but the rewards for bringing an extra sweater and raingear are great: an abundance of wildflowers and few tourists. January and February are the peak summer months, with days that are warm and long (the sun sets at 10 pm). March and April are good months to visit; the leaves of lenga and *ñire* trees brighten the rolling green forests with splashes of yellow and red, but rainy, cloudy days and cold nights can curtail some excursions.

GETTING HERE AND AROUND

The most efficient way to get here is by air from Buenos Aires or Calafate. The most scenic way to arrive is from Puerto Montt, Chile, by boat through the lakes. Buses are the new trains—fast, inexpensive, with varying degrees of luxury, including beds, meals, and attendants. A car or bus is the best way to travel between cities in the Lake District, and once you've settled in a destination, you can use local tours, buses, taxis, or a *remis* (a hired car with driver).

AIR TRAVEL

Aerolíneas Argentinas (⊕ *www.aerolineas.com.ar*) flies from Buenos Aires to Bariloche, Esquel, San Martín de los Andes, and Neuquén; it also connects Bariloche and Calafate. LATAM (⊕ *www.lan.com*) flies to Bariloche from Buenos Aires, as well as from Santiago, Chile.

BOAT TRAVEL

Traveling between Bariloche and Puerto Montt, Chile, by boat is one of the most popular excursions in Argentina. It requires three lake crossings and various buses, and can be done in a day or overnight. Travel agents and tour operators in Bariloche and Buenos Aires can arrange this trip.

BUS TRAVEL

Buses arrive in Bariloche from every corner of Argentina—from Jujuy in the north, Ushuaia in the south, and everywhere in between.

CAR TRAVEL

Driving to the Lake District from Buenos Aires is a long haul: the trip takes at least three days, and the route—extending for more than 1,500 km (930 miles)—has interminable stretches with few hotels, gas stations, or restaurants. In Bariloche, unless you're on a tour or a ski-only vacation, renting a car gives you the freedom to stop when and where you want. The Ruta de los Siete Lagos closes when weather is bad; for winter travel, rent a 4X4. Hiring a remis is another option.

RESTAURANTS

Restaurant reservations are seldom needed except during school, Easter, and summer holidays (July, January, and February). Attire is informal, and tipping is the same as in the rest of the country (about 10%). Most menus will feature regional dishes such as *trucha,*the salmon-like trout commonly found in the lakes and rivers of the district, as well as *cordero* (lamb), *ciervo* (venison), and *jabalí* (wild boar).

HOTELS

Idyllic lake-view lodges, cozy *cabañas* (cabins), vast *estancias* (ranches), and inexpensive *hospedajes* or *residenciales* (bed-and-breakfasts) are found in towns and in the countryside throughout northern Patagonia. Superluxurious hotels in Bariloche and Villa La Angostura attract outdoor enthusiasts from all over the world, as do small family-run hostels where backpackers squeeze five to a room. Fishing lodges in the San Martín de los Andes area and the Cholila Valley are not only for anglers; they make great headquarters for hiking, boating, or just getting away. Most of them include all meals. Guides are extra. "Apart-hotels" have small, furnished apartments with kitchenettes. Local tourist offices are helpful in finding anything from a room in a residence to a country inn or a downtown hotel. Advance reservations are highly recommended if you're traveling during peak times (December–March; July for the ski resorts). Note: lodging prices include tax (IVA—which is 21%) unless otherwise noted. *Hotel reviews have been shortened. For full information, visit Fodors.com.*

WHAT IT COSTS				
	$	**$$**	**$$$**	**$$$$**
Restaurants (in Pesos)	Under 300 pesos	301 pesos–500 pesos	501 pesos–750 pesos	over 750 pesos
Hotels (in USD)	Under $116	$116–$200	$201–$300	over $300

Restaurant prices are the average cost of a main course at dinner or, if dinner is not served, at lunch. Hotel prices are the lowest cost of a standard double room in high season.

TOURS

Alunco. Everything from hour-long tours in Bariloche to week-long excursions in the surrounding countryside can be arranged by Alunco. The company works with local guides who know the area well and have partnerships with many estancias and restaurants. Adventure and ski package are also available. ⊠ *Moreno 187, 1st fl., Bariloche* ☎ *2944/422–283* ⊕ *www.aluncoturismo.com.ar* ☜ *From 150 pesos.*

Causana Viajes. The team at Causana Viajes takes pride in providing tours that respect the natural surroundings. They've been offering excursions through Nahuel Huapi National Park for just over 30 years. ⊠ *Av. Guillermo Rawson 1331, Puerto Madryn* ☎ *2965/452–769* ⊕ *causanatour.com.ar.*

El Claro Turismo. For 25 years, El Claro Turismo has been leading excursions to Cerro Chapelco and Parque Nacional Lanín. Visitors can choose a half- or full-day tour to nearby attractions like Villa Quila Quina, or opt for a week-long package that includes accommodations, airport transfers, and some meals. ⊠ *Colonel Diaz 751, San Martín* *de los Andes* ☎ *2972/428–876, 2972/425–876* ⊕ *www.elclaroturismo. com.ar* ✉ *From 300 pesos for day trips; from 4,000 pesos for packages.*

Siete Lagos Turismo. This outfit provides a comprehensive range of tourism services including guided excursions, vehicle rentals, airport transfers, plus bus and hotel reservations. Its rafting adventures are particularly popular. ✉ *Villegas 313, San Martín de los Andes* ☎ *2972/427–877* ⊕ *sietelagosturismo.com.ar/empresa.html* ✉ *From 350 pesos.*

VISITOR INFORMATION

The comprehensive InterPatagonia website (⊕ *www.interpatagonia. com*), covering every city and region in Patagonia, is an excellent resource for travelers. Local tourist offices (Direcciónes de Turismo) are helpful, easy to find, and usually open late every day.

BARILOCHE

1,615 km (1,001 miles) southwest of Buenos Aires (2 hours by plane); 432 km (268 miles) south of Neuquén on R237; 1,639 km (1,016 miles) north of Río Gallegos; 876 km (543 miles) northwest of Trelew; 357 km (221 miles) east of Puerto Montt, Chile, via lake crossing.

Bariloche is the gateway to all the recreational and scenic splendors of the northern Lake District and the headquarters for Parque Nacional Nahuel Huapi. Although planes, boats, and buses arrive daily, you can escape on land or water—or just by looking out a window—into a dazzling wilderness of lakes, waterfalls, mountain glaciers, forests, and meadows.

The town of Bariloche hugs the southeastern shore of Lago Nahuel Huapi, expanding rapidly east toward the airport and west along the lake toward Llao Llao, as Argentineans and foreigners buy and build without any apparent zoning plan. Being the most popular vacation destination in Patagonia has not been kind to the town once called the "Switzerland of the Andes." Traffic barely moves on streets and sidewalks during holidays and the busy months (January, February, March, July, and August).

Nevertheless, the Centro Cívico (Civic Center) has not lost its architectural integrity. Designed by Alejandro Bustillo (1889–1982), the landmark square is as handsome as ever; and the buildings around it—with their gray-green local stone, brightly varnished wood, and decorative gable ends—are prime examples of the region's signature alpine style. With its view of the lake and mountains, the Centro Cívico is a good place to begin exploring Bariloche.

GETTING HERE AND AROUND

Many travelers choose to come via the Chilean Lakes crossing. If you're flying from Buenos Aires, regular nonstop flights take about two hours; by contrast, long-distance sleeper buses from the capital can take up to 23 hours. The airport is 30 minutes from the Centro Cívico, the bus terminal is 15; in either case, you can take a public bus into town (rutas 72 and 10, respectively) or grab a cab.

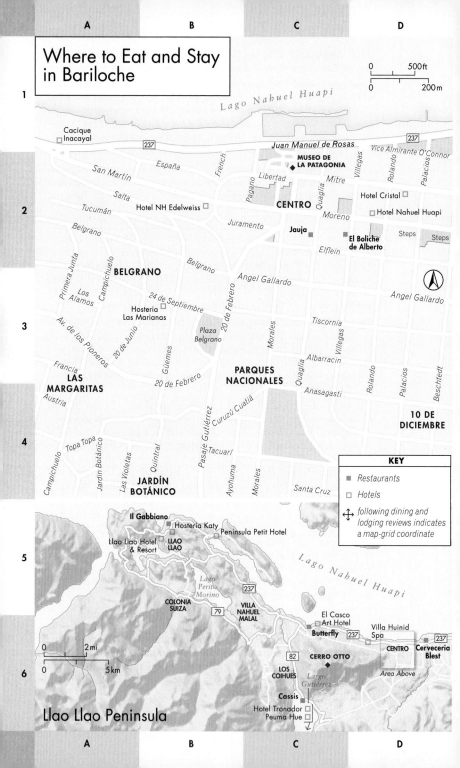

Where to Eat and Stay in Bariloche

A **B** **C** **D**

0 — 500ft
0 — 200m

1

Lago Nahuel Huapi

Cacique
□ Inacayal

237

Juan Manuel de Rosas

237

España

French

Vice Almirante O'Connor

San Martín

Pagano

Libertad

◆ MUSEO DE
LA PATAGONIA

Mitre

Villegas

Rolando

Palacios

2

Salta

Hotel NH Edelweiss □

Quaglia

CENTRO

Hotel Cristal □

Tucumán

Juramento

Moreno

□ Hotel Nahuel Huapi

Belgrano

■ Jauja

Elflein

■ El Boliche
de Alberto

Steps

Steps

Primera Junta

Campichuelo

BELGRANO

Belgrano

Angel Gallardo

Los
Alamos

24 de Septiembre

20 de Febrero

Angel Gallardo

3

Av. de los Pioneros

Hosteria
Las Marianas

Morales

Tiscornia

Villegas

Francia

20 de Junio

Güemes

Plaza
Belgrano

20 de Febrero

Quaglia

Albarracin

Rolando

Palacios

Beschtedt

LAS
MARGARITAS

20 de Febrero

PARQUES
NACIONALES

Anasagasti

Austria

Pasaje Gutiérrez

Curuzú Cuatiá

10 DE
DICIEMBRE

4

Campichuelo

Topa Topa

Jardín Botánico

Las Violetas

Quintral

Tacuarí

Ayohuma

Morales

Santa Cruz

JARDÍN
BOTÁNICO

KEY

■ *Restaurants*

□ *Hotels*

◆ *following dining and
lodging reviews indicates
a map-grid coordinate*

5

Il Gabbiano ■

■ Hosteria Katy

Llao Llao Hotel
& Resort

LLAO
LLAO

■ Peninsula Petit Hotel

*Lago
Nahuel Huapi*

*Lago
Perita
Morino*

237

COLONIA
SUIZA

79

VILLA
NAHUEL
MALAL

El Casco
□ Art Hotel

Villa Huinid
Spa

■ Butterfly

237

CENTRO

■ Cerveceria
Blest

237

6

0 — 2 mi
0 — 5 km

82

LOS
COIHUES

◆ CERRO OTTO

*Largo
Gutiérrez*

Area Above

■ Cassis

Hotel Tronador □
Peuma Hue □

Llao Llao Peninsula

A **B** **C** **D**

For long excursions, such as the Ruta de los Siete Lagos, Circuito Grande, or Tronadór, sign up for a tour through your hotel or with a local tour agency. The *Guía Busch,* available at car-rental agencies, kiosks, and hotels, has listings of the latter along with good maps. Fishing, rafting, and biking trips typically include transportation from your hotel; skiers can reach the slopes by public bus, although many hotels also have private shuttles. If you prefer the independence of figuring out maps and driving yourself, rent a car.

Bus Contacts Andesmar. ☎ *0261/405–0600* ⊕ *www.andesmar.com.* **Bariloche Bus Terminal.** ✉ *Av. 12 de Octubre* ☎ *2944/432–860.* **Don Otto.** ☎ *0810/333–7575.* **El Valle.** ☎ *0810/333–7575* ⊕ *www.elvalle.com. ar.* **Via Bariloche.** ☎ *2944/432–444* ⊕ *www.viabariloche.com.ar.* **VIATAC.** ☎ *0810/333–7575* ⊕ *www.viatac.com.ar.*

Rental Cars Baricoche. ✉ *Moreno 115, 1st fl., office 14* ☎ *2944/427–638* ⊕ *www.baricoche.com.ar.*

SAFETY AND PRECAUTIONS
Driving in Bariloche requires total attention to blind corners, one-way streets, and stop signs where no one stops. Be wary of road construction as avenues such as Bustillo regularly undergo maintenance work. Don't leave anything in your car. Bariloche's challenging sidewalks are riddled with uneven steps, broken pavement, and unexpected holes—all potential ankle breakers.

ESSENTIALS
Visitor and Tour Information Oficina Municipal de Turismo. ✉ *Centro Cívico, across from clock tower* ☎ *2944/429–850* ⊕ *www.barilocheturismo.gob.ar.*

EXPLORING

TOP ATTRACTIONS
Cerro Otto. For an aerial view of the area around Bariloche, ascend 1,405 meters (4,608 feet) to the top of Cerro Otto. A little red cable car owned by **Teleférico Cerro Otto** will carry you there in about 12 minutes, and all ticket proceeds go to local hospitals. ■TIP→ **A free shuttle bus leaves from the corner of Mitre and Villegas, and Perito Moreno and Independencia.** You can also hike or bike to the top, or drive up from Bariloche on a gravel road. In winter, cross-country skis and sleds are for rent at the cafeteria. In summer, hiking and mountain biking are the main activities. There is a revolving restaurant on the summit. For a real thrill, try soaring out over the lake in a paraplane. ✉ *Av. de los Pioneros, 5 km (3 miles) west of Bariloche* ☎ *2944/441–035 for information on schedules and equipment rental* ⊕ *www.telefericobariloche.com.ar* 🏷 *450 pesos* ⊙ *Cable car may close for a few wks in May for maintenance.*

Museo de la Patagonia. This small museum explains the social and geological history of northern Patagonia through displays of Indian and gaucho artifacts and exhibits on regional flora and fauna. The stories of the Mapuche and the Conquista del Desierto (Conquest of the Desert) are told in detail. ✉ *Centro Cívico, next to arch over Bartolomé*

CLOSE UP

Chilean Lakes Crossing

Cruce a Chile por Los Lagos (*Chile Lake Crossing*). This unique excursion by land and lakes can be done in one or two days in either direction.

Travelers board the boat at Puerto Pañuelo, west of Bariloche, then travel by bus up to Laguna Frías, a cold glacial lake frozen in winter. After crossing that lake to Puerto Fríos, you pass Argentine customs, then board another bus that climbs through lush rain forest over a pass before descending to Peulla. Clear Chilean customs just before a lodge by Lago Todos los Santos, where you stop for lunch. You may spend the night at the lodge (recommended) or head straight to Chile by catamaran from Peulla, with volcano views. An overnight stay is mandatory in winter. The boat trip ends at the port of Petrohué. Your final bus ride skirts Lago Llanquihue, stopping at the Petrohué waterfalls, and arriving at last in the the town of Puerto Varas. Guides usually speak English, but if you want to stay on the safe side, do this trip with a tour group. ⊠ *Mitre 219* ☎ *2944/426–228* ⊕ *www.cruceandino.com* ✉ *$280 (not including lunch)*.

If you're pressed for time, return to Bariloche by paved road via Osorno, crossing at Cardenal Samoré (aka Paso Puyehue) to Villa La Angostura, which is 125 km (78 miles) from the border to Bariloche on Ruta Nacional 231.

OTHER CROSSINGS

Paso Hua Hum is the only crossing open year-round. It may be the shortest route—only 47 km (29 miles) from San Martín de los Andes on Ruta Provincial 48—as the condor flies, but it's the longest journey by road, after factoring in the 1½-hour ferry ride across Lake Pirehueico on the Chilean side. There are three ferries daily, and buses leave regularly from San Martín de los Andes. You can also make this crossing by raft on the river Hua Hum.

Farther north, and accessible via Junín de los Andes, are two passes that require a longer excursion. Mamuil Malal (aka Paso Tromen) is 67 km (42 miles) northwest of Junín de los Andes on Ruta Provincial 60. This dirt road crosses Parque Nacional Lanín and passes through a forest of ancient araucaria trees as it heads for the foot of Volcán Lanín. Just before the park office, a road leads to good picnic spots and campsites on Lago Tromen. If you continue on to Chile, you'll see the Villarrica and Quetupil-lán volcanoes to the south and Pucón to the north.

Paso Icalma is 132 km (82 miles) west of Zapala on Ruta Nacional 13. Villa Pehuenia, 10 km (6 miles) before the pass, is a small village on the shore of Lake Alluminé with modern accommodations and restaurants. Rafting, fishing, or horse, bike, and raft rentals might tempt you to stay awhile.

No fresh fruits, meats, dairy products, or vegetables are allowed across the border, so bring a snack for long stretches without food. Lake crossings are not fun in driving rain and high waves. Snow may close some passes in winter. If driving, double-check with your rental agent that you have all the necessary paperwork. It's also good to have some Chilean pesos with you; it can be expensive to change them at the border.

Mitre ☎ 2944/422–309 ⊕ www.museodelapatagonia.nahuelhuapi.gov. ar ✉ 50 peso donation ⊙ Closed Sun. and Mon.

WHERE TO EAT

$$$$
INTERNATIONAL

✕ **Butterfly.** For an indulgent meal and direct views of Lake Nahuel Huapi, consider this intimate, modern restaurant. Every element is carefully thought out—from the tiny handmade salt spoons to the sublime degustation menus. **Known for:** shrimp in white chocolate sauce; picture-perfect desserts; lakeside views. $ *Average main: 1200 pesos* ✉ *Hua Huan 7831* ☎ *294/446–1441* ⊕ *www.butterflypatagonia.com. ar* ⊙ *Closed Sun., no lunch* ✛ *C6.*

$$$$
CONTEMPORARY
Fodor'sChoice
★

✕ **Cassis.** Chef Mariana Wolf combines the freshest seasonal ingredients, many from her own rural garden, in beautifully presented dishes that are both elegant and comforting. Savor standout dishes like prawns with rosehip relish, barley, and ginger while gazing at the tranquil shores of Lago Gutierrez. **Known for:** organic, homegrown ingredients; dazzling desserts; intimate service. $ *Average main: 1000 pesos* ✉ *Ruta 82, Km 5.5, Lago Gutiérrez* ☎ *294/459–3650* ⊕ *www.cassis.com.ar* ⊙ *Closed Mon. and Sun. for lunch* ✛ *C6.*

$$$$
ARGENTINE

✕ **Cerveceria Blest.** This lively spot claims that it was the first brewpub in Argentina, and its relaxed bustle hits the spot after a day on the slopes. You can come in just for an après-ski beer sampler or stay for pizzas, steak potpies, and other Anglophile dinner options. **Known for:** hearty goulash; extensive range of artisan beer; cozy atmosphere. $ *Average main: 250 pesos* ✉ *Av. Bustillo km 4* ☎ *2944/891–894* ⊕ *www.cervezablest.com.ar* ✛ *D6.*

$$$$
STEAKHOUSE

✕ **El Boliche de Alberto.** Leather place mats, calfskin menus, and the smell of beef all hint heavily at steak house. Alberto has the best beef in Bariloche. **Known for:** succulent beef; rich, creamy pastas; family-size servings. $ *Average main: 250 pesos* ✉ *Elflein 158* ☎ *2944/401–040* ⊕ *www.elbolichedealberto.com.ar* ✛ *C2.*

$$$$
ITALIAN

✕ **Il Gabbiano.** Staff at this cozy but elegant candlelit house on the Circuito Chico near Llao Llao boast, "we don't serve lunch because preparing dinner takes all day." It's hard to argue with that after you sample the exquisite Italian menu, which changes daily. Look for pumpkin ravioli or tortelli stuffed with wild boar; they also have a way with fresh trout. **Known for:** authentic, homemade pastas; charming bowtie wearing waiters; melt-in-your-mouth osso buco. $ *Average main: 870 pesos* ✉ *Av. Bustillo, Km 24.300* ☎ *2944/448–346* ⊙ *Closed Tues. No lunch* ✛ *B5.*

$$$$
ARGENTINE

✕ **Jauja.** Locals come to this friendly restaurant for its outstanding pastas and variety of entrées: expect meats from Patagonia to the pampas, fish from both oceans, local game, and fresh vegetables. Hearty portions make this an ideal place to end a long day on the slopes. **Known for:** delicious pastas; generous servings; regional dishes. $ *Average main: 450 pesos* ✉ *Elflein 148* ☎ *2944/422–952* ⊕ *www.restaurantejauja. com.ar* ✛ *C2.*

7

WHERE TO STAY

If you don't have a car, finding a place in town may be the most convenient option. That said, local buses run regularly and choosing a hotel or cabin en route to the Llao Llao Peninsula will give you better access to hiking trails and lake views. Many of the restaurants with the best views are also located away from the city center. Distances listed for out-of-town dining and lodging properties are measured in kilometers from the Bariloche Centro Cívico.

$$ HOTEL **Cacique Inacayal.** The waterside Cacique Inacayal has a spectacular spa and swimming pool with views overlooking Lake Nahuel Huapi. **Pros:** impressive views; central location; free shuttle to Cerro Catedral in season. **Cons:** rooms facing nearby disco can be noisy; no air-conditioning; dated decor. $ *Rooms from: US$180* ✉ *Juan Manuel de Rosas 625* ☎ *2944/433–888* ⊕ *www.hotelinacayal.com.ar* 🛏 *67 rooms* ❍| *Breakfast* ✚ *A1.*

$$$$ HOTEL Fodor's Choice ★ **El Casco Art Hotel.** At this stunning modern hotel all public spaces—halls, wine bar, gourmet restaurant, even the downstairs gym, indoor-out pool, and large Jacuzzi—face the lake, and a private launch docked at the pier makes getting out on the water easy. **Pros:** art everywhere; activities galore; the area's most stylish option. **Cons:** pricey; next to highway; transport required to get to city center. $ *Rooms from: US$350* ✉ *Av. Bustillo, Km 11.5* ☎ *2944/463–131* ⊕ *www.hotelelcasco. com* 🛏 *33 suites* ❍| *Breakfast* ✚ *C6.*

$ B&B/INN FAMILY **Hostería Katy.** This charming country cottage is surrounded by more than an acre of forest and offers simple rooms that are clean, quiet, and filled with natural light. **Pros:** stunning location surrounded by nature; car rental and airport transfers available; homemade bread and jams at breakfast. **Cons:** far from the center of Bariloche; difficult to get to and from without a car; basic rooms and amenities. $ *Rooms from: US$80* ✉ *Bustillo km 24.300* ☎ *2944/448–023* ⊕ *www.hosteriakaty. com* 🛏 *7 rooms* ❍| *Free Breakfast* ✚ *B5.*

$$ B&B/INN **Hostería Las Marianas.** On a quiet street surrounded by well-tended gardens, this perfectly proportioned Tyrolean villa in Barrio Belgrano (Bariloche's nicest neighborhood) is only four blocks from the city center, but it feels a world away. **Pros:** sunny hillside location; away from the crowds; friendly, multilingual staff. **Cons:** uphill haul from city center; tiny bathrooms; echoey hallways. $ *Rooms from: US$150* ✉ *24 de Septiembre 218* ☎ *2944/439–876* ⊕ *www.hosterialasmarianas.com. ar* 🛏 *16 rooms* ❍| *Breakfast* ✚ *B3.*

$$ HOTEL **Hotel Cristal.** This basic businesslike hotel lies in the center of Bariloche and has a fully equipped health club—complete with pool and spa. **Pros:** central location on a popular downtown street; good value; generous breakfast. **Cons:** small bathrooms; street-facing rooms can be noisy; frequented by tour groups. $ *Rooms from: US$190* ✉ *Mitre 355* ☎ *2944/422–442* ⊕ *www.hotel-cristal.com.ar* 🛏 *50 rooms* ❍| *Breakfast* ✚ *D2.*

$$ HOTEL **Hotel Nahuel Huapi.** This slick hotel on a busy downtown street in Bariloche has a spacious lobby with a wine bar in one corner and a sit-around fireplace in another; some rooms have a nice view into the neighboring garden. **Pros:** central location; good accessibility for people with disabilities; comfy bed. **Cons:** rooms overlooking street might be

noisy; elevator does not reach top floor; scatty Wi-Fi. $ *Rooms from: US$200* ✉ *Moreno 252* ☎ *2944/433–635* ⊕ *www.hotelnahuelhuapi. com.ar* ⌁ *74 rooms* ⊙ *Breakfast* ✛ *D2*.

$$$ ⊡ **Hotel NH Edelweiss.** This medium-size hotel is within walking distance
HOTEL   of everything in town and its top-floor rooms have stunning lake views
and bay windows. **Pros:** great location; spacious rooms; fancy fitness cen-
ter. **Cons:** windows don't open; so-so streetside restaurant; decor needs a
makeover. $ *Rooms from: US$230* ✉ *Av. San Martín 202* ☎ *2944/445–
500* ⊕ *www.edelweiss.com.ar* ⌁ *99 rooms* ⊙ *Breakfast* ✛ *B2*.

$$ ⊡ **Hotel Tronadór.** This all-inclusive stone-and-log lodge on Lago Mas-
HOTEL   cardi is the perfect springboard to explore the glaciers and waterfalls of
Monte Tronadór, which lies only 25 km (16 miles) up the road. **Pros:**
practically in the lap of the region's highest mountain glacier; amenities
include a game room, private beach, and organic garden; peaceful location. **Cons:** the road here is one-way heading toward the hotel 10:30
am–2 pm, one-way heading away 4 pm–7:30 pm, and two-way 7:30
pm–10:30 am only; activities not included in price; difficult to get to
and from. $ *Rooms from: US$130* ✉ *RN40 west from Bariloche 66
km, past Villa Masacardi, turn right on dirt road to west end of Lago
Mascardi* ☎ *2944/490–550* ⊕ *www.hoteltronador.com* ⊙ *Closed mid-
Apr.–mid-Nov.* ⌁ *36 rooms* ⊙ *All meals* ✛ *C6*.

$$$$ ⊡ **Llao Llao Hotel & Resort.** This masterpiece by architect Alejandro
RESORT   Bustillo, surrounded by three lakes and looking out to cliffs and snow-
covered mountains, caters to all tastes; the historic main building has
quirky rooms with locally crafted, one-of-a-kind furniture pieces, while
those in the newer Lake Moreno wing incorporate a more modern
aesthetic. **Pros:** gorgeous setting with dramatic lake views; helpful staff;
lots of activities. **Cons:** pricey; 40 minutes from Bariloche center; rooms
in historic wing a little dated. $ *Rooms from: US$478* ✉ *Av. Bustillo,
Km 25, 25 km (16 miles) west of Bariloche* ☎ *2944/448–530* ⊕ *www.
llaollao.com* ⌁ *218 rooms* ⊙ *Breakfast* ✛ *B5*.

$$ ⊡ **Península Petit Hotel.** Combining the amenities of a hotel with the
HOTEL   warmth of a home, this handsome lodge sitting at the edge of Lake
Nahuel Huapi is a great getaway spot for couples. **Pros:** all suites have
lake views; waterfront activities; homemade breakfast. **Cons:** limited
capacity; 25 minutes from center; walls are a bit thin. $ *Rooms from:
US$130* ✉ *Av. Campanario 493* ☎ *294/444–8537* ⊕ *www.peninsula-
petithotel.com.ar* ⊙ *Closed May* ⌁ *11 rooms* ⊙ *Breakfast* ✛ *B5*.

$$$$ ⊡ **Peuma Hue.** Inside Peuma Hue, a sense of rustic luxury prevails
HOTEL   (picture pine beams overhead, kilim rugs on wood floors, and guests
FAMILY   gathered around the stone fireplace); outside, Lago Gutiérrez shim-
mers through the trees across the lawn. **Pros:** lovely grounds; mas-
sage, yoga, and wine tastings are just the tip of the activities iceberg;
delicious organic meals. **Cons:** remote location; little to do when the
weather is bad; charges for extra activities. $ *Rooms from: US$410*
✉ *R40, Km 2014, Enter dirt road, about 2 miles to Lago Gutiérrez*
☎ *2944/501–030* ⊕ *www.peuma-hue.com* ⊙ *Closed June* ⌁ *16 rooms*
⊙ *All-inclusive; Breakfast* ☞ *30% deposit required* ✛ *C6*.

$$ ⊡ **Villa Huinid.** This peaceful complex consists of a grand hotel and
HOTEL   older two-story log-and-stucco cottages on the lawns below—the latter

Evening shoppers on Avenida Bartolomé Mitre, Bariloche

have stone chimneys, well-tended gardens, and wooden decks that give them the appearance of private homes. **Pros:** cabins have one-to-four bedrooms, combining privacy with hotel amenities; lake-view pool and spa; family and play areas on-site. **Cons:** outdoor hike from cabins to breakfast in hotel; 15–20 minute walk into town; can be busy with tour groups, particularly at breakfast. $ *Rooms from: US$190* ⊠ *Av. Bustillo, Km 2.6* ☎ *2944/523–523* ⊕ *www.villahuinid.com.ar* ↻ *91 rooms* ⦿ *Breakfast* ✛ *D6.*

SHOPPING

Along Bariloche's main streets, Calles Mitre and Moreno, and the cross streets from Quaglia to Rolando, you can find shops selling sports equipment, leather goods, hand-knit sweaters, and gourmet food like homemade jams, dried meats, and chocolate.

Ahumadero Familia Weiss. Come here to buy delicious pâtés, cheeses, smoked fish, and wild game. ⊠ *Mitre 131* ☎ *2944/435–874* ⊕ *www. ahumaderoweiss.com.*

Mamuschka. Crowned by giant mamuschka dolls, this renowned chocolate store is famous for its range of high quality, if slightly more expensive, chocolate and pastry products. Ask for the house specialty (a chocolate mousse "Timbal") or simply admire the beautifully decorated *bombones* (chocolate balls). ⊠ *Mitre 298* ☎ *0924/442–3294* ⊕ *www. mamuschka.com.*

Rapa Nui. A Willy Wonka land overflowing with chocolate, sweets, and ice cream, Rapa Nui has treats to delight adults and children alike.

Established in 1939, it is one of the longest-running *chocolaterías*. ⊠ *Mitre 202* ☏ *0924/442–3779* ⊕ *www.chocolatesrapanui.com.ar.*

Tito Testone. Local artisan and sculptor Tito Testone sells finely crafted bronze ornaments and decorations. ⊠ *Av. Bustillo 5709* ☏ *0294/452–5418.*

SPORTS AND THE OUTDOORS

FISHING

Fishing season runs November 15–April 15 (extended through May in certain areas), and guides are available by the day or the week. Nahuel Huapi, Gutiérrez, Mascardi, Correntoso, and Traful are the most accessible lakes in the Lake District. If you're seeking the perfect pool or secret stream for fly-fishing, you may have to do some hiking, particularly along the banks of the Chimehuín, Limay, Traful, and Correntoso rivers. Near Junín de los Andes the Malleo and Currihué rivers, and lakes Huechulafquen, Paimún, and Lácar are good fishing grounds. Note that catch-and-release is usually compulsory.

Baruzzi Deportes. Oscar Baruzzi at Baruzzi Deportes is a good local fishing guide. ⊠ *Urquiza 250* ☏ *2944/424–922* ⊕ *www.barilochefishing.com.*

Direcciones Provinciales de Pesca. Fishing licenses allowing you to catch brown, rainbow, and brook trout as well as perch and *salar sebago* (landlocked salmon) are obtainable in Bariloche at the Direcciones Provinciales de Pesca. You can also get licenses at the Nahuel Huapi National Park office and at most tackle shops. Nonresident license fees are $10/day and $100/season. ⊠ *Elfleín 10* ⊕ *www.maa.gba.gov.ar/sistemas/pesca/licencias/licencias00.php.*

Patagonia Anglers. This shop carries fishing and hunting equipment. ⊠ *Quaglia 259* ☏ *2944/427–353* ⊕ *www.patagoniaanglers.com.ar.*

Patagonia Fly Shop. Ricardo Almeijeiras, also a guide, owns the Patagonia Fly Shop. ⊠ *Quinchahuala 200, Av. Bustillo, Km 6.7* ☏ *2944/441–944* ⊕ *www.richard-ameijeiras.com.*

HIKING

For day hikes along the shores of Nahuel Huapi Lake, try the trails of the Circuito Chico in Parque Municipal Llao Llao. For altitude and grand panoramas, take the ski lift to the top of Cerro Catedral and follow the ridge trail to Refugio Frey, returning down to the base of the ski area. West of Bariloche, turn right at Villa Mascardi onto the dirt road to Pampa Linda; from there you can take a day-long hike to the Otto Meiling Refuge or make shorter forays to the glacier and nearby waterfalls. A three-day trek will take you right past Tronadór and its glacier, along the Alerce River, and over the Paso de los Nubes (Cloud Pass) to Puerto Blest, returning to Bariloche by boat.

Paseo de los Duendes. Looking for a child-friendly excursion? The 1-km (½-mile) Paseo de los Duendes—or Walk of the Elves—in Villa Los Coihues leads to a small but pretty waterfall. You can also hike onward for a view of the nearby Lago Gutiérrez or follow the 7½- km (5-mile) trail to Playa Muñoz. Once a campground, this area is still regenerating,

and while wide paths make it easy to navigate, it does not have the same impact as other hiking trails. ⊠ *Perito Moreno, Villa Los Coihues.*

Parque Municipal Llao Llao. Llao Llao Municipal Park has two main trails, each approximately 3 km (2 miles) long. One takes you through the mixed forest of coihues and mountain cypresses to the top of Cerro Llao Llao for a stunning view of Lake Nahuel Huapi. The other continues on to the small coastal beaches of Villa Tacul (Tacul Village), where you can paddle in the lake or explore the ruins of what is thought to be an abandoned World War II bunker. Access the park by taking the Route 20 bus to the end of the line or driving along Avenida Ezequiel Bustillo until you reach the beginning of the Circuito Chico. ⊠ *Av. Bustillo Km 27.5.*

HORSEBACK RIDING

Bastión del Manso. This outfitter combines riding and rafting over the border to Chile. ⊠ *Av. Bustillo, Km 13.491* ☎ *2944/456–111* ⊕ *www. bastiontravel.com/en* 🖾 *From 1190 pesos, includes transfers/pickup.*

Carol Jones. The granddaughter of an early pioneering family, Carol Jones's ranch north of town does day rides and overnights from the Patagonian steppes into the mountains. ⊠ *Modesta Victoria 5600* ☎ *2944/426–508* ⊕ *www.caroljones.com.ar* 🖾 *From 1300 pesos (cash only), includes transfers/pickup.*

Tom Wesley. Located at the Club Hípico Bariloche, Tom Wesley offers rides lasting from one hour to several days. ⊠ *Av. Bustillo, Km 15.5* ☎ *2944/448–193* ⊕ *www.cabalgatastomwesley.com* 🖾 *From 480 pesos* ☾ *Closed May–June.*

SKIING

Cerro Catedral (*Mount Cathedral*). Named for its Gothic-looking spires, Cerro Catedral is the oldest ski area in South America, with 38 lifts, 1,820 hectares (4,500 acres) of mostly intermediate terrain, and a comfortable altitude of 2,050 meters (6,725 feet). The runs are long, varied, and scenic. One side of the mountain has a vertical drop of 914 meters (3,000 feet), mostly in the fall line. Near the top of the highest chairlift at 2,250 meters (7,385 feet) is Refugio Lynch, a small restaurant on the edge of an abyss with a stupendous 360-degree view of Nahuel Huapi Lake. To the southwest, Monte Tronadór, an extinct volcano straddling the border with Chile, towers above lesser peaks that surround the lake. Other on-site facilities include a terrain park and picturesque cross-country ski trails. August and September are the best months to hit the slopes: avoid the first three weeks of July (school vacation).

Villa Catedral, at the base of the mountain, has numerous equipment retail and rental shops, information and ticket sales, ski-school offices, restaurants, and even a disco. Frequent buses transport skiers from Bariloche to the ski area. For information and trail maps, contact **La Secretaría de Turismo de Río Negro** (12 de Octubre 605 ☎ 2944/429–896). **Club Andino Bariloche** (20 de Febrero 30 ☎ 2944/422–266) also has information and trail maps. ⊠ *46 km (29 miles) west of Bariloche on R237; turn left at Km 8.5 just past Playa Bonita* ✛ *46 km (29 miles) west of town on Av. Bustillo (R237); turn left at Km 8.5 just past Playa Bonita* ☎ *2944/409–000* ⊕ *www.catedralaltapatagonia.com* 🖾 *From 1330 pesos (high season).*

SAN MARTÍN DE LOS ANDES AND NEARBY

SAN MARTÍN DE LOS ANDES

260 km (161 miles) north of Bariloche on R237, R40, and R234 via Junín de los Andes (a 4-hour drive); 158 km (98 miles) north of Bariloche on R237 and R63 over the Córdoba Pass (less than half is unpaved); 90 km (56 miles) northeast of Villa La Angostura on R234 (Ruta de los Siete Lagos, partly unpaved and closed for much of winter).

Surrounded by lakes, dense forests, and mountains, San Martín de los Andes lies in a natural basin at the foot of Lago Lácar. It's a small, easygoing town, much like Bariloche was many decades ago, with hotels and houses reflecting the distinctive Andean alpine architecture of Bustillo. Wide, flat streets lined with rosebushes run from the town pier on the eastern shore of Lago Lácar to the main square, Plaza San Martín, where two parallel streets—San Martín and General Villegas—teem with block after block of ski and fishing shops, chocolatiers, souvenir stores, clothing boutiques, and cafés.

The Mapuche lived in the area long before immigrants of Chilean, French, Dutch, and Italian descent founded the town in 1898. Because all of the water from this area runs into the Pacific, the territory was disputed by Chile, which claimed it as its own until 1902, when it was legally declared Argentine.

After Parque Nacional Lanín was established in 1937 and the ski area at Chapelco developed in the 1970s, tourism replaced forestry as the main source of income. Today San Martín is the major tourist center in Neuquén Province—the midpoint in the Ruta de los Siete Lagos and the gateway for exploring the Parque Nacional Lanín.

GETTING HERE AND AROUND

Aerolíneas Argentina and LATAM make the two-hour flight from Buenos Aires up to three times a day, but most people arrive from Bariloche via Junín de los Andes or along the Ruta de los Siete Lagos. El Valle buses make frequent daily trips between Bariloche and San Martín; the first typically leaves at 6 am and the last at 6 pm. The picturesque journey takes four hours with a brief stopover in Villa La Angostura. The centrally located San Martín bus terminal is within walking distance of most hotels.

Being flat, the town is pleasant for pedestrians. To access nearby beaches, hiking trails, or the ski area in winter, you need to rent a car, join a tour, or be an energetic cyclist. Taxis are inexpensive, and remises can be arranged through your hotel.

Bus Contacts El Valle. ☎ *0810/333–7575* ⊕ *www.elvalle.com.ar.* **San Martín de los Andes Bus Terminal.** ✉ *Villegas 251* ☎ *2972/427–044.*

Remis Del Oscar. ✉ *Av. San Martín 1254* ☎ *2972/428–774.*

ESSENTIALS

Visitor and Tour Information Dirección Municipal de Turismo. ✉ *J.M. Rosas 790, at Av. San Martín* ☎ *2972/427–347* ⊕ *www.sanmartindelosandes.gov.ar.*

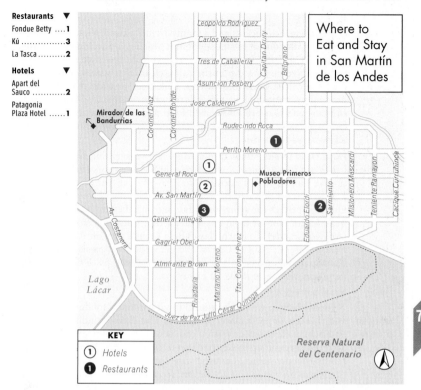

Restaurants ▼
Fondue Betty **1**
Kú **3**
La Tasca **2**

Hotels ▼
Apart del
Sauco **2**
Patagonia
Plaza Hotel **1**

Where to
Eat and Stay
in San Martín
de los Andes

KEY
① *Hotels*
❶ *Restaurants*

EXPLORING

Mirador de las Bandurrias (*Bandurrias Overlook*). From town you can hike, mountain bike, or drive 5 km (3 miles) up a steep hill through a dense forest of cypress and oak to the Mirador de las Bandurrias, where you'll be rewarded with a view of San Martín and the lake. The chance to visit **Paraje Trompul** —a Mapuche community that's home to about 40 families—is an added bonus. After taking a snack break in the *quincho* (café) and perusing the weavings and wood carvings sold here, you can continue another 5 km (3 miles) to see **Playa La Islita,** a small, rocky island in the middle of Lácar Lake.

If you're walking, take Avenida San Martín to the lake, turn right, cross the bridge behind the waterworks plant over Puahullo Creek, and then head uphill on a path around the mountain. By car, leave town on RP48 and drive about 4 km (3 miles) to a turnoff (no sign) on your left. Take the turn and continue to Comunidad Mapuche Curruhuinca, where you pay a fee for the lookout. ⊠ *San Martín de los Andes* ⊠ *15 pesos.*

Museo Primeros Pobladores (*Pioneer Museum*). Next to the tourist office, this museum occupies the tiny building that served as the original city council lodge. It is mainly dedicated to Mapuche ceramics and weavings; a collection of 13,000-year-old tools and fossils gives an idea of ancient life in the region. ⊠ *J.M. de Rosas 700* ☎ *2972/412–306* ⊠ *Free* ☉ *Closed Sun.*

BEACHES

FAMILY **Playa Catritre.** Easy access and a family-friendly atmosphere have made Playa Catritre one of the most popular beaches in San Martín. On the south side of Lago Lácar, 4 km (3 miles) from the town center, it's a great spot to enjoy a dip in the calm, clear lake waters, and admire the view of the Cerro Bandurrias. Oak trees provide shade for picnics, and water activities for children are available. A Mapuche-run campground is nearby. **Amenities:** food and drink; water sports. **Best for:** swimming; walking. ⊠ *4 km (3 miles) from San Martín on R234* 🚗 *70 pesos for parking.*

Playa Quila Quina. Situated in a Mapuche village, this small lakeside beach is a tourist hotspot with ferries bringing visitors from San Martín five times a day. It's possible to arrive by car, but be prepared for a steep descent down to the rocky beach. Although busy, Playa Quila Quina is perfect for swimming and enjoying the panoramic views of Lake Lácar. Not far from the shore, a trail leads to a small waterfall (Arroyo Grande). To reach Playa Quila Quina, turn off R234 2 km (1 mile) before the road to Catrite and get on R108. **Amenities:** food and drink; parking; toilets. **Best for:** swimming; walking. ⊠ *18 km (11 miles) from San Martín on R108* 🚗 *250 pesos.*

WHERE TO EAT

$$ ✕ **Fondue Betty.** It wouldn't be a ski town without a fondue restaurant,
ARGENTINE and this one is particularly appealing. The cheese fondue is smooth
FAMILY and rich, while the meat version comes with cubes of Argentine beef in assorted cuts and up to 12 condiments. **Known for:** abundant fondue; family-friendly service; fantastic wine list. $ *Average main: 200 pesos* ⊠ *Villegas 586* 🕿 *2972/422–522* ▭ *No credit cards* ⊗ *Closed May.*

$$$ ✕ **Kú.** Cozy dark-wood tables and booths, a friendly staff, a chalkboard
ARGENTINE listing tempting specials—these are good building blocks for a restau-
Fodor'sChoice rant. Order the smoked-meat plate with venison, boar, trout, salmon,
★ and cheese as a starter; then try the Patagonian lamb *al asador* (on the open fire). **Known for:** succulent steaks; extensive dessert menu; cozy atmosphere. $ *Average main: 300 pesos* ⊠ *Av. San Martín 1053* 🕿 *2972/427–039* ⊕ *www.facebook.com/kudelosandes.*

$$$ ✕ **La Tasca.** This is one of the traditional top-end choices in town for
ARGENTINE locals and tourists alike. With tables scattered about the black-stone floor, and wine barrels, shelves, and every other imaginable surface stacked with pickled vegetables, smoked meats, cheese rounds, dried herbs, olive oils, and wine bottles, you might think you're in a Patagonian deli. **Known for:** local wild game dishes; rustic charm; homemade pastas. $ *Average main: 300 pesos* ⊠ *Moreno 886* 🕿 *2972/428–663.*

WHERE TO STAY

$$ 🏨 **Apart del Sauco.** Accommodating up to eight guests, these clean, well-
RENTAL equipped apartments are a practical option for families and for any travelers considering longer stays. **Pros:** swimming pool; full kitchen; good base for exploring national parks. **Cons:** bland decor; basic hotel services; 15-minute walk to center. $ *Rooms from: US$160* ⊠ *Calderón 364* 🕿 *2972/411–900* ⊕ *www.delsauco.com.ar* ⬍ *15 rooms* ⦿| *Breakfast.*

$$ 📺 **Patagonia Plaza Hotel.** Located around the corner from shops, tourist
HOTEL   offices, and restaurants, this modern downtown hotel swaps genteel rusticity for state-of-the-art amenities and services. **Pros:** central location; big rooms with modern bathrooms with hydromassage baths; fitness center with swimming pool and sauna. **Cons:** restaurant lacks atmosphere; no air-conditioning; street-facing rooms can be noisy. $ *Rooms from: 130 pesos* ⊠ *Av. San Martín at Rivadavia* ☎ *2972/422–280* ⊕ *www.hotelpatagoniaplaza.com.ar* 📲 *90 rooms* 🍴 *Breakfast.*

SPORTS AND THE OUTDOORS

Tour agencies can arrange rafting trips on the Hua Hum or Aluminé rivers, guided mountain biking, horseback riding, and fishing tours, plus excursions to lakes in both Lanín and Nahuel Huapi national parks.

El Refugio. Active travelers can join this full service tour company and travel agency for rafting, trekking, mountain biking, fly-fishing, and skiing excursions. Overland road tours are available for the less intrepid. El Refugio can also book accommodations. ⊠ *Villegas 698* ☎ *2972/425–140* ⊕ *www.elrefugioturismo.com.ar* 🚗 *From 550 pesos.*

BOATING

Lacar and Nonthue. You can rent small boats, canoes, and kayaks at the pier from Lacar and Nonthue. You can also rent a bicycle and take an all-day excursion to the other side of Lake Lácar, where there is a nice beach and woods to explore. Another option is the boat tour to Hua Hum at the western end of the lake, where the river of the same name runs to the Chilean border. ⊠ *Av. Costanera 901* ☎ *2972/427–380* ⊕ *lagolacarynonthue.com.*

FISHING

During the fishing season (November 15–April 15, extended to the end of May in certain areas), local guides will take you to their favorite spots on lagos Lácar, Lolog, Villarino, and Falkner and on the ríos Caleufu, Quiquihue, Malleo, and Hermoso, or farther afield to the Chimehuín River and Lakes Huechulafquen and Paimún.

Intendencia de Parque Nacional Lanin. Permits for fishing are available at the Lanín National Park Office or any licensed fishing store along Avenida San Martín. Most stores and tour operators can suggest guides. ⊠ *Eduardo Elordi 600* ☎ *2972/420–664* ⊕ *www.pnlanin.org.*

Jorge Cardillo. Since opening his small Fly Shop in 1994, this well-known local guide has gained a reputation for his friendly, familial fishing trips to nearby rivers like Meliquina, Filo Hua-Hum, and Caleufu. ⊠ *Villegas 1061, behind casino* ☎ *2972/428–372* ⊕ *www.jorgecardillo.com.*

HORSEBACK RIDING

Cabalgatas Abuelo Enrique. These folks offer rides with a guide for two hours or all day, asado included. To get there, take Avenida Dr. Koessler (R234) toward Zapala, turn left at the polo field, and head toward Lago Lolog, then take a right past the military barracks to Callejón Ginsgins. ⊠ *Callejón Ginsgins, Campo 9* ☎ *2972/426–465* 🚗 *From 700 pesos per person* ⊗ *Closed Sun.* ☞ *Reservations required.*

MOUNTAIN BIKING

HG Rodados. San Martín itself is flat, but from there everything goes up. Dirt and paved roads and trails lead through forests to lakes and waterfalls. You can rent bikes in town at HG Rodados. ☒ *Av. San Martín 1061* ☏ *2972/427–345* ✉ *From 290 pesos per day.*

SKIING

Cerro Chapelco (*Chapelco Ski Resort*). The Chapelco Ski Resort is ideal for families and beginner-to-intermediate skiers. It has modern facilities and lifts, including a high-speed *telecabina* (gondola) from the base. On a clear day almost all the runs are visible from the top—a height of 1991 meters (6,534 feet)—and Lanín Volcano dominates the horizon. Lift tickets cost from 1,020 pesos per day in low season to 1,460 pesos in high season. Equipment rental facilities are available at the base camp (530–680 pesos per day for skis, boots, and poles). On some days cars need chains to get up to the mountain, so call and check the latest conditions before driving up. Taxis can also take you up or down for about 200 pesos each way. ■TIP➜ **In summer, the Adventure Center has mountain biking for experts and classes for beginners, plus horseback rides, hiking, archery, a swimming pool, an alpine slide, and children's activities.** ☒ *Information office:, San Martín at Elordi, 23 km (14 miles) southeast of San Martín de los Andes* ☏ *2972/427–845* ⊕ *www.chapelco.com* ☞ *5 km (3 miles) of road is unpaved.*

WHITE-WATER RAFTING

El Claro Turismo. Offering both short and long trips in the area, El Claro Turismo is a good rafting choice. ☒ *Col. Diaz 751* ☏ *2972/428–876, 2972/425–876* ⊕ *www.elclaroturismo.com.ar* ✉ *From 550 pesos (discount for cash).*

Siete Lagos Turismo. An all-day rafting trip that crosses into Chile on either Río Aluminé or Río Hua Hum can be arranged by Siete Lagos Turismo. Owner Fernando Aguirre, a lifelong resident of the area, also offers two- to four-day camping trips with combinations of rafting, hiking, riding, biking, and kayaking. ☒ *Villegas 313* ☏ *2972/427–877* ⊕ *www.sietelagosturismo.com.ar* ✉ *From 550 pesos.*

PARQUE NACIONAL LANÍN

The dramatically beautiful Parque Nacional Lanín contains 35 mountain lakes, countless rivers, ancient forests, and the Volcán Lanín. Tucked into the folds of the Andes along the Chilean border, it stretches 150 km (93 miles) north to south, covering 4,120 square km (1,590 square miles). The area is home to the Mapuche, and you can learn about their history and buy their handicrafts in one of the 50 communities throughout the park.

GETTING HERE AND AROUND

Three towns have access to the park. The northernmost section is reached from Aluminé: 145 km (90 miles) west of Zapala on Ruta Provincial 46, it's a typical Andean community with no paved streets but an abundance of nearby lakes (including Aluminé, Quillén, and Mohquehue). Junín de los Andes, in the middle section, is at the end of the paved road from Bariloche. Another paved road leads 41 km (25 miles) to San Martín, the park's major town, in the southern section. Daily buses run from San Martín and Junín to Lago Huechulafquen and Volcán Lanín; however, service can be unreliable and timetables change depending on the season. In Aluminé, public transport is largely nonexistent, so cars or remises are the only option. Note that all three of these towns have roads leading to the border with Chile *(See Chilean Lakes Crossing box).*

ESSENTIALS

Intendencia de Parques Nacionales (*National Park Office*). For information on the park, go to the Intendencia de Parques Nacionales in San Martín. The office has maps and information on all the parks and trails in the region, as well as fishing permits. ✉ *Eduardo Elordi 600, San Martín de los Andes* ☎ *2972/420–664* ⊕ *www.pnlanin.org.*

EXPLORING

Araucaria Araucana. Found only in this part of the Andes, the ancient Araucaria Araucana tree grows to 30 meters (100 feet) and has long spiny branches. Cones the size of bowling balls are full of pinon nuts that provided nourishment to the Mapuche, who call these trees *pehuenes*. The northern portion of the park near Lago Huechulafquen and Aluminé is one of the best places to view these peculiar giants. ✉ *Lago Huechulafquen.*

Volcán Lanín. Rising 3,773 meters (12,378 feet) in solitary snow-clad splendor on the western horizon, Volcán Lanín towers over the area and is visible from every direction. It sits on the Chilean border, with Lanín National Park on one side and Chile's Villarica National Park on the other. The closest Argentine access is from Junín, but the northern route to Paso Tromen also offers endless photo ops through the tangled branches of the araucaria trees. You can climb Lanín in three to four days round-trip with a guide. ⊕ *www.pnlanin.org.*

VILLA TRAFUL

60 km (37 miles) north of Villa La Angostura on R231 and R65; 39 km (23 miles) from Confluencia on R65; 100 km (60 miles) northwest of Bariloche on R237 and R65.

If there were a prize for the most beautiful lake in the region, Lago Traful would win for its clarity, serenity, and wild surroundings. Small log houses peek through the cypress forest along the way to Villa Traful, a village of about 500 inhabitants.

The tiny community consists of log cabins, horse corrals, shops for picnic and fishing supplies, a school, a post office, and a park ranger's office. Well-maintained campgrounds border the lake, and ranches and private fishing lodges are hidden in the surrounding mountains. By day swimmers play on rocky beaches, kayakers cut the still blue water, and divers go below to explore the mysteries of a submerged forest. Night brings silence, stars, and the glow of lakeside campfires.

GETTING HERE AND AROUND

On the Ruta de los Siete Lagos, Villa Traful can be reached by bus from Bariloche, San Martín, and Villa la Angostura (the nearest town); bus operators include Via Bariloche. Otherwise you can come by car or with a tour group. The waterside hamlet is contained within a single circuit, and most stores are in walking distance of the pier.

Bus Contacts Via Bariloche. ☎ 2944/432–444 ⊕ www.viabariloche.com.ar.

ESSENTIALS

Visitor Information Oficina Municipal de Turismo. ✉ *Across from municipal pier, Ruta provincial No. 65* ☎ *2944/838–974* ⊕ *www.turismoneuquen.com.ar/item/villa-traful-oficinas-de-turismo.*

WHERE TO STAY

$$$ **⛺ Cabañas Ruca Lico.** Intimate Ruca Lico hits the sweet spot between
RENTAL ranch and resort; the quaint, rustic interiors are very cozy, and you can admire views of Lago Traful from a private balcony or hot tub. **Pros:** close to lake, trails, and town center; self-catering facilities; price includes airport transfers. **Cons:** limited services; small bathroom; challenging walk to lake. $ *Rooms from: US$230* ✉ *RP65, Km 35* ☎ *2944/479–004* ⊕ *www.rucalico.com* 🔄 *6 rooms* ⛔ *No meals.*

SPORTS AND THE OUTDOORS
HIKING

Arroyo Blanco and Arroyo Coa Có. Drive, walk, or pedal about 3 km (2 miles) up from the village to the trailhead at Pampa de los Alamos, a clearing where the trail to Arroyo Blanco descends into a forest of 1,000-year-old coihué trees with ghostly naked trunks, gigantic lenga (deciduous beech), and ñires that grow only at high altitudes. The trail leads to a wooden walkway along a steep cliff—the only way one could possibly view the waterfall tumbling 20 meters (66 feet) into a dark chasm. Follow the wooden trail along the cliff for increasingly amazing glimpses of this wild gorge, then return up the same route. Arroyo Coa Có is in the opposite direction, with a view of both the waterfall and Lago Traful. ✉ *Villa Traful.*

Casacada Co Lemú. At the end of an arduous trail, the Casacada Co Lemú thunders down 20 meters (67 feet) with a deafening roar. Drive 8 km (5 miles) west toward the Seven Lakes Route to the bridge over Arroyo Cataratas. Before you cross the stream, on your left, the trail—covering 19 km (12 miles), round-trip—climbs slowly at first, then straight up to the falls. ✉ *Villa Traful.*

Cerro Negro. A strenuous seven-hour hike from the village to Cerro Negro climbs up through forests of cypress, coihué, lenga, and ñire, passing strange rock formations en route to the top. The summit—at 1,829 meters (6,000 feet)—promises a splendid view of Lago Traful and across the Andes all the way to Lanín. ✉ *Villa Traful.*

Laguna Las Mellizas y Pinturas Rupestres (*The Twins Lagoon and Cave paintings*). A 15-minute boat trip across the lake from the wharf takes you to a sandy beach on the northern shore. A two-hour walk down a trail into a steep gully leads to the pools. Nearby caves with

Continued on page 334

FLY FISHING

Chile and Argentina are the final frontier of fly fishing. With so many unexplored rivers, lakes, and spring creeks—most of which are undammed and free flowing to the ocean—every type of fishing is available for all levels of experience. You'll find many species of fish, including rainbow trout, browns, sea-run browns, brooks, sea trout, and steelhead

The Southern Cone has endless—and endlessly evolving—rivers, streams, and lakes, which is why they're so good for fly fishing. These waterways formed millions of years ago, as volcanic eruptions and receding glaciers carved out the paths for riverbeds and lakes that feed into the Pacific or Atlantic Oceans. With more than 2,006 volcanoes in Chile alone (including South America's most active mountain, Volcano Llaima, outside of Temuco), the Lake Districts of both countries are still evolving, creating raw and pristine fishing grounds.

Why choose Chile or Argentina for your next fly fishing adventure? If you're only after huge fish, stick to California. What these two South American countries offer is a chance to combine fishing, culture, and food in a unique package during the northern hemisphere's off season. With the right guide, you just might find yourself two hours down a dirt road, fishing turquoise water in the shadow of a glacial peak, with not a soul in sight but the occasional gaucho or huaso. It's an experience you will find nowhere else.

WHAT TO EXPECT ON THE GROUND

Fishing, Chile

LOGISTICS

You'll probably fly into Bariloche, Argentina, or Puerto Montt, Chile. You won't need more than two weeks for a good trip, and hiring a guide can make a big difference in the quality of your experience. Since most rivers are un-dammed, you'll need the extra help managing your drift boat or locating foot access for wading that stream you've spotted around the bend.

GUIDES VS. LODGES

You can purchase your trip package through either an independent guide or a specific lodge property. In both cases, packages usually last one week to 10 days, and include breakfast, lunch, and dinner. If you opt to purchase through a lodge, you have the benefit of property-specific guides who know every nook and cranny of stream surrounding the lodge. On the other hand, hiring an independent guide will give you more power to customize your trip and go farther afield.

TIMING

Contact your guide or lodge in October or November, during the southern hemisphere's spring; the upcoming season's peak fishing times depend on snow melt. Plan on traveling in February or March.

CHOOSING YOUR GUIDE

What type of fishing suits you best? Do you like to fish from a boat, or do you prefer wading the river as it rushes by? Ask guides these questions to find the best one for you.

WHAT TO ASK A GUIDE

- How early do you start in the morning?
- Do you mainly spin cast or fly fish?
- How long have you been in business?
- Do you always catch and release?
- Will I fish with you or another guide?
- Can I see pictures of your raft or drift boat?
- Do you supply the flies?
- Where do you get your flies?
- Can we fish a river twice if we like it?
- Which rivers and lakes do you float?
- Can we set an itinerary before I arrive?

WHAT TO BRING

5 to 7 Weight Rod: at least 9 foot (consider bringing 9½ foot for larger rivers, windy days, lakes, and sink-tip streamer fishing).

Floating Lines: for dry fly fishing and nymphing.

Streamers: for use while wading to or from the drift boat.

Lines: 15 to 20 foot sink-tip lines with a sink rate of 5.5 to 8 inches per second. It's good to carry two to four different sink rate lines.

Intermediate sink lines: for lakes and shallow depth fishing.

Line Cleaner: because low-ozone areas (the hole in the ozone is close to Antarctica) will eat up lines if you don't treat and clean the lines daily.

Hook sharpener: most guides don't have this very important item.

Small gifts: for the people you meet. Gift-giving can help you gain access to private rivers and lakes. Chocolates, such as Hershey Kisses, or some unique fly pattern, such as a dragon fly, always go over well.

Good map: Turistel, in Chile, puts out the best maps and internal information for that country (⊕ www.turistel.com). Check Argentina Tourism (⊕ www.turismo.gov.ar) for help with that country.

Coffee: Chile has Nescafé instant coffee just about everywhere you go. So if you like a good cup of joe, bring a filter and your favorite coffee. That way all you need is a cup and hot water, and you're all set for your morning fishing.

FLIES

■ Ask your guide where he or she gets flies. Those bought at a discount in countries outside of the United States are often sub-par, so get good guidance on this.

■ If you can, get a list of flies for the time of year you're scheduled to arrive and buy them in the United States before you go. Pay particular attention to the size as well type of insect.

■ The big fish and the quality catches are fooled by the flies that are tied by the guides

themselves, because the guides know the hatches and the times they occur.

■ Flies are divided up into similar categories in Chile and Argentina since South America has many of the same insects as we do in North America. Check and see what time each insect is hatching. Note their sizes and colors. **You'll need both dry and nymph versions of the following, in a variety of sizes, colors, and patterns:**

Royal Wulff	Bead Head Pheasant Tail	Mudder Minnow
Living Damsel	Bitch Creek	Adams

Lanín Volcano, an ice-clad, cone-shaped stratovolcano, in Parque Nacional Lanín

600-year-old Tehuelche cave paintings are worth exploring. The area is protected and registration with national park officials is required. ✉ *Villa Traful.*

SCUBA DIVING

Bosque Sumergido. In 1975 a violent earthquake caused half a mountain and its forest of cypress trees to slide to the bottom of the lake, creating the Bosque Sumergido. You can dive to 30 meters (98 feet) in crystalline water and explore this sunken forest. Boat trips can be arranged at **Cabañas Aiken** (☎ *9116/288–7018* ⊕ *www.aikencordoba. com*). ✉ *Villa Traful.*

VILLA LA ANGOSTURA

81 km (50 miles) northwest of Bariloche (an hour's drive on R231 around the east end of Lago Nahuel Huapi; also accessible by boat from Bariloche); 90 km (56 miles) southwest of San Martín de los Andes on R234 (the Ruta de los Siete Lagos, partly unpaved and closed for much of winter).

Sitting on a narrow *angostura* (isthmus) on the northern shore of Lake Nahuel Huapi, Villa La Angostura was once a mere hamlet. But, having benefited from thoughtful planning and strict adherence to business codes, it's now the second most popular tourist area in the Lake District. Its first hotel was built in 1923, 10 years before the town was founded, and today some of the most luxurious accommodations in Patagonia look out on the lake from discreet hiding places along its wooded shores.

Shops and restaurants line the Avenida Arrayanes, where you can stop for homemade ice cream or cakes while window-shopping in the three-block-long commercial zone. The tourist office and municipal buildings are at El Cruce (the Crossroads), where Ruta 231 from Bariloche to the Chilean border intersects with the road to the port and the Ruta de los Siete Lagos (Ruta 234) to San Martín de los Andes.

GETTING HERE AND AROUND

Fast and frequent El Valle buses make the two-hour trip from Bariloche at least six times a day; however, you'll want a car to get around the environs, which are creeping slowly from Lago Correntoso to Puerto Manzano.

Bus Contacts El Valle. ☎ *0810/333–7575* ⊕ *www.elvalle.com.ar.* **Villa La Angostura Bus Terminal.** ⊠ *Av. 7 Lagos 3* ☎ *2944/494–961.*

ESSENTIALS

Visitor and Tour Information Secretaría de Turismo y Cultura. ⊠ *Av. Array-anes 9* ☎ *2944/494–124* ⊕ *www.villalaangostura.gov.ar.*

WHERE TO EAT

$$$$ ✕ **Australis.** Easily one of the best microbreweries in Patagonia, the excel-
ARGENTINE lent cuisine at Australis integrates beer all the way through to dessert—a memorable flan is made with chocolate and a delicious stout. **Known for:** flavorful artisan beer; snug atmosphere; hearty German-inspired menu. ⑤ *Average main: 200 pesos* ⊠ *Ruta 231, Km 60, Av. Arrayanes 2490* ☎ *2944/495–645* ▭ *No credit cards* ⊘ *Closed May and June.*

$$$ ✕ **La Casita de la Oma.** Between the bay and the main street, this
ARGENTINE teahouse, with its award-winning garden, serves homemade cakes, pies, and scones. Moist chocolate brownie cake with dulce de leche (sweet caramelized milk) is a winner, as is a pile of filo leaves with dulce de leche and meringue on top. Jars of jam line the shelves. **Known for:** big desserts; fresh homemade jams; quaint tea-cozy charm. ⑤ *Average main: 150 pesos* ⊠ *Cerro Inacayal 303* ☎ *2944/494–602* ⊘ *Closed Easter–July.*

WHERE TO STAY

$$$$ ▦ **Costa Serena.** Every room at this complex in Puerto Manzano has a
HOTEL lake view; A-frame *cabañas* (cabins) with decks, kitchens, and outdoor
FAMILY barbecues sleep up to seven, while suites have huge wooden Jacuzzis with views to the water. **Pros:** stunning views; prime lakeside position; relaxing indoor-outdoor pool. **Cons:** far from town and tourist attrac-tions; limited restaurant services outside of high season; some rooms have low-running wooden beams. ⑤ *Rooms from: 3400 pesos* ⊠ *Los Pinos 435, Puerto Manzano* ☎ *2944/475–203* ⊕ *www.costaserenavla. com.ar* ⤳ *11 rooms* ⑩ *Breakfast.*

$$$$ ▦ **Hotel Correntoso.** Perched on a hill where the Correntoso River runs
HOTEL into Nahuel Huapi Lake, this landmark hotel is at once cozy and con-
Fodor's Choice temporary; from your bedroom window you can see the fish jumping.
★ **Pros:** great location, food, and spa facilities; well-organized excursions; the bar often has live music. **Cons:** expensive; no air-conditioning; rooms are a little cramped. ⑤ *Rooms from: US$350* ⊠ *RN231, Km*

86, Puente Correntoso ☎ 2944/15–619–728, 11/4803–0030 in Buenos Aires ⊕ www.correntoso.com ⥲ 49 rooms ⃝ Breakfast.

$$
HOTEL
Fodor'sChoice
★

🖵 **Puerto Sur.** Stone and wood merge throughout the angular space of this hillside hotel in Puerto Manzano, which has views of the lake and mountains from enormous windows. **Pros:** quiet, secluded spot; incredible lake views; spa, pool, and private beach on-site. **Cons:** far from town and tourist activities; difficult to get to and from without a car; no restaurant. ⑤ *Rooms from: US$160 ⊠ Los Pinos 221, Puerto Manzano ☎ 2944/825–351 ⊕ www.hosteriapuertosur.com.ar ☉ Closed mid-May and June ⥲ 14 rooms ⃝ Breakfast.*

SHOPPING

En El Bosque Chocolate. Follow your nose to En El Bosque, where the scent of delicious artisanal sweets wafts out onto the sidewalk. It ranks among the best of the many chocolate and ice cream shops here. ⊠ *Av. Arrayanes 218 ☎ 2944/495–738.*

SPORTS AND THE OUTDOORS

Visitors will be delighted by the variety of activities offered by this small, lakeside town, which has totally recovered from the 2011 eruption of the Puyehue volcano; a trip to the Secretaría de Turismo y Cultura will give you a good overview of the many outdoor excursions available.

BOATING

Patagonia Infinita. Full- and half-day kayaking tours of the Nahuel Huapi, Correntoso, and Espejo lakes are organized by Patagonia Infinita. Lunch is included in full-day trips, and snorkeling is available in summer. ⊠ *Arrayanes 204 ☎ 2944/553–954 ⊕ www.patagoniain-finita.com ⊡ From 1600 pesos.*

HORSEBACK RIDING

Cabalgatas Montahue. Short- and long-distance riding adventures can be arranged through Cabalgatas Montahue. Opt for a two-hour trip to the Lake Correntoso lookout point or a four-day excursion to Villa Traful. ⊠ *Av. 7 Lagos 402 ☎ 2944/511–345 ⊡ From 600 pesos.*

MOUNTAIN BIKING

Alquiles Rental & Outdoors. Mountain bikes can be rented by the day from Alquiles Rental. You can easily ride from the village to Laguna Verde, near the port, or off the Seven Lakes Route to Mirador Belvedere and on to the waterfalls at Inacayal. Kayaks and ski gear are also available. ⊠ *Av. Arrayanes 96 ☎ 2944/494–303 ⊕ www.aquilesrental.com. ar ⊡ From 330 pesos.*

PARQUE NACIONAL NAHUEL HUAPI

Created in 1934, Parque Nacional Nahuel Huapi is the oldest national park in Argentina. It's also one of the largest, encompassing more than 7,050 square km (2,720 square miles) along the eastern side of the Andes in the provinces of Neuquén and Río Negro, on the frontier with Chile. Because much of the park is covered by lakes—Lago Nahuel Huapi being the most sizable one—some of your exploration will be by boat to islands, down narrow fjords, or to distant shores on organized excursions. Multiple hiking trails also wind through the park, leading visitors from the thick undergrowth to open lakeside beaches. Nearby destinations such as the Circuito Chico, Circuito Grande, Tronadór, or the ski area at Catedral can be done in a day.

GETTING AROUND

The easy way to get around is to rent a car, hire a remis, or sign on with a local tour operator. When planning all-day or overnight trips, remember that distances are long and unpaved roads slow you down.

ESSENTIALS

Visitor Information Intendencia del Parque Nacional Nahuel Huapi. ✉ *Av. San Martín 24, at Civic Center, Bariloche* ☎ *2944/423–111* ⊕ *www.nahuelhuapi. gov.ar.*

EXPLORING

Isla Victoria. The most popular excursion on Lago Nahuel Huapi is the 30-minute boat ride from Puerto Pañuelo on the Península Llao Llao to Isla Victoria, the largest island in the lake. A grove of redwoods transplanted from California thrives in the middle of it. Walk on trails that lead to enchanting views of emerald bays and still lagoons; then board the boat to sail on to the Parque Nacional los Arrayanes. Boats go daily at 10 am and 2 pm (more frequently in high season). The earlier departure includes time for lunch on the island in a cafeteria-style restaurant. The later departure is a shorter trip. Vessels are run by **Cau Cau** (Mitre 139, Bariloche ☎ *2944/431–372* ⊕ *www.islavictoriayarrayanes.com*) and **Turisur** (Mitre 219 , *Bariloche* ☎ *2944/426–109* ⊕ *www.turisur.com.ar*).

Monte Tronadór (*Thunder Mountain*). A visit to Monte Tronadór requires an all-day outing, covering 170 km (105 miles) round-trip from Bariloche. This 3,658-meter (12,000-foot) extinct volcano—the highest mountain in the northern Lake District—straddles the frontier with Chile, with one peak on either side. Take R258 south along the shores of Lago Gutiérrez and Lago Mascardi. Between the two lakes the road crosses from the Atlantic to the Pacific watershed. At Km 35, turn off onto a road marked "Tronadór" and "Pampa Linda" and continue along the shore of Lago Mascardi, passing a village of the same name. Just beyond the village the road forks, and you continue on a gravel road, R254. Near the bridge the road branches left to Lago Hess and Cascada Los Alerces—a detour you might want to take on your way out.

As you bear right after crossing Los Rápidos Bridge, the road narrows: note that it's one-way heading up 10:30 am–2 pm, one-way heading down 4 pm–7:30 pm, and two-way 7:30 pm–10:30 am only. The lake ends in a narrow arm (Brazo Tronadór) at the Hotel Tronadór, which has a dock for tours arriving by boat. The road then follows the Río Manso to **Pampa Linda**, which has a lodge, restaurant, park ranger's office, campsites, and the trailhead for the climb up to the Refugio Otto Meiling at the snow line. Guided horseback rides are organized at the lodge. The road ends 7 km (5 miles) beyond Pampa Linda in a parking lot that was once at the tip of the receding **Glaciar Negro** (Black Glacier).

49

TO
JUNIN DE
LOS ANDES

234

San Martín
de Los Andes

48

Quila
Quina

*Parque
Nacional
Lanín*

CHILE

Lago Hermoso

63

234

64

237

Pichi
Traful

Pico Traful

Bayo o Alto
Mahuida

El Portezuelo

Lago Traful

Embalse
de Alicura

Puyehue

Ruca
Malen

A N D E S

215

65

Confluencia

*Parque
Nacional
Puyehue*

231

Villa La
Angostura

**Parque Nacional
Los Arrayanes**

**Parque Nacional
Nahuel Huapi**

S E R R A N I A   D E   L A   F R A G U A

Dormilón

Casablanca

**Isla
Victoria**

*Lago
Nahuel
Huapi*

237

Borcou

*Lago Todos
Los Santos*

231

Dina Huapi
Nahuel Huapi

23

Tronadór

Villa Cerro
Catedral

San Carlos
de Bariloche

Capitan

*Lago
Gutierrez*

80

MALLIN GRANDE

Bonete

Catedral

254

258

*Lago
Mascardi*

81

Villa Mascardi

Colorado

Torrecillas

Martín

A N D E S

Fuerte

Bastion

Río
Villegas

83

258

CHILE   ARGENTINA

0 ——— 4 mi
0 ——— 4 km

Parque Nacional
Nahuel Huapi

As the glacier flows down from the mountain, the dirt and black sediment of its lateral moraines are ground up and cover the ice. At first glance it's hard to imagine the tons of ice that lie beneath its black cap.

Parque Nacional los Arrayanes. Lago Nahuel Huapi's entire Quetrihue Peninsula, with its unique forest of *arrayanes* (myrtle trees), is protected by the Parque Nacional los Arrayanes. These trees absorb so much water through their thin skins that all other vegetation around them dies, leaving a barren forest of peeling cinnamon-color trunks. A stroll up and down wide wooden steps and walkways is a memorable experience, as light filters through the twisted naked trunks, reflecting a weird red glow. You can make this excursion from the pier at Bahía Brava in Villa La Angostura (or by boat from Bariloche via Isla Victoria). In summer, you can walk (three hours) or cycle, after registering at the *Guardaparque* office (ranger station) near the pier. ■ TIP→ **Leave in the morning, as the park entrance closes at 2 pm (noon in winter). A nice combination is to go by boat and return by bike (it's all downhill that way). If returning by boat, buy your return ticket at the pier before you leave.** ☎ *2944/423–111* ⊕ *www.parquesnacionales. gob.ar* ✉ *250 pesos.*

Parque Nacional Nahuel Huapi. This national park is notable for having the highest concentration of lakes in Argentina. The largest of them, Lago Nahuel Huapi, covers 897 square km (346 square miles) and has seven arms—the longest of which is 96 km (60 miles) long and 12 km (7 miles) wide—reaching deep into forests of coihue (a native beech), cypress, and lenga (deciduous beech) trees. Intensely blue across its vast expanse and aqua green in its shallow bays, the lake meanders into distant lagoons and misty inlets where the mountains, covered with vegetation at their base, rise straight up out of the water.

Inside the park, nearly every water sport invented can be arranged through local travel agencies, tour offices, or hotels. Boating is particularly popular, with options ranging from a placid Isla Victoria outing to challenging white-water-rafting adventures. Information offices throughout the park can also offer tips about tackling the miles of mountain and woodland trails. Small towns like Villa La Angostura and Villa Traful are excellent destinations for further explorations on foot or horseback. Since most of the park is at a low elevation (under 1,829 meters or 6,000 feet), getting around in winter is not difficult—just cold. Fall foliage, long, warm summer days, and spring flowers are the rewards of other seasons. ⊠ *Av. San Martín 24, Bariloche* ☎ *2944/423–111, 2944/423–121* ⊕ *www.nahuelhuapi.gov.ar* ✉ *250 pesos.*

WHERE TO STAY

$$$$
RESORT

▦ **Isla Victoria Lodge.** Poised dramatically on a cliff overlooking the lake and forests, this classic stone-and-wood lodge enjoys one of the most beautiful settings on earth: the architecture harmonizes with the natural surroundings, and the tranquil interior—with white walls, pine trim, leather upholstery, and fine Mapuche woven rugs—conveys a sense of peace. **Pros:** facilities include a heated outdoor pool and hiking trails; rates cover meals, alcoholic drinks, and on-site activities (including

Take in the view of Lago Nahuel Huapi on your way to Villa La Angostura.

horseback riding); gourmet meals. **Cons:** no nightlife; isolated; two-night minimum stay requirement. $ *Rooms from: US$315* ✉ *Isla Victoria CC 26, Nahuel Huapi National Park, Bariloche* ☎ *11/43–949–605* ⊕ *www.islavictoria.com* ⇌ *22 rooms* ❙❍❙ *All meals.*

$$ ⚍ **Río Mel Lodge.** Taking "off the beaten track" to a whole new level,
HOTEL this homey lodge sits on the banks of the Meliquina River in the middle of Parque Nacional Lanín and is a favorite with both fly fishermen and families. **Pros:** beautiful setting overlooking river; spacious suites; great spot for fishing. **Cons:** difficult to reach without a car; noise from adjacent rooms; no cell phone reception. $ *Rooms from: US$120* ✉ *Río Meliquina, 42 km (26 miles) south of San Martín de los Andes, San Martín de los Andes* ☎ *02972/427–199* ⊕ *www.riomellodge.com* ▭ *No credit cards* ⊘ *Closed May* ⇌ *6 rooms* ❙❍❙ *Some meals.*

SPORTS AND THE OUTDOORS

HIKING

Nahuel Huapi National Park has many forest trails near Bariloche, El Bolsón, and Villa La Angostura. Hiking guides can be recommended by local tour offices. For trail maps and information on all of the Lake District, look for the booklet (in Spanish) *Guía Sendas y Bosques* (*Guide to Trails and Forests*) sold at kiosks and bookstores.

Club Andino Bariloche. For ambitious treks, mountaineering, or information about mountain huts and climbing permits, contact Club Andino Bariloche. ✉ *20 de Febrero 30, Bariloche* ☎ *2944/422–266* ⊕ *www.clubandino.org/refugios-y-campings.*

MOUNTAIN BIKING

The entire park is ripe for all levels of mountain biking. Popular rides go from the parking lot at the Cerro Catedral ski area to Lago Gutiérrez and down from Cerro Otto. Local tour agencies can arrange guided tours by the hour or day and even international excursions to Chile. Rental agencies provide maps and suggestions and sometimes recommend guides.

Dirty Bikes. Day trips all over the Lake District (including long-distance ones to Chile and back) are organized by Dirty Bikes. Options for many ages and ability levels are available. ⊠ *Bariloche* ☎ *2944/529–821* ⊕ *www.dirtybikes.com.ar* ✉ *$45 per day.*

WHITE-WATER RAFTING

Thanks to all of its interconnected lakes and rivers, the national park offers rafters everything from a basic family float down the swift-flowing, scenic Río Limay to a wild and exciting ride down Río Manso (Class II), which carries you 16 km (10 miles) in three hours. If you're really adventurous, you can take the Manso all the way to Chile (Class IV).

Aguas Blancas. This outfit specializes in the Manso River and offers an overnight trip to Chile with asado and return by horseback. They also run guided inflatable kayak trips. ⊠ *Morales 564, Bariloche* ☎ *2944/432–799* ⊕ *aguasblancas.com.ar* ✉ *1750 pesos.*

Alunco. Mid-November through May, Alunco arranges rafting trips in the area. ⊠ *Moreno 187, 1st fl., Bariloche* ☎ *2944/422–283* ⊕ *www. aluncoturismo.com.ar* ✉ *From 1750 pesos (includes transfers, guide, lunch, and equipment).*

Extremo Sur. Trips on the Ríos Limay and Manso are arranged by Extremo Sur. ⊠ *Morales 765, Bariloche* ☎ *2944/427–301* ⊕ *www. extremosur.com* ✉ *From 2190 pesos for 2½ hrs.*

EL BOLSÓN AND NEARBY

EL BOLSÓN

131 km (80 miles) south of Bariloche via R40.

El Bolsón ("the purse") lies in a valley enclosed on either side by the jagged peaks of two mountain ranges. You catch your first glimpse of the valley about 66 km (41 miles) from Bariloche, with the glaciers of Perito Moreno and Hielo Azul—both more than 1,980 meters (6,500 feet) high—on the horizon south and west.

The first in Argentina to declare their town a nonnuclear zone, El Bolsón's residents have preserved the purity of its air, water, and land. In spring (late November–December), the roads are lined with ribbons of lupine in every shade of pink and purple imaginable. Red berry fruits, which are exported in large quantities, thrive on hillsides and in backyard *chacras* (farms); and huge fields of green hops support the exploding Patagonian microbrew industry.

Where to Eat and Stay in El Bolsón

CASCADA DE LA VIRGEN ◆
CASCADA MALLÍN AHÓGADO ◆
TO BARILOCHE
Del Agua
Parilla El Quincho de Danilo
Libano
Balcarce
Merino
Sgto. Cabral
Hotel Amancay
O'Connor
Plaza España
J. Hernández
Mascardi
Azcona
CABAÑA MICO
Larrea
Atte. Brown
Av. Sarmiento
Azcuénaga
Islas Malvinas
Dorrego
Uliedín
Ameghino
Gral. Roca
Plaza Pagano
La Gorda
P. Feliciano
Pellegrini
Islas Malvinas
BOSQUE TALLADO ◆→
Castelli
J.Y.P. Hube
French
Berutti
Güemes
TO ESQUEL
Lavalle
Lincoln Ranch
TO ESQUEL

KEY
■ Restaurants
□ Hotels
✛ following dining and lodging reviews indicates a map-grid coordinate

GETTING HERE AND AROUND

Most travelers come from Bariloche by car or bus; if you choose the latter, El Valle and Via Bariloche make the three-hour journey multiple times per day and deposit passengers downtown. The main street, San Martín, has shops, restaurants, and some lodgings within a two- to three-block area. A grassy plaza next to the tourist office is the center of activities; trails along the Río Azul or to nearby waterfalls and mountaintops are a short taxi or bike ride from it.

Bus Contacts El Valle. ☎ 0810/333–7575 ⊕ www.elvalle.com.ar. **Via Bariloche.** ☎ 0810/333–7575 ⊕ www.viabariloche.com.ar.

ESSENTIALS

Visitor and Tour Information Secretaría de Turismo. ⊠ Plaza Pagano at Av. San Martín ☎ 2944/492–604, 2944/455–336 ⊕ www.turismoelbolson.gob.ar.

EXPLORING

Bolsón International Jazz Festival. In February, the Bolsón International Jazz Festival brings music to streets and restaurants around town. The Fiesta Nacional de Lúpolo (National Hop Festival) is celebrated the same month. ⊠ El Bolsón.

Bosque Tallado (*Carved Forest*). About 1 km (½ mile) from the base of Piltriquitrón, you'll find fire-damaged beech trees that have been carved

Beer Sampling

This region has long been the biggest producer of hops in Argentina, and with a local population dedicated to agricultural pursuits, it's logical that entrepreneurial *cervecerías artesanales* (artisanal breweries) would become a growing industry.

Cervezería El Bolsón. About 2 km (1 mile) north of town, Cervezería El Bolsón is the brewery that started the Patagonian "cerveza artesanal craze," and even if it is now the least artisanal of the bunch, it's still a local landmark. Every night from December through March, and Fridays and Saturdays for the rest of the year, the brewery's tasting room turns into a hopping bar and restaurant, where *picadas* (kind of like tapas), pizzas, sausages with sauerkraut, and a hearty goulash are listed on one side of the menu with suggested beers on the other. For instance, black

beer is recommended with smoked meats; chocolate beer with dessert. There are 14 types of brew for you to taste, and descriptions of their ingredients are provided. A large campground is conveniently located by the river in back. ■ TIP➔ There is now a second location (Cervezeria El Bolsón Centro) in town at the corner of San Martin and Juez Fernandez. ⊠ *Ruta 258, Km 123.9* ☎ *2944/492–595* ⊕ *www.facebook. com/CerveceriaRestoCamping.*

Otto Tipp. Herr Tipp was a German immigrant who opened the first local brewery in 1890. Beers here include the classic triumvirate of blonde, red, and black—plus nonalcoholic malt beer and a fruity wheat beer. You can watch them being brewed and bottled from a bar stool. ⊠ *Islas Malvinas at Roca* ☎ *2944/493–700* ◷ *Closed Mon.*

over the years by 13 notable Argentine artists. Thirty-one monumental sculptures transform the dead forest into a living gallery. Tours can be arranged through Maputur. ⊠ *El Bolsón* ☎ *2944/491–440 Maputur.*

Cabaña Mico. Don't leave the El Bolsón area without a jar of jam! Not to be outdone by the beer tasting offered next door at Otto Tipp, Cabaña Mico has a long table lined with little jam pots (and disposable sticks), so you can sample the 40 different flavors before making your purchase. ⊠ *Islas Malvinas at Roca* ☎ *2944/492–691* ⊕ *www.mico.com. ar* ◷ *Closed Sun.*

Cascada de la Virgen (*Waterfall of the Virgin*). Venture 15 km (9 miles) north of El Bolsón to see the Cascada de la Virgen. It's most impressive in spring, when the runoff from the mountain falls in a series of three cascades visible from the road coming from Bariloche. ⊠ *El Bolsón.*

Cascada Mallín Ahogado (*Drowned Meadow Waterfall*). Four km (3 miles) north of El Bolsón on R258, the Cascada Mallín Ahogado makes a great picnic spot. ⊠ *El Bolsón.*

WHERE TO EAT

$$$$
ARGENTINE ✕ **La Gorda.** This centrally located restaurant offers generous servings of steaks and schnitzels, all presented on a wooden platter. Dig into *ojo de bife* and enjoy a side of sweet potatoes with Roquefort cheese. **Known**

for: juicy steaks; large portions; tasty desserts. $ *Average main: 300 pesos* ⊠ *25 de Mayo 2709, near corner of Feliciano* ☎ *2944/720–559* ✛ *C2.*

$$$$ ✕ **Parrilla El Quincho de Danilo.** About 10 minutes north of town, on the
ARGENTINE   bank of the river Arroyo del Medio, Parrilla El Quincho is the primo place to try *cordero patagónico al asador* (lamb roasted slowly on a metal cross over a fire), along with sizzling platters of beef. Vegetarian options are also available. **Known for:** lovely setting surrounded by trees; generous barbeque platters; coffee cooked on embers. $ *Average main: 350 pesos* ⊠ *Mallín Ahogado* ☎ *2944/492–870* ⊕ *elquincho. guiapatagonia.net* ▭ *No credit cards* ☉ *Closed in winter* ✛ *C1.*

WHERE TO STAY

The hotel selection in downtown El Bolsón is woefully inadequate. Numerous guesthouses take small groups, but the Hotel Amancay is the only full-service hotel worth recommending. You'll find more choices in **Villa Turismo,** a hillside community of cabins, bed-and-breakfasts, and small inns located about 2 km (1½ miles) south of town, off Avenida Belgrano. Lodges in the surrounding mountains open for fishing season in summer (November–April) and close in winter (May–October).

$ ⊞ **Hotel Amancay.** This yellow-stucco hotel, just three blocks from the cen-
HOTEL   ter of town, has fairly basic rooms, and showers are iffy, but it is about the best you can do in humble downtown El Bolsón. **Pros:** walking distance to restaurants; clean rooms; quiet. **Cons:** rooms and bathrooms are small and slightly run-down; basic breakfast; little natural light and ventilation. $ *Rooms from: US$50* ⊠ *Av. San Martín 3207* ☎ *2944/492–222* ⊕ *www. hotelamancay.com.ar* ⤳ *15 rooms* ⦿*Breakfast* ✛ *C1.*

$ ⊞ **Lincoln Ranch.** Perched higher than all the other cabin complexes, these
RENTAL   modern cottages have plenty of room and all the accoutrements of a vacation home. **Pros:** lots of space; easy walk up to Piltriquitrón; swimming pool. **Cons:** far from restaurants and downtown shops; outdated decor; hard to get to without a car. $ *Rooms from: US$69* ⊠ *Villa Turismo, Subida Los Maitenes* ☎ *2944/492–073* ▭ *No credit cards* ⤳ *6 cabins* ⦿*No meals* ✛ *C3.*

SPORTS AND THE OUTDOORS
HORSEBACK RIDING
Cabalgatas en Azul. Javier Eduardo offers guided horseback tours to the Azul Canyon, a gorge named for the river's deep blue waters. He also leads tours around Cascada Mallín Ahogado; more adventurous riders can opt to go all the way to the glaciers. ⊠ *El Bolsón* ☎ *2944/483–590* ▱ *1200 pesos for a full day or 250 pesos per hour.*

SKIING
Cerro Perito Moreno. Used mainly by local families, the ski area at Cerro Perito Moreno is owned and operated by Club Andino Piltriquitrón, which also runs a restaurant at the base where you can rent skis, snowboards, and sleds. Four short tows for beginners and one T-bar access the 750 meters (2,460 feet) of skiable terrain on east-facing slopes. ■TIP→ Since storms approach from the west, snowfall can be minimal; it's best to call the tourist office or Club Andino before you go. ⊠ *25 km (15 miles) northwest of El Bolsón* ☎ *2944/498–490* ▱ *Day passes from 450 pesos.*

Cerro Lindo, near El Bolsón, is a hiker's dream.

PARQUE NACIONAL LAGO PUELO

18 km (11 miles) south of El Bolsón on RN40 and RP16.

Parque Nacional Lago Puelo is one of the smallest national parks in the southern Andes and one of the warmest spots in the region. The oh-so-blue lake for which it's named (glacial sediment creates the distinctive color) offers a host of recreational opportunities. The land around it, meanwhile, is ideal for hiking and threaded with trails that lead all the way to the Chilean border.

GETTING HERE AND AROUND

To come by car, follow Ruta 16 to Villa Lago Puelo; from there, a 4-km (3-mile) gravel trail leads to the park entrance. If you don't have your own vehicle, your hotel will happily arrange transport with a local remis driver. You can get information on the park at the tourist office in El Bolsón; picnic and fishing supplies can be purchased in a roadside store at the turnoff to the trail.

EXPLORING

Parque Nacional Lago Puelo. Set more than 200 meters (656 feet) above sea level, this park's titular lake has warm water for swimmers, plentiful fish stocks for anglers, plus a selection of on-the-water excursions for boaters. Hiking options abound in the area as well—the most interesting of which are at the west end of the lake on the Chilean border.

SPORTS AND THE OUTDOORS
BOAT EXCURSIONS

Three launches, maintained by the Argentine navy, wait at the dock to take you out on Lago Puelo. The trip to El Turbio, an ancient settlement at the southern end of the lake on the Chilean border, is the longest. One side of the lake is inaccessible, as the Valdivian rain forest grows on steep rocky slopes right down into the water. Campgrounds are at the park entrance by the ranger's station, in a bay on the Brazo Occidental, and at the Turbio and Epuyén river outlets.

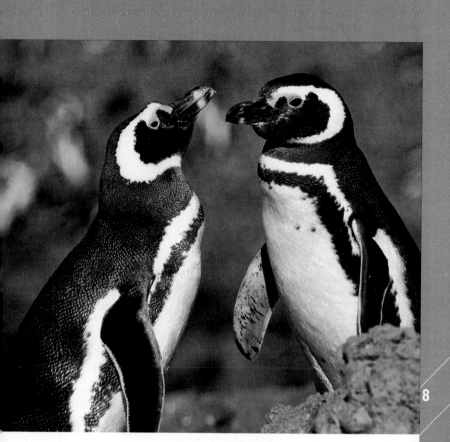

8

PATAGONIA

WELCOME TO PATAGONIA

TOP REASONS TO GO

★ **Glaciers and Mountains:** Set yourself opposite an impossibly massive wall of ice and contemplate the blue-green-turquoise spectrum trapped within. Meanwhile, stark granite peaks planted like spears in the Cordillera beckon extreme mountain climbers and casual trekkers alike.

★ **Marine Life:** Península Valdés is home to breeding populations of sea lions, elephant seals, orcas, and the star of the local sea show, the southern right whale. Punta Tombo is the world's largest Magellanic-penguin colony.

★ **Estancia Stay:** Visit an estancia, a working ranch where you can ride horses alongside tough-as-nails gauchos (cowboys) and dine on spit-roasted lamb under the stars.

★ **Earth, Sea, and Fire:** Patagonian cuisine has some of the most exquisite natural flavors in the world. Specialties include sumptuous king crab; flavorful Patagonian lamb; and indulgent Welsh teacakes.

Most of Patagonia is windswept desert steppe inhabited by rabbits, sheep, *guanacos* (a larger, woollier version of the llama), and a few hardy human beings. The population centers—and attractions—are either along the coast or in a narrow strip of land that runs along the base of the Andes mountain range, where massive glaciers spill into large turquoise lakes. In nearby Chile, Puerto Natales is the gateway town to Parque Nacional Torres del Paine.

At the bottom end of the continent, separated by the Magellan Strait, lies Tierra del Fuego. The resort town of Ushuaia, Argentina, base camp for explorations of the Beagle Channel and the forested peaks of the Cordillera Darwin mountain range, is the leading tourist attraction of the region.

1 Puerto Madryn and Península Valdés. Puerto Madryn provides easy access to Península Valdés, one of the world's best places for marine wildlife viewing.

2 Trelew, Gaiman, and Punta Tombo. Gaiman and Trelew's teahouses and rose gardens date back to the original 19th-century Welsh settlers. Head south to Punta Tombo, the largest penguin rookery in South America.

3 Sarmiento. This small, friendly town is a green oasis. Nearby are stunning petrified forests and a paleontology "park" with life-size dinosaur replicas.

4 El Calafate, El Chaltén, and Parque Nacional los Glaciares. The wild Parque Nacional los Glaciares dramatically contrasts with nearby boomtown El Calafate. North is El Chaltén, base camp for hikes to Cerros Torre and Fitzroy.

5 Puerto Natales and Torres del Paine, Chile. Border town Puerto Natales is the last stop before one of the finest national parks in South America, Parque Nacional Torres del Paine.

6 Ushuaia and Tierra del Fuego. This rugged, windswept land straddles Chile and Argentina. Ushuaia, in Argentina, is the world's southernmost city.

RÍO NEGRO

El Bolsón

Gastre

Cholila
Esquel
Trevelín

Sierra Grande

Golfo
San Matías

Puerto
Pirámides **1**

Puerto Madryn

2 Trelew

Gaiman

Rawson

PENÍNSULA
VALDÉS

Punta
Tombo

CHUBUT

Camarones

3 Sarmiento

Río
Mayo

CHILE

Perito
Moreno

Comodore
Rivadavía

Las Heras

Caleta Olivia

Golfo
San Jorge

Atlantic Ocean

Cabo Tres Puntas

Monumento Natural
Bosque Petrificado

Puerto
Deseado

SANTA CRUZ

Cerro Fitzroy
Cerro Torre
El Chaltén **4**
Cerro
Agassiz
Parque
Nacional
Los Glaciares
Mt. Stokes **5**

Tres Lagos

Punta del Lago

El Calafate

Reserva
Tehuelche

Bahía
Grande

Puerto
San Julián

Puerto Santa Cruz

Parque Nacional
Torres Del Paine

Yacimiento
Río Turbio
Puerto Natales

Cabo Buen Tiempo

Río Gallegos

Magellan Strait

Bahía Lomas

CHILE

TIERRA DEL FUEGO

Río Grande

6 TIERRA DEL
FUEGO

PENÍNSULA MITRE

Parque Nacional
Tierra Del Fuego

Ushuaia

Puerto
Williams

Canal
Beagle

Cape Horn

ISLA DE
LOS ESTADOS

0   100 mi
0   100 km

TO
FALKLAND ISLANDS
(ISLAS MALVINAS)

8

CALENDAR OF FAUNA ON PENÍNSULA VALDÉS

Although few wildlife-viewing experiences are as grandiose as seeing whales breach or witnessing orcas charge the beaches in a hunt for sea lions, there are numerous special moments throughout the yearly cycles of all Atlantic Patagonian fauna. Regardless of what time you visit, you'll be witnessing something memorable.

(above) Elephant seal bull with Snowy Sheathbill (top right) Dolphin Gull (bottom right) Southern Right Whale off Puerto Pirámides

Since practically everyone who visits Península Valdés is here for the wildlife, any guide we recommend will know where to go for the best views of the wildlife that's most active. Renting a car is a possibility, but going with a guide service makes things easier—your guide will be able to navigate the unpaved roads while you scan the land and water for creatures.

WHEN TO GO

Birds: June–December

Whales: May–December

Dolphins: December–March

Elephant Seals: year-round

Sea Lions: year-round

Orcas: September–April

Penguins: September–March

SCOPE IT OUT

Consider purchasing or renting binoculars or a scope.

LOOK TO THE WATER FOR ...

Southern Right Whales. The first southern right whales arrive in Golfo Nuevo at the end of April and can be observed from beaches in and along Puerto Madryn as well as the Península Valdés. Your best chance of seeing them will be from a whale-watching point at Puerto Pirámides. These whales are between 36 and 59 feet long, and have several endearing behaviors such as "sailing," where they hold their fins up in the air, and when a mother uses her flippers to teach calves how to swim.

Elephant Seals. Elephant seals are larger mammals than sea lions, and have a different way of moving—using their flippers to waddle along on land, whereas sea lions use both front and back flippers to thrust themselves forward. Adult males can reach up to 6 meters (20 feet) in length and weigh up to 4 tons, and after four years develop a proboscis, or elephant-like appendage on their noses, which inflates to help produce sounds. The biggest elephant-seal colonies are in Península Valdés, at Punta Cantor and Punta Delgada.

Sea Lions. In January and February sea lions begin to form "harems," with each dominant male taking up to a dozen females. The fights to maintain these harems can be violent, and it's possible to witness an invading male drag off one of the females from the harem with his teeth. Most of the year, however, sea-lion colonies appear peaceful: the animals sun themselves or swim, and the pups are curious and playful. They can be observed year-round all along the Atlantic Coast. From December through April sea lions and elephant seals are reproducing and raising pups.

Orcas. It's possible to see the black fins of orcas cutting through the water along the coastline, occasionally storming the beach in violent and spectacular chases. The best place to see orcas is at the extreme northern tip of Península Valdés, Punta Norte, in April.

LOOK TO THE AIR AND LAND FOR ...

Seabirds. Among the many seabirds found in Patagonia—including dolphin gulls, kelp geese, southern giant petrels, rock and blue-eyed cormorants, snowy sheathbills, blackish oystercatchers, and steamer ducks—one species, the arctic tern, has the longest migration—it flies over 21,750 miles annually from the Arctic to Antarctica and back.

Penguins. Along Atlantic Patagonia—most notably Punta Tombo—there are large rookeries of Magellanic penguins, with up to 500,000 of these flightless birds. The males arrive from the sea each August, followed by the females a month later when territorial battles begin. In October and into November the nesting pairs incubate the eggs. Once the chicks hatch in November, the parents make continual trips to the ocean for food. In January the chicks leave the nest, learning to swim in February. Their plumage matures throughout the fall, when the penguins begin migrating north to Brazil.

8

Updated
by Amanda
Barnes

Patagonia is a wild and rugged land filled with breathtaking landscapes and eye-catching wildlife. There are few other places in the world where you can feel such a great isolation and vast emptiness and yet see waters teeming with wildlife; visit gauchos living on windswept estancias; and get so close to ancient glaciers that you can actually walk inside these ice cathedrals. Spanning over a million square kilometers Patagonia has many worlds to discover.

Atlantic Patagonia is where the low pampas meet the ocean. It's a land of immense panoramic horizons and a coastline of bays, inlets, and peninsulas abounding with birds and marine wildlife. The region is most famous for Península Valdés, a UNESCO Natural World Heritage Site with southern right whales, orcas, elephant seals, and sea lions. There are seemingly endless dirt roads where you won't see another person or vehicle for hours—only guanacos, rheas, and other animals running across the steppe.

Farther south and inland to the Andes, the towns of El Calafate and El Chaltén come alive in summer (December through March) with the influx of visitors to the Parque Nacional los Glaciares, and climbers headed for Cerro Torre and Cerro Fitzroy. Imagine sailing across a blue lake full of icebergs, or traversing an advancing glacier in the shadow of the Andes mountain range, watching a valley being formed before your eyes. The Perito Moreno glacier attracts tourists continuously to this region.

Experiencing Patagonia, however, still means crossing vast deserts to reach isolated population centers, taking deep breaths of mountain air and draughts of pure stream water in the shadow of dramatic snow-capped peaks. Most of all, it means being embraced by independent, pioneering souls beginning to understand the importance of tourism as traditional industries—wool, livestock, fishing, and oil—are drying up.

PLANNING

WHEN TO GO

Late September to March—spring and summer in the Southern Hemisphere—is high season in Patagonia. Reservations are advised, especially in September and October in Atlantic Patagonia and December through February in Southern Patagonia. Although the summer sun can be strong, the winds whistle year-round, so always bring extra layers and a windbreaker. In Atlantic Patagonia many properties close in April and May to prepare for the first whale-watchers in June and July. While most of Southern Patagonia grinds almost to a halt from May to September, the ski season in Ushuaia is increasingly popular.

GETTING HERE AND AROUND

AIR TRAVEL

Flying is the best way to reach Patagonia from Buenos Aires (through which flights from most other parts of the country also pass). Always allow some buffer time when traveling to Patagonia: bad weather, heavy fog, and strikes can cause common delays on either side of the journey.

Aerolíneas Argentinas (⊕ www.aerolineas.com.ar) and LATAM (⊕ www.lan.com) have regular, direct flights to Trelew, Comodoro Rivadavía, Río Gallegos, El Calafate, and Ushuaia from Buenos Aires.

LADE (Líneas Aéreas del Estado ⊕ www.lade.com.ar) connects Comodoro Rivadavía to Rio Gallegos and Rio Grande with weekly flights in the summer. Andes Líneas Aéreas (⊕ www.andesonline.com) has direct flights between Buenos Aires and Puerto Madryn every day in peak season.

BUS TRAVEL

Comfortable overnight sleeper buses connect Patagonia to Buenos Aires (and other major cities). However, as getting to even the closest city in Atlantic Patagonia, Puerto Madryn, takes 20 hours, most travelers feel it's worth the price to fly. All the same, buses are a major form of transportation between destinations up to about 600 km (370 miles) apart. Don Otto (⊕ www.donotto.com.ar) is a reliable carrier.

CAR TRAVEL

If you truly enjoy the call of the open road, there are few places that can rival the vast emptiness and jaw-dropping beauty of Patagonia. Be prepared for miles and miles of semidesert steppes with no gas stations, towns, or even restrooms. Always carry plenty of water, snacks, a jack, and tire-changing tools, with at least one spare. Take extra care when driving on *ripios* (gravel roads): it's easy to flip small cars at speeds over 80 kph (55 mph). Fill your tank at every opportunity. If you're not driving, consider simply paying for a *remis* (car with driver) for day excursions.

RESTAURANTS

With so many miles of coastline, it's not surprising that Atlantic Patagonia is famous for its seafood, notably sole and salmon, *mejillones* (mussels), and *pulpo* (octopus). *Centolla* (king crab) is another specialty, especially south of Comodoro Rivadavía. Most restaurants are sit-down-and-take-your-time affairs that don't open for dinner until at least

8, and despite all the seafood on offer, steak still reigns supreme. The other carnivorous staple in the area is *cordero patagónico*, local lamb, usually served barbecued or stewed. Dining prices in most Patagonian cities rival those of upper-end Buenos Aires restaurants. Thankfully, so do the skills of local chefs, although expect more basic offerings of pizza, milanesas, and empanadas in smaller towns. Whenever possible, accompany your meal with a bottle of wine from one of the increasing number of Patagonian wineries.

Huge numbers of foreign visitors mean that vegetarian options are getting better, although vegan food is still scarce. Most cafés and bars serve quick bites known as *minutas*. The region is also famous for its stone fruits, which are used in various jams, preserves, sweets, and *alfajores* (a chocolate-covered sandwich of two cookies with jam in the middle). When in El Calafate, be sure to nibble on some calafate berries (or drink them in cocktails like the Calafate Sour)—legend has it if you eat them in El Calafate you are destined to return one day soon.

HOTELS

There aren't many budget accommodations in Patagonia; the luxury market, on the other hand, is booming. Patagonia is a "once-in-a-life-time" destination that most people are happy to splurge on, and the increasing cruise culture doesn't ease accommodation prices. In most cities and towns you'll find a mix of big, expensive hotels with comfortable resorts, local flavor estancias, and small B&B-style *hosterías*.

The terms *hospedaje* and *hostal* are used interchangeably in the region, so don't make assumptions based on the name. Many *hostals* are fine hotels—not youth hostels with multiple beds—just very small. By contrast, some *hospedajes* are little more than a spare room in someone's home. Campsites in the national parks often have shelter and can offer some of the best views in Patagonia. *Hotel reviews have been shortened. For full information, visit Fodors.com.*

WHAT IT COSTS				
	$	$$	$$$	$$$$
Restaurants	Under 300 pesos	300–500 pesos	501–750 pesos	over 750 pesos
Hotels in USD	Under $116	$116–$200	$201–$300	over $300

Restaurant prices are the average cost of a main course at dinner or, if dinner is not served, at lunch. Hotel prices are the lowest cost of a standard double room in high season.

HEALTH AND SAFETY

Most mountains are not high enough to induce altitude sickness, but the weather can turn nasty quickly. Sunglasses and sunscreen are essential. Although tap water is safe to drink throughout the region, most travelers still choose to drink bottled water. Do not approach or let your children approach sea lions, penguins, or any other animals, no matter how docile or curious they might seem.

CLOSE UP

Border Crossing

The border between Chile and Argentina is still strictly maintained, but crossing it doesn't present much difficulty beyond getting out your passport and waiting in a line to get the stamp. Most travelers end up crossing the border by bus, which means getting out of the vehicle for 30–45 minutes to go through the bureaucratic proceedings, then loading back in.

Crossing by car is also quite manageable (check with your car-rental company for restrictions on international travel). Chilean customs officers are extremely strict about bringing food into the country, especially compared with their Argentinean counterparts. Always declare food products (they are usually flexible once items are declared); otherwise, you face a hefty fine.

Emergency Services Coast Guard. ☎ *106.* **Fire.** ☎ *100.* **Forest Fire.** ☎ *103.* **Hospital.** ☎ *107.* **Police.** ☎ *101.*

CRUISING IN PATAGONIA

Cruising is a leisurely and comfortable way to take in the rugged marvels of Patagonia and the southernmost region of the world. Sailing through remote channels and reaching islands virtually untouched by man, you'll witness fjords, snowcapped mountains and granite peaks, and glacial lakes. You'll get a close look at elephant seals, migrating whales, colonies of Magellanic penguins, and cormorants from the comfort of your vessel and during shore excursions taken in Zodiacs (small motorized boats) led by naturalist guides. Far from the beaten path, you'll visit small fishing villages accessible only by sea, explore fantastic temperate rain forests, and enjoy the freshest seafood and local wines.

Most short cruises depart from Ushuaia, Argentina, or Punta Arenas, Chile. Longer and more luxurious itineraries typically depart from either Buenos Aires or Santiago.

WHEN TO GO

In the Southern Hemisphere, where the seasons are reversed, November through March is considered high season. However, the weather in Patagonia is unpredictable: strong winds and sudden storms are common. Summertime (December through February) is the best time to visit. Shoulder months—October, November, March, and April—tend to have cooler temperatures but also less wind. In winter, cruise companies all but hibernate for the season.

October (late spring). Best time to witness the whale migration and the immense colonies of elephant seals and sea lions in Península Valdés.

November (early summer). The natural nesting cycle of Magellanic penguins is November to February. Penguins arrive at the rookeries at the beginning of the month. Spring flowers are in full bloom. This is the best time to catch the bird nesting of finches, sparrows, condors, albatrosses, and other species.

December and January (high summer). The warmest months see penguin chicks hatch in Tierra del Fuego. Long daylight hours also mean great photography opportunities all over Patagonia.

February and March (late summer). Receding ice allows for easier exploration farther south. Whale-watching is at its best. Penguin colonies are very active, as the adults feed the chicks.

BOOKING YOUR CRUISE

The majority of cruisers plan their trips four to six months ahead of time. Book a year ahead if you're planning to sail on a small adventure vessel, as popular itineraries may be full six to eight months ahead.

Consider booking shore excursions when you book your cruise to avoid disappointment later. You can even book your spa services precruise to have your pick of popular times, such as sea days.

Although most travel is booked over the Internet nowadays, for cruises, booking with a travel agent who specializes in Patagonia cruises is still your best bet. Agents have strong relationships with the lines and have a better chance of getting you the cabin you want, possibly even a free upgrade. Cruise Lines International Association (⊕ *www.cruising.org*) lists recognized agents throughout the United States.

CRUISE ITINERARIES

Choosing an itinerary is as important as choosing a cruise line or tour operator that fits your tastes and budget. We highlight possibilities that focus on specific areas, as well as typical departure points, and the tour operators that can take you there.

ANTARCTIC CRUISES
Founded to promote environmentally responsible travel to Antarctica, the **International Association of Antarctica Tour Operators** (☎ *401/841–9700* ⊕ *www.iaato.org*) is a good source of information, including suggested readings. Most companies operating Antarctica trips are members of this organization and display its logo in their brochures.

Season: November–March.

Location: Most cruises depart from Ushuaia, in Argentine Patagonia.

Cost: From $5,495 from Ushuaia; prices can get quite high.

Tour Operators: Abercrombie & Kent; Adventure Center; Big Five Tours & Expeditions; ElderTreks; G Adventures; Lindblad Expeditions; Mountain Travel-Sobek; Quark Expeditions; Travcoa; Wilderness Travel; Zegrahm Expeditions.

Overview: Ever since Lars-Eric Lindblad operated the first cruise to the "White Continent" in 1966, Antarctica has exerted an almost magnetic pull for serious travelers. From Ushuaia, the world's southernmost city, you'll sail for two (often rough) days through the Drake Passage. Most visits are to the Antarctic Peninsula, the continent's most accessible region. Accompanied by naturalists, you'll travel ashore in motorized rubber crafts called Zodiacs to view penguins and nesting seabirds. Some cruises visit research stations, and many call at the Falkland, South Orkney, South Shetland, or South Georgia islands. Certain operators offer sea kayaking and, at an extra cost, the chance to camp for a night on the ice.

Expedition vessels have been fitted with ice-strengthened hulls; many originally were built as polar-research vessels. It's wise to inquire about the qualifications of the onboard naturalists and historians, the maximum number of passengers carried, the ice-readiness of the vessel, onboard medical facilities, whether there is an open bridge policy, and the number of landings attempted per day.

CRUISING THE TIP OF SOUTH AMERICA Cruising the southern tip of South America and along Chile's western coast north to the Lake District reveals fjords, glaciers, lagoons, lakes, narrow channels, waterfalls, forested shorelines, fishing villages, and wildlife. While many tour operators include a one- or two-day boating excursion as part of their Patagonia itineraries, the companies listed below offer 4 to 12 nights aboard ship.

Season: September–April.

Locations: Chilean fjords; Puerto Montt and Punta Arenas, Chile; Tierra del Fuego and Ushuaia, Argentina.

Cost: From $2,200 for a four-day, three-night cruise between Punta Arenas and Ushuaia.

Tour Operators: Abercrombie & Kent; Adventure Life; Big Five Tours & Expeditions; Cruceros Australis; International Expeditions; Lindblad Expeditions; Mountain Travel-Sobek; Wilderness Travel; Wildland Adventures.

Overview: Boarding your vessel in Punta Arenas, Chile, or Ushuaia, Argentina, you'll cruise the Strait of Magellan and the Beagle Channel, visiting glaciers, penguin rookeries, and seal colonies before heading north along the fjords of Chile's western coast. With Abercrombie & Kent and Wildland Adventures, you'll savor the mountain scenery of Torres del Paine National Park for several days before or following the cruise, while Lindblad Expeditions, Mountain Travel-Sobek, and International Expeditions visit Tierra del Fuego National Park. Cruceros Australis and some other companies also include Cape Horn National Park. Most itineraries begin or end in Santiago or Punto Arenas in Chile, or Buenos Aires, El Calafate, or Ushuaia in Argentina.

OCEAN CRUISES Some ships set sail in the Caribbean and stop at one or two islands before heading south; a few transit the Panama Canal en route. West Coast (U.S.) departures might include one or more Mexican ports before reaching South America. Fourteen- to 21-day cruises are the norm. Vessels vary in the degree of comfort or luxury as well as in what is or isn't included in the price. Guided shore excursions, gratuities, dinner beverages, and port taxes are often extra.

Season: October–April.

Locations: Many itineraries visit Argentina (Buenos Aires and Ushuaia), Brazil (Belém, Fortaleza, Rio de Janeiro, and Salvador), and Chile (Antofagasta, Arica, Cape Horn, Coquimbo, Puerto Montt, Punta Arenas, and Valparaíso).

Cost: Prices vary according to the ship, cabin category, and itinerary.

MAJOR CRUISE
LINES

Celebrity Cruises: Fjords, glaciers, and emerald lakes are the highlight of a cruise down the west coast of Chile and back up the Atlantic Coast to Buenos Aires. The 15-day cruise is offered December through February. ☎ 305/341–0205 ⊕ www.celebrity.com.

Fred.Olsen Cruise Lines: Their February cruise from Buenos Aires to Lima prides itself on being intimate, friendly, and catering to retired couples. ☎ 845/869–3330 ⊕ www.fredolsencruises.com.

Oceania Cruises: Patagonia (Buenos Aires to Valparaíso in January, and Lima to Buenos Aires in March) voyages with Oceania are as relaxed and elegant as a private country club—mahogany decor, plush carpeting and grand, sweeping staircases. ☎ 800/254–5067 ⊕ www.oceania-cruises.com.

Princess Cruises: Trips (in January and February) on this cruise line include eight ports of call in the Argentine and Chilean Patagonia regions. ☎ 800/774–6237 ⊕ www.princess.com.

Seabourn Cruise Line: Patagonia cruises with Seabourn include visits to the Beagle Channel and the Chilean fjords; a couple of cruises run November through February. ⊕ www.seabourn.com.

Silversea Cruises: Voyages with Silversea dock in Uruguay, the Falkland Islands, and Ushuaia, among others, running November through January. ☎ 954/607–2041 ⊕ www.silversea.com.

PUERTO MADRYN AND PENÍNSULA VALDÉS

Visiting populations of whales, orcas, sea lions, elephant seals, and penguins all gather to breed or feed on or near the shores of this unique peninsula, which comprises one of the lowest points in South America. The wildlife isn't only water-based; wandering the Patagonian scrub are guanacos, gray foxes, *maras* (Patagonian hares), skunks, armadillos, and rheas, while myriad bird species fill the air. There are also three inland salt lakes, and the curving gulf at Puerto Pirámides is one of the few places in Argentina where the sun sets over the water, not the land. With nature putting on such a generous display, it's not surprising that the 3,625-square-km (1,400-square-mile) peninsula has been designated a UNESCO World Heritage Site and is the main reason visitors come to Atlantic Patagonia.

Puerto Madryn is where you'll head first for organized excursions onto the peninsula. While a major part of the town's identity is a staging ground for these trips, it's also well worth exploring and has an interesting history. The first economic boom came in 1886, when the Patagonian railroad was introduced, spurring port activities along with the salt and fishing industries. Although it isn't likely that the original Welsh settlers who arrived here in 1865 could have imagined just how much Puerto Madryn would evolve, a large part of the town's success is owed to their hardworking traditions, which continue with their descendants today. The anniversary of their arrival is celebrated every July 28 here and in other Chubut towns. Only a statue—the Tehuelche Indian Monument—serves as a reminder of the indigenous people who once lived here and who helped the Welsh survive.

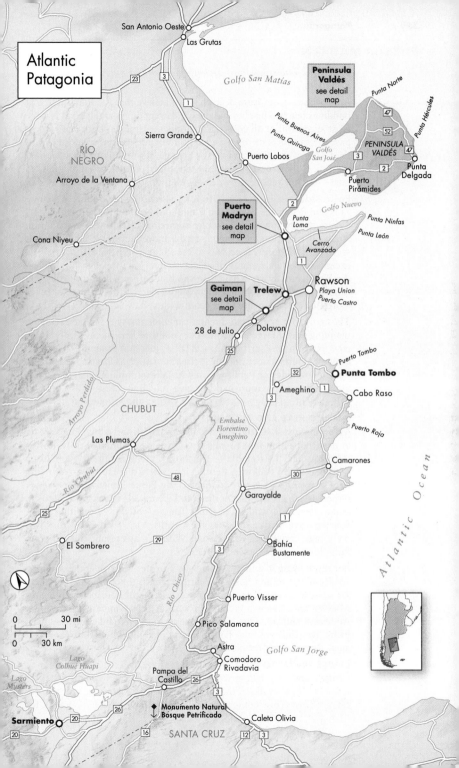

PUERTO MADRYN

67 km (42 miles) north of Trelew; 104 km (64 miles) west of Puerto Pirámides.

Approaching from Ruta 3, it's hard to believe that the horizon line of buildings perched just beyond the windswept dunes and badlands is the most successful of all coastal Patagonia settlements. But once you get past the outskirts of town and onto the wide coastal road known as the Rambla, the picture begins to change. Ranged along the clear and tranquil Golfo Nuevo are restaurants, cafés, dive shops, and hotels, all busy—but not yet overcrowded—with tourists from around the world.

Puerto Madryn is more a base for visiting nearby wildlife-watching sites like Península Valdés and Punta Tombo than a destination in its own right. The town's architecture is unremarkable, and beyond a walk along the coast there isn't much to do. Indeed, even the few museums serve mainly to introduce you to the fauna you'll see elsewhere. The exception is the beginning of whale season (May through July), when the huge animals cavort right in the bay before heading north—you can even walk out alongside them on the pier. During these months it's worth the extra expense for a room with a sea view.

The many tour agencies and rental-car companies here make excursion planning easy. Aim to spend most of your time here on one- or two-day trips exploring the surroundings. ■TIP→ Note that competition is fierce between tourism operators in destinations such as Puerto Madryn and Puerto Pirámides on Península Valdés. Take information that tour operators and even the tourism office give you about these with a grain of salt: they often exaggerate Madryn's virtues and other areas' flaws.

GETTING HERE AND AROUND

Madryn is just small enough to walk around in, and many hotels are on or near the 3½-km-long (2-mile-long) Avenida Almirante Brown—often referred to as "La Rambla"—which runs alongside the bay and has a wide pedestrian walkway. Renting a bicycle is a great way to reach the EcoCentro and (if you're feeling fit) the Punta Loma nature reserve. Otherwise, to get to either of these, to El Doradillo beach north of town, and to Península Valdés and Punta Tombo, you'll need to either rent a vehicle, travel with a tour, or take a remis. Mar y Valle also runs two daily bus services between Puerto Madryn's bus terminal and Puerto Pirámides on the Península Valdés.

For those flying in and out of Trelew, Transfer PMY operates a shuttle service direct to any hotel in Puerto Madryn (about US$15) or there are taxis available. There are services every half hour between Puerto Madryn and Trelew and Gaiman with the bus company 28 de Julio. Andesmar and Don Otto connect Puerto Madryn to Buenos Aires, Bariloche, Río Gallegos, and Puerto Montt in Chile. Numerous car rental agencies are along Avenida Roca.

CRUISE TRAVEL TO PUERTO MADRYN

Cruise ships land right next to the city center in Puerto Madryn, where it's only a short walk off the pier to the town's restaurants and tourism center. Most cruise companies will already have paid the port tax for

Continued on page 370

INTO THE PATAGONIAN WILD

Patagonia will shatter your sense of scale. You will feel very small, surrounded by an epic expanse of mountains and plains, sea, and sky. Whether facing down an advancing wall of glacial ice, watching an ostrich-like rhea racing across the open steppe, or getting splashed by a breaching right whale off the Valdez Peninsula, prepare to gasp at the majesty of the Patagonian wild.

GLACIERS OF PATAGONIA

Cruise on Lago Argentino, Santa Cruz province, Glaciers National Park, Argentina

The Patagonia ice field covers much of the southern end of the Andean mountain range, straddling the Argentina–Chile border. The glaciers that spill off the high altitude ice field are basically rivers of slowly moving ice and snow that grind and push their way across the mountains, crushing soft rock and sculpting granite peaks.

Most of Patagonia's glaciers spill into lakes, rivers, or fjords. Chunks of ice calve off the face of the glacier into the water, a dramatic display of nature's power that you can view at several locations. The larger pieces of ice become icebergs that scud across the water surface like white sailboats blown by the wind.

TRAVEL SHRINKS

The link between high-impact activities—such as air travel—and climate change is clear, leading to a disturbing irony: the more people come to see the glaciers of Patagonia, the more carbon is released into the atmosphere, and the more the glaciers shrink.

WEATHER
Weather is unpredictable around glaciers: it's not uncommon to experience sunshine, rain, and snow squalls in a single afternoon.

ICE COLORS
Although clear days are best for panoramas, cloudy days bring out the translucent blue of the glacial ice, creating great opportunities for magical photographs. You'll also see black or gray streaks in the ice caused by sediment picked up by the glacier as it grinds down the mountain valley. When that sediment is deposited into lakes, it hangs suspended in the water, turning the lake a pale milky blue.

ENVIRONMENTAL CONCERN
There's no question that human-induced climate change is taking its toll on Patagonia's glaciers. Although the famous Perito Moreno glacier is still advancing, nearly all the others have shrunk in recent years, some dramatically. You can find out more about the effects of climate change and their impact on the glaciers at Calafate's Glaciarium museum.

Right: Glacier Grey, Paine Circuit, Torres del Paine National Park, Chile

GLACIERS TO SEE

- Perito Moreno Glacier, Santa Cruz, Argentina
- Upsala Glacier, Santa Cruz, Argentina
- Martial Glacier, Tierra del Fuego, Argentina
- Serrano Glacier, Tierra del Fuego, Chile
- O'Higgins Glacier, Southern Coast, Chile

FIRE AND ICE: MOUNTAINS OF PATAGONIA

A trekker takes in the view of Cerro Torre (left) and Fitz Roy in Los Glaciares National Park, Patagonia.

In Patagonia, mountains mean the Andes, a relatively young range but a precocious one that stretches for more than 4,000 miles. The Patagonian Andes are of special interest to geologists, who study how fire, water, and ice have shaped the mountains into their present form.

CREATION
Plate tectonics are the most fundamental factor in the formation of the southern Andes, with the oceanic Nazca plate slipping beneath the continental South American plate and forcing the peaks skyward. Volcanic activity is a symptom of this dynamic process, and there are several active volcanoes on the Chilean side of the range.

GLACIAL IMPRINT
Glacial activity has also played an important role in chiseling the most iconic Patagonian peaks. The spires that form the distinctive skylines of Torres del Paine and the Fitzroy range are solid columns that were created when rising glaciers ripped away weaker rock, leaving only hard granite skeletons that stand rigid at the edge of the ice fields.

MOUNTAIN HIGH BORDERS
Because the border between Chile and Argentina cuts through the most impenetrable reaches of the ice field, the actual border line is unclear in areas of the far south. Even in the more temperate north, border crossings are often located at mountain passes, and the officials who stamp visas seem more like mountain guides than bureaucrats.

MOUNTAINS OF THE SEA
Tierra del Fuego and the countless islands off the coast of southern Chile were once connected to the mainland. Over the years the sea swept into the valleys, isolated the peaks, and created an archipelago that, viewed on a map, looks as abstract as a Jackson Pollack painting. From the water these island mountains appear especially dramatic, misty pinnacles of rock and ice rising from the crashing sea.

Right: Mt. Fitzroy

PROMINENT PEAKS AND RANGES

- Mt. Fitzroy and Cerro Torre, Santa Cruz, Argentina
- Cuernos of Torres del Paine, Chile
- Beagle Channel Mountains, Tierra del Fuego, Chile/ Argentina
- Cerro Piltriqitron, El Bolson, Argentina
- Osorno Volcano, Lake District, Chile

PENGUINS OF PATAGONIA

Magellanic Penguin walking to his nest in Peninsula Valdes

Everyone loves penguins. How could you not feel affection for such cute, curious, and loyal little creatures? On land, their awkward waddle is endearing, and you can get close enough to see the inquisitive gaze in their eyes as they turn their heads from side to side for a good look at you. In the water, penguins transform from goofballs into Olympic athletes, streaking through the waves and returning to the nest with mouthfuls of fish and squid for their chicks.

TYPES

Most of the penguins you'll see here are Magellanic penguins, black and white colored birds that gather in large breeding colonies on the beaches of Patagonia in the summer and retreat north to warmer climes during winter. Also keep an eye out for the red-beaked Gentoo penguins that nest among the Magellanics.

If your image of penguins is the large and colorful Emperor penguins of Antarctica that featured in the documentary *March of the Penguins*, you might be slightly underwhelmed by the little Magellanics. Adults stand about 30 inches tall and weigh between 15 and 20 pounds. What they lack in glamour, Patagonia's penguins make up in vanity—and numbers. Many breeding sites are home to tens of thousands of individuals, all preening and strutting as if they were about to walk the red carpet at the Academy Awards.

PENGUIN RELATIONS

Male and female penguins form monogamous pairs and share the task of raising the chicks, which hatch in small burrows that the parents return to year after year. If you sit and observe a pair of penguins for a little while you'll notice how affectionate they appear, grooming each other with their beaks and huddling together on the nest.

HUMAN CONTACT

Although penguins are not shy of humans who keep a respectful distance (about 8 feet is a good rule of thumb), the history of penguin-human relations is not entirely one of peaceful curiosity. Early pioneers and stranded sailors would raid penguin nests for food, and in modern times, oil spills have devastated penguin colonies in Patagonia.

Magellanic Penguins

WHERE & WHEN

The best time to see penguins is from November through February, which coincides with the best weather in coastal Patagonia. Some of the most convenient and impressive colonies to visit are:

- Punta Tombo, Chubut, Argentina
- Cabo Virgenes, Santa Cruz, Argentina
- Isla Madalena, Chile
- Martillo Island, Tierra del Fuego, Argentina
- Puerto San Julian, Santa Cruz, Argentina

IN THE SEA

The Patagonian coast teems with marine life, including numerous "charismatic megafauna" such as whales, dolphins, sea lions, and seals.

❶ Seals and Sea Lions

In the springtime massive elephant seals and southern sea lions drag themselves onto Patagonian beaches for mating season—hopefully out of range of hungry orcas. These giant pinnipeds form two groups in the breeding colonies. Big, tough alpha bulls have their own harems of breeding females and their young, while so-called bachelor males hang out nearby like freshman boys at a fraternity party, hoping to entice a stray female away from the alpha bull's harem.

❷ Orcas

Orcas aren't as common as dolphins, but you can spot them off the Valdez Peninsula, Argentina, hunting seals and sea lions along the shore. Sometimes hungry orcas will chase their prey a few feet too far and beach themselves above the tide line, where they perish of dehydration.

❸ Whales

The Valdez Peninsula is also one of the best places to observe right whales, gentle giants of the ocean. Although the name right whale derives from whalers who designated it as the "right" whale to kill, the right whale is now protected by both national legislation and international agreements.

❹ Dolphins

Dolphins are easy to spot on tours, because they're curious and swim up to the boat, sometimes even surfing the bow wake. Commerson's dolphins are a common species in coastal Argentina and the Straights of Magellan. Among the world's tiniest dolphins, their white and black coloring has earned them the nickname "skunk dolphin" and prompted comparisons with their distant cousins, orcas.

IN THE AIR

Patagonia is a twitcher's paradise. Even non-bird-lovers marvel at the colorful species that squawk, flutter, and soar through Patagonia's skies.

❺ Albatross

You can spot several species of albatross off the Patagonian coast, gliding on fixed wings above the waves. The albatross lives almost entirely at sea, touching down on land to breed and raise its young. Unless you're visiting Antarctica or the Falklands, your best bet for seeing an albatross is to take a cruise from Punta Arenas or Ushuaia.

❻ Andean Condor

You probably won't see a condor up close. They nest on high-altitude rock ledges and spend their days soaring in circles on high thermals, scanning mountain slopes and plains for carrion. With a wing span of up to 10 feet, however, the king of the Andean skies is impressive even when viewed from a distance. Condors live longer than almost any other bird. Some could qualify for Social Security.

❼ Magellanic Woodpecker

You can hear the distinctive rat-tat of this enormous woodpecker in nothofagus forests of Chilean Patagonia and parts of Argentina. Males have a bright red head and a black body, while females are almost entirely black.

❽ Rhea (Nandu)

No, it's not an ostrich. The rhea is an extremely large flightless bird that roams the Patagonian steppe. Although they're not normally aggressive, males have been known to charge humans who get too close to their partner's nests.

❾ Kelp Goose

As the name implies, kelp geese love kelp. In fact, kelp is the only thing they eat. The geese travel along the rocky shores of Tierra del Fuego in search of their favorite seaweed salad.

you, so simply bring your ID and some layered clothing when exploring Puerto Madryn by foot.

If you have a full day here you should head to the Península Valdés (100 km northeast). If you have only a couple of hours, head out to the Sea Lion Reserve (17 km southeast) or simply enjoy the city and try spotting whales from the coastline.

ESSENTIALS

Bus Contacts Andesmar. ⊠ *Terminal de Ómnibus* ☎ *0280/447–3764* ⊕ *www.andesmar.com.* **Don Otto.** ⊠ *Terminal de Ómnibus* ☎ *0280/445–1675, 0810/333–7575.* **Mar y Valle.** ⊠ *Terminal de Ómnibus* ☎ *0280/445–0600.* **Transfer PMY.** ⊠ *Ruta Nacional 250* ☎ *280/15–4873–000.* **28 de Julio.** ⊠ *Terminal de Ómnibus, Doctor Ávila 350* ☎ *2804/472–056.*

Visitor Information Puerto Madryn. ⊠ *Av. Roca 223* ☎ *0280/445–3504* ⊕ *www.madryn.gob.ar/turismo.*

TOURS

Puerto Madryn is a useful base for exploring nearby wildlife sites such as Península Valdés and Punta Tombo. If time is tight, or you don't feel like driving the several hundred kilometers round-trip, consider taking an organized day tour. The regular services offered by the many agencies around town vary little in price and content. Try to book a couple of days ahead if you can, although midweek many companies accept bookings the night before the tour leaves.

Note that the English spoken by most guides can vary wildly, so read up on the area first. Drinks, snacks, and meals are rarely included: bring plenty of your own along, and be prepared to spend a long, long time on your minibus.

Standard tours to Península Valdés typically include a stop at the visitor center, a whale-watching boat trip (June through December), and a visit to two other wildlife spots on the peninsula. Time is often tight, and tours can feel more like working through a fauna checklist than getting close to nature. Companies can drop you off in Puerto Pirámides on the way back if you've decided to stay there overnight.

Day trips to Punta Tombo stop off at Rawson for dolphin-watching (not always included in the tour price), then continue south to the penguin reserve, where you get a scant hour or so. They usually return via Gaiman (with a visit to a Welsh teahouse) or Trelew (to see the dinosaur museum). Most companies are happy to drop you at the Trelew airport on the way back if you have an evening flight.

For more information, see the Getting Here and Around sections for Península Valdés and Punta Tombo.

Argentina Vision. With more than 35 years of experience, this tour company offers excursions including visiting Península Valdés, kayaking and diving with seals in Punta Loma, bird-watching boat tours, whale-spotting, and horseback riding. They also do a half-day 4X4 outing to Punta Loma. ⊠ *Av. Roca 536* ☎ *0280/445–5888* ⊕ *www.argentinavision.com* 🖃 *From 1200 pesos.*

Bottazzi. One of the first whale-watching operators in Puerto Madryn, Bottazzi specializes in whale-watching from its own fleet of 20-, 50-, and 80-passenger boats from Puerto Pirámides. Guided trips last about an hour and a half. When it isn't whale season, they offer dolphin-watching trips at Puerto Rawson, where you can watch toninas, the world's smallest dolphins, at play. One of the most popular tours combines a full-day Punta Tombo excursion (which includes transport from Puerto Madryn) to see penguins with dolphin-watching. Bottazzi also offers other sightseeing tours and activities. ✉ *Av. Roca 31* ☎ *0280/447–4110* ⊕ *www.bottazzi.com.ar* ✉ *From 1300 pesos.*

Causana Viajes. Custom-tour operator Causana Viajes will organize the tour or schedule you want with your own chauffeur and guide. The most requested tours are full-day excursions to Península Valdés with whale-watching, and full-day tours to Punta Tombo for penguins and dolphin-spotting. ✉ *Rawson 1331* ☎ *0280/447–5919* ⊕ *www.causana-tour.com.ar* ✉ *From 6000 pesos.*

Miras del Mar. The most popular tour through this outfitter is the full-day Punta Tombo excursion, which includes a stopover for Welsh tea at Gaiman and Trelew's paleontology museum and includes transport from Puerto Madryn. ✉ *Moreno 38* ☎ *0280/447–4316* ⊕ *www.miras-delmar.com* ✉ *From 1000 pesos.*

Nievemar. As well as full-day tours to Punta Tombo and Península Valdés, Nievemar offers private day tours to the Petrified Forest, half days visiting the tonina dolphins, and whale-spotting visits from Playa el Doradillo. You can book tours from their Puerto Madryn and Trelew offices. ✉ *Av. Roca 493* ☎ *0280/445–5544* ⊕ *www.nievemartours.com. ar* ✉ *From 1100 pesos.*

EXPLORING

FAMILY **EcoCentro.** From its perch on a windswept outcrop 4 km (3 miles) south of the town center, this museum and research center affords excellent views of Madryn's bays and desolate coastline. Inside, thoughtful, well-translated displays introduce you to the area's ocean fauna and seek to promote marine conservation. An invertebrates "touch pool" and a whale-sounds exhibit—which you reach by walking through a curtain imitating baleen plates—are especially good for kids. ✉ *Julio Verne 3784* ☎ *0280/488–3173* ⊕ *www.ecocentro.org.ar* ✉ *From 260 pesos* ⊙ *Closed June.*

El Doradillo. Following the coastal road 14 km (9 miles) north from Puerto Madryn brings you to this whale-watching spot. The ocean floor drops away steeply from the beach, so between June and mid-December you can stand on the sand almost alongside southern right whales, usually mothers teaching their young to swim. During the rest of the year it's just a regular beach. It's a pleasant 1½ hours' bike ride from Puerto Madryn. Alternatively, taxis charge about 500 pesos for the round-trip including a 45-minute stay. ✉ *Puerto Madryn* ✉ *Free.*

Fodor's Choice **Museo Provincial del Hombre y el Mar (Ciencias Naturales y Oceanografía).**
★ This whimsical collection of taxidermied animals, shells, skeletons, and engravings examines humankind's relationship with the sea. Housed in a restored 1915 building, the beautifully displayed exhibits evoke the marine myths of the Tehuelche (the area's indigenous people), imagined

Puerto Madryn

Golfo Nuevo

Luis Perlotti

KEY

❶ *Exploring sights*

① *Hotels &*
Restaurants

European sea monsters, the ideas of 19th-century naturalists, through to modern ecology. It's more about experience than explanation, so don't worry about the scarcity of English translations, although the excellent room on orca behavior is a welcome exception. Finish by looking out over the city and surrounding steppes from the tower. ✉ *Domecq García at José Menéndez* ☎ *0280/445–1139* 🎟 *35 pesos* ⊘ *Closed weekends.*

Punta Loma Sea Lion Reserve. Some 600 South American sea lions lounge on the shore below a tall, crescent bluff at Punta Loma, 17 km (11 miles) southeast of the city. Aim to visit during low tide. You can reach the reserve by car (follow signs toward Punta Ninfas); by bicycle, if the wind is not too strong; or by taxi—expect to pay about 500 pesos for the return trip, including a 45-minute stay. ✉ *Punta Loma* 🎟 *160 pesos.*

WHERE TO EAT

$$$$
INTERNATIONAL

✕ **Cantina El Náutico.** Photos of visiting Argentine celebrities mingle with the marine-themed doodads that cover the walls at this local favorite serving up large portions of fish dishes and traditional Argentine cuisine. **Known for:** big portions; simple fish and seafood; homemade pasta. 💲 *Average main: 300 pesos* ✉ *Av. Roca 790* ☎ *0280/447–1404* ⊕ *www. cantinaelnautico.com.ar.*

$$$$ ✕ **En Mis Fuegos.** Chef Gustavo Rapretti gets playful in this intimate
ARGENTINE eatery with a tasting menu that changes regularly (it's written on a
blackboard) but always incorporates local ingredients (from freshly
picked seaweed to local sheep's cheese). **Known for:** creative cuisine;
fire-cooking; locally sourced ingredients. $ *Average main: 400 pesos*
⊠ *Av. Gales 32* ☎ *0280/445–8740* ⊕ *www.gustavorapretti.com.ar*
☾ *Closed Sun. and Mon.*

WHERE TO STAY

$ ⛏ **Australis Yene Hue.** Overlooking the bay, this hotel has a great loca-
HOTEL tion and while the interiors need a bit of TLC you'll be plenty pleased
for the price, which includes access to the terrace pool and small spa.
Pros: terrace pool; great location; great views over bay. **Cons:** service is
rough around the edges; a bit dated; simple breakfast. $ *Rooms from:*
US$115 ⊠ *Av. Roca 33* ☎ *0280/447–1214* ⊕ *www.australisyenehue.*
com.ar ⇨ *71 rooms* ⦿ *Breakfast.*

$$ ⛏ **Dazzler.** Right on the beachfront in the city center, Dazzler's sea
HOTEL views will keep you eagerly hunting for whales, while the comfy beds
and generous amenities will pull you away from the window for just
a little while. **Pros:** central beachfront location; friendly staff; gym,
sauna, and sun terrace. **Cons:** centralized temperature control; no
bathtubs; parking costs extra. $ *Rooms from: US$120* ⊠ *Bul. Almi-*
rante Brown 637 ☎ *0280/447–5758* ⊕ *www.dazzlerpuertomadryn.*
com ⇨ *95 rooms* ⦿ *Breakfast.*

$$ ⛏ **Hotel Península Valdés.** The minimal gray-and-taupe lobby and slick,
HOTEL wooden-walled breakfast bar are the result of the gradual renovation of
this well-established hotel; some rooms are cramped and still outdated
but the *panorámicos* have bigger beds and fabulous views of the bay,
and the Peninsula Suite has an outdoor balcony and a Jacuzzi tub with
a bay view. **Pros:** oceanfront location; good service; disabled access.
Cons: older rooms not worth the price; gym is tiny; cramped spaces.
$ *Rooms from: US$175* ⊠ *Av. Roca 155* ☎ *0280/447–1292* ⊕ *www.*
hotelpeninsula.com.ar ⇨ *76 rooms* ⦿ *Breakfast.*

SPORTS AND THE OUTDOORS
BICYCLING
Napra Club. Cycling is a great way to reach El Doradillo and Punta
Loma. You can rent mountain bikes by the hour or the day from this
windsurf school on the beach. ⊠ *Av. Almte. Brown 860* ☎ *0280/445–*
5633 ⊕ *www.napraclub.com.*

DIVING
Lobo Larsen. If you've every fancied getting up close and personal with
giant sea lions, Lobo Larson offers a chance to snorkel with them as
they play around you in the crystal clear waters. Their English-speaking
dive masters also offer snorkeling and introductory dives and courses
to nondivers, and wreck and reef outings to certified divers. Equipment
and transport from Puerto Madryn is provided; special polar dry suits
allow for winter diving. ⊠ *Av. Roca 885* ☎ *0280/447–0277* ⊕ *www.*
lobolarsen.com.

8

Experienced divers might be lucky enough to swim near a right whale calf like the one in the foreground here.

KAYAKING AND WINDSURFING

FAMILY **Escuela Windsurf Napra Club.** This outfit rents sea kayaks and Windsurfers, and runs guided nature-watching kayak tours to nearby bays. During their summer Sea School, local instructors work with children on snorkeling, windsurfing, bait and lure fishing, and identification of local fauna. ⊠ *Av. Almte. Brown 860* ☎ *0280/445–5633* ⊕ *www.napraclub.com.*

PENÍNSULA VALDÉS

Puerto Pirámides is 104 km (64 miles) northeast of Puerto Madryn.

Fodor'sChoice The biggest attraction in Península Valdés is the *ballena franca* (south-
★ ern right whale) population, which feeds, mates, and gives birth here. The protected mammals attract more than 120,000 visitors every year from June, when they first arrive, through December. Especially during the peak season of September and October, people crowd into boats at Puerto Pirámides to observe at close range as the 30- to 35-ton whales breach and blast giant V-shape spouts of water from their blowholes.

GETTING HERE AND AROUND

About 60 km (37 miles) northeast along the coast on Ruta 2 from Puerto Madryn, the land narrows to form an isthmus. A ranger's station here marks the entrance to the Península Valdés Area Natural Protegida (Protected Natural Area), where you pay a park entry fee of about US$20. A further 22 km (14 miles) down the road is the remodeled Centro de Visitantes Istmo Ameghino (Ameghino Isthmus Visitor Center). A series of rather dry displays provides a basic introduction to the marine, coastal, and continental flora and fauna ahead of you.

More exciting are the complete skeleton of a southern right whale and the views over the isthmus from the lookout tower.

From the visitor center it's another 24 km (15 miles) to the junction leading to Puerto Pirámides, 2 km (3 miles) to the south. By following the road 5 km (3 miles) east, you reach the start of the circuit of the interconnected 32- to 64-km (20- to 40-mile) dirt roads around the peninsula.

There are different ways to explore the peninsula. If you prefer natural surroundings to cityscapes and really want to see all the area has to offer, plan on spending at least a night or two here rather than using Puerto Madryn as your base. The accommodations in Puerto Pirámides easily rival those in town, and when the tour parties leave, you get the rugged, windswept coastal landscape to yourself. Hearing whales splashing offshore at night is a particularly magical experience. By staying you also have time to do an additional whale-watching trip at sunset, and to go hiking, kayaking, or snorkeling with sea lions.

However, if your schedule is tight, consider one of the many organized day trips that operate out of Puerto Madryn. A minibus typically picks you up at your hotel around 8 am, stops briefly at the visitor center, then continues to Puerto Pirámides for whale-watching (June through December only) and lunch. During the afternoon you visit two other spots on the peninsula before returning to Puerto Madryn by about 7 pm. These tours are reasonably priced (starting at 1,400 pesos per person) and pack a lot in. However, you spend most of the day crammed in the minibus, don't get to visit the entire peninsula, and have little time to linger at wildlife spots.

To visit the peninsula more extensively at your own pace, you need to rent a car and stay overnight. Having your own wheels also gives you the freedom to stay in the beautiful but remote lodgings at Punta Delgada and Punta Norte. Bear in mind, though, that you'll have to drive several hundred kilometers on dirt and gravel roads in varying states of repair. Stock your vehicle well with drinks, snacks, and gas (the only station is at Puerto Pirámides), and don't try to overtake the tour buses: cars are much lighter, and flipping is unfortunately a common accident here. Economy vehicle rental starts at about $60 per day; the nearest place to rent from is Puerto Madryn—there are numerous car rentals along Avenida Roca.

If all you want to do is whale-watch, you can reach Puerto Pirámides on the daily public bus service from Puerto Madryn run by Mar y Valle (in high season they shuttle back and forth twice a day). Tickets cost $140 each way.

For the freedom of having your own car without the responsibility of driving, arrange for a remis. You can do this as a day trip from Puerto Madryn through most local tour operators (prices vary), or from Puerto Pirámides, if you're staying there, with El Gauchito. Expect to pay about 2,400 pesos for a full day (six hours) exploring the peninsula.

Finally, you can combine some of the above approaches and get an overview of the peninsula on a tour, but then get off at Puerto Pirámides on the way back and stay overnight, do other excursions, and then return on the public bus.

Península
Valdés

Golfo San Matías

Punta Norte

Punta Quiroga

Punta Buenos Aires

Golfo San José

Isla de los Pájaros

Entrance

Visitor
Center   Puerto Pirámides

Lobería Puerto Pirámide

Punta Pardelas

Punta Flecha

Golfo San Nuevo

Puerto
Madryn   Punta Loma

CERRO AVANZADO

Punta Ninfas

Caleta Valdés

El
Salitral

Península Valdés
Area Natural Protegida

Salina
Grande   Salina
Chica

Punta
Cantor

Punta
Hércules

Punta
Delgada

Atlantic Ocean

Punta León

Rawson

0   15 mi

0   15 km

ESSENTIALS
Bus Contacts Mar y Valle. ⊠ *Terminal de Ómnibus, Puerto Madryn*
☎ *0280/445–0600.*

Remis Tours El Gauchito. ☎ *0280/449–5014.*

**Visitor Information Centro de Visitantes Istmo Ameghino (Ameghino
Isthmus Visitor Center).** ⊠ *At entrance to Península* ☎ *0280/445–0489.*

EXPLORING
PUERTO PIRÁMIDES
The only settlement on Península Valdés is tiny Puerto Pirámides, which
transforms into Argentina's whale-watching capital between June and
December. The main street, Avenida de las Ballenas, runs parallel to
the shore about 200 meters inland, and is lined with pretty tin-roofed
buildings among dunes and scrubby flowers. Two streets run down from
it to the sea; all the whale-watching operations are clustered around the
first of these, known as La Primera Bajada.

For ecological reasons, only 350 people are allowed to live here permanently, but there is a good selection of hotels and restaurants.
■ TIP→ **Bring plenty of money with you, as the one ATM may be out of
cash.** In addition to whale-watching and lounging around with a beer
while looking out on the pyramid-shape cliffs that gave the town its

name, you can go scuba diving or snorkeling with sea lions, kayaking, sand boarding, and mountain biking.

Lobería Puerto Pirámides. Some 4 km (3 miles) from Puerto Pirámides lies the Lobería Puerto Pirámides, a sea-lion colony that is also a great bird-watching spot. A signposted turnoff from the main road into town leads here, or you can follow the coastal path on foot. ⊠ *Puerto Pirámides*.

WHERE TO EAT

PUERTO PIRÁMIDES

For quick sandwiches or burgers before a whale-watching trip, try one of the snack bars that are interspersed with the tour operators on the Primera Bajada. All close at about 7 pm. Aside from the food joints on the main drag, check out the hotel restaurants for good options, too.

$$$$ ✕**La Covacha.** A seaside feel and menu is what this sunny spot prides
ARGENTINE itself on, serving up pizzas, fried calamari, and chilled brews with a view to the ocean. **Known for:** relaxed pace; afternoon beers on the seafront; pub grub. ⑤ *Average main: 280 pesos* ⊠ *Osvaldo Bayern, Puerto Pirámides* ☎ *0280/460–1712* ⊗ *Closed Tues.*

$$$$ ✕**La Estación Pub.** The coolest bar in Pirámides is also the town's best
ARGENTINE seafood restaurant where amid nets, nautical gear, and glam-rock posters the requisite fish and steak dishes are offered alongside pizzas and homemade pastas. **Known for:** cozy, unpretentious vibe; comfort food; good beer range. ⑤ *Average main: 240 pesos* ⊠ *Av. de las Ballenas s/n, Puerto Pirámides* ☎ *0280/449–5047* ⊗ *Closed Tues.*

WHERE TO STAY

PUERTO PIRÁMIDES

$ ⊡**Cabañas en el Mar.** Skip the aging A-frame cabins and try to book
RENTAL one of the apartments—their living rooms look down the street to the ocean and include fully equipped kitchens, making them popular with families and biologists here on extended stays. **Pros:** stylish; good value, especially for groups; great location. **Cons:** day noise; cabins are less attractive than apartments; poor Wi-Fi. ⑤ *Rooms from: US$105* ⊠ *Av. de las Ballenas s/n, Puerto Pirámides* ☎ *0280/449–5049* ⊕ *www.cabañasenelmar.com* ⇆ *2 cabañas, 4 apartments.*

$$ ⊡**Hostería Ecológica del Nómade.** When you're staying in a wildlife
HOTEL reserve, taking care of Mother Nature seems only right; while this eco-
Fodor'sChoice friendly hotel uses solar panels, low-energy fittings, and recycles its
★ water, they don't skimp on style or luxury. **Pros:** eco-awareness at no loss to comfort; book expeditions through informed staff; fabulous breakfasts. **Cons:** slightly removed from the restaurants on the main drag; patchy Wi-Fi; some rooms have limited views. ⑤ *Rooms from: US$150* ⊠ *Av. de las Ballenas s/n, Puerto Pirámides* ☎ *0280/449–5044* ⊕ *www.ecohosteria.com.ar* ⊗ *Closed mid-Apr.–mid-Aug.* ⇆ *8 rooms* ⫩ *Breakfast.*

$$$ ⊡**Las Restingas.** The powder-blue clapboard facade of Puerto Pirámides's
HOTEL most upmarket hotel stretches along the beachfront: squint and you can see whales from the huge picture windows in the front-facing rooms and lobby lounge. **Pros:** restaurant with deck overlooking the sea; sea (and whale) views from some rooms; large rooms. **Cons:** rooms facing the village are very overpriced; tiny bathrooms; inconsistent service.

8

General Julio Argentino Roca

Look at the street signs in any Patagonian city and you're sure to spot the name General Julio Argentino Roca. (To see what he looks like, whip out your wallet: he's riding along the 100-peso note, too). But look a little closer and you may well find stickers or stencils changing the street's name to "Pueblos Originarios" ("First Peoples").

The history books celebrate Roca as the man who "civilized" Patagonia and extended Argentine territory south, but the real story is much darker. In the late 1870s the bottom half of Argentina was still largely controlled by various indigenous peoples who resisted the European colonization of their territory. Funded by rich landowners from Buenos Aires anxious to extend their estates, war minister Roca led a series of brutal military attacks—euphemistically known as the "Desert Campaigns"— which led to the massacre of over a thousand Mapuche, Tehuelche, and Ranquel warriors and the enslavement of countless indigenous women and children.

Despite repeated attempts by indigenous rights groups to rename the streets and reprint the banknotes, for the time being these continue to honor the man behind the massacre.

⑤ *Rooms from: US$229* ⊠ *Primera Bajada at beach, Puerto Pirámides* ☎ *0280/449–5101* ⊕ *www.lasrestingas.com* ☾ *Closed Apr. and May* ⤴ *12 rooms* ⦿| *Breakfast.*

PUNTA DELGADA

$$

HOTEL

Fodor'sChoice

★

⚏ **Faro Punta Delgada.** This remote complex of buildings on the tip of Península Valdés offers luxuries that are simple and old-fashioned: comfortable beds with chintz covers, a pleasant pub with pool and darts, board games, utter tranquility under starry night skies, horseback rides, and guided nature walks among the sea lions and elephant seals on its private beaches. **Pros:** peaceful location in touch with nature; private beaches afford great wildlife experiences; good restaurant on-site. **Cons:** rooms don't have water views; basic rooms and few amenities; busy with tour buses at midday. ⑤ *Rooms from: US$140* ⊠ *Península Valdés, Punta Delgada* ☎ *0280/445–8444* ⊕ *www.puntadelgada.com* ☾ *Closed Apr.–June* ⤴ *27 rooms* ⦿| *Breakfast; Some meals.*

SPORTS AND THE OUTDOORS

From June to December the main attractions at Puerto Pirámides are whale-watching boat trips into the Golfo Nuevo to see southern right whales. Experienced captains pilot the boats between the huge mammals while bilingual guides tell you about their habits and habitats. Expect to use up lots of your camera memory as the graceful creatures dive, spout water, and salute you with their tails.

Most whale-watching companies operate several trips a day while the whales are in town, especially during the peak months of September and October. Standard daytime excursions last about 1¼ hours, and the price is set each year by the municipality. Trips in smaller boats and longer tours are usually more expensive. Although no boat is allowed closer than 15 meters to the whales (the animals themselves sometimes break the rules by diving under your boat), you certainly feel closer from smaller vessels. On clear days the magical sunset tours are definitely worth paying extra for: you see the whales frolic as the sun sets over the water around them. It's best to call a day or two ahead to reserve, although many companies will fit you in if you show up on the day.

BOAT TOURS

Bottazzi. Although trips tend to be more expensive with Bottazzi, they tend to be longer than other companies' and have excellent English-speaking guides. The sunset trips are on very small boats, and include wine and cheese back at their office afterwards. ⊠ *Primera Bajada, Puerto Pirámides* ☎ *0280/449–5050* ⊕ *www.bottazzi.com.ar.*

Hydrosport. Ecological commitment is the foremost priority at Hydro-sport, a reliable, long-running operator with three different boat sizes. ⊠ *Primera Bajada, Puerto Pirámides* ☎ *0280/449–5065.*

Southern Spirit. This outfitter allows you not only to see but also to hear the whales, thanks to their underwater sound-detection system. They use large but fairly low boats and operate up to five 90-minute trips a day, including a sunset outing. ⊠ *Av. de las Ballenas at Primera Bajada, Puerto Pirámides* ☎ *0280/15–4572–340* ⊕ *www.southernspirit.com.ar.*

KAYAKING

Patagonia Explorers. Kayaking in the Golfo Nuevo and the Golfo San José is offered by Patagonia Explorers, who also have English-speaking guides. ⊠ *Av. de las Ballenas at Primera Bajada, Puerto Pirámides* ☎ *0280/15–4340–619* ⊕ *www.patagoniaexplorers.com.*

8

TRELEW, GAIMAN, AND PUNTA TOMBO

When the Welsh settlers landed on the desertlike Patagonian coast in 1865, they realized they would need to move inland to find suitable land for farming. Some 25 km (15 miles) inland, in the fertile Chubut River valley, they founded Trelew and Gaiman. Both retain Welsh traditions to this day: Trelew holds an Eisteddfod (festival of Welsh poetry, song, and dance) each October, and Gaiman is the largest Welsh settlement outside of Wales.

With almost 100,000 inhabitants, Trelew is now a large city by Patagonian standards, and its airport is the gateway to Atlantic Patagonia. Beyond the excellent dinosaur museum, however, the dusty, windswept center is of little interest to tourists. With its teahouses, rose gardens, and chapels, Gaiman retains a country-town feel. Indeed, farms and stone-fruit orchards still fill the countryside surrounding it.

On the coast 120 km (74 miles) south of Trelew lies the Punta Tombo penguin reserve, which you can easily visit on a day trip from Trelew, Gaiman, or Puerto Madryn.

Trelew's Museo Paleontológico Egidio Feruglio, or Paleontology Museum, is bursting with fossil treasures.

TRELEW

11 km (6 miles) east of Gaiman; 67 km (42 miles) south of Puerto Madryn.

Trelew (pronounced Tre- *leh*-ew) is a commercial, industrial, and service hub that contains the region's main airport. Its biggest attractions are its paleontology museum (with enormous dinosaur fossils on exhibit) and its proximity to the Punta Tombo reserve (though both can also be reached on day trips from Gaiman and Puerto Madryn). Otherwise, the city has little to recommend it: its mediocre hotels are notoriously overpriced, and aside from rental-car firms its tourism infrastructure is far less organized than Puerto Madryn's. If you come in the second half of October you can watch part of the Eisteddfod, a Welsh literary and music festival first held in Patagonia in 1875.

Trelew was founded in 1886 as a result of the construction of the now-defunct Chubut railway line, which connected the Chubut River valley with the Atlantic coast. The town is named after its Welsh founder, Lewis Jones (*Tre* means "town" in Welsh, and *Lew* stands for Lewis), who fought to establish this railroad.

GETTING HERE AND AROUND

If you're driving, from the Ruta Nacional 3, take Ruta Nacional 25 to Avenida Fontana. The long-distance bus terminal is at Urquiza and Lewis Jones, along the Plaza Centenario. Most of what you'll visit is found in the half-dozen blocks between Plaza Centenario and Plaza Independencia, which is also where you'll find the tourist office.

ESSENTIALS

Bus Contacts Andesmar. ✉ *Terminal de Ómnibus, Urquiza and Lewis Jones* ☎ *0280/443–3535.* **Don Otto.** ✉ *Terminal de Ómnibus, Urquiza and Lewis Jones* ☎ *0280/442–9496.* **TAC.** ✉ *Terminal de Ómnibus, Urquiza and Lewis Jones* ☎ *0810/333–7575.*

Car Rental Hertz. ✉ *Aeropuerto de Trelew* ☎ *0280/442–4421* ⊕ *www.hertz. com.ar.*

Visitor and Tour Information Tourist Office. ✉ *Mitre 387* ☎ *0280/442–0139* ⊕ *www.trelewpatagonia.gov.ar.*

EXPLORING

FAMILY

Fodor'sChoice

★

Museo Paleontológico Egidio Feruglio (MEF). Trelew's star attraction is the paleontology museum, where four hushed and darkened galleries of fossils both real and replica take you back in time. You start among the South American megafauna (giant armadillos and the like) that may have cohabited with the first humans here, then plunge back to a time before the Andes existed. Back then Patagonia was a subtropical rain forest filled with dinosaurs, including one of the largest creatures ever to walk the earth: the 70-ton, 120-foot-long Argentinosaurus. Replicas of its massive leg bones are on display, along with countless other dino skeletons, including the latest discovery of the largest dinosaur in the world—a 130-foot-long herbivore. Other highlights include a 290-million-year-old spider fossil with a 3-foot leg span and the 70-million-year-old petrified eggs of a Carnotaurus. The visit ends with a peek into the workshop where paleontologists study and preserve newly unearthed fossils. Tours in English are available—they're a good idea, as only the introductions to each room are translated. ✉ *Av. Fontana 140* ☎ *0280/443–2100* ⊕ *www.mef.org.ar* 🎟 *Approx. 140 pesos.*

Museo Regional Pueblo de Luis (*Trelew Regional Museum*). Across the street from MEF is Trelew's old train station, which now contains a small museum of the town's history. Photos, clothing, and objects from local houses, offices, and schools form the mishmash of displays on the European influence in the region, the indigenous populations of the area, and wildlife. ✉ *Av. 9 de Julio at Av. Fontana* ☎ *0280/442–4062* 🎟 *14 pesos.*

WHERE TO EAT AND STAY

$$$$

ITALIAN

Fodor'sChoice

★

✕**Miguel Angel/Raices.** With its paneled walls, sleek black tables, and vintage photos, this retro Italo-Argentine diner is popular with locals and visitors alike for its pasta specialties. Try the stuffed gnocchi and the good prix-fixe menus. **Known for:** excellent pasta; one of Trelew's liveliest restaurants; succulent roast meat. $ *Average main: 290 pesos* ✉ *Av. Fontana 246* ☎ *0280/443–0403* 🕐 *Closed Mon.*

$$$$

CAFÉ

✕**Touring Club.** Legend has it that Butch Cassidy and the Sundance Kid once stayed here—search long enough and you might find them among the old photos cluttering the walls. This cavernous old *confitería* (café) was founded in 1895, and became Chubut's first hotel in 1926. **Known for:** historic spot; great bar; barely comfortable rooms. $ *Average main: 180 pesos* ✉ *Av. Fontana 240* ☎ *0280/443–3997* ⊕ *www.touringpatagonia.com.ar.*

8

$$$$ ✕ **Sugar.** This central restaurant serves up every meal of the day and
FUSION while the chocolate fondue has some fame in the town, it's really the
Fodor's Choice fusion cuisine in the evening that keeps punters returning. There's a
★ relaxed but professional bistro vibe to Sugar and the chef has an eye
for smart presentation. **Known for:** international flavors in Welsh Patagonia; chocolate fondue; enviable Plaza-side location. $ *Average main:
340 pesos* ✉ *25 de Mayo 247* ☎ *0280/442–1210* ☼ *Closed Sun.*

$ ⊡ **Hotel Libertador.** This big hotel has definitely seen better days, and
HOTEL while rooms are clean (if worn around the edges), the faded bedcov-
ers and scuffed furnishings of the standard rooms really aren't up to
the price, although it still remains one of the best of the rather limited
options in town. **Pros:** on-site parking; amenable staff; superior rooms
are a bit more modern. **Cons:** outdated rooms; simple breakfast; lacking
amenities. $ *Rooms from: US$85* ✉ *Av. Rivadavia 31* ☎ *0280/442–
0220* ⊕ *www.hotellibertadortw.com.ar* ⮑ *90 rooms* ⦿ *Breakfast.*

GAIMAN

17 km (11 miles) west of Trelew.

The most Welsh of the Atlantic Patagonian settlements, sleepy Gaiman
(pronounced *Guy*-mon) is far more charming than nearby Trelew and
Rawson. A small museum lovingly preserves the history of the Welsh
colony, and many residents still speak Welsh (although day-to-day com-
munication is now in Spanish). A connection to Wales continues with
teachers, preachers, and visitors going back and forth frequently (often
with copies of family trees in hand). Even the younger generation maintains an interest in the culture and language.

Perhaps the town's greatest draws are its five Welsh teahouses (*casas de
té*)—Ty Gwyn, Plas-y-Coed, Ty Nain, Ty Cymraeg, and Ty Té Caerdydd.
Each serves a similar set menu of tea and home-baked bread, scones,
and a dazzling array of cakes made from family recipes, although the
odd dulce de leche–filled concoction is testament to Argentine cultural
imperatives. Most teahouses are open daily 3–8 and charge about
US$15 per person for tea (the spreads are generous enough to replace
lunch or dinner, and you can usually take away a doggy bag of any
cake you don't finish). Each establishment has its own family history
and atmosphere, and there's healthy competition between them as to
which is the most authentically Welsh.

GETTING HERE AND AROUND

Gaiman is easily walkable: nearly all the teahouses and other attractions
are within a five-block radius of the town square at Avenue Eugenio
Tello and M.D. Jones. If you don't have a car, you can access the few
sites outside of town—such as the Bryn Gwyn Paleontology Park—by
taking an inexpensive remis from one of the *remiserías* on the square.

Although their English isn't great, the friendly young staff at the tourist
office give enthusiastic advice on what to visit in Gaiman and hand out
detailed maps of the town and its surroundings.

8

ESSENTIALS

Visitor and Tour Information Tourist Office. ☒ *Belgrano 574, at Rivadavía*
☏ *0280/449–1571.*

EXPLORING

Capilla Bethel. Throughout the Chubut Valley there are three dozen or
so chapels where the Welsh settlers prayed, went to school, and held
meetings, trials, and social events. Two of these simple brick chapels
stand alongside each other just over the river from Gaiman—they're
usually closed to the public, but are interesting to see from the outside.
To reach the chapels, walk south from the square on J.C. Evans and
cross the pedestrian bridge. Locals take a shortcut by ducking through
the fencing where the bridge ends and walking 100 meters to the right
along the riverside. Otherwise take the first right into Morgan and follow the dirt road around several bends. ☒ *Gaiman.*

Capilla Vieja (*Old Chapel*). The aptly named Capilla Vieja, next to
Capilla Bethel, was built in 1880 and is used each year for the traditional Welsh Eisteddfod, when townspeople gather to celebrate—and
compete with each other in—song, poetry, and dance under the chapel's
wooden vaulted ceiling. ☒ *Gaiman.*

Museo Histórico Regional (*Regional Historical Museum*). Photographs
and testimonies of Gaiman's original 160 Welsh settlers are on display

CLOSE UP

Gaiman's Teahouses

Gaiman's Welsh teahouses have been famous among travelers for decades. The first teahouse, Plas y Coed, opened in 1944, and figured in Bruce Chatwin's *In Patagonia.*

Each of Gaiman's teahouses serves up its own unique family recipes for all manner of baked goodies, including *torta galesa* (a rich dried-fruit cake), seasonal fruit tarts, buns and sponges, *torta de crema* (a rich baked cream cake), as well as homemade bread, scones, and jam. The tea is always served in big china pots dressed for the occasion in deliciously kitsch hand-knitted tea cozies to ensure your brew stays warm.

Just as the recipes and tastes differ slightly from teahouse to teahouse, so do their interiors. But common to all the teahouses are tapestries and ornamental tea towels, often inscribed with Welsh words and with intricate Celtic designs around the borders. Hanging from the walls—and often for sale, too—are heart-shape

wooden spoons with intricately carved handles. Known as love spoons, they're a Welsh tradition that dates to the 16th century: a young man would carve a spoon from a single piece of wood and give it to the girl he wished to marry.

Most of Gaiman's teahouses are owned and run by descendants of the original Welsh settlers, who are happy to recount their family history if you ask about it. There's a strong sense of appreciation for how easy things are today compared to just a couple of generations ago. Ana, of Plas y Coed, whose great-grandmother was featured in Bruce Chatwin's book, told us, "Imagine making everything from scratch and running this place without refrigerators."

There's an Alice in Wonderland effect as you nibble various cakes and look out on the vast Atlantic Patagonian steppe (which would make anyone feel small).

in the Museo Histórico Regional, along with household objects they brought with them or made on arrival. The staff are passionate about their history and will happily show you round the tiny building, which used to be Gaiman's train station. ✉ *28 de Julio 705, at Sarmiento* ☎ *0280/449–1007* 🖃 *3 pesos.*

Parque Paleontológico Bryn Gwyn (*Bryn Gwyn Paleontology Park*). Just south of Gaiman the green river valley gives way to arid steppes where clearly visible strata reveal more than 40 million years of geological history. Some 600 acres of these badlands—many of them bursting with fossils—make up the Parque Paleontológico Bryn Gwyn, a branch of the Museo Paleontológico Egidio Feruglio in Trelew where a fossil trail and botanical gardens await. Confirm with the museum before going as the Park can close periodically after heavy rain. ✉ *8 km (5 miles) south of town* ☎ *0280/443–2100* 🌐 *www.mef.org.ar/exhibiciones/geoparque-bryn-gwyn* 🖃 *30 pesos* 🕐 *Closed Mon.*

WHERE TO EAT

$$$$
ARGENTINE
✕**Cornel Wini.** For decades the Jones family, owners of this stately red-brick corner building, ran a hotel and bar (complete with a boxing ring in the basement) here, but switched to serving steaks, pizzas, and pasta in between the tea cakes. The decision has been a success: on weekends locals pack themselves around the wooden tables to devour the generous *parilladas* (mixed grills). **Known for:** comfort food; large portions; old-school decor. $ *Average main: 240 pesos* ✉ *Av. Eugenio Tello 199* ☎ *0280/449–1397* ▭ *No credit cards* ☾ *Closed Tues. (and Wed. in winter).*

$$$$
ARGENTINE
FAMILY
✕**Gwalia Lân.** Homemade pastas are the specialty here but locals also tuck into hearty grilled dishes of steak, pork, and chicken at this lively restaurant with exposed brick, low lighting, wooden booths, and a traditional publike atmosphere. Some come just for a beer while others come to dine. **Known for:** large pasta dishes; juicy steaks drizzled in creamy sauce; jovial atmosphere. $ *Average main: 300 pesos* ✉ *M.D. Jones 418, at Tello on plaza* ☎ *2965/15–682–352* ▭ *No credit cards* ☾ *Closed Mon. No dinner Sun.*

$$$$
CAFÉ
✕**Ty Nain.** The matriarch who presides over the kitchen here, Mirna Jones, is a proud descendant of the first woman born in Gaiman. Her ivy-covered teahouse on the main square looks like a knickknack shop: it's stuffed with doodads and hung with crochet, and there are gramophones, carriage lamps, and antique radios on display above the four original chimneys, which date to 1890, although Formica paneling detracts slightly from the old-world style. **Known for:** Welsh tea; friendly service; unreliable opening hours. $ *Average main: 310 pesos* ✉ *Hipólito Yrigoyen 239* ☎ *0280/449–1126* ▭ *No credit cards* ☾ *Closed weekdays in winter.*

$$$$
CAFÉ
Fodor's Choice
★
✕**Ty Té Caerdydd.** A short way out of town lies Gaiman's largest teahouse (where Lady Di famously took tea in the 1990s), surrounded by cypress trees, sculpted gardens, and a giant tea pot. It stands apart from its rivals culturally, too: it's run by descendents of a Spanish family, which shows in the sprawling colonial-style architecture. **Known for:** peaceful and picturesque location; indulgent tea cakes; Lady Diana shrine. $ *Average main: 360 pesos* ✉ *Finca 202, Zona de Chacras* ☎ *0280/449–1510.*

WHERE TO STAY

$
B&B/INN
🏠**Hostería Yr Hen Ffordd.** Gaiman's best budget accommodation is this family-run B&B, where rooms are simple but spacious and warm, with comfy beds, bright feather quilts, good bathrooms, and free Wi-Fi (quite a find in Gaiman). **Pros:** great breakfasts; friendly owners with local advice; good value. **Cons:** dated decor; simple rooms; poor water pressure. $ *Rooms from: US$55* ✉ *Miguel de Jones 342* ☎ *0280/449–1394* ⊕ *www.yrhenffordd.com.ar* ▭ *No credit cards* ⤴ *5 rooms* ❑ *Breakfast.*

$
B&B/INN
🏠**Plas y Coed.** Gaiman's oldest teahouse has also been a bed-and-breakfast since 1997, and a stay here is rather like visiting with a favorite aunt: the rooms are simple but immaculate, have polished wooden floors and pastel bedspreads, and there's a comfy lounge area for relaxing in. **Pros:** family atmosphere; great teahouse and cakes; comfortable common room. **Cons:** no credit cards; simple amenities; some rooms

8

CLOSE UP

Pandas of the Sea

You've watched the whales, seen the seals, and admired the penguins. But how about *toninas* (dolphins)? The southern coast of Argentina is home to a particularly attractive species, *Cephalorhynchus commersonii,* whose black-and-white coloring has earned them the nickname "pandas of the sea." **Toninas Adventure** (Av. Marcelino González at docks, Puerto Rawson ☎ 0280/15-467-5741 ⊕ www.enpuertorawson.com.ar/ toninas, Boat trip 1000 pesos, Daily 9–6), the only dolphin-watching enterprise in the area, operates hour-long boat trips from the port at Rawson. They guarantee sightings of their playful namesake creatures, who love to race alongside the boats in packs of three or four, regularly jumping up in perfect arcs. Puerto Rawson is on the coast 30 km (20 miles) east of Trelew, and is an easy detour on trips south to Punta Tombo or beyond. Most organized tours to Punta Tombo stop here.

a bit tight. ⑤ *Rooms from: US$80* ⊠ *Irigoyen 320* ☎ *0280/469–7069* ⊕ *www.plasycoed.com.ar* ▤ *No credit cards* ➦ *5 rooms* ⏐◎⏐ *Breakfast.*

$$
B&B/INN ⊡ **Posada Los Mimbres.** Wandering the nature trail alongside the Chubut River, picking fruit from the orchard, and helping at milking time are just some of the joys of staying on this working century-old farm where the family fills you with homemade treats and you'll rest nicely on the comfy beds. **Pros:** you don't need to go back into town for meals; most ingredients are sourced from the farm; rural setting and historic farmhouse. **Cons:** isolated from town if you don't have a vehicle; poor Wi-Fi; simple lodgings. ⑤ *Rooms from: US$170* ⊠ *Chacra 211* ☎ *0280/449–1299* ⊕ *www.posadalosmimbres.com.ar* ▤ *No credit cards* ➦ *7 rooms, 1 cottage* ⏐◎⏐ *Breakfast; Some meals.*

$
B&B/INN ⊡ **Ty Gwyn.** The soaring ceilings, wooden rafters, and cobbled white walls of this cavernous teahouse make it seem like you're eating in a medieval dining hall; an interior garden leads to the staircase that takes you to four lovely bedrooms with wood floors, heavy drapes, and dressers fashioned from antique sewing-machine tables. **Pros:** rooms overlook the river; generous breakfasts include fruit and eggs; well-kept lawn. **Cons:** cruise-ship groups arrive regularly in high season; simple rooms; dated decor. ⑤ *Rooms from: US$85* ⊠ *Av. 9 de Julio 111* ☎ *0280/449–1009* ⊕ *www.tygwyn.com.ar* ➦ *4 rooms* ⏐◎⏐ *Breakfast.*

PUNTA TOMBO

120 km (74 miles) south of Trelew.

This protected area is home to one of the world's biggest colonies of Magellenic penguins; they come for the season to lay eggs and feed their newly hatched young. The park is also a great spot for observing other seabirds along with guanacos, seals, and hares.

EXPLORING

Fodor's Choice
★ **Area Natural Protegido Punta Tombo** (*Punta Tombo Protected Natural Area*). From the middle of September through March, up to half a million penguins live in the Area Natural Protegido Punta Tombo, the world's largest colony of Magellanic penguins and one of the most varied seabird rookeries. From the park entrance, a series of trails, boardwalks, and bridges lead you 3½ km (3 miles) through the scrubby landscape where the penguins nest to the sea. The quizzical creatures seem unafraid of humans, and peer up at you from under the bushes where, between September and November, both males and females incubate eggs, often right beside the trail. Look for the bald vertical strips on the penguins' abdomens: they pluck out feathers so the eggs can sit warm against their skin. Come December, the ground is teeming with fluffy gray young, and the adult penguins waddle back and forth from the sea to feed them. They may move comically on land, but once you reach the rocky outcrops overlooking the water you'll see how graceful and powerful these creatures become when they enter the water. You may also spot guanacos, seals, and Patagonian hares in the reserve, as well as cormorants and a host of other seabirds.

The last 22 km (14 miles) of the road from Trelew is fairly bumpy gravel. If you're not driving, you can easily reach Punta Tombo on a day tour from Trelew, Gaiman, or Puerto Madryn, although note that these often give you a scant 1½ hours in the reserve. A small restaurant next to the carpark serves good lamb empanadas and also has burgers, coffee, cakes, and cold beverages. ✉ *Punta Tombo* ⊕ *www.puntatombo. com* ✉ *160 pesos.*

8

SARMIENTO AND THE BOSQUE PETRIFICADO

545 km (339 miles) southwest of Gaiman.

Built in a fertile valley formed by the Río Senguer and its two interconnected lakes, Lago Musters and Lago Colhué Huapi, the Sarmiento area is a green oasis in the middle of the hard Patagonian steppe. The town itself—home to about 13,000 people—is relatively unattractive, but a visit here gives you a taste of what is undeniably and unpretentiously the "real Patagonia." Relatively few foreign travelers come here, even though the lakes and river, petrified forest, and paleontology park are great attractions, and the rolling farmland outside of town is truly striking, with its tall windbreaks of Lombardy poplars twisting in the strong wind.

GETTING HERE AND AROUND

There are several daily bus services between Sarmiento and Comodoro Rivadavía run by ETAP and Don Otto. The latter also has services to Esquel and Bariloche. Buses arrive at the bus station at 12 de Octubre and Avenida San Martín, which runs through the center of town.

Sarmiento is only 15 blocks long and 8 blocks wide, and can be walked easily, but if you get tired or would like to arrange a trip outside of town, there are various remiserías along Avenida San Martín.

You're not the only visitor to Punta Tombo: guanacos might join you as you scope out the Magellanic penguins.

ESSENTIALS

Bus Contacts Don Otto. ✉ *Terminal de Ómnibus, Sarmiento* ☎ *0810/333–7575* ⊕ *www.donotto.com.ar.* **ETAP.** ✉ *Terminal de Ómnibus, Sarmiento* ☎ *297/489–3058.*

Visitor and Tour Information Sarmiento. ✉ *Av. Regimiento de Infanteria 25 at Pietrobelli, Sarmiento* ☎ *297/489–2105* ⊕ *www.coloniasarmiento.gob.ar.*

EXPLORING

Monumento Natural Bosque Petrificado Sarmiento (*Sarmiento Petrified Forest Natural Monument*). An eerie and vast landscape scattered with hundreds of petrified trees takes you more than 75 million years back in time. The palm and conifer trees originally arrived here by river when the area was a tropical delta, although now the sun-bleached and striated badlands are anything but tropical. Dry, parched, and whipped by winds, this place requires a jacket any time of year. Entrance is free, but consider paying for a guide to help you understand exactly what you are looking at. The Monumento Natural Bosque Petrificado Sarmiento is about 30 km (19 miles) from Sarmiento following R26 until you reach the access road on the right. If you don't have your own vehicle, book a remis from Sarmiento: most will charge you for the return trip, including an hour's waiting time. ✉ *30 km (19 miles) from Sarmiento, Sarmiento* ☎ *297/489–8282* 💳 *20 pesos.*

FAMILY **Parque Paleontológico Valle de los Gigantes** (*Valley of the Giants Paleontology Park*). Walk among life-size and scientifically accurate replicas of a dozen different dinosaurs whose fossils were discovered in the region.

Guided visits in English leave directly from the tourist office every hour on the hour—arrive 10 minutes ahead to get your ticket. ⊠ *200 meters from tourist office, Sarmiento* ☎ *297/489–2105* 🖅 *20 pesos.*

While you're in the area, stop at **Lago Musters,** 7 km (4 miles) from Sarmiento, and **Lago Colhué Huapi,** a little farther on. At Lago Musters you can swim, and there's fishing year-round.

WHERE TO STAY

$ 🖼 **Los Lagos.** The new section in this small, affordable hotel has updated
HOTEL   carpets, furnishings, and bathrooms; the staff doesn't speak much English but they're friendly and helpful. **Pros:** affordable; free Wi-Fi; one of few options in Sarmiento. **Cons:** can get hot in summer; street noise; old part is considerably worse than new section. $ *Rooms from: US$65* ⊠ *Av. Roca at Alberdi, Sarmiento* ☎ *2974/893–046* ▭ *No credit cards* 🖘 *20 rooms* ⏸◯⏸ *Breakfast.*

EL CALAFATE, EL CHALTÉN, AND PARQUE NACIONAL LOS GLACIARES

The Hielo Continental (Continental Ice Cap) spreads its icy mantle from the Pacific Ocean across Chile and the Andes into Argentina, covering an area of 21,700 square km (8,400 square miles). Approximately 1½ million acres of it are contained within the Parque Nacional los Glaciares (Glaciers National Park), a UNESCO World Heritage Site. The park extends along the Chilean border for 350 km (217 miles), and 40% of it is covered by ice fields that branch off into 47 glaciers feeding two enormous lakes—the 15,000-year-old **Lago Argentino** (Argentine Lake, the largest body of water in Argentina and the third largest in South America) at the park's southern end, and **Lago Viedma** (Lake Viedma) at the northern end near **Cerro Fitzroy,** which rises 11,138 feet.

Plan on a minimum of two to three days to see the glaciers and enjoy El Calafate—more if you plan to visit El Chaltén or any of the other lakes. Entrance to the southern section of the park, which includes Perito Moreno Glacier, costs 500 pesos for non-Argentineans.

EL CALAFATE

320 km (225 miles) north of Río Gallegos via R5; 253 km (157 miles) east of Río Turbio on Chilean border via R40; 213 km (123 miles) south of El Chaltén via R40.

Founded in 1927 as a frontier town, El Calafate is the base for excursions to the Parque Nacional Los Glaciares, which was created in 1937 as a showcase for one of South America's most spectacular sights, the Glaciar Perito Moreno. Because it's on the southern shore of Lago Argentino, the town enjoys a microclimate much milder than the rest of southern Patagonia.

To call El Calafate a boomtown would be a gross understatement. In the first decade of this millennium the town's population exploded

Southern Patagonia

Atlantic Ocean

TO FALKLAND ISLANDS (ISLAS MALVINAS) →

C. San Vicente

TIERRA DEL FUEGO

Tolhuin
Estancia Harberton
Puerto Williams

Ushuaia
see detail map

Puerto San Julián

Río Grande

San Sebastián

TIERRA
DEL FUEGO

Puerto Santa Cruz

Punta Quilla

Bahía
Grande

Cabo Vírgenes

Puerto Beta

Cameron

Estancia La Julia

Puerto Coig
Punta Montes

Cabo Buen Tiempo

Río Gallegos

Magellan
Strait

Punta Espora

Comandante
Luis Piedrabuena

Gobernador
Gregores

SANTA CRUZ

Guer Aike

Punta Delgada

Punta Arenas

Porvenir

Esperanza

Estancia
La Primera
Argentina

Tres Lagos
Punta del Lago

Río Santa Cruz

Río Coig

Río Gallegos

Yacimiento
Río Turbio

Morro Chico

Villa Tehuelches

Puerto Hambre

Lago
Cardiel

El Calafate
see detail map

Lago
Viedma

Cerro
Fitzroy
Cerro
Torre

El Chaltén

Lago
Argentino

Monumento
Natural
Cueva de
Milodón

Puerto Natales

CHILE

Laguna del Desierto

Parque Nacional
los Glaciares
see detail map

Parque Nacional
Torres del Paine
see detail map

Pacific Ocean

50 mi

50 km

from 4,000 to more than 25,000, and it shows no signs of slowing down; at every turn you'll see new construction, with many boutique hotels and new cafés cropping up. As a result, the downtown has a new sheen to it, although most buildings are constructed of wood and corrugated iron with a rustic aesthetic.

Now with a paved road between El Calafate and the glacier, the visitors continue to flock in to see the creaking ice sculptures. These visitors include luxury-package

CASH WOES

For a town that lives and dies on tourism, one of the most infuriating elements of the boom is the cash shortage that strikes El Calafate during high season. ATMs in town frequently run out of money, especially over the weekend, and credit cards are not always accepted in restaurants. Stock up on pesos before you arrive.

tourists bound for handsome estancias in the park surroundings, backpackers over from Chile's Parque Nacional Torres del Paine, and *porteños* (from Buenes Aires) in town for a long weekend.

GETTING HERE AND AROUND

Daily flights from Buenos Aires, Ushuaia, and Río Gallegos, and direct flights from Bariloche transport tourists to El Calafate's 21st-century glass-and-steel airport with the promise of adventure and discovery in distant mountains and glaciers. El Calafate is so popular that the flights sell out weeks in advance, so don't plan on booking at the last minute.

If you can't get on a flight or are looking for a cheaper option, there are daily buses between El Calafate, El Chaltén, Río Gallegos, Ushuaia, and Puerto Natales in Chile—all of which can be booked at the bus terminal. El Calafate is also the starting (or finishing) point for the legendary Ruta 40 journey to Bariloche. If you can bear the bus travel for a few days, you'll pass some exceptional scenery, and most operators allow you to hop on and hop off at canyons, lakes, and the famous handprint-covered caves en route.

Driving from Río Gallegos takes about four hours across desolate plains enlivened by occasional sightings of a gaucho, his dogs, and a herd of sheep, and *ñandú* (rheas), shy llama-like guanacos, silver-gray foxes, and fleet-footed hares the size of small deer. Esperanza is the only gas, food, and bathroom stop halfway between the two towns. Driving from Puerto Natales is similar, although snow-topped mountains line the distance; arriving by road from Ushuaia requires four border crossings and more than 18 hours.

Avenida del Libertador San Martín (known simply as Libertador) is El Calafate's main street, with tour offices, restaurants, and shops selling regional specialties, sportswear, camping and fishing equipment, and food.

A staircase ascends from the middle of Libertador to Avenida Julio Roca, where you'll find the bus terminal and a very busy Oficina de Turismo with a board listing available accommodations and campgrounds; you can also get brochures and maps, and there's a multilingual staff to help plan excursions. The tourism office has another location on the

Where to Eat and Stay in El Calafate

A

NIMEZ LAGOON ECOLOGICAL RESERVE

Antonio P Zupic

Egidio Feruglio

TO CENTRO DE INTERPRETACÍON HISTÓRICO EL CALAFATE

B

Los Tehuelches

9 de Julio

25 de Mayo

E. Bustillo

Comandante Tomas Espora

Los Gouchos

Perito Moreno

C

Coronel Rosales

Puerto Deseado

Puerto San Julian

D

TO AIRPORT →

1

Madre Tierra □

Isabel ■

Gobernador Moyano □

Hotel Posada Los Alamos

Olivia Coffee Shop ■

Gobernador Gregores

■ La Zaina

Casimiro

Biguá ■

Nibepo Aike □

Avenida del Libertador General San Martín

Pantin

Arroyo Calafate

2

◆ GLACIAR PERITO MORENO

← ◆ GLACIARIUM

◆ GLACIAR UPSALA

←□ Mirador del Lago

11

La Lechuza ■

San Juan Bosco

■ La Tablita

11

■ Pura Vida

□ Eolo

□ Estancia Cristina

←□ Los Ponchos Apart Boutique

1 de Mayo

Julio A. Roca

Campaña del Desierto

José Formenti

Campana del Desierto

Helsingfors □

Hotel Kau-Yatun □

José Formenti

Olavarría

3

KEY

□ Hotels

■ Restaurants

✦ following dining and lodging reviews indicates a map-grid coordinate

Buenos Aires

TO LAGO ROCA

Avenida Juan Domingo Peron

0   220 yards

0   200 meters

corner of Rosales and Libertador; both locations are open daily from 8 to 8 (during high season). The Oficina Parques Nacionales, open weekdays 8 to 4, has information on the Parque Nacional Los Glaciares, including the glaciers, area history, hiking trails, and flora and fauna.

TIMING

During the long summer days between December and February (when the sun sets around 10 pm), and during Easter vacation, tens of thousands of visitors come from all corners of the world and fill the hotels and restaurants. This is the area's high season, so make reservations well in advance. October, November, March, and April are less crowded and less expensive periods to visit, although some estancias might still be closed. March through May can be rainy and cool, but it's also less windy and often quite pleasant, and the autumn colors can be quite stunning. The only bad time to visit is winter, particularly May, June, July, and August, when many of the hotels and tour agencies are closed.

TOURS

In El Calafate, each tour has to be approved by the local government and is assigned to one tour operator only. On the upside you'll never fall foul of a shady operator, but on the downside there is no competition to keep prices low. Whether you book a tour directly with the operator who leads it, with another operator, or through your hotel

Near Parque Nacional Los Glaciares and El Calafate you'll find some of the most remote-feeling estancias in Argentina.

or other tour agency, the price should remain the same. Take note that most tour prices do not include the park entrance fee, an extra 500 pesos for foreigners.

ESSENTIALS

Bus Contacts Cal Tur. ⊠ *Terminal Ómnibus* ☎ *2902/491-842* ⊕ *www.caltur. com.ar* ✉ *Av. Libertador 1080* ☎ *2902/491-368* ⊕ *www.caltur.com.ar.* **TAQSA.** ⊠ *Bus terminal* ☎ *2902/491-843* ⊕ *www.taqsa.com.ar.* **Turismo Zaahj.** ⊠ *Bus terminal* ☎ *2902/491-631* ⊕ *www.turismozaahj.com.*

Remis El Calafate. ⊠ *Av. Roca 1004* ☎ *2966/1538-9034.*

Rental Cars Fiorasi. ⊠ *Av. Libertador 1319* ☎ *0280/15-430-2958* ⊕ *www. fiorasirentacar.com.* **ServiCar.** ⊠ *Av. Libertador 695* ☎ *2902/492-541.*

Visitor and Tour Information Oficina de Turismo. ⊠ *Rosales at Libertador* ☎ *2902/491-090* ⊕ *www.elcalafate.gov.ar* ✉ *Bus terminal* ☎ *2902/491-476.* **Oficina Parques Nacionales.** ⊠ *Av. Libertador 1302* ☎ *2902/491-005* ⊕ *www. parquesnacionales.gob.ar.*

EXPLORING

Glaciarium. This out-of-town glacier museum gives you an educational walk through the formation and life of glaciers (particularly in Patagonia) and the effects of climate change, as well as temporary art exhibitions. A 3-D film about the national park and plenty of brightly lit displays, along with the stark glacier-shape architecture, give it a modern appeal. Don't miss the Glaciobar—the first ice bar in Argentina—where you can don thermal suits, boots, and gloves, and where a whisky on the rocks means 200-year-old glacier rocks from Perito

Moreno. ✉ *Ruta 11, Km 6* ⊕ *Arrive by taxi (200 pesos each way), 1 hr walking, or by shuttle service from tourism office leaving every hr (100 pesos return)* ☎ *2902/497–912* ⊕ *www.glaciarium.com* ✉ *Museum 400 pesos; bar 280 pesos for 25 minutes with 1 drink.*

FodorsChoice **Glaciar Perito Moreno.** Eighty km (50 miles) away on R11, the road to
★ the Glaciar Perito Moreno has now been entirely paved. From the park entrance the road winds through hills and forests of lenga and ñire trees, until all at once the glacier comes into full view. Descending like a long white tongue through distant mountains, it ends abruptly in a translucent azure wall 5 km (3 miles) wide and 240 feet high at the edge of frosty green Lago Argentino.

Although it's possible to rent a car and go on your own (which can give you the advantage of avoiding large tourist groups), virtually everyone visits the park on a day trip booked through one of the many travel agents in El Calafate. The most basic tours start at 1,000 pesos for the round-trip (excluding entrance) and take you to see the glacier from a viewing area composed of a series of platforms wrapped around the point of the Península de Magallanes. The platforms, which offer perhaps the most impressive view of the glacier, allow you to wander back and forth, looking across the Canal de los Tempanos (Iceberg Channel). Here you listen and wait for nature's number-one ice show—first, a cracking sound, followed by tons of ice breaking away and falling with a thunderous crash into the lake. As the glacier creeps across this narrow channel and meets the land on the other side, an ice dam sometimes builds up between the inlet of Brazo Rico on the left and the rest of the lake on the right. As the pressure on the dam increases, everyone waits for the day it will rupture again.

In recent years the surge in the number of visitors to Glaciar Perito Moreno has created a crowded scene that is not always conducive to reflective encounters with nature's majesty. Although the glacier remains spectacular, savvy travelers would do well to minimize time at the madhouse that the viewing area becomes at midday in high season, and instead encounter the glacier by boat or on a mini-trekking excursion. Better yet, rent a car and get an early start to beat the tour buses, or visit Perito Moreno in the off-season when a spectacular rupture is just as likely as in midsummer and you won't have to crane over other people's heads to see it. ✉ *El Calafate* ✉ *500 pesos park entrance.*

Glaciar Upsala. The largest glacier in South America, Glaciar Upsala is 55 km (35 miles) long and 10 km (6 miles) wide, and accessible only by boat. Daily cruises depart from Puerto Banderas (40 km [25 miles] west of El Calafate via R11) for the 2½-hour trip. Dodging floating icebergs (*tempanos*), some as large as a small island, the boats maneuver as close as they dare to the wall of ice that rises from the aqua-green water of Lago Argentino. The seven glaciers that feed the lake deposit their debris into the runoff, causing the water to cloud with minerals ground to fine powder by the glacier's moraine (the accumulation of earth and stones left by the glacier). Condors and black-chested buzzard eagles build their nests in the rocky cliffs above the lake. When the boat stops for lunch at Onelli Bay, don't miss the walk behind the restaurant into

VISITING LAGO ROCA

Camping Lago Roca. There are gorgeous campsites, simple cabins, fishing-tackle rentals, hot showers, and a basic restaurant at Camping Lago Roca. Make reservations in advance if visiting over the Christmas holidays; at other times the campground is seldom crowded. In high season Cal Tur offer shuttles from Lago Roca to Perito Moreno. For more comfortable accommodations, you can arrange to stay at the Nibepo Aike Estancia at the western end of Lago Roca, about 5 km (3 miles) past the campground. The national park entrance fee is collected only on the road to Perito Moreno Glacier or at Puerto Banderas, where cruises depart, so admission to the Lago Roca corner of the park is free. ⊠ *El Calafate* ☎ *2902/499–500* ⊗ *Closed May–Sept.*

Lago Roca. This little-visited lake is inside the national park just south of Brazo Rico, 46 km (29 miles) from El Calafate. The area receives about five times as much annual precipitation as El Calafate, creating a relatively lush climate of green meadows by the lakeshore, where locals come to picnic and cast for trophy rainbow and lake trout. Don't miss a hike into the hills behind the lake—the view of dark-blue Lago Roca backed by a pale-green inlet of Lago Argentino with the Perito Moreno glacier and jagged snowcapped peaks beyond is truly outstanding. ⊠ *El Calafate.*

a wild landscape of small glaciers and milky rivers carrying chunks of ice from four glaciers into Lago Onelli. Glaciar Upsala has diminished in size in recent years. ⊠ *El Calafate* ✉ *Cruises start from 1000 pesos.*

Nimez Lagoon Ecological Reserve. A marshy area on the shore of Lago Argentino just a short walk from downtown El Calafate, the Nimez Lagoon Ecological Reserve is home to many species of waterfowl, including black-necked swans, buff-necked ibises, southern lapwings, and flamingos. Road construction along its edge and the rapidly advancing town threaten to stifle this avian oasis, but it's still a haven for bird-watchers and a relaxing walk in the early morning or late afternoon. Strolling along footpaths among grazing horses and flocks of birds may not be as intense an experience as, say, trekking on a glacier, but a trip to the lagoon provides a good sense of the local landscape. Don't forget your binoculars and a telephoto lens. ⊠ *1 km (½ mile) north of downtown, just off Av. Alem* ☎ *2902/495–536* ✉ *40 pesos.*

WHERE TO EAT

$$$$
ARGENTINE

✕ **Casimiro Biguá.** This restaurant and wine bar boasts a hipper-than-thou interior and modern menu serving such delights as Patagonian lamb with *calafate* sauce (calafate is a local wild berry). The Casimiro Biguá Parrilla, down the street from the main restaurant, has a similar trendy feel but you can recognize the *parrilla* by the *cordero al asador* (spit-roasted lamb) displayed in the window. **Known for:** fantastic roast lamb; big portions; typical asado atmosphere. Ⓢ *Average main: 440 pesos* ⊠ *Av. Libertador 963* ☎ *2902/492–590* ⊕ *www.casimirobigua.com* ✛ *C2.*

$$$$ ✕ **Isabel.** It takes a lot of moxie to open a restaurant not serving *cordero,*
ARGENTINE barbecue, or pizza in Patagonia, and former "fancy" chefs José and Leandro show they have just that with their homey restaurant, Isabel, which
uses vintage plow wheels to cook a traditional and ultimately delicious
stew-style dish known as *al disco*. The *al disco* menu offers all sorts of
meats and veggies cooked in beer, red wine, or white wine; more creative
and quasi-modern options like Bife al Napolitana; or you can create your
own. And you've got to love a restaurant that tells you not to bother with
starters but rather just dunk your bread in the disco sauce. **Known for:**
signature stew dish cooked several creative ways; charming and lively
atmosphere; massive portions. ⑤ *Average main: 300 pesos* ⊠ *Gobernador
Moyano 1020, at 25 Mayo* ☎ *2902/489–000* ✛ *B2.*

$$$$ ✕ **La Lechuza.** This bustling spot is where locals go for their pizza joint
ARGENTINE fix, thanks to the typical Argentine-style pizza of thick crust, and lay-
FAMILY ered with stringy cheese. Their empanadas are just as good—pick up a
few and you have the perfect pastry pick-me-up during a long day of
exploring. **Known for:** fantastic empanadas; classic Argentine pizza;
crowds of locals. ⑤ *Average main: 300 pesos* ⊠ *Av. Libertador at 1 de
Mayo* ☎ *2902/491–610* ✛ *B2.*

$$$$ ✕ **La Tablita.** It's a couple of extra blocks from downtown and across a
ARGENTINE little white bridge, but this *parrilla* is where the locals go for a special
night out to watch their food as it's cooking; Patagonian lamb and beef
ribs roast gaucho-style on frames hanging over a circular asador, and an
enormous grill along the back wall is full of steaks, chorizos, and *morcilla* (blood sausage). The whole place is filled with a warm glow despite
the lackluster decor. **Known for:** great traditional parrilla; tasty empanadas; big crowds on weekends. ⑤ *Average main: 500 pesos* ⊠ *Coronel
Rosales 28* ☎ *2902/491–065* ⊕ *www.la-tablita.com.ar* ✛ *D2.*

$$$$ ✕ **La Zaina.** This trendy bistro is filled with seductive cocktails, colorful
ARGENTINE plates, and fusion flavors. It might be located in a rural Patagonian town
Fodor'sChoice at the end of the world, but these dishes could easily come straight out
★ of a trendy Buenos Aires restaurant—served with edible flowers, spirit
infusions, and plenty of attitude. **Known for:** creative cuisine; trendy bar
service; Instagram-worthy plates. ⑤ *Average main: 400 pesos* ⊠ *Gobernador Gregores 1057* ☎ *2902/496–789* ✛ *B2.*

$$$$ ✕ **Olivia Coffee Shop.** For a chilled out cuppa and delicious sweet
CAFÉ treats, this modern and calm café off the main strip offers a moment
of peace with a caffeine boost. **Known for:** decent coffee; good playl-
ist; scrumptious muffins. ⑤ *Average main: 200 pesos* ⊠ *9 de Julio 131*
☎ *2902/488–038* ☉ *Closed mornings in winter* ✛ *B2.*

$$$$ ✕ **Pura Vida.** Bohemian music, homey cooking, and colorful patchwork
ARGENTINE cushions set the tone for this unpretentious, vegetarian-friendly restaurant several blocks from downtown. You'll be surrounded by funky
artwork, couples whispering under low-hung lights, and laid-back
but efficient staff as you try to decide which big-enough-to-share dish
you'll order while working your way through a great dome of steaming
bread. **Known for:** signature pumpkin stew; great vegetarian options;
fun and eclectic decor. ⑤ *Average main: 300 pesos* ⊠ *Av. Libertador
1876* ☎ *2902/493–356* ☉ *Closed Wed. No lunch* ✛ *A3.*

8

WHERE TO STAY

$$$$ | 🏨 **Eolo.** A luxury lodge on the road to Perito Moreno, Eolo offers full-
HOTEL | board stays in handsome accommodations where you can take in the beauty of Patagonia's vast, empty lands and see Lago Argentino in the distance. **Pros:** beautiful location; luxury service; endless acres of estate to explore. **Cons:** expensive; no drinks included in meal plans; far from town or any services. $ *Rooms from: US$980* ✉ *Ruta Provincial N 11, Km 23,000* ☎ *2902/492–042* ⊕ *www.eolo.com.ar* ⊗ *Closed mid-Apr.– mid-Oct.* ⮌ *17 rooms* ⦿ *All-inclusive; Some meals* ✛ *A3.*

$$$$ | 🏨 **Estancia Cristina.** Arriving at Estancia Cristina by catamaran on Lago
HOTEL | Argentina past fields of ice and imposing mountains is just the begin-
Fodor's Choice | ning of a remarkable Patagonian adventure: on arrival you'll be treated
★ | to cozy accommodation, delicious cuisine, and unbeatable excursions to little-explored corners of the park. **Pros:** fantastic excursions; excellent restaurant; incredible views from well-appointed rooms. **Cons:** patchy Wi-Fi; expensive; no alcoholic drinks included in (high) price. $ *Rooms from: US$1360* ✉ *Punta Bandera* ☎ *2902/491–133* ⊕ *www. estanciacristina.com* ⊗ *Closed mid-Apr.–mid-Nov.* ⮌ *20 rooms* ⦿ *All-inclusive* ✛ *A3.*

$$$$ | 🏨 **Helsingfors.** You couldn't dream of a more beautiful location for this
ALL-INCLUSIVE | luxurious converted ranch house on the shore of Lago Viedma: you
Fodor's Choice | wake up to stellar views across the lake and onto the Fitz Roy massif,
★ | while inside you'll be treated to cozy fireplaces, comfortable en suite rooms, and exceptional four-course meals in the intimate restaurant. **Pros:** unique and breathtaking location; wonderful personal excursions; fantastic restaurant. **Cons:** three hours by dirt road from El Calafate; rooms are dated; expensive (and doesn't include alcoholic drinks). $ *Rooms from: US$800* ✉ *Lago Viedma, 3 hrs by dirt road from El Calafate* ☎ *11/2021–506927* ⊕ *www.helsingfors.com.ar* ⊗ *Closed May–Oct.* ⮌ *9 rooms* ⦿ *All-inclusive* ✛ *D3.*

$$ | 🏨 **Hotel Kau-Yatún.** This converted ranch is nestled in a quiet tree-lined
HOTEL | valley by a stream yet lies just six blocks from the main street and offers a full schedule of mountain biking, horseback riding, and four-wheel-drive expeditions in the 42,000-acre Estancia 25 de Mayo that lies just behind the hotel. **Pros:** good value; nice details; central location. **Cons:** water pressure is only adequate; lost a bit of personality from chain takeover; Wi-Fi and modern amenities sparse. $ *Rooms from: US$140* ✉ *25 de Mayo* ☎ *2902/491–059* ⊕ *www.kauyatun.com* ⊗ *Closed Apr.– Sept.* ⮌ *44 rooms* ⦿ *Breakfast* ✛ *D3.*

$$ | 🏨 **Kosten Aike.** Lined with wooden balconies, high-beamed ceilings,
HOTEL | and a slate floor, this hotel is a paragon of Andean Patagonian architecture, while a sunny rooftop spa, gym, and spacious Jacuzzi offer great views over town to Lago Argentino. **Pros:** large rooms and spa; central location; good value at this price point. **Cons:** dining room decor is uninspired; rooms are simply furnished; some rooms get outside noise. $ *Rooms from: US$160* ✉ *G. Moyano 1243, at 25 de Mayo* ☎ *2902/492–424* ⊕ *www.kostenaike.com.ar* ⊗ *Closed May–Sept.* ⮌ *80 rooms* ⦿ *Breakfast* ✛ *B2.*

"We walked from our hotel in the center of town to the Laguna Nimez Reserve. Wild horses grazed lazily amid the white wildflowers. It was a magical moment ... So unexpected!" –Lois Zebelman, Fodors.com member

$$$
B&B/INN
🏠 **Los Ponchos Apart Boutique.** Cozy and handsomely designed two-floor apartments in this boutique complex have beautiful views over Lago Argentina and offer some independence and privacy with a self-catering kitchen and homey, gaucho-chic decoration. **Pros:** warm service; cozy atmosphere; private. **Cons:** a long walk from town; street dogs noisy at night; pricey compared to local competition. $ *Rooms from: US$230* ✉ *Los Alamos 3321* ☎ *2902/496–330* ⊕ *www.losponchosapart.com.ar* ⊙ *Closed June–mid-Sept.* ↝ *8 rooms, 2 double apartments, 1 cabin* 🍴 *Breakfast* ⊹ *A3.*

$$
B&B/INN
FAMILY
🏠 **Madre Tierra.** The friendly welcome from the owners makes staying at this B&B feel like visiting a friend's home (with great attention to detail in design and well-chosen furnishings). **Pros:** personalized and friendly service; central location; authentic. **Cons:** walls are thin and noise travels; expensive and cash only; small rooms for price. $ *Rooms from: US$170* ✉ *9 de Julio 239* ☎ *2902/489–880* ⊕ *www.madretierrapatagonia.com* ☰ *No credit cards* ↝ *7 rooms* 🍴 *Breakfast* ⊹ *B1.*

$$
HOTEL
🏠 **Mirador del Lago.** Great views across the lake are the main selling point of this smartly kept hotel, where each lakeside vista has a seated window or armchair so you can watch the beautiful sunset colors dance across the sky. **Pros:** good value; modern; open all year. **Cons:** a bit of a walk from town; impersonal service; lots of steps. $ *Rooms from: US$160* ✉ *Av. del Libertador 2047* ☎ *2902/493–213* ⊕ *www.mirador-dellago.com.ar* ↝ *68 rooms* 🍴 *Breakfast.* ⊹ *A2.*

$$$$
ALL-INCLUSIVE
FAMILY
🏠 **Nibepo Aike.** This lovely estancia is an hour and a half from El Calafate in a bucolic valley overlooking Lago Roca and backed by snow-capped mountain peaks; where sheep and horses graze, friendly gauchos give horse-racing and sheep-shearing demonstrations, and every evening

a communal table is laid for a supper of spit-roast locally reared lamb. **Pros:** spectacular scenery; classic estancia experience; friendly guides and excellent horse-riding. **Cons:** expensive for simple amenities; restaurant has limited offerings; patchy Wi-Fi. $ *Rooms from: US$375* ✉ *For reservations:, Av. Libertador 1215* ☎ *11/5272–0341 reservations (Buenos Aires), 2902/492–797 day visits* ⊕ *www.nibepoaike.com.ar* ⊗ *Closed May–Sept.* ⇆ *10 rooms* ⦿ *All-inclusive; Breakfast* ✛ *B2.*

$$ ⊡ **Posada los Alamos.** Surrounded by tall, leafy alamo trees, this enor-
HOTEL mous complex incorporates a country manor house, half a dozen con-
FAMILY vention rooms, a spa, and an indoor swimming pool, but for what it has in amenities Los Alamos lacks in service and attention. **Pros:** spa and gym; beautiful gardens; long breakfast hours. **Cons:** tired furnishings and decor; small rooms; inattentive staff. $ *Rooms from: US$150* ✉ *Guatti 1135* ☎ *2902/491–144* ⊕ *www.posadalosalamos.com* ⇆ *144 rooms* ⦿ *Breakfast* ✛ *A2.*

SPORTS AND THE OUTDOORS
BOAT TOURS
Glaciares Gourmet. If fine dining and sipping wine while admiring the glaciers is more your style, this is the no-effort-required cruise for you. With a maximum of 28 passengers, the deluxe cruise liner visits Spegazzini and Upsala glaciers and stops for a short leg-stretching walk at beauty spot Puesto de las Vacas before the six-course gourmet lunch with wine. If a full day isn't enough, you can opt for the two-night cruise option. ✉ *Cruceros Marpatag, 9 de Julio (Local 4, Galleria de los Pajaros)* ☎ *2902/492–118* ⊕ *www.crucerosmarpatag.com* ⊠ *From 1400 pesos.*

Safari Náutico. Boats depart from a small port 7 km (4 miles) from Perito Moreno glacier and take tourists on an hour-long cruise around the glacier's south face for a closer inspection of the advancing glacier and floating icebergs. On a good day, you can stand on the deck for the best up-close photo opportunities. Tours happen all year and can be reserved at the port or in advance in the downtown office or other tour agencies. ✉ *Hielo y Aventura, Av. Libertador 935* ☎ *2902/492–205* ⊕ *www.hieloyaventura.com* ⊠ *From USD$30.*

Solo Patagonia. With two different full-day boat excursions, Solo Patagonia has been navigating the milky waters for years. Their fleet of large cruisers offers access to some of the best views of the Perito Moreno, Upsala, and Spegazzini glaciers from October to March. ✉ *Av. Libertador 867* ☎ *2902/491–155* ⊕ *www.solopatagonia.com* ⊠ *From $70.*

HORSEBACK RIDING AND ESTANCIAS
Estancia El Galpón del Glaciar. This estancia welcomes guests overnight or for the day—for a horseback ride, bird-watching, or an afternoon program that includes a demonstration of sheep dogs working, a walk to the lake with a naturalist, sheep-shearing, and dinner in the former sheep-shearing barn served right off the asador by knife-wielding gauchos. ✉ *Ruta 11, Km 22* ☎ *11/5217–6720* ⊕ *www.elgalpondelglaciar.com.ar.*

Nibepo Aike. This pretty estancia an hour and a half from El Calafate offers a range of horseback experiences from hour-long excursions to

Great views of Cerro Fitzroy seem to wait at every bend on the trail in Parque Nacional Los Glaciares.

full-day, nine-hour rides to view glaciers in the distance. It's possible to visit Nibepo Aike by booking a day trip at the office in downtown El Calafate, or you can stay overnight at the estancia. ✉ *53 km (31 miles) from El Calafate near Lago Roca on Ruta 15* ☎ *2902/492–797, 11/5272–0341 reservations from Buenos Aires* ⊕ *www.nibepoaike.com.ar.*

ICE TREKKING

Hielo y Aventura. For the most up-close-and-personal experience with Perito Moreno glacier, book yourself onto an ice trekking day where you'll don crampons and walk over the glacier studying crevasses and ice lakes before finishing with a whisky on the rocks using ice from the glacier. The full day Mini Trekking excursion includes a 90-minute ice trek, a short trek in the forest, a 20-minute boat ride, and a transfer to the park from your hotel. You'll have to pay your own park entrance, bring a packed lunch, and wear the right clothing (crampons are provided), but you also get over an hour to enjoy the view of Perito Moreno Glacier from the park. For a more in-depth and challenging ice day, opt for the Big Ice trek, which includes more time on the ice and ducking through bright-blue ice tunnels. ✉ *Av. Libertador 935* ☎ *2902/492–205* ⊕ *www.hieloyaventura.com* ✉ *From 3000 pesos.*

KAYAKING

Mil Outdoor. Those brave enough to get in the milky ice waters can get dropped off by a boat on the glacier's edge and take a two-hour guided kayaking excursion with this outfitter, weather permitting (not available in June and July). ✉ *Av. Libertador 1037* ☎ *2902/491–446* ⊕ *www. miloutdoor.com.ar* ✉ *From 4000 pesos.*

Laguna del Desierto

Lago San Martín

Parque Nacional Bernardo O'Higgins

Pier Giorgio

Cerro Fitzroy 11,286 ft.
Cerro Torre 10,174 ft.
Adela Sur
Chorillo del Salta
El Chalten

Cordón
Pana
Congrejo

MESETA DEL QUEMADO
MESETA DEL VIENTO
MESETA CHICA
MESETA BASALTICA

CHILE

Dos Cuernos
Dos Cumbres
Padre De Agostini
Puntudo

San Jose Ranch
23

Los Alamos Ranch

Huemul

Glaciar Viedma

Viedma Glacier Ice Trekking

Lago Viedma

23

CORDILLERA DE LOS ANDES

PARQUE NACIONAL LOS GLACIARES

Mascarello

Helsingfors (Hotel)

Pico Negro

21

40

La Leona

Norte

Mesón

Planchón

Las Tetas o Dos Picos

69

Estación Astronómica Austral

Glaciar Upsala

Murallón

Pintado

Guardaparque

Estancia Cristina (Hotel)

Loyola o Mirador

Río La Leona

ARGENTINA

Bertrand
Agassiz

Lago Onelli

Onelli

Castillo

Horqueta

19

40

Peineta

Spegazzini Glacier

Brazo Norte

San Ernesto Ranch

Lago Argentino

Charles Fuhr

Puesto la Diana

Boat Tours to Upsala
Punta Bandera

11

PENÍNSULA AVELLANEDA

Mayo Sound

SIERRA CATTLE

Frías

El Calafate

Negro

Mayo Glacier

SIERRA BUENOS AIRES

11

60

15

Perito Moreno Glacier Ice Trekking

Témpanos Canal

Mt. Peritobelli

Glaciar Perito Moreno

Lago Roca (w/camping)

Cervantes

Adriana

Brazo Rico

Brazo Sur

CORCON DE LOS CRISTALES

Mesa de Truco

Centinela o Alfiler

SIERRA BAGUALES

Verlika

15

Río Bote

CHILE

Parque Nacional Bernardo O'higgins

Mt. Stokes
Parque Nacional Torres Del Paine

SIERRA CONTRERAS

0   10 mi
0   10 km

Parque Nacional los Glaciares

LAND ROVER EXCURSIONS

Mil Outdoor. If pedaling uphill sounds like too much work, check out the Land Rover expeditions offered by Mil Outdoor October to April. These trips use large tour trucks to follow dirt tracks into the hills above town for stunning views of Lago Argentino. On a clear day, you can even see the peaks of Cerro Torre and Cerro Fitzroy on the horizon. During the winter, the same company (also known as Calafate Mountain Park) runs a children's snow park with sledding and snowmobiling. ✉ *Av. Libertador 1037* ☎ *2902/491–446* ⊕ *www.miloutdoor.com.ar* 💳 *From 1300 pesos.*

MOUNTAIN BIKING

Bike Rental. Mountain biking is popular along the dirt roads and mountain paths that lead to the lakes, glaciers, and ranches. There are several places to rent bikes in town; two options are **HLS** (Perito Moreno 95) and **E Bike** (Av. Libertador 1319). ✉ *El Calafate.*

EL CHALTÉN

222 km (138 miles) north of El Calafate (35 km [22 miles] east on R11 to R40, then north on R40 to R23 north).

Founded in 1985, El Chaltén is Argentina's newest town, and it's growing at an astounding rate. Originally just a few shacks and lodges built near the entrance to Parque Nacional Los Glaciares, the town is starting to fill a steep-walled valley in front of Cerro Torre and Cerro Fitzroy, two of the most impressive peaks in Argentina.

Famous for the exploits of rock climbers who started their pilgrimage to climb some of the most difficult rock walls in the world in the 1950s, the range is now drawing hikers whose more earthbound ambitions run to dazzling mountain scenery and unscripted encounters with wildlife including condors, Patagonian parrots, red-crested woodpeckers, and the *huemul*, an endangered deer species.

8

GETTING HERE AND AROUND

The three-hour car or bus trip to El Chaltén from El Calafate makes staying at least one night here a good idea. The only gas, food, and restroom facilities en route are at La Leona, a historically significant ranch 110 km (68 miles) from El Calafate where Butch Cassidy and the Sundance Kid once hid from the long arm of the law.

Before you cross the bridge into town over Río Fitzroy, stop at the Parque Nacional office. It's extremely well organized and staffed by bilingual rangers who can help you plan your mountain treks and point you to accommodations and restaurants in town. It's an essential stop; orientation talks are given in coordination with arriving buses, which automatically stop here before continuing on to the bus depot.

There's only one ATM in town (it's in the bus station), and it's in high demand; because of servicing schedules, on the weekend El Chaltén runs into the same cash availability problems that El Calafate does, though on a smaller scale. ■ TIP→ **During the week, stockpile the cash you'll need for the weekend, or bring it with you if you're arriving between midday Friday and midday Monday.**

ESSENTIALS

Visitor Information Parque Nacional Office. ⌂ *Av. M.M. de Güemes 21*
☎ *2962/493–004* ⊕ *www.losglaciares.com/en.*

EXPLORING

Cerro Torre and Cerro Fitzroy. You don't need a guide to do the classic
treks to Cerro Torre and Cerro Fitzroy, each about six to eight hours
round-trip out of El Chaltén. If your legs feel up to it the day you do
the Fitzroy walk, tack on an hour of steep switchbacks to Mirador Tres
Lagos, the lookout with the best views of Mt. Fitzroy and its glacial
lakes. Both routes, plus the Mirador and various side trails, can be
combined in a two- or three-day trip. ⌂ *El Chaltén.*

Chorillo del Salta (*Trickling Falls*). Just 4 km (3 miles) north of town
on the road to Lago del Desierto, the Chorillo del Salta waterfall is no
Iguazú, but the area is extremely pleasant and sheltered from the wind.
A short hike uphill leads to secluded river pools and sun-splashed rocks
where locals enjoy picnics on their days off. If you don't feel up to a
more ambitious hike, the short stroll to the falls is an excellent way
to spend the better part of an afternoon. Pack a bottle of wine and a
sandwich and enjoy the solitude. ⌂ *El Chaltén.*

Laguna del Desierto (*Lake of the Desert*). A lovely lake surrounded by
lush forest, complete with orchids and mossy trees, the Laguna del
Desierto is 37 km (23 miles) north of El Chaltén on R23, a dirt road.
Hotels in El Chaltén can arrange a trip for about $50 for the day. Locals
recommend visiting Lago del Desierto on a rainy day, when more ambitious hikes are not an option and the dripping green misty forest is extra
mysterious. ⌂ *El Chaltén.*

WHERE TO EAT AND STAY

$$$$
ARGENTINE
FAMILY

✕**Aonikenk.** In a dark wooden dining hall you'll share hearty steaks,
warming soups, and wine poured from penguin-shaped ceramic jugs
in a family restaurant that includes a hostel upstairs. It's rustic, and the
food is not spectacular, but you can't beat the friendly atmosphere in
what is easily El Chaltén's largest and most popular restaurant. **Known
for:** family-friendly atmosphere; standard Chilean cuisine; open hours
even in the off-season. ⑤ *Average main: 340 pesos* ⌂ *Av. M.M. de
Güemes 23* ☎ *2962/493–070* ⊟ *No credit cards.*

$$$$
ARGENTINE
Fodor's Choice
★

✕**La Cervecería.** While El Chaltén is still building all it needs to become
a full-fledged town, it already has a successful microbrewery that is
famous in the region for its brews and comfort food. Of course, it's
not just the hops bringing in the crowds; they also cook up delicious
soups, snacks, empanadas, and a great *locro* (hearty traditional northern Argentine stew). **Known for:** impressive craft beer; hearty comfort
food; welcoming atmosphere. ⑤ *Average main: 240 pesos* ⌂ *San Martín
320* ☎ *2962/493–109* ⊘ *Closed June–Oct.*

$$$$
HOTEL

▢ **Aguas Arriba Lodge.** Accessible only by boat or a three-hour trek,
Aguas Arriba has a privileged location right on the Lago del Desierto, with a glimmer of Mt. Fitzroy in the distance. **Pros:** fantastic
location; attended by owners; excellent excursions. **Cons:** noise travels
between rooms; private shuttle to lake required in addition to walk/
boat; no phone signal. ⑤ *Rooms from: US$800* ⌂ *Lago del Desierto*

☎ *11/4152–5697 Buenos Aires ⊕ www.aguasarribalodge.com ⊘ Closed mid-Apr.–Sept. ➾ 6 rooms* ⦿ *Breakfast.*

$ 🛏 **Nothofagus.** A simple B&B off the main road, Nothofagus is named
B&B/INN after the southern beech tree, and the lodge has a rough-hewn, woodsy feel with exposed beams and leaves stamped into the lampshades. **Pros:** great views; bright and sunny breakfast room; good value. **Cons:** staff energy too low for some; spartan rooms and bathrooms, some of which are shared; simple breakfast. ⑤ *Rooms from: US$90 ✉ Hensen, at Riquelme ☎ 2962/493–087 ⊕ www.nothofagusbb.com.ar ▭ No credit cards ⊘ Closed May–Sept. ➾ 9 rooms* ⦿ *Breakfast.*

$$ 🛏 **Posada Lunajuim.** A traditional A-frame roof keeps the lid on a
HOTEL funky, modern lodge filled with contemporary artwork, exposed brick masonry, and a spacious lounge and dining room complete with a roaring fireplace and a library stacked with an intriguing mix of travel books. **Pros:** great lounge area; friendly staff; awesome food and wine list. **Cons:** not all rooms have views; baths are quite small; slow Wi-Fi. ⑤ *Rooms from: US$140 ✉ Trevisan 45 ☎ 2962/493–047 ⊕ www.lunajuim.com ➾ 26 rooms* ⦿ *Breakfast.*

SPORTS AND THE OUTDOORS

El Chaltén owes its existence to those who wanted a base for trekking into this corner of Los Glaciares National Park, specifically Cerro Torre and Cerro Fitzroy. It's no surprise that nearly everyone who comes here considers hiking up to those two mountains to be the main event—though the locro and microbrews at the end of the day are a plus.

MOUNTAIN CLIMBING

Casa de Guias. A guide is required if you want to enter the ice field or trek on any of the glaciers in Los Glaciares National Park. Casa de Guias is a group of professional, multilingual guides who offer fully equipped multiday treks covering all the classic routes in the national park, and longer trips exploring the ice field. They even offer a taste of big-wall climbing on one of the spires in the Fitzroy range. ✉ *Av. San Martín 310 ☎ 2962/493–118 ⊕ www.casadeguias.com.ar.*

El Chaltén Mountain Guides. Five mountain guides offer expeditions in and around El Chaltén, as well as many other destinations in Argentina. One-day and multiday treks and ascents to rock and ice-climbing expeditions are available. In the winter they also offer backcountry skiing tours. ✉ *Rio de las Vueltas 212 ☎ 2962/493–329 ⊕ www.ecmg.com.ar.*

PUERTO NATALES AND TORRES DEL PAINE, CHILE

Serious hikers often come to this area and use Puerto Natales as their base for hiking the classic "W" or circuit treks in **Torres del Paine,** which take between four days and a week to complete. Others choose to spend a couple of nights in one of the park's luxury hotels and take in the sights during day hikes.

If you have less time, however, it's possible to spend just one day touring the park, as many people do, with Puerto Natales as your starting

Picadas, or light snacks, reach a new level of delicious after an excursion in the wilds of Patagonia; a selection may include peanuts, pistacios, marinated baby onions, or a local cheese.

point. In that case, rather than drive, you'll want to book a one-day Torres del Paine tour with one of the many tour operators here. Most tours pick you up at your hotel between 8 and 9 am and follow the same route, visiting several lakes and mountain vistas, seeing Lago Grey and its glacier, and stopping for lunch in Hostería Lago Grey or one of the other hotels inside the park. These tours return around sunset. A budget option is the daily bus tour (year-round) from the bus station with Transportes María José, which also offers hop-on, hop-off options for hikers and campers.

While visiting Torres del Paine remains the most popular excursion, nearby Parque Bernardo O'Higgins is also ripe for exploration with popular boat tours to glaciers with companies Turismo 21 de Mayo (year-round) and Agunsa (September through April).

Argentina's magnificent **Glaciar Perito Moreno,** near El Calafate, can be visited on a popular (but extremely long) one-day tour, leaving at the crack of dawn and returning late at night—don't forget your passport. It's a four-hour-plus trip in each direction; some tours sensibly include overnights in El Calafate.

Please note, if calling outside of Chile, you will require the international dialing code (+56). From within Chile you need to add 0 before dialing any local code.

Prices for restaurants and hotels in Puerto Natales and Torres del Paine are given in Chilean pesos. As of this writing, the exchange rate was US$1 to 595 Chilean pesos.

PUERTO NATALES, CHILE

242 km (150 miles) northwest of Punta Arenas.

Puerto Natales has become the main base for exploring a number of southern Patagonia's top attractions, including Parque Nacional Torres del Paine and Parque Nacional Bernardo O'Higgins. The medium-sized fishing town offers picturesque views of the Seno Última Esperanza (Last Hope Sound) channel, which was named so by Spanish navigator Juan Ladrillero in the 16th century as it was his last hope to reach the Strait of Magellan.

As a launching point for many touristic sites, Puerto Natales has recently seen a large increase in tourism and development with a new surge of luxury accommodation offering all-inclusive stays with excursions. The town has added a string of hip eateries, cafés, and boutique hotels recently, and is starting to challenge the more staid larger city of Punto Arenas as a hub for exploring the entire region.

GETTING HERE AND AROUND

The trip to Puerto Natales from El Calafate is a beautiful journey through color-washed Patagonian landscapes with white peaked mountains in the distance and picturesque estancias and cattle ranches dotted along the way.

Puerto Natales centers on the Plaza de Armas, a lovely, well-landscaped sanctuary. A few blocks west of the plaza on Avenida Bulnes you'll find the small Museo Histórico Municipal. On a clear day, an early morning walk along Avenida Pedro Montt, which follows the shoreline of the Seno Última Esperanza (or Canal Señoret, as it's called on some maps), can be a soul-cleansing experience. The rising sun gradually casts a glow on the mountain peaks to the west.

ESSENTIALS

Bus Contacts Buses Fernández. ⊠ *Eleuterio Ramirez 399* ☎ *612/411–111* ⊕ *www.busesfernandez.com.* **Cootra.** ⊠ *Bus station* ☎ *612/412–785* ⊕ *www. cootra.com.ar.* **Transportes María José.** ⊠ *Av. España 1455* ☎ *612/410–951* ⊕ *www.busesmariajose.com.*

Rental Cars Avis (Emsa). ⊠ *Barros Arana 118* ☎ *612/614–388* ⊕ *www. emsarentacar.com.*

EXPLORING

Iglesia Parroquial. Across from the Plaza de Armas is the squat little Iglesia Parroquial. The ornate altarpiece in this church depicts the town's founders, indigenous peoples, and the Virgin Mary all in front of the Torres del Paine. ⊠ *Arturo Prat and Eberhard.*

Museo Historico Municipal. A highlight in the small but interesting Museo Historico Municipal is a room filled with antique prints of Aonikenk and Kaweshkar indigenous peoples. Another room is devoted to the exploits of Hermann Eberhard, a German explorer considered the region's first settler. Check out his celebrated collapsible boat. In an adjacent room you will find some vestiges of the old Bories sheep plant, which processed the meat and wool of more than 300,000 sheep a year. ⊠ *Av. Bulnes 285* ☎ *61/220–9548* 🎟 *1000 pesos* ☉ *Closed Sun.*

8

Monumento Natural Cueva de Milodón. In 1896, Hermann Eberhard stumbled upon a gaping cave that extended 200 meters (650 feet) into the earth. Venturing inside, he discovered the bones and dried pieces of hide (with deep red fur) of an animal he could not identify. It was later determined that what Eberhard had discovered were the extraordinarily well-preserved remains of a prehistoric herbivorous mammal, *mylodon darwini,* about twice the height of a man, which they called a *milodón.* The discovery of a stone wall in the cave, and of neatly cut grass stalks in the animal's feces led researchers to conclude that 10,000 years ago a group of Tehuelche Indians captured this beast. The cave is at the Monumento Natural Cueva de Milodón. The cathedral-size space was carved out of a solid rock wall by rising waters. Its dusty floor and barren walls are unspectacular, and the tacky life-size fiberglass model at the cave mouth is useful only as a reference to the size of the gigantic animal that lived here. ⊠ *5 km (3 miles) off Ruta 9 signpost, 28 km (17 miles) northwest of Puerto Natales ⊕ www.cuevadelmilodon.cl ☜ 5000 pesos.*

Plaza de Armas. A few blocks east of the waterfront overlooking Seno Última Esperanza is the not-quite-central Plaza de Armas. An incongruous railway engine sits prominently in the middle of the square. ⊠ *Arturo Prat at Eberhard.*

WHERE TO EAT

$$$
CHILEAN

✕ **Asador Patagónico.** This bright spot in the Puerto Natales dining scene is zealous about meat; so zealous, in fact, that there's no seafood on the menu. Incredible care is taken with the excellent *lomo* and other grilled steaks, and the room is filled with the smell of roasting meat. **Known for:** mouthwatering meats; cozy open fire; friendly service. ⑤ *Average main: 10000 pesos* ⊠ *Prat 158* ☎ *61/241–3553* ☉ *Closed June.*

$$
SEAFOOD

✕ **Cangrejo Rojo.** Although it requires a taxi drive to the other side of town, this nautical-chic café is worth it for its maritime feel, good music and atmosphere, and the tasty, feel-good food prepared lovingly by the marine biologist owners, Francisco and Nuriys. As well as a plethora of sea dwellers, you'll find lamb and other meats on the contemporary menu. **Known for:** excellent king crab; homemade waffles; organic wine menu. ⑤ *Average main: 9000 pesos* ⊠ *Santiago Bueras Av. 782* ☎ *612/412–436* ☉ *Closed Sun.*

$
CAFÉ
Fodor's Choice
★

✕ **The Coffee Maker.** It is no exaggeration to say that this coffee bar is the best spot for a steaming cup of joe in Patagonia, thanks to its well-sourced beans, expert baristas, and some of the best views in town. The Coffee Maker also serves breakfasts, cakes, afternoon snacks, and cocktails, making it a good spot to enjoy the view and take advantage of the Wi-Fi anytime of the day. **Known for:** the area's best coffee; unique pisco sours; great views. ⑤ *Average main: 4000 pesos* ⊠ *Kau, Pedro Montt 161* ☎ *61/241–4611* ⊕ *www.the-coffeemaker.com* ☉ *No lunch in winter.*

$$
VEGETARIAN

✕ **El Living.** This bohemian, loft-style café offers comfy couches and tables covered in gossip magazines and tour info. The gluten-free and vegetarian options on the menu will tick the box in comfort and health. **Known for:** healthy juices; tasty curries; huge salads. ⑤ *Average main: 6000 pesos* ⊠ *Arturo Prat 156* ⊕ *www.el-living.com* ☉ *Closed Apr.–Oct. and Sun.*

$$ ✕ **Espacio Ñandu.** Right on the corner of the plaza, this modern artisan
CHILEAN shop doubles as a restaurant, bar, café, post office, and the best Wi-Fi
FAMILY spot in town, where you can surf on your own computer or rent one
of theirs. With empanadas, tacos, seafood, and salads, you've got all
bases covered for lunch, dinner, or just coffee and a snack. **Known for:**
quick bites; souvenir shopping over lunch; local beers. ⑤ *Average main:
7000 pesos* ✉ *Eberhard and Arturo Prat* ☎ *61/241–031.*

$$$$ ✕ **Kosten.** You'll watch the wind whip the Seno Última Esperanza from
CHILEAN a comfortable lounge in front of the fireplace at this modern café and
bar attached to Indigo Hotel. With a well-stocked bar upstairs, this is
a nice spot for a calafate sour, and if you are feeling lazy, just amble
downstairs to the small restaurant where they serve simple, modern
Chilean cuisine. **Known for:** good views; fun cocktail list; simple but
tasty Chilean food. ⑤ *Average main: 14000 pesos* ✉ *Indigo Hotel,
Ladrilleros 105* ☎ *612/740–670* ⊕ *www.indigopatagonia.cl* ⊙ *Closed
in winter; months vary.*

$$ ✕ **Restaurant Última Esperanza.** Named for the strait on which Puerto
CHILEAN Natales is located, Restaurant Última Esperanza is perhaps your last
chance to try Patagonian seafood classics in a town being overrun by
hip eateries. This traditional restaurant is well known for attentive,
if formal, service, and top-quality, typical dishes. **Known for:** classic
king crab stew; poached conger eel in shellfish sauce; old-school service. ⑤ *Average main: 9000 pesos* ✉ *Av. Eberhard 354* ☎ *61/241–1391*
⊙ *Closed July.*

WHERE TO STAY

$$ 🛏 **Hostal Lady Florence Dixie.** Named after an aristocratic English immi-
B&B/INN grant and tireless traveler, this long-established hotel with an alpine-
inspired facade is on the town's main street; its bright, spacious upstairs
lounge is a good people-watching perch. **Pros:** convenient location;
relaxed atmosphere; good value. **Cons:** simple amenities; dowdy
rooms; basic breakfast. ⑤ *Rooms from: 85000 pesos* ✉ *Av. Bulnes 655*
☎ *612/411–158* ⊕ *www.hotelflorencedixie.cl* ⟿ *19 rooms* ⎮◎⎮ *Breakfast.*

$$$$ 🛏 **Hotel CostAustralis.** This old grande dame of Puerto Natales has been
HOTEL somewhat superseded by more modern, eye-catching hotels, but its
peaked, turreted roof and distinctive architecture still dominate the
waterfront. **Pros:** great views from bay-facing rooms; courteous and
professional staff; startlingly low off-season rates. **Cons:** rooms are
somewhat bland; endless corridors a little impersonal; wind and
street noise. ⑤ *Rooms from: 150000 pesos* ✉ *Av. Pedro Montt 262,
at Av. Bulnes* ☎ *612/412–000* ⊕ *www.hotelcostaustralis.com* ⟿ *112
rooms* ⎮◎⎮ *Breakfast.*

$$$ 🛏 **Hotel Martín Gusinde.** Don't let the dowdy exterior put you off—inside
HOTEL is a modern hotel with a good downtown location and simple but well-
equipped rooms. **Pros:** urbane atmosphere; comfortable beds; central
location. **Cons:** weak Wi-Fi; simple breakfast; noise travels. ⑤ *Rooms
from: 115000 pesos* ✉ *Carlos Bories 278* ☎ *61/271–2100* ⊕ *www.hotel-
martingusinde.com* ⟿ *28 rooms* ⎮◎⎮ *Breakfast.*

$$$$ 🛏 **Índigo.** Chilean architect Sebastian Irarrazabel was given free rein to
HOTEL redesign this building along a nautical theme; inside, a maze of gang-
planks, ramps, and staircases shoot out across cavernous open spaces,

8

minimalist wood panels line walls and ceilings, and water burbles down a waterfall that borders the central walkway. **Pros:** rooftop spa; great views; excellent guiding on excursions. **Cons:** weak Wi-Fi; standard rooms do not have bathtubs; can get noisy. $ *Rooms from: 164000 pesos* ⊠ *Ladrilleros 105* ☎ *61/274–0670* ⊕ *www.indigopatagonia.cl* ➬ *29 rooms* ⦿ *Breakfast.*

$$
B&B/INN ⌂ **Kau Lodge.** One of the best B&B offerings in town comes with excellent views over the lake, comfy and large beds draped in wool throws, and insider touring tips from the mountain-guide owner. **Pros:** cozy rooms; good value; fantastic coffee. **Cons:** wind can be noisy on windows; basic breakfast; small showers. $ *Rooms from: 61,000 pesos* ⊠ *Pedro Montt 161* ☎ *612/414–611* ⊕ *www.kaulodge.com* ➬ *9 rooms* ⦿ *Breakfast.*

OUTSIDE PUERTO NATALES

Several lodges have been constructed on a bluff overlooking the Seno Ultima Esperanza, about a mile outside of town. The views at these hotels are spectacular, with broad panoramas and unforgettable sunsets. While some might complain about the 10- to 30-minute trek into town, it is an easy walk along the seafront. A taxi will set you back around 2,000–2,500 Chilean pesos.

$$$
HOTEL ⌂ **Altiplánico Sur.** This is the Patagonian representative of the Altiplánico line of thoughtfully designed eco-hotels, and nature takes center stage: the hotel blends so seamlessly with its surroundings, it's almost subterranean. **Pros:** eco-friendly; stellar views; outdoor Jacuzzi on request. **Cons:** slow service; few technological amenities, including television; patchy Wi-Fi. $ *Rooms from: 115000 pesos* ⊠ *Ruta 9 Norte, Km 1.5, Huerto 282* ☎ *61/241–2525* ⊕ *www.altiplanico.cl* ☉ *Closed May–Sept.* ➬ *22 rooms* ⦿ *Breakfast.*

$$$$
HOTEL
Fodor's Choice
★
⌂ **Remota.** The eye-catching architecture of Remota competes with stunning views over the Última Esperanza for your attention, especially at night when the soft orange lighting beckons. **Pros:** great spa area; restaurant menu of delicious, native ingredients; inspiring design. **Cons:** wind noises can be wild in the common areas; no Wi-Fi in rooms; expensive. $ *Rooms from: 225000 pesos* ⊠ *Ruta 9 Norte, Km 1.5, Huerto 279* ☎ *612/414–040* ⊕ *www.remota.cl* ➬ *72 rooms* ⦿ *All-inclusive; Breakfast.*

$$$$
HOTEL
Fodor's Choice
★
⌂ **The Singular Patagonia.** Inhabiting the former Bories Cold-Storage Plant, which used to process and export more than 250,000 sheep a year and practically built Puerto Natales as a town, the Singular may well be Puerto Natales's most luxurious and tasteful hotel. **Pros:** one-of-a-kind historic setting; expeditions and tours for all levels of fitness; fantastic restaurant. **Cons:** taxi ride from town; super pricey; breakfast can get busy. $ *Rooms from: 530000 pesos* ⊠ *Y-300 Rd., toward Torres del Paine National Park, Puerto Bories* ☎ *61/722–030* ⊕ *www.thesingular. com* ➬ *57 rooms* ⦿ *All-inclusive; Breakfast.*

$$$$
HOTEL ⌂ **Weskar Patagonian Lodge.** Weskar stands for "hill" in the language of the indigenous Kaweskar, to whom owner Juan José Pantoja, a marine biologist, pays homage in creating and maintaining this cozy lodge, which is high on a ridge overlooking the Ultima Esperanza fjord. **Pros:**

great views from your room; cozy log-cabin decor; rustic and cozy design. **Cons:** less luxurious than neighbors; no lunch offerings; poor temperature regulation. $ *Rooms from: 145000 pesos* ✉ *Ruta 9 Norte, Km 1/Puerto Natales* ☎ *612/414–168* ⊕ *www.weskar.cl* ☉ *Closed May–Sept.* ➦ *30 rooms* ⍾ *Breakfast.*

PARQUE NACIONAL TORRES DEL PAINE, CHILE

80 km (50 miles) northwest of Puerto Natales.

A top global destination for hikers and nature spotters, Torres del Paine National Park is, quite simply, outstanding. With breathtaking mountains, glaciers, and lakes, along with wildlife like guanacos, rheas, and pumas, the Park offers plenty of picture-perfect moments. Frequently changeable Patagonian weather is the only blemish in this UNESCO World Heritage Site, which attracts more than 150,000 visitors a year.

ESSENTIALS

Visitor Information CONAF. ✉ *CONAF station in southern section of the park past Hotel Explora* ☎ *61/269–1931* ⊕ *www.conaf.cl* ✉ *Baquedano 847, Puerto Natales* ☎ *61/241–1438* ✉ *Av. Bulnes 0309, 4th fl., Punta Arenas* ☎ *61/223–8581.*

EXPLORING

Fodor's Choice
★
Parque Nacional Torres del Paine. About 12 million years ago, lava flows pushed up through the thick sedimentary crust that covered the southwestern coast of South America, cooling to form a granite mass. Glaciers then swept through the region, grinding away all but the twisted ash-gray spire, the "towers" of Paine (pronounced "pie-nay"; it's the old Tehuelche word for "blue"), which rise over the landscape to create one of the world's most beautiful natural phenomena, now the Parque Nacional Torres del Paine. The park was established in 1959. Snow and rock formations dazzle at every turn of road, and the sunset views are spectacular. The 2,420-square-km (934-square-mile) park's most astonishing attractions are its lakes of turquoise, aquamarine, and emerald waters; and the Cuernos del Paine ("Paine Horns"), the geological showpiece of the immense granite massif.

Another draw is the park's unusual wildlife; creatures like the guanaco and the ñandú abound. They are acclimated to visitors, and don't seem to be bothered by approaching cars and people with cameras. Predators like the gray fox make less frequent appearances. You may also spot the dramatic aerobatics of falcons and the graceful soaring of endangered condors. The beautiful puma, celebrated in a National Geographic video filmed here, is especially elusive, but sightings have grown more common.

The vast majority of visitors come during the summer months of January and February, which means the trails can get congested. Early spring, when wildflowers add flashes of color to the meadows, is an ideal time to visit because the crowds have not yet arrived. In summer, the winds can be incredibly fierce. During the wintertime of June to September, the days are sunnier yet colder (averaging around freezing) and shorter, but the winds all but disappear. The park is open all year,

Parque Nacional
Bernardo O'higgins

ARGENTINA
Parque Nacional
Los Glaciares

Glaciar
Dickson

Mt. Stokes

Glaciar Grey

Paine Chico
Norte

Lago
Dickson

Lago
Paine

Refugio
Las Cumbres

Refugio Las Chinas

Refugio
La Chilenita

Lago
Azul

9

CORDILLERA PAINE

Blanco
Sur

Catedral

Fortaleza
Hojo

Máscara

Paine
Grande

Cuerno
Norte

Torre Norte
Torre Central
Torre de Agostini
(Torre Sur)

Cuerno Principal

Refugio Las Torres

Refugio Guardería
Laguna Amarga

Dirt

Lago Pingo

Lago Grey

Zapata

Refugio Paine
Grande

Refugio Pudeto

Lago Sermiento

9

PARQUE
NACIONAL
TORRES DEL PAINE

Lago
Pehoe

Ferrier

Lagun
Verde

Guardería Laguna Verde

SIERRA DEL TORO

Dirt

KEY

Foot Trails

Horse Trails

Glaciar Tyndall

Donoso

Lago
Tyndall

Refugio
Lago Toro

Lago del Toro

Dirt

TO
RÍO GALLEGOS
(ARGENTINA)

Cerro Castillo

Lago
Geike

Tenerife

Refugio Juvenil
Maravilla

Lago
Porteño

Balmaceda

Punto Toro

Dirt

CHILE

Seno Ultima Esperanza

Dirt

ARG.

Río Turbio

Dirt

Parque Nacional
Torres del Paine

0   6 mi
0   6 km

9

Punto
Bories

Puerto Natales

TO PUNTA
↓ ARENAS

but some trails are not accessible in winter. Storms can hit without warning, so be prepared for sudden rain or snow. The sight of the Paine peaks in clear weather is stunning; if you have any flexibility in your itinerary, visit the park on the first clear day.

EXPLORING THE PARK

There are three entrances to the park: Laguna Amarga (all bus arrivals), Lago Sarmiento, and Laguna Azul. You are required to sign in when you arrive, and pay your entrance fee (around US$35 in high season). *Guardaparques* (park rangers) staff six stations around the reserve, and can provide a map and up-to-the-day information about the state of various trails. A regular minivan service connects Laguna Amarga with the Hostería Las Torres, 7 km (4½ miles) to the west. Alternatively, you can walk approximately two hours before reaching the starting point of the hiking circuits.

Although considerable walking is necessary to take full advantage of Parque Nacional Torres del Paine, you need not be a hard-core trekker. Many people choose to hike the **"W" route,** which takes four days, but others prefer to stay in one of the comfortable lodges and hit the trails in the morning or afternoon. **Glaciar Grey,** with its fragmented icebergs, makes a rewarding and easy hike; equally rewarding is the spectacular boat or kayak ride across the lake, past icebergs, and up to the glacier, which leaves from Hostería Lago Grey *(below)*. Another great excursion is the 900-meter (3,000-foot) ascent to the sensational views from **Mirador Las Torres,** four hours one way from Las Torres Patagonia *(below)*. Even if you're not staying at the Hostería, you can arrange a morning drop-off there, and a late-afternoon pickup, so that you can see the Mirador while still keeping your base in Puerto Natales or elsewhere in the park; alternatively, you can drive to the Hostería and park there for the day.

If you do the "W," you'll begin (or end, if you reverse the route) at Laguna Amarga and continue to Mirador Las Torres and Los Cuernos, then continue along a breathtaking path up Valle Frances to its awe-inspiring and fiendishly windy lookout (hold on to your hat!) and finally Lago Grey. The W runs for 100 kilometers (62 miles), but always follows clearly marked paths, with gradual climbs and descents at relatively low altitude. The challenge comes from the weather. Winds whip up to 90 mph, and a clear sky can suddenly darken with storm clouds, producing rain, hail, or snow in a matter of minutes. An even more ambitious route is the "Circuito," which essentially leads around the entire park and takes from a week to 10 days. Along the way some people sleep at the dozen or so humble *refugios* (shelters) evenly spaced along the trail, and many others bring their own tents.

Driving is an easy way to enjoy the park: a new road cuts the distance to Puerto Natales from a meandering 140 km (87 miles) to a more direct 80 km (50 miles). Inside the national park more than 100 km (62 miles) of roads leading to the most popular sites are safe and well maintained, though unpaved. ■TIP➜ If you stick to the road, you won't need four-wheel drive.

You can also hire horses from the Hostería Las Torres and trek to the Torres, the Cuernos, or along the shore of Lago Nordenskjold (which offers the finest views in the park, as the lake's waters reflect the chiseled massif). Alternatively, many Puerto Natales–based operators offer multiday horseback tours. Water transport is also available, with numerous tour operators offering sailboat, kayak, and inflatable Zodiac speedboat options along the Río Serrano toward the Paine massif and the southern ice field. Additionally, the Hostería Lago Grey operates the *Grey II*, a large catamaran making a three-hour return trip to Glaciar Grey four times daily as well as dinghy runs down the Pingo and Grey rivers. Another boat runs between Refugio Pudeto and Refugio Lago Pehoé.

EN ROUTE **Erratic Rock.** For anyone seriously contemplating trekking the W or the full Circuit around Torres del Paine, the Erratic Rock hostel in Puerto Natales offers a free seminar on how best to make the journey. Rustyn Mesdag, the hostel's Oregonian co-owner, is a rambunctious, opinionated guide who gives the not-to-be-missed "Three O'Clock Talk" describing all the routes, tips, and tricks you need to complete one of South America's most challenging treks. His hour-long presentation to a room full of eager hikers starts promptly at 3 pm every day of the high season, and is full of advice on camping, equipment, food, and provisions, including the latest reports on weather and trail conditions inside the park. It's a great introduction to possible trekking partners, as CONAF doesn't allow you to complete the walk on your own. The irrepressible Mr. Mesdag also publishes the ubiquitous Black Sheep newspaper in English. ⊠ *Baquedano 719, Puerto Natales* ☎ *61/414–317* ⊕ *www.erraticrock.com.*

WHERE TO STAY

$$$$
HOTEL
🏨 **Hostería Lago Grey.** The panoramic view from the restaurant and bar, past the lake dappled with floating icebergs to the glacier beyond, is worth the somewhat difficult journey here. **Pros:** great views in communal areas; excellent location; heated bathroom floors. **Cons:** thin walls; older rooms are not very attractive; hard to access without own transport. Ⓢ *Rooms from: 178000 pesos* ⊠ *Lago Grey* ☎ *612/712–100* ⊕ *www.lagogrey.com* 🛏 *60 rooms* ⦿ *Breakfast.*

$$$$
HOTEL
Fodor'sChoice
★
🏨 **Hotel Explora—Salto Chico.** There's no better location in the park than Hotel Explora: on top of a gently babbling waterfall on the southeast corner of Lago Pehoé with a shimmering lake offset by tiny rocky islets and a perfect view of Torres del Paine. **Pros:** the grande dame of Patagonian hospitality; heart-stopping views from the center of the national park; adventurous park excursions. **Cons:** a bank breaker; poor Wi-Fi and none in rooms; simple breakfast. Ⓢ *Rooms from: 1300000 pesos* ⊠ *Lago Pehoé, Parque Nacional Torres Del Paine* ☎ *2/2395–2800 in Santiago, 2/395–2580 in Lake Pehoé* ⊕ *www. explora.com* 🛏 *49 rooms* ⦿ *All-inclusive.*

$$$$
HOTEL
🏨 **Hotel Río Serrano.** The main draw of this grand hotel are the views, which take in the entire Torres del Paine mountain range, with the Serrano River and a wind-stunted forest in the foreground. **Pros:** stunning location and all-encompassing views; comfortable rooms; Wi-Fi in rooms. **Cons:** standard rooms are tight on space; pricey for facilities; not always good water temperature. Ⓢ *Rooms from: 220000 pesos* ⊠ *Lago*

Toro, Torres del Paine ☎ *61/222–4181 for reservations (Puerto Natales)*
⊕ *www.hotelrioserrano.cl* ⬑ *95 rooms* ⦿ *All-inclusive; Breakfast.*

$$$$ ⚎ **Las Torres Patagonia.** Owned by one of the earliest families to settle
HOTEL   in what eventually became the park, Las Torres has a long history, and
is the closest hotel to the main trails into the heart of the Torres del
Paine itself. **Pros:** friendly and efficient; homey atmosphere; couldn't
be closer to the mountains. **Cons:** not cheap and prices keep rising;
poor Wi-Fi; noisy bar. $ *Rooms from: 310000 pesos* ⊠ *Lago Amarga*
☎ *61/261–7450* ⊕ *www.lastorres.com* ☉ *Closed mid-Apr.–mid-Sept.*
⬑ *84 rooms* ⦿ *All-inclusive; Breakfast.*

USHUAIA AND TIERRA DEL FUEGO

Tierra del Fuego, a more or less triangular island separated from the
southernmost tip of the South American mainland by the twists and
bends of the Estrecho de Magallanes, is indeed a world unto itself. The
vast plains on its northern reaches are dotted with trees bent low by
the savage winds that frequently lash the coast. The mountains that rise
in the south are equally forbidding, traversed by huge glaciers slowly
making their way to the sea.

The first European to set foot on this island was Spanish explorer Her-
nando de Magallanes, who sailed here in 1520. The smoke that he
saw coming from the fires lighted by the native peoples prompted him
to call it Tierra del Humo (Land of Smoke). King Charles V of Spain,
disliking that name, rechristened it Tierra del Fuego, or Land of Fire.

Tierra del Fuego is split in half. The island's northernmost tip, well
within Chilean territory, is its closest point to the continent. The
only town of any size here is Porvenir. Its southern extremity, part of
Argentina, points out into the Atlantic toward the Falkland Islands.
Here you'll find Ushuaia, the main destination, on the shores of the
Canal Beagle. Farther south is Cape Horn, the southernmost point
of land before Antarctica (still a good 500 miles across the brutal
Drake Passage).

USHUAIA

*230 km (143 miles) south of Río Grande; 596 km (370 miles) south
of Río Gallegos; 914 km (567 miles) south of El Calafate; 3,580 km
(2,212 miles) south of Buenos Aires.*

At 55 degrees latitude south, Ushuaia (pronounced oo-swy-ah) is closer
to the South Pole than to Argentina's northern border with Bolivia. It
is the capital and tourism base for Tierra del Fuego, the island at the
southernmost tip of Argentina.

The city rightly (if perhaps too loudly) promotes itself as the southernmost city in the world (Puerto Williams, a few miles south on the
Chilean side of the Beagle Channel, is a small town). You can make
your way to the tourism office to get your clichéd, but oh-so-necessary,
"Southernmost City in the World" passport stamp. Ushuaia feels like
a frontier boomtown, at heart still a rugged, weather-beaten fishing
village, but exhibiting the frayed edges of a city that quadrupled in

size in the '70s and '80s and just keeps growing. Unpaved portions of Ruta 3, the last stretch of the Pan-American Highway, which connects Alaska to Tierra del Fuego, are finally being paved. The summer months (December through March) draw more than 120,000 visitors, and dozens of cruise ships. The city is trying to extend those visits with events like March's Marathon at the End of the World and by increasing the gamut of winter activities buoyed by the excellent snow conditions.

A terrific trail winds through the town up to the Martial Glacier, where a ski lift can help cut down a steep kilometer of your journey. The chaotic and contradictory urban landscape includes a handful of luxury hotels amid the concrete of public housing projects. Scores of "sled houses" (wooden shacks) sit precariously on upright piers, ready for speedy displacement to a different site. But there are also many small, picturesque homes with tiny, carefully tended gardens. Many of the newer homes are built in a Swiss-chalet style, reinforcing the idea that this is a town into which tourism has breathed new life. At the same time, the weather-worn pastel colors that dominate the town's landscape remind you that Ushuaia was once just a tiny fishing village, snuggled at the end of the Earth.

As you stand on the banks of the Canal Beagle (Beagle Channel) near Ushuaia, the spirit of the farthest corner of the world takes hold. What stands out is the light: at sundown the landscape is cast in a subdued, sensual tone; everything feels closer, softer, and more human in dimension despite the vastness of the setting. The snowcapped mountains reflect the setting sun back onto a stream rolling into the channel, as nearby peaks echo their image—on a windless day—in the still waters.

Above the city rise the last mountains of the Andean Cordillera, and just south and west of Ushuaia they finally vanish into the often-stormy sea. Snow whitens the peaks well into summer. Nature is the principal attraction here, with trekking, fishing, horseback riding, wildlife spotting, and sailing among the most rewarding activities, especially in the Parque Nacional Tierra del Fuego (Tierra del Fuego National Park).

GETTING HERE AND AROUND

Arriving by air is the preferred option. Ushuaia's Aeropuerto Internacional Malvinas Argentinas (Peninsula de Ushuaia ☏ 2901/431–232) is 5 km (3 miles) from town and is served daily by flights to and from Buenos Aires, Río Gallegos, El Calafate, Trelew, and Comodoro Rivadavia. There are also flights to Santiago via Punta Arenas in Chile. A taxi into town costs about US$8.

Arriving by road on the Ruta Nacional 3 involves Argentine and Chilean immigrations/customs, a ferry crossing, and a lot of time. Buses to and from Punta Arenas make the trip five days a week in summer, four in winter. Daily buses to Río Gallegos leave in the predawn hours, and multiple border crossings mean an all-day journey. Check prices on the 55-minute flight, which can be a much better value. There is no central bus terminal, just individual company locations.

There is no regular passenger transport (besides cruises) by sea.

Where to Eat and Stay in Ushuaia

KEY

☐ Hotels

■ Restaurants

✛ following dining and lodging reviews indicates a map-grid coordinate

CRUISE TRAVEL TO USHUAIA

As you sail into Ushuaia, the captain almost always takes you around the picturesque lighthouse at the "end of the world": a beacon for the southernmost city perched on the edge of the Canal Beagle. The port is just two blocks from the main street, leaving you in a central location once you disembark.

Before undertaking the five-minute walk into town, stop at the Tourism Office (right in front of the port), where you can gather information and take advantage of the free Wi-Fi. Most city attractions can be reached on foot, although if you're spending the night here, you may need to take a taxi to your hotel. If you're in Ushuaia only for the day, lace on some good shoes, as the city is built on a hill and requires calves of steel.

ESSENTIALS

Bus Services Tecni-Austral. ✉ Roca 157 ☎ 2901/437–005.

Visitor Information Ushuaia Tourist Office. ✉ Prefectura Naval 470
☎ 2901/437–666, 2901/432–001 ⊕ www.turismoushuaia.com.

Crab really is king in Tierra del Fuego; king crab, or centolla, is delicious and readily available.

EXPLORING
TOP ATTRACTIONS

Fodor's Choice ★ **Canal Beagle.** Several tour operators run trips along the Canal Beagle, on which you can get a startling close-up view of sea mammals and birds on **Isla de los Lobos, Isla de los Pájaros,** and near **Les Eclaireurs Lighthouse.** Catamarans, motorboats, and sailboats usually leave from the tourist pier at 9:30, 10, 3, and 3:30 (trips depend on weather; few trips go in winter). Some trips include hikes on the islands. Check with the tourist office for the latest details; you can also book through any of the local travel agencies or scope out the offers yourself by walking around the kiosks on the tourist pier. ⊠ *Ushuaia* 🛥 *From 1400 pesos.*

Estancia Harberton (*Harberton Ranch*). This property—50,000 acres of coastal marshland and wooded hillsides—was a late-19th-century gift from the Argentine government to Reverend Thomas Bridges, who authored a Yamana–English dictionary and is considered the patriarch of Tierra del Fuego. His son Lucas wrote *The Uttermost Part of the Earth,* a memoir about his frontier childhood. Today the ranch is managed by Bridges's great-grandson, Thomas Goodall, and his American wife, Natalie, a scientist and author who has cooperated with the National Geographic Society on conservation projects and operates the impressive marine mammal museum, **Museo Acatushun.** Most people visit as part of organized tours, but you'll be welcome if you arrive alone. They serve up a tasty tea in their house, the oldest building on the island. For safety reasons, exploration of the ranch can be done only on guided tours (45–90 minutes). Lodging is available, either in the Old Shepherd's House or the Old Cook's House. Additionally, you can arrange a three-course lunch at the ranch by calling two days ahead for a reservation. Most tours reach the estancia by boat, offering a rare opportunity to explore the Isla Martillo penguin colony and a sea-lion refuge on Isla de los Lobos (Seal Island) along the way. ⊠ *85 km (53 miles) east of Ushuaia* ☎ *2901/422–742* ⊕ *www.estanciaharberton.com* ▭ *$240.*

Fodor'sChoice   **Glaciar Martial.** It might pale in comparison to the glaciers in El Cala-
★   fate, but a visit to the shrinking Glaciar Martial in the mountain range just above Ushuaia offers a nice walk. Named after Frenchman Luís F. Martial, a 19th-century scientist who wandered this way aboard the warship *Romanche* to observe the passing of the planet Venus, the glacier is reached via a panoramic *aerosilla* (ski lift) or by foot. Take the Camino al Glaciar (Glacier Road) 7 km (4 miles) out of town until it ends (this route is also served by the local tour companies). Stop off at one of the teahouses en route (at the foot of the ski lift, when it is functioning) because this is a steep, strenuous 90-minute hike to the top. You can cool your heels in one of the many gurgling, icy rivulets that cascade down water-worn shale shoots or enjoy a picnic while you wait for sunset (you can walk all the way down if you want to linger until after the *aerosilla* closes). When the sun drops behind the glacier's jagged crown of peaks, brilliant rays beam over the mountain's crest, spilling a halo of gold-flecked light on the glacier, valley, and channel below. Moments like these are why this land is so magical. Note that temperatures drop dramatically after sunset, so come prepared with warm clothing. ⊠ *Glaciar Martial.*

Fodor'sChoice   **Museo Marítimo** (*Maritime Museum*). Part of the original penal colony, the
★   Presidio building was built to hold political prisoners, murderous estancia owners, street orphans, and a variety of Buenos Aires' most violent criminals. Some even claim that singer Carlos Gardel landed in one of the cells for the petty crimes of his misspent youth. In its day it held 600 inmates in 380 cells. Today it's on the grounds of Ushuaia's naval base and holds the Museo Marítimo, which starts with exhibits on the canoe-making skills of the region's indigenous peoples, tracks the navigational history of Tierra del Fuego and Cape Horn and the Antarctic, and even has a display on other great jails of the world. You can enter cell blocks and read about the grisly crimes of the prisoners who lived in them and measure yourself against their eerie life-size plaster effigies. Of the five wings spreading out from the main guard house, one has been transformed into an art gallery and another has been kept untouched—and unheated. Bone-chattering cold and bleak, bare walls powerfully evoke the desolation of a long sentence at the tip of the continent. Well-presented tours (in Spanish only) are conducted at 11:30 am, 4:30 pm, and 6:30 pm daily. ⊠ *Gobernador Paz at Yaganes* ☎ *2901/437–481* ⊕ *www.museomaritimo.com* ▭ *300 pesos (valid for 2 days).*

Tren del Fin del Mundo (*End of the World Train*). Heavily promoted but a bit of a letdown, the Tren del Fin del Mundo purports to take you inside the Parque Nacional Tierra del Fuego, 12 km (8 miles) away from town, but you have to drive to get there, and it leaves visitors a long way short of the most spectacular scenery in the national park. The touristy 40-minute train ride's gimmick is a simulation of the trip El Presidio prisoners were forced to take into the forest to chop wood; but unlike them, you'll also get a good presentation of Ushuaia's history (in Spanish and English). The train departs daily at 9:30, noon, and 3 (only 10 and 3 in low season). One common way to do the trip is to hire a remis that will drop you at the station for a one-way train ride and pick you up at the other end, then drive you around the Parque Nacional for two or three hours of sightseeing (which is far more scenic than the train ride itself). ⊠ *Ruta 3, Km 3042* ☎ *2901/431–600* ⊕ *www.trendelfindelmundo.com.ar* ⊠ *840 pesos, one-way or round-trip.*

WORTH NOTING

Antigua Casa Beban (*Old Beban House*). One of Ushuaia's original houses, the Antigua Casa Beban long served as the city's social center. Built between 1911 and 1913 by Fortunato Beban, it's said he ordered the house through a Swiss catalog. In the 1980s the Beban family donated the house to the city to avoid demolition. It was moved to its current location along the coast and restored, and is now a cultural center with art exhibits. ⊠ *Maipú at Pluschow* ☎ *2901/431–386* ⊠ *Free* ⊘ *Closed weekends.*

Canal Fun. This unconventional tour goes to Monte Olivia, the tallest mountain along the Canal Beagle, rising 1,358 meters (4,455 feet) above sea level. You also pass the Five Brothers Mountains and go through the Garibaldi Pass, which begins at the Rancho Hambre, climbs into the mountain range, and ends with a spectacular view of Lago Escondido. From here you continue on to Lago Fagnano through the countryside past sawmills and lumber yards. To do this tour in a four-wheel-drive truck with an excellent bilingual guide, contact Canal Fun; you'll drive *through* Lago Fagnano (about 3 feet of water at this point) to a secluded cabin on the shore and have a delicious asado, complete with wine and dessert. In winter they can also organize tailor-made dogsledding and cross-country-skiing trips. ⊠ *Roca 136* ☎ *2901/435–777* ⊕ *www.canalfun.com.*

Lago Escondido (*Hidden Lake*). One good excursion in the area is to Lago Escondido and Lago Fagnano (Fagnano Lake). The Pan-American Highway out of Ushuaia goes through deciduous beech forests and past beavers' dams, peat bogs, and glaciers. The lakes have campsites and fishing and are good spots for a picnic or a hike. This can be done on your own or as a seven-hour trip, including lunch, booked through the local travel agencies (around 1,500 pesos for standard tour or 2,200 pesos with lunch and 4X4 transportation). ⊠ *Ushuaia.*

Museo del Fin del Mundo (*End of the World Museum*). Here you can see a large taxidermied condor and other native birds, indigenous artifacts, maritime instruments, a reconstruction of an old Patagonian general store, and such seafaring-related objects as an impressive mermaid figurehead taken from the bowsprit of a galleon. There are also photographs and histories of El Presidio's original inmates, such as Simon Radowitzky, a Russian immigrant anarchist who received a life sentence for killing an Argentine police colonel. The museum is split across two buildings—the first, and original, is in the 1905 residence of a Fuegonian governor at Maipú 173. The newer museum building is farther

8

down the road at Maipú 465, where you can see extended exhibitions of the same style. ✉ *Maipú 173, at Rivadavía* ☎ *2901/421–863* 💲 *240 pesos* ⊗ *Closed Mon. in winter.*

OFF THE
BEATEN
PATH

Tres Marias Excursions. Although there are a number of boat tours through the Canal Beagle or around the bays to Tierra del Fuego National Park, one offers an experience that will put you in the shoes of the earliest explorers to visit the far south. The operators of Tres Marias Excursions offer a half-day sailing trip to Island H, an outcrop in the middle of the channel, with cormorant colonies, families of snow geese, seaweed stands, and a weather station that records the howling winds blowing in from the misnamed Pacific Ocean. The guides are skillful sailors and storytellers. On a gusty day you'll marvel at the hardiness of the Yamana people, who survived frigid winters wearing little or no clothing by setting fires behind natural and man-made windbreaks. You'll find the same plant and moss species that grow in the high Andes; they thrive here at sea level because the conditions kill off less hardy, temperate species. On the way back you visit a sea lion colony, but won't soon forget arriving in Ushuaia under full sail as the late sun hits the mountains. It's only a little more expensive, and a lot more adventurous, than the motorized alternatives trawling for business at the dock. Tours only October to March. ✉ *Port* ☎ *2901/582–060* ⊕ *www.tresmariasweb.com* 💲 *1500 pesos.*

WHERE TO EAT

$$$$
ARGENTINE

✕ **Bodegón Fueguino.** A mustard-yellow pioneer house that lights up the main street, this traditional eatery is driven by its ebullient owner Sergio Otero, a constant presence bustling around the bench seating, making suggestions, and revving up his staff. Sample the *picada* plate (king crab rolls, Roma-style calamari, marinated rabbit) over an artisanal Beagle Beer—the dark version is the perfect balm on a cold windy day. **Known for:** large and hearty portions; famous Patagonian lamb; no-reservations but a quick wait. 💲 *Average main: 440 pesos* ✉ *San Martín 859* ☎ *2901/431–972* ⊕ *www.tierradehumos.com* ⊗ *Closed Mon.* ✛ *B2.*

$$$$
SEAFOOD
Fodor's Choice
★

✕ **Chez Manu.** *Herbes de provence* in the greeting room, a tank of lively king crabs in the dining room: French chef Manu Herbin gives local seafood a French touch and creates some of Ushuaia's most memorable meals with views to match. The first-rate wine list includes Patagonian selections, while all dishes are created entirely with ingredients from Tierra del Fuego. **Known for:** amazing views of Beagle Channel; excellent king crab gratin and other fresh seafood; fantastic wine list. 💲 *Average main: 760 pesos* ✉ *Camino Luís Martial 2135* ☎ *2901/432–253* ⊕ *www.chezmanu.com* ⊗ *Closed Mon. No lunch Tues. Closed 2 wks in May and June* ✛ *A1.*

$$$$
MODERN
ARGENTINE

✕ **Kalma Resto.** Beautiful dishes and a contemporary twist on traditional Patagonian flavors meet at this funky little restaurant at the end of the world. Owner and chef Jorge says that recipes are inspired by his grandma's classics, but there is also a hint of Peruvian and Mediterranean with signature dishes like octopus ceviche, centolla, and Beagle Channel mussels, and paella. **Known for:** creative cuisine with wines to match; fantastic tasting menu; sophisticated service. 💲 *Average main:*

460 pesos ⊠ Gobernador Valdez 293 ☎ 2901/425–786 ⊕ www.kal-maresto.com.ar ⊗ Closed Sun. and May and June ✛ D2.

$$$$ ✕**Kaupé.** The white picket fence, manicured lawns, and planter boxes
ARGENTINE play up the fact that this out-of-the-way restaurant used to be a family
home. Inside, the star ingredient is *centolla* (king crab), best presented
as chowder with a hint of mustard. **Known for:** seafood served with
elegance and sophistication; sunset views over the city; hard-to-find
location. ⑤ *Average main: 580 pesos ⊠ Roca 470 ☎ 2901/422–704
⊕ www.kaupe.com.ar ⊗ Closed Sun. ✛ C1.*

$$$$ ✕**La Cabaña Casa de Té.** This impeccably maintained riverside cottage
ARGENTINE is nestled in a verdant stand of lenga trees and overlooks the Beagle
Channel and provides a warm, cozy spot for delicious loose leaf tea or
comforting snacks before or after a hike to the Martial Glacier (conveniently located at the end of the Martial road that leads up from
Ushuaia). An afternoon tea with all the trimmings will satiate any peck-
ish trekker, fondues are served at lunchtime, and at 8 pm in summer
the menu shifts to pricier dinner fare with dishes like salmon in wine
sauce (mainly for the guests at the adjoining cabin accommodation).
Known for: countryside setting and views; traditional afternoon tea
menu; lunchtime fondue. ⑤ *Average main: 280 pesos ⊠ Camino Luís
Martial 3560 ☎ 2901/424–779 ⊕ www.lacabania.com.ar ⊗ Closed Apr.
and May ✛ A1.*

$$$$ ✕**Ramos Generales.** Entering this café on the waterfront puts you in
ARGENTINE mind of a general store from the earliest frontier years of Ushuaia,
which is why locals call it the *viejo almacen* (old grocery store). Burgers and picada platters are uninspiring; choose fresh-baked bread or
scrumptious lemon croissants instead, and try the *submarino*—a mug
of hot milk in which you plunge a bar of dark chocolate (goes well with
a panini). **Known for:** old-school frontier vibe; sweet treats like lemon
croissants; good hot chocolate. ⑤ *Average main: 360 pesos ⊠ Maipú
749 ☎ 2901/424–317 ⊗ Closed 3 wks in May ✛ C2.*

$$$$ ✕**Tia Elvira.** On the street that runs right along the Beagle Channel,
ARGENTINE Tia Elvira is a good place to sample the local catch. Garlicky shellfish
appetizers and centolla are delicious; even more memorable is the tender
merluza negra (black sea bass). **Known for:** good local seafood; attentive service; kitschy decor. ⑤ *Average main: 540 pesos ⊠ Maipú 349
☎ 2901/424–725 ⊗ Closed Sun. ✛ C2.*

$$$$ ✕**Volver.** A giant king crab sign beckons you into this red-tin-walled
ARGENTINE restaurant, where the maritime bric-a-brac hanging from the ceiling
can be a little distracting. The name means "return" and it succeeds
in getting repeat visits on the strength of its seafood; the culinary
highlight is the centolla, which comes served with a choice of five different sauces. **Known for:** great place to try signature dish of Tierra
del Fuego, centolla (king crab); waterfront views; cozy maritime atmosphere. ⑤ *Average main: 560 pesos ⊠ Maipú 37 ☎ 2901/423–977
⊗ No lunch Sun. Closed Mon. ✛ D2.*

8

Can't beat the view in Ushuaia, the world's southernmost city.

WHERE TO STAY

Choosing a place to stay depends in part on whether you want to spend the night in town, several miles west toward the national park, or uphill in the hotels above town. The hotels with the best views all require a taxi ride or the various complimentary shuttle services to reach Ushuaia.

$$$$
RESORT
Arakur. You can see this luxury hotel towering in the distance in front of Monte Olivia; it's one of the most extensive spa-and-resort complexes in Ushuaia and overlooks the entire bay and town from its own nature reserve out of town on the road to Cerro Castor. **Pros:** modern design with luxury fittings; sweeping views; nature reserve at doorstep. **Cons:** expensive; sterile atmosphere; far from town. $ *Rooms from: US$320* ⊠ *Cerro Alarken, Access via Av. Héroes de Malvinas 2617* ☎ *2901/442–900* ⊕ *www.arakur.com* ⇄ *131 rooms* ⫢⊙⫢ *Breakfast* ✛ *D1.*

$$$
B&B/INN
Cumbres de Martial. This charming complex of cabins and bungalows, painted a deep berry purple, is high above Ushuaia in the woods at the base of the ski lift to the Martial Glacier; each spacious room has an extremely comfortable bed and a small wooden deck with terrific views down to the Beagle Channel. **Pros:** easy access to the glacier and nature trails; romantic cabins; lovely spa. **Cons:** you need to cab it to and from town; few restaurant options or services within walking distance; slow service. $ *Rooms from: US$205* ⊠ *Camino Luís Martial 3560* ☎ *2901/424–779* ⊕ *www.cumbresdelmartial.com.ar* ⊙ *Closed Apr. and May* ⇄ *6 rooms, 4 cabins* ⫢⊙⫢ *Breakfast* ✛ *A1.*

$
B&B/INN
Hostería Patagonia Jarké. Jarké means "spark" in a local native language, and this B&B is a bright, electric addition to Ushuaia; the three-story lodge cantilevers down a hillside on a dead-end street in the heart

of town. **Pros:** warm, welcoming rooms with decent views; good price for Patagonia; friendly staff. **Cons:** steep walk home; can't compete with the views from the larger hotels farther uphill; noise travels through walls. *$ Rooms from: US$115 ✉ Gobernador Paz 1305 ☎ 11/6385–4226 ⊕ www.patagoniajarke.com.ar ⤴ 15 rooms ⦿ Breakfast ⊕ A2.*

$$
HOTEL
☷ **Hotel Fueguino.** In downtown Ushuaia, the Fueguino boasts all the modern amenities: a conference center; a gym; a spa; shuttle service; outgoing, professional, multilingual staff; and one of the better Wi-Fi signals in town. **Pros:** all the modern conveniences; central location; friendly staff. **Cons:** some street noise; small rooms; weak Wi-Fi in rooms. *$ Rooms from: US$175 ✉ Gobernador Deloqui 1282 ☎ 2901/424–894 ⊕ www.fueguinohotel.com.ar ⤴ 53 rooms ⦿ Breakfast ⊕ B2.*

$$$
HOTEL
☷ **Hotel Los Yámanas.** This cozy hotel 4 km (3 miles) from the center of town is named after the local tribe and offers a rustic mountain aesthetic. **Pros:** some stunning views from rooms; peaceful location; sauna is very nice. **Cons:** far from town; questionable taste in decoration; Wi-Fi not strong in rooms. *$ Rooms from: US$230 ✉ Costa de los Yámanas 2850, Km 4 ☎ 2901/446–809 ⊕ www.hotelyamanas.com.ar ⊙ Closed May ⤴ 41 rooms ⦿ Breakfast ⊕ A3.*

$$
HOTEL
☷ **Hotel y Resort Las Hayas.** In the wooded foothills of the Andes, Las Hayas is slightly dated in its facilities, but the views overlooking the town and channel below still make it worth the trip. **Pros:** great views; delicious restaurant; relaxing spa. **Cons:** decor doesn't suit everyone; facilities dated; rooms could use some revamping. *$ Rooms from: US$170 ✉ Camino Luís Martial 1650, Km 3 ☎ 2901/442–000 ⊕ www.lashayashotel.com ⤴ 88 rooms ⦿ Breakfast ⊕ A1.*

$$
B&B/INN
☷ **La Tierra de Leyendas.** This adorable B&B is a honeymooners' delight, thanks to the multiple personal touches, from home-cooked cuisine to family photos on the walls. **Pros:** tasty food in restaurant; enthusiastic, personal, and attentive service; all seven rooms have views. **Cons:** the street name is no joke—it's insanely windy; immediate surroundings are a bit barren; closed during winter. *$ Rooms from: US$200 ✉ Tierra de Vientos 2448 ☎ 2901/446–565 ⊕ www.tierradeleyendas.com.ar ⊙ Closed mid-Apr.–mid-July ⤴ 7 rooms ⦿ Breakfast ⊕ A3.*

$$
HOTEL
FAMILY
☷ **Los Acebos.** From the owners of Las Hayas (just around the corner on the winding mountain road), Los Acebos is a modern hotel on a forested ridge with a commanding view over the Beagle Channel; spacious and superclean rooms feature the same iconoclastic decor as Las Hayas, including the trademark fabric-padded walls, only this time with a '60s-style color scheme. **Pros:** spacious rooms; expansive views of the channel; friendly staff. **Cons:** out of town; no spa; simple breakfast. *$ Rooms from: US$175 ✉ Luis F. Martial 1911 ☎ 2901/442–200 ⊕ www.losacebos.com.ar ⤴ 60 rooms ⊕ A1.*

$$$$
HOTEL
Fodor'sChoice
★
☷ **Los Cauquenes Resort and Spa.** Right on the shore of the Beagle Channel about 8 km (5 miles) west of town, this resort is in a private community with privileged beach access and a nature hike that starts right outside your room. **Pros:** luxurious spa offers comprehensive range of treatments and massages; free transfer into city; private boat excursions offered. **Cons:** rooms can get uncomfortably hot; thin walls can make

8

for noisy nights; outside of town. ⑤ *Rooms from: US$320* ✉ *De la Ermita 3462, Barrio Bahía Cauquén* ☎ *2901/441–300* ⊕ *www.loscauquenes.com* 🗩 *54 rooms* ⦿| *Breakfast* ✛ *A3.*

NIGHTLIFE

Ushuaia has lively nightlife in summer, with its casino, discos, and intimate cafés all close to each other.

Bar Ideal. This cozy and historic bar and café opens from 9 am onward. ✉ *San Martín 393, at Roca* ☎ *2901/437–860* ⊕ *www.elbarideal.com.*

El Náutico. The biggest and most popular pub in town, El Náutico attracts a young crowd with disco and techno music. ✉ *Belgrano 21* ⊙ *Closed Sun.–Thurs.*

Tante Sara. This popular café-bar in the heart of town has a casual, old-world feel. Locals kick back with a book or a beer; they pour the local artisanal brews, too. During the day it's one of the few eateries to defy the 3–6 pm siesta and stays open late. Their other branch, at San Martín 175, closes at 8:30 pm. ✉ *San Martín 701* ☎ *2901/423–912, 2901/433–710* ⊕ *www.tantesara.com.*

SHOPPING

Boutique del Libro–Antartida y Patagonia. Part of a bookstore chain, this branch specializes in Patagonian and polar exploration. Along with dozens of maps and picture books, postcards, and posters, it offers adventure classics detailing every Southern expedition from Darwin's Voyage of the Beagle to Ernest Shackleton's incredible journeys of Antarctic survival. While books in English are hard to come by in the rest of Argentina, here you're spoiled for choice, and the Antarctica trip logbooks on sale at the counter might inspire you to extend your travel farther south. ✉ *San Martín 1120* ☎ *2901/4245–750* ⊙ *Closed Sun.*

Laguna Negra. If you can't get to South America's chocolate capital Bariloche, pop into this chocolate boutique for planks of homemade chocolate and a selection of artisanal beers, chutneys, and spices. In the small coffee shop at the back, drop a glorious slab of dark chocolate into a mug of piping hot milk—one of the best *submarinos* in town. ✉ *San Martín 513* ☎ *2901/431–144* ⊕ *www.lagunanegra.com.ar.*

PARQUE NACIONAL TIERRA DEL FUEGO

21 km (13 miles) west of Ushuaia.

This park is one of the main reasons that travelers make a trip to the tip of Argentina. Its deep forests, glistening lakes, and wind-whipped trees will not disappoint. An easy day trip from Ushuaia, this 60,000-hectare park offers varied outdoor experiences and many wildlife-spotting opportunities.

EXPLORING

Fodor'sChoice ★ **Parque Nacional Tierra del Fuego.** The pristine park offers a chance to wander through peat bogs, stumble upon hidden lakes, trek through native *canelo, lenga,* and wild cherry forests, and experience the wonders of wind-whipped Tierra del Fuego's rich flora and fauna. Everywhere,

The banner tree, or *Tuta complementaria*, is whipped by Patagonian winds from the time it's a mere shoot; the result has a bannerlike effect, hence the name.

lichens line the trunks of the ubiquitous lenga trees, and "chinese lantern" parasites hang from the branches.

Another thing you'll see everywhere are the results of government folly, in the form of *castoreros* (beaver dams) and lodges. Fifty beaver couples were first brought here from Canada in 1948 so that they would breed and create a fur industry. In the years since, without any predators, the beaver population has exploded to plague proportions (more than 100,000) and now represents a major threat to the forests, as the dams flood the roots of the trees; you can see their effects on parched dead trees on the lake's edge. Believe it or not, the government used to pay hunters a bounty for each beaver they killed (they had to show a tail and head as proof). To make matters worse, the government, after creating the beaver problem, introduced weasels to kill the beavers, but the weasels killed birds instead; they then introduced foxes to kill the beavers and weasels, but they also killed the birds. With eradication efforts failing, some tour operators have accepted them as a permanent presence and now offer beaver-viewing trips.

Visits to the park, which is tucked up against the Chilean border, are commonly arranged through tour companies. Trips range from bus tours to horseback riding to more adventurous excursions, such as canoe trips across Lapataia Bay. Entrance to the park is about 420 pesos.

Several private bus companies travel through the park making numerous stops; you can get off the bus, explore the park, and then wait for the next bus to come by or trek to the next stop (the service operates only in summer; check providers with the tourism office). Another option is to drive to the park on R3 (take it until it ends and you see the famous sign indicating the end of the Pan-American Highway, which starts 17,848 km [11,065 miles] away in Alaska, and ends here). If you don't have a car, you can also hire a private *remis* (taxi) to spend a few hours driving through the park, including the Pan-American terminus, and perhaps combining the excursion with the Tren del Fin del Mundo. Trail and camping information is available at the park-entrance ranger station or at the Ushuaia tourist office. At the park entrance is a gleaming restaurant and teahouse set amid the hills, Patagonia Mia (⊕ *www.patagoniamia.com*); it's a great place to stop for tea or coffee, or a full meal of roast lamb or Fuegian seafood. A nice excursion in the park is by boat from lovely Bahía Ensenada to **Isla Redonda,** a wildlife refuge where you can follow a footpath to the western side and see a wonderful view of the Canal Beagle. This is included on some of the day tours; it's harder to arrange on your own, but you can contact the tourist office to try. While on Isla Redonda you can send a postcard and get your passport stamped at the world's southernmost post office. You can also see the Ensenada bay and island (from afar) from a point on the shore that is reachable by car.

Other highlights of the park include the spectacular mountain-ringed lake, **Lago Roca,** as well as **Laguna Verde,** a lagoon whose green color comes from algae at its bottom. Much of the park is closed from roughly June through September, when the descent to Bahía Ensenada is blocked by up to 6 feet of snow. Even in May and October, chains for your car are a good idea. No hotels are within the park—the only one burned down in the 1980s, and you can see its carcass as you drive by—but there are three simple camping areas around Lago Roca. Tours to the park are run by **All Patagonia** (⊕ *www.allpatagonia.com*). ⊕ *www. parquesnacionales.gob.ar* ⊠ *400 pesos.*

SPORTS AND THE OUTDOORS
FISHING
The rivers of Tierra del Fuego are home to trophy-size freshwater trout—including browns, rainbows, and brooks. Both fly- and spin-casting are available. The fishing season runs November through April; license fees range from 1,000 pesos per week to 1,200 pesos per season for nonresidents. Fishing expeditions are organized by the various local companies.

Asociación de Caza y Pesca. Founded in 1959, the Asociación de Caza y Pesca is the principal hunting and fishing organization in the city. ⊠ *Av. Maipú 822* ☎ *2901/423–168* ⊕ *www.cazaypescaushuaia.org.*

Rumbo Sur. The city's oldest travel agency can assist in setting up fishing trips. ⊠ *Av. San Martín 350* ☎ *2901/421–139* ⊕ *www.rumbosur.com.ar.*

Wind Fly. In summer this outfitter is dedicated exclusively to fishing, and offers classes and arranges trips. ⊠ *Av. 25 de Mayo 155, Ushuaia* ☎ *2901/431–713* ⊕ *www.windflyushuaia.com.ar.*

MOUNTAIN BIKING

A mountain bike is an excellent mode of transport in Ushuaia, giving you the freedom to roam without the rental-car price tag. Good mountain bikes normally cost about US$10 for a half day or US$15 for a full day. Guided tours are about the same price.

All Patagonia. Guided bicycle tours (including rides through the national park) are organized by All Patagonia. ⊠ *Juana Fadul 58, Ushuaia* ☎ *2901/433–622* ⊕ *www.allpatagonia.com.*

Rumbo Sur. One of the city's biggest travel agencies, Rumbo Sur can arrange cycling trips. ⊠ *San Martín 350, Ushuaia* ☎ *2901/421–139* ⊕ *www.rumbosur.com.ar.*

Ushuaia Extreme. You can rent bikes or do a tour with Ushuaia Extreme. ⊠ *San Martín 830, Ushuaia* ☎ *2901/434–373* ⊕ *www.ushuaiaextremo. com.*

SCENIC FLIGHTS

The gorgeous scenery and island topography of the area is readily appreciated on a Cessna tour.

Aeroclub Ushuaia. Half-hour- and hour-long trips are available through Aeroclub Ushuaia. The half-hour flight ($95 per passenger with a group; $125 for single passengers) with a local pilot takes you over Ushuaia, Tierra del Fuego National Park, and the Beagle Channel with views of area glaciers, waterfalls, and snowcapped islands south to Cape Horn. A 60-minute flight ($155 per passenger with a group; $205 for single passengers) crosses the Andes to Escondida and Fagnano lakes. ⊠ *Antiguo Aeropuerto, Luis Pedro Fique 151, Ushuaia* ☎ *2901/421–717* ⊕ *www.aeroclubushuaia.org.ar.*

Heli-Ushuaia. All sorts of helicopter trips are available from Heli-Ushuaia, beginning with a seven-minute spin at $99 per person. There are plenty of longer trips and excursions if you have money to burn. ⊠ *Luis Pedro Fique 119, Ushuaia* ☎ *2901/444–444* ⊕ *www.heliushuaia.com. ar.*

SKIING

Canopy Ushuaia. Located at the Martial Glaciar, Canopy Ushuaia offers skiing in winter and canopy lines in summer. ⊠ *Cerro Martial, Luis Fernando Martial 3551, Ushuaia* ☎ *2901/1550–3767* ⊕ *www.canopyushuaia.com.ar.*

Cerro Castor. With off-piste and alpine skiing and almost guaranteed snow, this has become a popular ski haunt for European Olympic teams looking for summer snow. Pistes range from beginners to black-diamond runs with more than 31 trails and four high-speed lifts. You can rent skis and snowboards and take ski lessons at this resort 26 km (17 miles) northeast of Ushuaia on R3. Day passes are around $50 USD in high season, and there are restaurants, bars, and a ski lodge on-site. The resort is open June to October, depending on snow. ⊠ *Ruta 3, Km 26, Ushuaia* ☎ *2901/499–301* ⊕ *www.cerrocastor.com.*

8

Club Andino. Ushuaia is the cross-country skiing (*esqui de fondo* in Spanish) center of South America, thanks to enthusiastic Club Andino members who took to the sport in the 1980s and made the forested hills of a high valley about 20 minutes from town a favorite destination for skiers. It's a magnet for international ski teams who come from Europe to train in the northern summer. ⊠ *Alem 2873, Ushuaia* ☎ *2901/440–732* ⊕ *www.clubandinoushuaia.com.ar.*

Haruwen. Here, you can snowmobile in the winter, and ride a buggie in the summer. Countryside lamb cookouts are offered all year-round. ⊕ *www.haruwen.com.ar.*

TRAVEL SMART
ARGENTINA

GETTING HERE AND AROUND

TRAVEL TIMES FROM BUENOS AIRES		
TO	BY AIR	BY BUS
Montevideo, Uruguay	45 minutes	8 hours
Atlantic Coast	1 hour	5–6 hours
Córdoba	1¼ hours	9–11 hours
Mendoza	1¾ hours	12–14 hours
Puerto Iguazú	1¾ hours	17–20 hours
Salta	2¼ hours	18–20 hours
Bariloche	2¼ hours	21–23 hours
El Calafate	3¼ hours	40 hours

Argentina extends approximately 3,650 km (2,268 miles) from tip to tail, and many of its attractions are hundreds of miles apart. So you can save a lot in terms of both time and money by carefully plotting your course. Buenos Aires lies about two-thirds of the way up Argentina's eastern side, on the banks of the Río de la Plata. It's the country's capital and its main transportation hub.

Three of the country's main draws are about 1,000 km (621 miles) from Buenos Aires as the crow flies: Puerto Iguazú, the base for exploring Iguazú Falls, in northeastern Misiones Province; Salta, the gateway to the Andean Northwest; and Mendoza, in the Wine Region, near the Chilean border. Slightly farther, this time southwest of Buenos Aires, is Bariloche, the hub for the Lake District of northern Patagonia. El Calafate, the hub for southern Patagonia and the launch pad for the Glaciar Perito Moreno, is a whopping 2,068 km (1,285 miles) southwest of Buenos Aires.

Flying within the country makes sense given these huge distances. That said, domestic flights are expensive, and flight delays are fairly regular occurrences.

Many visitors opt to take the more reliable overnight sleeper buses for trips of up to 1,000 km (621 miles). A well-developed network of long-distance buses connects Buenos Aires with cities all over Argentina; buses also operate between many urban centers without passing through the capital.

❚ AIR TRAVEL

TO ARGENTINA

There are direct daily flights between Buenos Aires and several North American cities, with New York and Miami being primary departure points. Many airlines also serve Buenos Aires via Santiago de Chile, Lima, or São Paulo in Brazil, which adds only a little to your trip time.

Aerolíneas Argentinas, the flagship airline, is part of SkyTeam and operates direct flights between Buenos Aires and JFK once a day and Miami twice a day. Aerolíneas' reputation for chronic delays has greatly improved, although strikes do still ground planes.

Chilean airline LATAM is Aerolíneas' biggest local competition. LATAM flies direct from Buenos Aires to Miami, and via Santiago de Chile, São Paulo, or Lima to JFK, Dallas, Washington, D.C., and Los Angeles, often in partnership with Brazilian airline TAM. LATAM also allows you to bypass Buenos Aires by flying into Mendoza and Córdoba from JFK and Miami, both via Santiago de Chile, and into Bariloche via São Paulo.

U.S. carriers serve Buenos Aires, too. There are direct flights from Atlanta on Delta and from Houston and Newark on United; American flies nonstop from JFK, Miami, and Dallas.

Flying times to Buenos Aires are 11–12 hours from New York, 10½ hours from Atlanta, Dallas, or Houston, and 9 hours from Miami.

WITHIN ARGENTINA

Most domestic flights operate from Buenos Aires, so to fly from the extreme south of the country to the extreme north, you often have to change planes here.

Aerolíneas Argentinas and its partner Austral link Buenos Aires to more Argentinean cities than any other airline, with flights running to Puerto Iguazú, Salta, Mendoza, Córdoba, Bariloche, Ushuaia, and El Calafate at least once a day. Austral also provides direct service between Puerto Iguazú and Salta and Córdoba, bypassing Buenos Aires; LATAM also flies to these cities. Small, Salta-based Andes Líneas Aéreas operates flights between Buenos Aires, Bariloche, Jujuy, Mendoza, Salta, and Puerto Madryn. A new local low-cost airline, FlyBondi, has started operating between El Palomar, a western suburb of Buenos Aires, and Puerto Iguazú, Córdoba, Mendoza, Salta, and Bariloche. It also connects Mendoza and Córdoba direct to Bariloche and Puerto Iguazú, among other routes that bypass Buenos Aires.

Airline Contacts Aerolíneas Argentinas. ⊕ *www.aerolineas.com.ar.* **American Airlines.** ⊕ *www.aa.com.* **Andes Líneas Aéreas.** ⊕ *www.andesonline.com.* **Delta Airlines.** ⊕ *www.delta.com.* **FlyBondi.** ⊕ *www.flybondi. com.* **LATAM.** ⊕ *www.latam.com.* **United Airlines.** ⊕ *www.united.com.*

Airline Security Issues Transportation Security Administration. ⊕ *www.tsa.gov.*

AIRPORTS

Airports in Argentina are mostly small, well maintained, and easy to get around. Security at most isn't as stringent as it is in the States—computers stay in cases, shoes stay on your feet, and there are no random searches.

BUENOS AIRES

Buenos Aires' Aeropuerto Internacional de Ezeiza Ministro Pistarini (EZE)—known as Ezeiza—is 35 km (22 miles) southwest of the city center. Ezeiza is the base for international flights operated by Aerolíneas Argentinas and its partner Austral; these and LATAM run a limited number of domestic flights to Puerto Iguazú, El Calafate, Bariloche, Trelew, Córdoba, Ushuaia, and Rosario from here as well, although most domestic services operate from Aeroparque Jorge Newbery. All international flights arrive at newly renovated Terminal A, and most international services also depart from here. The exceptions are international departures on Aerolíneas Argentinas and SkyTeam-member airlines (including Delta), which go from the newest terminal, C. The small number of domestic Aerolíneas and LATAM flights in and out of Ezeiza also operate from Terminal C. At this writing, Terminal B had recently been demolished ahead of a large-scale overhaul of the entire airport, although no dates have been announced for construction work.

A covered walkway connects terminals A and C. Both have a few small snack bars, a small range of shops—including a pharmacy—a public phone center with Internet services, and a tourist information booth. The ATM, 24-hour luggage storage, and car-rental agencies are in Terminal A. There is free public Wi-Fi throughout the airport.

■ TIP➔ Avoid changing money in the baggage claim area. The best exchange rates are at the small Banco de la Nación in the Terminal A arrivals area; it's open round the clock but expect a 15-minute wait.

Most domestic flights and some flights to or via Chile and Brazil operate out of Aeroparque Jorge Newbery (AEP). It's next to the Río de la Plata in northeast Palermo, about 8 km (5 miles) north of the city center. Low-cost airline FlyBondi has recently started operating out of El Palomar, a tiny airport in a western suburb of Buenos Aires about 25 km (15 miles) from downtown. Aeroparque, El Palomar, and Ezeiza are all run by the private company Aeropuertos Argentinos 2000.

ELSEWHERE IN ARGENTINA

Several other airports in Argentina are technically international, but only because they have a few flights to neighboring countries; most flights are domestic.

Aeropuerto Internacional de Puerto Iguazú (IGR) is close to Iguazú Falls; it's 20 km (12 miles) from Puerto Iguazú and 10 km (6 miles) from the park entrance. There's another nearby airport just over the border in Brazil, Foz do Iguaçu/Cataratas International Airport (IGU), 10 km (6 miles) from the Brazil–Argentina border. The northwest is served by Salta's Aeropuerto Internacional Martín Miguel de Güemes (SLA), 7 km (5 miles) west of the city of Salta.

The airport for the Wine Region and western Argentina is Aeropuerto Internacional de Mendoza Francisco Gabrieli (MDZ), usually known as El Plumerillo. It's 10 km (6 miles) north of Mendoza. Northern Patagonia's hub is Bariloche, 13 km (8 miles) west of which is the Aeropuerto Internacional San Carlos de Bariloche Teniente Luis Candelaria (BRC), known as the Aeropuerto de Bariloche. The gateway to southern Patagonia is Aeropuerto Internacional de El Calafate Comandante Armando Tola (ECA), 18 km (11 miles) east of El Calafate itself.

Airport Information Aeropuerto El Palomar. ☏ 11/4758–7963 ⊕ www.aa2000. com.ar. **Aeropuerto Internacional de Ezeiza Ministro Pistarini.** ☏ 11/5480–6111 ⊕ www. aa2000.com.ar. **Aeroparque Jorge Newbery.** ☏ 11/5480–6111 ⊕ www.aa2000.com.ar.

▌ BOAT TRAVEL

Ferries run frequently across the Río de la Plata between Buenos Aires and the Uruguayan cities of Colonia and Montevideo. Buquebus operates several high-speed ferries to and from Colonia per day, which take 1¼ hours, and one direct ferry to Montevideo, which takes 2¼ hours. Round-trip tickets cost 1,100 pesos to Colonia and 2,100 pesos to Montevideo, but there are substantial off-peak and midweek discounts. Seacat or Colonia Express catamarans, which take an hour or less to Colonia and connect with a two-hour bus service to Montevideo, offer the best value. Full-price round-trip tickets cost around 1,250 and 1,500 pesos, respectively, but they often drop as low as 700 and 850 pesos if you book online (midweek same-day return tickets are sometimes even less).

All three companies also sell packages that include bus tickets to other destinations in Uruguay, including Carmelo, La Paloma, La Pedrera, and Punta del Este direct from Colonia's ferry terminal. You can order tickets by phone or online. All three companies leave from Puerto Madero: Buquebus and Seacat leave from a terminal at the northern end and Colonia Express from one at the southern end.

Contacts Buquebus. ⊠ Av. Antártida Argentina 821, Puerto Madero ☏ 11/4316–6550 ⊕ www.buquebus.com. **Colonia Express.** ⊠ Av. Elvira Rawson de Dellepiane 155, Puerto Madero ☏ 11/4317–4100 ⊕ www.coloniaexpress.com. **Seacat.** ⊠ Av. Antártida Argentina 821, Puerto Madero ☏ 11/4314–5100 ⊕ www. seacatcolonia.com.

▌ BUS TRAVEL

Frequent, comfortable, and dependable long-distance buses connect Buenos Aires with cities all over Argentina and with neighboring countries. Falling airfares and rising bus prices mean that more locals and visitors now opt to fly to far-flung destinations rather than take overnight sleeper buses. All the same, tickets on basic bus services can still be substantially cheaper than last-minute air travel and buses are less prone to delays.

The Plataforma 10 website lets you assess routes, compare prices, and buy tickets for long-distance bus rides throughout Argentina, as well as ones to top international destinations like Montevideo. Most major bus companies have their own online timetables; some allow you to purchase tickets online or by phone. Websites also list alternative *puntos de venta* (sales offices)—in many cases you can buy tickets from booths in shopping malls or subway stations, though outside of peak season you can usually buy them at the terminal right up until departure time. Many now accept credit cards; even so, you should be prepared to pay in cash. In January, February, and July, get your ticket as far in advance as possible (a week or more, at least) and arrive at the terminal extra early.

Most long-distance buses depart Buenos Aires from the Terminal de Omnibus de Retiro, which is often referred to as the Terminal de Retiro or simply Retiro. Ramps and stairs from the street lead you to a huge concourse where buses leave from more than 60 numbered platforms. There are restrooms, restaurants, public phones, lockers, news kiosks, and a tourist office on this floor.

If you didn't buy tickets in advance, you can get them from the *boleterías* (ticket offices) on the upper level; there are also two ATMs here. Each company has its own ticket booth; they're arranged in zones according to the destinations served, which makes price comparisons easy. The terminal's comprehensive Spanish-language website lists bus companies by destination, including their phone number and ticket booth location, as does the more user-friendly ⊕ *www.retiro.com.ar. (See individual chapters for information about local bus stations.)* ⚠ **Stay alert in the terminal: pickpockets and bag-snatchers often prey on distracted travelers. Be particularly wary when using the ATMs.**

Long-distance buses have toilets, air-conditioning, videos, and snacks. The most basic service is *semi-cama*, which has minimally reclining seats and often takes a little longer than more luxurious services. It's worth paying the bit extra for *cama ejecutivo*, which has large, business-class-style seats and, sometimes, pillows and blankets.

On routes between nearby towns you can usually choose between regular buses (*común*) and air-conditioned or heated ones with reclining seats (*diferencial*). The companies that run local services rarely have websites—you buy tickets directly from the bus station.

Contacts Plataforma 10. ⊕ *www.plataforma10.com.* **Terminal de Ómnibus Retiro.** ✉ *Av. Antártida Argentina at Av. Ramos Mejía, Retiro* ☎ *11/4310–0700* ⊕ *www.tebasa.com.ar.*

▌ CAR TAVEL

Argentina's long highways and fabulous scenery make it a great place for road trips. However, if you're only going to be staying in Buenos Aires and other big cities, parking limitations and downright crazy traffic make renting a car more trouble than it's worth. Stick with public transportation, including taxis or Uber.

TAXIS, REMISES, AND UBER

There are licensed, metered taxi services in all of Argentina's major cities. You can hail cabs on the street or call or, in Buenos Aires, book them via the city government's BA Taxi app. Taxi drivers speak little to no English: the standard way to state your destination is to give the name of the nearest two intersecting streets (*Córdoba y Malabia*, for example). *Remises* are unlicensed taxi services that operate longer routes such as from downtown to airports or for trips to the countryside, usually for a flat, preagreed fare.

Ridesharing apps Uber (⊕ *www.uber.com*) and Cabify (⊕ *www.cabify.com*) are popular in Buenos Aires and other major cities. Both are substantially cheaper than official metered taxis and are particularly useful if you don't speak much Spanish. Services are limited beyond downtown areas.

Taxi drivers in big cities are usually honest, but occasionally they decide to take people for a ride, literally. All official cabs have meters, so make sure this is turned on. It helps to have an idea where you're going and how long it will take. Local lore says that if you're hailing taxis on the street, those with lights on top (usually labeled "Radio Taxi") are more trustworthy. Late at night, try to call for a cab—all hotels and restaurants, no matter how cheap, have a number and will usually call for you.

GASOLINE

Gas stations (*estaciones de servicio*) are in and near most towns and along major highways. Most are open 24 hours and include full service, convenience stores, and sometimes ATMs. In rural areas, stations have small shops and toilets; however, they are few and far between and have reduced hours.

On long trips, fill your tank whenever you can, even if you've still got gas left, as the next station could be a long way away (signs at stations often tell you how far). Attendants always pump the gas and don't expect a tip, though most locals add 10–20 pesos for a full tank. Credit cards often aren't accepted even in major cities—look for signs reading *Tarjetas de crédito suspendidas* ("No credit cards") or *Solo efectivo* ("Cash only"). It's safest to check with attendants before filling up: *¿Se puede pagar con tarjeta?* ("Can I pay by credit card?").

The major service stations are YPF, Shell, Petrobras, and Axion. YPF gas tends to be the cheapest. Prices are often higher in the north of Argentina. South of an imaginary line between Bariloche and Puerto Madryn, gas is heavily subsidized and costs roughly half what it does elsewhere. There are three grades of unleaded fuels, as well as diesel and biodiesel. GNC

is compressed natural gas, an alternative fuel. Stations with GNC signs may sell only this, or both this and regular gas.

PARKING

On-street parking is limited in big cities. Some have meter systems or tickets that you buy from kiosks and display on the dashboard and others use parking apps or SMS-based systems. In meter-free spots there's often an informal "caretaker" who guides you into your spot and charges 10–20 pesos to watch your car, which you pay when you leave.

Car theft is common, so many agencies insist that you park rental cars in a guarded lot. Many hotels have their own lots, and there are plenty in major cities: look for a circular blue sign with a white "E" for *estacionamiento* (parking). In downtown Buenos Aires, expect to pay 60–70 pesos per hour, or 250–290 pesos for 12 hours. Rates are lower elsewhere. Illegally parked cars are towed only from restricted parking areas in city centers, especially in Buenos Aires. Getting your car back is a bureaucratic nightmare and costs around 1,000 pesos.

ROAD CONDITIONS

The streets of many Argentinean cities are notorious for potholes, uneven surfaces, and poorly marked intersections. Most major cities have a one-way system whereby parallel streets run in opposite directions: never going the wrong way along a street is one of the few rules that Argentineans abide by. Where there are no traffic lights at an intersection, you give way to drivers coming from the right, but have priority over those coming from the left.

Two kinds of roads connect major cities: *autopistas* (two- or three-lane freeways) and *rutas* (single or dual carriageways) or *rutas nacionales* (main "national routes," usually indicated with an "RN" before the route number). Both types of roads are subject to regular tolls. Autopistas are well maintained, but the state of rutas varies hugely. In more remote locations even rutas that look like major highways on maps may be narrow roads with no central division. Always travel with a map or GPS, as signposts for turnoffs are scarce and often downright confusing.

Night driving can be hazardous: some highways and routes are poorly lighted, routes sometimes cut through the center of towns, cattle or sheep often get onto the roads, and in rural areas farm trucks and old cars seldom have all their lights working. Outside of the city of Buenos Aires, be especially watchful at traffic lights, as crossing on red lights at night is common practice. A useful road-trip website is ⊕ *www.ruta0.com* , which calculates distances and tolls between places and offers several route options.

ROADSIDE EMERGENCIES

All rental-car agencies have an emergency help line in case of breakdowns or accidents—some services take longer than others to arrive. The best roadside assistance is usually that of the Automóvil Club Argentina (ACA), which sends mechanics and tow trucks to members traveling anywhere in the country. The ACA also offers free roadside assistance to members of North American clubs and automobile associations. However, bear in mind when you call for assistance that most operators speak only Spanish.

Contacts American Automobile Association (*AAA*). ☎ *800/222–4357* ⊕ *www.aaa. com.* **Automóvil Club Argentino** (*ACA*). ☎ *800/888–9888, 800/777–2894 emergencies* ⊕ *www.aca.org.ar.* **Police.** ☎ *101.*

RULES OF THE ROAD

You drive on the right in Argentina, as in the United States. Seatbelts are required by law for front-seat passengers. You must use your headlights on highways at all times. The use of cell phones while driving is forbidden, and turning left on two-way avenues is prohibited unless there's a left-turn signal or left-turn traffic light; there are no right turns on red. Traffic lights turn yellow before they turn red, but also before turning green, which

is interpreted by drivers as an extra margin to get through the intersection, so take precautions.

The legal blood-alcohol limit is 500 mg of alcohol per liter of blood, but in practice breathalyzing is common only in Buenos Aires and along the highways of the Atlantic coast during January and February. In towns and cities a 40-kph (25-mph) speed limit applies on streets and a 60-kph (37-mph) limit is in effect on avenues. On autopistas the limit is 130 kph (80 mph), and on rutas it ranges between 100 kph (62 mph) and 120 kph (75 mph). On smaller roads and highways out of town it's 80 kph (50 mph). Locals take speed-limit signs, the ban on driving with cell phones, and drunk driving lightly, so drive very defensively.

Police tend to be forgiving of foreigners' driving faults and often waive tickets and fines when they see your passport. If you do get a traffic ticket, don't argue. Most tickets aren't payable on the spot, but some police officers offer "reduced" on-the-spot fines in lieu of a ticket: it's bribery, and you'd do best to insist on receiving the proper ticket. During peak local holiday times (January, February, and July), police often check drivers' licenses, registration, and proof of insurance on highways—rental companies should provide the latter two; it's illegal to drive without them.

In Buenos Aires, buses and taxis have exclusive lanes on major avenues. On other streets they often drive as though they have priority, and it's good to defer to them for your own safety.

Paved highways run from Argentina to the Chilean, Bolivian, Paraguayan, and Brazilian borders. Most rental agencies do not allow you to take their cars out of the country. If you do cross the border by land, you'll be required to present your passport, documentation of car ownership, and insurance paperwork at immigration and customs checkpoints. It's also common for cars and bags to be searched for contraband, such as food, livestock, and drugs.

RENTAL CARS

Daily rates range from around 900 pesos to 3,000, depending on the type of car and the distance you plan to travel. This generally includes tax and at least 200 free km (125 free miles) daily—unlimited mileage deals are common. Note that most cars have manual transmissions; if you need an automatic, request one in advance and be prepared to pay extra—usually only the more expensive vehicle categories have them.

Reputable firms don't rent to drivers under 21, and drivers under 23 often have to pay a daily surcharge. Children's car seats are not compulsory, but are available for about 150 pesos per day. Some agencies charge a 10% surcharge for picking up a car from the airport.

A collision damage waiver (CDW) is mandatory and is usually included in standard rental prices. However, you may still be responsible for a deductible fee (known locally as a *franquicia* or *deducible*)—a maximum amount that you'll have to pay if damage occurs. It ranges from 6,000 to 30,000 pesos for a car and can be much higher for a four-wheel-drive vehicle. You can reduce the figure substantially or altogether by paying an insurance premium (anywhere from 100 to 1,000 pesos per day); some companies have lower deductibles than others.

In general, you cannot cross the border in a rental car. Many rental companies don't insure you on unpaved roads and have special insurance clauses that make you responsible for most of the value of the car if it flips over in an accident, which is commonplace on unpaved roads in Patagonia. Discuss your itinerary with the agent to be certain you're always covered.

Rental Agencies Alamo. ☏ *810/999-2526, 11/4811-9993 in Buenos Aires* ⊕ *www.alamoargentina.com.ar.* **Avis.** ☏ *810/9991-2847, 11/4326-5542 in Buenos Aires* ⊕ *www.avis.com.ar.* **Budget.** ☏ *810/999-2834, 11/4326-3825 in Buenos Aires* ⊕ *www.budget.com.ar.* **Hertz.** ☏ *810/222-43789, 11/4816-0899 in Buenos Aires* ⊕ *www.hertz.com.ar.*

ESSENTIALS

■ ACCOMMODATIONS

Argentina has a broad variety of hotels, and the healthy competition between them generally translates into high quality and reasonable rates. Nearly all hotels—even hostels—include breakfast in the room price, but not all include the 21% tax in their quoted rates. Prices are also linked to municipality-run rating systems, which are based on a checklist of amenities (often outdated) rather than detailed evaluation. You can get wildly different things for your money, so do your homework. In destinations popular with locals, room prices soar in high season (usually January, February, and July), and some establishments won't take bookings for less than seven days. In the off-season the same places can be a steal.

Airbnb lists more than 300 furnished rentals in Buenos Aires and plenty more in other parts of Argentina. International outfit Oasis Collections specializes in luxury rental properties and has 150 Buenos Aires properties on its books. Both process payments through their website.

When choosing your rental, remember that air-conditioning is a must in central and northern Argentina, including Buenos Aires, between December and March. Always check exact street locations on a map, as listings sometimes exaggerate a property's proximity to particular neighborhoods, landmarks, or subway stations.

Rental Contacts Air BnB. ⊕ *www.airbnb. com.* **ByT Argentina.** ☎ *11/4876–5006* ⊕ *www.bytargentina.com.* **HomeAway.** ⊕ *www.homeaway.com.* **Oasis Collection.** ☎ *855/686–2747 in U.S., 11/5217–5932 in Argentina* ⊕ *www.oasiscollections.com.*

ESTANCIAS

You get a taste of traditional Argentinean country life—including home-cooked meals and horseback riding or polo—when you stay at an *estancia* (ranch or country estate). Estancias Travel and Estancias Argentinas are two good booking services, but you usually get better rates if you call the estancia directly.

When booking, ask specifically about what activities and drinks are included in rates, and bear in mind that many establishments accept only cash payments. Be sure to factor in travel times and costs when planning your stay: remote locations may be reachable only by private transport, often at a hefty cost.

Estancia Reservations Estancias Argentinas. ☎ *11/4343–2366* ⊕ *www. estanciasargentinas.com.* **Estancias Travel.** ☎ *11/5236–1054* ⊕ *www.estanciastravel.com.*

■ COMMUNICATIONS

INTERNET

Free or inexpensive Internet access is widely available in major urban centers. Both budget establishments and high-end hotels tend to have free Wi-Fi, though connection quality varies greatly. Many bars and restaurants in big cities also have free Wi-Fi—look for stickers on their windows. Network names and passwords are often displayed on the menu or on signs on the table, otherwise you need to ask waitstaff for them—*¿Me podrías decir la clave del Wi-Fi?* ("Could you give me the Wi-Fi password?").

In the capital, wider coverage comes courtesy of BA WiFi, a free service provided by the city government in many subte stations, Metrobus shelters, public libraries, museums, cultural centers, and even major streets and squares. The BA WiFi website list an ever-growing number of hot spots, which you can also find through their app (⊕ *www.buenosaires.gob.ar/aplicacionesmoviles/ba-wifi*). Civic and provincial governments elsewhere in the country offer similar services on major public thoroughfares or in libraries. You can also find Wi-Fi in many business and event centers, some airports, and in other public spaces—piggybacking is common practice.

Contact **BA WiFi.** ⊕ *www.buenosaires.gob.ar/ innovacion/ciudadinteligente/proyectos/bawifi.*

PHONES

The country code for Argentina is 54. To call landlines in Argentina from the United States, dial the international access code (011) followed by the country code (54), the two- to four-digit area code without the initial 0, then the six- to eight-digit phone number. For example, to call the Buenos Aires number 011/4123–4567, you would dial 011/54–11–4123–4567.

Any number that is prefixed by a 15 is a cell-phone number. To call cell phones from the United States, dial the international access code (011) followed by the country code (54), Argentina's cell-phone code (9), the area code without the initial 0, then the seven- or eight-digit cell-phone number *without* the initial 15. For example, to call the Buenos Aires cell phone (011) 15/5123–4567, you would dial 011/54–9–11–5123–4567.

CALLING WITHIN ARGENTINA

Cell phones are king in Argentina: public phones and phone centers, called *locutorios* or *telecentros*, are quickly becoming a thing of the past. Businesses and hotels still use landlines but many now also list a WhatsApp number, by far the favorite local messaging service. Public Wi-Fi is usually good enough for you to make calls using services like WhatsApp or Skype. You can usually also make local and long-distance calls straight from your hotel room, but hefty surcharges often apply.

MOBILE PHONES

All cell phones in Argentina are GSM 850/1900 Mhz. Cell numbers use a local area code, then the cell-phone prefix (15), then a seven- or eight-digit number. To call a cell in the same area as you from a landline, dial 15 and the number. To call a cell in a different area from a landline, dial the area code, including the initial 0, then 15, then the number. If you're calling from another cell phone, you don't need to include the 15.

There are three main phone companies: Movistar, Claro, and Personal. Although they're similar, Claro has the most users and is said to have the best rates, while Movistar has the best coverage, and Personal the best customer service. All three offer 4G, but service is patchy outside of big cities, so don't be surprised when your signal indicator switches from 4G to H+ and occasionally to E.

There are two ways to use your smartphone in Argentina: activate an international plan or get it unlocked before you travel, then purchase a local pay-as-you-go SIM card (*tarjeta SIM prepaga*) once you land. You can buy one for 20 to 50 pesos from any of the companies' offices and sales stands, which are easy to find countrywide, including at airports. The main three companies offer different pay-as-you-go services that include good-value data packages: expect to pay around 7 pesos per day for 50MB; 7-day and 30-day plans are also available. Most now allow you to use WhatsApp even if you run out of credit. You choose your plan (ask sales staff about the different options) then top up credit as necessary by *carga virtual* (virtual top-ups) at *kioscos* (convenience stores), where sales clerks add credit to your line directly while you wait.

■ TIP→ **Pickpockets often target tourists for their cell phones, so consider leaving your latest-generation model at home and packing an older or cheaper one instead.**

Local charges for calling a cell phone from a landline depend on factors like the company and time of day, but most around 1.50 pesos per minute. In general, you pay only for outgoing calls from cell phones, which cost around 6 pesos a minute. Calls from pay-as-you-go phones are the most expensive and calls to phones from the same company as yours are usually cheaper. Pay-as-you-go services usually include free calls to at least one other number on the same network and some include a small number of free minutes per day.

Contacts **Claro.** ☎ *800/123–2527* ⊕ *www. claro.com.ar.* **Movistar.** ☎ *800/321–1111* ⊕ *www.movistar.com.ar.* **Personal.** ☎ *800/444–4100* ⊕ *www.personal.com.ar.*

▌ CUSTOMS AND DUTIES

Customs uses a random inspection system that requires you to push a button at the inspection bay—if a green light appears, you walk through; if a red light appears, your bags are X-rayed (and very occasionally opened). Officially, foreign tourists are allowed to bring up to 2 liters of alcoholic beverages, 400 cigarettes, and 50 cigars into the country duty-free. You are also allowed another $300 worth of purchases from the duty-free shops, which most of Argentina's international airports have, after you land. In practice, however, most officials wave foreigners through customs controls and are rarely interested in alcohol or tobacco. Fishing gear and skis present no problems.

If you enter the country by bus from Bolivia, Brazil, or Paraguay, you, your bags, and the vehicle may be subject to lengthy searches by officials looking for drugs and smuggled goods.

Argentina has strict regulations designed to prevent the illicit trafficking of antiques, fossils, and other items of cultural and historical importance and a license system for exporting artworks. For more information, contact the Dirección Nacional de Bienes y Sitios Culturales (National Department of Cultural Property and Sites).

Information in Argentina Dirección Nacional de Bienes y Sitios Naturales. ☎ *11/4381–7275* ⊕ *www. cultura.gob.ar/institucional/organismos/ direccion-nacional-de-bienes-y-sitios-culturales.*

U.S. Information U.S. Customs and Border Protection. ⊕ *www.cbp.gov.*

▌ ELECTRICITY

The electrical current is 220 volts, 50 cycles alternating current (AC), so most North American appliances can't be used without a converter. Older wall outlets take continental-type plugs, with two round prongs, whereas newer buildings take plugs with three flat, angled prongs or two flat prongs set at a "v" angle.

Brief power outages (and surges when the power comes back) are fairly regular occurrences, especially outside of Buenos Aires, so it's a good idea to use a surge protector with your laptop.

▌ EMERGENCIES

In a medical emergency, taking a taxi to the nearest hospital can be quicker than waiting for an ambulance. If you do call any emergency services, operators speak only Spanish. Ambulances transport you to the nearest hospital—possibly a public one that may well look run-down; don't worry, though, as the medical care will be excellent. Alternatively, you can call a private hospital directly.

For theft, wallet loss, small road accidents, and minor emergencies, contact the nearest police station. Expect all dealings with the police to be a lengthy, bureaucratic business—it's probably only worth bothering if you need the report for insurance claims. Check the website of the U.S. Embassy in Argentina for information on potential safety concerns.

American Embassy U.S. Embassy in Argentina. ✉ *Av. Colombia 4300, Palermo* ☎ *11/5777–4354 emergency assistance, 11/5777–4533 general inquiries* ⊕ *ar. usembassy.gov.*

General Contacts Ambulance and Medical. ☎ *107.* **Fire.** ☎ *100.* **Police.** ☎ *101.*

LOCAL DO'S AND TABOOS

CUSTOMS OF THE COUNTRY

Outside Buenos Aires, siestas are still sacrosanct: most shops and museums close between 1 and 4 or 5 pm. Locals are usually fashionably late for all social events—don't be offended if someone keeps you waiting over half an hour for a lunch or dinner date. However, tardiness is frowned upon in the business world.

GREETINGS

One kiss on the right cheek is the customary greeting between both male and female friends, although men—especially older men—often shake hands the first time they meet someone. Other than that, handshaking is seen as very cold and formal, and not greeting people "properly" (with a kiss or handshake) is seen as rude.

When you leave a party it's normal to say good-bye to everyone in the room (or, if you're in a restaurant, to everyone at your table), which means kissing everyone once again. Unlike other Latin Americans, Argentineans use the formal "you" form, *usted*, only with people much older than they or in very formal situations, and the casual greeting *¡Hola!* often replaces *buen día, buenas tardes,* and *buenas noches.* In small towns, formal greetings and the use of *usted* are more widespread.

LANGUAGE

Argentina's official language is Spanish, known locally as *castellano* (rather than *español*). It differs from other varieties of Spanish in its use of *vos* (instead of *tú*) for the informal "you" form, and there are lots of small vocabulary differences, especially for everyday things like food. Intonation varies greatly around Argentina, but it is markedly singsong in Buenos Aires. Another *porteño* peculiarity is pronouncing the letters "y" and "ll" as a "sh" sound. Elsewhere these same letters are pronounced "y" or "j" and "ly." In the northern half of Argentina, the typical Spanish "r" is trilled much more softly.

In hotels, restaurants, and shops that cater to visitors, many people speak at least some English. All the same, attempts to speak Spanish are usually appreciated. Basic courtesies like *por favor* (please) and *gracias* (thank you) are a good place to start.

OUT ON THE TOWN

A firm nod of the head or raised eyebrow usually gets waiters' attention; *disculpa* (excuse me) also does the trick. You can ask your waiter for *la cuenta* (the check) or make a signing gesture in the air from afar.

Alcohol—especially wine and beer—is a big part of life in Argentina. Social events usually end in general tipsiness rather than all-out drunkenness.

Smoking is fairly common in Argentina. Antismoking legislation in several cities—including Buenos Aires, Mendoza, and Córdoba—has banned it indoors, but expect smoke with your steak at sidewalk tables, where smoking is allowed. Smoking is prohibited on public transport and in government offices, banks, and cinemas.

Public displays of affection between heterosexual couples attract little attention in most parts of the country. Although same-sex marriage is now legal throughout Argentina, beyond downtown Buenos Aires same-sex couples may attract hostile reactions.

If you're invited to someone's home for dinner, a bottle of good Argentinean wine, a shop-bought cake or dessert, or chocolates are all good gifts to take the hosts.

▌ HEALTH

MEDICAL CONCERNS

No vaccinations are required for travel to Argentina. However, the National Centers for Disease Control & Prevention (CDC) recommend vaccinations against hepatitis A and typhoid for all travelers and against hepatitis B, rabies, and yellow fever for travelers to the northeast of the country, which includes Iguazú. Each year there are cases of cholera in northern Argentina, mostly in the indigenous communities near the Bolivian border; your best protection is to avoid eating raw seafood.

The Zika virus is present in Argentina although relatively few cases have been reported to date. The CDC thus recommends that pregnant women avoid traveling to Argentina and that women planning to get pregnant inform themselves of the risks the virus poses before deciding to travel there. Malaria is a threat only in low-lying rural areas near the borders of Bolivia and Paraguay. There have been periodic outbreaks of dengue fever (another mosquito-borne disease) in northern Argentina, especially in Misiones Province (where Iguazú Falls is), and cases are regularly reported as far south as Buenos Aires. The best preventive measure against both dengue and malaria is to cover your arms and legs, use a good mosquito repellent containing DEET, and stay inside at dusk. American trypanosomiasis, or Chagas' disease, is present in remote rural areas.

The CDC recommends chloroquine as a preventive antimalarial for adults and infants in Argentina. To be effective, the weekly doses must start a week before you travel and continue four weeks after your return. There is no preventive medication for Zika, dengue, or Chagas'. Children traveling to Argentina should have current inoculations against measles, mumps, rubella, and polio.

In most urban areas in Argentina, including Buenos Aires, people drink tap water and eat uncooked fruits and vegetables. However, if you're prone to tummy trouble, stick to bottled water. Take standard flu-avoidance precautions such as hand-washing and cough-covering, and consider contacting your doctor for a flu shot if you're traveling during the austral winter.

OTHER ISSUES

Apunamiento, or altitude sickness, which results in shortness of breath and headaches, may be a problem when you visit high altitudes in the Andes. To remedy any discomfort, walk slowly, eat lightly, and drink plenty of fluids (avoid alcohol). In northwestern Argentina, coca leaves are widely available (don't worry, it's totally legal). Follow the locals' example and chew a wad mixed with a dab of bicarbonate of soda on hiking trips: it does wonders for altitude problems. You can also order tea made from coca leaves (*mate de coca*), which has the same effect. If you experience an extended period of nausea, dehydration, dizziness, or severe headache or weakness while in a high-altitude area, seek medical attention. Dehydration, sunstroke, frostbite, and heatstroke are all dangers of outdoor recreation at high altitudes. Awareness and caution are the best preventive measures.

Health Warnings National Centers for Disease Control & Prevention (*CDC*). ☎ *800/232–4636* ⊕ *www.cdc.gov/travel.* **World Health Organization** (*WHO*). ⊕ *www. who.int.*

HEALTH CARE

Argentina has free national health care that also provides foreigners with free outpatient care. Although the medical practitioners working at *hospitales públicos* (public hospitals) are first-rate, the institutions themselves are often chronically underfunded: bed space and basic supplies are at a minimum. Except in emergencies you should consider leaving these resources for the people who really need them. World-class private clinics and hospitals are plentiful, and consultation and treatment fees are low compared with those in North America. Still, it's good to have some kind of medical insurance.

In nonemergency situations you'll be seen much quicker at a private clinic or hospital, and overnight stays are more comfortable. Many doctors at private hospitals speak at least some English. Note that only cities have hospitals; smaller towns may have a *sala de primeros auxilios* (first-aid post).

OVER-THE-COUNTER REMEDIES

Towns and cities have a 24-hour pharmacy system: each night there's one *farmacia de turno* (on-duty pharmacy) for prescriptions and emergency supplies.

In Argentina, *farmacias* (pharmacies) carry painkillers, first-aid supplies, contraceptives, diarrhea treatments, and a range of other over-the-counter treatments, including some drugs that would require a prescription in the United States (many antibiotics, for example). Note that acetaminophen—or Tylenol—is known as *paracetamol* in Spanish. If you think you'll need to have prescriptions filled while you're in Argentina, be sure to have your doctor write down the generic name of the drug, not just the brand name.

Farmacity is a supermarket-style drugstore chain with branches all over Buenos Aires and other major cities, including Córdoba, Mendoza, and Salta; many of them are open 24 hours and offer a delivery service.

Pharmacies Farmacity. ⊕ *www.farmacity. com.ar.*

▌ HOLIDAYS

January through March is summer holiday season for Argentineans. Winter holidays fall toward the end of July. Most public holidays are celebrated on their actual date, except June 17, August 17, October 12, and November 20, which move to the nearest Monday. When public holidays fall on a Thursday or Tuesday, the following Friday or preceding Monday, respectively, is sometimes declared a holiday, creating a four-day weekend known as a *feriado puente.*

Año Nuevo (New Year's Day), January 1. **Carnaval** (Carnival), Monday and Tuesday six weeks before Easter. **Día Nacional de la Memoria por la Verdad y la Justicia** (National Memorial Day for Truth and Justice; commemoration of the start of the 1976–83 dictatorship), March 24. **Día del Veterano y de los Caídos en la Guerra de Malvinas** (Malvinas Veterans' Day), April 2. **Jueves Santo** (Maundy Thursday), March or April. **Viernes Santo** (Good Friday), March or April. **Día del Trabajador** (Labor Day), May 1. **Día de la Revolución de Mayo** (Anniversary of the 1810 Revolution), May 25. **Paso a la Inmortalidad del General Martín Miguel de Güemes** (Anniversary of General Martín Miguel de Güemes's Death), June 17. **Paso a la Inmortalidad del General Manuel Belgrano** (Anniversary of General Manuel Belgrano's Death; Flag Day), June 20. **Día de la Independencia** (Independence Day), July 9. **Paso a la Inmortalidad del General José de San Martín** (Anniversary of General José de San Martín's Death), August 17. **Día del Respeto a la Diversidad Cultural** (Day of Respect for Cultural Diversity), October 12. **Día de la Soberanía Nacional** (National Sovereignty Day; Anniversary of the Battle of Vuelta de Obligado), November 20. **Inmaculada Concepción de María** (Immaculate Conception), December 8. **Christmas,** December 25.

▌ MAIL

Correo Argentino, the mail service, has an office in most towns or city neighborhoods; some locutorios also serve as collection points and sell stamps. Older postboxes are dark blue and yellow, newer ones dark and light blue: most are found either inside or directly outside post offices. Mail delivery isn't dependable: it can take 6 to 21 days for standard letters and postcards to get to the United States. Regular airmail letters cost 83 pesos for up to 20 grams.

If you want to be sure something will arrive, send it by *correo certificado* (registered mail), which costs 220 pesos for international letters up to 20 grams. Valuable items are best sent with express services like DHL, UPS, or FedEx—delivery within one to two days for a 5-kilogram (11-pound) package starts at about 5,500 pesos. A similar size package would cost 2,680 pesos to send *expreso* (express) with Correo Argentino and would take up to a week to arrive.

Argentina's post-code system is based on a four-digit code. Each province is assigned a letter (the city of Buenos Aires is "C," for instance) that goes before the number code, and each city block is identified by three letters afterward (such as ABD). In practice, however, only big cities use these complete postal codes (which look like C1234ABD; the rest of Argentina uses the basic number code (1234, for example).

Contacts Correo Argentino. ⊕ *www.correo-argentino.com.ar.*

▌ MONEY

Prices go up almost by the day in Argentina: since 2015, annual inflation rates have ranged between 20% and 45%. The number of pesos you get for your dollar has been steadily increasing as well, but even so, Argentina is not as good value as it once was—eating out and accommodation are on a par with U.S. prices.

ITEM	AVERAGE COST
Cup of coffee and three *medialunas* (croissants)	75–90 pesos
Glass of wine	80–100 pesos
Liter bottle of local beer at a bar	150–180 pesos
Steak and fries in a cheap restaurant	200–250 pesos
One-mile taxi ride in Buenos Aires	50 pesos
Museum admission	Free–120 pesos

Cash remains king for day-to-day dealings in Argentina, although more and more establishments now take debit and credit cards. This change is partly a response to the unpredictability of the banking system: regular strikes in recent years have meant that ATMs often run out of money, especially over weekends or during holiday season. Always withdraw more cash well before your current supply is spent, particularly in small towns. U.S. dollars can be changed at any bank and are often accepted as payment in clothing stores, souvenir shops, and supermarkets.

Note that there's a perennial shortage of change in Argentina. Five-hundred-peso bills can be hard to get rid of, so ask for 100s when you change money.

You can usually pay by debit and credit card in hotels countrywide and in nicer restaurants and stores in big cities. But be advised that even establishments displaying stickers from different card companies may suddenly stop accepting them: look out for signs reading *tarjetas de crédito suspendidas* (credit card purchases temporarily unavailable). Outside of urban areas, plastic is less widely accepted. Most establishments use traditional credit card terminals, but TodoPago card readers, which stores insert into a cell phone to swipe your card, are also common.

Nonchain stores often display two prices for goods: *precio de lista* (the standard price, valid if you pay by credit card) and a discounted price if you pay in *efectivo* (cash). Many travel services and even some hotels also offer hefty cash discounts—it's always worth asking about.

Prices throughout this guide are given for adults. Substantially reduced fees are almost always available for children.

ATMS AND BANKS

ATMs, called *cajeros automáticos,* are found all over Buenos Aires and other big cities. Most smaller towns have at least one ATM; gas stations on major highways also sometimes have them. If you plan to be away from urban areas or major tourist destinations for long, take ample cash with you. There are two main systems. Banelco, indicated by a burgundy-color sign with white lettering, is used by Banco Comafi, BBVA Banco Francés, HSBC, Banco Galicia, ICBC, Banco Itaú, Banco Macro, Banco Santander Río, Supervielle, and Banco Patagonia. Link, recognizable by a green-and-yellow sign, is the system used by Banco Provincia, Credicoop, Banco Hipotecario, and Banco de la Nación, as well as nearly all banks belonging to other provinces. Cards on the Cirrus and Plus networks can be used on both systems.

Many banks have daily withdrawal limits of 5,000 pesos or less. Sometimes ATMs will impose unexpectedly low withdrawal limits (say, 1,500 pesos) on international cards—this is more common on Banelco than Link machines. You can get around it by requesting a further transaction before the machine returns your card, but first check whether your bank back home charges high per-withdrawal fees. Always make withdrawals from ATMs in daylight hours and keep your wits about you when leaving.

ATM Locations Banelco. ⊕ *www.banelco. com.ar.* **Link.** ⊕ *www.redlink.com.ar.*

CURRENCY AND EXCHANGE

Argentina's currency is the peso, which equals 100 centavos. Bills come in denominations of 1,000 (ocher), 500 (green), 100 (violet), 50 (navy blue), 20 (red), 10 (ocher), 5 (green), and 2 (light blue) pesos, although the 2-peso note is being phased out. Check your change when using high-denomination notes: the color of the 1,000-peso note is fairly similar to the 10-peso note, and that of the 500-peso note to the 5-peso note. Coins are in denominations of 2 pesos and 1 peso (both heavy and bimetallic), as well as 50, 25, and 10 centavos. U.S. dollars are widely accepted in big-city stores, supermarkets, and at hotels and top-end restaurants (usually at a slightly worse exchange rate than you'd get at a bank). You always receive change in pesos, even when you pay with U.S. dollars.

Following a series of devaluations, the official exchange rate at this writing is around 20 pesos to the U.S. dollar. You can change dollars at this rate at most banks (between 10 am and 3 pm), at a *casa de cambio* (money changer), or at your hotel. All currency exchange involves fees, but as a rule banks charge the least and hotels the most. You need to show your passport to complete the transaction.

On busy streets (like Calle Florida in Buenos Aires), you'll likely be propositioned by touts from small currency-exchange shops that are referred to locally as "*cuevas,*" or caves. Most are safe, but try to change relatively small amounts regularly to minimize any possible trouble.

■ TIP➜ **You may not be able to change currency in rural areas at all, so don't leave major cities without adequate amounts of pesos in small denominations.**

Exchange-Rate Information Oanda.com. ⊕ *www.oanda.com.* **XE.com.** ⊕ *www.xe.com.*

▌ PASSPORTS

As a U.S. citizen, you need a passport valid for at least six months to enter Argentina as a tourist. Argentina no longer operates its reciprocal entry fee scheme for U.S. citizens, so you don't need a visa for visits of up to 90 days.

If you need to stay longer, you can apply for a 90-day extension (*prórroga*) to your tourist visa at the Dirección Nacional de Migraciones (Department of Immigration). The process takes a morning and costs about 1,000 pesos. Alternatively, you can exit the country (by taking a boat trip to Uruguay from Buenos Aires, or crossing into Brazil near Iguazú, for example); upon reentering Argentina, your passport will be stamped allowing an additional 90 days. Overstaying your tourist visa is illegal and incurs a fine of 1,500 pesos, which you must pay at the Dirección Nacional de Migraciones. Once you have done so, you must leave the country within 10 days. You should carry your passport or other photo ID with you at all times: you need it to make credit-card purchases, change money, and send parcels, as well as in the unlikely event that the police stop you.

Officially, children visiting Argentina with only one parent do not need a signed and notarized permission-to-travel letter from the other parent. However, as Argentinean citizens *are* required to have such documentation, it's worth carrying a letter just in case laws change or border officials get confused.

For information on passport and visa requirements to visit the Brazilian side of Iguazú Falls, see the Planner pages at the start of Chapter 3, Side Trips from Buenos Aires.

Contacts Dirección Nacional de Migraciones (*Department of Immigration*). ✉ *Av. Antártida Argentina 1355, Retiro* ☎ *11/4317–0234* ⊕ *www.migraciones.gov.ar.* **Embassy of Argentina in the U.S.** ☎ *202/238–6400* ⊕ *www.eeeuu.mrecic.gov.ar.*

U.S. Passport Information U.S. Department of State. ☎ *877/487–2778* ⊕ *www.travel.state.gov.*

▌ SAFETY

Argentina is safer than many Latin American countries. However, street crime is still a concern—mainly pickpocketing, bag snatching, and occasionally mugging—especially in Buenos Aires. Taking a few precautions when traveling in the region is usually enough to keep you out of harm's way.

CRIME

As in any major city, walk with purpose; if you don't look like a target, you'll likely be left alone. Avoid wearing flashy jewelry. Keep a grip on your purse or bag, and keep it in your lap if you're sitting (never leave it hanging on the back of a chair or on the floor); many restaurants mount hooks under their tables for you to hang purses on. Try to keep your cash and credit cards in different places about your person (and always leave one card in your hotel safe, if possible), so that if one gets stolen you can fall back on the other.

Other valuables are best left in hotel safes, too. Avoid carrying large sums of money around, but always keep enough to have something to hand over in the unlikely event of a mugging. Another time-honored tactic is to keep a dummy wallet (an old one containing an expired credit card and a small amount of cash) in your pocket, with your real cash in an inside or vest pocket: if your "wallet" gets stolen you have little to lose.

Women can expect pointed looks, the occasional *piropo* (catcalls, usually alluding to some physical aspect), and some advances. These catcalls rarely escalate into actual physical harassment, although a wave of violence against women in recent years means that local women feel more threatened by them than in the past. The best reaction is to follow their example and ignore them and move on; reply only if you're really confident with

Spanish curse words. If you're heading out for the night, it's wise to take a taxi.

There's usually a notable police presence in areas popular with tourists, such as San Telmo and Palermo in Buenos Aires. This deters potential pickpockets and hustlers somewhat. However, Argentineans have little faith in their police forces: officers are often corrupt, and at best, the police are well-meaning but underequipped.

SCAMS

Beware of scams such as a kindly passer-by offering to help you clean a stain that has somehow appeared on your clothes: while your attention is occupied, an accomplice picks your pocket or snatches your bag.

When asking for price quotes while shopping in touristy areas, always confirm whether the amount is given in dollars or pesos. Some salespeople, especially street vendors, have found that they can take advantage of confused tourists by charging dollars for goods that are actually priced in pesos.

Advisories and Other Information Transportation Security Administration. ⊕ *www.tsa.gov.* **U.S. Department of State.** ⊕ *www.travel.state.gov.*

▌ TAXES

Argentina has a $29 departure tax for international flights and an $8 departure tax for domestic flights. These are included in your ticket price when you fly from some airports, including those in Buenos Aires. Otherwise you can pay by credit card or in cash at booths in airports (pesos, dollars, and euros are accepted). Hotel rooms carry a 21% tax. Cheaper hotels and hostels tend to include this in their quoted rates; more expensive hotels add it to your bill. At this writing, Buenos Aires was automatically refunding VAT on accommodation in the city if you pay using your credit card from back home.

Argentina has 21% VAT (known as IVA) on most consumer goods and services. The tax is usually included in the price of goods and noted on your receipt. You can get nearly all the IVA back on locally manufactured goods if you spend more than 70 pesos at stores displaying a Global Blue duty-free sign. You'll be given a Global Blue refund check for the amount you're entitled to; then, after getting it stamped by a customs official at the airport, you can cash it at the clearly signed tax refund booths. Allow an extra hour to complete the process.

Tax refunds Global Blue. ⊕ *www.globalblue.com.*

▌ TIME

Argentina is three hours behind G.M.T., or three hours ahead of U.S. Central Standard Time. Although Argentina does not currently observe Daylight Saving, it has in the past, so double-check time differences when you travel.

Time-Zone Information Timeanddate.com. ⊕ *www.timeanddate.com/worldclock.*

▌ TIPPING

Propinas (tips) are a question of rewarding good service rather than an obligation. Restaurant bills—even those that have a *cubierto* (bread and service charge)—don't include gratuities; locals usually add 10% to 15%. Bellhops and maids expect tips only in the very expensive hotels, where a tip in dollars is appreciated. You can also give a small tip (10%) to tour guides. Porteños round off taxi fares (paying, say, 100 pesos for a 94-peso ride), though some cabbies who frequent hotels popular with tourists seem to expect more. Tipping is a nice gesture with beauty and barbershop personnel—5% to 10% is fine.

TIPPING GUIDELINES FOR ARGENTINA

Bellhop at high-end hotels	$1–$5 per bag, depending on the level of the hotel
Hotel maid at high-end hotels	$1–$3 a day (either daily or at the end of your stay, in cash)
Hotel room-service waiter	$1 to $2 per delivery, even if a service charge has been added
Taxi driver	5%–10% to round up the fare
Tour guide	10% of the cost of the tour if service was good
Waiter	10%–15%, depending on service
Restroom attendants	2–5 pesos

▮ TRIP INSURANCE

Comprehensive trip insurance is an excellent investment. Such policies typically cover cancellation and interruption, letting you cancel or cut your trip short because of a personal emergency, illness, or, in some cases, acts of terrorism in your destination. They also include evacuation and medical care, typically reimbursing you for medical care (excluding that related to preexisting conditions) and hospitalization abroad, and providing for evacuation. You usually have to pay the bills yourself and await reimbursement from the insurer, though. Most schemes also cover you for travel delays because of bad weather or mechanical problems, as well as for lost or delayed baggage. Before buying insurance, check with your credit card provider: higher-level cards (typically platinum and above) often include reasonable insurance coverage for trips abroad. Allianz, TravelSafe, and AXA Assistance are popular travel insurance providers.

Always read the fine print of your policy to make sure that you are covered for the risks that are of most concern to you. Compare several policies to make sure you're getting the best price and range of coverage available:

⊕ *InsureMyTrip.com* and ⊕ *SquareMouth. com* are useful sites for this.

Insurance Comparison Sites Allianz Global Assistance. ☎ 866/884–3556 ⊕ *www.allianztravelinsurance.com.* **AXA Assistance USA.** ☎ 855/327–1441 ⊕ *www.axatravelinsurance. com.* **IM Global.** ☎ 800/628–4664 ⊕ *www. imglobal.com.* **InsureMyTrip.com.** ☎ 800/487–4722 ⊕ *www.insuremytrip.com.* **Square Mouth. com.** ☎ 800/240–0369 ⊕ *www.squaremouth. com.* **TravelSafe.** ☎ 888/885–7233 ⊕ *www. travelsafe.com.*

▮ VISITOR INFORMATION

All major cities and most smaller tourist destinations have tourist offices that can provide maps as well as information on accommodation and sightseeing. The quality of these offices varies according to local funding, but employees are usually friendly and helpful. The city of Buenos Aires has several tourist information centers and booths around the city where you can fill up your water bottle, charge your phone, and buy SUBE travel cards, which you need to use public transport (bring photo ID). Its extensive website includes downloadable maps, an online shop selling tickets for tours and events, a trip planner, and insightful articles on porteño culture, translated into questionable though largely comprehensible English. You can access most of this information on the go via the BA Turismo app; the city's other useful apps include a transportation planner (BA Cómo Llego) and a Wi-Fi hotspot finder (BA WiFi). For more information on these, visit ⊕ *turismo.buenosaires.gob.ar/en/article/downloadable-apps.*

Each Argentinean province has its own tourism website and also operates a tourist office in Buenos Aires, usually called the "Casa de [Province Name] en Buenos Aires."

Limited tourist information is also available at Argentina's embassy and consulates in the United States.

Contacts Embassy of Argentina in the U.S. ⊕ *www.eeeuu.mrecic.gob.ar.* **Turismo Buenos**

Aires (*Tourism Department of the Government of the City of Buenos Aires*). ☎ 0800/999–2838 in Argentina ⊕ www.turismo.buenosaires.gob.ar/en.

ONLINE RESOURCES

Argentina's main national newspapers are the conservative *La Nación*, mainstream *Clarín*, and progressive *Página12*, all of which publish daily print and digital editions in Spanish. There are no longer any English-language newspapers in Argentina and the expat-run blogs and online papers that once proliferated have also shut down. Instagram is a great source of inspiration for trip planning—and shopping, of course. Useful Instagram accounts to follow before you travel include @*VisitArgentina*, the official Argentinian tourism promotion feed; @*TravelBuenosAires*, the official B.A. travel feed; @*BridgetGlee*, Buenos Aires–based writer and artist offering watercolor explanations of local life; @*FrancisMallmann*,legendary Argentinean chef; and @*TripArgentina*, gorgeous views from a local travel agency. Like-minded travelers on the Travel Talk Forums at Fodors.com are eager to answer questions and swap travel tales. The crudely translated regional information and itinerary ideas on the government-run Argentina Travel website are a useful planning resource.

The Museo Nacional de Bellas Artes contains the world's biggest digital collection of Argentinean art and has lots of background on Argentinean artists. Todo Tango is a visually unarresting but comprehensive bilingual tango site with lyrics, history, and free downloads.

Wines of Argentina is overflowing with information about Argentina's best beverage. For insight into local cooking, restaurants, and ingredients, head to Saltshaker, the blog of American food writer Dan Perlman. Another food-obsessed American, Allie Lazar, is the sassy voice behind the unflinchingly detailed—and usually hilarious—restaurant and bar reviews at Pick Up the Fork.

All About Argentina Argentina Travel. ⊕ www.argentina.travel. **Clarín.** ⊕ www.clarin.com. **Embassy of Argentina in the U.S.** ⊕ www.eeeuu.mrecic.gov.ar. **Fodors.com.** ⊕ www.fodors.com/community. **La Nación.** ⊕ www.lanacion.com.ar. **Página 12.** ⊕ www.pagina12.com.ar.

Culture and Entertainment Museo Nacional de Bellas Artes. ⊕ www.bellasartes.gob.ar. **Todo Tango.** ⊕ www.todotango.com.

Food and Drink Pick Up the Fork. ⊕ www.pickupthefork.com. **Saltshaker.** ⊕ www.saltshaker.net. **Wines of Argentina.** ⊕ www.winesofargentina.org.

Great Reads Sample the work of Argentina's greatest writers with Jorge Luis Borges's *Labyrinths: Selected Stories and Other Writings* and Julio Cortázar's *Blow-Up and Other Stories*. Bruce Chatwin's *In Patagonia* is the classic piece of travel writing on Argentina. Delve deeper into the lives of two (in)famous Argentineans with Tomás Eloy Martínez's *Santa Evita*, a fictional look at Eva Perón's life and death, and Jon Lee Anderson's excellent biography *Che Guevara: A Revolutionary Life*. Contemporary literary legends include César Aira, who publishes one to two acclaimed novellas a year—*Ghosts* is a good one to start with. The landscape of the Pampas thrums with menace in Samanta Schweblin's literary thriller *Fever Dream*. The 1982 Falklands/Malvinas war is the starting point for Carlos Gamerro's *The Islands*.

On-screen Vengeance is the thread that runs through the six shorts in Oscar-nominated *Wild Tales*, directed by Damián Szifrón and shot in Buenos Aires, Salta, and Jujuy. The snow-covered Andes are the backdrop for a Latin American presidential summit in Santiago Mitre's drama *The Summit*. Two thrillers take you to Buenos Aires' recent past: Juan José Campanella's Oscar-winning *The Secret in Their Eyes* is set in the politically troubled early 1970s, while Pablo Trapero's true-crime story *The Clan* unfolds in the 1980s. Colonial-era Argentina was recreated in Corrientes and Formosa for Lucrecia Martel's arty period drama *Zama*. A remorse-struck gaucho is the stormy star of Fernando Spiner's *Aballay*, an arty Argentinean Western filmed in Tucumán Province.

SPANISH VOCABULARY

	ENGLISH	SPANISH	PRONUNCIATION
BASICS			
	Yes/no	Sí/no	see/noh
	Please	Por favor	por fah-vor
	Thank you (very much)	(Muchas) gracias	(**moo**-chas) **grah**-see-ass
	You're welcome	De nada	deh **nah**-da
	Excuse me	Con permiso	con pehr- **mee**-so
	Pardon me	¿Perdón?	pehr- **don**
	Could you tell me?	¿Podría decirme?	po- **dree**-ah deh- **seer**-me
	I'm sorry	Lo siento/Perdón	lo see- **en**-to/pehr- **don**
	Hello!/Hi!	¡Hola!	**o**-la
	Good morning!	¡Buen día!	bwen **dee**-a
	Good afternoon!	¡Buenas tardes!	**bwen**-as **tar**-des
	Good evening/Good night!	¡Buenas noches!	**bwen**-as **no**-ches
	Goodbye!	¡Chau!/¡Adiós!	chow/a-dee- **os**
NUMBERS			
	0	Cero	seh-ro
	1	Un, uno	oon, **oo**-no
	2	Dos	doss
	3	Tres	tress
	4	Cuatro	**kwah**-troh
	5	Cinco	**sin**-koh
	6	Seis	**say**-iss
	7	Siete	see- **yet**-eh
	8	Ocho	och-oh
	9	Nueve	nweh-veh
	10	Diez	dee- **ess**
DAYS OF THE WEEK			
	Sunday	domingo	doh- **ming**-oh
	Monday	lunes	**loo**-ness
	Tuesday	martes	**mar**-tess
	Wednesday	miércoles	mee- **er**-koh-less

ENGLISH	SPANISH	PRONUNCIATION
Thursday	jueves	**hweh**-vess
Friday	viernes	vee- **er**-ness
Saturday	sábado	**sah**-bad-oh

USEFUL PHRASES

Do you speak English?	¿Habla usted inglés? / ¿Hablás inglés?	**ab**-la oo- **sted** ing- **less** / **ab**-las ing- **less**
I don't speak Spanish	No hablo castellano	No **ab**-loh cas- **teh**-sha-no
I don't understand	No entiendo	No en-tee- **en**-doh
I understand	Entiendo	en-tee- **en**-doh
I don't know	No sé	No seh
What's your name?	¿Cómo se llama usted? / ¿Cómo te llamás?	ko-mo seh **shah**-mah oo- **sted** / ko-mo teh **shah**-mass
My name is.	Me llamo.	meh **shah**-moh.
What time is it?	¿Qué hora es?	keh **o**-rah ess
It's one o'clock	Es la una	ess la **oo**-na
It's two/three/four. o'clock	Son las dos/tres/cuatro	son lass doss/tress/ **kwah**-troh
Yes, please/	Si, gracias.	see, **grah**-see-ass
No, thank you	No, gracias.	noh, **grah**-see-ass
How?	¿Cómo?	**ko**-mo
When?	¿Cuándo?	kwan-doh
Tonight	Esta noche	**ess**-tah **noch**-eh
What?	¿Qué?	Keh
What is this?	¿Qué es esto?	keh ess **ess**-toh
Why?	¿Por qué?	por keh
Who?	¿Quién?	kee- **yen**
Telephone	teléfono	tel- **eff**-on-oh
I am ill	Estoy enfermo(a)	ess- **toy** en- **fer**-moh(mah)
Please call a doctor	Por favor, llame a un médico	Por fah- **vor**, **shah**-meh a oon **meh**-dik-oh
Help!	¡Auxilio!	owk- **see**-lee-oh
Fire!	¡Incendio!	in- **sen**-dee-oh

ENGLISH	SPANISH	PRONUNCIATION
Look out!	¡Cuidado!	kwee- **dah**-doh

OUT AND ABOUT

ENGLISH	SPANISH	PRONUNCIATION
Where is?	¿Dónde está?	**don**-deh ess- **tah**.
the train station	la estación de tren	la ess-tah-see- **on** deh tren
the subway station	la estación de subte	la ess-tah-see- **on** deh **soob**-teh
the bus stop	la parada del colectivo	la pah- **rah**-dah del col-ek- **tee**-voh
the post office	el correo	el cor- **reh**-yoh
the bank	el banco	el **ban**-koh
the hotel	el hotel	el oh- **tel**
the museum	el museo	el moo- **seh**-yoh
the hospital	el hospital	el oss-pee- **tal**
the elevator	el ascensor	el ass- **en**-sor
the bathroom	el baño	el **ban**-yoh
Left/right	izquierda/derecha	iss-kee- **er**-dah/ deh- **rech**-ah
Straight ahead	derecho	deh- **rech**-oh
Avenue	avenida	av-en- **ee**-dah
City street	calle	**cah**-sheh
Highway	carretera/ruta	cah-ret- **eh**-rah
Restaurant	restaurante/restorán	rest-ow- **ran**-teh/ rest-oh- **ran**
Main square	plaza principal	**plass**-ah prin-see- **pal**
Market	mercado	mer- **kah**-do
Neighborhood	barrio	**bah**-ree-oh

MENU GUIDE

With so much meat on the menu, you'll need to know how to order it: *jugoso* (juicy) means medium rare, *vuelta y vuelta* (flipped back and forth) means rare, and *vivo por adentro* (alive inside) is barely warm in the middle. Argentineans like their meat *bien cocido* (well cooked).

aceite de olivo: olive oil

alfajores: Argentine cookies, usually made with dulce de leche and often covered with chocolate, though there are hundreds of varieties

arroz: rice

bife de lomo: filet mignon

bife de chorizo: like a New York strip steak, but double the size (not to be confused with *chorizo,* which is a type of sausage)

budín de pan: Argentine version of bread pudding

cabrito: roasted kid

cafecito: espresso

café con leche: coffee with milk

centolla: King crab, a Patagonian specialty

chimichurri: a sauce of oil, garlic, and salt, served with meat

chinchulines: small intestines

chorizo: thick, spicy pork-and-beef sausages, usually served with bread (*choripan*)

churros: baton-shaped doughnuts for dipping in hot chocolate

ciervo: venison

chivito: kid

cordero: lamb

cortado: coffee "cut" with a drop of milk

dulce de leche: a sweet caramel concoction made from milk and served on pancakes, in pastries, on cookies, and on ice cream

empanadas: pockets stuffed with meat—usually beef—chicken, or cheese

ensalada de fruta: fruit salad (sometimes fresh, sometimes canned)

estofado: beef stew

facturas: small pastries

huevos: eggs

humitas: steamed cornhusks wrapped around cornmeal and cheese

jamón: ham

lechón: roast suckling pig

lengua: tongue

licuado: milk shake

locro: local stew, usually made with hominy and beans, that's cooked slowly with meat and vegetables; common in northern Argentina

medialuna: croissant

mejillones: mussels

merluza: hake

milanesa: breaded meat cutlet, usually veal, pounded thin and fried; served as a main course or in a sandwich with lettuce, tomato, ham, cheese, and egg

milanesa a la napolitana: a breaded veal cutlet with melted mozzarella cheese and tomato sauce

mollejas: sweetbreads; the thymus glands, usually of the cow but also can be of the lamb or the goat

morcilla: blood sausage

pejerrey: a kind of mackerel

pollo: chicken

provoleta: grilled provolone cheese sprinkled with olive oil and oregano

puchero: boiled meat and vegetables; like pot-au-feu

queso: cheese

salchichas: long, thin sausages

sambayon: an alcohol-infused custard

tamales: ground corn stuffed with meat, cheese, or other fillings and tied up in a corn husk

tenedor libre: all-you-can-eat meat and salad bar

tinto: red wine

trucha: trout

INDEX

PHOTO CREDITS